Oracle Database 10g PL/SQL Programming

ORACLE®

Oracle Press™

Oracle Database 10g PL/SQL Programming

Scott Urman
Ron Hardman
Michael McLaughlin

McGraw-Hill/Osborne

New York   Chicago   San Francisco
Lisbon   London   Madrid   Mexico City   Milan
New Delhi   San Juan   Seoul   Singapore   Sydney   Toronto

*The **McGraw·Hill** Companies*

McGraw-Hill/Osborne
2100 Powell Street, 10th Floor
Emeryville, California 94608
U.S.A.

To arrange bulk purchase discounts for sales promotions, premiums, or fund-raisers, please contact **McGraw-Hill/Osborne** at the above address. For information on translations or book distributors outside the U.S.A., please see the International Contact Information page immediately following the index of this book.

Oracle Database 10*g* PL/SQL Programming

1234567890 DOC DOC 01987654

ISBN 0-07-223066-5

Publisher
  Brandon A. Nordin

Vice President & Associate Publisher
  Scott Rogers

Acquisitions Editor
  Lisa McClain

Project Editor
  Carolyn Welch

Acquisitions Coordinator
  Athena Honore

Technical Editor
  Cheryl Riniker

Copy Editor
  Bob Campbell

Proofreader
  Susie Elkind

Indexer
  Claire Splan

Computer Designers
  Lucie Ericksen, John Patrus, Dick Schwartz

Illustrators
  Melinda Lytle, Kathleen Edwards

Cover Series Design
  Damore Johann Design, Inc.

This book was composed with Corel VENTURA™ Publisher.

About the Authors

Scott Urman is a Principal Member of Technical Staff in the Diagnostics and Defect Resolution (DDR) team in Oracle's Server Technology division. He currently focuses on the internals of Oracle Text and Oracle Ultrasearch, and has worked with JSP, JDBC, PL/SQL, and OCI. Prior to joining DDR, he was a Senior Analyst in the Languages division of Oracle Worldwide Technical Support, focusing on all of Oracle's language tools. He has been with Oracle since 1989. He is also the best-selling author of *Oracle8i Advanced PL/SQL Programming*, *Oracle8 PL/SQL Programming*, and *Oracle9i PL/SQL Programming*.

Ron Hardman, OCP, is a Senior Technical Specialist with Oracle Worldwide Technical Support. Prior to joining Oracle Corporation, he was an Oracle Database Developer and Consultant. He is a frequent presenter on the topics of Oracle Text and Ultrasearch at Oracle User Group conferences, teaches classes on SQL and PL/SQL, and has published articles with Oracle Magazine and other online magazines on subjects related to information retrieval.

Michael McLaughlin, D. CS., is the Senior Application Upgrade Manager for Oracle Applications Release Engineering. He is currently working on the upgrade architecture for the next release of Oracle Applications. He has worked with PL/SQL since its first version in Oracle 6, and has authored customer support notes on customizing Oracle Applications with Pro*C and PL/SQL. He has taught computer science and information technology at Regis University and Colorado Technical University, including courses in database development, SQL, PL/SQL, and Java.

About the Technical Editor

Cheryl Riniker is a Senior Technical Specialist with Oracle Worldwide Support in Oracle's Bug Diagnosis and Escalation division. She currently works with Oracle Applications' Financials Suite of products. She has used PL/SQL in development projects since 1997, and received her DBA OCP in 2001. She graduated magna cum laude with an M.A. in English/ESL from Utah State University.

This book is dedicated to our
daughter Almarah Rose Urman,
born May 1st, 2004.

—*Scott Urman*

To my wife Susan, you inspire me.
Thank you for your patience and encouragement.
To my daughter Jessica, and son Joshua, thank you for
your hugs and kisses. They never ran out.
To my parents, thank you for your example.

—*Ron Hardman*

To my wife Lisa, who is my constant,
and our children Sarah, Joseph, Elise,
Ian, Ariel, Callie, Nathan, and Spencer.
Thank you for your inspiration, patience,
and sacrifice that made my efforts
on this book possible.

—*Michael McLaughlin*

Contents at a Glance

PART III
Appendixes

Contents

PART II
Advanced PL/SQL Features

PART III
Appendixes

Acknowledgments

book like this takes quite a lot of work. Many thanks go to Lisa McClain at McGraw-Hill/Osborne for keeping the book moving forward and for providing guidance throughout the publishing process; Cheryl Riniker, our wonderful technical editor, whose input was invaluable; and project editor Carolyn Welch and copy editor Robert Campbell, whose work is greatly appreciated. Special mention goes to Craig Hollister for his contribution to this book. Thanks also to Athena Honore for running us down and keeping us on schedule until she went off to work in politics. Finally, to McGraw-Hill/Osborne's production department, your efforts to pull the book together have not gone unnoticed. Thank you all so much for your hard work.

We welcome any comments about this book, or suggestions for topics to include in the next release. Please e-mail us at Feedback@PLSQLBook.com. Let us know what you think!

Introduction

Oracle is an extremely powerful and flexible relational database system. Along with this power and flexibility comes complexity, however. In order to design useful applications that are based on Oracle, it is necessary to understand how Oracle manipulates the data stored within the system. PL/SQL is an important tool that is designed for data manipulation, both internally within Oracle and externally in your own applications. PL/SQL is available in a variety of environments, each of which has different advantages.

The first PL/SQL book in this series was *Oracle PL/SQL Programming*, published in 1996. This first edition covered releases up to PL/SQL version 2.3 with Oracle7 Release 7.3—at the time the most recent version of the database and PL/SQL. The second edition, *Oracle8 PL/SQL Programming*, published in 1997, expanded on the material in the first edition and included information up to Oracle8 Release 8.0. The third edition, *Oracle8i Advanced PL/SQL Programming*, was published in 2000. That edition focused on advanced features, up to and including Oracle8i. The fourth edition, *Oracle 9i PL/SQL Programming*, was published in 2002, and served as an introduction to PL/SQL up to and including Oracle9i.

This fifth edition is principally rewritten, and includes all new examples and coverage of advanced topics like object oriented programming with PL/SQL, external routines, job scheduling, and more. This book covers both introductory and advanced material, and provides complete coverage of the PL/SQL language including new 10g features.

What's New

This fifth release adds not only new features for Oracle 10g, but includes content we believe will make you a more efficient PL/SQL programmer. The following list highlights some of the changes:

- Oracle JDeveloper supports PL/SQL development, and we walk you through examples developing and debugging code through this IDE.

xxiii

- Completely new and expanded coverage of PL/SQL Records and Collections provides the most complete coverage of the topics you will find in any book.

- Advanced features such as External Routines, Dynamic SQL, Object Types, and LOBs take you beyond the basics of the language.

- Job scheduling using DBMS_JOB and the new Oracle 10*g* Scheduler are demonstrated.

New features of the book are not restricted to just the advanced topics, however. Sections covering basic PL/SQL topics answer the *why* and *how* questions that are most often overlooked in technical documentation. We don't just discuss transactions. We teach you how transaction processing works and demonstrate what the database is doing behind the scenes. We don't just discuss how to create a cursor. We teach you what happens in the database when the cursor is used, and how to avoid problems when they are used improperly. Data retrieval is not limited to basic SELECT statements in PL/SQL. We demonstrate the use of hierarchical queries, Regular Expressions, and Oracle Text for advanced methods of retrieval.

How to Use This Book

There are 17 chapters and two appendixes in this book. Chapters 1 through 10 include topics that are absolutely critical for all PL/SQL programmers to understand. Chapters 11 through 17 cover advanced topics. We recommend that you read the first ten chapters thoroughly before jumping into the advanced topics.

The chapters are as follows:

Chapter 1: Introduction to PL/SQL

In this chapter you are introduced to programming, and how PL/SQL compares to some of the other languages you may be used to like Java and Perl. It provides a release-by-release recap of major PL/SQL enhancements through the years and highlights some of the new 10*g* features that are discussed in greater detail in later chapters.

Chapter 2: Using SQL*Plus and JDeveloper

Chapter 2 discusses the most commonly used interface to the database, SQL*Plus. We also introduce JDeveloper as a PL/SQL development environment, and walk you through examples editing and debugging PL/SQL.

Chapter 3: PL/SQL Basics

In Chapter 3 we introduce the basic concepts of the language including block structure, anonymous and named blocks, error messages and compile time warnings, language rules and conventions, variables, and more.

Chapter 4: Using SQL with PL/SQL

In this chapter we discuss transaction processing, data retrieval including the use of hierarchical queries, Oracle Text, and Regular Expressions. We discuss how DML can be used, and how restrictions on the use of DDL inside PL/SQL can be overcome. We cover how to use cursors, and how cursors work in Oracle. Built-in SQL functions are covered, as well as how to use ROWID and ROWNUM in your PL/SQL.

Chapter 5: Records

In Chapter 5 we discuss records by covering their use as structures and types within the database. We illustrate these by comparing and contrasting development methods using traditional PL/SQL program record structures and object types.

Chapter 6: Collections

In Chapter 6 we compare and contrast varrays, nested tables, and associative arrays. We illustrate how to use base types, PL/SQL record structures, and object types. We supplement the PL/SQL details by providing key DML access methods. We demonstrate how to use the Collections API and teach you how to navigate the new Oracle 10*g* unique string indexed associative arrays.

Chapter 7: Error Handling

Chapter 7 discusses what an exception is, and how exception handlers can be declared. We show how the EXCEPTION_INIT pragma can be used, and discuss exception propagation in detail.

Chapter 8: Creating Procedures, Functions, and Packages

In Chapter 8 we show you how to create procedures, functions, and packages, paying particular attention to various types of parameter passing. Differences between these types of objects are discussed. Package overloading is demonstrated.

Chapter 9: Using Procedures, Functions, and Packages

In Chapter 9 we show you how to use subprograms and stored packages. These are well-paced examples of the fundamentals required for effective PL/SQL coding.

Chapter 10: Database Triggers

In Chapter 10 we delve into how to write triggers. We cover how you can use them for local and remote instance management. We also include how to leverage stored Java libraries with the necessary setup steps to compile and load your first Java library.

Chapter 11: Intersession Communication

In Chapter 11 we show you how to use DBMS_PIPE and DBMS_ALERT to manage intersession communications. We discuss the benefits and pitfalls of each and give you working examples so that you can begin using these Oracle built-in packages.

Chapter 12: External Routines

In Chapter 12 we demonstrate how to use external procedures. We include the details necessary to configure your environment to take advantages of these, including how to configure the Oracle Heterongeneous Server to support multithreaded external procedures. We compare and contrast external procedures with stored Java libraries.

Chapter 13: Dynamic SQL

In Chapter 13 we provide examples of leveraging the features of Native Dynamic SQL (NDS) and the traditional DBMS_SQL package. The examples illustrate work with standard Oracle data types and collections.

Chapter 14: Introduction to Objects

Chapter 14 introduces the concept of object oriented programming, and how PL/SQL has changed over the last few releases to support it. This chapter describes the basic concepts of Objects and Object Types, and discusses where you might take advantage of these great features. Inheritance, dynamic method dispatch, and type evolution are shown.

Chapter 15: Objects in the Database

This chapter extends Chapter 14 by discussing how Objects can be stored in the database. Object views, object tables, and column objects are just a few of the topics discussed.

Chapter 16: Large Objects

Chapter 16 discusses the different types of LOBs and how they work with PL/SQL. We show you how they can be used, under what circumstances they should be used over other datatypes, and how LOB storage works in Oracle.

Chapter 17: Scheduling Tasks

In Chapter 17 we show how tasks can be scheduled using the built-in package DBMS_JOB, and demonstrate the UTL_SMTP supplied package in the process. Oracle 10g introduced job scheduling using the DBMS_SCHEDULER package. We show how jobs created with DBMS_JOB can be created using DBMS_SCHEDULER, and demonstrate the UTL_MAIL supplied package as well.

Appendix A

This appendix contains a list of reserved words. These words have a special meaning to Oracle; therefore, they cannot be used by developers as identifiers in code.

Appendix B

Appendix B provides a list of Oracle supplied packages, with creation script names and descriptions of each. In addition to SYS owned packages, Oracle Text supplied packages are included.

PART
I

Introduction

CHAPTER
1

Introduction to
PL/SQL

 e've seen some really well-written code make some really lousy applications. Look at some of the beautifully written viruses that are out there, or some of the now-defunct software companies that turned out flashy but useless applications! Programming is more than just syntax. It is a profession where knowledge can be combined with ingenuity, communication, attitude, and discipline to build a successful career and world-class applications.

Throughout this book, we focus on more than syntax and rules. We answer the "Why would I use that?" question we all ask when shown new capabilities. Our discussions go beyond the fact that Oracle *can* do something. We show *how* and *why* it does it.

In this first chapter we set the stage for the rest of the book. The following points are discussed:

- SQL and its interaction with the relational database

- How PL/SQL uses SQL to increase capabilities

- Programming concepts, comparing procedural languages to object-oriented programming

- PL/SQL history and features

- The benefits (and drawbacks) of the language

- How to approach the remainder of this book and get the most out of this fully revised text

Introduction to Programming Languages

Java, C++, PL/SQL, and Visual Basic are some of the most popular programming languages in use today. Each one is quite different from the next, having its own unique characteristics. Even though they are distinct languages, some of them share common traits. Programming languages can be categorized according to these commonalities. The languages just listed fit into two categories: procedural and object-oriented.

Procedural languages, such as PL/SQL and Visual Basic, are linear. They *begin* at the beginning, and *end* at the end. This is a simplistic definition, but nevertheless a primary differentiator between procedural and object-oriented languages. Each statement must wait for the preceding statement to complete before it can run. For many beginning programmers, cutting their teeth on a procedural language is the best way to learn. You have a series of steps your program must perform, and that is exactly how the code works—step-by-step.

Object-oriented programming (OOP) languages such as Java and C++ are more abstract in nature. OOP languages work with structures called *objects.* For example, instead of writing code to pull together information about a book directly from the data structures, we can create an *object* called BOOK. Each *object* has *attributes*: number of pages, price, title, etc. Attributes describe the object. *Methods* are more action oriented. They operate on the data, retrieving it or modifying it. Should you want to change the price, for example, you call a method to perform this task. This differs from a procedural language, where you would execute a series of steps to produce the same effect.

In a rare dual-category listing, PL/SQL can now be considered both procedural and object-oriented. Oracle 8 introduced objects, though in the initial releases the support for advanced features such as inheritance, type evolution, and dynamic method dispatch were not provided. With Oracle 9*i*R1, Oracle began a major push to fully support object-oriented programming with PL/SQL. As of Oracle 10*g*, most major OO features are fully supported.

NOTE
The object-oriented features mentioned here are explained in detail in Chapters 14 and 15.

Note to Beginning Programmers

Like many developers, I cut my teeth on Basic. The syntax was easily learned, yet the programming "truths" that applied to Basic applied to most other languages. I believe you will find the same true with PL/SQL.

My favorite feature of PL/SQL is not its tight integration with the database (though it is tightly integrated), advanced language concepts and capabilities (by the end of this book, you will be amazed at what can be done), or any other type of functionality it provides. My favorite feature is its structured approach to programming. For every BEGIN, there is an END. For every IF, there is an END IF.

As an instructor teaching PL/SQL to many students new to programming (not just new to PL/SQL), I know that you can learn this language. It is structured, linear, and not very forgiving. This is a good thing! You will learn structure and rules. If you do not follow the rules, you get instant feedback when trying to run your code.

```
Warning: Procedure created with compilation errors.
```

TIP
Obviously, structure does not guarantee good code. It simply makes the language easier to learn. Take caution to use good form, adopt proper naming conventions, document your actions, and practice, practice, practice. Do not allow yourself to take shortcuts that make your code inefficient and difficult to maintain. As with any language, you can write terrible code that compiles.

You may have noticed that the best programmers are not necessarily the most technically gifted. The best programmers are good communicators who have the ability to put themselves in the shoes of their users and customers. The design phase is where this is especially critical. You meet with project managers, other developers, DBAs, end users, QA engineers, and management. Each group of people has different objectives during the systems development life cycle, and each group will place different demands on you. Your attitude and ability to communicate spells the success or failure of the project and ultimately determines how far you can go in this industry.

PL/What?

So, what is PL/SQL? It is the procedural (and sometimes object-oriented) programming extension to SQL, provided by Oracle, exclusively for Oracle. If you are familiar with another programming language called Ada, you will find striking similarities in PL/SQL. The reason they are so similar is that PL/SQL grew from Ada, borrowing many of its concepts from it.

The PL in PL/SQL stands for *procedural language.* PL/SQL is a proprietary language not available outside the Oracle Database. It is a third-generation language (3GL) that provides programming constructs similar to other 3GL languages, including variable declarations, loops, error handling, etc. Historically, PL/SQL was procedural only. As discussed in the preceding section, however, PL/SQL can now be considered part of the object-oriented category of languages. Should we change the name to PL/OO/SQL?

Structured Query Language (SQL)

The SQL in PL/SQL stands for *structured query language.* We use SQL to SELECT, INSERT, UPDATE, or DELETE data. We use it to create and maintain objects and users, and to control access rights to our instances.

SQL (pronounced as *sequel* or by its letter abbreviation) is the entrance, or window, to the database. It is a fourth-generation language (4GL) that is intended to be easy to use and quick to learn. The basic SQL syntax is not the creation of Oracle. It actually grew out of the work done by Dr. E.F. Codd and IBM in the early 1970s. The American National Standards Institute (ANSI) recognizes SQL and publishes standards for the language.

Oracle supports ANSI-standard SQL but also adds its own twist in its SQL*Plus utility. Through SQL*Plus, Oracle supports additional commands and capabilities that are not part of the standard. SQL*Plus is a utility available in multiple forms:

■ **Command line** From the Unix prompt or DOS prompt

- **GUI**   SQL*Plus Client, SQL Worksheet, Enterprise Manager

- **Web Page**   iSQL*Plus, Enterprise Manager in 10*g*

With just a client installed, we can configure a network connection to remote databases. Oracle 10*g* makes configuration even easier with a browser-based Enterprise Manager and iSQL*Plus, both configured at install time.

Relational Database Overview

SQL is the window to the database, but what is the database? A *database* in general terms is anything that stores data. Electronic databases can be as simple as a spreadsheet or word processing document.

As you might imagine, storing large amounts of data in a spreadsheet or word processing document can become overwhelming very quickly. These one-dimensional databases have no efficient way of filtering redundant data, ensuring consistent data entry, or handling information retrieval.

Oracle is a *relational database management system,* or RDBMS. Relational databases store data in tables. *Tables* are made up of columns that define the type of data that can be stored in them (character, number, etc.). A table has a minimum of one *column*. When data is placed in the table, it is stored in *rows*. This holds true for all relational database vendors (see Figure 1-1).

In Oracle, tables are owned by a user, or schema. The schema is a collection of objects, like tables, that the database user owns. It is possible to have two tables in one database that have the same name as long as they are owned by different users.

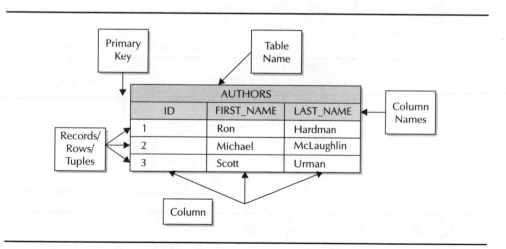

FIGURE 1-1.   *Table structure*

Other vendors do not necessarily follow this approach. SQL Server, for example, applies different terminology. The SQL Server database is more like an Oracle schema, and the SQL Server *server* more resembles the Oracle database. The result is the same, however. Objects, such as tables, always have an owner.

It is possible to store all of our data in a single table, just like the spreadsheet, but that does not take advantage of Oracle's relational features. For example, a table containing data about Oracle Press books is incomplete without author information. It is possible that an author has written multiple titles. In a flat-file, or single-table, model, the author is listed multiple times. This redundancy can be avoided by splitting the data into two tables with a column that links related data together. Figure 1-2 illustrates how we can break this into two separate tables.

In Figure 1-2 there are two tables, AUTHORS and BOOKS. Author information stores the first and last names of authors one time. Each row of data is given an ID that is guaranteed unique and not null (null means empty, so not null means not empty).

Since we have the AUTHORS table, we don't have to repeat author information over and over for every title each person writes. We add a single AUTHOR1 column in the BOOKS table and insert the appropriate ID value from the AUTHORS table for each title in the BOOKS table. Using a FOREIGN KEY on the BOOKS.AUTHOR1 column, we can relate the two tables together using SQL. Let's take a look at an example:

NOTE
You may wish to use the CreateUser.sql *script located in this chapter's directory on the web site. It creates a user called plsql and grants required permissions to the user.*

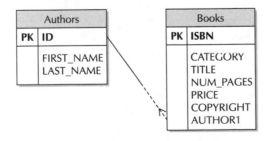

FIGURE 1-2. *ERD for Books and Authors*

```
-- Available online as part of PlsqlBlock.sql
CREATE TABLE authors (
   id           NUMBER PRIMARY KEY,
   first_name VARCHAR2(50),
   last_name  VARCHAR2(50)
);

CREATE TABLE books (
   isbn        CHAR(10) PRIMARY KEY,
   category  VARCHAR2(20),
   title       VARCHAR2(100),
   num_pages NUMBER,
   price       NUMBER,
   copyright NUMBER(4),
   author1    NUMBER CONSTRAINT books_author1
              REFERENCES authors(id)
);
```

After inserting a few records into the tables, we can perform a SELECT, joining the tables according to their relationship.

```
SELECT b.title, a.first_name, a.last_name
FROM authors a, books b
WHERE b.author1 = a.id;
```

This joins the two tables together and retrieves data just as you would have seen it had it been stored in a flat file. The differences are less redundancy, fewer opportunities for error, and greater flexibility. To add publisher information, all I would need to do is create a table called PUBLISHER that contains an ID, then add a column to the BOOKS table with a FOREIGN KEY pointing back to the PUBLISHER.ID column.

NOTE
For expanded coverage of SQL, refer to the
online documentation at http://otn.oracle.com.

PL/SQL vs. SQL

SQL gives us complete access to our data. By complete, I mean we can get to everything. . . eventually. . . in less than ideal ways in many cases. There is no guarantee of efficiency, and few actual programming capabilities found in most languages are possible. SQL provides no ability to

- Loop through records, manipulating them one at a time.
- Keep code secure by offering encryption, and storing code permanently on the server rather than the client.
- Handle exceptions.
- Work with variables, parameters, collections, records, arrays, objects, cursors, exceptions, BFILEs, etc.

While SQL is powerful, and SQL*Plus (Oracle's proprietary SQL interface) includes commands and built-in functions not found in the ANSI standard, SQL remains more of a method of access to the database than a programming language. PL/SQL takes over where SQL leaves off by adding the features mentioned here and more.

NOTE
Do not worry if you do not know what all of the programming features mentioned here are! That is what this book is for. They are explained in detail in later chapters.

Virtually all SQL capabilities are possible with PL/SQL. In fact, as of Oracle 9*i*R1, the PL/SQL parser is the same as the SQL parser, ensuring that commands are treated the same regardless of where they are executed. Prior to Oracle 9*i*R1, you would find some cases where a SQL statement was treated completely differently. Not so anymore.

Let's take the query of the BOOKS and AUTHORS tables that we did earlier and use it in a PL/SQL example.

```
-- Available online as part of PlsqlBlock.sql
SET SERVEROUTPUT ON
DECLARE
    v_title books.title%TYPE;
    v_first_name authors.first_name%TYPE;
    v_last_name authors.last_name%TYPE;

    CURSOR book_cur IS
        SELECT b.title, a.first_name, a.last_name
        FROM authors a, books b
        WHERE a.id = b.author1;
BEGIN
```

```
DBMS_OUTPUT.ENABLE(1000000);
OPEN book_cur;
LOOP
    FETCH book_cur INTO v_title, v_first_name, v_last_name;
    EXIT WHEN book_cur%NOTFOUND;

    IF v_last_name = 'Hardman'
    THEN
        DBMS_OUTPUT.PUT_LINE('Ron Hardman co-authored '||v_title);
    ELSE
        DBMS_OUTPUT.PUT_LINE('Ron Hardman did not write '||v_title);
    END IF;
END LOOP;

CLOSE book_cur;

EXCEPTION
    WHEN OTHERS
        THEN
        DBMS_OUTPUT.PUT_LINE(SQLERRM);
END;
/
```

This example includes the select statement we used earlier, but it loops through all of the query results, determines if 'Hardman' is the last name of the author, and formats the output accordingly. The power of SQL 4GL is combined with the features of a procedural 3GL language.

NOTE
Take note of the structure in the last block.
For every begin, there is an end.

PL/SQL vs. Java

Oracle 8*i* introduced support for Java, and Java Stored Procedures, in the database. Why not just use Java, then?

PL/SQL is, and has always been, tightly integrated with the Oracle database. Oracle continues to improve PL/SQL performance by adding integration features such as native compilation of PL/SQL code. This means that when the code is compiled, it is converted to C (the language Oracle is written in). At run time, no interpretation between PL/SQL syntax and C is required. Performance is greatly improved—up to 30 percent over interpreted mode (the default).

Another advantage of PL/SQL is that it is very compact. You can turn a SQL statement into a PL/SQL block (blocks are discussed in Chapter 3) by simply adding a BEGIN before the statement, and an END after it. The same cannot be said for Java. The following block of code is the most basic you can create with PL/SQL:

```
BEGIN
    NULL;
END;
/
```

Try it—it works. It does absolutely nothing, but it runs.

Here are some other distinctive features of PL/SQL:

- PL/SQL now shares the same parser as SQL, so there is guaranteed consistency between interfaces.

- PL/SQL can be executed from SQL.

- OO features are constantly being added to PL/SQL, removing many of the reasons to switch to Java.

This is not to say that you should *always* use PL/SQL and *never* use Java. Java includes a whole host of features not yet available in PL/SQL. Java is not a replacement for PL/SQL, though. It is simply an alternative.

NOTE
Since Java's introduction to the database, I have repeatedly heard a rumor that PL/SQL was on the way out and Java is taking over—not true.

PL/SQL History and Features

What you see as a rich feature set in the most recent releases of PL/SQL is actually 13 years (as of the time of this writing) of constant development and improvement of the language by Oracle. PL/SQL is a language developed out of need, both internal and external to Oracle. Though many of the features were created to satisfy the demands of database developers in the user community, a large number were also prompted by Oracle's need for functionality in their own application development and consulting efforts. As a developer, I find it encouraging to know that Oracle is heavily using the same technologies I rely on in my career.

It is hard to imagine the Oracle database without PL/SQL, but it was not that long ago when it was first introduced.

Version 1.x

PL/SQL 1.0 was introduced in 1991 with the 6.0 release of the data server. As you might expect with a new programming language, it was lacking in most features you might expect from a more mature release. The Oracle development community, however, appreciated it because it gave capabilities such as IF-THEN logic that were not possible with SQL at the time.

Version 2.x

By PL/SQL version 2.3 (released with version 7.3 of the database), Oracle added support for stored procedures and functions, and added numerous built-in packages. PL/SQL was key to the success of Oracle's developer tools, and Oracle Applications relied heavily on tight integration of PL/SQL to the data server.

Version 8.0

Oracle 8.0 included support for objects. Though object support was not exactly feature-rich in this introductory release, it gave us an indication of where Oracle was taking the language. OO enhancements continue through the most recent release of 10gR1. One other change in 8.0 is the versioning for PL/SQL and the data server. PL/SQL began following the same version sequence as the data server it was integrated with.

Version 8.1

With Oracle 8*i*, marketing of PL/SQL features took a back seat to Java integration in the "Database for the Internet." This did not mean that there was nothing new with PL/SQL, though. One of my favorite enhancements: Native Dynamic SQL (NDS) gave us EXECUTE IMMEDIATE! I love this command—in fact, you will see it in nearly every schema creation script in the examples for this book.

Version 9.0

Oracle 9*i*R1 was a huge release for PL/SQL. The following list summarizes some of the major improvements:

- SQL and PL/SQL now share the same parser, ensuring consistency. Prior to this improvement, a statement that succeeded in the SQL*Plus window would not be guaranteed to work in PL/SQL.

- Character semantics, which allows us to define our variable or column precision in characters or bytes, was added in 9*i*R1. Unicode characters are not all created equal. They can differ in byte size. Precision in Oracle is actually in bytes, not characters! A variable declaration specifying VARCHAR2(2) means that the variable can hold two bytes, not two characters. Some Asian characters are up to three bytes, which means that an assignment of a single Chinese character may not fit into a variable with a precision of two. Now that is annoying!

- Support for objects now includes inheritance and type evolution. These were glaring weaknesses in PL/SQL's OO support.

- Native compilation allows PL/SQL code to be compiled as C code (Oracle is written in C), reducing time to execute, since no interpretation is required at run time.

Version 9.2

Many of the Oracle 9*i*R2 features were improvements of 9*i*R1 enhancements. Object features were improved, adding built-in functions and support for user-defined constructors. Oracle Text introduced the CTXXPATH, providing improved PL/SQL access to XML documents stored in the XMLTYPE datatype.

Version 10.0

PL/SQL 10.0 added a number of new features:

- Arguably the most important addition to 10*g*R1 PL/SQL is support for regular expressions. Regular expressions have long been a staple of Unix and Perl scripting, and they are now available with Oracle and supported in PL/SQL. The short definition: Regular expressions find, retrieve, and manipulate patterns in text.

- Another great feature added in 10*g*R1 is the ability to receive warnings when code is compiled. I don't mean errors—we get these already. We can get warnings now using the plsql_warnings parameter, or the DBMS_WARNING package. They give us hints about potential performance problems and minor problems that do not result in errors at compile time.

- New datatypes—BINARY_FLOAT and BINARY_DOUBLE—are native floating-point datatypes that are an alternative to using the NUMBER type.

- DBMS_LOB offers support of large LOBs—between 8 and 128 terabytes (depending on block size). See Chapter 16 for more information.

- String literal customization. If you get tired of having to put two single quotes inside of a string literal, you can use q' !...! ', with the string placed inside the exclamation points. This lets you use one single quote in your string rather than requiring two. Here's a quick example using an anonymous block:

```
SET SERVEROUTPUT ON
BEGIN
    DBMS_OUTPUT.PUT_LINE('Ron's');
END;
/
```

This returns the following error:

```
ORA-01756: quoted string not properly terminated
```

To fix it, we used to have to use two single quotes in place of the apostrophe, as in `Ron''s`. 10*g*R1 provides another alternative:

```
BEGIN
    DBMS_OUTPUT.PUT_LINE(q'!Ron's!');
END;
/
```

This completes successfully and displays Ron's as intended.

Language Fundamentals

In this section we look at some of the basic features of PL/SQL, such as the ability to execute code without storing it, storing code for later use, and the differences between various types of stored objects. We discuss them at a high level, just to introduce the concepts. They are discussed in much greater detail in Chapters 3, 4, 8, and 9.

Anonymous Blocks

Anonymous blocks of code are not stored, and not named. They are executed in-session and cannot be called from another session. To execute the same code again, you must save the anonymous block to an OS file and run it, type it in again, or include it in a program that executes the block when needed.

You will find throughout the examples that anonymous blocks are used extensively. Anonymous blocks are perfect for scripting, or activities that you do not wish to repeat frequently. The following example is an anonymous block:

```
SET SERVEROUTPUT ON
DECLARE
    v_Date TIMESTAMP;
BEGIN
    SELECT systimestamp - 1/24
    INTO v_Date
    FROM dual;
    DBMS_OUTPUT.PUT_LINE('One hour ago: '||v_Date);
END;
/
```

The block begins with DECLARE or BEGIN and is not stored anywhere once executed.

NOTE
A PL/SQL block is a complete section of PL/SQL code. A PL/SQL program is made up of one or more blocks that logically divide the work. Blocks can even be nested within other blocks. Chapter 3 includes a full discussion on block structure.

Procedures

Procedures are named and stored. They can return a *value* when executed, but they *do not* have to. The only thing that must be returned is the success or failure of the execution.

Stored procedures, or named procedures, are given a unique name at creation time. They are owned by the user that created them unless otherwise stated in the creation script.

You can execute procedures from the SQL*Plus prompt, from within a SQL script, or from another PL/SQL block of code.

Functions

Functions differ from procedures in that they *must* return a value. Their structure is very similar to procedures, with the mandatory RETURN clause being the biggest difference. Functions are named and can be called from the SQL*Plus prompt, from within a SQL script, or from another PL/SQL block of code. When executing a function, you must have the ability to handle the value returned, though.

Packages

Packages are logical groupings of procedures and functions. They have two parts: the specification and the body.

The *specification,* or *spec,* is public and shows the structure of the package. When a package is described in SQL*Plus, it is the spec that is shown. The spec is always created or compiled before the body. In fact, it is possible to create the spec without ever creating the body.

Object Types

Oracle's object types allow you to write object-oriented code using PL/SQL. Object types are similar in structure to packages, having both a specification and a body. They provide a level of abstraction to your underlying data structure.

Object types may include attributes and methods. *Attributes* are defining characteristics of your object. A book, for example, might have attributes of title, number of pages, etc.

Methods act upon the underlying data structures for the object. All interaction between the application and object data should be done using methods.

Some of the advantages of using object types include

- **Abstraction** The application developer is removed from the relational data structures and thinks in terms of real-world structures.

- **Consistency** If all application interaction is done through objects rather than directly against the data structures, data corruption becomes much less likely to be introduced.

- **Simplicity** Instead of taking a real-world model and converting it to code, the model stays in the real world. If I want to know something about a book object, I look to the *book* object.

Features introduced since Oracle 9*i*R1 include inheritance, dynamic method dispatch, and type evolution. They make object-oriented programming using PL/SQL much more robust.

PL/SQL Statement Processing

When you execute a PL/SQL block, the code is passed to the PL/SQL engine. The engine may be in the data server itself or in one of the tools (like Oracle Reports) that bundles the PL/SQL engine with it. Next, the code is parsed, and the SQL is passed to the SQL engine, or SQL Statement Executor. The procedural statements are passed to the Procedural Statement Executor for processing.

Interpreted

Interpreted is the default mode for Oracle. This means that stored procedures, functions, and packages are compiled and stored as PL/SQL and are interpreted by Oracle (written in C) at run time. In interpreted mode, PL/SQL compilation is quicker, but code execution may be slower than if native compilation was used.

Native Compilation

Native compilation, first introduced in Oracle 9*i*R1 and improved in 10*g*R1, converts PL/SQL to C at compile time. This makes execution up to 30 percent faster, since no interpretation is required at run time.

Getting the Most from This Book

This book is fully revised and includes beginning, intermediate, and advanced topics. Sample code is used throughout to demonstrate features, and all of it is available online for download. The web site includes chapter directories, where all code referenced in the book is stored. The code for each chapter is intended to run independent of other chapters—no cross-chapter dependencies. Schema creation scripts are included for ease of testing. You will need to modify them as appropriate for your environment and database access.

There are some topics that require more space than we could possibly allocate inside the book. Instead of reducing coverage to fit the book, we have created supplemental papers for download that are extensions to chapter topics. We hope you will find this added coverage useful.

Audience

This book is written for new and experienced PL/SQL application developers, as well as for DBAs who would like to take advantage of all PL/SQL has to offer. Advanced chapters (11–17) require that you understand Chapters 1–10. If you are an experienced PL/SQL programmer, you may still want to peruse the first few chapters. We include discussions on new features, and example code that may generate some new ideas for your applications.

Regardless of your level of experience, we are confident that you will find something you had not yet discovered in each chapter.

Objective

PL/SQL is a mature, robust language that continues to improve with every release. As complexity increases, keeping up with new features becomes a daunting task. We aim to help you

- Learn PL/SQL if you are new to the language.

- Develop good form and efficient code.

- Understand features only referenced in passing in other texts, or not covered at all.

- Discover how powerful this language is!

Scope

Every book includes limitations. Ours are as follows:

■   There is only limited coverage of database administration topics. If you wish to learn more about database administration, I will refer you to http://otn.oracle.com, or one of the excellent database administration books by Oracle Press.

■   Performance tuning coverage is limited to making your PL/SQL efficient. It does not cover database performance tuning.

■   We can only provide you with information, advice, and examples. It is up to you to take advantage of them, and write good code.

Assumptions

The base release for this book is Oracle 8.1.7.4, the terminal release of the Oracle 8*i* database. Coverage includes 8.1.7, 9*i*R1, 9*i*R2, and 10*g*R1. To take full advantage of this book, and the new features in Oracle, we recommend you download and install Oracle 10*g*R1 from OTN (http://otn.oracle.com). You can download the data server for free as long as you register (registration is also free).

TIP
10gR1 is a single-disk install, so the download will be much quicker than for any version of 9i.

At a minimum, it is recommended that you have access to an Oracle instance, and that you have the necessary permissions to create a user and the required objects. It is important that you are aware of your version of PL/SQL, since it impacts feature availability.

Since Oracle 8, PL/SQL versions have coincided with the database versions. In texts that cover releases prior to Oracle 8, you will see versioning like PL/SQL 1.1, 2.X, etc. To find the version you are running, query the V$VERSION view.

```
SELECT banner
FROM v$version;
```

The select returns the following in my current environment:

```
BANNER
---------------------------------
Oracle Database 10g Enterprise Edition Release 10.1.0.2.0 - Prod
PL/SQL Release 10.1.0.2.0 - Production
CORE    10.1.0.2.0      Production
TNS for 32-bit Windows: Version 10.1.0.2.0 - Production
NLSRTL Version 10.1.0.2.0 - Production
```

So I am using version 10.1.0.2.0 of the database, and PL/SQL version 10.1.0.2 as well.

Conventions

We use different fonts through the book to highlight and differentiate certain text. Code examples, and external references to database objects in the text, are in COURIER. References to variables in the text are also in COURIER. Items of particular interest in a code example are placed in **bold** letters. Take special note of the Note and Tip sections in the book.

Examples

User creation scripts are included in each chapter that grant permissions required by the examples in that chapter alone. Do not use a schema creation script from one chapter for the examples in another.

Most chapters use example objects related to a bookstore. The base tables for most examples are BOOKS and AUTHORS, as shown earlier in this chapter in Figure 1-1. There are slight differences in the schema design between chapters in order to demonstrate different features.

The BOOKS table structure is

```
DESC books
 Name                                     Null?     Type
 ---------------------------------------- --------- ------------
 ISBN                                     NOT NULL  CHAR(10)
 CATEGORY                                           VARCHAR2(20)
 TITLE                                              VARCHAR2(100)
 NUM_PAGES                                          NUMBER
 PRICE                                              NUMBER
 COPYRIGHT                                          NUMBER(4)
 AUTHOR1                                            NUMBER
 AUTHOR2                                            NUMBER
 AUTHOR3                                            NUMBER
```

The AUTHORS table structure is as follows:

```
DESC authors
 Name                                     Null?     Type
 ---------------------------------------- --------- ------------
 ID                                       NOT NULL  NUMBER
 FIRST_NAME                                         VARCHAR2(50)
 LAST_NAME                                          VARCHAR2(50)
```

The schema creation script in Chapter 16, called `CreateLOBUser.sql`, creates two tablespaces to use for the storage parameter on a `create table` statement. The tablespace names and datafile names and locations can be modified as needed for your environment.

Finally, take time to review the different methods used to create the schemas and examples. We tried to employ different techniques throughout the book in order to demonstrate there is more than one way to accomplish the same task. As you look through the examples, think about how you can employ some of the same techniques, naming conventions, and strategies in your application design. Ingenuity, communication, attitude, discipline, and knowledge will propel you in your career using Oracle PL/SQL and aid in whatever task you apply yourself to.

Summary

In this chapter we introduced programming concepts, described how PL/SQL fits in both object-oriented and procedural programming categories, and previewed some of PL/SQL's features that are covered in this book. We reviewed the basics of relational databases and SQL, and looked at how PL/SQL compares with SQL and Java. Finally, we discussed this book, and how you can get the most out of it.

We hope you find this book helpful and discover things you never thought possible with PL/SQL.

CHAPTER
2

Using SQL*Plus
and JDeveloper

K
nowing how to develop and run PL/SQL doesn't do much good unless you have a place to run it. Oracle provides GUI and command-line utilities to create and debug PL/SQL code, and then run and maintain it.

In this chapter we discuss PL/SQL execution and development using SQL*Plus and JDeveloper. SQL*Plus, the most widely used utility shipped with the data server, provides an interface to the database that is flexible and always available. JDeveloper, once strictly a Java development tool, now includes features for managing database objects and developing PL/SQL.

The section on SQL*Plus covers

- Connecting to the instance

- Using SQL*Plus from the command line, GUI client, SQL Worksheet, and iSQL*Plus

- Changing SQL*Plus settings

- Running scripts from files

- Displaying output to the screen using DBMS_OUTPUT

The section on JDeveloper covers

- Installation and configuration

- Loading a program

- Creating a program

- Compiling code

- Stepping through code to debug

To run the examples in this chapter, you should first run the CreateUser.sql script included in the online files for this chapter. This script provides all necessary permissions to successfully complete the examples.

SQL*Plus

SQL*Plus is the main interface to the database regardless of release. It is included with all versions of the data server and is available from the server or client via command line, GUI, or browser. Oracle extends ANSI standard SQL with built-in packages (see Appendix B for a list of supplied packages) and additional commands.

Connecting to the Instance

To connect to the instance from the client, configure your `tnsnames.ora` file in your `$ORACLE_HOME/network/admin` directory. This file can be modified with any text editor or configured using the Net Assistant or Net Manager (the same utility, the name is different depending on release). To configure the connection, you will need the name or IP address of the host machine, the port the data server is using for connections, and the name of the service name (instance name). For an example string, see the `tnsnames.ora` entry for our instance in Figure 2-1.

NOTE
You must have installed the Oracle client, data server, or other Oracle development tool on the machine you are connecting from in order to configure your `tnsnames.ora` file. Depending on your release, the `tnsnames.ora` file may be located in your `$ORACLE_HOME/net80/admin` directory.

The first highlighted entry in Figure 2-1 is called the *net service name*. This is an alias and is the name we refer to when connecting to our instance. We could have called this entry "ron," and if all other information in the entry remained the same, we could still connect to the same instance (ORCL) by referring to the instance as "ron." In the following example we do just that:

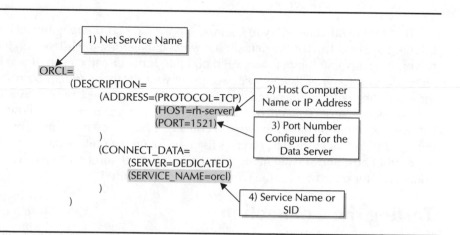

FIGURE 2-1. *TNSNAMES.ORA configuration*

```
sqlplus plsql/oracle@ron

SQL*Plus: Release 10.1.0.2.0 - Production on Sun Jul 4 15:09:15 2004
Copyright (c) 1982, 2004, Oracle. All rights reserved.
Connected to:

Oracle Database 10g Enterprise Edition Release 10.1.0.2.0 - Production
With the Partitioning, OLAP and Data Mining options

SQL>
```

We are still connected to the `orcl` instance, though. As a general rule, we keep our net service name the same name as our instance. We would be unable to reference the "ron" instance in communications between developers if it were called that name only from our client. The *Keep It Simple* principle applies here.

The *host computer name* or *IP address* is the second entry highlighted in Figure 2-1. We can't very well connect to a location on our network without first identifying where that computer resides. On most work networks this is a no-brainer. Simply put the name given to the server here. For some networks and remote connections there is no DNS server to translate the computer name into the IP address. In these cases, put the IP address as the host, or make an entry in the client's *hosts* file. The hosts file maps aliases to IP addresses like the DNS server, but it does so just for the client where the file resides. On a Windows machine you will find this file at `C:\[Windows|WINNT]\system32\drivers\etc`. The following entry in our hosts file allows me to refer to *rh-server* rather than the IP address or *localhost* to connect to 127.0.0.1:

```
127.0.0.1        rh-server
```

The third highlighted entry in Figure 2-1 is for the *port number* the data server is listening on. Port 1521 is the default, but when configuring the listener on the host server, the entry can be set to any valid port that is not already taken. If you do not know the port for your listener, please contact your database administrator, or check for an existing entry in the host server's `tnsnames.ora` or `listener.ora` file.

Finally, the *service name,* or *SID,* is entered in our `tnsnames.ora` entry. This is the name of our instance. In order to connect, this service name must be included in the list of instances the data server is listening for on the port specified. If we enter the correct host and service name, but the port for a different listener that is not configured for our instance, the connection will be refused.

Testing the Connection

If you are using the Net Manager to create your `tnsnames.ora` connection string, there is a Test button at the end of the configuration. By default, the test uses the username of "scott" and password of "tiger." We actually do not have this sample schema in our instance, so when testing the connection, we receive the following exception:

```
The test did not succeed.
ORA-01017: invalid username/password; logon denied
```

While it is possible to change the login and retest, is it really necessary? How could our client have determined that a username or password was invalid if it didn't at least make the connection? Even with this failure, we consider the test successful, since the goal was to reach the instance and verify a connection could be made.

If we modify the `tnsnames.ora` file directly, we can run a simple test from the command line by logging into SQL*Plus. The following tests our connection:

```
c:\>sqlplus system@orcl
SQL*Plus: Release 10.1.0.2.0 - Production on Mon Jun 21 22:46:22 2004
Copyright (c) 1982, 2004, Oracle. All rights reserved.

Enter password:

Connected to:
Oracle Database 10g Enterprise Edition Release 10.1.0.2.0 - Production
With the Partitioning, OLAP and Data Mining options

SQL>
```

Our client connection to Net Service Name `orcl` on host `rh-server` with a Service Name of `orcl` is successful.

Another quick way to verify the connection is to use TNSPING to ping the instance. Here is an example testing our ability to connect to the `orcl` instance:

```
tnsping orcl

Used TNSNAMES adapter to resolve the alias
Attempting to contact (DESCRIPTION = (ADDRESS = (PROTOCOL = TCP)
(HOST = rh-laptop)(PORT = 1521)) (CONNECT_DATA =
(SERVER = DEDICATED) (SERVICE_NAME = orcl)))
OK (40 msec)
```

The connection is successful. If it were not successful, it would show

```
tnsping notaninstancename

TNS Ping Utility for 32-bit Windows: Version 10.1.0.2.0 -
Production on 04-JUL-2004 14:42:12
Copyright (c) 1997, 2003, Oracle. All rights reserved.

Used parameter files:
```

```
sqlnet.ora
TNS-03505: Failed to resolve name
```

We passed an invalid instance name resulting in a failure.

Using SQL*Plus

When we use SQL*Plus, we prefer to use the command-line version of the utility in most cases. The command-line version has the advantage of not changing, and it is always available. When we work on different machines at various locations around the country, we see different utilities and configurations from site to site, but SQL*Plus from the command line is always present. SQL*Plus has the following types of implementations, all included with the purchase of the data server:

- Command-line SQL*Plus

- SQL*Plus GUI Client

- SQL Worksheet

- iSQL*Plus

Additional third-party utilities offer interfaces to SQL*Plus as well, but they are beyond the scope of this book.

Command Line

By command line, we are referring to a Unix or DOS prompt. To connect to an instance, type **sqlplus** at the prompt, then type the username and password separated by a forward slash (/), and follow that immediately with an **@** and the net service name you are connecting to. The following example shows a connection to our instance with all connection information shown on a single line:

```
sqlplus system/oracle@orcl
```

While this connects, it is not the best way to type your connection because your password is displayed. A better way to connect is to type the username followed by an **@** and the net service name as follows:

```
sqlplus system@orcl

SQL*Plus: Release 10.1.0.2.0 - Production on Wed Jun 23 18:44:13 2004
Copyright (c) 1982, 2004, Oracle. All rights reserved.
Enter password:
```

Oracle prompts for the password and then connects to the instance.

To change to a different schema or another instance, it is not necessary to disconnect from the current session. CONNECT allows a new connection from the current session.

```
SQL> connect ctxsys@orcl
Enter password:
Connected.
```

TIP
Instead of typing CONNECT, use the abbreviation
CONN. It does the same thing.

The sqlplus binary is located in the $ORACLE_HOME/bin directory. This directory is included in the PATH environment variable. If you receive an error that the sqlplus program cannot be found, check your PATH settings to ensure the $ORACLE_HOME/bin directory is there.

SQL*Plus provides editing commands to modify the contents of the buffer without requiring the full text to be re-entered. The following example selects a value, but there is a typo:

```
SELECT systimestamp
   FROM duall;
```

This results in the following exception:

```
FROM duall
      *
ERROR at line 2:
ORA-00942: table or view does not exist
```

To correct this mistake, we can either retype the text in its entirety or edit only the value that needs to be changed. We'll demonstrate the latter here:

```
c /11/1
```

We used c to change the last line in the buffer. If we needed to change a different line, we just type the number of the line to edit, and it moves to that line in the buffer. Our change modifies duall to dual and reprints the altered line.

```
FROM dual
```

To rerun the contents of the buffer, use a forward-slash, */.*

`/`

```
SYSTIMESTAMP
-------------------
04-JUN-04 06.08.57.102000 PM -07:00
```

As you might imagine, this approach can come in very handy when working with larger blocks of code and PL/SQL. Some other useful editing commands include **a**, which appends whatever follows to the end of the line currently in the buffer, and **l**, which reprints the contents of the buffer. Typing **ed** at the SQL prompt opens the default editor with the text from the buffer loaded. You can edit and save the contents, and rerun by typing a forward-slash, **/**, at the SQL prompt.

SQL*Plus GUI

The SQL*Plus GUI does not include any advanced features not offered by the command-line version, but it does provide a look and feel that is more comfortable for some users. To launch it in a Windows environment, navigate to Start | All Programs | *YourOraHome*| Application Development || SQL Plus.

SQL Worksheet

The SQL*Plus Worksheet adds features that are not included in either command-line or GUI versions. One of the biggest differences is the ability to recall past statements from history and reload them into the buffer for execution. Another great feature is that it displays the explain plan for SQL statements that it runs.

NOTE
Explain plans, *or execution plans, are the methods of access chosen by Oracle to most efficiently run a SQL statement. Oracle generates multiple explain plans for every statement and assigns a cost to each of them based on statistics in the database. The cost measures how expensive each execution plan is, so the lowest-cost plan can be chosen. This is how Oracle optimizes SQL execution.*

iSQL*Plus

Though we are still partial to the command line, we have been using iSQL*Plus more and more, especially when working with applications that support multiple languages (globalization). DOS (and most other applications for that matter) does not render Asian characters without loading extra fonts and going through configuration changes.

iSQL*Plus provides the means to display multibyte characters, like Japanese, with very little modification. To modify the encoding for Internet Explorer, navigate to View | Encoding | Unicode(UTF-8). Log into iSQL*Plus using the URL provided during instance creation, and any UTF-8 supported font can be rendered.

Changing SQL*Plus Session Settings

SQL*Plus runs a script called `glogin.sql` at login. This script, found at `$ORACLE_HOME/sqlplus/admin`, sets the environment for the session. While it is possible to change the settings once logged into SQL*Plus, we find it much easier to add the most common settings to the `glogin.sql` script so that they are set automatically. For example, the following SHOW command lists the current settings for *long, pages, feedback,* and *echo*:

```
SQL> show long pages feedback echo
```

This results in the following in our environment:

```
long 80
pagesize 14
echo OFF
```

We change these settings frequently when logging in, so changing the `glogin.sql` script to automate these changes makes sense. Here are the changed settings as they appear in our `glogin.sql` script:

```
-- Custom settings
SET pages 9999 - pages is short for pagesize
SET echo OFF
SET long 64000
```

Checking our settings again after reconnecting to SQL*Plus, we see the altered settings without explicitly making the changes in our session:

```
SQL> show long pages echo
long 64000
pagesize 9999
echo OFF
```

These are just a few of the changes that can be made. If you wish, modify other settings the SQL prompt, run a script, or print a message to the screen at each login.

Running a Script from a File

SQL*Plus provides the ability to run scripts stored in external files. To execute the contents of a file, log in to SQL*Plus as the user you need and type an @ followed by the name of the file (provide the full path if you are not currently in the correct directory).

We'll demonstrate this using the `CreateUser.sql` script that is available online for this chapter. This script creates the user PLSQL with a password of ORACLE. After modifying the script header for our environment, we are ready to run it. Follow these steps to run the script:

1. Assuming you are using a Windows machine, open a command prompt (Start | Run and type **cmd**).

2. When the command window opens, **cd** to the directory where the chapter scripts are stored.

   ```
   cd C:\book\Chapter2\Examples
   ```

3. Log in to SQL*Plus as **SYS** or **SYSTEM**.

   ```
   C:\book\Chapter2\Examples>sqlplus system@orcl
   SQL*Plus: Release 10.1.0.2.0 - Production on Sat Jun 26 11:47:12 2004

   Copyright (c) 1982, 2004, Oracle. All rights reserved.
   Enter password:
   Connected to:
   Oracle Database 10g Enterprise Edition Release 10.1.0.2.0 - Production
   With the Partitioning, OLAP and Data Mining options

   SQL>
   ```

4. At the SQL prompt, run the script.

   ```
   SQL> @CreateUser.sql
   ```

The same steps are followed for Unix, with the exception of the file structure for the directory storage, of course.

If you have forgotten the filename, or the file's case when using Unix, it is possible to view the host machine's directory contents without leaving the SQL prompt. For Unix, type the following:

```
SQL> !ls
```

The exclamation point, or bang, allows Unix commands to be used from the SQL prompt. Once the command is complete, control will be passed back to the SQL prompt once again without requiring you to log in again. The same can be done from a Windows machine using the `host` command:

```
SQL> host dir
```

The directory contents are displayed, and then control is returned to the SQL prompt once again.

Output to the Screen Using SQL*Plus and PL/SQL

We won't put you through the standard "Hello, World" example first program, but we will tell you how it can be done. Oracle provides a built-in package called DBMS_OUTPUT. This package includes a number of subprograms, including a procedure called PUT_LINE. Using DBMS_OUTPUT.PUT_LINE, we can write a simple program that displays text when running a program from SQL*Plus.

Let's take a look at a simple example. The following PL/SQL code prints a line of text to the screen:

```
-- Available online as part of DbmsOutput.sql
BEGIN
    DBMS_OUTPUT.PUT_LINE('Oh Beautiful for Spacious Skies...');
END;
/
```

This doesn't have the intended effect, however. The following is all that is shown when the code is run from the SQL prompt:

```
PL/SQL procedure successfully completed.
```

So, the text wasn't printed to the screen. This is because of another setting called SERVEROUTPUT. By default, this is set to OFF. We can set it to ON by typing the following:

```
SET SERVEROUTPUT ON
```

Now, when we run the same code, we get a different result:

```
/
Oh Beautiful for Spacious Skies...
PL/SQL procedure successfully completed.
```

The text is displayed to the screen.

NOTE
The / in the preceding code block executes the code already in the buffer. If you have run any other statement in this session, you will need to rerun the complete block.

JDeveloper

SQL*Plus is handy because it is built into every current version of the database and is the primary interface to the data server. It isn't considered a development environment, though. Since the 9*i* release, Oracle JDeveloper added the ability to develop, debug, and maintain PL/SQL. It is not just for Java anymore. Features in JDeveloper 10*g* include

- Framed display of all database objects
- The ability to edit PL/SQL in the database with JDeveloper
- Code templates for faster code generation
- SQL tuning advice
- Debug capabilities, including stepping through code

JDeveloper does require an additional license to own as part of a corporate solution, but developers can download complete versions of the tool from http://otn.oracle.com for noncommercial use.

Installing JDeveloper

As mentioned, JDeveloper can be downloaded from http://otn.oracle.com. In order to download software from Oracle Technology Network (OTN), users must first register and create a username and password. OTN membership costs nothing. Once registered, users are free to download all downloadable software, courses, sample code, and labs posted on the site.

Oracle has three ways to download the software. Unless you are familiar with Java and have the correct version of JDK on your system according to the web site, we recommend users get the *full* download. This includes the correct version of all files in a single Zip file. The Zip file can be downloaded to any directory on the system.

JDeveloper does not include an installer. Instead, all files are stored in the Zip file and are placed in the correct directories when uncompressed. Unzipping the file installs the application. Once files are unzipped to a local directory, navigate to

```
$ cd JDEVELOPER_HOME/jdev
```

This directory includes the `readme.html` and `install.html` files. Refer to these documents for any additional steps required by your version of JDeveloper.

To start JDeveloper, execute `jdevw.exe` on Windows, or `jdev` on other platforms, in the `JDEVELOPER_HOME/jdev/bin` directory. If there are any problems launching JDeveloper, make certain the size of the Zip file on your system matches the number of bytes shown on the OTN site, and double-check the `install.html` and `readme.html` files for version-specific requirements.

Connecting to the Database

Many PL/SQL developers consider vi and Notepad development environments. If you are in that camp, JDeveloper might be a little overwhelming at first. The good news is that PL/SQL developers who are not going to jump right into Java can ignore many of the buttons and menu items in JDeveloper. Figure 2-2 shows the integrated development environment (IDE) for JDeveloper 10g (9.0.5.2).

In order to use the examples in this section, run the `CreateUser.sql` script available online with this book.

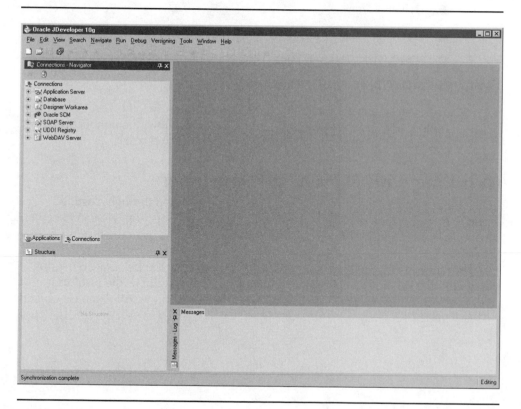

FIGURE 2-2. *The JDeveloper IDE*

Open JDeveloper and do the following to establish a connection to the database:

1. In the Connections – Navigator window (shown on the top-left side of the page in Figure 2-2), right-click the Database menu item, and click New Database Connection.

2. The first step of the connection wizard prompts for the Connection Name. Enter **PLSQL** and leave the Connection Type as Oracle (jdbc). Click Next.

3. The next screen prompts for the Username, Password, and Role. Enter **plsql** for the username and **oracle** for the password. Leave Role empty, and click Deploy Password. With Deploy Password checked, you will not need to reauthenticate when running PL/SQL against this instance.

4. The third step requires much of the same information as the `tnsnames.ora` entry we created earlier. Use the following settings and click Next.

   - **Driver** Thin
   - **Host** The machine name or IP address where the instance resides
   - **JDBC Port** The port name for the connection. The default is 1521
   - **SID** The name of the instance

5. The final step of the wizard tests the connection. Click the Test Connection button, and if it shows Success! in the Status window, the connection is good. If the connection fails, correct the settings and retest.

Working with PL/SQL in JDeveloper

JDeveloper provides the ability to create new code and step through existing code to debug. When provided with a valid database connection, we can execute the code in debug mode directly against the data server, so even the results can be verified.

Throughout this section we use the objects created by the `Debug.sql` script located in the online examples for this chapter. Run this script as the plsql user created by the `CreateUser.sql` script, also included online. All database objects created by Debug.sql can be seen in JDeveloper. Figure 2-3 shows the procedure AUTHOR_BOOKS_SEL.

Edit Stored Code

The procedure AUTHOR_BOOKS_SEL, as created by the Debug.sql script, does not successfully compile. Double-click the procedure name in the JDeveloper Connections window to load the procedure from the database. As shown in Figure 2-4, navigate to Run | Compile to compile the code.

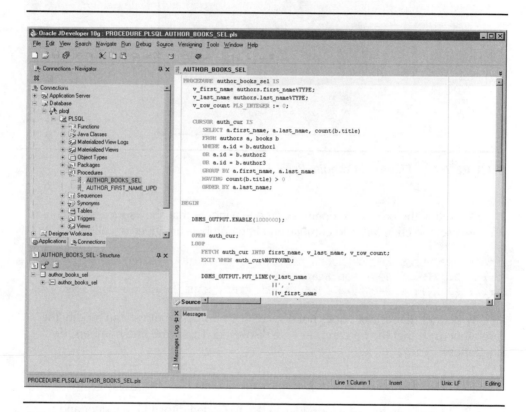

FIGURE 2-3. *The AUTHOR_BOOKS_SEL procedure*

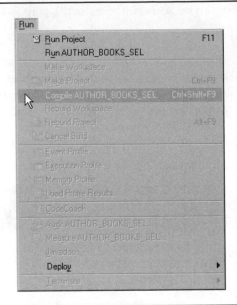

FIGURE 2-4. *Figure 4: Compile PL/SQL*

Compiling the procedure opens a Compile window that shows success or failure. In our case, the code failed to compile and line numbers are given as follows:

```
PROCEDURE.PLSQL.AUTHOR_BOOKS_SEL.pls
Error(22,7): PL/SQL: SQL Statement ignored
Error(22,27): PLS-00201: identifier 'FIRST_NAME' must be declared
```

By default, JDeveloper does not display line numbers, but we can modify the preferences so that the line numbers are displayed. To set the line numbers, do the following:

1. From the main menu (top of the screen), select Tools | Preferences.

2. In the Preferences window, navigate to Code Editor | Line Gutter and select Show Line Numbers.

3. Click OK to save the settings and return to the main window.

4. Verify that your screen looks like Figure 2-5.

The compile error shows line 22 is the problem, and the column numbers point to the variable named `first_name`. Change the variable name `first_name` to `v_first_name` and recompile. This should now result in the following message in the Compile window at the bottom of the screen:

```
Compiling...
[12:37:54 PM] Successful compilation: 0 errors, 0 warnings.
```

The change is saved to the database.

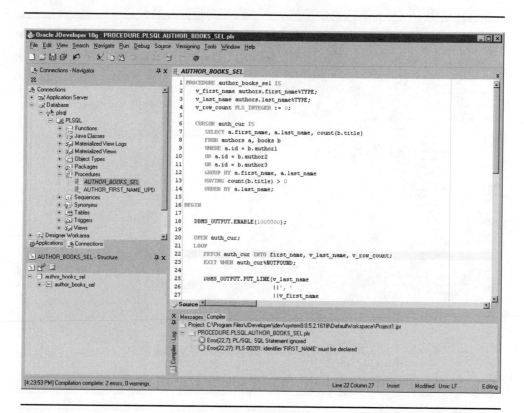

FIGURE 2-5.   *Compile error with line numbers*

Step Through PL/SQL Code

To debug PL/SQL, the user you are connected as must have the DEBUG CONNECT
SESSION and DEBUG ANY PROCEDURE user privileges. These privileges were
granted to the plsql user in the CreateUser.sql script for these examples.

Follow these steps to debug the AUTHOR_BOOKS_SEL procedure:

1. In the Connections Navigator, double-click the AUTHOR_BOOKS_SEL
   procedure.

2. Click directly on the number 22 to set a break point on the FETCH
   (see Figure 2-6).

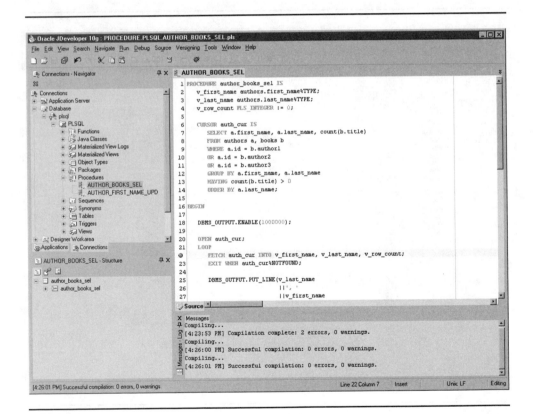

FIGURE 2-6. *A break point*

3. In the Connections Navigator window, right-click the AUTHOR_BOOKS_ SEL procedure and click Debug from the menu (see Figure 2-7).

4. When the Debug PL/SQL window opens, click OK. If any parameters were required for this procedure, you would be able to enter them here to fully test the code.

5. JDeveloper returns control back to the main window, and a new View is shown. The Smart Data window at the bottom right of Figure 2-8 displays the results of the fetch into variables. The main code window shows a blue line over the break point, indicating the code has completed up to that point but has not gone past it.

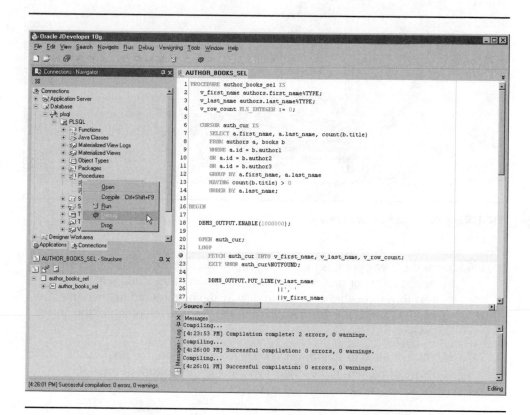

FIGURE 2-7.   *The Debug menu*

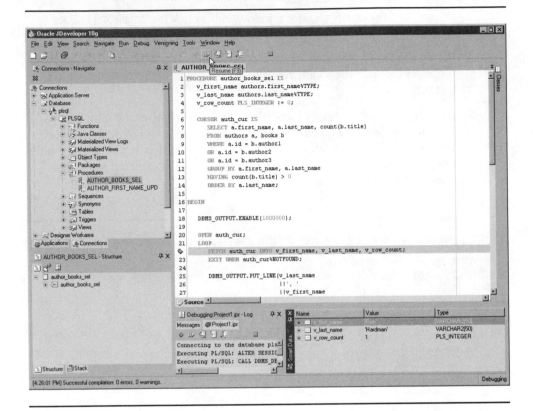

FIGURE 2-8. *Smart Data view*

6. Since the break point is inside the loop, if we resume (click the green arrow in the top menu or project window), execution of the code will break on its next turn through the loop and display the next record fetched into the variables. Compare Figures 2-8 and 2-9 to see the difference in the Smart Data view.

7. As you continue to step through code to completion, the final results of the code are displayed in the Project window at the bottom of the IDE.

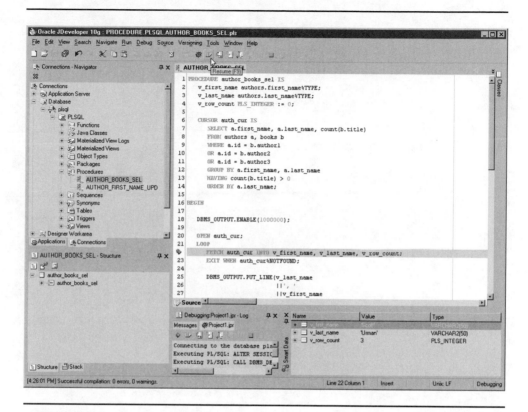

FIGURE 2-9.   *Step through code*

Summary

In this chapter we reviewed SQL*Plus, including connecting to an instance, different implementations of SQL*Plus, running scripts from files, and displaying output using the DBMS_OUTPUT package.

We also covered how to use JDeveloper with PL/SQL, including installation and configuration, editing code, and debugging features.

The next chapter covers PL/SQL Basics, including block structure, datatypes, PL/SQL expressions, and recommended programming styles.

CHAPTER
3

PL/SQL Basics

yntax and rules govern what you can and cannot do in PL/SQL. While following syntax and programming standards alone do not make a program good, failure to understand the rules of the language can certainly make a program bad. In this chapter, we discuss the basic principles of the language, including

- PL/SQL block structure

- Variable declarations

- Literals, characters, and reserved words

- Data types available for PL/SQL

- Wrapper utility to hide code

TIP
*If you are new to PL/SQL, learn the contents of this chapter
well before moving on to more advanced chapters.*

The PL/SQL Block

The basic program unit in PL/SQL is called a *block*. Blocks contain sets of instructions for Oracle to execute, display information to the screen, write to files, call other programs, manipulate data, and more. All PL/SQL programs are made of at least one block. Methods of implementation range from programs that executed one time only and are not stored anywhere, to blocks that are stored in the database for later use. Blocks support all DML statements, and using Native Dynamic SQL (NDS) or the built-in DBMS_SQL (see Appendix B for more information on DBMS_SQL), they can run DDL statements.

NOTE
*DML stands for Data Manipulation Language and
includes INSERT, UPDATE, and DELETE commands.
DDL stands for Data Definition Language and
includes ALTER, CREATE, DROP, TRUNCATE,
GRANT, and REVOKE commands.*

The Basic Structure

The minimum structure for a PL/SQL block is a BEGIN and an END with at least one executable command in between. The following block successfully compiles and runs, and is the most basic statement you can create:

```
BEGIN
    NULL;
END;
/
```

If we were to omit the NULL from the preceding statement, it would generate the following exception:

```
BEGIN
END;
/
END;
*
ERROR at line 2:
ORA-06550: line 2, column 1:
PLS-00103: Encountered the symbol "END" when expecting one of the following:
begin case declare exit for goto if loop mod null pragma
raise return select update while with <an identifier>
...
```

So, a block *must* contain some set of instructions, even if those instructions say to do nothing, or NULL. As shown in Figure 3-1, the section between the BEGIN and END commands is called the EXECUTION section. All types of PL/SQL blocks support two other optional sections; the DECLARATION and EXCEPTION sections. All three are discussed in detail next.

The Declaration Section

The DECLARATION section is optional. It is used to list the variables used in the block along with the types of data they support. Cursors (discussed in Chapter 4) are also declared in this section. This is the place where all local variables used in the program are defined and documented.

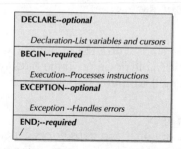

FIGURE 3-1. *Basic block*

The following declaration section lists variables that will be used later in the block, defines the type of data that will be stored in each variable, and in one case, initializes the variable:

```
-- Available online as part of BlockStructure.sql
DECLARE
    v_date_time TIMESTAMP;
...
```

The block begins with DECLARE, telling the PL/SQL compiler the type of code that comes next. The variable V_DATE_TIME is of type TIMESTAMP, so only compatible data can be stored in it.

The Execution Section

This section is the only one required. The contents must be complete to allow the block to compile. By complete, we mean that a complete set of instructions for the PL/SQL engine must be between the BEGIN and END keywords. As you saw earlier with an execution section of NULL, compiled code does not mean it must actually perform an action.

The execution section supports all DML commands and SQL*Plus built-in functions. It supports DDL commands using Native Dynamic SQL (NDS) and/or the DBMS_SQL built-in package.

The following example shows just the EXECUTION section of a block:

```
-- Available online as part of BlockStructure.sql
...
BEGIN
    -- Retrieve the timestamp into a variable
    SELECT systimestamp
    INTO v_date_time
    FROM dual;

    -- Display the current time to the screen
    DBMS_OUTPUT.PUT_LINE(v_date_time);
...
```

The EXECUTION section starts with BEGIN. In this example, the system time is retrieved and stored in the variable declared in the DECLARATION section. It is then displayed on the screen using the built-in package DBMS_OUTPUT.

The Exception Section

The EXCEPTION section is optional and traps errors generated during program execution. This section can trap for specific errors using functions provided in the STANDARD or DBMS_STANDARD packages or using EXCEPTION_INIT pragma statements (for an example of using the EXCEPTION_INIT pragma, see the CreateUser.sql script included online with this chapter). Chapter 7 covers exceptions in detail.

The following exception section uses WHEN OTHERS to trap any error and perform an action:

```
-- Available online as part of BlockStructure.sql
...
EXCEPTION
   WHEN OTHERS
   THEN
      DBMS_OUTPUT.PUT_LINE(sqlerrm);
END;
/
```

The action in this case was to display the error message to the screen.

Anonymous Blocks

Anonymous blocks are not given a name and are not stored in the database. They can call other programs, but they cannot be called themselves (how do you call something without a name!). Anonymous blocks use the basic structure shown in Figure 3-1. The next example is an anonymous block that performs a row count of the number of books each author has written, and displays the output to the screen.

> **NOTE**
> *All chapters in the book have user creation scripts and example files available online. The* CreateUser.sql *script in this chapter must be run as SYS or SYSTEM. Modify the script to set the tablespace values appropriately for your environment. Each example file can be run without dropping and re-creating the user. It cleans up after itself!*

```
-- Available online as part of AnonymousBlock.sql
SET SERVEROUTPUT ON

DECLARE

   -- variable declaration
   v_first_name authors.first_name%TYPE;
   v_last_name authors.last_name%TYPE;
```

```
   v_row_count PLS_INTEGER := 0;

   -- cursor declaration
   CURSOR auth_cur IS
      SELECT a.first_name, a.last_name, count(b.title)
      FROM authors a, books b
      WHERE a.id = b.author1
        OR a.id = b.author2
        OR a.id = b.author3
      GROUP BY a.first_name, a.last_name
      HAVING count(b.title) > 0
      ORDER BY a.last_name;

BEGIN

   -- start mandatory execution section
   DBMS_OUTPUT.ENABLE(1000000);

   -- open the cursor from the declaration section
   OPEN auth_cur;

   -- loop through all records retrieved by the cursor
   --  passing the values into the variables declared earlier
   LOOP
      FETCH auth_cur INTO v_first_name, v_last_name, v_row_count;
      EXIT WHEN auth_cur%NOTFOUND;

      -- send results from each record retrieved to the screen
      DBMS_OUTPUT.PUT_LINE(v_last_name
                           ||', '
                           ||v_first_name
                           ||' wrote '
                           ||v_row_count
                           ||' book(s).');
   END LOOP;

   -- close the cursor
   CLOSE auth_cur;

EXCEPTION

   -- start optional exception section
   WHEN OTHERS
      THEN
      -- print any errors to the screen
      DBMS_OUTPUT.PUT_LINE(SQLERRM);
END;
/
```

NOTE
The '--' preceding some of the text indicate inline comments. The text following the dashes is not used in the execution of the code. Comments are used to document the code. They are discussed later in this chapter, in the section titled "Documenting Code Using Comments."

This block does the following:

■ It declares three variables for use in the execution section.

■ It declares a cursor for use in the execution section (more about cursors in Chapter 4).

■ It executes the cursor SELECT statement when it is opened and loops through the results one line at a time.

■ It traps any errors that are thrown and prints the resulting error message to the screen.

This block used all three sections. While we could have removed the exception section with no ill effects on the code execution, any error messages that occurred during the execution of the block would have been a mystery. Unless we are just running an ad hoc block of code, we always prefer to include the exception section.

Running Anonymous Blocks

Anonymous blocks are not named and are not stored for execution. So, how is the code executed? An anonymous block of code can be run either from a file or by typing the code at the SQL> prompt. To run the last example from the file, do the following:

■ Save the script from its online location to your client or server (wherever you are connecting to SQL*Plus).

■ From the command prompt, cd to the directory where you saved the script.

■ Log in to SQL*Plus as the plsql user.

```
sqlplus plsql/oracle@<<your SID>>
```

■ Run the AnonymousBlock.sql script.

```
SQL> @AnonymousBlock.sql
```

The following is abbreviated output from the execution of the script:

```
Abbey, Michael wrote 3 book(s).
Abramson, Ian wrote 2 book(s).
Adkoli, Anand wrote 2 book(s).
Allen, Christopher wrote 1 book(s).
Armstrong-Smith, Darlene wrote 1 book(s).
Armstrong-Smith, Michael wrote 1 book(s).
Bo, Lars wrote 1 book(s).
Brown, Brad wrote 2 book(s).
Burleson, Donald wrote 2 book(s).
Carmichael, Rachel wrote 2 book(s).
Chang, Ben wrote 1 book(s).
Coekaerts, Wim wrote 1 book(s).
Corey, Michael wrote 3 book(s).
Cox, Kelly wrote 1 book(s).
Deshpande, Kirtikumar wrote 1 book(s).
Devraj, Venkat wrote 1 book(s).
Dorsey, Paul wrote 2 book(s).
Freeman, Robert wrote 3 book(s).
Gerald, Bastin wrote 1 book(s).
Haisley, Stephan wrote 1 book(s).
Hardman, Ron wrote 1 book(s).
Hart, Matthew wrote 2 book(s).
...
```

For additional examples of anonymous blocks, refer to the `CreateUser.sql` script included online with this chapter.

Named Blocks

Named blocks differ from anonymous blocks in the most obvious of ways: they are given a name. There are some other differences as well, of course, chief of which is the structure. The basic structure for a block shown earlier in the chapter provides no way to name the block or to distinguish a procedure from a function.

NOTE
Functions are named blocks that always return a value, while procedures may or may not return a value. Procedures and functions are covered in detail in Chapters 8 and 9.

Named blocks add a fourth section to the structure referred to as the HEADER section. The HEADER section tells Oracle the name of the block and whether the block is a procedure or a function; if it is a function, it declares the type of value it will be returning. When the block is run, it does not execute immediately. Instead, it is compiled and stored in the database for later use.

NOTE
Procedures and Functions are covered in detail in Chapter 8.

Here we modified the first part of the anonymous block shown earlier to be a named block:

```
-- Available online as part of NamedBlock.sql
CREATE OR REPLACE PROCEDURE Named_Block
AS
    v_first_name authors.first_name%TYPE;
    v_last_name authors.last_name%TYPE;
    v_row_count PLS_INTEGER := 0;
...
```

The header begins with PROCEDURE or FUNCTION and is followed by the object name. The DECLARATION section follows the AS keyword. The remainder of the block is the same as the anonymous block.

To execute the procedure, run it as follows:

```
-- Available online as part of NamedBlock.sql
exec named_block
```

This returns the same result set as the anonymous block.

Compile Errors

One big advantage of named blocks is that syntax-, dependency-, and permission-related errors are caught when the procedure or function is compiled instead of at execution time. The first time Oracle sees an anonymous block is at execution, so it cannot provide advanced warning of a problem. When a procedure or function is created, Oracle compiles the code and checks for dependencies and proper syntax. If there is a violation, it returns a message and the named block is marked as invalid.

The following example creates a stored procedure that references a table that does not exist:

```
-- Available online as part of CompileError.sql
CREATE OR REPLACE PROCEDURE Compile_Error
    AS
    v_timestamp timestamp;
BEGIN
    SELECT systimestamp
```

```
      INTO v_timestamp
    FROM duall;

  DBMS_OUTPUT.PUT_LINE(v_timestamp);
EXCEPTION
  WHEN OTHERS
  THEN
      DBMS_OUTPUT.PUT_LINE(SQLERRM);
END;
/
```

When this procedure creation is compiled, it returns the following message:

```
Warning: Procedure created with compilation errors.
```

To see the complete error message, type SHOW ERRORS at the SQL prompt.

```
SHOW ERRORS
```

The output shows the problem that was found, as well as the line and column that needs to be corrected.

```
-- Available online as part of CompileError.sql
Errors for PROCEDURE COMPILE_ERROR:
LINE/COL ERROR
-------- -------------------------------------------------
5/4      PL/SQL: SQL Statement ignored
7/11     PL/SQL: ORA-00942: table or view does not exist
```

To see the line of text that is causing the problem (line 7 in this case), we can query the USER|DBA|ALL_SOURCE view and retrieve the line number and text for that line.

```
-- Available online as part of CompileError.sql
SELECT line||' '||text PROCEDURE
FROM user_source
WHERE name = 'COMPILE_ERROR';
```

This returns the following:

```
PROCEDURE
------------------------------------------
1 PROCEDURE Compile_Error
2   AS
3     v_timestamp timestamp;
4 BEGIN
5   SELECT systimestamp
6   INTO v_timestamp
```

```
 7    FROM duall;
 8
 9    DBMS_OUTPUT.PUT_LINE(v_timestamp);
10 EXCEPTION
11    WHEN OTHERS
12    THEN
13       DBMS_OUTPUT.PUT_LINE(SQLERRM);
14 END;
```

From this we can see that line 7 (referred to in the output of SHOW ERRORS) has a typo with the table name, and we know what needs to be corrected.

The data dictionary view USER|DBA|ALL_OBJECTS shows that the procedure is marked as invalid.

```
-- Available online as part of CompileError.sql
COL object_name FORMAT A15
COL status FORMAT A10
SELECT object_name, status
  FROM user_objects
  WHERE object_name = 'COMPILE_ERROR';


OBJECT_NAME      STATUS
---------------  ----------
COMPILE_ERROR    INVALID
```

If we try to execute the procedure in this state, we get the following exception:

```
-- Available online as part of CompileError.sql
EXEC compile_error
BEGIN compile_error; END;
      *
ERROR at line 1:
ORA-06550: line 1, column 7:
PLS-00905: object PLSQL.COMPILE_ERROR is invalid
ORA-06550: line 1, column 7:
PL/SQL: Statement ignored
```

To fix the problem, correct the table name in the procedure creation script and rerun.

```
-- Available online as part of CompileError.sql
CREATE OR REPLACE PROCEDURE Compile_Error
   AS
   v_timestamp timestamp;
BEGIN
   SELECT systimestamp
     INTO v_timestamp
     FROM dual;
```

```
EXCEPTION
    WHEN OTHERS
    THEN
        DBMS_OUTPUT.PUT_LINE(SQLERRM);
END;
/
```

This time the procedure compiles.

```
Procedure created.
```

If we execute the procedure, it returns the correct results:

```
-- Available online as part of CompileError.sql
EXEC compile_error

04-JUN-04 09.16.52.206000 PM
PL/SQL procedure successfully completed.
```

The compile-time error saved us the trouble of diagnosing the problem when people needed to use the procedure, and provided some assurance that the procedure will work when used. Anonymous blocks do not provide this kind of assurance.

Compile-Time Warnings

A named block that compiles provides some level of comfort that our syntax does not violate any rules, and that dependent objects exist and are valid. It does not guarantee that the execution will go smoothly, or that our code is efficient.

Compile-time warnings provide additional feedback when named blocks are compiled (warnings are not available for anonymous blocks). They do not cause a named block to be marked invalid if a potential problem is identified, but they do provide feedback indicating a runtime problem may exist.

Warning Messages   Warning messages can be any of the following:

- **ALL**   This includes all available warning conditions and messages.

- **PERFORMANCE**   Only performance-related warnings are returned.

- **INFORMATIONAL**   This flags code that may not be useful to the program that can be moved or corrected. The condition is not performance related and will not generate an error. It is intended to assist developers in making code more maintainable.

- **SEVERE**   Problems identified as severe indicate there may be a problem with code logic.

- **Specific Error**   The warning can be specific to an error message.

It is possible to enable warnings by these categories for the compilation of a single named block, for all named blocks that are compiled in the current session, or for the entire instance. Individual warnings can also be configured to generate an error. This might be helpful during the development cycle in particular, to differentiate between warnings that you do not care about and messages that are more critical to the application. If a warning is treated as an error, the problem must be corrected before it can be compiled successfully.

PLSQL_WARNINGS Parameter   PLSQL_WARNINGS is an init.ora parameter used to set warning levels. The parameter can be set in the init.ora file, or at the SQL> prompt for each subprogram, the session, or the entire system. To see the current setting, log in as SYS or SYSTEM and type

```
SHOW PARAMETER PLSQL_WARNINGS
```

This displays the current setting for your system.

```
NAME                                   TYPE        VALUE
-------------------------------------- ----------- ----------------
plsql_warnings                         string      DISABLE:ALL
```

In the following example, we set the parameter in the init.ora file and bounced our instance:

```
PLSQL_WARNINGS='ENABLE:PERFORMANCE'
```

If we wanted to list multiple settings for PLSQL_WARNINGS, we simply provide a comma-delimited list:

```
PLSQL_WARNINGS='ENABLE:PERFORMANCE', 'ENABLE:SEVERE'
```

To set the parameter from the SQL> prompt for the system, type the following:

```
ALTER SYSTEM SET PLSQL_WARNINGS='ENABLE:PERFORMANCE', 'ENABLE:SEVERE';
```

After altering the system, we can type SHOW PARAMETER PLSQL_WARNINGS again and see the change reflected.

```
SQL> show parameter plsql_warnings
NAME                                   TYPE        VALUE
-------------------------------------- ----------- --------------------------
plsql_warnings                         string      DISABLE:INFORMATIONAL,
                                                   ENABLE:PERFORMANCE,
                                                   ENABLE:SEVERE
```

We are going to run a quick test to see if the warning message is generated on compilation. In this example, we create a procedure (a procedure is a form of named block discussed in Chapter 8) that inserts a record into the BOOKS table:

```
-- Available online as part of PLSQL_Warnings.sql
CREATE OR REPLACE PROCEDURE BOOK_INS (
    i_ISBN VARCHAR2,
    i_Category VARCHAR2,
    i_Title VARCHAR2,
    i_Num_Pages NUMBER,
    i_Price VARCHAR2,
    i_Copyright NUMBER,
    i_Author1 NUMBER,
    i_Author2 NUMBER,
    i_Author3 NUMBER)
IS
BEGIN

    INSERT INTO BOOKS (
        isbn, category, title, num_pages,
        price, copyright, author1, author2, author3)
    VALUES (
        i_ISBN, i_Category, i_Title, i_Num_Pages,
        i_Price, i_Copyright, i_Author1, i_Author2, i_Author3);

EXCEPTION
    WHEN OTHERS
    THEN
        DBMS_OUTPUT.PUT_LINE('Error: '||sqlerrm);
END;
/
```

The i_Price variable is of type VARCHAR2, and the PRICE column in the BOOKS table is of type NUMBER. While Oracle does an implicit conversion on INSERT, it is not optimal and takes additional processing. When this procedure is created in the PLSQL schema after PLSQL_WARNINGS has been set to 'ENABLE:PERFORMANCE', it generates a PERFORMANCE warning.

NOTE
If the same procedure creation script is rerun, no warning is delivered the second time. If the ALTER command is used to compile the procedure, the warning is given each time it is run.

```
-- Available online as part of PLSQL_Warnings.sql
SP2-0804: Procedure created with compilation warnings
```

```
Errors for PROCEDURE BOOK_INS:
LINE/COL ERROR
-------- -----------------------------------------------------------
14/4     PLW-07202: bind type would result in conversion away
         from column type
```

Even though the compilation shows there is a warning, the procedure is valid in the database, as can be seen with the following query:

```
-- Available online as part of PLSQL_Warnings.sql
COL object_name FORMAT A30
COL status FORMAT A10
SELECT object_name, status
  FROM user_objects
  WHERE object_name = 'BOOK_INS';


OBJECT_NAME                      STATUS
------------------------------   ----------
BOOK_INS                         VALID
```

If we determine that this warning should prevent our procedure from compiling, we can set the message number so that it is treated as an error rather than a warning. The following example includes the PLSQL_WARNINGS setting in the ALTER command and establishes that warning 07202 should be treated as an error:

```
ALTER PROCEDURE book_ins COMPILE PLSQL_WARNINGS='ERROR:07202';
```

Now instead of returning a warning, the compilation shows an error.

```
Warning: Procedure altered with compilation errors.
```

Now the procedure is marked as invalid until we fix the problem.

```
-- Available online as part of PLSQL_Warnings.sql
COL object_name FORMAT A30
COL status FORMAT A10
SELECT object_name, status
  FROM user_objects
  WHERE object_name = 'BOOK_INS';


OBJECT_NAME                      STATUS
------------------------------   ----------
BOOK_INS                         INVALID
```

DBMS_WARNING Package   Oracle 10*g*R1 introduced the DBMS_WARNING package that modifies the PLSQL_WARNINGS init.ora parameter. All of the settings available with PLSQL_WARNINGS can be used with the DBMS_WARNING package.

By modifying the PLSQL_WARNINGS parameter using the DBMS_WARNING package, we can control the level of debug and warning messages made available for our compiled code. The following example procedure compiles with no errors if DBMS_WARNING is set to DISABLE:ALL:

```
-- Available online as part of CompileWarning.sql
CALL DBMS_WARNING.SET_WARNING_SETTING_STRING('DISABLE:ALL', 'SESSION');

CREATE OR REPLACE PROCEDURE compile_warning
AS
    v_title VARCHAR2(100);
    CURSOR dbms_warning_cur
    IS
    SELECT title
    FROM books;
BEGIN
    OPEN dbms_warning_cur;
    LOOP
    FETCH dbms_warning_cur INTO v_title;
    -- there should be a line to exit here
    -- like: EXIT WHEN dbms_warning_cur%NOTFOUND;

    DBMS_OUTPUT.PUT_LINE('Titles Available: '||v_title);
    END LOOP;
    CLOSE dbms_warning_cur;
END;
/
```

This produces no errors when compiled even though it does have a problem. To get warnings for the procedure that may only be seen on execution, we can set the warning level as follows:

```
-- Available online as part of CompileWarning.sql
CALL DBMS_WARNING.SET_WARNING_SETTING_STRING('ENABLE:ALL', 'SESSION');
```

To see the warning level, we can call the GET_WARNING_SETTING_STRING function.

```
-- Available online as part of CompileWarning.sql
SELECT DBMS_WARNING.GET_WARNING_SETTING_STRING() WARNING_LEVEL
FROM dual;
```

This returns the correct results based on our setting:

```
-- Available online as part of CompileWarning.sql
WARNING_LEVEL
--------------
ENABLE:ALL
```

To test out the warning messages, recompile the same procedure.

```
-- Available online as part of CompileWarning.sql
ALTER PROCEDURE compile_warning COMPILE;

SP2-0805: Procedure altered with compilation warnings
```

Type **SHOW ERRORS** to see what the problem is.

```
-- Available online as part of CompileWarning.sql
SHOW ERRORS

Errors for PROCEDURE COMPILE_WARNING:
LINE/COL ERROR
-------- -----------------------------------------------------
24/4     PLW-06002: Unreachable code
```

If not for the warning message, we would not be aware of this problem until the procedure is executed.

Why would DBMS_WARNING be used instead of just changing the PLSQL_ WARNINGS parameter? We have started to use DBMS_WARNING in our build script, for example. There are times during the execution of the build where modifying system settings is not feasible, and session settings are lost on disconnect. We also do not want to turn the warning messages on for the entire build. Using DBMS_WARNING, we can easily toggle the parameter to whatever value we need as our scripts run.

Before moving on to the next section, we recommend you disable warnings again. If this step is missed, you will be wondering why code that previously compiled without any messages is now returning warning messages. To disable, run the following:

```
CALL DBMS_WARNING.SET_WARNING_SETTING_STRING('DISABLE:ALL', 'SESSION');
```

Also, make sure to disable the settings for the PLSQL_WARNINGS init.ora parameter.

TIP
Consider this part of your unit testing (everyone does unit testing, right?), and it will save time and aggravation for yourself and your testers.

Nested Blocks

Blocks can contain other sub-blocks. This is referred to as nesting and is allowed in the EXECUTION and EXCEPTION sections of the block. Nested blocks are not allowed in the DECLARATION section.

For the following example, we are creating an anonymous block with two nested blocks that are one level deep. The purpose of nesting in this case is to provide feedback regarding an exception should it occur, but continue to the second nested block even if the first SELECT statement causes an exception.

```
-- Available online as part of NestedBlock.sql
DECLARE
    v_author AUTHORS.FIRST_NAME%TYPE;
BEGIN
    -- the first nested block
    BEGIN
        SELECT first_name
        INTO v_author
        FROM authors
        WHERE UPPER(last_name) = 'HARTMAN';
    EXCEPTION
        WHEN NO_DATA_FOUND
        THEN
            DBMS_OUTPUT.PUT_LINE('EXCEPTION HANDLER for nested block 1');
            DBMS_OUTPUT.PUT_LINE('====================================');
            NULL;
    END;

    -- the second nested block
    BEGIN
        SELECT first_name
        INTO v_author
        FROM authors
        WHERE UPPER(last_name) = 'HARDMAN';
    EXCEPTION
        WHEN TOO_MANY_ROWS
        THEN
            DBMS_OUTPUT.PUT_LINE('====================================');
            DBMS_OUTPUT.PUT_LINE('EXCEPTION HANDLER for nested block 2');
            DBMS_OUTPUT.PUT_LINE('If this is printing, then the both nested');
            DBMS_OUTPUT.PUT_LINE('blocks'' exception handlers worked!');
    END;
END;
/
```

Let's take a closer look at what this example does, and how nesting benefits us in this scenario.

Both nested blocks have exception handlers. For the first nested block, we select an author name into a variable where the `last_name` for the author does not exist in the table. This results in no data being returned. When selecting into a variable, passing a null result set to the variable causes an `ORA-1403 no data found` exception. The built-in exception `NO_DATA_FOUND` helps us here, and we can trap that exception should it occur.

> **NOTE**
> *Variables are discussed in more detail later in this chapter in the section titled "Using Variables."*

For this code, we want to continue with the second statement should the first one fail. The exception section concludes with a `NULL` indicating that the exception should be ignored. Oracle continues to process the second statement as if nothing happened. If this were one big block instead, the failure would have happened on the first statement, causing all other code to be skipped.

Triggers

Triggers offer a unique implementation of PL/SQL. They are stored in the database but are not stored procedures or functions. Triggers are event driven and are attached to certain actions performed in the database.

For example, if an `AFTER UPDATE` trigger is created on the `AUTHORS` table and there is an update performed, the trigger will fire. PL/SQL that is written for that trigger will be executed. The following example is on the `AUTHORS` table and fires whenever the `FIRST_NAME` column is updated.

```
-- Available online as part of Trigger.sql
CREATE OR REPLACE TRIGGER author_trig
    AFTER UPDATE OF first_name
    ON authors
    FOR EACH ROW
WHEN (OLD.first_name != NEW.first_name)
BEGIN
    DBMS_OUTPUT.PUT_LINE('First Name '
                        ||:OLD.first_name
                        ||' has change to '
                        ||:NEW.first_name);
END;
/
```

Notice the `BEGIN` and `END` showing where the PL/SQL block is in relation to the trigger creation. This trigger sends a message to the screen using the built-in package

DBMS_OUTPUT whenever the FIRST_NAME column is updated in the AUTHORS table. To test the trigger, simply update the first name of one of the authors.

```
-- Available online as part of Trigger.sql
SET SERVEROUTPUT ON
UPDATE authors
SET first_name = 'Ronald'
WHERE first_name = 'Ron';
```

The trigger immediately fires and displays the following on the screen:

```
First Name Ron has change to Ronald
```

The trigger fired as expected, and the PL/SQL was executed.

NOTE
Triggers are discussed in detail in Chapter 10.

Object Types

PL/SQL began support for object-oriented programming (OOP) in version 8 of PL/SQL. Since then, a number of enhancements have been made that make PL/SQL a true object-oriented language. For a detailed discussion of OOP, see Chapters 14–16.

The essence of OOP is to make code abstract. In the model of a bookstore, a book is considered an object. Instead of writing application code to work directly against the data structures to find and manipulate information about books, it works through a predefined object called BOOKS. ATTRIBUTES to define what a book is, and METHODS perform actions on the book objects.

Methods

Methods work directly against the object's underlying data structures. Since object methods do the work, application developers simply pick and choose the methods they need for their application design and call the appropriate methods to do the job.

Language Rules and Conventions

PL/SQL includes rules and conventions just like any other languages. In this section, we take a look at lexical units (including identifiers, literals, special characters, reserved words, delimiters, white space, and comments) and using variables.

Lexical Units

Lexical units are the characters that make up PL/SQL text. Table 3-1 shows a valid string of characters and its lexical units.

We discuss the main components of PL/SQL Lexical Units in the following sections.

Identifiers

Identifiers provide a named reference to PL/SQL objects such as variables and cursors, and to database objects, including procedures, functions, and packages. The identifier allows the object to be referenced by name rather than by some Oracle internal reference.

Restrictions on identifier names include:

- Names must be 30 characters or less.

- Names *must* start with a letter.

- Names can contain the following characters as long as they are not the first character in the name: $, #, _, and any number.

- Names cannot contain punctuation, spaces, or hyphens.

TIP
PL/SQL is not case sensitive. Two identifiers with the same name but different case are the same, so use unique names, or unique prefixes for identifiers to avoid reusing the same name.

The following identifier names are valid:

```
My_Procedure
Variable1
cursor_#1
Function_4_$
```

Lexical Unit	Characters
Arithmetic symbols	+ - * / > < = **
ASCII letters	A–Z, a–z
Numbers	0–9
White space	Tab, Space, Carriage Return
Special characters	. ? ~ ! @ { } [ ] # $ % ^ & ( ) _ ,	: ; ' "

TABLE 3-1. *Lexical Units*

The following identifiers are not valid:

My-Procedure
1Variable
cursor #1
Function_@_name

Identifier names should be self-explanatory. There are 30 characters to work with, leaving plenty of space to create a descriptive name.

Quoted Identifiers   Identifiers can include nonstandard characters and spaces when they are enclosed in double quotes. The following *quoted identifiers* are supported:

```
"Susan's Procedure"
"Mine/Yours"
"Begin"
```

Quoted identifiers are case sensitive and can even include reserved words that are not otherwise allowed. We highly recommend against using these nonstandard identifiers. Unless working with an extreme situation where they are somehow required, they will only cause problems.

Special Characters   *Special characters* are identifiers that PL/SQL interprets as a command or that have some other special purpose. Using these characters in PL/SQL in a way that is contrary to their purpose will result in an error or incorrect processing of code.

To see a list of reserved characters for your version, run the following SELECT statement:

```
-- Available online as part of Reserved.sql
SET PAGES 9999

SELECT keyword
  FROM v_$reserved_words
  WHERE length = 1
  AND keyword != 'A'
  OR keyword = '<<';
```

You must run this script as SYSDBA or SYSOPER, as access to the view is not granted to PUBLIC.

Reserved Words   *Reserved words* are identifiers that Oracle sets aside for internal use. If they are used in application development, Oracle will interpret them as defined by Oracle, not according to your definition. This can cause some serious problems if the reserved words are used for purposes such as variable names.

We find the best way to avoid using a reserved word in variable declaration is to use naming conventions similar to those outlined at the end of this chapter. This way, even if a reserved word is used, it includes a prefix that allows Oracle to differentiate variable name from reserved word.

Just like the rest of Oracle and PL/SQL, reserved words change from release to release. Rather than reading a huge laundry list of words and characters in this section, run the following script in your database to get a list of all reserved words:

```
-- Available online as part of Reserved.sql
SET PAGES 9999
COL keyword FORMAT A30

SELECT keyword, length
  FROM v_$reserved_words
  WHERE (length > 1
  OR keyword = 'A')
  AND keyword != '<<'
  ORDER BY keyword;
```

You must run this script as SYSDBA or SYSOPER, as access to the view is not granted to PUBLIC. A list of reserved words for Oracle 10gR1 is available in Appendix A.

Delimiters

Delimiters are symbols used by Oracle for a special purpose. They act as separators, database link indicators, mathematical operators, and concatenation operators. Table 3-2 lists the delimiters available.

Delimiters are used in every example script created for this book, so to see them in action, look to any online script.

Delimiter	Description
+, –, *, /, **	Mathematical operators
..	Range operator, frequently used in for-loops
<, >, <>, =, !=, ~=, ^=, <=, >=	Relational operators (greater than, less than, etc.)
--, /*, */	Comment indicators (single line and multiline)
<<, >>	Label delimiters

TABLE 3-2. *Delimiters*

Delimiter	Description
%	Attribute indicator, used with TYPE, ROWTYPE, NOTFOUND, and other attributes
(,)	Expression delimiters, often used in the WHERE clause with AND and OR operators
:	Bind variable indicator—bind variables are used for performance reasons in PL/SQL to reduce the number of parses required for SQL where only the values of the variables change and not the structure of the SQL itself
,	Item separator—a comma separates lists whenever present in PL/SQL
'	Character string delimiter—strings or character literals between two single quotes are case sensitive
"	Quoted identifier delimiter—quoted identifiers are case sensitive and can contain spaces and special characters
@	Database link delimiter—in a SQL statement the string following this symbol is the database name that is linked to the current instance
;	Statement terminator, used at the completion of every statement or declaration in PL/SQL to signify the completion of the command
:=	Assignment delimiter—this delimiter initializes variables (to the left of the operator) with values (to the right of the operator)
=>	Association operator, used when calling a procedure or function, passing values to the parameters
||	Concatenation operator, combines the string on the left with the string on the right of the operator

TABLE 3-2. *Delimiters* (continued)

Literals

Literals are Character, String, Number, Boolean, and Date/Time values not represented by an identifier. The following sections detail the differences between each type of literal.

Character   *Character* literals are single characters in quotes. They are case sensitive and include any alphanumeric character or special character. Numbers that are treated as character literals (whenever they are in quotes) are not treated as numbers unless used in arithmetic and converted. Examples of character literals are

```
'C'   'c'   '1'   '%'   '~'
```

Character literals are similar to string literals except they are single-character.

String   String literals include all alphanumeric characters, special characters, and punctuation. One of the biggest areas of confusion we have witnessed teaching classes on PL/SQL is in the handling of apostrophes in a string literal. For example, the following string includes an apostrophe in one of the words:

```
-- Available online as part of StringLiteral.sql
SET SERVEROUTPUT ON
BEGIN
    DBMS_OUTPUT.PUT_LINE('Colorado's National Parks are BEAUTIFUL');
END;
/
```

This results in the following error:

```
ERROR:
ORA-01756: quoted string not properly terminated
```

The reason this fails is the handling of the apostrophe and the confusion regarding where the end of the string is. For all versions, a valid work-around for this is to use two single quotes (*not a double quote*), as follows:

```
-- Available online as part of StringLiteral.sql
BEGIN
    DBMS_OUTPUT.PUT_LINE('Colorado''s National Parks are BEAUTIFUL');
END;
/
```

This time the string successfully prints, and does so with a single apostrophe.

```
Colorado's National Parks are BEAUTIFUL
```

Oracle 10*g*R1 introduces a new way to handle the single-quote/double-quote problem when working with apostrophes. The new quoting syntax is q'[...]', where the brackets are the user-defined delimiters. The [] can be any character not present in the string literal. The string literal is placed between the user-defined delimiters. The following example shows a few ways to handle the apostrophe:

```
-- Available online as part of StringLiteral.sql
BEGIN
    DBMS_OUTPUT.PUT_LINE('Colorado''s National Parks are BEAUTIFUL');
    DBMS_OUTPUT.PUT_LINE(q'!Colorado's National Parks are BEAUTIFUL!');
    DBMS_OUTPUT.PUT_LINE(q'[Colorado's National Parks are BEAUTIFUL]');
```

```
    DBMS_OUTPUT.PUT_LINE(q'<Colorado's National Parks are BEAUTIFUL>');
    DBMS_OUTPUT.PUT_LINE(q'%Colorado's National Parks are BEAUTIFUL%');
END;
/
```

The output is shown here:

```
Colorado's National Parks are BEAUTIFUL
Colorado's National Parks are BEAUTIFUL
Colorado's National Parks are BEAUTIFUL
Colorado's National Parks are BEAUTIFUL
Colorado's National Parks are BEAUTIFUL
```

All of these are handled correctly.

Number   *Numeric* literals can be divided into integer values and real values. Integer values are whole numbers with no decimals. Real values are numbers with one decimal point. Both integer and real values can use scientific notation to represent the number.

Integer value examples:

```
1000
-5
+3
```

Integers can include signs indicating plus (+) or minus (–).

Real value examples:

```
1000.0
-5.
+3.1
```

Real values can also include signs indicating plus (+) or minus(–).

Scientific notation examples:

```
1.125E3
3.24e-4
-2.32E+5
```

The E (or e) in this type of notation indicates ten to the power of the number that follows. The preceding examples can be interpreted as follows:

```
1.125E3 = 1.125 times 10 to the 3rd power
        = 1.125 times 1000
```

```
         = 1125

3.24e-4 = 3.24 times 10 to the -4th power
        = 3.24 times .0001
        = 0.000324

-2.32E+5 = -2.32 times 10 to the 5th power
         = -2.32 times 100000
         = -232000
```

Globalization may require changes to the preceding examples. Reference the Globalization documentation at http://otn.oracle.com for detailed National Language Support (NLS) requirements for numeric literals.

Boolean TRUE, FALSE, and NULL are the *Boolean* values available in PL/SQL. We can declare a variable of type Boolean and assign the literal value to it. The following block demonstrates the use of Boolean literals:

```
-- Available online as part of BooleanLiteral.sql
SET SERVEROUTPUT ON
DECLARE
    v_true BOOLEAN := TRUE;
    v_false BOOLEAN := FALSE;
    v_null BOOLEAN := NULL;
BEGIN
    IF v_true
    THEN
        DBMS_OUTPUT.PUT_LINE('true');
    END IF;

    IF v_false
    THEN
        DBMS_OUTPUT.PUT_LINE('false');
    END IF;

    IF v_null
    THEN
        DBMS_OUTPUT.PUT_LINE('null');
    END IF;
END;
/
```

This returns the following to the screen:

```
true
```

This example shows a few important aspects of Boolean literals and variables:

- The Boolean literals are not in quotes. They are not strings. In fact, if the assignment of the value to the Boolean variable had strings, it would result in the following exception:

  ```
  PLS-00382: expression is of wrong type
  ```

- Boolean variables, when combined with an IF-THEN block, do not need to be provided with a comparison value if only comparing to TRUE. If they are comparing to FALSE or NULL, a value must be provided in the comparison. For example, the following two IF-THEN statements are identical:

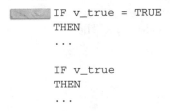

```
IF v_true = TRUE
THEN
...

IF v_true
THEN
...
```

NOTE
IF-THEN procedural constructs are discussed in detail later in this chapter in the section titled "IF-THEN-ELSE."

Date/Time   *Date/Time* literals include four different data types:

- DATE
- TIMESTAMP
- TIMESTAMP WITH TIMEZONE
- TIMESTAMP WITH LOCAL TIMEZONE

The following example demonstrates the Date/Time literals:

```
-- Available online as part of DateTimeLiteral.sql
SET SERVEROUTPUT ON
DECLARE
    v_date DATE := DATE '2004-06-05';
    v_timestamp TIMESTAMP := TIMESTAMP '2004-06-05 22:14:01';
    v_timestamp_tz TIMESTAMP WITH TIME ZONE :=
              TIMESTAMP '2004-06-05 22:14:01 +06:00';
```

```
    v_timestamp_ltz TIMESTAMP WITH LOCAL TIME ZONE :=
                TIMESTAMP '2004-06-05 22:14:01';
BEGIN
    DBMS_OUTPUT.PUT_LINE(v_date);
    DBMS_OUTPUT.PUT_LINE(v_timestamp);
    DBMS_OUTPUT.PUT_LINE(v_timestamp_tz);
    DBMS_OUTPUT.PUT_LINE(v_timestamp_ltz);
END;
/
```

This example prints the following:

```
05-JUN-04
05-JUN-04 10.14.01.000000 PM
05-JUN-04 10.14.01.000000 PM +06:00
05-JUN-04 10.14.01.000000 PM
```

DATE and TIMESTAMP types are discussed in greater detail in the section titled "PL/SQL Data Types."

Documenting Code Using Comments

Documentation is not just for technical writers. Good programming requires two kinds of code documentation with every program written.

The first and easiest type of documentation is referred to as self-documentation. Self-documentation means that, just by looking at the code, anyone should be able to determine what is being done by the identifier names chosen. For example, a procedure that updates book prices might be called BOOK_PRICE_UPD. This leaves very little doubt as to what that procedure does.

The second type of documentation is a comment that describes the program or statement. The comments are written in the program either as single-line or multiline documentation. Single-line and multiline comments are set apart from the rest of the program by delimiters, so the PL/SQL engine effectively ignores them.

In Line Comments   Inline comments begin with a double-hyphen (single-line comment delimiter). The comment begins after the hyphens and includes a single line of text only. If a second line is required, the next line must also include the delimiter at the beginning. The following example shows two single-line comments in an anonymous block:

```
-- Available online as part of SingleLineComment.sql
DECLARE
    v_price BOOKS.PRICE%TYPE;
BEGIN
```

```
    -- Retrieve the price of a book into a local variable
    SELECT price
    INTO v_price
    FROM books
    WHERE isbn = '72230665';

    DBMS_OUTPUT.PUT_LINE('The original price for isbn 72230665 was: '
         ||v_price);

    -- Discount the price by 10 percent
    v_price := v_price * .9;

    -- Update the price in the books table to reflect the discount
    UPDATE books
    SET price = v_price
    WHERE isbn = '72230665';

    DBMS_OUTPUT.PUT_LINE(CHR(0)); -- This outputs a blank line
    DBMS_OUTPUT.PUT_LINE('The discounted price for isbn 72230665 is: '
         ||v_price);

EXCEPTION
    WHEN OTHERS
        THEN DBMS_OUTPUT.PUT_LINE (SQLERRM);
END;
/
```

Take note of the comment placed after the statement. Single-line comments do not require their own line. The comment begins with the double-hyphen delimiter, even if that is part way through the line, and extends to the end of the line.

TIP
Single-line hyphens are great for commenting out lines of code for testing.

Multiline Comments   Multiline comments use '/*' as a beginning comment delimiter and '*/' as an ending comment delimiter. The comments span multiple lines or paragraphs. Multiline comments are great for including headers or version control notes in the PL/SQL directly. Multiline comments can be used for

- Header information in the PL/SQL object
- Header information for scripts (see the headers in the example scripts for this chapter)

- Commenting out blocks of code. This is useful for test purposes, or to effectively remove the code while still leaving it for future use should it be required

- Code documentation, especially comments that extend beyond single lines

The following example comments out a block of code that is not needed and includes a reference to the date it was removed:

```
-- Available online as part of MultiLineComment.sql
SET SERVEROUTPUT ON
DECLARE
    v_price BOOKS.PRICE%TYPE;
BEGIN

    SELECT price
    INTO v_price
    FROM books
    WHERE isbn = '72230665';
    DBMS_OUTPUT.PUT_LINE('The original price for isbn 72230665 was: '
        ||v_price);

/*

    v_price := v_price * .9;

    UPDATE books
    SET price = v_price
    WHERE isbn = '72230665';

    DBMS_OUTPUT.PUT_LINE(CHR(0));
    DBMS_OUTPUT.PUT_LINE('The discounted price for isbn 72230665 is: '
        ||v_price);
*/

EXCEPTION
    WHEN OTHERS
        THEN DBMS_OUTPUT.PUT_LINE (SQLERRM);
END;
/
```

This is great for debugging or for adding comments when it is known that the text will exceed one line.

Character Spacing and White Space

Do not skimp on the white space! We're not saying to double-space all of your code, but use a reasonable amount of space (lines, tabs, spaces, and so on) to separate code. Nested blocks, IF-THEN blocks, LOOPs, and other types of programming constructs that are logically separate from other code should be physically separated in the code for clarity.

Spacing and indentation is another separator that makes code much more readable. Take the following example:

```
-- Available online as part of WhiteSpace.sql
DECLARE
v_first_name authors.first_name%TYPE;
v_last_name authors.last_name%TYPE;
v_row_count PLS_INTEGER := 0;
CURSOR auth_cur IS
SELECT a.first_name, a.last_name, count(b.title)
FROM authors a, books b
WHERE a.id = b.author1
OR a.id = b.author2
OR a.id = b.author3
GROUP BY a.first_name, a.last_name
HAVING count(b.title) > 0
ORDER BY a.last_name;
BEGIN
DBMS_OUTPUT.ENABLE(1000000);
OPEN auth_cur;
LOOP
FETCH auth_cur INTO v_first_name, v_last_name, v_row_count;
EXIT WHEN auth_cur%NOTFOUND;
DBMS_OUTPUT.PUT_LINE(v_last_name||', '||v_first_name||' wrote '||v_row_
count||' book(s).');
END LOOP;
CLOSE auth_cur;
EXCEPTION
WHEN OTHERS
THEN
DBMS_OUTPUT.PUT_LINE(SQLERRM);
END;
/
```

Now, multiply the number of lines of code by ten and imagine maintaining this. Making code readable does not need to be a difficult task. There are tools like Formatter Plus and PL/Formatter that provide automated indentation and line spacing. These tools can format entire projects so that there is consistency from one file to the next, and they can do it much quicker than you can by hand.

Even if automated formatting tools are not possible, it is still important to make code readable and consistent with the use of white space. Put yourself in the shoes of the person that will eventually maintain your code, because it just might be you!

PL/SQL Data Types

In this section, we discuss data types used with PL/SQL. These types should not be confused with database types. In most cases, capabilities and limitations between database and PL/SQL types are identical, but some have dramatically different storage capabilities that can pop up to bite you.

PL/SQL data types can be broken down into the following categories:

- Scalar
- Reference
- Composite
- LOB

The Scalar category is broken down further into subcategories, or families of types. The next few sections discuss each category, subcategory, and PL/SQL data type.

Scalar

A *Scalar* type is a data type that holds a single value. Scalar types can be broken down into subcategories, or families, that include

- Character/String
- Number
- Boolean
- Date/Time

We'll review each of these in detail in the following sections.

Character/String

PL/SQL character or string types include everything from single character values to large strings up to 32K in size. These types can store letters, numbers, and binary data, and they can store any character supported by the database character set. They all define their precision as an integer with units in bytes (the default setting of bytes can be changed, as you will see in the next section on "Character Semantics") at the time the variable is declared.

Character Semantics

Character/string types define precision, or storage, with an integer. The number provided actually specifies the number of bytes allowed rather than the number of characters. Prior to Oracle 9i, this was a real problem when working with multibyte characters. It was possible that a variable precision of 2 could not even handle a single three-byte Asian character. Oracle introduced character semantics in 9i to solve this problem.

Character semantics can be specified for the system using the NLS_LENGTH_SEMANTICS init.ora parameter, or for each variable in the declaration. The following example shows a normal declaration of a variable of type VARCHAR2:

```
DECLARE
    v_string VARCHAR2(10);
```

By default, this declaration means that the variable v_string can store up to ten bytes. Here we modified the declaration to use character semantics:

```
DECLARE
    v_string VARCHAR2(10 CHAR);
```

The addition of the CHAR to the precision means that the v_string variable will now store up to ten characters, regardless of the number of bytes per character.

Character/String Types

Table 3-3 lists scalar types and offers a description of each type.

Type	Description
CHAR	Fixed-length character data type. The precision is specified as an integer. Storage is in bytes rather than characters by default. Use character semantics to override.
LONG	The LONG PL/SQL type is different than the LONG database type. It is a variable-length type with a limit of 32K (32,760 bytes). It is possible for a column of type LONG to not fit in a variable of type LONG. Because of the difference between the PL/SQL and database types, use of the LONG PL/SQL type is limited.
LONG RAW	LONG RAW holds binary data up to 32K (32,760 bytes). Just like the LONG type, the LONG RAW differs in size restriction between PL/SQL type and database type. It is possible for a column of type LONG RAW to not fit in a variable of type LONG RAW. Because of the difference between the PL/SQL and database types, use of the LONG RAW PL/SQL type is limited.

TABLE 3-3. *Character Types*

Type	Description
NCHAR	NCHAR holds fixed-length national character data. It is identical to the CHAR type but takes on the character set specified by the National Character Set.
NVARCHAR2	NVARCHAR2 holds variable-length character data. It is identical to the VARCHAR2 type, but takes on the character set specified by the National Character Set.
RAW	The RAW type stores fixed-length binary data and can hold up to 32K (32,760 bytes). The RAW type for the database can hold only 2K, so the problem is the opposite of that experienced with the LONG and LONG RAW types. If a RAW variable holds more than 2K, it cannot insert it into the database column of the same type.
ROWID	Every record in a table contains a unique binary value called a ROWID. The rowid is an identifier of the row in the table. The PL/SQL type is the same and stores the ROWID of a database record without conversion to a character type. The ROWID type supports physical rowids, but not logical rowids.
UROWID	UROWID supports both physical and logical rowids. Oracle recommends using the UROWID PL/SQL type when possible.
VARCHAR	VARCHAR is an ANSI-standard SQL type, synonymous with VARCHAR2. Oracle recommends VARCHAR2 be used to protect against future modifications to VARCHAR impacting code.
VARCHAR2	The VARCHAR2 PL/SQL data type can store up to 32K (32,767) bytes in Oracle 10g. The database VARCHAR2 type can store only 4K. This can be a problem, of course, when a variable of type VARCHAR2 holds data that exceeds 4K and attempts to insert the contents into a database column of type VARCHAR2.

TABLE 3-3. *Character Types* (continued)

TIP
LONG and LONG RAW types, while still supported, are not advantageous to use. Instead, migrate legacy applications to a LOB type. LONG types can be converted to CLOBs, while LONG RAW types can be converted to BLOBs. For more information on how to migrate LONG and LONG RAW data to CLOBs and BLOBs, see Chapter 16.

Number Types

Number types include basic integer data types that hold whole numbers, the new-to-10*g* BINARY_FLOAT and BINARY_DOUBLE types that are intended primarily for complex calculations, and basic number data types that support real numbers. Table 3-4 shows the most common number types and provides a description of each.

Type	Description
BINARY_DOUBLE	New to 10gR1, BINARY_DOUBLE is an IEEE-754 double-precision floating-point type. This type is generally used for scientific calculations where its performance gains can be seen.
BINARY_FLOAT	Also new to 10gR1, the BINARY_FLOAT type is a single-precision floating-point type. Like BINARY_DOUBLE, this type is generally used for scientific calculations where its performance gains can be seen.
BINARY_INTEGER	This type has a range of –2147483647 to +2147483647. Storage is in a two's complement binary format (hence the binary in the name). This type is used when a whole number will not be stored in the database but will be used in arithmetic operations.
NUMBER	The NUMBER PL/SQL type is identical to the database NUMBER type. This type can hold floating-point values or integers. Total maximum precision is 38, which is its default if no precision is declared. Since NUMBER accepts floating-point values as well, the declaration can include a scale, or number of digits to the right of the decimal. The scale can range from –84 to 127. NUMBER is discussed in greater detail later in this section.
PLS_INTEGER	PLS_INTEGER supports values from –2147483647 to +2147483647. Subtypes include NATURAL, NATURALN, POSITIVE, POSITIVEN, and SIGNTYPE. For new application development, Oracle recommends the use of PLS_INTEGER over BINARY_INTEGER. Just as with the BINARY_INTEGER type, use PLS_INTEGER when the value stored in it will be used within the context of the block but will not be stored in the database.

TABLE 3-4. *Number Types*

Aside from the new BINARY_DOUBLE and BINARY_FLOAT types, number types have not changed since before Oracle 8*i*. This consistency will make converting applications to 10g much easier.

NUMBER Data Type

The NUMBER data type supports both integer and floating-point values. The precision for integers is easily defined, but setting precision and scale is often a point of confusion when working with floating-point values. Let's take a look at how to handle decimal places when defining precision and scale for floating-point values. Precision and scale are defined as

- Precision—The number of total digits allowed for the value. The maximum precision for the NUMBER type is 38.

- Scale—The number of digits allowed to the right of the decimal place (if scale is positive), or number of digits to round to the left of the decimal place (if scale is negative). Scale can range from –84 to 127.

In this example, we have an anonymous block that pulls values from a table called PRECISION and prints how each variable handles the assignment. If you wish to test other assignments, simply insert the records into the precision table and modify the following block of code:

```
-- Available online as part of Number.sql
SET SERVEROUTPUT ON
DECLARE
    v_integer NUMBER(5);
    v_scale_2 NUMBER(5,2);
    v_real NUMBER;

    CURSOR scale_0_cur
    IS
        SELECT value
        FROM precision
        WHERE scale = 0;

    CURSOR scale_2_cur
    IS
        SELECT value
        FROM precision
        WHERE scale = 2;
BEGIN
    DBMS_OUTPUT.PUT_LINE('====== PRECISION 5 SCALE 0 =====');
    OPEN scale_0_cur;
```

```
     -- Loop through all records that have a scale of zero
     LOOP
     FETCH scale_0_cur INTO v_real;
     EXIT WHEN scale_0_cur%NOTFOUND;

     -- Assign different values to the v_integer variable
     --  to see how it handles it
     BEGIN
        DBMS_OUTPUT.PUT_LINE('===================');
        DBMS_OUTPUT.PUT_LINE('Assigned: '||v_real);

        v_integer := v_real;
        DBMS_OUTPUT.PUT_LINE('Stored: '||v_integer);
     EXCEPTION
        WHEN OTHERS
        THEN
           DBMS_OUTPUT.PUT_LINE('Exception: '||sqlerrm);
     END;
     END LOOP;
     CLOSE scale_0_cur;

     DBMS_OUTPUT.PUT_LINE('==================================');
     DBMS_OUTPUT.PUT_LINE('====== PRECISION 5 SCALE 2 =====');
     OPEN scale_2_cur;

     -- Loop through all records that have a scale of 2
     LOOP
     FETCH scale_2_cur INTO v_real;
     EXIT WHEN scale_2_cur%NOTFOUND;

     -- Assign different values to the v_scale_2 variable
     --  to see how it handles it
     BEGIN
        DBMS_OUTPUT.PUT_LINE('===================');
        DBMS_OUTPUT.PUT_LINE('Assigned: '||v_real);

        v_scale_2 := v_real;
        DBMS_OUTPUT.PUT_LINE('Stored: '||v_scale_2);
     EXCEPTION
        WHEN OTHERS
        THEN
           DBMS_OUTPUT.PUT_LINE('Exception: '||sqlerrm);
     END;
     END LOOP;
     CLOSE scale_2_cur;
END;
/
```

This block shows the following results given current seeded values in the
`PRECISION` table.

```
====== PRECISION 5 SCALE 0 =====
Assigned: 12345
Stored: 12345

Assigned: 123456
Exception: ORA-06502: PL/SQL: numeric or value error:
     number precision too large

Assigned: 123.45
Stored: 123

====== PRECISION 5 SCALE 2 =====
Assigned: 12345
Exception: ORA-06502: PL/SQL: numeric or value error:
     number precision too large

Assigned: 123.45
Stored: 123.45

Assigned: 12.345
Stored: 12.35

Assigned: 1234.5
Exception: ORA-06502: PL/SQL: numeric or value error:
     number precision too large
```

Notice the assigned value of 12.345 to a variable of precision 5 and scale 2 is
rounded, not truncated. If scale were negative, the number would be rounded
to the left of the decimal by the number of digits specified by scale.

Boolean

The Boolean Scalar category includes a single type called BOOLEAN. Boolean
accepts values of TRUE, FALSE, and NULL. When assigning one of these three
values to a variable of type BOOLEAN, do not use quotes. If quotes are used,
they cause an error condition:

```
-- Available online as part of Boolean.sql
DECLARE
    v_boolean BOOLEAN;
BEGIN
    v_boolean := 'TRUE';
END;
```

```
      /
        v_boolean := 'TRUE';
                       *
ERROR at line 4:
ORA-06550: line 4, column 17:
PLS-00382: expression is of wrong type
ORA-06550: line 4, column 4:
PL/SQL: Statement ignored
```

BOOLEAN types are discussed later in this chapter in the section titled "IF-THEN-ELSE."

Date/Time

Date/Time PL/SQL types include the DATE, TIMESTAMP, and INTERVAL types. They are identical to the database data types of the same names. The next few sections discuss them in much greater detail.

DATE

The DATE PL/SQL type stores the century, year, month, day, hour, minute, and second. No fractional seconds are available. Dates can be converted between Character types and the DATE type using TO_DATE and TO_CHAR built-in functions. Using these functions, date formatting can be adjusted to include or exclude relevant date/time details and to show the time in either 12-hour or 24-hour increments.

TIMESTAMP Types

There are three PL/SQL types that fall under the heading of TIMESTAMP:

- TIMESTAMP

- TIMESTAMP WITH TIMEZONE

- TIMESTAMP WITH LOCAL TIMEZONE

TIMESTAMP   The TIMESTAMP type provides for date/time storage much like the DATE type, except that TIMESTAMP provides subsecond times up to nine digits (the default is six). If we were accessing a database in New York at 17:00 EST, TIMESTAMP would show us the value retrieved from the database server, or 17:00. The following example illustrates the use of TIMESTAMP:

```
-- Available online as part of Timestamp.sql
SET SERVEROUTPUT ON
```

```
DECLARE
    v_datetime TIMESTAMP (9) := SYSTIMESTAMP;
BEGIN
    DBMS_OUTPUT.PUT_LINE(v_datetime);
END;
/
```

This returns the following result:

```
05-JUN-04 06.51.47.051000000 PM
```

There are nine digits beyond the second because we set precision to the maximum value of 9.

TIMESTAMP WITH TIME ZONE   This PL/SQL type returns the date/time in the same format as TIMESTAMP, but it includes the local timestamp relative to UTC (formerly GMT). We can determine the local time relative to UTC this way. In this example, TIMESTAMP WITH TIME ZONE is used:

```
-- Available online as part of Timestamp.sql
SET SERVEROUTPUT ON
DECLARE
    v_datetime TIMESTAMP (3) WITH TIME ZONE := SYSTIMESTAMP;
BEGIN
    DBMS_OUTPUT.PUT_LINE(v_datetime);
END;
/
```

This returns a slightly different result than TIMESTAMP:

```
05-JUN-04 07.03.46.926 PM -07:00
```

Only three digits to the right of the second spot are shown. In addition, a –07.00 is returned, indicating our machine is seven hours behind UTC.

TIMESTAMP WITH LOCAL TIME ZONE   The last date/time PL/SQL type also returns data in the same format as the TIMEZONE type, but it returns the time corresponding to the location of the client accessing the data server. For example, if we were accessing a database server in New York from Denver at 17:00 EST, TIMESTAMP WITH LOCAL TIME ZONE would show us the time as 15:00, matching the time zone setting of our client.

The following example illustrates TIMESTAMP WITH LOCAL TIME ZONE:

```
-- Available online as part of Timestamp.sql
SET SERVEROUTPUT ON
```

```
DECLARE
   v_datetime TIMESTAMP (0) WITH LOCAL TIME ZONE := SYSTIMESTAMP;
BEGIN
   DBMS_OUTPUT.PUT_LINE(v_datetime);
END;
/
```

This results in:

```
05-JUN-04 07.15.48 PM
```

Note that precision was set to zero, so there are no digits to the right of the second.

Interval

An INTERVAL type comes in two varieties: INTERVAL YEAR TO MONTH and INTERVAL DAY TO SECOND. Both types provide the difference between two dates, but do so in years/months or days/seconds.

The following example uses INTERVAL YEAR TO MONTH to calculate the amount of time I have before my daughter leaves for college:

```
-- Available online as part of Interval.sql
DECLARE
   v_college_deadline TIMESTAMP;
BEGIN
   v_college_deadline := TO_TIMESTAMP('06/06/2004', 'DD/MM/YYYY')
                         + INTERVAL '12-3' YEAR TO MONTH;

   DBMS_OUTPUT.PUT_LINE('My daughter leaves for college in '
                        ||v_college_deadline);
END;
/
```

This returns the following result:

```
My daughter leaves for college in 06-SEP-16 12.00.00.000000
```

In this example, I added '12-3', or 12 years 3 months to today's date. I was only able to be accurate within a month using the INTERVAL YEAR TO MONTH. I can use the INTERVAL DAY TO SECOND type to get it a bit more accurate.

```
-- Available online as part of Interval.sql
DECLARE
   v_college_deadline TIMESTAMP;
BEGIN
   v_college_deadline := TO_TIMESTAMP('06/06/2004', 'DD/MM/YYYY')
                         + INTERVAL '12-3' YEAR TO MONTH
```

```
                                    + INTERVAL '19 9:0:0.0' DAY TO SECOND;

        DBMS_OUTPUT.PUT_LINE('My daughter leaves for college in '
                              ||v_college_deadline);
    END;
    /
```

I added 19 days and 9 hours to the time shown previously, and it displays
as follows:

```
My daughter leaves for college in 25-SEP-16 09.00.00.000000 AM
```

TIP
*Would I use INTERVAL instead of other ways to
calculate dates? Yes, especially if I need precision
down to subsecond times. I probably would not use
this all of the time, however. There are still occasions
where using MONTHS_BETWEEN and the TO_DATE
function is just quicker to write than using INTERVAL.*

Composite

Composite types differ from Scalar types in that they have internal components. They
can contain multiple scalar variables that are referred to as attributes. Composite
types include records, nested tables, index-by tables, and varrays. These are
covered in detail in the following chapters:

- **Records**   Chapter 5
- **Nested Tables, Index-By Tables, Varrays**   Chapter 6

Object Types

Object types are a unique composite type. While they can contain multiple scalar
variables like other composite types, they also include subprograms referred to as
methods. For more information on Object types, refer to Chapters 14–16.

Reference

Oracle includes two PL/SQL types in the *Reference* category, called REF CURSOR
and REF. Reference types differ from other types primarily in the way they handle
memory and storage. Reference types provide memory structures, but unlike Scalar
and Composite types, they can point to different storage locations throughout the
program.

REF CURSOR

A variable of type REF CURSOR is referred to as a *cursor* variable. We can define a cursor variable as type SYS_REFCURSOR and retrieve a record set from a procedure or function. SYS_REFCURSOR is a weakly typed REF CURSOR type that was provided with PL/SQL beginning with Oracle 9iR1.

The following example is a simple procedure that returns a record set from the AUTHORS table:

Available as part of Ref_Cursor.sql
```
CREATE OR REPLACE PROCEDURE authors_sel (
    cv_results IN OUT SYS_REFCURSOR)
IS
BEGIN
    OPEN cv_results FOR
    SELECT id, first_name, last_name
    FROM authors;
END;
/
```

To test the procedure, run it as follows:

```
-- Available online as part of Ref_Cursor.sql
VARIABLE x REFCURSOR
EXEC authors_sel(:x)
PRINT x
```

This returns the contents of the AUTHORS table.

```
        ID FIRST_NAME
---------- ------------
LAST_NAME
----------------------
         1 Marlene
Theriault
         2 Rachel
Carmichael
         3 James
Viscusi
...
```

Chapter 4 expands on the coverage of cursor variables in the section titled "Cursors."

REF

REFs are used with Object types. Think of a REF value simply as a pointer to an object instance in an object table or object view. For a detailed explanation of REFs, refer to Chapter 15.

LOB

Oracle provides LOB (*large object*) data types to work with binary and character data up to 4 gigabytes in database releases prior to Oracle 10g. In 10gR1, LOBs can store from 8 to 128 terabytes, depending on the block size of the database and its use. Aside from storage capabilities, LOBs provide another great advantage over LONG and LONG RAW types: the data stored in LOBs can be manipulated piecewise, where LONG and LONG RAW must be manipulated in their entirety. Chapter 16 addresses LOBs in much greater detail.

Using Variables

Variables are memory regions used in a PL/SQL block to hold data. They are defined in the DECLARATION section of the block, where they are assigned a specific data type and are often initialized with a value. The syntax for declaring a variable is

variable_name [CONSTANT] type [NOT NULL] [:= value];

Variable_name is the name you give to the variable. Type is the data type the variable needs to support. Value is used to initialize a variable.

The following example shows some different ways to declare variables:

```
DECLARE
    v_first_name VARCHAR2(50);
    v_author_count PLS_INTEGER := 0;
    v_date DATE NOT NULL DEFAULT SYSDATE;
...
```

The declaration of type 'AUTHORS.LAST_NAME%TYPE' is an anchored type that takes on whatever data type is assigned to the AUTHORS.LAST_NAME column.

A variable can also be made constant, or unchanging from its initial value, as defined in the DECLARATION section. The following example creates a variable as a constant and then tries to change the value in the EXECUTION section:

```
-- Available online as part of Variables.sql
DECLARE
    v_first_name CONSTANT VARCHAR2(50) := 'Ron';
BEGIN
    v_first_name := 'Ronald';
EXCEPTION
    WHEN OTHERS
    THEN
```

```
        DBMS_OUTPUT.PUT_LINE(SQLERRM);
END;
/
```

This fails on execution with the following:

```
    v_first_name := 'Ronald';
    *
ERROR at line 4:
ORA-06550: line 4, column 4:
PLS-00363: expression 'V_FIRST_NAME' cannot be used as an assignment target
ORA-06550: line 4, column 4:
PL/SQL: Statement ignored
```

Variable names can be any identifier. See the section titled "Identifiers" for the name restrictions of variables.

%TYPE

If the variable we are declaring maps directly to a column in the database, we can anchor our variable type to the database type given to that column with %TYPE. The declaration look like this:

```
DECLARE
    v_last_name AUTHORS.LAST_NAME%TYPE;
...
```

AUTHORS is the table name, and LAST_NAME is the column name. If the AUTHORS.LAST_NAME column is VARCHAR2(50), then our v_last_name variable is of the same type.

This is especially handy when data types change. If we have to make a change to the column precision, all variables anchored to that column automatically change with it. If the declaration were not anchored and the variables were of type VARCHAR2(50), we would have to make the same change to all objects individually. Using anchored types, the adjustment is automatic.

%ROWTYPE

%ROWTYPE is similar to %TYPE in that it anchors a variable to the table it is tied to. %ROWTYPE anchors the variable to all columns in the table, though, not just one. The following example declares a variable as AUTHORS.%ROWTYPE, declaring that the record should take on the attributes of a row in the AUTHORS table.

```
DECLARE
    v_author AUTHORS%ROWTYPE,
...
```

The variable v_author has the following definition based on this declaration:

```
id            NUMBER(38)
first_name    VARCHAR2(50)
last_name     VARCHAR2(50)
```

When any of the column data types are modified, the change will be reflected in the structure of the variable the next time it is run or compiled.

Variable Scope

Scope refers to accessibility and availability of a variable within a block. Variables are available only as long as they are in scope. A variable declared in a block, for example, is local to that block only. It is a local variable. When variables are no longer in scope, the memory used for them is released, and they can no longer be used until they are once again declared and initialized.

Figure 3-2 shows that a variable declared in a nested block is not available in the outer block. Its scope is limited to the nested block. The variables declared in the outer block, however, are available for use in the nested block.

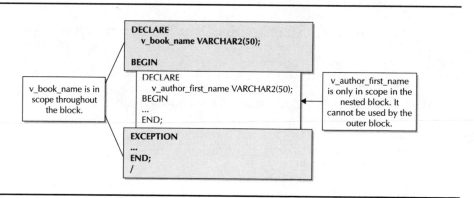

FIGURE 3-2. *Variable scope*

Variable Visibility

It is possible for a variable that is in scope to not be visible in the current block. This happens when a nested block declares a variable by the same name, causing the new definition to be visible and the old one to be hidden. Take the following example:

```
-- Available online as part of Visibility.sql
SET SERVEROUTPUT ON
DECLARE
    v_visible VARCHAR2(30);
    v_hidden VARCHAR2(30);
BEGIN
    v_visible := 'v_visible in the outer block';
    v_hidden := 'v_hidden in the outer block';

    DBMS_OUTPUT.PUT_LINE('*** OUTER BLOCK ***');
    DBMS_OUTPUT.PUT_LINE(v_visible);
    DBMS_OUTPUT.PUT_LINE(v_hidden);
    DBMS_OUTPUT.PUT_LINE('================');

    DECLARE
        v_hidden NUMBER(10);
    BEGIN
        DBMS_OUTPUT.PUT_LINE('*** INNER BLOCK ***');
        v_hidden := 'v_hidden in the inner block';
        DBMS_OUTPUT.PUT_LINE(v_hidden);
    EXCEPTION
        WHEN OTHERS
        THEN
            DBMS_OUTPUT.PUT_LINE('v_hidden of type VARCHAR2 was...hidden');
    END;
END;
/
```

Executing this anonymous block returns the following result:

```
*** OUTER BLOCK ***
v_visible in the outer block
v_hidden in the outer block

*** INNER BLOCK ***
v_hidden of type VARCHAR2 was...hidden
```

The v_hidden variable of type VARCHAR2 was hidden in the inner block. Oracle provides a way around this by using a label. Labels are markers, allowing us to refer to an outer block in this case, or to use a GOTO statement should we require. They use the << and >> delimiters and can be used inside programs, or just before them, as you will see in our next example. Here we add a label just before the DECLARE:

```
-- Available online as part of Visibility.sql
SET SERVEROUTPUT ON
<<l_outer_block>>
DECLARE
    v_visible VARCHAR2(30);
    v_hidden VARCHAR2(30);
BEGIN
    v_visible := 'v_visible in the outer block';
    v_hidden := 'v_hidden in the outer block';

    DBMS_OUTPUT.PUT_LINE('*** OUTER BLOCK ***');
    DBMS_OUTPUT.PUT_LINE(v_visible);
    DBMS_OUTPUT.PUT_LINE(v_hidden);
    DBMS_OUTPUT.PUT_LINE('==============');

    DECLARE
        v_hidden NUMBER(10);
    BEGIN
        DBMS_OUTPUT.PUT_LINE('*** INNER BLOCK ***');
        l_outer_block.v_hidden := 'v_hidden in the inner block';
        DBMS_OUTPUT.PUT_LINE(l_outer_block.v_hidden);
    EXCEPTION
        WHEN OTHERS
        THEN
            DBMS_OUTPUT.PUT_LINE('v_hidden of type VARCHAR2 was...hidden');
    END;
END;
/
```

This time, we used a label to qualify our variable name so that the PL/SQL engine knew we were trying to use the variable in the outer block.

Bind Variables

Queries go through three main phases when they are run: PARSE, EXECUTE, and FETCH. In the PARSE phase, a statement is broken down into a hash value, and both the query itself (letter-for-letter syntax) and the hash value of the statement are compared with other recently run queries to determine if the statement matches any of them. If it does, Oracle skips the process of generating an execution (explain) plan because it has already done the work. If it does not match any of them, Oracle creates a new set of execution plans, determines the cost of each, and chooses what it believes to be the lowest-cost plan for accessing the required data.

The following queries are treated as different queries by Oracle:

```
-- Available online as part of BindVariables.sql
ALTER SESSION SET SQL_TRACE = TRUE;
SELECT last_name
```

```
FROM authors
WHERE first_name = 'Ron';

SELECT last_name
FROM authors
WHERE first_name = 'Mike';
ALTER SESSION SET SQL_TRACE = FALSE;
```

The difference can be seen in the tkprof:

```
SELECT last_name
FROM authors
WHERE last_name = 'Ron'

call      count       cpu     elapsed
-------  ------   --------  ----------
Parse        1       0.00        0.00
Execute      1       0.00        0.00
Fetch        1       0.00        0.00
-------  ------   --------  ----------
total        3       0.00        0.00

SELECT last_name
FROM authors
WHERE last_name = 'Mike'

call      count       cpu     elapsed
-------  ------   --------  ----------
Parse        1       0.00        0.00
Execute      1       0.00        0.00
Fetch        1       0.00        0.00
-------  ------   --------  ----------
total        3       0.00        0.00
```

NOTE
The tkprof utility is shipped with the data server. It can be found in the $ORACLE_HOME/bin directory. To generate the tkprof file, locate the trace file created in the udump directory on your machine, and tkprof as follows:

`tkprof trace_name.trc tkprof_filename.txt explain=system`

where `trace_name.trc` *is the name of the trace file that was generated, and* `tkprof_filename.txt` *is what you want to call the tkprof file.*

The queries are identical, except for the value being used in the WHERE clause. The solution? We can use bind variables in place of hard-coded values so that Oracle sees the statements as identical during the PARSE phase. With bind variables, the preceding queries might be written as

```
SELECT last_name
FROM authors
WHERE first_name = :v;
```

When a value is assigned to variable 'v', it is done so after the execution plan is already generated, and we have saved time. To run the preceding query, do the following:

```
-- Available online as part of BindVariables.sql
ALTER SESSION SET SQL_TRACE = TRUE;
VARIABLE v VARCHAR2(10)
BEGIN
    :v := 'Ron';
END;
/

SELECT last_name
FROM authors
WHERE first_name = :v;
```

Without logging out of our session, if we change the value assigned to the variable and rerun the select, we get a new result.

```
-- Available online as part of BindVariables.sql
BEGIN
    :v := 'Mike';
END;
/

SELECT last_name
FROM plsql.authors
WHERE first_name = :v;

ALTER SESSION SET SQL_TRACE = FALSE;
```

The tkprof output shows the query once even though it was run twice.

```
SELECT last_name
FROM authors
WHERE first_name = :v
```

call	count	cpu	elapsed
Parse	1	0.00	0.00
Execute	1	0.00	0.00
Fetch	2	0.00	0.00
total	4	0.00	0.00

Take notice of the count values: 1 Parse, 1 Execute, and 2 Fetches. Also note the bind variable represented in the query shown in the trace.

Local Variables and Binds

When a block assigns a value to a variable and that variable is used in the query, it is treated as a bind variable. Take the following example using a named block:

```
-- Available online as part of BindVariables.sql
CREATE OR REPLACE PROCEDURE bind_test (
    i_author_first_name IN AUTHORS.FIRST_NAME%TYPE)
IS
    v_author_last_name AUTHORS.LAST_NAME%TYPE;
BEGIN
    SELECT last_name
    INTO v_author_last_name
    FROM authors
    WHERE first_name = i_author_first_name;

    DBMS_OUTPUT.PUT_LINE(i_author_first_name
                        ||' has a last name of '
                        ||v_author_last_name);
EXCEPTION
    WHEN OTHERS
    THEN
        DBMS_OUTPUT.PUT_LINE(sqlerrm);
END;
/
```

This named block takes a first name in as a parameter and uses that in the WHERE clause. Let's take a look at what happens when it is run multiple times with different names.

```
-- Available online as part of BindVariables.sql
ALTER SESSION SET SQL_TRACE = TRUE;
EXEC bind_test('Ron')
EXEC bind_test('Mike')
ALTER SESSION SET SQL_TRACE = FALSE;
```

The tkprof shows the following result:

```
SELECT last_name
    FROM authors
    WHERE first_name = :b1

call      count        cpu      elapsed
-------  ------    --------   ----------
Parse         1      0.00         0.00
Execute       2      0.00         0.00
Fetch         2      0.00         0.00
-------  ------    --------   ----------
total         4      0.00         0.00
```

The local variable is shown as :b1, a bind variable. The statement is present only one time in the tkprof, so on the second execution Oracle recognized that it was the same statement, even though the value passed to the parameter was different.

Cursor Sharing

Oracle 8*i* introduced the init.ora parameter CURSOR_SHARING. This setting determines how exact a query needs to be in order to be treated as identical to a previously parsed query. The available settings are

■ **EXACT**   The default setting, this requires that the syntax (including literals) be identical.

■ **SIMILAR**   Provides for some differences in SQL statement literals, but the differences cannot be enough to modify the statement's purpose or the execution plan.

■ **FORCE**   This setting is like the SIMILAR setting, but it is a bit more lax in that it allows the differences between statements to impact the execution plan or optimization. Using this setting, our first two statements with literals would only show up once in a tkprof.

While this sounds great, keep in mind that it adds overhead to the processing of queries. Anytime Oracle must rewrite a query, it takes away from other processing that can be taking place. If you plan to use this setting, we recommend you only do so until the code can be changed to use binds.

Hiding Code

One thing you may have noticed with all of the examples is that they are viewable and can be easily modified. This suits our needs perfectly for this book, but as application developers we do not always want our code displayed to the world when writing an application. In some cases, the features are proprietary and we need to protect the intellectual capital that is invested in them. In other cases, we simply want to prevent the code from being modified by the user in order to avoid problems down the road.

Oracle provides a way to hide code with the PL/SQL Wrapper utility. When source code has been wrapped, not only is the file unreadable, but also when it is loaded into the database, the code cannot be read in the data dictionary.

The wrapper utility does not encrypt the code. Instead, it converts it to hexadecimal digits so that it cannot be read or edited. To run the utility, use the following syntax:

```
wrap iname=input_file.sql oname=output_file.plb
```

where `wrap` is the name of the utility found at ORACLE_HOME/bin, *input_file*.sql is the source file, and *output_file.plb* is the destination file. The following example is the source file:

```
-- Available online as part of WrapBefore.sql
CREATE OR REPLACE PROCEDURE author_book_count
AS
    v_first_name authors.first_name%TYPE;
    v_last_name authors.last_name%TYPE;
    v_row_count PLS_INTEGER := 0;

    CURSOR auth_cur IS
        SELECT a.first_name, a.last_name, count(b.title)
        FROM authors a, books b
        WHERE a.id = b.author1
        OR a.id = b.author2
        OR a.id = b.author3
        GROUP BY a.first_name, a.last_name
        HAVING count(b.title) > 0
        ORDER BY a.last_name;

BEGIN
    DBMS_OUTPUT.ENABLE(1000000);

    OPEN auth_cur;
    LOOP
        FETCH auth_cur INTO v_first_name, v_last_name, v_row_count;
        EXIT WHEN auth_cur%NOTFOUND;

        DBMS_OUTPUT.PUT_LINE(v_last_name
                            ||', '
                            ||v_first_name
```

```
                                ||' wrote '
                                ||v_row_count
                                ||' book(s).');
      END LOOP;
      CLOSE auth_cur;
EXCEPTION
      WHEN OTHERS
          THEN
          DBMS_OUTPUT.PUT_LINE(SQLERRM);
END;
/
```

To hide this code, cd to the directory where the source file resides and type the following:

```
wrap iname=WrapBefore.sql oname=WrapAfter.plb
```

The following is displayed on execution:

```
PL/SQL Wrapper: Release 10.1.0.2.0- Production on Tue Jul 06 22:37:34 2004
Copyright (c) 1993, 2004, Oracle. All rights reserved.
Processing WrapBefore.sql to WrapAfter.plb
```

The converted file appears here:

```
-- Available online as part of WrapAfter.plb
CREATE OR REPLACE PROCEDURE author_book_count wrapped
a000000
b2
abcd
abcd
abcd
abcd
abcd
abcd
abcd
abcd
abcd
abcd
abcd
abcd
abcd
abcd
abcd
7
3bc 21b
aobxOtpNeS716UcMqnjDRDT7FFIwgwIJ2SdqfC+KMQ8tnC/9X6GDui6eP35+zJMK8sAcSYRr
```

sBzheWucz88BOvNJIfRnyt6Agoyz8umIiw3mWide8ScJUbEbjKMElrMcpn7sKl6DIWYmOchK
3ICCA5wEv2dBcQbUtz5Zs2Fepvoyakav4ZR6ZHDzEmJmCo0bQ1ermDmLz7Rr9wvJyliFB594
GEaPEXMhZUe4dJL29uk9j+fxL4NJJ1r4/GHbM4Hz2ThE3nfupxAtDVKHQjSjQvzVAlGj5kWd
uQNbp/pA9AYVgjTd4ImFedFKETQntvItcBVEjbCNSE3fwt/zGBRDfZYfSDZM8RTMX61F0q33
duA1t423iQJrA3LLsCSr3LViuYi4xlkTmqELG4XYYhS70pZ6gzG4G1BPL/5LqsYIVyg4P/1/
Ms8HmT+dyyQs/r3GvxmGEiR2InO7yuxb0fOOvtmxeXHvxyVX+ppqTEAlfNOHsTDhhbQz/ZIF
4pU7tNL9gGPFCsljBgckntJVaw==

/

To test the converted file, first run the seed script.

```
SQL>@WrapSeed.sql
```

Next, run the wrapped file.

```
SQL> @wrapafter.plb

Procedure created.
```

Even though the code is unreadable, it compiles without error.

Expressions

Expressions are a composite of operators and operands. In the case of a mathematical expression, the operand is the number and the operator is the symbol such as + or – that acts on the operand. The expression value is the evaluated total of the operands using the operators.

Here is a simple expression:

```
1 + 2
```

The operands are the values 1 and 2, and the operator is the +. The evaluated total of 3 is the value of the expression. An expression always returns one, and only one, value.

To extend this to PL/SQL, operands can be numbers just as in the last example or any combination of literals, constants, or variables. Operators are divided into categories that describe the way they act upon operands.

- Comparison operators are binary, meaning they work with two operands. Examples of comparison operators are the *greater than (>)*, less than (<), and equal (=) signs, among others.

- Logical operators include *AND*, OR, and NOT.

- Arithmetic operators include *addition/positive (+),* subtraction/negative (–), multiplication (*), and division (/).

- The assignment operator is specific to PL/SQL and is written as *colon-equal (:=)*. This is discussed in greater detail in the text that follows.

- The lone character operator is a *double pipe (||)* that joins two strings together, concatenating the operands. This is discussed in greater detail in the text that follows.

- Other basic SQL operators include *IS NULL*, IN, and BETWEEN.

Two of these categories warrant additional coverage in the context of this book because they are of particular use to PL/SQL.

Assignment Operator

The assignment operator is specific to PL/SQL. Its primary function is to set a variable equal to the value or expression on the other side of the operator. If we wanted to set the variable v_price equal to 54.95 * .90, we would write it as follows:

```
v_price := 54.95 * .9;
```

An assignment can take place in the declaration section when a variable is first declared, or in the execution or exception sections at any time. For example, to declare the variable v_price, we would write

```
DECLARE
    v_price books.price%TYPE;
...
```

The variable is not yet initialized, and its value is NULL. To initialize the variable to zero, we can use the assignment operator in the declaration section as follows:

```
DECLARE
    v_price books.price%TYPE := 0;
...
```

In the execution section, the assignment operator is used for assigning constants, literals, other variables, or expressions to a variable. Another use is to assign a function call to a variable where the return value of the function is ultimately stored. With the introduction of Native Dynamic SQL (NDS), we often use an assignment operator to store the command we will execute to a variable, and then pass the variable to the EXECUTE IMMEDIATE command. This improves the readability of the code.

```
...
BEGIN
    EXECUTE IMMEDIATE ('CREATE TABLE authors(id NUMBER PRIMARY KEY,  first_name
```

```
VARCHAR2(50), last_name  VARCHAR2(50))');
...
```

Using the assignment operator, we can rewrite this as

```
...
BEGIN
    v_string := 'CREATE TABLE authors(id NUMBER PRIMARY KEY,  first_name
VARCHAR2(50), last_name  VARCHAR2(50))';

    EXECUTE IMMEDIATE (v_string);
...
```

This becomes even more of an issue as the statements become larger and more NDS commands are used. NDS is discussed in detail in Chapter 13.

Concatenation Operator

To further improve the readability of the last example, we can combine the assignment operator with a character operator that concatenates two strings, values, or expressions together. The earlier example can be rewritten as

```
...
BEGIN
    v_string := 'CREATE TABLE authors('
                ||'id NUMBER PRIMARY KEY, '
                ||'first_name VARCHAR2(50), '
                ||'last_name  VARCHAR2(50))';

    EXECUTE IMMEDIATE (v_string);
...
```

Ultimately, Oracle sees no difference between this example and the one shown earlier, but it does improve the readability of the code.

Concatenation goes beyond this example, of course, to include all of its uses with SQL. For more information on the concatenation operator, or any other operator, and how they work with SQL, please see the *Oracle Database SQL Reference* on the OTN web site.

Controlling Program Flow

PL/SQL programs run sequentially, from the top of the block to the bottom, unless acted upon by a control structure. Like many other third-generation languages, PL/SQL provides the ability to divert code execution in accordance with certain conditions, execute code repeatedly until a condition is met, or jump to various sections of the block as needed.

The control structures described in this section are divided into three categories.

- **Conditional evaluation**   Run code only if certain conditions are met.

- **Circular execution**   Run code repeatedly until some end-point is reached.

- **Sequential navigation**   Jump to different sections of the block.

These control structures give PL/SQL much of its power and flexibility. In the remainder of this section we will demonstrate each control structure and discuss scenarios where each is used.

Conditional Evaluation

Conditional evaluation refers to the ability to process a portion of code depending on whether certain criteria are met. We use conditional evaluation for activities every day. IF it is raining outside, THEN get an umbrella, ELSIF it is sunny outside, get sunscreen, ELSE get outside ASAP and enjoy the day.

Using this type of logic in PL/SQL gives the programmer control over what code gets run and under what conditions it is run. In the `CreateUser.sql` script for this chapter we use conditional evaluation to test whether the PLSQL user exists or not. If it does exist, then drop it. If it does not exist, continue with the user creation.

IF-THEN
The most basic conditional evaluation is an IF-THEN statement. IF a condition is met, THEN do something. Implicit with this logic is IF a condition is not met, skip the code that follows and continue with the rest of the program.

The syntax for an IF-THEN statement is

IF *condition*
THEN
 action;
END IF;

The *condition* can be any expression, variable, constant, or identifier compared to any other expression, variable, constant, or identifier. The condition must evaluate to TRUE, FALSE, or NULL.

If a *condition* is met (evaluates to TRUE), an action is performed. The action can be any valid statement, or even another nested IF-THEN statement. If separate exception handling is required inside the IF-THEN section, a nested block can be used. If a condition is not met (evaluates to FALSE or NULL), the action is skipped.

The following example demonstrates the use of the basic IF-THEN logic:

```
-- Available online as part of If.sql
DECLARE
    v_count NUMBER(10) := 0;
BEGIN
    SELECT count(1)
    INTO v_count
    FROM authors
    WHERE id = 54;

    IF v_count = 0
    THEN
        INSERT INTO authors
        VALUES (54, 'Randy', 'Stauffacher');
    END IF;
    COMMIT;
EXCEPTION
    WHEN OTHERS
    THEN
        DBMS_OUTPUT.PUT_LINE(SQLERRM);
END;
/
```

The *condition* being tested here is whether a record exists in the AUTHORS table with an ID of 54. If one does not exist, INSERT the record. If the *condition* in this case evaluates to FALSE, then do nothing.

IF-THEN-ELSE

Using IF-THEN logic, a condition that evaluates to FALSE or NULL does nothing. The program is skipped. IF-THEN-ELSE adds another layer to the logic, allowing us to specify what to do if the condition evaluates to FALSE or NULL. The syntax is

IF *condition*
THEN
 action;
ELSE
 action
END IF;

Modifying the last example to use ELSE, we can write

```
-- Available online as part of If.sql
SET SERVEROUTPUT ON
```

```
DECLARE
    v_count PLS_INTEGER := 0;
BEGIN
    SELECT COUNT(1)
    INTO v_count
    FROM authors
    WHERE id = 55;

    IF v_count = 0
    THEN
        INSERT INTO authors
        VALUES (54, 'Roger', 'Wootten');
        DBMS_OUTPUT.PUT_LINE('Added author');
    ELSE
        DBMS_OUTPUT.PUT_LINE('Author already exists');
    END IF;
    COMMIT;
EXCEPTION
    WHEN OTHERS
    THEN
        DBMS_OUTPUT.PUT_LINE(SQLERRM);
END;
/
```

Now, if the record does exist and the condition evaluates to FALSE, a message is printed to the screen letting us know that the author already exists in the table.

IF-THEN-ELSIF

The previous two examples are great for single-condition statements, but not all logic falls into such concise terms. For example, if we wanted to modify a book's price, but the percentage discount depends on the price of the book, we might require multiple IF-THEN statements. This is highly inefficient, since all IF statements must be evaluated even if one of them has already evaluated to TRUE.

Oracle provides a way to chain IF conditions together so that if one is met, the rest are assumed to be false and are skipped. The syntax is as follows:

IF *condition*
THEN
 action
ELSIF condition
THEN
 action
[ELSE
 action]
END IF;

Take special note that the term is ELSIF, not ELSEIF. Also, ELSE can optionally be included at the end to handle all conditions not met by the prior evaluations.

In this example, we query the books table, retrieving the price of the book into a variable. We will then use the price in an IF-THEN-ELSIF evaluation to determine the discount to apply:

```
-- Available online as part of If.sql
SET SERVEROUTPUT ON
DECLARE
    v_price books.price%TYPE;
    v_isbn books.isbn%TYPE := '72230665';
BEGIN
    SELECT price
    INTO v_price
    FROM books
    WHERE isbn = v_isbn;

    DBMS_OUTPUT.PUT_LINE('Starting price: '||v_price);

    IF v_price < 40
    THEN
        DBMS_OUTPUT.PUT_LINE('This book is already discounted');
    ELSIF v_price BETWEEN 40 AND 50
    THEN
        v_price := v_price - (v_price * .10);

        UPDATE books
        SET price = v_price
        WHERE isbn = v_isbn;
    ELSIF v_price > 50
    THEN
        v_price := v_price - (v_price * .15);

        UPDATE books
        SET price = v_price
        WHERE isbn = v_isbn;
    END IF;

    DBMS_OUTPUT.PUT_LINE('Ending price: '||v_price);
    ROLLBACK;
EXCEPTION
    WHEN OTHERS
    THEN
        DBMS_OUTPUT.PUT_LINE(SQLERRM);
        ROLLBACK;
END;
/
```

Since the price is more than 50.00, the first two conditions evaluate to FALSE, and the price is updated in the final ELSIF section to have a 15 percent discount.

CASE

CASE, introduced in Oracle 9*i,* provides a different approach to conditional evaluation. It simplifies the syntax a bit by requiring the condition to be passed only one time. The syntax is

CASE *expression*
  WHEN test1 THEN action;
  WHEN test2 THEN action;
  ...
END CASE;

In this example, we determine the discount to apply by testing the category of a book:

```
-- Available online as part of Case.sql
SET SERVEROUTPUT ON
DECLARE
    v_category books.category%TYPE;
    v_discount NUMBER(10,2);
    v_isbn books.isbn%TYPE := '72230665';
BEGIN
    SELECT category
    INTO v_category
    FROM books
    WHERE isbn = v_isbn;

    -- Determine discount based on category
    CASE v_category
    WHEN 'Oracle Basics'
       THEN v_discount := .15;
    WHEN 'Oracle Server'
       THEN v_discount := .10;
    END CASE;

    DBMS_OUTPUT.PUT_LINE('The discount is '
                         ||v_discount*100
                         ||' percent');
EXCEPTION
    WHEN OTHERS
    THEN
        DBMS_OUTPUT.PUT_LINE(SQLERRM);
END;
/
```

This works just like an IF-THEN-ELSIF statement as long as only the book falls into those two categories. Unlike an IF-THEN-ELSIF statement, however, CASE throws an exception if unable to evaluate the condition to TRUE. For example, If we update ISBN 72230665 to be in a category called 'Oracle Programming', the code would return an error.

```
-- Available online as part of Case.sql
UPDATE books
SET category = 'Oracle Programming'
WHERE isbn = '72230665';
COMMIT;
```

Now rerun the CASE statement and the following error is returned:

```
ORA-06592: CASE not found while executing CASE statement
```

This is resolved by adding ELSE to handle all cases that are not evaluated explicitly. For example, the prior CASE statement can be rewritten as

```
...
    CASE v_category
    WHEN 'Oracle Basics'
        THEN v_discount := .15;
    WHEN 'Oracle Server'
        THEN v_discount := .10;
    ELSE v_discount := .5;
    END CASE;
...
```

Now the code completes without error.

Searched CASE

Searched CASE statements differ from traditional test CASE statements in that the expression is not passed at the beginning. Instead, each WHEN clause can accept an expression to evaluate. In the context of a single case statement, either a single expression can be repeated in each WHEN clause or different expressions can be evaluated.

We'll first rewrite the IF-THEN-ELSIF example used earlier to use CASE syntax instead. The output that follows shows only the CASE statement itself, since the rest of the block has not changed. The complete example is available in the online script.

```
-- Available online as part of Case.sql
...
CASE -- Notice that there is no expression here...
    WHEN v_price < 40 THEN
        DBMS_OUTPUT.PUT_LINE('This book is already discounted');
```

```
      WHEN v_price BETWEEN 40 AND 50  THEN
          v_price : v_price - (v_price ^ .10);

          UPDATE books
          SET price = v_price
          WHERE isbn = v_isbn;

      WHEN v_price > 50 THEN
          v_price := v_price - (v_price * .10);

          UPDATE books
          SET price = v_price
          WHERE isbn = v_isbn;
      ELSE
         DBMS_OUTPUT.PUT_LINE('Price not found');
      END CASE;

   ...
```

In this case, the same variable is used for each condition. We can also use CASE to evaluate different variables or expressions in each WHEN clause. For example,

```
-- Available online as part of Case.sql
SET SERVEROUTPUT ON
DECLARE
    v_name1 VARCHAR2(30) := 'Steve';
    v_name2 VARCHAR2(30) := 'Jim';
    v_name3 VARCHAR2(30) := 'Kathy';
    v_name4 VARCHAR2(30) := 'Ron';
BEGIN

    CASE
    WHEN v_name1 = 'Steve' THEN
       DBMS_OUTPUT.PUT_LINE('Steve');
    WHEN v_name2 = 'Jim' THEN
       DBMS_OUTPUT.PUT_LINE('Jim');
    WHEN v_name3 = 'Kathy' THEN
       DBMS_OUTPUT.PUT_LINE('Kathy');
    WHEN v_name4 = 'Ron' THEN
       DBMS_OUTPUT.PUT_LINE('Ron');
    END CASE;
EXCEPTION
    WHEN OTHERS
    THEN
        DBMS_OUTPUT.PUT_LINE(SQLERRM);
        ROLLBACK;
END;
/
```

Four different variables were used in this CASE statement. The syntax makes evaluating this statement easy for the developer, in turn making the code easier to maintain and troubleshoot.

TIP
When should CASE be used in place of IF-THEN style syntax? While there is no "rule", we find CASE statements easier to read when the logic gets complex.

Circular Execution

Circular execution refers to the ability to repeatedly execute code until some condition is met. PL/SQL uses loops to accomplish this, and we cover three different types here.

- **Simple loops**   The most basic kind of loop, they include LOOP, END LOOP, and some method of EXIT.
- **Numeric FOR loops**   With this loop structure we can define the number of times the loop will cycle before exiting.
- **While loops**   This type of loop executes only while a certain condition is met. When it no longer meets the condition, the loop ends.

These categories are discussed in greater detail in the following sections.

Simple Loops

Simple loops provide a simple interface for circular execution. The basic syntax is

```
LOOP
  action;
END LOOP;
```

Action is any valid statement. In theory, we can run the following loop (DO NOT RUN THIS):

```
-- DO NOT RUN
SET SERVEROUTPUT ON
BEGIN
    LOOP
        DBMS_OUTPUT.PUT_LINE('I WARNED YOU!');
    END LOOP;
END;
/
```

If our warning was ignored, and you ran this code, expect your DBA to stop by your desk in a few minutes. The reason? This is an infinite loop. At no point did we tell the loop if/when/how to exit. While the syntax is valid, the logic is not.

To resolve this dilemma, PL/SQL uses the following syntax:

EXIT [WHEN *condition*]

We can rewrite the last example with a few modifications to allow a specific number of iterations.

```
-- Available online as part of Loop.sql
SET SERVEROUTPUT ON
DECLARE
    v_count PLS_INTEGER := 0;
BEGIN
    LOOP
        DBMS_OUTPUT.PUT_LINE('Ah -- Much better');
        v_count := v_count + 1;
        EXIT WHEN v_count = 20;
    END LOOP;
END;
/
```

Now this runs for 20 iterations.

An alternative to EXIT WHEN *condition* is the use of EXIT. EXIT steps out of the loop without requiring any condition be met. It is typically seen in the context of CASE or IF-THEN statements where a condition is evaluated in some other way.

Numeric FOR Loop

Numeric for-loops have a predefined number of iterations built into the syntax.

FOR *counter* IN *low_number .. high_number*
LOOP
 action;
END LOOP;

This makes specifying the number of iterations more natural than the way we showed you in the example for simple loops. To rewrite the simple loop example, we can do the following:

```
-- Available online as part of Loop.sql
SET SERVEROUTPUT ON
BEGIN
    FOR v_count IN 1 .. 20
    LOOP
```

```
        DBMS_OUTPUT.PUT_LINE('Iteration: '||v_count);
    END LOOP;
END;
/
```

There are no variables to declare, counters to increment, or exits to worry about. We use the numeric FOR loop whenever we need to load mass amounts of data. If there is a primary key or unique constraint, use the counter V_COUNT to increment the data. For an example, look at the output of this statement:

```
Iteration: 1
Iteration: 2
Iteration: 3
Iteration: 4
Iteration: 5
...
```

The number is incrementing as the counter does. This same concept can be applied to the insertion of unique numbers or values into a table.

WHILE Loop

The WHILE loop executes as long as the stated expression evaluates to TRUE. The syntax is as follows:

WHILE *condition*
LOOP
 action;
END LOOP;

Every iteration of the loop revisits the Boolean *condition* to determine if it evaluates to TRUE. If it does, the action is performed again. If it evaluates to FALSE or NULL, the loop is ended.

The example using the counter variable can be rewritten as

```
-- Available online as part of Loop.sql
SET SERVEROUTPUT ON
DECLARE
    v_count PLS_INTEGER := 1;
BEGIN
    WHILE v_count <= 20
    LOOP
        DBMS_OUTPUT.PUT_LINE('While loop iteration: '||v_count);
        v_count := v_count + 1;
    END LOOP;
END;
/
```

In this example, we are back to using the counter variable and incrementing the counter. We do not need to specify an `EXIT` point though. This is taken care of as soon as the `WHILE` condition evaluates to `FALSE`.

Loops and Labels

Labels provide a marker of sorts; a way to name the unnamable in PL/SQL. Loops cannot be explicitly named, but they can be given a label that allows them to be referenced as if they were named. For example,

```
-- Available online as part of Loop.sql
SET SERVEROUTPUT ON
BEGIN
<<l_For_Loop>>
    FOR v_count IN 1 .. 20
    LOOP
        DBMS_OUTPUT.PUT_LINE('Iteration: '||v_count);
    END LOOP l_For_Loop;
END;
/
```

The double-angle brackets are label delimiters, and `l_For_Loop` is the label name. Ending the loop with the label name is optional.

Sequential Navigation using GOTO

So far, we have demonstrated *conditional evaluation* using IF-THEN and CASE syntax and *circular execution* using three types of loops. PL/SQL also provides the ability to jump through a program using GOTO.

In my very first programming class (Basic), I was told to never use GOTO. My instructor believed any use of GOTO turned code into a "meandering jumble of code snippits prone to err and fraught with danger."

Besides being a bit melodramatic, he was also not entirely correct. I still avoid using GOTO when not necessary (which is most of the time), but in certain circumstances GOTO is the correct solution.

For example, I used GOTO when working with complex exception handlers in nested blocks to make the execution section more readable. In that case, creating a separate procedure or function to handle the exceptions was not the best choice (its use would have been limited to a single procedure and would not have been consistent with the rest of the code in the system). Keeping all of the code in each exception section of each nested block cluttered the code. I instead used a GOTO, pointing to the appropriate label at the end of the block. This is truly a rare circumstance where GOTO is ultimately the best choice, but it provides an example of why it should not be removed from consideration completely.

GOTO syntax is as follows:

GOTO *label_name*;

Label_name is the name of the label created with the syntax

<<*label_name*>>

Labels are created for use with GOTOs just as they were with loops in the last section. The double-angle brackets are label delimiters, and the *label_name* acts as a pointer available during program execution.

The following example shows how a GOTO is used in an anonymous block:

```
-- Available online as part of Goto.sql
SET SERVEROUTPUT ON
BEGIN
    DBMS_OUTPUT.PUT_LINE('BEGINNING OF BLOCK');
    GOTO l_Last_Line;

    DBMS_OUTPUT.PUT_LINE('GOTO didn''t work!');
    RETURN;

    <<l_Last_Line>>
    DBMS_OUTPUT.PUT_LINE('Last Line');
END;
/
```

In this example, the section between the GOTO and the *label* is skipped.

There are a few rules to remember regarding GOTOs:

- GOTO cannot reference a label in a nested block.

- GOTO cannot be executed outside an IF clause to a label inside the IF clause.

- GOTO cannot be executed from inside an IF clause to a label inside another IF clause.

- GOTO cannot navigate from the EXCEPTION section to any other section of the block.

Summary

In this chapter we reviewed PL/SQL basics, including

- Block structure
- Variables including bind variables
- Literals, characters, and reserved words
- Data types
- The PL/SQL Wrapper utility

Chapter 4 continues the introduction to PL/SQL by reviewing transaction processing, data retrieval options, data manipulation, built-in SQL functions, and cursors.

CHAPTER
4

Using SQL with
PL/SQL

PL/SQL is Oracle's procedural language extension to the Structured Query Language (SQL). SQL is used to select data from the database, manipulate that data, and return the results to the end user and/or write it to the data source. As was mentioned in Chapter 1, SQL is the window to the database, and PL/SQL helps us exploit what it can do.

This chapter focuses on how SQL can be used in PL/SQL and presents some advanced features that improve application performance and design. In this chapter, we discuss the following:

- Transaction processing

- Retrieving data with basic select statements, Oracle Text information retrieval, regular expressions, and cursors.

- Advanced data retrieval techniques using hints, ROWID, and ROWNUM.

- Manipulating data using SQL

- Built-in SQL functions

As these features are demonstrated, think about how they can be used to improve the functionality, performance, and design of your applications.

Transaction Processing

Imagine that you are entering an order into an online catalog. You add the items to the shopping cart, you enter your credit card number into the form, and when the button to submit the order is pressed, the site crashes. Were you charged for the items? Was only a portion of the information saved before the crash?

In business, transactions involve multiple dependent operations that all must be complete for the entire transaction to be successful. If one part fails and another is allowed to succeed, the entire transaction is corrupt. In Oracle, a *transaction* is a complete unit of work. It can be a single DML statement or multiple DML statements that are not yet made permanent. If successful, the entire transaction is recorded to the database. If there is a failure, the entire transaction is reverted or rolled back. Even though a transaction may have completed its work, the changes are not reflected in the database until the commit is complete.

Transactions provide read consistency for the database. A set of properties that describe how transactions should work in a database are described by the acronym *ACID. ACID* stands for

- **A**tomicity   Transactions either succeed or fail as a unit.

- **C**onsistency   The database is always kept in a consistent state. No partial transactions.

- **I**solation   Changes made by the transaction can be seen only by the session making the change until they are committed.

- **D**urability   When the transaction is complete, it cannot be undone.

ACID properties prevent transactional data corruption. They ensure each session has a complete view of the data.

Transactions and Locking

Transactions are not tied to PL/SQL blocks, or PL/SQL for that matter. Transactions involve any DML change to the database. There is no specific statement that starts a transaction in Oracle. Instead, a transaction begins whenever a DML command locks an object. Whenever DML is used, Oracle locks the objects being modified until the transaction is complete. This can be seen with a simple UPDATE statement against the AUTHORS table, and a query of the data dictionary.

```
-- Available online as part of LockSession1.sql
-- SESSION 1
UPDATE authors
SET first_name = 'Ronald'
WHERE id = 44;

1 row updated
```

We have yet to commit this, so the transaction is waiting for an action on our part to either commit or rollback the statement. We can see the transaction lock by querying either the DBA_LOCKS or V$LOCK views.

```
-- Available online as part of LockSession1.sql
-- SESSION 1
SELECT d.session_id sid, d.lock_type, d.mode_requested,
       d.mode_held, d.blocking_others
FROM dba_locks d, v$session v
WHERE v.username = 'PLSQL'
AND d.session_id = v.sid;
```

This returns the following result:

```
      SID LOCK_TYPE        MODE_REQUESTED  MODE_HELD       BLOCKING_
OTHERS
----- -------- -------- -------- --------
```

| 204 | **Transaction** | None | **Exclusive** | Not Blocking |
| 204 | **DML** | None | **Row-X (SX)** | Not Blocking |

Two locks are held for our session. The first record displayed is a `Transaction` lock, which is held in `Exclusive` mode. It is not currently blocking any other users from their tasks. The transaction lock will prevent other sessions from modifying the row.

NOTE
Your SID value will be different,
since it is session specific.

The second record returned is a lock on the object being modified. In this case, the `AUTHORS` table has a row lock against it, as can be seen by the `MODE_HELD` value of `Row-X` (row exclusive). It is not blocking anyone either. This lock prevents modifications to the structure of the object it is locking. To see the object held, run the following query:

```
-- Available online as part of LockSession1.sql
-- SESSION 1
SELECT dbl.lock_type, dbl.mode_held, dbl.blocking_others,
    dbo.object_name object_locked, dbo.object_type
FROM dba_locks dbl, v$session v, dba_objects dbo
WHERE v.username = 'PLSQL'
AND dbl.session_id = v.sid
AND dbo.object_id = dbl.lock_id1;
```

The results of the query contain the name and type of the object being held, along with the lock information shown earlier.

```
LOCK_TYPE       MODE_HELD       BLOCKING_OTHERS OBJECT_LOCKED OBJECT_TYPE
--------- --------- --------- ------- ------
DML             Row-X (SX)      Not Blocking    AUTHORS       TABLE
```

These locks are held for the duration of the transaction. While held, they prevent another user from updating the same record from a different session.

Here, we start another SQL*Plus session while leaving the first open. We can query the `AUTHORS` table and see that the change is not yet viewable to other sessions:

```
-- Available online as part of LockSession2.sql
-- SESSION 2
SELECT first_name
FROM authors
WHERE id = 44;
```

This returns the FIRST_NAME value showing no change.

```
FIRST_NAME
------
Ron
```

When we attempt to run the same SQL statement, it simply hangs.

```
-- Available online as part of LockSession2.sql
-- SESSION 2
UPDATE authors
SET first_name = 'Ronald'
WHERE id = 44;
```

There is no error, and no messages are shown to let us know what is happening. We can run the following query to see what is happening:

```
-- Available online as part of LockSession1.sql
-- SESSION 1
SELECT d.session_id sid, d.lock_type, d.mode_requested,
       d.mode_held, d.blocking_others
FROM dba_locks d, v$session v
WHERE v.username = 'PLSQL'
AND d.session_id = v.sid;
```

TIP
*Do this from the first session, since
the second one is hanging.*

This shows a lock that was previously not blocking others as a blocking lock now.

SID	LOCK_TYPE	MODE_REQUESTED	MODE_HELD	BLOCKING_OTHERS
202	Transaction	Exclusive	**None**	Not Blocking
202	DML	None	Row-X (SX)	Not Blocking
204	Transaction	None	Exclusive	**Blocking**
204	DML	None	Row-X (SX)	Not Blocking

The first two records are the new locks obtained. The new Transaction lock is unable to obtain the lock, so it is in queue. It shows it has requested an exclusive lock but is not currently holding one. Another change can be seen in the third record. It was previously not blocking others, but now it is blocking. The second transaction cannot complete until the first one does.

COMMIT

The number one purpose for a commit is to write all redo log buffer information to the online redo logs. It does not force a write of data from the database buffer cache to the physical data files—a common misconception. Other operations performed during a commit include SCN generation and writing of the SCN to online redo logs.

> **NOTE**
> *If you are unfamiliar with what an SCN is, or the way redo log buffers, database buffer cache, redo log files, and data files work and are curious, see the Oracle Concepts guide on the OTN web site (http://otn.oracle.com).*

The syntax for commit is

COMMIT [*WORK*]

WORK is optional and is not typically used.

To continue with our last example, we type the following to commit the transaction in session 204:

```
-- SESSION 1
commit;
```

Once we commit the transaction, we can re-query the DBA_LOCKS view. Here we can see that the locks for SESSION_ID 204 are gone and that session 202 is now able to obtain an Exclusive lock.

SID	LOCK_TYPE	MODE_REQUESTED	MODE_HELD	BLOCKING_OTHERS
202	Transaction	None	Exclusive	Not Blocking
202	DML	None	Row-X (SX)	Not Blocking

The first transaction is now complete, and the second session is now able to process the request.

ROLLBACK

Where committing a transaction makes changes permanent, issuing a ROLLBACK reverts the modifications. The syntax for rollback is

ROLLBACK [*WORK*]

WORK is an optional term and adds nothing to the command beyond readability. To illustrate, the following example issues a rollback:

```
-- SESSION 2
rollback;
```

This ends the transaction, just like the COMMIT, but no change is made to the data. We can see that the locks are no longer held on re-query of the DBA_LOCKS view.

```
-- Available online as part of LockSession1.sql
-- SESSION 2
SELECT d.session_id sid, d.lock_type, d.mode_requested,
       d.mode_held, d.blocking_others
FROM dba_locks d, v$session v
WHERE v.username = 'PLSQL'
AND d.session_id = v.sid;

no rows selected
```

Both locks are released.

Partial ROLLBACK Using SAVEPOINT   As demonstrated, a rollback reverts entire transactions. Using a command called *savepoint,* rollback is able to revert partial transactions, too. Savepoint provides a marker for rollback, enabling rollback to revert only to a particular point in the transaction. Work completed in the transaction before the savepoint is left intact. DML after the savepoint is reverted. Savepoint syntax is

SAVEPOINT *name*;

Name can be any valid identifier (see Chapter 3 for identifier naming rules). To use rollback with a savepoint, modify the rollback syntax as follows:

ROLLBACK [*WORK*] TO SAVEPOINT *name*;

The following example performs two INSERTs and an UPDATE; it includes two savepoints:

```
-- Available online as part of Savepoint.sql
BEGIN
    INSERT INTO books (ISBN, CATEGORY,
                  TITLE, NUM_PAGES,
                  PRICE, COPYRIGHT, AUTHOR1)
```

```
VALUES ('12345678', 'Oracle Server',
      'Oracle Information Retrieval with Oracle Text', 440,
      35.99, 2005, 44);

SAVEPOINT A;

INSERT INTO inventory (isbn, status, status_date, amount)
VALUES ('12345678', 'BACKORDERED', null, 1100);

SAVEPOINT B;

UPDATE inventory
SET status = 'IN STOCK'
WHERE isbn = '12345678';

ROLLBACK TO SAVEPOINT B;

COMMIT;
END;
/
```

NOTE
*If you have been following along with the examples,
you may need to issue a commit in your sessions
prior to proceeding. This releases the locks held
from the earlier examples.*

We can see the impact of the ROLLBACK TO SAVEPOINT command with the
following select:

```
-- Available online as part of Savepoint.sql
SELECT b.title, i.status
FROM books b, inventory we
WHERE b.isbn = '12345678'
AND b.isbn = i.isbn;
```

This returns the name of the book, as well as the status.

```
TITLE                                    STATUS
------------------------- ------
Oracle Information Retrieval with Oracle Text  BACKORDERED
```

From the SELECT, we can see that the rollback worked. The first two SQL
statements completed and are committed. The third, which updated the STATUS
column to IN-STOCK, was rolled back.

Autonomous Transactions

Autonomous transactions are started by a *parent,* or *main,* transaction but operate independently of the parent for transaction control. If a commit or rollback is used in the autonomous or main transaction, or if a failure occurs for any reason, it does not impact the other transaction.

Our favorite use of this feature is for logging application events. If the need is to log activity, regardless of the outcome, but the logging success or failure should not impact the application, autonomous transactions are the perfect solution.

To create an autonomous transaction, use a pragma called AUTONOMOUS_ TRANSACTION. The pragma is placed in the declaration section of the block. When the code is executed, the PL/SQL compiler sees the pragma (instructions for the compiler), and handles the block as autonomous.

We tend to group our code for event logging and auditing in a package, but the autonomous transaction code can be created in procedures, functions, triggers, and object types. All of these program types are discussed in detail later in this book.

In this example, we create a procedure using the pragma AUTONOMOUS_ TRANSACTION:

```
-- Available online as part of Autonomous.sql
CREATE OR REPLACE PROCEDURE logging_ins (
    i_username IN VARCHAR2,
    i_datetime IN TIMESTAMP)
IS
    PRAGMA AUTONOMOUS_TRANSACTION;
BEGIN

    INSERT INTO logging (username, datetime)
    VALUES (i_username, i_datetime);

    commit;
END;
/
```

This procedure, when called, will operate independently of the parent transaction calling it. Here we create a procedure that inserts a record into the books table, calls the LOGGING_INS procedure we just created, and then performs a rollback.

```
-- Available online as part of Autonomous.sql
CREATE OR REPLACE PROCEDURE book_ins (
    i_isbn IN BOOKS.ISBN%TYPE,
    i_category IN BOOKS.CATEGORY%TYPE,
    i_title IN BOOKS.TITLE%TYPE,
    i_num_pages IN BOOKS.NUM_PAGES%TYPE,
```

```
    i_price IN BOOKS.PRICE%TYPE,
    i_copyright IN BOOKS.COPYRIGHT%TYPE,
    i_author1 IN BOOKS.AUTHOR1%TYPE,
    i_author2 IN BOOKS.AUTHOR1%TYPE,
    i_author3 IN BOOKS.AUTHOR1%TYPE)
IS
BEGIN
    -- Parent transaction begins
    INSERT INTO books (ISBN, CATEGORY,
                 TITLE, NUM_PAGES,
                 PRICE, COPYRIGHT, AUTHOR1,
                 AUTHOR2, AUTHOR3)
    VALUES (i_isbn, i_category,
         i_title, i_num_pages,
         i_price, i_copyright, i_author1,
         i_author2, i_author3);

    -- Call is made to procedure to begin autonomous transaction
    LOGGING_INS('PLSQL', systimestamp);

    -- The rollback is for the parent transaction only
    ROLLBACK;

EXCEPTION
    WHEN OTHERS
    THEN
        DBMS_OUTPUT.PUT_LINE(sqlerrm);
END;
/
```

To test this out, we execute the BOOK_INS procedure as follows:

```
-- Available online as part of Autonomous.sql
BEGIN
 BOOK_INS('12345678',
 'Oracle Server', 'Oracle Information Retrieval with Oracle Text',
 440, 35.99, 2005, 44, NULL, NULL);
END;
/
```

The BOOK_INS procedure inserted a record into the BOOKS table with an ISBN value of 12345678. Next, it logged the event in the LOGGING table by calling an autonomous transaction in the form of the LOGGING_INS procedure. Finally, back in the parent procedure, it performed a ROLLBACK. This is illustrated in Figure 4-1.

To test how well the autonomous transaction worked, we can select the records from the BOOKS and LOGGING tables.

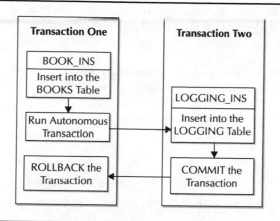

FIGURE 4-1. *Autonomous transaction*

```
-- Available online as part of Autonomous.sql
COL username FORMAT A10
COL datetime FORMAT A30
SELECT *
FROM logging;
```

This returns

```
USERNAME    DATETIME
-----  ----------------
PLSQL       13-JUL-04 09.58.13.050000 PM
```

The record inserted from the autonomous transaction is in the LOGGING table, so the commit was successful. We can run the following select to check the BOOKS table:

```
-- Available online as part of Autonomous.sql
SELECT *
FROM books
WHERE isbn = '12345678';

no rows selected
```

This returns no rows, so the rollback was successful.

Be careful to always terminate autonomous transactions with a commit or rollback! Neglecting transaction control statements in basic PL/SQL objects is sloppy. Doing so in objects declared as autonomous transactions will lead to errors. Next we create a procedure identical to the LOGGING_INS procedure used earlier, except we have no commit or rollback:

```
-- Available online as part of Autonomous.sql
CREATE OR REPLACE PROCEDURE logging_ins_error (
    i_username IN VARCHAR2,
    i_datetime IN TIMESTAMP)
IS
    PRAGMA AUTONOMOUS_TRANSACTION;
BEGIN

    INSERT INTO logging (username, datetime)
    VALUES (i_username, i_datetime);

    -- NO COMMIT OR ROLLBACK

END;
/
```

There is *no* error when compiling this code. We will try running it and see what happens.

```
-- Available online as part of Autonomous.sql
EXEC LOGGING_INS_ERROR('PLSQL', systimestamp)
```

Executing this procedure results in the following error:

```
BEGIN LOGGING_INS_ERROR('PLSQL', systimestamp); END;
*
ERROR at line 1:
ORA-06519: active autonomous transaction detected and rolled back
ORA-06512: at "PLSQL.LOGGING_INS_ERROR", line 13
ORA-06512: at line 1
```

Use transaction control statements COMMIT and ROLLBACK appropriately, and avoid this error.

Set Transaction

While most transaction processing properties cannot be modified, Oracle does provide some level of control. Table 4-1 lists the commands available, and a description of what each does.

Command	Description
SET TRANSACTION READ ONLY	When set, the transaction that follows operates on essentially a snapshot of the database at the time the command was issued. This is especially useful when multiple select statements are executed over the course of a transaction, and data must be consistent.
SET TRANSACTION READ WRITE	This changes the transaction to a writable state. This is the default state of a transaction.
SET TRANSACTION ISOLATION LEVEL READ COMMITTED	As in the example in the section "Transactions and Locking" earlier, if we try to modify a record that already has a DML Row Exclusive lock on that record, the attempt to update will wait until the locks are released.
SET TRANSACTION ISOLATION LEVEL SERIALIZABLE	Identical to READ COMMITTED, except the second session fails with errors instead of waiting for the locks to be released.
SET TRANSACTION USE ROLLBACK SEGMENT	Prior to Oracle 9i, all DML statements use rollback segments to provide read consistency for the database. They must be sized large enough to accommodate an entire transaction, since space used in a rollback segment is not released until the transaction is committed or rolled back. This command provides the ability to specify which rollback segment will be used for a given transaction. Oracle 9i introduced Automatic Undo Management. If that is used, this setting is not generally necessary.

TABLE 4-1. *SET TRANSACTION*

TIP
The SET TRANSACTION command must be the first statement in a transaction, and it is terminated by a semicolon. If you try this and get an exception, place a commit prior to the SET command to ensure you are not already in a transaction.

Retrieving Data

Data retrieval options range from basic SELECT statements to pattern matching with regular expressions, and Information Retrieval (IR) using Oracle Text. While we do cover the basic SELECT statement in this section, it is assumed that you have a working knowledge of SQL. We will quickly move into advanced features that may be difficult to understand otherwise.

We begin this section by looking at a basic SELECT statement. Next, we examine the use of LEVEL, a pseudo-column that gives the ability to retrieve a hierarchical data set, providing the appropriate position of each row in the relationship. We introduce a feature new to Oracle 10*g* called Regular Expressions that provides advanced pattern-matching capabilities. Finally, we explore Information Retrieval (IR) using Oracle Text. As you read through this section, think of the ways these different data/information retrieval options can help you.

SQL SELECT Statement

ANSI-standard SQL requires that a SELECT statement be made of two parts—the SELECT and FROM clauses. Additional clauses are available but are optional. The following is the basic syntax for a select statement:

```
SELECT select_list
[INTO variable_list]
FROM table_list
[WHERE where_clause]
[ORDER BY column_list]
```

The *select_list* can be columns, strings, built-in SQL functions, or a * to retrieve the entire record. Arithmetic operations are allowed in the *select_list*. Aliases can be used to display a name other than what is specified in the list, but they do not change the values that are returned.

The *variable_list* in the INTO clause is a variable, or set of variables, that match the number and data types of values in the *select_list*. Variables can be declared as a single data type, such as VARCHAR2 or NUMBER, or as an anchored type using %TYPE. They can also be declared as entire records, so a single variable can accommodate a SELECT * select clause.

The *table_list* can be one or more tables, views, or in-line views (subqueries in the FROM clause). If column names are supplied in the *select_list,* they must exist in the objects represented in the *table_list*.

The *where_clause* restricts the result set and provides a way to link, or relate, objects in the *table_list* together. Comparison operators used in the WHERE clause are discussed later in this chapter.

NOTE
*This is only a partial list of available clauses for
SQL. Refer to the* Oracle Database SQL Reference
at http://otn.oracle.com for a complete list.

In the following example, we SELECT the title of a book INTO a variable and
display it to the screen using the built-in package DBMS_OUTPUT:

```
-- Available online as part of BasicSelect.sql
SET SERVEROUTPUT ON
DECLARE
   v_title BOOKS.TITLE%TYPE;
BEGIN

   SELECT title
   INTO v_title
   FROM books
   WHERE isbn = '72230665';

   -- display the results to the screen
   DBMS_OUTPUT.PUT_LINE(v_title);

EXCEPTION
   WHEN OTHERS
   THEN
      -- display any exception to the screen
      DBMS_OUTPUT.PUT_LINE(sqlerrm);
END;
/
```

This anonymous block returns the following output:

```
Oracle Database 10g PL/SQL Programming
```

When selecting a value into a variable, be sure one and only one value is returned.
If no rows are returned, the following exception is returned:

```
ORA-01403: no data found
```

If more than one record is returned for a SELECT . . . INTO statement, the following
is error is returned:

```
ORA-01422: exact fetch returns more than requested number of rows
```

For methods of trapping these errors using predefined exceptions, refer to Chapter 7.

Hierarchical Data Retrieval

The data in the prior example was a simple table and required nothing special to retrieve the record we wanted. Some data is stored in a hierarchical fashion, though. For example, your family tree is hierarchical. It begins at a root, or starting point, you specify and branches out, with each branch dependent on the one before it. Data that is used every day, such as manager/employee or company organizational units, has this same hierarchical structure.

How can we represent a hierarchical data set in a select statement so that each level is known and displayed? Using a pseudo-column called LEVEL, we can see where each record fits into the tree.

In this example, we added a column to the books table called PARENT_ISBN. This column references the book that preceded it in the series. The table is structured as follows:

```
DESC books
  Name                Null?      Type
  --------- ---- -------
  ISBN               NOT NULL  VARCHAR2(10)
  PARENT_ISBN                  VARCHAR2(10)
  SERIES                       VARCHAR2(20)
  CATEGORY                     VARCHAR2(20)
  TITLE                        VARCHAR2(100)
  NUM_PAGES                    NUMBER
  PRICE                        NUMBER
  COPYRIGHT                    NUMBER(4)
```

The first book in the series has a NULL PARENT_ISBN because it has no predecessor. Subsequent books in the series contain the ISBN of the book released before them in the series. The seed data contains two book series. The first series of books is for Oracle PL/SQL, and contains three titles. The second book series contains only one book. The records are inserted into the table in random order to how demonstrate data order does not come into play.

For this example, we want to retrieve each book in the table, showing its position in the hierarchy. Notice that the table does not contain a column showing a release order, date released, or position in the tree. We want to determine the position solely based on the parent/child hierarchy established by the PARENT_ISBN number. In this example, we do just that using the LEVEL pseudocolumn along with the START WITH and CONNECT BY PRIOR clauses:

```
-- Available online as part of Level.sql
SET SERVEROUTPUT ON
DECLARE
    v_level PLS_INTEGER;
    v_title BOOKS.TITLE%TYPE;
```

```
        -- use a cursor to point to the data I wish to use in my query
        CURSOR cur_tree
        IS
            SELECT isbn, title, series
            FROM books;
    BEGIN

    -- Loop through the cursor, one record at a time
    FOR l IN cur_tree
    LOOP

        -- Retrieve the level of each record relative to the tree
        --  and store it in the v_level variable
        SELECT max(LEVEL)
        INTO v_level
        FROM books
        START WITH isbn = l.isbn
        CONNECT BY PRIOR parent_isbn = isbn;

        -- display the title and level to the screen
        DBMS_OUTPUT.PUT_LINE(l.title||' is book '
                        ||v_level||' in the '||l.series||' series');

    -- stop looping through the cursor when no more records exist
    END LOOP;

    EXCEPTION
        WHEN OTHERS
        THEN
            DBMS_OUTPUT.PUT_LINE(sqlerrm);
    END;
    /
```

NOTE
For this section, focus on the text in **bold** *that demonstrates the use of LEVEL. We will use the same example when showing cursors and cursor for-loops later in this chapter.*

Execution of this anonymous block results in the following:

```
Oracle9i PL/SQL Programming is book 2 in the Oracle PL/SQL series
Oracle8i Advanced PL/SQL Programming is book 1 in the Oracle PL/SQL series
Oracle Database 10g PL/SQL Programming is book 3 in the Oracle PL/SQL series
Oracle E-Business Suite Financials Handbook is book 1 in the Oracle
    Ebusiness series
```

The LEVEL is shown in bold, as is the correct placement of each title with respect to its hierarchy.

If the LEVEL is needed as a hard-coded value, simply add a position/level column to the table. The preceding example block can be modified to include an insert or update statement that sets the correct level in terms of current data in the system. This allows for data changes while maintaining a current hard-coded value for each record's position in the hierarchy. There is a complete example of this provided online in LevelUpdate.sql.

Pattern Matching

Any SELECT statement whose WHERE clause compares a text column to a string is performing *pattern matching.* It may match an exact string when performing an equijoin, or just part of the string by using the LIKE operator. Pattern matching differs from information retrieval in that there is no interpretation of the data's meaning or relevance. Either a pattern of text is found in the data, or it is not.

LIKE

The LIKE operator makes pattern matching a much more forgiving task by allowing for unknown characters (using an underscore, _) and partial strings (using a wildcard, %). The LIKE operator is used in the WHERE clause. It takes as input any string or partial string and attempts to find a match in the data being searched. Pattern matching using LIKE is great for small strings—names, cities, countries, etc.

Here we create a procedure to search the AUTHORS table:

```
-- Available online as part of Like.sql
CREATE OR REPLACE PROCEDURE author_sel (
   i_last_name IN AUTHORS.LAST_NAME%TYPE,
   cv_author IN OUT SYS_REFCURSOR)
IS
   v_last_name AUTHORS.LAST_NAME%TYPE;
BEGIN

   /* Place wildcards on either side of the string provided
      and convert it to uppercase */
   v_last_name := '%'||UPPER(i_last_name)||'%';


   OPEN cv_author FOR
   SELECT id, first_name, last_name
   FROM authors
   WHERE UPPER(last_name) LIKE v_last_name;

EXCEPTION
   WHEN OTHERS
```

```
   THEN
        DBMS_OUTPUT.PUT_LINE(sqlerrm);
END;
/
```

This procedure takes a string as input and attempts to match the value to any last name in the AUTHORS table. To test, enter a partial value for a name:

```
-- Available online as part of Like.sql
COL first_name FORMAT A20
COL last_name FORMAT A20

VARIABLE x REFCURSOR
EXEC author_sel('rin', :x)

print x
```

The result is as follows:

```
      ID FIRST_NAME          LAST_NAME
----- ---------- ---------
      28 Sumit              Sarin
      54 Cheryl             Riniker
```

The string occurs in a different position in the name, but both match the string 'rin' that was passed to the procedure.

Regular Expressions

Oracle 10g introduced a new pattern-matching feature called Regular Expressions (RE). If you have a Unix or Perl background, you may already be familiar with it. RE has long been a part of Perl and Unix scripting languages, and now Oracle supports the IEEE POSIX (Portable Operating System Interface) ERE (Extended Regular Expression) standard as well.

The basic concept is surprisingly similar to that of the LIKE operator. Strings, or characters, are matched against the data source looking for the same text pattern. Metacharacters and built-in functions provide a boost to RE capabilities that far exceeds anything available with LIKE, though. The metacharacters have special meaning to Oracle, similar to the reserved words discussed in Chapter 3. They determine how Oracle parses the strings and matches or replaces patterns of text. Built-in functions include

- REGEXP_LIKE

- REGEXP_INSTR

- REGEXP_REPLACE

■ REGEXP_SUBSTR

The tasks these functions perform map closely to their root functions/operators of LIKE, INSTR, REPLACE, and SUBSTR.

RE works with the following data types:

■ CHAR

■ VARCHAR2

■ NCHAR

■ NVARCHAR

■ CLOB

■ NCLOB

Any of these types can be searched using RE.

Metacharacters   Table 4-2 includes a list of commonly used metacharacters and their descriptions. A call to a regular expression function can be a bit intimidating if never seen before. Remember, they are simply a sum of their individual components. Break down the command into each literal and/or metacharacter, and apply the meaning of each until the whole string makes sense.

Character	Description
*	Matches zero or more values.
.	A valid character.
^	Pattern-matches at the beginning of the line.
[ ]	Groups characters. Individual characters are treated as if separated by an OR.
$	Pattern-matches at the end of the line.
\	Escape character. Used when a metacharacter should be treated as a literal.
( )	Groups strings. Frequently used with l.
l	Separates expressions that are part of a group. Equal to OR.

TABLE 4-2.   *Regular Expression Metacharacters (subset)*

TIP
When I (Ron Hardman) first started working with Regular Expressions (using Perl), I found it much easier when I wrote out the meaning of each command—in longhand, not code. This reduced the complexity of the commands until they began flowing naturally.

For this chapter, we am going to focus our attention on the REGEXP_LIKE function. This function is similar to the LIKE operator. You may see this referred to as an operator, and different than the other functions, but that is done primarily for SQL. For PL/SQL, REGEXP_LIKE works like a function.

Syntax for using REGEXP_LIKE is

REGEXP_LIKE(*column, string* [,*parameter*])

Column is the database column being searched. *String* is the expression, including literals and metacharacters, that we are searching for, and *parameter* is an optional parameter.

The following example performs a search on the AUTHORS.LAST_NAME column:

```
-- Available online as part of RegexpLike.sql
CREATE OR REPLACE PROCEDURE author_sel_regexp_like (
   cv_author IN OUT SYS_REFCURSOR)
IS
BEGIN

   -- Search for hardman or hartman
   OPEN cv_author FOR
   SELECT id, first_name, last_name
   FROM authors
   WHERE REGEXP_LIKE(last_name, '^har(d|t)man$', 'i');

EXCEPTION
   WHEN OTHERS
   THEN
      DBMS_OUTPUT.PUT_LINE(sqlerrm);
END;
/
```

The search string indicates the value returned should match the string 'hartman' or 'hardman', have no text before the name and no text after it, and perform a case-insensitive search. Refer to Figure 4-2 for the breakdown of the REGEXP_LIKE command.

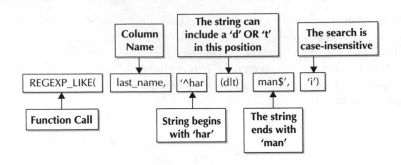

FIGURE 4-2. *REGEXP_LIKE*

To test the procedure, run it as follows:

```
-- Available online as part of RegexpLike.sql
COL first_name FORMAT A20
COL last_name FORMAT A20

VARIABLE x REFCURSOR
EXEC author_sel_regexp_like(:x)

PRINT x
```

This returns the following result:

```
   ID FIRST_NAME          LAST_NAME
----- ---------- -------   -------
   44 Ron                  Hardman
   55 Robert               Hartman
```

The search was successful, and did what we wanted it to do. Both `Hardman` and `Hartman` were returned, and the search was case-insensitive.

Information Retrieval

Information retrieval (IR) technologies aim to return the data that is needed, while weeding out the data that will not be of benefit. The following definitions may help distinguish the differences between data and information:

- **Data** Characters, strings, or numbers stored in the database. Simple SELECT statements return data.

- **Information** Data that is filtered according to meaning and reliably and accurately represents the search criteria. It is immediately useful in business. Some level of intelligence can be applied to the filtration process to determine "meaning" of the user and/or the data.

The core component of Oracle's IR solution is Oracle Text. Oracle Text, called interMedia in 8*i* and ConText in 8.0, is a full-featured IR solution.

Oracle Text

Oracle Text is a document/text indexing solution. It can index over 150 different document formats and provides full-text search capabilities. It also indexes the contents of all LOB types. See Chapter 16 for an example of Oracle Text indexing of LOBs. These are some of the search features:

- Relevance ranking

- Fuzzy searches

- Stemming

- Wildcard searches

- Case-insensitive searches by default

- Support for multiple languages, stored and indexed in the same table, enabling multiple language search capabilities against a single table

- Plus many more!

Oracle Text is useful for PL/SQL developers working on data warehouse applications, catalogs, knowledge repositories, and any application that requires a user search. It can index text stored in the database, documents stored in the database, or documents on the file system when links to the files are provided.

This is advantageous for developers because it provides access to data not otherwise available via traditional retrieval methods. In addition, it provides case-insensitive queries by default, and the index is always used.

Oracle Text has four different types of indexes that are specifically targeted to different applications. Table 4-3 lists the four index types available from Oracle 9*i* Release 1 on. Oracle 8*i* included all but the CTXXPATH index.

Index Type	Description
CONTEXT	Traditional full-text retrieval. Best for static catalog and warehouse applications where data change is infrequent but search requirements are high.
CTXCAT	Specifically designed for e-business catalogs, this index is best for more applications whose data is frequently updated. Search functions are restricted more than the CONTEXT index.
CTXRULE	Best index for knowledge repositories, or other classification-style applications. Document routing based on predefined rules can be done.
CTXXPATH	The first full-text index designed for XML, this index improves performance and search features when searching XML documents.

TABLE 4-3. *Oracle Text Indexes*

The next section demonstrates the use of the CONTEXT index in PL/SQL development. For more information on Oracle Text and its features, refer to the *Oracle Text Application Developer's Guide* available on OTN.

CONTAINS   To use the CONTEXT index, we must use the CONTAINS operator in our queries. CONTAINS signals Oracle that there is an Oracle Text index available for the data. For this example, we have a seed table called BOOK_DESCRIPTIONS. We created an Oracle Text index on the DESCRIPTIONS column and will test search functionality against that column.

The syntax for using the CONTAINS operator is as follows:

SELECT [*score(label),*]*column_list*
[INTO *variable_list*]
FROM *table_list*
WHERE CONTAINS (*column_name,* '*search_string*'[, *label*]) > 0;

The portions in bold are what differentiate this syntax from a basic SELECT statement. These differences are defined as follows:

- The *score(label)* is related to relevance ranking. *Label* must match the label provided in the WHERE clause. This is required only if relevance ranking is desired. The value provided as the label has no bearing on the score returned.

- The CONTAINS operator requires a ***column name*** that must have a CONTEXT index on it that is valid. It also requires a ***search_string*** to use in its search. If provided, ***label*** must match the label in the SELECT clause. Finally, a comparison operator is required to complete the query. The > 0 means that the result is returned as long as the score is greater than zero. The score is determined regardless of whether it is provided in the SELECT clause.

In this first example, we will demonstrate a case-insensitive query using the CONTAINS operator:

```
-- Available online as part of TextIndex.sql
SET SERVEROUTPUT ON
DECLARE
    v_isbn BOOK_DESCRIPTIONS.ISBN%TYPE;
    v_score NUMBER(10);
BEGIN
    SELECT score(1), isbn
    INTO v_score, v_isbn
    FROM book_descriptions
    WHERE CONTAINS (description, '10G or oracle', 1) > 0;

    DBMS_OUTPUT.PUT_LINE('Score: '||v_score||' and ISBN: '||v_isbn);

EXCEPTION
    WHEN OTHERS
    THEN
        DBMS_OUTPUT.PUT_LINE(sqlerrm);
END;
/
```

The string '10G' is stored in the database with a lowercase *g,* but the preceding query includes uppercase. Also, the string 'oracle' has a lowercase *o* in the search string, but is stored with an uppercase *O* in the database. The query returns the record as expected.

```
Score: 3 and ISBN: 72230665
```

This next example tests proximity searches where one term is NEAR another in the text:

```
-- Available online as part of TextIndex.sql
SET SERVEROUTPUT ON
DECLARE
    v_isbn BOOK_DESCRIPTIONS.ISBN%TYPE;
    v_score NUMBER(10);
```

```
BEGIN
    SELECT score(1), isbn
    INTO v_score, v_isbn
    FROM book_descriptions
    WHERE CONTAINS (description, '10g near Oracle', 1) > 0;

    DBMS_OUTPUT.PUT_LINE('Score: '||v_score||' and ISBN: '||v_isbn);
EXCEPTION
    WHEN OTHERS
    THEN
        DBMS_OUTPUT.PUT_LINE(sqlerrm);
END;
/
```

Even though the search string contains the same terms as the prior example, the score is noticeably different.

```
Score: 14 and ISBN: 72230665
```

The reason for the difference is the addition of the proximity term NEAR. 10g is close to the term Oracle, and therefore it has a high degree of relevance.

TIP
We have just touched the tip of the Oracle Text iceberg. Play around with the examples, and look for ways to use this powerful technology in your application design. You may have already noticed that Oracle itself is relying more on Oracle Text in recent years, building UltraSearch, IFS, XML DB, and Oracle Applications with Oracle Text as a core component.

Cursors

I am directionally challenged when it comes to driving. Drop me off in a strange city and I can get lost just going around the block. If I have to drive, I refuse to leave the airport without a detailed map of the area.

Imagine yourself getting dropped off in a new city with a map where every street was included. The map is not just for that city, though. It is a map of the entire country. Every highway, every back street and alley, 99.9999 percent of which you don't care about because you just want to find your hotel! How long would it take you to find your destination? How efficient would your search be? This map of the entire country is like SQL to the Oracle database, and the world of information contained in it.

Detailed city maps provide a much more focused data set. They provide details relevant to your situation and exclude details that are not. They direct you to the areas within the city and provide an efficient way to process the information. In the same way, the cursor reduces the data a transaction has to process, while providing direct access to that information for improved efficiency.

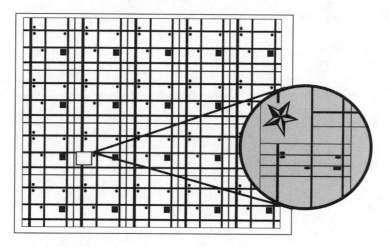

How Cursors Work

A *cursor* provides a subset of data, defined by a query, retrieved into memory when opened, and stored in memory until the cursor is closed. When I first began learning PL/SQL, my instructor described a cursor as a pointer to records in the database. This description to me was confusing as I began to use PL/SQL more and more. To me, a pointer that is directly against the data in the tables is nothing more than an index. If it were like an index where changes to data would be reflected in the cursor result set during processing, database read consistency would be thrown out the window.

A cursor is not just a pointer to the data in the table. It points to a memory region in the Process Global Area (PGA) called the context area that holds the following:

- Rows returned by the query

- Number of rows processed by the query

- A pointer to the parsed query in the Shared Pool

So, the pointer is to memory, not to the data directly. Since records are retrieved into memory at the time the cursor is opened, we are guaranteed a consistent view of data throughout the transaction.

If data is added, deleted, or modified after the cursor is opened, the new or changed data is not reflected in the cursor result set. Opening the cursor is literally like taking a snapshot of the data as it currently exists. Take the following example:

```
-- Available online as part of ContextArea1.sql
SET SERVEROUTPUT ON
DECLARE

    v_rowid ROWID;
    v_rowcount NUMBER := 0;

    CURSOR author_cur1
    IS
        SELECT rowid
        FROM authors
        WHERE id > 50;

    CURSOR author_cur2
    IS
        SELECT rowid
        FROM authors
        WHERE id > 50;
BEGIN
    OPEN author_cur1;

    DELETE FROM authors
    WHERE id > 50;

    OPEN author_cur2;

    -- Check cursor #1
    FETCH author_cur1 INTO v_rowid;
    IF author_cur1%ROWCOUNT > 0
    THEN
        DBMS_OUTPUT.PUT_LINE('Cursor 1 includes the deleted rows');
    ELSE
        DBMS_OUTPUT.PUT_LINE('Cursor 1 does not include the deleted rows');
    END IF;

    v_rowcount := 0;
    -- Check cursor #2
    FETCH author_cur2 INTO v_rowid;
    IF author_cur2%ROWCOUNT > 0
    THEN
        DBMS_OUTPUT.PUT_LINE('Cursor 2 includes the deleted rows');
```

```
    ELSE
        DBMS_OUTPUT.PUT_LINE('Cursor 2 does not include the deleted rows');
    END IF;

    CLOSE author_cur1;
    CLOSE author_cur2;

    ROLLBACK;
EXCEPTION
    WHEN OTHERS
    THEN
        DBMS_OUTPUT.PUT_LINE(sqlerrm);
END;
/
```

The following steps are taken through the block:

- We create two identical cursors. Each cursor selects the rowid of any record with an ID greater than 50.

- The first cursor is opened, retrieving the rowid for authors 51, 52, and 53 into memory.

- Next, all records with an ID greater than 50 are deleted from the physical table.

- The second cursor is opened, retrieving any records into memory where the ID is greater than 50.

- An attempt is made to fetch a record from each cursor, and the %ROWCOUNT attribute is used to determine if any records are retrieved.

- A message is displayed stating whether records were available for each cursor.

This block returns the following output on execution:

```
Cursor 1 includes the deleted rows
Cursor 2 does not include the deleted rows
```

This demonstrates that once opened, cursors maintain an image of the data the way it was, and do not simply act as a dynamic pointer to live data. Cursors opened after a change to the data do reflect the change, even when part of the same block. Another example is available online that provides an even more drastic example, where a cursor is opened, the table is dropped, and still we are able to loop through the records in the table. The file is called ContextArea2.sql.

In this section we demonstrate the following four different kinds of cursors, and discuss cursor attributes, loops, and the OPEN_CURSORS parameter:

- **Explicit cursors**   The cursor is declared, using a SELECT statement, in the declaration section of any block. The developer controls almost all operations involving the cursor.

- **Implicit cursors**   Implicit cursors are controlled by PL/SQL, and are created whenever any DML or SELECT...INTO statement is run.

- **Cursor variables**   A cursor variable is a declared type that can be associated with multiple queries in the same PL/SQL block.

- **Cursor subqueries**   Cursor subqueries, sometimes called nested cursor expressions, provide the ability to embed cursors in SQL statements.

Explicit Cursors

Explicit cursors provide control over cursor processing that is not possible with other types of cursors. They are meant to work with SELECT statements that return more than one record at a time. While providing more control than implicit cursors, they require additional steps to operate. We compare the use of implicit vs. explicit cursors in the section titled "Implicit Cursors."

To use an explicit cursor, it must be declared, opened, fetched from, and closed.

Declare the Cursor

Name the cursor, and provide the SELECT statement to use for the cursor, in the DECLARATION section of the block. The following syntax is used:

```
CURSOR cursor_name [parameter_list]
[RETURN return_type]
IS query
[FOR UPDATE [OF (column_list)][NOWAIT]];
```

The *cursor_name* can be any valid identifier, though we recommend following a standard naming convention for consistency. *Parameter_list* is optional and can be any valid parameter used for query execution. The optional RETURN clause specifies the type of data to be returned as defined by *return_type*. The *query* can be any SELECT statement. Finally, the optional FOR UPDATE clause locks the records when the cursor is opened. These records are still available to other sessions as READ ONLY. FOR UPDATE ensures these things:

- As the program loops through the cursor's records, they are available for update and are not locked by any other session.

- The data is consistent with what is in the context area.

- If NOWAIT is specified, the program will exit immediately on open if an exclusive lock cannot be obtained.

The cursor declaration from the "How Cursors Work" section is

```
CURSOR author_cur1
    IS
        SELECT rowid
        FROM authors
        WHERE id > 50;
```

If we wanted to create the cursor to accept the ID value as a parameter, we could rewrite this declaration as

```
CURSOR author_cur1 (i_id IN NUMBER)
    IS
        SELECT rowid
        FROM authors
        WHERE id > i_id;
```

Open the Cursor

Cursors are opened in the EXECUTION or EXCEPTION sections of the block. The syntax is

OPEN *cursor_name* [(*parameter_values*)];

The OPEN command prepares the cursor for use. When executed, the query is parsed, the bind values are evaluated, the rows are recorded in the context area, and the result set is made ready.

There can be only one active record in a cursor at a time. On OPEN, the active record is the first one returned by the cursor's query. See Figure 4-3 for a visual example of what happens on an OPEN.

The following line opens the AUTHOR_CUR1 cursor without a parameter list:

```
OPEN author_cur1;
```

That's it! If we were to use the same cursor with a parameter list as shown in the Declare the Cursor section, the OPEN would appear as

```
OPEN author_cur1(50);
```

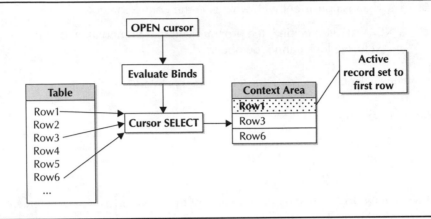

FIGURE 4-3. *OPEN process*

In this case, the value is passed on OPEN and the bind value is determined. This value will not change, so neither will the result set, unless the cursor is closed and then reopened.

Fetch Records from the Cursor

FETCH is what retrieves records from the context area into a variable so that it can be used. The FETCH command operates on the current record only and proceeds through the result set one record at a time. The exception to this is the use of the BULK COLLECT clause that can retrieve all cursor records at once. For more information on this feature, refer to Chapter 6.

The syntax for FETCH is

FETCH *cursor_name* INTO *variable_name(s)* | *PL/SQL_record*;

Cursor_name is the name of the open cursor, and *variable_name(s)* can be one or more comma-delimited variables that match the number and type of columns included in the result set. *PL/SQL_record* can be used as an alternative to the variable list if each row of the result set includes a complete record.

A fetch of a single-column result set into a single variable might look like this:

```
FETCH author_cur1 INTO v_rowid;
```

A fetch where the cursor returns multiple rows and requires multiple variables might look like the following:

```
FETCH author_cur INTO v_first_name, v_last_name;
```

In this case, the SELECT statement for AUTHOR_CUR must include the first name and last_name columns in that order. The cursor cannot include any other columns.

If the cursor includes a complete record, a PL/SQL record can be used as an alternative to individual variables.

```
DECLARE
    v_author authors%ROWTYPE;
BEGIN
...
    FETCH author_cur INTO v_author;
...
```

The v_author variable includes a complete record. To reference values, use the following syntax:

```
variable_name.column_name
```

To reference the ID, for example, type the following:

```
v_author.id
```

Close the Cursor

Always, always close your explicit cursors! The comparison that is most frequently used is to equate forgetting to close a cursor to intentionally introducing a memory leak into code. I love this analogy. Remember, the context area is memory (part of the PGA) used for the cursor. Until the cursor is closed, the memory is not released.

Oracle does check for *abandoned* cursors when the last block is finished, and it does automatically close the cursors when the outermost block completes. *Do not* rely on this to close your cursors, however.

To close a cursor, use the following syntax:

CLOSE *cursor_name*;

Cursor_name is the name of the opened cursor. If a CLOSE is used on a cursor that is not currently open, the following exception is raised:

```
ORA-01001: invalid cursor
```

The next section demonstrates how to test whether a cursor is currently open so that this error can be avoided.

Cursor Attributes

Oracle provides six attributes that are used with cursors. They are listed in Table 4-4 along with their descriptions.

Attribute Name	Description
%BULK_EXCEPTIONS	This attribute is used for array or Bulk Collect operations. It provides information regarding exceptions encountered during such operations.
%BULK_ROWCOUNT	Also used for Bulk Collect operations, this attribute provides information regarding the number of rows changed during the operation.
%FOUND	The %FOUND attribute tests whether a FETCH returned a record. The return value is of Boolean type. If TRUE, a row was returned by the FETCH. If FALSE, a row was not returned.
%ISOPEN	This attribute tests to see if a cursor is already open. If TRUE, the cursor is open. If FALSE, it is not open.
%NOTFOUND	%NOTFOUND is the opposite of %FOUND. It returns TRUE if a row was *not* returned by the FETCH and FALSE if one was returned.
%ROWCOUNT	This tests for the number of rows fetched from the cursor at any given time and returns a number.

TABLE 4-4. *Cursor Attributes*

NOTE
*The attributes related to bulk collect
are covered in Chapter 6.*

The following example demonstrates the use of the %FOUND, %ISOPEN, %NOTFOUND, and %ROWCOUNT attributes:

```
-- Available online as part of ExplicitAttribute.sql
SET SERVEROUTPUT ON
DECLARE
    v_first_name AUTHORS.FIRST_NAME%TYPE;
    v_last_name AUTHORS.LAST_NAME%TYPE;
    v_row_count PLS_INTEGER := 0;
    v_book_count PLS_INTEGER := 0;

    CURSOR auth_cur IS
        SELECT a.first_name, a.last_name, count(b.title)
```

```
            FROM authors a, books b
            WHERE a.id = b.author1
            OR a.id = b.author2
            OR a.id = b.author3
            GROUP BY a.first_name, a.last_name
            HAVING count(b.title) > 0
            ORDER BY a.last_name;
  BEGIN
      DBMS_OUTPUT.ENABLE(1000000);

      OPEN auth_cur;
      LOOP
          FETCH auth_cur INTO v_first_name, v_last_name, v_book_count;
          EXIT WHEN auth_cur%NOTFOUND;
          -- Alternatively use EXIT WHEN NOT auth_cur%FOUND;

          v_row_count := auth_cur%ROWCOUNT;
          DBMS_OUTPUT.PUT_LINE(v_row_count||' rows processed so far');

          DBMS_OUTPUT.PUT_LINE(v_last_name
                              ||', '
                              ||v_first_name
                              ||' wrote '
                              ||v_book_count
                              ||' book(s).');
      END LOOP;
      CLOSE auth_cur;

      IF auth_cur%ISOPEN = FALSE
      THEN
          DBMS_OUTPUT.PUT_LINE('Cursor closed');
      ELSE
          DBMS_OUTPUT.PUT_LINE('The cursor is still open');
      END IF;
  EXCEPTION
      WHEN OTHERS
          THEN
          DBMS_OUTPUT.PUT_LINE(SQLERRM);
  END;
  /
```

Navigate Cursors with Loops

Cursors are most often used with *LOOPS* (as you may have noticed in the last
example) to provide a way to navigate through the active record set. As you will
see later, this is unnecessary with implicit cursors but very useful for all other
kinds of cursors.

Simple Loop   The simple loop has the following syntax:

LOOP ... END LOOP;

Inside the loop, each record in the active set is retrieved and used. If not using Bulk Collect as described in Chapter 6, each loop iteration advances the pointer by one record in the active set.

The following example demonstrates how a simple loop works:

```
-- Available online as part of SimpleLoop.sql
SET SERVEROUTPUT ON
DECLARE
    v_author AUTHORS%ROWTYPE;

    CURSOR auth_cur IS
        SELECT *
        FROM authors;
BEGIN
    OPEN auth_cur;
    LOOP
        FETCH auth_cur INTO v_author;
        EXIT WHEN auth_cur%NOTFOUND;

        DBMS_OUTPUT.PUT_LINE(v_author.last_name);
    END LOOP;
    CLOSE auth_cur;
END;
/
```

The EXIT WHEN statement is necessary inside the loop to ensure the loop completes when the last record has been fetched.

While Loop   The WHILE loop is similar to the simple loop in function, though the method of execution is slightly different. Here we rewrote the last example to use the WHILE loop instead of the simple loop:

```
-- Available online as part of WhileLoop.sql
SET SERVEROUTPUT ON
DECLARE
    v_author AUTHORS%ROWTYPE;
    CURSOR auth_cur IS
        SELECT *
        FROM authors;
BEGIN
    OPEN auth_cur;
```

```
    FETCH auth_cur INTO v_author;
    WHILE auth_cur%FOUND LOOP
        DBMS_OUTPUT.PUT_LINE(v_author.last_name);
        FETCH auth_cur INTO v_author;
    END LOOP;

    CLOSE auth_cur;
END;
/
```

This block, though using different syntax, returns the same results as the
`SimpleLoop.sql` example. There is also no need to include an `EXIT WHEN`
statement, since `%FOUND` is integrated into the `WHILE` loop syntax.

Cursor For-Loop   The cursor for-loop is unique in that it does not require an
explicit OPEN, FETCH, or CLOSE. Although the cursor is declared as an explicit
cursor, PL/SQL handles its processing. In addition, the for-loop uses a variable that
is never declared in the *DECLARATION* section of the block. Using the same example
as the other loops, we have rewritten the query to use the cursor for-loop instead.

```
-- Available online as part of CursorForLoop.sql
SET SERVEROUTPUT ON
DECLARE
    CURSOR auth_cur IS
        SELECT *
        FROM authors;
BEGIN
    FOR v_author IN auth_cur
    LOOP
        DBMS_OUTPUT.PUT_LINE(v_author.last_name);
    END LOOP;
END;
/
```

As you can see, this type of loop is by far the most compact. This returns the
same results as the last two anonymous blocks, but it does so without an explicit
OPEN, FETCH, or CLOSE.

Implicit Cursors

Implicit cursors are opened and closed automatically by Oracle. In fact, every DML
SQL statement executed is provided a context area in the PGA and in turn has a
cursor. No interaction is required on the part of the developer to use implicit cursors.
OPEN, FETCH, and CLOSE commands are not used, but the same six attributes

available for explicit cursors can be used for implicit cursors as well (see earlier Table 4-4).

This example performs an update and uses cursor attributes to test the outcome:

```
-- Available online as part of ImplicitAttribute.sql
SET SERVEROUTPUT ON
BEGIN
    DBMS_OUTPUT.ENABLE(1000000);

    UPDATE books
    SET price = price * .90
    WHERE isbn = '78824389';

    DBMS_OUTPUT.PUT_LINE(SQL%ROWCOUNT||' rows updated');

    IF SQL%NOTFOUND
    THEN
        DBMS_OUTPUT.PUT_LINE('Unable to update isbn 78824389');
    END IF;

    COMMIT;
EXCEPTION
    WHEN OTHERS
        THEN
        DBMS_OUTPUT.PUT_LINE(SQLERRM);
END;
/
```

> **NOTE**
> *Using %ISOPEN with implicit cursors always return a value of FALSE, since they are closed automatically. While there is no error, using %ISOPEN is not useful with implicit cursors.*

Cursor Variables

Cursor *variables* offer a dynamic and persistent cursor alternative to the static explicit cursors we demonstrated earlier. Cursor variables are evaluated at run time instead of compile time and can be opened for multiple SELECT statements in the same block.

Cursor variables can be implemented in different ways, depending on the need. For the most part, they share the same level of control as explicit cursors. That said, they do not always need to be explicitly closed, and FETCH is not required to retrieve records, though it can be used. One more great feature of cursor variables is that they provide a way for procedures (discussed in Chapter 8) to return a result set.

The following anonymous block declares a cursor variable and then opens, fetches from, and closes the cursor:

```
-- Available online as part of CursorVariable1.sql
SET SERVEROUTPUT ON
DECLARE
    TYPE book_typ IS REF CURSOR RETURN BOOKS%ROWTYPE;
    cv_books book_typ;
    v_books BOOKS%ROWTYPE;
BEGIN

    DBMS_OUTPUT.ENABLE(1000000);

    OPEN cv_books FOR
    SELECT *
    FROM books
    WHERE isbn = '78824389';

    FETCH cv_books INTO v_books;

    DBMS_OUTPUT.PUT_LINE(v_books.title||' is '||v_books.price);

    CLOSE cv_books;
END;
/
```

For this example, we declared a type named book_typ as a REF CURSOR. We then declared a cursor variable of that type and declared a local variable to receive the record during the FETCH. Finally, the cursor is closed.

This example does not show some of my favorite features of cursor variables, though. The following example is a stored procedure that returns a result set to the SQL*Plus prompt. In the example, the cursor variable declaration uses the built-in SYS_REFCURSOR type (available in Oracle 9*i*):

```
-- Available online as part of CursorVariable2.sql
SET SERVEROUTPUT ON
CREATE OR REPLACE PROCEDURE authors_sel (
    cv_results IN OUT SYS_REFCURSOR)
IS
BEGIN
    OPEN cv_results FOR
    SELECT id, first_name, last_name
    FROM authors;
END;
/
```

In the procedure, we declared the cursor variable and associated it with a SELECT statement when it was opened. We did not FETCH from the cursor, nor did we close it, because we want the result set available to our client application even after the program is complete. To run this, we type

```
-- Available online as part of CursorVariable2.sql
COL first_name FORMAT A12
VARIABLE x REFCURSOR
EXEC authors_sel(:x)
PRINT x
```

This returns the results as expected:

```
   ID FIRST_NAME   LAST_NAME
----- ------ ------
    1 Marlene      Theriault
    2 Rachel       Carmichael
    3 James        Viscusi
```

Had we closed the cursor variable inside the procedure, it would have compiled just fine. We would have been unable to retrieve the output from the SQL*Plus prompt, however.

Cursor Subqueries

Cursor *subqueries,* sometimes called nested cursor expressions, were made available in Oracle 9*i* with the integration of SQL*Plus and PL/SQL parsers. They were a feature first introduced to SQL in Oracle 8*i,* but without integration to PL/SQL, their use was severely limited.

Cursor subqueries use a cursor expression inside a SQL SELECT statement. They can be used with all types of cursors defined thus far, except implicit cursors. The return type is always of type REF CURSOR.

This example uses a cursor subquery in an explicit cursor:

```
-- Available online as part of CursorSubquery.sql
SET SERVEROUTPUT ON
DECLARE
    cv_author SYS_REFCURSOR;
    v_title BOOKS.TITLE%TYPE;
    v_author AUTHORS%ROWTYPE;
    v_counter PLS_INTEGER := 0;

    CURSOR book_cur
    IS
        SELECT b.title,
```

```
        CURSOR (SELECT *
                FROM authors a
                WHERE a.id = b.author1
                OR a.id = b.author2
                OR a.id = b.author3)
    FROM books b
    WHERE isbn = '78824389';

BEGIN
    OPEN book_cur;
    LOOP
        FETCH book_cur INTO v_title, cv_author;
        EXIT WHEN book_cur%NOTFOUND;

        DBMS_OUTPUT.PUT_LINE('Title from the main cursor: '||v_title);
        LOOP
            FETCH cv_author INTO v_author;
            EXIT WHEN cv_author%NOTFOUND;

            v_counter := v_counter + 1;
            DBMS_OUTPUT.PUT_LINE('Author'||v_counter||': '
                                 ||v_author.first_name||' '
                                 ||v_author.last_name);
        END LOOP;
    END LOOP;

    CLOSE book_cur;

END;
/
```

When executed, this block returns the following:

```
Title from the main cursor: Oracle PL/SQL Tips and Techniques
Author1: Brad Brown
Author2: Rich Niemic
Author3: Joe Trezzo
```

Open Cursors

The number of open cursors allowed at any given time is controlled by the
init.ora parameter called OPEN_CURSORS. To determine the maximum
number, run the following query:

```
SELECT value
FROM v$parameter
WHERE name = 'open_cursors';
```

We have ours set to a very low value of 20 to show what happens when this number is exceeded. To test this, we will modify the example we used for the cursor subquery so that it returns all records. The cursor is modified as follows:

```
-- Available online as part of OpenCursor.sql
    CURSOR book_cur
    IS
        SELECT b.title,
            CURSOR (SELECT *
                    FROM authors a
                    WHERE a.id = b.author1
                    OR a.id = b.author2
                    OR a.id = b.author3)
        FROM books b;
```

All we removed is the WHERE clause. Running this anonymous block again, it loops through each book and prints all authors associated with it, but it ends with the following error:

```
DECLARE
*
ERROR at line 1:
ORA-01000: maximum open cursors exceeded
ORA-06512: at line 25
```

DML and DDL

Data Manipulation Language (DML) includes INSERT, UPDATE, and DELETE statements that modify data. PL/SQL supports DML commands directly. The following example is an anonymous block that does an update to the dual table (well, not really...notice the WHERE clause).

```
-- Available online as part of UpdateDual.sql
BEGIN
    UPDATE dual
    SET dummy = 'x'
    WHERE 1=2;
END;
/
```

TIP
Never, ever really update the dual table! This is a common method to initiate a transaction without doing anything. The WHERE clause never evaluates to TRUE because 1 cannot equal 2.

This block compiles without error. Now consider another simple example using DDL. This example creates a table with a single column:

```
-- Available online as part of DDL.sql
BEGIN
    CREATE TABLE ddl_table (
        id NUMBER(10));
EXCEPTION
    WHEN OTHERS
    THEN
        DBMS_OUTPUT.PUT_LINE(sqlerrm);
END;
/
```

This fails!

```
    CREATE TABLE ddl_table (
    *
ERROR at line 2:
ORA-06550: line 2, column 4:
PLS-00103: Encountered the symbol "CREATE" when expecting one of the following:
begin case declare exit for goto if loop mod null pragma
raise return select update while with <an identifier>
...
```

Why did it fail?

Pre-Compilation

PL/SQL objects are precompiled. All dependencies are checked prior to execution, making program execution much faster. Dependencies are not related to data. They are on other database objects, such as tables, views, synonyms, and other program structures. As such, DML that is run in a PL/SQL block stands no chance of changing a dependency that would cause a program failure. DDL, on the other hand, which supports CREATE, DROP, and ALTER commands, as well as permission control statements GRANT and REVOKE, can change the dependencies during execution, if allowed.

For example, if we have a block that first drops a table and then attempts to update that same table, it would of course fail to execute properly. That dependency cannot be checked ahead of time, though. Until the time of execution, the UPDATE would look as if it would be successful, since the table currently exists. It fails only when the block is run because of the dropped object.

DDL statements are therefore not allowed directly in PL/SQL. As we will discuss later in this section, and in Chapter 13 as well, Oracle provides a way around this restriction.

Manipulating Data with DML

As discussed at the beginning of this chapter in the section titled "Transaction Processing," DML statements require an explicit COMMIT before changes become permanent. DML also supports ROLLBACK and SAVEPOINT to revert changes prior to commit when they should not be permanent.

NOTE
Not all clauses available for these DML statements are presented. For a complete list of available clauses, refer to the Oracle Database SQL reference at http://otn.oracle.com.

INSERT

INSERT statements add records to tables. The basic syntax for an INSERT is

INSERT INTO *table_name* [(*column_list*)]
VALUES *select_statement* | (*value_list*);

The *table_name* can be a table, a synonym, or an updatable view. The *column_list* is optional, but we highly recommend including it to prevent problems with values being inserted into the wrong columns. It also helps readability and maintenance. The VALUES clause can include a SELECT statement that retrieves the same number of columns of the same type as the destination table, or a list of values. If a *value_list* is used, it must be in parentheses, and it can include literals or variables. A *value_list* can be any valid expression (as defined in Chapter 3).

The following example includes both literals and variables in its list of VALUES:

```
-- Available online as part of Insert.sql
SET SERVEROUTPUT ON
DECLARE
    v_isbn BOOKS.ISBN%TYPE := '12345678';
    v_category BOOKS.CATEGORY%TYPE := 'Oracle Server';
    v_title BOOKS.TITLE%TYPE := 'Oracle Information Retrieval';
BEGIN
    INSERT INTO books (ISBN,CATEGORY,TITLE,NUM_PAGES,PRICE,
                       COPYRIGHT,AUTHOR1)
    VALUES (v_isbn, v_category, v_title, 450, 39.95,
            2005, 44);

    COMMIT;
EXCEPTION
    WHEN OTHERS
```

```
    THEN
        DBMS_OUTPUT.PUT_LINE(SQLERRM);
        ROLLBACK;
END;
/
```

Take special note of the transaction control (COMMIT and ROLLBACK) used with all of the DML examples. This will be covered to a greater extent in Chapter 7.

UPDATE

An UPDATE statement modifies existing data, following the same transaction control rules as INSERT. The syntax for UPDATE is

UPDATE *table_name*
SET *column_name* = *select_statement* | *value* [, column_name = value]
[WHERE *where_clause* | WHERE CURRENT OF *cursor*];

The *table_name* can be any table, synonym, or updatable view. *Column_name* is any column in the *table_name* specified. The SET clause can include more than one *column_name* in a comma-delimited list. Columns can be set equal to an integer, a variable, or any valid expression. They can also be set equal to the result of a subselect. The optional WHERE CURRENT OF clause is useful when working with a cursor that is declared with a FOR UPDATE clause. The *where_clause* can be any column in the table compared to any expression. The WHERE CURRENT OF clause works with UPDATEs and DELETEs, and says to operate against the current record from the *cursor*.

The first example performs an update against a table, with its value derived from a variable of the same type as the column.

```
-- Available online as part of Update.sql
SET SERVEROUTPUT ON
DECLARE
    v_num_pages BOOKS.NUM_PAGES%TYPE;
    v_isbn BOOKS.ISBN%TYPE := '72230665';
BEGIN
    SELECT num_pages
    INTO v_num_pages
    FROM books
    WHERE isbn = v_isbn;

    DBMS_OUTPUT.PUT_LINE('Number of pages before: '||v_num_pages);

    v_num_pages := v_num_pages + 200;
```

```
    UPDATE books
    SET num_pages = v_num_pages
    WHERE isbn = v_isbn;

    DBMS_OUTPUT.PUT_LINE('Number of pages after: '||v_num_pages);

    COMMIT;
EXCEPTION
    WHEN OTHERS
    THEN
        DBMS_OUTPUT.PUT_LINE(SQLERRM);
        ROLLBACK;
END;
/
```

This second example uses a WHERE CURRENT OF clause.

```
-- Available online as part of WhereCurrentOf.sql
SET SERVEROUTPUT ON
DECLARE
    v_isbn INVENTORY.ISBN%TYPE;
    v_amount INVENTORY.AMOUNT%TYPE;

    CURSOR inventory_cur
    IS
        SELECT isbn, amount
        FROM inventory
        WHERE status = 'IN STOCK'
        AND isbn IN (SELECT isbn
                     FROM books
                     WHERE price > 40)
        FOR UPDATE OF amount;

BEGIN
    FOR y IN inventory_cur
    LOOP
        FETCH inventory_cur INTO v_isbn, v_amount;
        EXIT WHEN inventory_cur%NOTFOUND;

        DBMS_OUTPUT.PUT_LINE(v_isbn||'Amount IN STOCK before: '||v_amount);

        v_amount := v_amount + 250;

        UPDATE inventory
        SET amount = v_amount
        WHERE CURRENT OF inventory_cur;
```

```
        DBMS_OUTPUT.PUT_LINE(v_isbn||'Amount IN STOCK after: '||v_amount);

    END LOOP;
    COMMIT;

EXCEPTION
    WHEN OTHERS
    THEN
        DBMS_OUTPUT.PUT_LINE(SQLERRM);
        ROLLBACK;
END;
/
```

The UPDATE statement modifies only the current record of the cursor.

DELETE

DELETE statements remove data, following the same transaction rules as INSERTs and UPDATEs. Syntax for a DELETE statement is

DELETE FROM *table_name*
[WHERE *where_clause* | WHERE CURRENT OF *cursor*]

The *table_name* can be any table, synonym, or updatable view where the user has DELETE permissions. If no WHERE clause is provided, all records will be deleted. The *where_clause* can be any column in the table compared to any expression. The WHERE CURRENT OF clause works with UPDATEs and DELETEs, and says to operate against the current record from the *cursor*.

The following example performs a DELETE from the AUTHORS table:

```
-- Available online as part of Delete.sql
SET SERVEROUTPUT ON
DECLARE
    v_author AUTHORS%ROWTYPE;
BEGIN

    SELECT *
    INTO v_author
    FROM authors
    WHERE id = 54;

    DELETE FROM authors
    WHERE id = v_author.id;

    DBMS_OUTPUT.PUT_LINE('Author '||v_author.first_name
```

```
                            ||' '||v_author.last_name
                            ||' has been deleted');
    COMMIT;

EXCEPTION
    WHEN OTHERS
    THEN
        DBMS_OUTPUT.PUT_LINE(SQLERRM);
        ROLLBACK;
END;
/
```

The delete is successful:

```
Author Charles Moffett has been deleted
```

Introduction to Dynamic SQL

So far, the SQL statements we have shown you have been static. They are precompiled with the code and are inflexible. Dynamic SQL is built and run during the execution of the block. It does this using either the built-in package called DBMS_SQL or Native Dynamic SQL (NDS).

We mentioned earlier that DDL is not directly supported in PL/SQL. The built-in package DBMS_SQL provides a few dozen procedures and functions that enable the use of dynamic SQL, including DDL. Though not terribly efficient, it has been available since Oracle 7.1 and includes a few features not available with NDS (though not many).

Newer development is likely taking advantage of Native Dynamic SQL (NDS). NDS was introduced in Oracle 8*i* and requires far fewer steps to execute. The next section provides an overview of NDS. Chapter 13 provides full coverage of both DBMS_SQL and NDS.

Native Dynamic SQL

NDS uses a single command, EXECUTE IMMEDIATE, to run statements dynamically within the PL/SQL block. I cannot tell you how excited I was to see this feature come in Oracle 8*i*. While DBMS_SQL is a useful package, it just cannot compare to the simplicity and performance of NDS for most operations.

This example shows how to build a statement dynamically and use the EXECUTE IMMEDIATE command to run it in PL/SQL.

```
-- Available online as part of NDS.sql
SET SERVEROUTPUT ON
DECLARE
```

```
    v_statement VARCHAR2(500);

    CURSOR trigger_cur
    IS
        SELECT trigger_name
        FROM user_triggers;
BEGIN
    FOR y IN trigger_cur
    LOOP
        -- Build the statement
        v_statement := 'ALTER TRIGGER '||y.trigger_name||' DISABLE';

        -- Run the statement
        EXECUTE IMMEDIATE v_statement;
END LOOP;
END;
/
```

This block does the following:

■ It loops through a trigger with all trigger names in the current schema.

■ It builds a DDL statement to alter each trigger retrieved by the cursor to disable it.

■ It executes the statement inside the loop, once for each record in the cursor.

For another example, refer to the `CreateUser.sql` script available online.

Using ROWID and ROWNUM

Similar to the `LEVEL` column discussed earlier, `ROWID` and `ROWNUM` are pseudocolumns that can be used in application development. Just from the names it is easy to tell that both are related to individual rows, or records, in a table. They have very distinct purposes and structures, however.

ROWID

A `ROWID` is a system-generated unique identifier that is created for every record in the database. This binary value is the address, or location of the data in the system. A `ROWID` can be physical, as is the case with records in a standard database table. As discussed in Chapter 3, `ROWID`s can be logical as well, as is the case with rows in an index-organized table.

In my system, the ROWID for the record in the AUTHORS table with my name returns the following result:

```
SELECT rowid
  FROM authors
  WHERE first_name = 'Ron';
```

This returns the following result:

```
ROWID
---------
AAAMZzAAEAAAAB/Aau
```

> **NOTE**
> *Your rowid will differ from mine. It is a system-generated number and cannot be predicted.*

That is the physical location for the record containing my name in the AUTHORS table. It is unique to that record in the database. The structure is broken down in Figure 4-4.

ROWIDs use base-64 encoding and return the ten-byte value as a string when selected from SQL*Plus. Although the structure of the ROWID is fairly easy to understand, deciphering the actual location of the row with the human eye is akin to recognizing a person after seeing their DNA pattern.

Fortunately, we do not have to understand the value as long as Oracle does. We just get to take advantage of the performance edge it provides when accessing data.

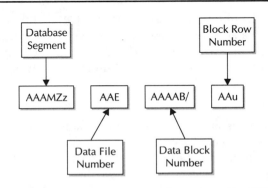

FIGURE 4-4. *ROWID DNA*

ROWID and Performance

One of the biggest benefits of ROWID is the performance improvement it provides when using it to reference a record. No index is necessary, no determination needs to be made whether a full scan of the table is better, and there is no question of cardinality. ROWID provides the address to the record, so no interpretation is required at all.

The following example illustrates how ROWID can be used in an UPDATE. First, we will select the records based on the cursor used later to show the current state of the data:

```
-- Available online as part of RowID.sql
COL first_name FORMAT A10
COL last_name FORMAT A10
SELECT a.rowid, a.first_name, a.last_name
FROM authors a, books b
WHERE b.isbn = '72230665'
AND (
        a.id = b.author1 OR
        a.id = b.author2 OR
        a.id = b.author3);
```

This returns the ROWID, FIRST_NAME, and LAST_NAME of the authors on this book, as follows:

```
ROWID                FIRST_NAME LAST_NAME
---------            ----- -----
AAAMaHAAEAAAAIHAAZ Scott      Urman
AAAMaHAAEAAAAIHAAu Ron        Hardman
AAAMaHAAEAAAAIHAAv Mike       McLaughlin
```

The names are stored in initcap, but we want to convert them to uppercase. Running the following anonymous block does exactly that:

```
-- Available online as part of RowID.sql
SET SERVEROUTPUT ON
DECLARE
/* Retrieve the rowid of the authors
   of this book into the cursor */

   CURSOR author_rowid_cur
   IS
     SELECT a.rowid
     FROM authors a, books b
     WHERE b.isbn = '72230665'
     AND (
```

```
          a.id = b.author1
          OR
          a.id = b.author2
          OR
          a.id = b.author3);
BEGIN
   /* Loop through the records retrieved by the cursor and convert
      the first and last names to uppercase */

   FOR y IN author_rowid_cur
   LOOP
      UPDATE authors
      SET first_name = UPPER(first_name),
          last_name = UPPER(last_name)
      WHERE rowid = y.rowid;
   END LOOP;

   COMMIT;
EXCEPTION
   WHEN OTHERS
   THEN
      DBMS_OUTPUT.PUT_LINE(sqlerrm);
END;
/
```

This block does the following:

- It retrieves the ROWID of the three authors on this book in the AUTHOR_ROWID_CUR.

- It loops through the cursor (pointer to the three rows that match).

- It runs an update that uses the ROWID of each record to restrict the update.

This is a small data set to work with, and we could have used the AUTHORS.ID column without any noticeable performance degradation. However, in a larger application using the same logic, the performance gain would be noticeable, especially if there were no unique key created in the table that could be used as an alternative.

Checking the data one more time, the results are as expected.

```
ROWID                 FIRST_NAME LAST_NAME
--------- ----- -----
AAAMaHAAEAAAAIHAAZ SCOTT      URMAN
AAAMaHAAEAAAAIHAAu RON        HARDMAN
AAAMaHAAEAAAAIHAAv MIKE       MCLAUGHLIN
```

To confirm only these records were updated, we will check the first record in the table.

```
SELECT rowid, first_name, last_name
  FROM authors
  WHERE rownum = 1;
```

This returns

```
ROWID              FIRST_NAME LAST_NAME
---------- ----- -----
AAAMaHAAEAAAAIHAAA Marlene    Theriault
```

Since this name is not all uppercase, we can be certain our update did restrict according to ROWID. As for the use of ROWNUM in that last query, we address it next.

ROWNUM

The ROWNUM pseudocolumn returns the row number of the record. In the last example in the ROWID section, we used ROWNUM to retrieve the very first record in the AUTHORS table. This is a logical number, determined at the time a query is run. As such, a delete or insert can cause a different ROWNUM assignment. Row numbers do not stick to a particular record, so never rely on them as you would a physical ROWID.

One common use of ROWNUM is to restrict the number of records returned. We can run the following SELECT so that it returns only the top ten records in the table:

```
SELECT title
FROM books
WHERE ROWNUM <= 10;
```

This type of query might be used in a function or procedure (using a REFCURSOR) to limit a possible large result set.

NOTE
See Chapter 9 for more information on how to use procedures and functions.

Using ROWNUM with ORDER BY

Using ROWNUM with an ordered result set does not yield the results you might expect. For example, if we want to pull the author names in alphabetical order, but retrieve only the top ten of the ordered list, we cannot use a basic ORDER BY and ROWNUM query.

Here, procedure AUTHOR_SEL performs a select of author names, ordering them by last name, and restricting by ROWNUM:

```
CREATE OR REPLACE PROCEDURE author_sel (
    cv_authors IN OUT SYS_REFCURSOR)
IS
BEGIN
   OPEN cv_authors FOR
   SELECT id, last_name||', '||first_name NAME
   FROM authors
   WHERE rownum <= 10
   ORDER BY last_name;
EXCEPTION
   WHEN OTHERS
   THEN
       DBMS_OUTPUT.PUT_LINE(sqlerrm);
END;
/
```

You may think that this would sort all results and return the first ten ordered by last name in ascending order, but that is not what happens. To run the procedure, we type

```
VARIABLE x REFCURSOR
EXEC author_sel(:x)
```

The result set is now stored in x, so to print it to the screen we type

```
COL name FORMAT A30
PRINT x
```

Notice the results return the top ten rows in the table, then order them by last name instead of sorting the rows, and then restrict them by the top ten.

```
   ID NAME
----- ------------
    4 Abbey, Michael
    9 Abramson, Ian
    2 Carmichael, Rachel
    5 Corey, Michael
    7 Deshpande, Kirtikumar
    8 Kostelac, John
   10 Smith, Kenny
    1 Theriault, Marlene
    6 Vaidyanatha, Gaja
    3 Viscusi, James
```

This does not return what we wanted. Think of this in terms of other business applications, where maybe orders are displayed by date, but only the ten most recent are displayed. The results would contain the first ten rows in the table ordered by date, but never date ordered, with the ten most recent orders.

Inline View The problem with using ROWNUM and ORDER BY can be solved by using an inline view. Inline views are subselects in the FROM clause that act as a view at execution time. They are not named views, stored in the database.

The following alteration to the procedure AUTHOR_SEL handles the problem:

```
CREATE OR REPLACE PROCEDURE author_ordered_sel (
    cv_authors IN OUT SYS_REFCURSOR)
IS
BEGIN
    OPEN cv_authors FOR
    SELECT *
    FROM (
            SELECT id, last_name||', '||first_name NAME
            FROM authors
            ORDER BY last_name) SORTED_AUTHORS
    WHERE rownum <= 10;
EXCEPTION
    WHEN OTHERS
    THEN
        DBMS_OUTPUT.PUT_LINE(sqlerrm);
END;
/
```

We run the procedure just as before, supplying the new procedure name.

```
VARIABLE x REFCURSOR
EXEC author_ordered_sel(:x)
COL name FORMAT A30
PRINT x
```

This procedure delivers exactly what we wanted; an ordered set of data, restricted to the top ten of the ordered list.

```
   ID NAME
----- -------------
    4 Abbey, Michael
    9 Abramson, Ian
   33 Adkoli, Anand
   14 Allen, Christopher
   30 Armstrong-Smith, Michael
   31 Armstrong-Smith, Darlene
```

```
12 Bo, Lars
51 Boudreaux, Scott
36 Brown, Brad
35 Burleson, Donald
```

The ordered inline view solved the problem and allows us to use ROWNUM to achieve the intended result.

Built-in SQL Functions

In addition to SQL commands, PL/SQL supports most SQL built-in functions. Though complete coverage of the functions is out of the scope of this book, we have divided the most used functions into categories.

These built-in functions are actually part of a PL/SQL package called STANDARD. This package, owned by the user SYS, groups the functions together for easier maintenance and use. If the structure of the function is ever needed, simply do a DESC STANDARD and all parameter names and data types are displayed. Packages are discussed in detail in Chapters 8 and 9.

> **NOTE**
> *For additional information on each SQL function, see the Oracle Database SQL reference available on the OTN web site (http://otn.oracle.com).*

Character Functions

Character functions take VARCHAR2 or CHAR values as input and return either characters or numbers. An example of a character function is the LOWER function, which takes a string as input and returns a string in lowercase in return.

```
-- Available online as part of Lower.sql
SET SERVEROUTPUT ON
BEGIN
    DBMS_OUTPUT.PUT_LINE(LOWER('CaSe Is nOt AlWAyS ImpoRtaNt'));
END;
/
```

Refer to Table 4-5 for a list of character functions.

Numeric Functions

Numeric functions take a number as an argument and return a number as a result. The ROUND function, for example, takes a number as an input, and

ASCII	INSTRC	NLS_LOWER	SUBSTR
ASCIISTR	LENGTH	NLS_UPPER	SUBSTR2
CHR	LENGTH2	NLSSORT	SUBSTR4
COMPOSE	LENGTH4	REGEXP_LIKE	SUBSTRB
CONCAT	LENGTHB	REGEXP_INSTR	SUBSTRC
DECOMPOSE	LENGTHC	REGEXP_REPLACE	TRANSLATE
INITCAP	LOWER	REGEXP_SUBSTR	TRIM
INSTR	LPAD	REPLACE	UNISTR
INSTR2	LTRIM	RPAD	UPPER
INSTR4	NCHR	RTRIM	
INSTRB	NLS_INITCAP	SOUNDEX	

TABLE 4-5. *Character Functions*

rounds to the number of digits specified. The syntax is as follows:

ROUND (*a* [, *b*])

where *a* is the number to be rounded and *b* is the number of decimal places to round to. The following example shows how the function works:

```
-- Available online as part of Round.sql
SET SERVEROUTPUT ON
DECLARE
    v_round NUMBER (10,4) := 12345.6789;
BEGIN
    DBMS_OUTPUT.PUT_LINE('Default: '||ROUND(v_round));
    DBMS_OUTPUT.PUT_LINE('+2: '||ROUND(v_round, 2));
    DBMS_OUTPUT.PUT_LINE('-2: '||ROUND(v_round, -2));
END;
/
```

This results in the following:

```
Default: 12346
+2: 12345.68
-2: 12300
```

Other numeric functions are listed in Table 4-6.

ABS	CEIL	LOG	SIN
ACOS	COS	MOD	SINH
ASIN	COSH	POWER	SQRT
ATAN	EXP	REMAINDER	TAN
ATAN2	FLOOR	ROUND	TANH
BITAND	LN	SIGN	TRUNC

TABLE 4-6. *Numeric Functions*

Date Functions

Date functions take dates as arguments and return either a date or a number. The functions in this category range from SYSDATE and SYSTIMESTAMP, which return the current date/time value from the instance, to arithmetic functions like ADD_MONTHS that calculate date/time.

This example shows the use of SYSDATE, SYSTIMESTAMP, MONTHS_BETWEEN, and LAST_DAY:

```
-- Available online as part of DateTime.sql
DECLARE
   v_sysdate DATE := SYSDATE;
   v_systimestamp TIMESTAMP := SYSTIMESTAMP;
   v_date DATE;
   v_number NUMBER(10);
BEGIN

   -- Print the current date
   DBMS_OUTPUT.PUT_LINE('Today''s Date: '||v_sysdate);

   -- Print the current date and timestamp
   DBMS_OUTPUT.PUT_LINE('Today''s Date: '||v_systimestamp);

   -- Calculate the months between two dates
   v_number := MONTHS_BETWEEN('13-JUN-1973', '23-JAN-1973');
   DBMS_OUTPUT.PUT_LINE('Months Between Dates: '||v_number);

   -- Determine the number of days left in the month from today
   v_date := LAST_DAY(v_sysdate);
```

```
    DBMS_OUTPUT.PUT_LINE('Last Day Of This Month: '||v_date);

END;
/
```

This returns the following result:

```
Today's Date: 15-JUN-04
Today's Date: 15-JUN-04 11.57.42.637000 PM
Months Between Dates: 5
Last Day Of This Month: 30-JUN-04
```

Refer to Table 4-7 for additional functions.

Conversion Functions

Conversion functions are divided into two categories: implicit and explicit. Most PL/SQL data types are converted implicitly, or automatically, by Oracle when required. In cases where the output requires a specific format, the default is used. Explicit conversion requires a specific call to one of these functions, but the format of the output is controllable.

Two of the most commonly used conversion functions, TO_DATE and TO_CHAR, work with dates. TO_DATE takes a string as input and returns output as a DATE data type. When working with dates, TO_CHAR takes a date as input and returns the output in a VARCHAR2 format.

ADD_MONTHS	MONTHS_BETWEEN	SYSTIMESTAMP
CURRENT_DATE	NEW_TIME	TO_DSINTERVAL
CURRENT_TIME	NEXT_DAY	TO_TIME
CURRENT_TIMESTAMP	NUMTODSINTERVAL	TO_TIME_TZ
DBTIMEZONE	NUMTOYMINTERVAL	TO_TIMESTAMP
EXTRACT	ROUND	TO_TIMESTAMP_TZ
FROM_TZ	SESSIONTIMEZONE	TO_YMINTERVAL
LAST_DAY	SYS_EXTRACT_UTC	TRUNC
LOCALTIMESTAMP	SYSDATE	TZ_OFFSET

TABLE 4-7.   *Date Functions*

The following example converts between TO_DATE and TO_CHAR, modifying the format along the way:

```
-- Available online as part of Conversion.sql
SET SERVEROUTPUT ON
DECLARE
    v_sysdate DATE := SYSDATE;
    v_date DATE;
    v_char VARCHAR2(20);
BEGIN

    -- Print the current date
    DBMS_OUTPUT.PUT_LINE('Today''s Date: '||v_sysdate);

    -- Print the current date/time as a character string
    --  and modifies the format
    v_char := TO_CHAR(v_sysdate, 'DD:MM:YYYY HH24:MI:SS');
    DBMS_OUTPUT.PUT_LINE('Display as CHARACTER DD:MM:YYYY HH24:MI:SS: '||
                        v_char);

    -- Convert the character string back to date format
    v_date := TO_DATE(v_char, 'DD:MM:YYYY HH24:MI:SS');
    DBMS_OUTPUT.PUT_LINE('Convert back to DATE format: '||v_date);

END;
/
```

This returns the following output:

```
Today's Date: 16-JUN-04
Display as CHARACTER DD:MM:YYYY HH24:MI:SS: 16:06:2004 07:42:33
Convert back to DATE format: 16-JUN-04
```

Table 4-8 includes a listing of additional conversion functions.

Error Functions

Error functions are unique in that they cannot be used in SQL. They provide PL/SQL developers with a way to display any errors that are received during program

CASE	RAWTONHEX	TO_CHAR	TO_NCLOB
CHARTOROWID	ROWIDTOCHAR	TO_CLOB	TO_NUMBER
CONVERT	TO_BINARY_DOUBLE	TO_DATE	TO_SINGLE_BYTE
HEXTORAW	TO_BLOB	TO_MULTI_BYTE	
RAWTOHEX	TO_BINARY_FLOAT	TO_NCHAR	

TABLE 4-8. *Conversion Functions*

execution. SQLERRM returns the error message text received, and SQLCODE returns the error code. The following block illustrates this:

```
-- Available online as part of Error.sql
SET SERVEROUTPUT ON
DECLARE
    v_error VARCHAR2(10);
BEGIN
    SELECT dummy
    INTO v_error
    FROM dual
    WHERE 1=2;
EXCEPTION
    WHEN OTHERS
    THEN
        DBMS_OUTPUT.PUT_LINE('SQLERRM: '||SQLERRM);
        DBMS_OUTPUT.PUT_LINE('SQLCODE: '||SQLCODE);
END;
/
```

The results of the block show the difference between these two functions:

```
SQLERRM: ORA-01403: no data found
SQLCODE: 100
```

These error functions are discussed in more detail in Chapter 7.

Other Functions

The functions in this section don't fit into a nice category listing. Many of them are discussed in detail in other chapters of this book because of their relationship to specific technologies. For example, DEREF, REF, TREAT, and VALUE are all related to object types and are discussed in Chapters 14 and 15. BFILENAME, EMPTY_ BLOB, and EMPTY_CLOB are all LOB related and are demonstrated in Chapter 16.

This example shows the use of the GREATEST and LEAST functions in a PL/SQL block:

```
-- Available online as part of GreatestLeast.sql
SET SERVEROUTPUT ON
DECLARE
    v_char VARCHAR2(10);
    v_number NUMBER(10);
BEGIN

    v_char := GREATEST('A', 'B', 'C');
    v_number := GREATEST(1,2,3);

    DBMS_OUTPUT.PUT_LINE('Greatest Character: '||v_char);
    DBMS_OUTPUT.PUT_LINE('Greatest Number: '||v_number);

    v_char := LEAST('A', 'B', 'C');
    v_number := LEAST(1,2,3);

    DBMS_OUTPUT.PUT_LINE('Least Character: '||v_char);
    DBMS_OUTPUT.PUT_LINE('Least Number: '||v_number);

END;
/
```

The output for GREATEST character returns 'C', or the greatest letter provided to the function, while the GREATEST number returns '3', or the highest value. LEAST provides the exact opposite.

```
Greatest Character: C
Greatest Number: 3
Least Character: A
Least Number: 1
```

Table 4-9 displays a complete list of SQL functions not included in the other tables.

BFILENAME	EMPTY_CLOB	NLS_CHARSET_NAME	TREAT
COALESCE	GREATEST	NULLIF	UID
DECODE	LEAST	NVL	USER
DEREF	NANVL	REF	USERENV
DUMP	NLS_CHARSET_DECL_LEN	SYS_CONTEXT	VALUE
EMPTY_BLOB	NLS_CHARSET_ID	SYS_GUID	VSIZE

TABLE 4-9.   *Other Functions*

Summary

In this chapter we demonstrated how to use SQL in PL/SQL, including

- Data retrieval with SELECT, Regular Expressions, and Oracle Text
- Cursor use
- Manipulating data with DML
- Built-in functions
- The use of ROWID and ROWNUM
- Dynamic SQL

The next chapter focuses on PL/SQL records.

CHAPTER
5

Records

ecords and collections are powerful structures that enable you to develop programs that manage large sets of data. Records let you manage sets of variable types; collections let you manage groups of a variable type. You need to have a command of records to use collections. In this chapter, we will explain records and show you how to use them in your PL/SQL programming code. Collections will be covered in Chapter 6.

We will cover topics as follows. The chapter assumes you read it sequentially. If you feel comfortable with an area, please feel free to move to the section of interest. However, the chapter assumes you have mastery of earlier sections.

- Introducing records

- Working with records

Introducing Records

Records were introduced in the Oracle 7 database. They have grown in utility with each release of the Oracle database. Oracle 8 provided object types, but they were feature limited. Oracle 10g changed that. Object types now have user-defined constructors. The constructors enable object types to mimic record types. Record and object types are compared and contrasted in their roles as types.

What Is a Record?

A *record* provides the means of defining a programming structure. A programming structure is a set of variable types. They are grouped together and managed as a unit. Record types map to a stored definition of the structure.

For example, a database table or view contains rows of information. The table's columns define each row. A record type is a programming structure that mirrors a single row in a table. Since there is only a single row in any record, a record contains fields rather than columns. Field types may be any Oracle 10g data type or user-defined data type. As you will see in Chapter 6, the data types can be collections. Collections become multiple row fields in record types.

Working with Records

Oracle 9i and Oracle 10g increase the flexibility and complexity of records. Most of the change is due to enhancements to the two collection types introduced in Oracle 8, varrays and nested tables.

As discussed, records are structures. Structures are sets of variable types that are grouped together. The grouping of variable types and naming of variables is meaningful in the context of a programming problem. Often record structures are created to mimic the structure of tables in a database. We will examine this approach first.

We will use the ERD diagram (see Figure 5-1) to define our case study for the chapter. It defines three tables. One contains individual records; the others contain an address and phone numbers, respectively. The small ERD model has the following relationships. The code for the tables is found in the `create_addressbook1.sql` script.

- An individual may have one to many addresses or telephone numbers.

- One or more telephone numbers may be related to an address.

Defining Record Types

There are three ways to define records in PL/SQL. One uses the `%ROWTYPE` attribute. Another uses explicit definition in the declaration section of a PL/SQL program. Last, a record type may be defined as a database structure or object type.

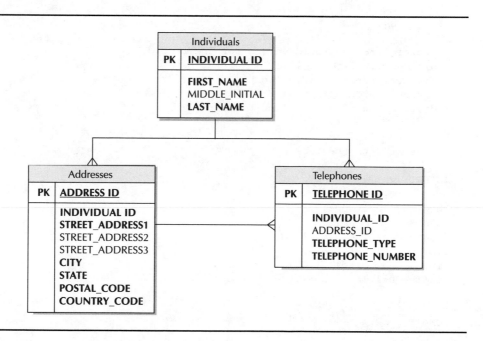

FIGURE 5-1. *Address book entity relationship diagram*

A record type is like a single row in a table. You know one or more columns define tables. Since record types have only one row, fields define them. One or more fields define a record type.

Defining Implicity with the %ROWTYPE Attribute

The %ROWTYPE attribute may be applied to or reference a PL/SQL cursor, table, object, or view in the database. It inherits the definition of a row for any of those objects. Within the row all fields are implicitly defined as the column data types of the table being referenced. The field names are likewise those of the columns defined in the table. The following program shows the use of the %ROWTYPE attribute. The individuals%ROWTYPE defines the record variable individual. Using the variable and field name separated by a dot, you can access record variable types. That syntax is shown in this example:

```
-- Available online as part of create_record1.sql
DECLARE

  -- Define a variable with an implicit record type.
  individual individuals%ROWTYPE;

BEGIN

  -- Initialize the field values for the record.
  individual.individual_id := 1;
  individual.first_name := 'John';
  individual.middle_initial := 'D';
  individual.last_name := 'Rockefeller';


  -- Insert into the table.

  INSERT

  INTO     individuals
  VALUES
  (individual.individual_id
  ,individual.first_name
  ,individual.middle_initial
  ,individual.last_name);

  -- Commit the work.
  COMMIT;
```

```
END;
/
```

The sample program does the following:

- It defines and declares a variable `individual` using the `%ROWTYPE` attribute. The `%ROWTYPE` attribute maps the `individuals` table structure for a record type.

- It initializes the field values for the `individual` variable.

- It uses an insert statement to populate a row in the `individuals` table.

- It commits the work.

The column definitions for the table are the field definitions for the record type. A dot notation references the field values. The generalized assignment syntax is

```
RECORD_TYPE.FIELD_TYPE := VALUE;
```

It then uses the dot notation of record and field type to insert a row into the `individuals` table.

Defining Record Types Explicitly as PL/SQL Structures

You may build a record explicitly by defining a record type in the declaration section of a PL/SQL program. You may use explicit variable typing or the `%TYPE` attribute to define variables. Both styles are used in the example. The following program shows how to define a record type.

Unlike when using the implicit definition technique illustrated in the prior example, you must define a record type. You then define the variable as a record type. You can then use it in the execution section of a PL/SQL program as shown in the following sample program.

```
-- Available online as part of create_record2.sql

DECLARE

  -- Define a record type.
  TYPE individual_record IS RECORD
  (individual_id  INTEGER
  ,first_name     VARCHAR2(30 CHAR)
```

```
  ,middle_initial individuals.middle_initial%TYPE
  ,last_name      VARCHAR2(30 CHAR));

-- Define a variable of the record type.
individual INDIVIDUAL_RECORD;

BEGIN

-- Initialize the field values for the record.
individual.individual_id := 2;
individual.first_name := 'John';
individual.middle_initial := 'P';
individual.last_name := 'Morgan';

-- Insert into the table.
INSERT
INTO       individuals
VALUES
(individual.individual_id
,individual.first_name
,individual.middle_initial
,individual.last_name);

-- Commit the work.
COMMIT;

END;
/
```

The sample program does the following:

■ It defines a record-type variable, `individual_record`. This is an explicitly defined record type. It explicitly defines data types for three of the fields. The data type definitions mirror the equivalent column definitions in the `individuals` table. The `middle_initial` field data type is implicitly assigned. It uses the `%TYPE` style. The `%TYPE` inherits the data type of a column in a table. The variable is defined by the generalized syntax (and the details may be found in Chapter 3):

```
VARIABLE TABLE.COLUMN%TYPE;
```

- It defines an `individual` variable that uses the `individual_record` record type.

- It initializes the field values for the `individual` variable.

- It uses an insert statement to populate a row in the `individuals` table.

- It commits the work.

The column definition becomes the field definition with a `%TYPE`. As the column definitions for the table change, so does the field definition of the record type. The same cannot be said for those columns defined explicitly in PL/SQL programs.

You need to define a variable of the record type to use it. This was not required in the prior example when defining a variable of an object with the `%ROWTYPE` attribute. Otherwise, the code using the explicit technique is a mirror of the prior example file.

You may build on the techniques of explicitly defined record types. You can create a compound record type. Using your two defined record types, you can create a compound record type. Your two record types will then become subtypes of the compound record type. Compound record types are most useful when combined with collections, as will be seen in Chapter 6. Figure 5-2 shows the hierarchy of the compound record types used in the example.

When you build compound record types, you can use *only* record types that are explicitly defined. You cannot use the `%ROWTYPE` attribute to define either of the base record types. They must be explicitly defined.

Compound record types nest record types. When you nest record types, you increase the complexity of the syntax to access record type elements. Adding a layer to the dot notation enables this.

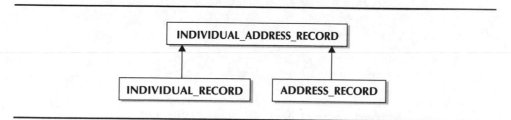

FIGURE 5-2. *Compound record type hierarchy*

The following example program demonstrates the definition and referencing of nested record types in a compound record type:

```
-- Available online as part of create_record3.sql
DECLARE

   -- Define a record type.
   TYPE individual_record IS RECORD
   (individual_id    INTEGER
   ,first_name       VARCHAR2(30 CHAR)
   ,middle_initial   VARCHAR2(1 CHAR)
   ,last_name        VARCHAR2(30 CHAR));

   -- Define a record type.
   TYPE address_record IS RECORD
   (address_id       INTEGER
   ,individual_id    INTEGER
   ,street_address1  VARCHAR2(30 CHAR)
   ,street_address2  VARCHAR2(30 CHAR)
   ,street_address3  VARCHAR2(30 CHAR)
   ,city             VARCHAR2(20 CHAR)
   ,state            VARCHAR2(20 CHAR)
   ,postal_code      VARCHAR2(20 CHAR)
   ,country_code     VARCHAR2(10 CHAR));

   -- Define a record type of two user-defined record types.
   TYPE individual_address_record IS RECORD
   (individual       INDIVIDUAL_RECORD
   ,address          ADDRESS_RECORD);

   -- Define a user-defined compound record type.
   individual_address INDIVIDUAL_ADDRESS_RECORD;

BEGIN

   -- Initialize the field values for the record.
   individual_address.individual.individual_id := 3;
   individual_address.individual.first_name := 'Ulysses';
   individual_address.individual.middle_initial := 'S';
   individual_address.individual.last_name := 'Grant';

   -- Initialize the field values for the record.
   individual_address.address.address_id := 1;
   individual_address.address.individual_id := 3;
   individual_address.address.street_address1 :=
     'Riverside Park';
   individual_address.address.street_address2 := '';
```

```
individual_address.address.street_address3 := '';
individual_address.address.city := 'New York City';
individual_address.address.state := 'New York';
individual_address.address.postal_code := '10027-3914';
individual_address.address.country_code := 'USA';

-- Insert the values into the target object.
INSERT
INTO       individuals
VALUES
(individual_address.individual.individual_id
,individual_address.individual.first_name
,individual_address.individual.middle_initial
,individual_address.individual.last_name);

-- Insert the values into the target object.
INSERT
INTO       addresses
VALUES
(individual_address.address.address_id
(individual_address.address.individual_id
,individual_address.address.street_address1
,individual_address.address.street_address2
,individual_address.address.street_address2
,individual_address.address.city
,individual_address.address.state
,individual_address.address.postal_code
,individual_address.address.country_code);

-- Commit the record.
COMMIT;

END;
/
```

The sample program does the following:

- It defines a record-type variable, individual_record. All fields are explicitly defined in the PL/SQL program equivalent to the related table.

- It defines a record-type variable, address_record. All fields are explicitly defined in the PL/SQL program equivalent to the related table.

- It defines a record-type variable, individual_address_record. This new record type is a compound record type. It has two fields, which are the earlier individual_record and address_record record types. Each of the record types becomes a subtype of the compound record type.

- It defines an `individual_address` variable using the `individual_ address_record` compound record type as the data type.

- It initializes the `individual_address` variable field values for the `individual` subtype. Initialization is carried out by assigning values to the field-level elements in the record type. You initialize by using a two-dot notation. On the left side of the assignment operator, the two-dot notation separates the variable from subtype record and the subtype record from the field values as shown here:

  RECORD_TYPE.NESTED_RECORD_TYPE.FIELD_TYPE := VALUE;

- It initializes the field values for the `address` subtype. Initialization is accomplished by assigning values to the field-level elements in the record type.

- It inserts a row into the `individuals` table, which is a parent table in the ERD model. The table is a parent table because of a referential integrity constraint found in the `addresses` table.

- It inserts a row into the `addresses` table, which is a child table in the ERD model.

- It commits the work.

While PL/SQL does not impose a limit that constrains nesting, you should carefully consider when it is appropriate to do it. Ideal situations for nesting involve nested record sets that have two or more database tables related to the record set. For example, in the prior example, the subsets belong to two tables. After initializing the set, the two subsets are inserted into their respective tables.

Defining Record Types Explicitly as Object Types

You may construct a record explicitly by defining an object type within the database. Your object type will be referenced in your program's declaration section. The techniques of working with Oracle 10*g* objects are covered in Chapters 14–16. The programs that follow leverage database object types and use the Oracle 10*g* user-defined constructor feature.

The following program illustrates defining the object type and a variable that uses it. The syntax can be counterintuitive to programmers who have not done object-oriented programming. It is recommended that you look at Chapter 14 for generalized syntax and coverage of object construction.

-- Available online as part of create_record4.sql

```
-- Create a database object type.
CREATE OR REPLACE TYPE individual_record AS OBJECT
```

```
  (individual_id   INTEGER
  ,first_name      VARCHAR2(30 CHAR)
  ,middle_initial VARCHAR2(1 CHAR)
  ,last_name       VARCHAR2(30 CHAR)
  ,CONSTRUCTOR FUNCTION individual_record
  (individual_id   INTEGER
  ,first_name      VARCHAR2
  ,middle_initial VARCHAR2
  ,last_name       VARCHAR2)
  RETURN SELF AS RESULT)
  INSTANTIABLE NOT FINAL;
/

-- Create a database object body.
CREATE OR REPLACE TYPE BODY individual_record AS
  CONSTRUCTOR FUNCTION individual_record
  (individual_id   INTEGER
  ,first_name      VARCHAR2
  ,middle_initial VARCHAR2
  ,last_name       VARCHAR2)
  RETURN SELF AS RESULT IS
  BEGIN
    self.individual_id := individual_id;
    self.first_name := first_name;
    self.middle_initial := middle_initial;
    self.last_name := last_name;
    RETURN;
  END;
END;
/

DECLARE

  -- Define a variable of the record type.
  individual INDIVIDUAL_RECORD;

BEGIN

  -- Construct an instance of the object type.
  individual :=
    individual_record(4,'Klaes','M','van Roosevelt');

  -- Insert the values into the table.
  INSERT
  INTO      individuals
  VALUES
  (individual.individual_id
  ,individual.first_name
```

```
    ,individual.middle_initial
    ,individual.last_name);

    -- Commit the work.
    COMMIT;

END;
/
```

The sample program does the following:

- It defines an object-type variable, `individual_record`. All fields are explicitly defined in the database object type and are equivalent to the related table. It also contains a user-defined constructor. You can see the structure of the object by issuing a `DESCRIBE` command at the SQL*Plus prompt. Also, you can query the object by using the `USER_OBJECTS` view.

- It defines an object body for the `individual_record` object type. The constructor acts like a function with a parameterized list of formal parameters that match the object type. The return value for the constructor is an instance, or copy, of the object type. The constructor function assigns the formal parameters to variables of the same name. They are prefaced with the keyword SELF. The SELF keyword references what is termed an instance variable of an object type. You can read more on the SELF keyword in Chapter 14.

- In the PL/SQL anonymous block, it defines an `individual_address` variable using the `individual_address_record` compound object type as the data type.

- Also in the PL/SQL anonymous block, it initializes the `individual` variable by constructing an instance of an `individual_record` object type. Using a special syntax initializes it. On the left side of the assignment operator, you have the variable name. The right side uses the object construction process, which uses the object body constructor function to initialize the field-level values. The generalized syntax uses the object type name and a comma-delimited set of actual parameters. It is shown here:

  ```
  OBJECT_CONSTRUCTOR( [ attr1, … attr(n+1) ] );
  ```

- It inserts a row into the `individuals` table, which is a parent table in the ERD model. The table is a parent table because of a referential integrity constraint found in the `addresses` table.

- It commits the work.

A DESCRIBE of the `individual_record` object will provide the following output:

```
-- Available in the database after running create_record4.sql

individual_record is NOT FINAL
 Name                                  Null?    Type
 ----------------------------------- -------- ------------------
 INDIVIDUAL_ID                                  NUMBER(38)
 FIRST_NAME                                     VARCHAR2(30 CHAR)
 MIDDLE_INITIAL                                 VARCHAR2(1 CHAR)
 LAST_NAME                                      VARCHAR2(30 CHAR)

METHOD
------
 FINAL CONSTRUCTOR FUNCTION INDIVIDUAL_RECORD RETURNS SELF AS RESULT
 Argument Name                 Type                 In/Out Default?
 --------------------------- -------------------- ------ --------
 INDIVIDUAL_ID                 NUMBER               IN
 FIRST_NAME                    VARCHAR2             IN
 MIDDLE_INITIAL                VARCHAR2             IN
 LAST_NAME                     VARCHAR2             IN
```

Building on the techniques of compound record types, you can now examine how one works using compound object types. The example illustrates extending an object by constructing nested object types in the constructor of a compound object type. These features are introduced here to help you understand the new flexibility of object types as record types, and they are explained in Chapters 4–16.

You may recall that the base record types need to be explicitly defined. These can be defined in a number of ways. For example, they can be defined in the declaration section, as done earlier in this chapter. Alternatively, they can be defined in a package specification, which you can check in Chapter 8. Finally, they can be defined as object types in the database.

As seen in the last example, the syntax for leveraging object types to build records is less than intuitive. It is just a bit less intuitive for compound objects. This is why the syntax coverage is incorporated here and in Chapter 14. If you have done object-oriented programming, you will notice this is a form of composition. Composition is the process by which a program structure or unit contains another program structure or unit.

In the next example, you will build another base object type for the `addresses` table. You will then build a compound object. In it, the object types for `individuals` and `addresses` become subtypes. The individual object type is included in the prior example but is not repeated here.

You gain reusability and access by leveraging object types. The alternative is defining record types in package specifications. Object types stand on their own merits in the database and are generally more intuitive to access and use, while declaring record types in package specifications may limit reuse to application programming interfaces. However, if you want to hide a record type, doing so in a package specification is an excellent choice.

The following program demonstrates using a compound object type as a record structure. While `create_record5.sql` has a dependency on the prior example, it can be run independently. If you compare this against the example of compound record types earlier in the chapter, you should find it simpler. At least, you should find it simpler once the newness of constructor syntax has worn away. As we move through the collection section in Chapter 6, you will see how object features become more helpful in building effective solutions.

```
-- Available online as part of create_record5.sql
-- Create a database object type.
CREATE OR REPLACE TYPE address_record AS OBJECT
  (address_id      INTEGER
  ,individual_id   INTEGER
  ,street_address1 VARCHAR2(30 CHAR)
  ,street_address2 VARCHAR2(30 CHAR)
  ,street_address3 VARCHAR2(30 CHAR)
  ,city            VARCHAR2(20 CHAR)
  ,state           VARCHAR2(20 CHAR)
  ,postal_code     VARCHAR2(20 CHAR)
  ,country_code    VARCHAR2(10 CHAR)
  ,CONSTRUCTOR FUNCTION address_record
  (address_id      INTEGER
  ,individual_id   INTEGER
  ,street_address1 VARCHAR2
  ,street_address2 VARCHAR2
  ,street_address3 VARCHAR2
  ,city            VARCHAR2
  ,state           VARCHAR2
  ,postal_code     VARCHAR2
  ,country_code    VARCHAR2)
  RETURN SELF AS RESULT)
  INSTANTIABLE NOT FINAL;
/

-- Create a database object body.
CREATE OR REPLACE TYPE BODY address_record AS
  CONSTRUCTOR FUNCTION address_record
  (address_id      INTEGER
  ,individual_id   INTEGER
  ,street_address1 VARCHAR2
```

```
      ,street_address2 VARCHAR2
      ,street_address3 VARCHAR2
      ,city            VARCHAR2
      ,state           VARCHAR2
      ,postal_code     VARCHAR2
      ,country_code    VARCHAR2)
      RETURN SELF AS RESULT IS
      BEGIN
        -- Instantiate object attributes.
        self.address_id := address_id;
        self.individual_id := individual_id;
        self.street_address1 := street_address1;
        self.street_address2 := street_address2;
        self.street_address3 := street_address3;
        self.city := city;
        self.state := state;
        self.postal_code := postal_code;
        self.country_code := country_code;
        RETURN;
      END;
    END;
    /


-- Create a database object type.
CREATE OR REPLACE TYPE individual_address_record AS OBJECT
  (individual       INDIVIDUAL_RECORD
  ,address          ADDRESS_RECORD
  ,CONSTRUCTOR FUNCTION individual_address_record
  (individual       INDIVIDUAL_RECORD
  ,address          ADDRESS_RECORD)
  RETURN SELF AS RESULT)
  INSTANTIABLE NOT FINAL;
/


-- Create a database object body.
CREATE OR REPLACE TYPE BODY individual_address_record AS
  CONSTRUCTOR FUNCTION individual_address_record
  (individual       INDIVIDUAL_RECORD
  ,address          ADDRESS_RECORD)
  RETURN SELF AS RESULT IS
  BEGIN
    -- Assign an instance of INDIVIDUAL_RECORD.
    self.individual := individual;

    -- Assign an instance of ADDRESS_RECORD.
    self.address := address;
    RETURN;
```

```
  END;
END;
/

DECLARE

  -- Define a variable of the record type.
  individual_address INDIVIDUAL_ADDRESS_RECORD;

BEGIN

  -- Construct an instance of the object type.
  -- It uses two nested constructors in the constructor.
  individual_address :=
    individual_address_record(
      individual_record(5,'Kermit','','Roosevelt'),
      address_record(2,5,'20 Sagamore Hill','',''
                     ,'Oyster Bay','NY'
                     ,'11771-1899','USA'));

  -- Insert the values into the table.
  INSERT
  INTO        individuals
  VALUES
  (individual_address.individual.individual_id
  ,individual_address.individual.first_name
  ,individual_address.individual.middle_initial
  ,individual_address.individual.last_name);

  -- Insert the values into the target object.
  INSERT
  INTO        addresses
  VALUES
  (individual_address.address.address_id
  ,individual_address.individual.individual_id
  ,individual_address.address.street_address1
  ,individual_address.address.street_address2
  ,individual_address.address.street_address3
  ,individual_address.address.city
  ,individual_address.address.state
  ,individual_address.address.postal_code
  ,individual_address.address.country_code);

  -- Commit the record.
  COMMIT;

END;
/
```

The sample program does the following:

■ It defines an object-type variable, `address_record`. All fields are explicitly defined in the database object type and are equivalent to the related table. It also contains a user-defined constructor.

■ It defines an object body for the `address_record` object type. The constructor acts like a function with a parameterized list of formal parameters that match the object type. The return value for the constructor is an instance, or copy, of the object type. The constructor function assigns the formal parameters to variables of the same name. They are prefaced with the keyword SELF. The SELF keyword references what is termed an instance variable of an object type. You will read more on the SELF keyword in Chapter 14.

■ It defines an object-type variable, `individual_record`. All fields are explicitly defined in the database object type and are equivalent to the related table.

■ It defines an object body for the `individual_record` object type.

■ It defines a record-type variable, `individual_address_record`. This new record type is a compound record type. It has two fields, which are the earlier `individual_record` and `address_record` record types. Each of the record types becomes a subtype of the compound record type.

■ It defines an object body for the `individual_address_record` object type. Its constructor function assigns an instance of `address_record` and `individual_record` to self-contained instances.

■ In the PL/SQL anonymous block, it defines an `individual_address` variable using the `individual_address_record` compound object type as the data type.

■ Also in the anonymous block, it initializes the `individual_address` variable fields of the objects. You initialize by using a nesting syntax. On the left side of the assignment operator, you have the variable name. The right side uses a nested object construction process. The nesting construction process is often called *run-time construction*. Run-time construction leverages the subtype object body constructors to initialize field-level values. The generalized syntax uses a comma-delimited set of object constructors. Each object constructor uses the object type name and a comma-delimited set of actual parameters. It is shown here:

```
OBJECT_CONSTRUCTOR(
  [ OBJECT_CONSTRUCTOR( [ attr1, … attr(n+1) ] ),
    OBJECT_CONSTRUCTOR( [ attr1, … attr(n+1) ] ) ] );
```

- It inserts a row into the `individuals` table, which is a parent table in the ERD model. The table is a parent table because of a referential integrity constraint found in the `addresses` table.

- It inserts a row into the `addresses` table, which is a child table in the ERD model.

- It commits the work.

An alternative to the nested construction used in the example exists. You can first define and initialize the two independent object-type variables. Then you can use those variables to construct an instance of the compound object type.

The two inserts based on the new compound object type use a more complex dot notation, which includes the object type, the nested object type, and then the attribute or field. You see that more than one or two levels of nesting can become very complex. You should consider your business model when working with nesting. As a rule of thumb, one or two levels of nesting are generally manageable.

The compound object type mimics a record type. As the syntax becomes more familiar, you will appreciate how object types simplify syntax in your declaration sections.

These object-type examples have illustrated key concepts that you should consider. You have seen the basics of record and object types. Now, the chapter will show you how they can be used in the context of function parameter and return types.

Defining and Using Record Types as Formal Parameters

Record types and object types are defined as formal parameters in much the same way. You must define a record or object type before using it as a formal parameter in cursors, functions, or procedures. You define the physical size of the object externally to the cursor, function, or procedure. The size is implicitly inherited when you pass it as actual parameter(s). If the concept of subprograms is new to you, please refer to Chapters 8 and 9. Likewise, if formal and actual parameters are new, please refer to same chapters. The following example uses a subprogram within an anonymous-block PL/SQL program. If you do not understand how functions are used in PL/SQL, you should read Chapters 8 and 9 first.

You will examine the method with record types first. The example that follows extends the solution demonstrated in `create_record3.sql` earlier in the chapter. It uses two local procedures to do inserts. One inserts into the `addresses` table. Another inserts into the `individuals` table. You will see a compound record type in the example. Subtypes of the compound record type are passed as the actual parameter to the local procedures. A two-dot notation does this. The first element is the compound record type, and the second is the record subtype.

```
-- Available online as part of create_record6.sql
DECLARE

  -- Define a record type.
  TYPE individual_record IS RECORD
  (individual_id    INTEGER
  ,first_name       VARCHAR2(30 CHAR)
  ,middle_initial   VARCHAR2(1 CHAR)
  ,last_name        VARCHAR2(30 CHAR));

  -- Define a record type.
  TYPE address_record IS RECORD
  (address_id       INTEGER
  ,individual_id    INTEGER
  ,street_address1  VARCHAR2(30 CHAR)
  ,street_address2  VARCHAR2(30 CHAR)
  ,street_address3  VARCHAR2(30 CHAR)
  ,city             VARCHAR2(20 CHAR)
  ,state            VARCHAR2(20 CHAR)
  ,postal_code      VARCHAR2(20 CHAR)
  ,country_code     VARCHAR2(10 CHAR));

  -- Define a record type of two user-defined record types.
  TYPE individual_address_record IS RECORD
  (individual       INDIVIDUAL_RECORD
  ,address          ADDRESS_RECORD);

  -- Define a user-defined compound record type.
  individual_address INDIVIDUAL_ADDRESS_RECORD;

  -- Define a local procedure to manage addresses inserts.
  PROCEDURE insert_address
    (address_in ADDRESS_RECORD) IS

BEGIN

  -- Insert the values into the target object.
  INSERT
  INTO      addresses
  VALUES
  (address_in.address_id
  ,address_in.individual_id
  ,address_in.street_address1
  ,address_in.street_address2
  ,address_in.street_address3
  ,address_in.city
  ,address_in.state
  ,address_in.postal_code
```

```
      ,address_in.country_code);

   END insert_address;

   -- Define a local procedure to manage addresses inserts.
   PROCEDURE insert_individual
      (individual_in INDIVIDUAL_RECORD) IS

   BEGIN

      -- Insert the values into the table.
      INSERT
      INTO      individuals
      VALUES
      (individual_in.individual_id
      ,individual_in.first_name
      ,individual_in.middle_initial
      ,individual_in.last_name);

   END insert_individual;

BEGIN

   -- Initialize the field values for the record.
   individual_address.individual.individual_id := 6;
   individual_address.individual.first_name := 'Ruldolph';
   individual_address.individual.middle_initial := '';
   individual_address.individual.last_name := 'Gulianni';

   -- Initialize the field values for the record.
   individual_address.address.address_id := 3;
   individual_address.address.individual_id := 6;
   individual_address.address.street_address1 := '89th St';
   individual_address.address.street_address2 := '';
   individual_address.address.street_address3 := '';
   individual_address.address.city := 'New York City';
   individual_address.address.state := 'NY';
   individual_address.address.postal_code := '10028';
   individual_address.address.country_code := 'USA';

   -- Create a savepoint.
   SAVEPOINT addressbook;

   -- Process object subtypes.
   insert_individual(individual_address.individual);
   insert_address(individual_address.address);

   -- Commit the record.
```

```
  COMMIT;

EXCEPTION

  -- Rollback to savepoint on error.
  WHEN OTHERS THEN
    ROLLBACK to addressbook;
    RETURN;

END;
/
```

The sample program does the following:

- It defines a record-type variable, `individual_record`. All fields are explicitly defined in the PL/SQL program equivalent to the related table.

- It defines a record-type variable, `address_record`. All fields are explicitly defined in the PL/SQL program equivalent to the related table.

- It defines a record-type variable, `individual_address_record`. This new record type is a compound record type. It has two fields, which are the previously defined `individual_record` and `address_record` record types. Each of the record types becomes a subtype of the compound record type.

- It defines an `individual_address` variable that uses the compound record type `individual_address_record`.

- It defines a local procedure, `insert_address`. The procedure takes a single formal parameter, a variable of the `address_record` record type. The local `insert_address` procedure inserts a row into the addresses table.

- It defines a local procedure, `insert_individual`. The procedure takes a single formal parameter, a variable of the `individual_record` record type. The local `insert_individual` procedure inserts a row into the addresses table.

- It initializes the `individual_address` variable field values for the `individual` subtype. Initialization is performed by assigning values to the field-level elements in the record type.

- It initializes the field values for the `address` subtype. Initialization is performed by assigning values to the field-level elements in the record type.

- It sets a save point for transaction control.

- It calls the local `insert_individual` procedure and passes an actual parameter of the `individual` subtype.

- It calls the local `insert_address` procedure and passes an actual parameter of the `address` subtype.

- It commits the work.

You can read more about transaction control management in Chapter 2. An exception handler is also added to illustrate a rollback if either of the table inserts failed. When we use two or more insert statements, transaction controls are required for an all-or-nothing process. You can read more about exception handlers in Chapter 7.

You have now seen how record types can be used as parameters to local program units. While you have seen only an example of using local procedures, the process does not differ much in stored functions, procedures, or packages.

Defining and Using Object Types as Parameters

The method changes very little with the use of objects. However, the declaration block becomes much smaller because the object types are defined in the database. They need not be redefined with each program. Next is an example extending the solution presented in `create_record5.sql`. Leveraging object types previously defined, we have avoided reprinting the object type definitions. The example demonstrates passing variables with user-defined object types. You will notice that they also use the two-dot notation to pass subtypes to the local procedures.

```
-- Available online as part of create_record7.sql
DECLARE

  -- Define a variable of the record type.
  individual_address INDIVIDUAL_ADDRESS_RECORD;

  -- Define a local procedure to manage addresses inserts.
  PROCEDURE insert_address
    (address_in ADDRESS_RECORD) IS

  BEGIN

    -- Insert the values into the target object.
    INSERT
    INTO     addresses
    VALUES
    (address_in.address_id
    ,address_in.individual_id
```

```
      ,address_in.street_address1
      ,address_in.street_address2
      ,address_in.street_address3
      ,address_in.city
      ,address_in.state
      ,address_in.postal_code
      ,address_in.country_code);

  END insert_address;

  -- Define a local procedure to manage addresses inserts.
  PROCEDURE insert_individual
    (individual_in INDIVIDUAL_RECORD) IS

  BEGIN

    -- Insert the values into the table.
    INSERT
    INTO      individuals
    VALUES
    (individual_in.individual_id
    ,individual_in.first_name
    ,individual_in.middle_initial
    ,individual_in.last_name);

  END insert_individual;

BEGIN

  -- Construct an instance of the object type.
  -- It uses two nested constructors in the constructor.
  individual_address :=
    individual_address_record(
      individual_record(7,'Quentin','','Roosevelt'),
      address_record(4,7,'20 Sagamore Hill','',''
                  ,'Oyster Bay','NY'
                  ,'11771-1899','USA'));

  -- Create a savepoint.
  SAVEPOINT addressbook;

  -- Process object subtypes.
  insert_individual(individual_address.individual);
  insert_address(individual_address.address);

  -- Commit the record.
  COMMIT;
```

```
EXCEPTION

  -- Rollback to savepoint on error.
  WHEN OTHERS THEN
    ROLLBACK to addressbook;
    RETURN;

END;
/
```

While the sample program does more than is displayed, it uses the same object types as earlier in the chapter. Please refer to the prior examples if you would like to review their structure or explanation. The sample program does the following:

- It defines an object-type variable, `individual_address_record`, in the anonymous block program. The object type is a compound object type and can be used as an alternative implementation to a record type.

- It defines a local procedure, `insert_address`. The procedure takes a single formal parameter, a variable of the `address_record` object type. The local `insert_address` procedure inserts a row into the `addresses` table.

- It defines a local procedure, `insert_individual`. The procedure takes a single formal parameter, a variable of the `individual_record` object type. The local `insert_individual` procedure inserts a row into the `addresses` table.

- It initializes the `individual_address` variable field values for the `individual` subtype. Initialization is performed by assigning values to the field-level elements in the record type.

- It initializes the field values for the `address` subtype. Initialization is performed by assigning values to the field-level elements in the record type.

- It sets a save point for transaction control.

- It calls the local `insert_individual` procedure and passes an actual parameter of the `individual` subtype.

- It calls the local `insert_address` procedure and passes an actual parameter of the `address` subtype.

- It commits the work.

You have now seen how object types can be used as parameters to local program units. You can see that object types and record types are interchangeable as formal parameter types. While you have seen only an example of using local procedures, the process will not differ much in stored functions, procedures, or packages.

The choice of implementing one or the other depends on several factors. Record types have been the traditional approach, but object types in Oracle 10g have become very powerful. As Chapters 14–16 cover objects, all that needs to be said here is that objects can encapsulate and localize access methods. Prior to Oracle 10g, many developers built record structures within packages to support their user-defined application programming interfaces (APIs). Some of these record structures were duplicated or propagated to other APIs. When multiple versions of record types proliferate to support APIs, they present version control and maintenance programming problems. Using object types can eliminate this risk and extra work.

Returning Record Types from Functions

The following example uses subprograms within an anonymous block PL/SQL program. Like the prior discussion on using record types as return values, the discussion assumes that you understand subprograms. If you do not understand how functions are used in PL/SQL, you should read Chapters 8 and 9 first.

Formal and actual parameters will be discussed in the respective contexts of defining and using function return types. The examples in this section use anonymous block programs with functions as subprograms. You should note that there are other possible implementations. Please refer to Chapter 8 and 9 for greater detail on potential implementation methods.

As done previously in the chapter, you will be presented with traditional handling of record types and then object types. In Oracle 10g, you now have a better choice between record- and object-type implementations. While these methods are very similar, you will benefit from clear examples of both.

Defining and Using Record Types as Return Values

When defining record types as function return values, you have only one choice of implementation. You must define an explicit record type before the function definition. You cannot use the %ROWTYPE definition method.

The following example program uses an explicit record type before the function in the declaration section. (As mentioned, functions are covered in Chapters 8 and 9.) You can see that a variable of the same record type is also defined. In the execution section, you see the assignment of the return type to the variable of the same type. The attributes of the record type are then printed to the console with the built-in DBMS_OUTPUT utility and dot notation.

```
-- Available online as part of create_function1.sql
DECLARE

   -- Define a record type.
   TYPE individual_record IS RECORD
   (individual_id   INTEGER
```

```
        ,first_name       VARCHAR2(30 CHAR)
        ,middle_initial   individuals.middle_initial%TYPE
        ,last_name        VARCHAR2(30 CHAR));

      -- Define a variable of the record type.
      individual INDIVIDUAL_RECORD;

      -- Define a local function to return a record type.
      FUNCTION get_row
        (individual_id_in INTEGER)
      RETURN INDIVIDUAL_RECORD IS

        -- Define a cursor to return a row of individuals.
        CURSOR c (individual_id_cursor INTEGER) IS
          SELECT   *
          FROM individuals
          WHERE    individual_id = individual_id_cursor;

      BEGIN

        -- Loop through the cursor for a single row.
        FOR i IN c(individual_id_in) LOOP

          -- Return a %ROWTYPE from the INDIVIDUALS table.
          RETURN i;

        END LOOP;

      END get_row;

    BEGIN

      -- Demonstrate function return variable assignment.
      individual := get_row(1);

      -- Display results.
      dbms_output.put_line(CHR(10));
      dbms_output.put_line('INDIVIDUAL_ID  : '
      ||                      individual.individual_id);
      dbms_output.put_line('FIRST_NAME     : '
      ||                      individual.first_name);
      dbms_output.put_line('MIDDLE_INITIAL : '
      ||                      individual.middle_initial);
      dbms_output.put_line('LAST_NAME      : '
      ||                      individual.last_name);

    END;
    /
```

The sample program does the following:

- It defines a record type, `individual_record`.
- It defines a variable `individual` of the `individual_record` record type.
- It defines a local `get_row` function. The function takes a single formal parameter of an integer and returns a variable of the `individual_record` record type. In the local `get_row` function, there is a cursor that takes a single formal parameter and returns a `%ROWTYPE` from the `individuals` table.
- It uses a cursor for-loop to retrieve a single row from the `individuals` table. It then returns the `%ROWTYPE` selected by the cursor.
- It assigns the return value from the local `get_row` function to an individual variable that uses the same record-type variable.
- It uses `DBMS_OUTPUT` utility to print the data.

The program will generate the following output to console:

 `-- Available as output from online create_function1.sql`

```
INDIVIDUAL_ID   : 1
FIRST_NAME      : John
MIDDLE_INITIAL  : D
LAST_NAME       : Rockefeller
/
```

The local function returns a `%ROWTYPE` from the `individuals` table. The return type of the local function is the same as the `individual` variable record type. The conversion of the cursor data type is implicitly managed in the local function because they are mutually assignable when they share equivalent row structures.

NOTE
You must enable SERVEROUTPUT to see the results printed by the DBMS_OUTPUT utility.

Defining and Using Object Types as Return Values

Object types also perform as function return values. They work like record types. You must define an explicit object type before the function definition.

The following example program uses an explicit object type. It was introduced in the `create_record4.sql` example earlier in this chapter. The function in the declaration section defines its formal return parameter as an object type. As in the record-type example earlier, you will find a variable of the same object type defined in the declaration section. The execution section has the same assignment of the function return type to a variable of the equivalent type.

```
-- Available online as part of create_function2.sql

DECLARE

  -- Define a variable of the record type.
  individual INDIVIDUAL_RECORD;

  -- Define a local function to return a record type.
  FUNCTION get_row
    (individual_id_in INTEGER)
  RETURN INDIVIDUAL_RECORD IS

    -- Define a cursor to return a row of individuals.
    CURSOR c (individual_id_cursor INTEGER) IS
      SELECT    *
      FROM      individuals
      WHERE     individual_id = individual_id_cursor;

  BEGIN

    -- Loop through the cursor for a single row.
    FOR i IN c(individual_id_in) LOOP

      -- Return a constructed object from a %ROWTYPE.
      RETURN    individual_record(i.individual_id
                                 ,i.first_name
                                 ,i.middle_initial
                                 ,i.last_name);
    END LOOP;

  END get_row;

BEGIN

  -- Demonstrate function return variable assignment.
  individual := get_row(1);

  -- Display results.
  dbms_output.put_line(CHR(10));
  dbms_output.put_line('INDIVIDUAL_ID   : '
```

```
||                         individual.individual_id);
dbms_output.put_line('FIRST_NAME      : '
||                         individual.first_name);
dbms_output.put_line('MIDDLE_INITIAL : '
||                         individual.middle_initial);
dbms_output.put_line('LAST_NAME       : '
||                         individual.last_name);
END;
/
```

The sample program uses an object type defined in a prior example that is not reprinted. The program does the following:

- It defines a variable `individual` of the `individual_record` object type.

- It defines a local `get_row` function. The function takes a single formal parameter of an integer and returns a variable of the `individual_record` object type. In the local `get_row` function, there is a cursor that takes a single formal parameter and returns a `%ROWTYPE` from the `individuals` table.

- It uses a cursor for-loop to retrieve a single row from the `individuals` table. It constructs an instance of the `individual_record` object type from the `%ROWTYPE` field values. It then assigns that as the return value.

- It assigns the return object instance to the `individual` variable of the same object type.

- It uses `DBMS_OUTPUT` utility to print the data.

In the local `get_row` function, there is a syntax difference between handling an object type and a record type. While both programs have the same structure for the local function, the return statements are different. The return types of the functions drive the difference.

If you examine the preceding row-type example, you will see that it returns a row from the cursor. When the cursor returns a row, it implicitly returns a `%ROWTYPE` structure. In the `create_function1.sql` example, the `%ROWTYPE` structure matches the defined record type. When the cursor row is returned, PL/SQL manages the run-time conversion implicitly. This simplifies coding but can introduce problems. For example, if the underlying table structure changes and the record structure remains unchanged, the program will generally fail. It will succeed only if the changes leave a record called a *signature* that contains the same count of fields with the same data types or subtypes. Another caveat is that the columns must be physically large enough to handle the run-time data.

If you examine the object-type example, you will see it returns a row from the cursor. When the cursor returns a row, it implicitly returns a %ROWTYPE structure, as did the record-type example. Unfortunately, the PL/SQL engine does not implicitly cast a %ROWTYPE to an object type. Therefore, you must explicitly use an object constructor in the for-loop. There are advantages and disadvantages to both approaches. You need to examine when one approach is superior to the other.

This behavior is the expected behavior. Prior to Oracle 10g, the PL/SQL engine saw %ROWTYPE and object types as mutually assignable when they shared equivalent row structures. Explicit construction is now required when moving from record types to object types. It does not matter whether they are explicitly or implicitly defined (the latter by using %ROWTYPE). You can use online create_function2e.sql to raise an ORA-00382 error by attempting to assign a %ROWTYPE.

```
-- Available as output from online create_function2e.sql

        individual_type := i;
                          *
ERROR at line 24:
ORA-06550: line 24, column 26:
PLS-00382: expression is of wrong type
ORA-06550: line 24, column 7:
PL/SQL: Statement ignored
```

The successful output of create_function2.sql is a mirror of what you saw for the prior record-type example, so it is not redisplayed in the text.

You have learned how to use record and object types as function return variables. While they are similar, you should also know when and where one is more appropriate than the other. The next section will demonstrate verifying the record- and object-type examples used.

Verifying Work with Record Types

The following query will enable us to see the success of the three record type methods and their variations. If you have not run the individual scripts along the way, you can run runset1.sql to obtain the full results. The SQL*Plus formatting is useful to avoid line wrapping.

```
-- Available online as part of query_records1.sql
COL individual_id    FORMAT 9,999
COL first_name       FORMAT A14
```

```
COL middle_initial   FORMAT A1
COL last_name        FORMAT A14

SELECT    individual_id
,         first_name
,         middle_initial
,         last_name
FROM      individuals
ORDER BY 1;

COL address_id       FORMAT 9,999
COL individual_id    FORMAT 9,999
COL street_address1  FORMAT A16
COL city             FORMAT A14
COL state            FORMAT A2
COL country_code     FORMAT A3

SELECT    address_id
,         individual_id
,         street_address1
,         city
,         state
,         country_code
FROM      addresses
ORDER BY 1;
```

The query_record1.sql generates the following output to console:

```
INDIVIDUAL_ID FIRST_NAME       M LAST_NAME
------------- --------------   - -------------
            1 John             D Rockefeller
            2 John             P Morgan
            3 Ulysses          S Grant
            4 Klaes            M van Roosevelt
            5 Kermit             Roosevelt
            6 Ruldolph           Gulianni
            7 Quentin            Roosevelt

ADDRESS_ID INDIVID STREET_ADDRESS1  CITY          ST COU
---------- ------- ---------------- -------------- -- ---
         1       3 Riverside Park   New York City  NY USA
         2       5 20 Sagamore Hill Oyster Bay     NY USA
         3       6 89th Street      New York City  NY USA
         4       7 20 Sagamore Hill Oyster Bay     NY USA
```

Summary

You now have a working knowledge of record and object types. You have seen that they are powerful utilities in Oracle 10*g* and how to use them. Hopefully, you know when and why to use one or the other.

The skills you have developed studying record and object types will help you leverage the collection features of Oracle 10*g*. Collections are covered in Chapter 6.

CHAPTER

6

Collections

s discussed in Chapter 5, records and collections are powerful structures. They enable you to develop programs that manage large sets of data. Records let you manage sets of variable types. Collections let you manage groups of a variable type. Collections also avoid the complexity of indirect reference by pointers in C/C++. Since you have developed a working understanding of records, we will now build on that knowledge base. We will explain collections and show you how to use them in your PL/SQL programming code.

We will cover topics as follows. The chapter assumes you read it sequentially. If you feel comfortable with an area, please feel free to move to the section of interest. However, the chapter assumes you have mastery of earlier sections.

- Introducing collections
- Working with collections
- Oracle 10*g* Collection API

Introducing Collections

Records are necessary structures to manage single rows of data. Collections are necessary structures to manage multiple rows of data.

The first collections were PL/SQL tables, introduced in the Oracle 7 database. Oracle 8 added two new types, both known as collections. PL/SQL tables were renamed index-by tables. Collections let you store data sets in a row within a table. Oracle 8*i* improved the access and management of collections. Oracle 9*i* introduced multilevel collections.

Oracle 10*g* improves collections by adding ANSI functionality, globalization, multiset operations, and unique string indexes for associative arrays. Index-by tables were again renamed; now they are known as associative arrays.

What Is a Collection?

Collections are lists, which may be ordered or unordered. Ordered lists are indexed by unique subscripts; unordered lists are indexed by unique identifiers, which may be numbers, hash values, or string names.

Working with Collections

Oracle 10*g* provides three types of collections. None of these are technically new to Oracle 10*g*. However, you might argue that associative arrays are new because of the significant subscript changes. Instead of unique number subscripts, Oracle 10*g* allows you to use either a unique number or a string.

These are key structures that you will use frequently in PL/SQL programming. You should take time to develop a clear understanding of what they are, when to use them, and how to use them.

Each of the collection types will be explained and demonstrated. If you have read the discussion in Chapter 5 on record and object types, you will have a solid foundation for the discussion of collections. If you skipped the record and object type discussion, it is assumed you have command of those topics. The three Oracle 10*g* collection types and their descriptions are shown in Table 6-1.

Collection Type	Description	Subscript	Size
Associative arrays (index-by tables)	Associative array is the new name for a familiar structure. You may have known these as index-by tables in Oracle 8 to Oracle 9*i* and possibly as PL/SQL tables in Oracle 7. They have mutated forward in Oracle 10*g* and deserve a new name. They are still sparsely populated arrays, which means the numbering does not have to be sequential, only unique. They now support subscripts that are unique numbers or strings. This change moves a familiar and powerful structure from a sparsely populated array to a standard structured programming language data type, known as lists or maps.	Sequential numbers or unique strings	Dynamic
Nested tables	Nested tables were introduced in Oracle 8. They are initially defined as densely populated arrays but may become sparsely populated as records are deleted. They may be stored in permanent tables and accessed by SQL. They also may be dynamically extended and act more like traditional programming bags and sets than arrays.	Sequential numbers	Dynamic
Varrays	Varrays were introduced in Oracle 8. They are densely populated arrays and behave like traditional programming arrays. They may be stored in permanent tables and accessed by SQL. At creation, they have a fixed size that cannot change.	Sequential numbers	Fixed

TABLE 6-1. *Collection Type Comparison*

All of the collections are single dimensional, which means that they are a list of like data types. Data types may be standard Oracle 10g data types, subtypes, or user-defined types. You may think of a list of like data types as a column of data, like numbers or strings. A single column of like data types is a dimension of data.

You may define single-dimensional user collections by using standard data types. Alternatively, you may create user-defined record or object types. While record and object types act like multiple-dimensional collections, they are treated as single-dimensional collections by the Oracle database. Record and object types are also called data structures. Qualifying this helps explain why you worked through record and object types before dealing with collection types.

Oracle 10g collections deliver set operators. These act and function like SQL set operators in select statements. The difference is that they are used in assignments between collections of matching signature types. Table 6-2 describes the multiset operators.

Multiset Operator	Description
MULTISET EXCEPT	The MULTISET EXCEPT operator removes one set from another. It works like the SQL MINUS set operator.
MULTISET INTERSECT	The MULTISET INTERSECT operator evaluates two sets and returns one set. The return set contains elements that were found in both original sets. It works like the SQL INTERSECT set operator.
MULTISET UNION	The MULTISET UNION operator evaluates two sets and returns one set. The return set contains all elements of both sets. Where duplicate elements are found, they are returned. It functions like the UNION ALL set operator. You may use the DISTINCT operator to eliminate duplicates. The DISTINCT operator follows the MULTISET UNION operator rule. It functions like the SQL UNION operator.
SET	The SET operator removes duplicates from a collection. It acts like a DISTINCT operator in a SQL statement.

TABLE 6-2. *Set Operators for Collections*

TIP
*The SET operator can be used to eliminate
DISTINCT operators from your DQL select
statements. Using BULK COLLECT (covered in the
later section "Working with Associative Arrays")
in a nested table or associative array, you can
then do the following assignment:*

```
collection_variable := SET(collection_variable);
```

*It will eliminate duplicate records from the set in
memory.*

Deciding on the collection type that best meets your programming need is critical. You should carefully consider the strengths and weaknesses of each collection type. Here is a thumbnail guide to selecting the right collection:

- Use a varray when the physical size of the collection is static and the collection may be used in tables. Varrays are the closest thing to arrays in other programming languages, such as Java, C, C++, or C#.

- Use nested tables when the physical size is unknown due to run-time variations and when the type may be used in tables. Nested tables are like lists and bags in other programming languages.

- Use associative arrays when the physical size is unknown due to run-time variations and when the type will not be used in tables. Associative arrays are ideal for standard programming solutions, such as using maps and sets.

While Table 6-1 introduced collections in alphabetical order, you will cover them in descending alphabetical order. The discussion will start with varrays and end with associative arrays. Coverage will include access methods in both SQL and PL/SQL. It is hard to imagine how you would use them in PL/SQL without knowing how to leverage these methods in your tables.

Working with Varrays

Varrays are single-dimensional structures of an Oracle 10*g* data type or a user-defined record/object type. This section focuses on single-dimensional structures of an Oracle 10*g* data type.

Varrays may be used in table, record, and object definitions and may be accessed in SQL and PL/SQL. They are arrays in the traditional sense of programming languages such as Java, C, C++, and C#. They use sequential index values to reference elements in the structure.

Defining and Using Varrays as PL/SQL Program Constructs

The syntax to define a varray in a PL/SQL program unit is

TYPE *type_name* IS {VARRAY | VARYING ARRAY} (*size_limit*)
  OF *element_type* [NOT NULL];

The *type name* is often a string followed by an underscore and the word varray. Many programmers and configuration management people find it a useful pattern to improve code readability. It is also the convention used in the chapter.

Either VARRAY or VARYING ARRAY syntax may be used, but the former is much more common. The size limit is a required value. It is a positive integer giving the maximum number of elements in the varray. Element type may be any Oracle 10*g* data type or a user-defined data type. Allowing null values in varrays is the default. If null values should be disallowed, the fact must be specified when they are defined.

The following example program demonstrates defining, declaring, and initializing a varray of integers in a PL/SQL program unit. An integer is a subtype of the Oracle 10*g* number data type.

Subscript index values begin at 1, not zero. This is consistent with the long-standing behavior of index-by tables in Oracle 8 to Oracle 9*i* and PL/SQL tables in Oracle 7. Most programming languages, including Java, C, C++, and C#, use subscript index values that begin with zero.

```
-- Available online as part of create_varray1.sql

DECLARE
  -- Define a varray of integer with 3 rows.
  TYPE integer_varray IS VARRAY(3) OF INTEGER;

  -- Declare and initialize a varray that allows nulls.
  varray_integer INTEGER_VARRAY :=
    integer_varray(NULL,NULL,NULL);

BEGIN

  -- Print title.
  dbms_output.put_line('Varray initialized as nulls.');
  dbms_output.put_line('--------------');

  -- Loop through the three records.
  FOR i IN 1..3 LOOP

    -- Print the contents.
    dbms_output.put     ('Integer Varray ['||i||'] ');
    dbms_output.put_line('['||varray_integer(i)||']');

  END LOOP;
```

```
-- Assign values to subscripted members of the varray.
varray_integer(1) := 11;
varray_integer(2) := 12;
varray_integer(3) := 13;

-- Print title.
dbms_output.put        (CHR(10)); - Visual line break.
dbms_output.put_line('Varray initialized as values.');
dbms_output.put_line('--------------');

-- Loop through the three records.
FOR i IN 1..3 LOOP

  -- Print the contents.
  dbms_output.put_line('Integer Varray ['||i||'] '
  ||                    '['||varray_integer(i)||']');

END LOOP;

END;
/
```

As shown in the preceding example, three steps are required to enable a varray for use by your PL/SQL program. The steps are defining, declaring, and initializing the varray data type.

- It defines a varray data type. The varray is named `integer_varray`. It has a maximum size of 3 and a data type of an integer. An integer is a subtype of the number data type.

- It declares and initializes a variable `varray_integer`. The variable is an `integer_varray` varray data type. It is initialized as a three-element collection with null values in each element.

- It prints a title with the DBMS_OUTPUT utility.

- It uses a range for-loop and the DBMS_OUTPUT utility to print the null values initialized when the `varray_integer` variable was declared.

- It assigns elements the numeric values of 1 to 3, respectively.

- It uses a range for-loop and the DBMS_OUTPUT utility to print the values.

- It uses a range for-loop and the DBMS_OUTPUT utility to print the newly assigned values.

Here is the output from `create_varray1.sql` program:

`-- Available online as output from create_varray1.sql`

```
Varray initialized as nulls.
--------------
Integer Varray [1] []
Integer Varray [2] []
Integer Varray [3] []

Varray initialized as values.
---------------
Integer Varray [1] [11]
Integer Varray [2] [12]
Integer Varray [3] [13]
```

If you skip any of the steps, you will encounter exceptions. The one that most new developers encounter is an uninitialized collection, as shown here:

```
DECLARE
*
ERROR at line 1:
ORA-06531: Reference to uninitialized collection
ORA-06512: at line 11
```

It is raised when you forget to initialize the varray. The example program initializes the varray with null values because nulls are allowed. It is also possible to initialize the variable with values. You initialize the variable by using the varray type name and parentheses around the values. When you initialize a varray, you set the actual number of initialized rows. Using the Collection API COUNT method returns the number of elements with allotted space. Use of this method will be shown in the next example program.

If you fail to initialize all values in varray, you initially constrain your variable to a smaller row size. You can test this by editing `create_varray1.sql` and changing the initialization from three null values to two. (Please consider making a copy of `create_varray1.sql` to test the changes.) When you run the program, you will raise the following exception:

```
DECLARE
*
ERROR at line 1:
ORA-06533: Subscript beyond count
ORA-06512: at line 13
```

The exception means that subscript 3 is unavailable. It does not exist. While you defined the varray as three elements in size, you initialized it as only two elements in size. Therefore, the variable has only two valid subscripts, one and two.

If you encountered the error, you might check the Oracle 10*g* documentation. You would find that there is a Collection API EXTEND method for collections and that it is overloaded. The Collections API *requires us to initialize a row and then assign a value.*

You add a row using the Collection API EXTEND method without an actual parameter or with a single actual parameter. If you use the single parameter, it is the number of elements to initialize. It cannot exceed the difference between the number of possible and actual elements defined by the varray. You will read more on using these methods in the section "Oracle 10*g* Collection API" at the end of this chapter.

The following program illustrates initialization with zero rows in the declaration section. Then, it demonstrates dynamic initialization and assignment in the execution section:

```
-- Available online as part of create_varray2.sql

DECLARE

  -- Define a varray of integer with 3 rows.
  TYPE integer_varray IS VARRAY(3) OF INTEGER;

  -- Declare and initialize a null set of rows.
  varray_integer INTEGER_VARRAY := integer_varray();

BEGIN

  -- Loop through the three records.
  FOR i IN 1..3 LOOP

    -- Initialize row.
    varray_integer.EXTEND;

    -- Assign values to subscripted members of the varray.
    varray_integer(i) := 10 + i;

  END LOOP;

  -- Print title.
  dbms_output.put_line('Varray initialized as values.');
  dbms_output.put_line('---------------');
```

```
   -- Loop through the records to print the varrays.
   FOR i IN 1..3 LOOP

     -- Print the contents.
     dbms_output.put      ('Integer Varray ['||i||'] ');
     dbms_output.put_line('['||varray_integer(i)||']');

   END LOOP;

END;
/
```

The example program does the following:

■ It defines a varray data type. The varray is named `integer_varray`.
   It has a maximum size of 3 and a data type of integer.

■ It declares and initializes a variable `varray_integer`. The variable is
   an `integer_varray` varray data type. It is initialized as a null element
   collection. A null element collection has not allocated space to any elements.

■ It uses a range for-loop and the Collection API `EXTEND` method to allocate
   space. Then, it allocates space to the maximum number of possible
   elements in the varray. After each space allocation with the `EXTEND` method,
   it assigns a value to each element in the varray.

■ It prints a title with the `DBMS_OUTPUT` utility.

■ It uses a range for-loop and the `DBMS_OUTPUT` utility to print the newly
   assigned values.

The output is shown here:

-- Available online as output from create_varray2.sql

```
Varray initialized as values.
---------------
Integer Varray [1] [11]
Integer Varray [2] [12]
Integer Varray [3] [13]
```

You now have the fundamentals to build varray structures within PL/SQL
program units. The power and management utilities of the collection methods will
enhance your ability to use these. While this section has touched on the Collection
API methods to illustrate initialization issues, they are covered in depth later in the

chapter. By doing so, you will be able to see how you can apply these methods across collection types.

Defining and Using Varrays as Object Types in PL/SQL

The syntax to define an object type of varray in the database is

CREATE OR REPLACE TYPE *type_name*
  AS {VARRAY | VARYING ARRAY} (*size_limit*)
  OF *element_type* [NOT NULL];

As discussed, the type name is often a string followed by an underscore and the word varray. Many programmers and configuration management people find this a useful pattern to improve code readability. It is also the convention used in the chapter for PL/SQL structure and object types.

As with a PL/SQL type structure, either VARRAY or VARYING ARRAY syntax may be used. The former is much more common. The size limit is a required value. It is a positive integer, the maximum number of elements in the varray. The element type may be any Oracle 10*g* data type or a user-defined data type. Allowing null values in varrays is the default. If null values should be disallowed, that fact must be specified when they are defined.

The following example program demonstrates defining an object type of varray with a limit of three elements. The anonymous-block PL/SQL program then uses the varray object type by declaring and initializing a variable:

`-- Available online as part of create_varray3.sql`

```
CREATE OR REPLACE TYPE integer_varray
  AS VARRAY(3) OF INTEGER;
/

DECLARE

  -- Declare and initialize a null set of rows.
  varray_integer INTEGER_VARRAY :=
    integer_varray(NULL,NULL,NULL);

BEGIN

  -- Loop through the three records.
  FOR i IN 1..3 LOOP

    -- Assign values to subscripted members of the varray.
    varray_integer(i) := 10 + i;

  END LOOP;
```

```
  -- Print title.
  dbms_output.put_line('Varray initialized as values.');
  dbms_output.put_line('---------------');

  -- Loop through the three records.
  FOR i IN 1..3 LOOP

    -- Print contents.
    dbms_output.put       ('Integer Varray ['||i||'] ');
    dbms_output.put_line('['||varray_integer(i)||']');

  END LOOP;

END;
/
```

The example program does the following things:

- It defines a varray data type in SQL as an object type in the database. The varray is named `integer_varray`. It has a maximum size of 3 and a data type of integer.

- It declares and initializes in PL/SQL a variable `varray_integer`. The variable is an `integer_varray` varray object type. It is initialized as a three-element collection with null values in each element.

- It uses a range for-loop to assign elements the numeric values of 1 to 3, respectively.

- It prints a title with the `DBMS_OUTPUT` utility.

- It uses a range for-loop and the `DBMS_OUTPUT` utility to print the newly assigned values.

The output is shown here:

-- Available online as output from create_varray3.sql

```
Varray initialized as values.
---------------
Integer Varray [1] [11]
Integer Varray [2] [12]
Integer Varray [3] [13]
```

The benefit of defining the varray object type is that it may be referenced from any programs that have permission to use it, whereas a PL/SQL varray type structure is limited to the program unit. Program units may be anonymous-block programs like the example or stored procedures or packages in the database. Only the latter enables reference by other PL/SQL programs that have permissions to the package. Please refer to Chapter 8 for details on creating packages and Chapter 9 for using them.

All the varrays to this point leverage the default behavior that allows null values. It is always a bit clearer to start with the default behavior. After you master the basic syntax and default for defining, declaring, and initializing varrays, there is a question that needs to be resolved: When, why, and how do you allow or disallow null rows?

This is a good question. In the small example programs in the book, it seems that it may not matter too much. In fact, it does matter a great deal. Varrays are the closest structure related to standard programming language arrays. Arrays are structures that require attentive management. As a rule of thumb, arrays should always be dense. Dense means that there should not be any gaps in the sequencing of index values. It also means you should not have gaps in data. You should not allow nulls when you want a varray to act like a standard array structure.

Allowing nulls in varrays ensures that you may encounter them in the data stream. Oracle 10g does not allow you to create gaps in index values. If you *do not* want to write a host of error handling routines for arrays with missing data, you should consider overriding the default behavior. Disallow null values in varrays. Simplifying data access and error handling is why you should disallow null values in varrays.

You will now learn how to disallow null values in varrays. The main impact of disallowing null values in varrays is felt when you initialize them. For example, if you redefined the varray object type used in the previous program to disallow null values, the program would fail. You would see the following errors when attempting to initialize the varray object type:

```
    varray_integer INTEGER_VARRAY :=
      integer_varray(NULL,NULL,NULL);
                                        *
ERROR at line 4:
ORA-06550: line 4, column 51:
PLS-00567: cannot pass NULL to a NOT NULL constrained
          formal parameter
ORA-06550: line 4, column 56:
PLS-00567: cannot pass NULL to a NOT NULL constrained
          formal parameter
ORA-06550: line 4, column 61:
PLS-00567: cannot pass NULL to a NOT NULL constrained
          formal parameter
```

A problem with programming books is that concepts need to be illustrated with an economy of space. To do so, they are limited to small, workable examples. Small workable arrays seldom illustrate the real world and the high demands placed on these structures.

When you use varrays as arrays, it will be to do large transaction processing in memory because the I/O costs are too high. You will define varrays that contain hundreds of elements. Some may be dynamically defined by counting rows in a table before being built as dynamic structures.

When you initialize varrays that contain 100 percent of the data, doing so is straightforward because the constructor can do that. However, when you initialize varrays that contain less than all the data, adding elements requires additional programming.

The following example allocates the 100 possible records. It does so without initializing the data as null values by leveraging the Collection API. You will find the Collection API covered later in the chapter.

-- **Available online as part of create_varray4.sql**

```
CREATE OR REPLACE TYPE integer_varray
  AS VARRAY(100) OF INTEGER NOT NULL;
/

DECLARE

  -- Declare and initialize a null set of rows.
  varray_integer INTEGER_VARRAY := integer_varray();

BEGIN

  -- Loop through all records.
  FOR i IN 1..varray_integer.LIMIT LOOP

    -- Initialize row.
    varray_integer.EXTEND;

  END LOOP;

  -- Print to console how many rows are initialized.
  dbms_output.put     ('Integer Varray Initialized ');
  dbms_output.put_line('['||varray_integer.COUNT||']');

END;
/
```

The example program creates an object type as a varray with three members or rows. It then uses an anonymous-block PL/SQL program to test the varray object type. The example program's declaration defines and initializes a varray.

The example program does the following:

- It defines a varray data type in SQL as an object type in the database. The varray is named `integer_varray`. It has a maximum size of 100 and a data type of integer.

- It declares and initializes a variable `varray_integer`. The variable is an `integer_varray` varray object type. It is initialized as a null element collection. A null element object collection mirrors the varray data type you worked with earlier in the chapter.

- It uses a range for-loop and the Collection API `LIMIT` method to set the upward range value. Within the for-loop, it uses the Collection API `EXTEND` method to allocate space to the maximum size defined by the `integer_varray` varray object type.

- It prints the number of elements for which space has been allocated with the `DBMS_OUTPUT` utility. Using the Collection API `COUNT` method does this.

The output is shown here:

```
-- Available online as output from create_varray4.sql
```

```
Integer Varray Initialized [100]
```

You have developed skills with using varrray object types. The next section will use those varray object types to define tables that use them as column data types.

Defining and Using Varrays as Column Data Types in Tables

The power of varrays is not limited to procedural programming. Varrays provide Oracle 8 through Oracle 10*g* with unique capabilities for representing data. This is why Oracle's database became known as an object relational database management system (ORDBMS). It is a standard that many have moved to adopt.

Relational databases work on a principal of normalization. *Normalization* is the process of grouping related data into sets that are unique. It relies on two basic premises. One is that data may be positioned by semantic evaluation into third normal form or higher. Another is that data may be positioned by domain normal key. For the purposes of the discussion on Oracle 10*g* collections, the book will advocate only that each table should possess a primary key that uniquely identifies each row.

The book uses a pseudokey as the primary key. A *pseudokey* is an artificial key, that is, a key or column that it is not part of the data in the row.

In the first figure in Chapter 5, an ERD was introduced. It presented the three principal tables for the chapter. At this point, one of the tables needs to change to take advantage of collections. If you compare Figure 5-1 in Chapter 5 with Figure 6-1, you will notice that the three street addresses have now become a single list.

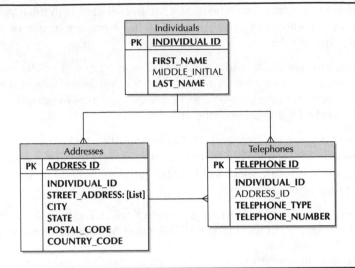

FIGURE 6-1. *List-enabled ERD*

In a very rigid definition of third normal form, the three columns of street address should have been in another table. That table would consist of three or more columns: a primary key, a foreign key, and data columns. An instantiated row would contain the following:

- A unique pseudokey in the primary key column

- A copy of a valid primary key from the base table, which is addresses

- A string value for the street address

The ability to include the list in the base table reduces the complexity of physical implementation. It eliminates the need to join the base table and the subordinate table. This changes because the latter becomes a list within a row of the base table.

Defining Varrays in Database Tables

The `create_addressbook2.sql` script changes the table definition to the new model. The following varray object type definition is provided, which supports globalization by using a Unicode standard.

-- Available online as part of create_addressbook2.sql

```
CREATE OR REPLACE TYPE address_varray
  AS VARRAY(3) OF VARCHAR2(30 CHAR);
/
```

After creating the object type, the addresses table is redefined to conform to the new ERD model. As you can see, the ERD list is implemented as a varray of a known type. The table is also maintaining referential integrity through database constraints. This was also done in the base case.

-- Available online as part of create_addressbook2.sql

```
CREATE TABLE addresses
   (address_id              INTEGER          NOT NULL
   ,individual_id           INTEGER          NOT NULL
   ,street_address          ADDRESS_VARRAY   NOT NULL
   ,city                    VARCHAR2(20 CHAR) NOT NULL
   ,state                   VARCHAR2(20 CHAR) NOT NULL
   ,postal_code             VARCHAR2(20 CHAR) NOT NULL
   ,country_code            VARCHAR2(10 CHAR) NOT NULL
   ,CONSTRAINT address_pk   PRIMARY KEY (address_id)
   ,CONSTRAINT addr_indiv_fk FOREIGN KEY (individual_id)
    REFERENCES individuals  (individual_id));
```

You will notice that the street_address column uses the address_varray object type. The varray is a single-dimensioned array of three variable-length strings. The variable-length strings are defined as noted to support Unicode.

Using Varrays in Database Tables

After creating a table with a column of a varray data type, you need to know how to use it. Using it requires understanding data manipulation language (DML) access methods to varrays. Varrays present no unique conditions for deleting, since deletion is at the row level. However, there are substantive differences when it comes to using insert and update statements.

NOTE
DML access involves inserting, updating, and deleting data from tables.

Insert statements have one type of access. It is an all-or-nothing approach to the data type. Insert statements allocate space necessary to the construction of the varray. For example, in the three-element array for street_address, it is possible to insert one to three rows of data. When the insert is made to the row, an instance of the collection type is built with the number of rows used.

`-- Available online as part of varray_dml1.sql`

```
INSERT
INTO       addresses
VALUES
(11
,11
,address_varray
  ('Office of Senator McCain'
  ,'450 West Paseo Redondo'
  ,'Suite 200')
,'Tucson'
,'AZ'
,'85701'
,'USA');
```

The example program inserts a full set of three rows into the varray data type. It is important to note that in the values clause, the varray data type name is used as the constructor name. The constructor uses the syntax previously presented with a list of comma-delimited actual parameters in a set of parentheses.

If you were to query the street_address column from the table, you would see a return set of the constructor with its actual parameters. This is illustrated by running a query like the following:

`-- Available online as part of varray_dml1.sql`

```
SELECT    street_address
FROM      addresses;
```

The shortened output from the query is noted.

`-- Available online as output from varray_dml1.sql`

```
STREET_ADDRESS
------------------------------
ADDRESS_VARRAY('Office of Senator McCain','450 West Paseo ...
```

This type of output is not very useful. It is also very different than what you might expect. Using data query language (DQL) to select a result from a varray data type requires specialized syntax. You need to define a nested table collection structure to actually access the varray data meaningfully.

NOTE
DQL is a new acronym to some. Select statements were previously classified as DML statements.

The following example illustrates how you build a nested table collection for the immediate problem at hand. Later in the chapter you will cover this in more detail when studying nested tables. Here, it illustrates a rather unintuitive syntax for querying the data.

```
-- Available online as part of varray_dml1.sql

-- Create a PL/SQL table data type.
CREATE OR REPLACE TYPE varray_nested_table
IS TABLE OF VARCHAR2(30 CHAR);
/

-- Use SQL*Plus to format the output.
COL column_value FORMAT A30

-- Print a list of the varray elements.
SELECT    column_value
FROM      THE (SELECT    CAST(street_address AS
                              varray_nested_table)
               FROM      addresses
               WHERE     address_id = 11);
```

In the example program, a nested table collection is built to mirror the element definition for the varray. Nested tables are not upwardly bound as are varrays but can be used to temporarily hold the contents of varrays. Using a nested table is the *only* way to meaningfully display the contents of a varray using a select statement.

There is a quick formatting line to dress up the output. The select statement is a bit complex. It will be covered in more detail later in this chapter. Here, however, are the basics of the select statement:

- The reserved word `column_value` is an access method for rows in a nested table. (You should know there is also a hidden column, `nested_table_id`, which is a foreign key that maps to the row in the parent table.)

- `THE` is a reserved word in SQL that enables a `column_value` to be selected from a query of a nested table.

- In the query of the addresses table, an object method `CAST` explicitly converts the `street_address` varray to the nested table. The nested table was defined as a collection type in the database. It is the casting that enables the nested table syntax to work against the varray collection type. Please check Chapter 4 for coverage of the CAST function.

The formatted output from the query is

-- Available online as output from varray_dml1.sql

```
COLUMN_VALUE
---------------
Office of Senator McCain
450 West Paseo Redondo
Suite 200
```

You must ensure that your varray is a mirror of your nested table structure. If they are not data type mirrors, you will encounter an ORA-00932 error. The error complains that the source for the CAST is the wrong type to convert to a nested table.

You can create this error by running create_addressbook2e.sql and varray_dml1.sql. The first script will create a varray of integers. It then uses that type to define the street_address column of the addresses table. The second script attempts the cast to a nested table of variable strings, which raises the inconsistent data types exception.

-- Available online as output from varray_dml1.sql

```
FROM      THE (SELECT    CAST(street_address AS
                              *
ERROR at line 2:
ORA-00932: inconsistent datatypes: expected - got
          PLSQL.ADDRESS_VARRAY
```

After constructing a varray collection, allocating new elements requires specialized syntax. As you have seen earlier in the chapter, this is done in PL/SQL and uses the Collection API. Unfortunately, this is also the case with update statements to varray data types in database tables. The only exception is when you are replacing the entire set of contents.

After restoring the now-invalid data structures, you use the following example program to replace the entire content of the street_address varray data type. You restore the environment by running create_addressbook2.sql script before varray_dml2.sql.

-- Available online as part of varray_dml2.sql

```
-- Insert into address using the varray structure.
UPDATE   addresses
```

```
SET        street_address =
               address_varray('Office of Senator McCain'
                             ,'2400 E. Arizona Biltmore Cir.'
                             ,'Suite 1150')
WHERE      address_id = 11;
```

The update statement assigns the value of a newly constructed `address_varray` collection type. Using the same complex select statement to query the new data, you will see the following output:

`-- Available online as output from varray_dml2.sql`

```
COLUMN_VALUE
---------------
Office of Senator McCain
2400 E. Arizona Biltmore Cir.
Suite 1150
```

You cannot update a portion of a varray column by any direct or indirect method in SQL. You *must* update portions of varray collections by using PL/SQL programs. The following anonyomous-block program enables the update of first element of the varray collection:

`-- Available online as part of varray_dml3.sql`

```
DECLARE

  -- Define a record type for a row of the addresses table.
  TYPE address_type IS RECORD
  (address_id            INTEGER
  ,individual_id         INTEGER
  ,street_address        ADDRESS_VARRAY
  ,city                  VARCHAR2(20 CHAR)
  ,state                 VARCHAR2(20 CHAR)
  ,postal_code           VARCHAR2(20 CHAR)
  ,country_code          VARCHAR2(10 CHAR));

  -- Define a variable of the addresses table record type.
  address               ADDRESS_TYPE;

  -- Define a cursor to return the %ROWTYPE value.
  CURSOR get_street_address
    (address_id_in        INTEGER) IS
    SELECT   *
    FROM     addresses
    WHERE    address_id = address_id_in;
```

```
BEGIN

  -- Open the cursor.
  OPEN  get_street_address(11);

  -- Fetch a into the record type variable.
  FETCH get_street_address
  INTO  address;

  -- Close the cursor.
  CLOSE get_street_address;

  -- Reset the first element of the varray type variable.
  address.street_address(1) :=
    'Office of Senator John McCain';

  -- Update the varray column value.
  UPDATE   addresses
  SET      street_address = address.street_address
  WHERE    address_id = 11;

END;
/
```

The example program does the following:

- It defines an `address_type` record type.

- It defines a variable named `address` of the `address_type` record type.

- It defines a cursor that takes one formal parameter and returns a `%ROWTYPE` from the `addresses` table.

- It opens the cursor by passing an actual `address_id` value.

- It fetches the `%ROWTYPE` value into the `address` variable.

- It closes the open cursor.

- It assigns a new variable-length string to the first indexed row of the `street_address` varray data type.

- It updates the `street_address` varray in the `addresses` table with the `address.street_address` varray.

You can see that it has only changed the first element of the varray collection column. This is done using our nested table syntax, which was discussed in a prior example. The results are in the following output file:

-- Available online as output from varray_dml3.sql

```
COLUMN_VALUE
---------------
Office of Senator John McCain
2400 E. Arizona Biltmore Cir.
Suite 1150
```

Another update scenario remains for you to examine. This example shows how a varray collection column may be grown from one element to two or more elements. Adding elements to a varray collection column requires PL/SQL. This is like the case of updating a single element of the varray collection column. You should recall from the prior discussion that an insert statement constructs a varray collection column.

The insert statement for this example inserts only one element into the street_address column, initializing only one element in the varray collection for the row. The following example shows the insert statement:

-- Available online as part of varray_dml4.sql

```
-- Insert into address using the varray structure.
INSERT
INTO       addresses
VALUES
(12
,12
,address_varray('Office of Senator Kennedy')
,'Boston'
,'MA'
,'02203'
,'USA');
```

You can use the following solution to add the missing elements to the varray collection column:

-- Available online as part of varray_dml4.sql

```
DECLARE

   -- Define a record type for a row of the addresses table.
   TYPE address_type IS RECORD
   (address_id          INTEGER
   ,individual_id       INTEGER
   ,street_address      ADDRESS_VARRAY
   ,city                VARCHAR2(20 CHAR)
   ,state               VARCHAR2(20 CHAR)
```

```
    ,postal_code           VARCHAR2(20 CHAR)
    ,country_code          VARCHAR2(10 CHAR));

    -- Define a variable of the addresses table record type.
    address                ADDRESS_TYPE;

    -- Define a cursor to return the %ROWTYPE value.
    CURSOR get_street_address
      (address_id_in       INTEGER) IS
      SELECT   *
      FROM     addresses
      WHERE    address_id = address_id_in;

BEGIN

    -- Open the cursor.
    OPEN  get_street_address(12);

    -- Fetch a into the record type variable.
    FETCH get_street_address
    INTO  address;

    -- Close the cursor.
    CLOSE get_street_address;

    -- Add element space.
    FOR i IN 2..3 LOOP
      address.street_address.EXTEND;
    END LOOP;

    -- Reset the first element of the varray type variable.
    address.street_address(2) := 'JFK Building';
    address.street_address(3) := 'Suite 2400';

    -- Update the varray column value.
    UPDATE    addresses
    SET       street_address = address.street_address
    WHERE     address_id = 12;

END;
/
```

The program does the following:

- It defines a record type that mirrors the addresses table.

- It defines a variable of the record type.

- It defines a cursor that takes a single formal parameter for the primary key of the `addresses` table.

- It opens a cursor, passing the required actual parameter.

- It fetches the `%ROWTYPE` value into the defined variable.

- It closes the open cursor.

- It uses a range for-loop and the Collection API to create space for two additional rows.

- It assigns values to the second and third elements in the nested table.

- It finally uses a DML update statement to replace the entire contents of the `street_address` varray data type column.

You can see that the column now has three elements, using our nested table syntax again. The following output file shows the results:

```
-- Available online as output from varray_dml4.sql
```

```
COLUMN_VALUE
---------------
Office of Senator Kennedy
JFK Building
Suite 2400
```

You have now covered the features of varrays in Oracle 10*g*. You have seen that varrays are highly structured collection types. The advantages and disadvantages of varrays have been covered. Moreover, you will now know when and how to use this collection type.

The discussion on varrays has set a foundation for moving to the next collection type, nested tables. You saw in the select statements that varrays depend on nested table structures in some cases. While varrays have a place in database design, they do present challenges that can be avoided by using unbounded nested tables. You may conclude that varrays are better suited to PL/SQL processing than they are to defining tables.

Working with Nested Tables

Nested tables are single-dimensional structures of an Oracle 10*g* data type or a user-defined record/object type. This section focuses on single-dimensional structures of an Oracle 10*g* data type.

Nested tables may be used in table, record, and object definitions. They may be accessed in SQL and PL/SQL. They are different than arrays in the traditional sense of programming languages such as Java, C, C++, and C#. While they use sequential index values to reference elements in the structure, their size is unconstrained. The closest corollaries to standard programming languages are bags and sets.

Defining Nested Tables as Object Types as PL/SQL Program Constructs

The syntax to define an object type of nested tables in the database is

CREATE OR REPLACE TYPE *type_name*
 AS TABLE OF *element_type* [NOT NULL];

As discussed, the type name is often a string followed by an underscore and the word table. Some programming traditions prefer the suffix of tab to that of table. It does not matter what you choose to do. It does matter that you do it consistently.

The following example program demonstrates defining, declaring, and initializing a nested table of cards in a PL/SQL program unit. The cards will be limited to a single suit. They will be defined as variable-length strings:

-- **Available online as part of create_nestedtable1.sql**

```
DECLARE

  -- Define a nested table of variable-length strings.
  TYPE card_table IS TABLE OF VARCHAR2(5 CHAR);

  -- Declare and initialize a nested table with three rows.
  cards          CARD_TABLE := card_table(NULL,NULL,NULL);

BEGIN

  -- Print title.
  dbms_output.put_line(
    'Nested table initialized as null values.');
  dbms_output.put_line(
    '--------------------');

  -- Loop through the three records.
  FOR i IN 1..3 LOOP

    -- Print the contents.
    dbms_output.put      ('Cards Varray ['||i||'] ');
    dbms_output.put_line('['||cards(i)||']');

  END LOOP;

  -- Assign values to subscripted members of the varray.
  cards(1) := 'Ace';
```

```
cards(2) := 'Two';
cards(3) := 'Three';

-- Print title.
dbms_output.put      (CHR(10)); - Visual line break.
dbms_output.put_line(
  'Nested table initialized as 11, 12 and 13.');
dbms_output.put_line(
  '--------------------');

-- Loop through the records to print the varrays.
FOR i IN 1..3 LOOP

  dbms_output.put_line('Cards ['||i||'] '
  ||                   '['||cards(i)||']');

END LOOP;

END;
/
```

As shown in the preceding example, three steps are required to enable a nested table for use by your PL/SQL program: you must define, declare, and initialize a nested table data type.

- It defines a nested table data type. The nested table is named `card_table`. It has no maximum size and a data type of a globalized variable string that is five characters in length.

- It declares and initializes a variable `cards` as a `card_table` nested table type.

- It prints a title with the DBMS_OUTPUT utility.

- It uses a range for-loop and the DBMS_OUTPUT utility to print the null values initialized when the `cards` variable was declared.

- It assigns elements 1 to 3 values Ace, Two, and Three, respectively.

- It prints a title with the DBMS_OUTPUT utility.

- It uses a range for-loop and the DBMS_OUTPUT utility to print the newly assigned values.

The execution section uses a for-loop to check and print the contents of the nested table structure. Then it individually assigns values according to the subscript index. Finally, it uses another for-loop to check and print the modified contents of the varray. Here is the output from create_nestedtable1.sql program:

```
-- Available online as output from create_nestedtable1.sql

Nested table initialized as nulls.
-----------------
Cards Varray [1] []
Cards Varray [2] []
Cards Varray [3] []

Nested table initialized as Ace, Two and Three.
-----------------------
Cards [1] [Ace]
Cards [2] [Two]
Cards [3] [Three]
```

If you skip any of the steps, you will encounter exceptions. The one that most new developers encounter is an unitialized collection, as shown next. You should notice that the behavior of nested tables is very much like that of varrays, as covered earlier.

```
DECLARE
*
ERROR at line 1:
ORA-06531: Reference to uninitialized collection
ORA-06512: at line 11
```

It is raised when you forget to initialize the nested table. The example program initializes the nested table with null values because nulls are allowed. It is also possible to initialize the variable with actual values. You initialize the variable by using the nested table type name and parentheses around the values. When you initialize a varray, you set the actual number of initialized rows. You can use the Collection API COUNT method to see how many rows have been initialized.

Since nested tables are unbounded structures, when you initialize a variable, you set the initial size. If you attempt to access an element beyond the number of initialized rows, you will encounter the following error message. This behavior is a mirrored behavior to the varray type covered earlier.

```
DECLARE
*
ERROR at line 1:
ORA-06533: Subscript beyond count
ORA-06512: at line 13
```

The exception means that subscript is unavailable. It does not exist. When you defined the nested table as three rows in size, you set its size. Therefore, the variable has three valid subscripts, 1, 2, and 3.

If you encountered the error, you might check the Oracle 10*g* documentation. You would find that there is the Collection API EXTEND method to allocate space, and that it is overloaded. It is also covered later in this chapter in the section "Oracle 10*g* Collection API."

As discussed in the varrays section, use of the Collection API EXTEND(n,i) method to insert a row beyond the subscripted range will fail. It will raise the subscript beyond count error.

You add a row using the Collection API EXTEND method without an actual parameter or with a single actual parameter. If you use the single parameter, it is the number of rows to initialize. It cannot exceed the difference between the number of possible and actual rows for the varray. More on using these methods is in the section "Oracle 10*g* Collection API."

The following program illustrates initialization with zero rows in the declaration section. Then it demonstrates dynamic initialization and assignment in the execution section.

```
-- Available online as part of create_nestedtable2.sql

DECLARE

  -- Define a nested table of variable-length strings.
  TYPE card_suit IS TABLE OF VARCHAR2(5 CHAR);

  -- Declare and initialize a null set of rows.
  cards CARD_SUIT := card_suit();

BEGIN

  -- Loop through the three records.
  FOR i IN 1..3 LOOP

    -- Initialize row.
    cards.EXTEND;

    -- Assign values to subscripted members of the varray.
    IF    i = 1 THEN
      cards(i) := 'Ace';
    ELSIF i = 2 THEN
      cards(i) := 'Two';
    ELSIF i = 3 THEN
      cards(i) := 'Three';
    END IF;
```

```
END LOOP;

-- Print title.
dbms_output.put_line(
   'Nested table initialized as Ace, Two and Three.');
dbms_output.put_line(
   '--------------------');

-- Loop through the records to print the nested tables.
FOR i IN 1..3 LOOP

   -- Print the contents.
   dbms_output.put      ('Cards ['||i||'] ');
   dbms_output.put_line('['||cards(i)||']');

END LOOP;

END;
/
```

The example program does the following:

- It defines the nested table type of variable-length strings that are five characters in length.

- It defines a variable `cards` using the nested table type and initializes it as a null collection.

- It uses a range for-loop to allocate space and assign values. Space allocation is done by using the Oracle 10*g* Collection API extend method. Values are assigned in an if-then-else block.

- It prints a title with the DBMS_OUTPUT utility.

- It uses a range for-loop and the DBMS_OUTPUT utility to print the newly assigned values.

The output is shown here:

-- Available online as output from create_nestedtable2.sql

```
Nested table initialized as Ace, Two and Three.
-----------------------
Cards [1] [Ace]
Cards [2] [Two]
Cards [3] [Three]
```

You now have the fundamentals to build nested table structures within PL/SQL program units. The power and management utilities of the collection methods will enhance your ability to use these. This section has further touched on the same Collection API methods used in the varray discussion. They help illustrate initialization issues and are covered in depth later in the chapter. By using these in simple examples, you will be able to see opportunities to apply the methods across collection types.

Defining and Using Nested Tables as Object Types in PL/SQL

The syntax to define an object type of varray in the database is

```
CREATE OR REPLACE TYPE type_name
  AS TABLE OF element_type [ NOT NULL ];
```

The type name is often a string followed by an underscore and the word table. As discussed, many programmers and configuration management people find it a useful pattern to improve code readability. It is also the convention used in the chapter for PL/SQL structure and object types.

The element type may be any Oracle 10*g* data type or a user-defined data type. Allowing null values in varrays is the default. If null values should be disallowed, it must be specified when they are defined.

The following example program demonstrates defining a nested table object type. The anonymous-block PL/SQL program then uses it by declaring and initializing a variable.

-- **Available online as part of create_nestedtable3.sql**

```
CREATE OR REPLACE TYPE card_table
  AS TABLE OF VARCHAR2(5 CHAR);
/

DECLARE

  -- Declare and initialize a nested table with three rows.
  cards CARD_TABLE := card_table(NULL,NULL,NULL);

BEGIN

  -- Print title.
  dbms_output.put_line(
    'Nested table initialized as nulls.');
  dbms_output.put_line(
    '-------------------');

  -- Loop through the three records.
  FOR i IN 1..3 LOOP
```

```
  -- Print the contents.
  dbms_output.put      ('Cards Varray ['||i||'] ');
  dbms_output.put_line('['||cards(i)||']');

END LOOP;

-- Assign values to subscripted members of the table.
cards(1) := 'Ace';
cards(2) := 'Two';
cards(3) := 'Three';

-- Print title.
dbms_output.put      (CHR(10)); - Visual line break.
dbms_output.put_line(
  'Nested table initialized as Ace, Two and Three.');
dbms_output.put_line(
  '-----------------------');

-- Loop through the records to print the nested table.
FOR i IN 1..3 LOOP

  dbms_output.put_line('Cards ['||i||'] '
  ||                   '['||cards(i)||']');

END LOOP;

END;
/
```

The example program does the following:

- It defines a nested table object type of variable-length strings that are five characters in length.

- It defines a `cards` variable using the `card_table` object type.

- It defines a variable `cards` using the nested table type and initializes it as a collection of three null-value elements.

- It prints a title with the `DBMS_OUTPUT` utility.

- It uses a range for-loop to print the null values with the `DBMS_OUTPUT` utility.

- It assigns values to the `cards` variable elements, using the indexes 1 to 3 and the values Ace, Two, and, Three, respectively.

- It uses a range for-loop and the `DBMS_OUTPUT` utility to print the newly assigned values.

The output is shown here:

```
Nested table initialized as null values.
--------------------
Cards Varray [1] []
Cards Varray [2] []
Cards Varray [3] []

Nested table initialized as Ace, Two and Three.
-----------------------
Cards [1] [Ace]
Cards [2] [Two]
Cards [3] [Three]
```

The benefit of defining the nested table object type is that it may be referenced from any programs that have permission to use it, whereas a PL/SQL nested table type structure is limited to the program unit. Program units may be anonymous-block programs like the example or stored procedures or packages in the database. Only the latter enables reference by other PL/SQL programs that have permissions to the package. Please refer to Chapter 8 for details on creating packages and Chapter 9 for using them.

The nested table type uses the default behavior that allows null values. After you master the basic syntax and defaults for defining, declaring, and initializing varrays, there is a question that needs to be resolved. When, why, and how do you allow or disallow null rows?

This is a good question and one that you initially covered in the varray section. In these small example programs, it seems that it may not matter too much, though it will matter when you implement nested table collections. Nested tables start as dense arrays, like varrays. However, it is possible to remove elements from nested tables. As elements are removed, nested tables become sparse. Sparse means that there are gaps in the sequencing of index values.

While index sequencing has gaps, logically there should not be any data gaps. If your application design allows nulls in nested tables, you should carefully review it. You should consider why you want to allow nulls in a nested table, because there should never be data gaps in nested tables.

Allowing nulls in nested tables guarantees you will encounter them in the data stream. Combined with index sequence gaps, allowing null values will increase the amount of required error handling. You should consider overriding the default behavior and disallowing null values in nested tables. Essentially, nested tables and varrays are ill-suited to fill the traditional programming role of lists or maps. If you need the functionality of a list or map, you should use an associative array.

You will now learn how to disallow null values in nested tables. The main impact of disallowing null values in nested tables comes when initializing them. This is a mirror of the issue you saw in varrays earlier. For example, if you redefined the nested table object type used in the previous program to disallow null values, the program would fail. You would see the following errors when attempting to initialize the varray object type:

```
    cards CARD_TABLE := card_table(NULL,NULL,NULL);
                                    *
ERROR at line 4:
ORA-06550: line 4, column 34:
PLS-00567: cannot pass NULL to a NOT NULL constrained
           formal parameter
ORA-06550: line 4, column 39:
PLS-00567: cannot pass NULL to a NOT NULL constrained
           formal parameter
ORA-06550: line 4, column 44:
PLS-00567: cannot pass NULL to a NOT NULL constrained
           formal parameter
```

When you use nested tables as bags or sets, you will define structures that contain hundreds of rows. Some may be dynamically defined by counting rows in a table before being built as dynamic structures.

When you initialize nested tables that contain 100 percent of the data, doing so is straightforward because the constructor can do that. However, when you initialize nested tables that contain less than all the data, adding rows will require some additional programming techniques. These are more or less equivalent to what you worked through with varrays.

The following example allocates a full playing deck of cards. To do so, you will work with varrays that contain the value sets. You will use varrays because the problem is a natural fit to traditional structured arrays. There are thirteen cards in a suit and there are four suits. We will see the use of these structures as in the following program along with nested loops. If you are not comfortable with loop structures, you can review them in Chapter 3.

-- Available online as part of create_nestedtable4.sql

```
-- Define a varray of four rows of variable-length strings.
CREATE OR REPLACE TYPE card_unit_varray
  AS VARRAY(13) OF VARCHAR2(5 CHAR);
/

-- Define a varray of four rows of variable-length strings.
CREATE OR REPLACE TYPE card_suit_varray
```

```
    AS VARRAY(4) OF VARCHAR2(8 CHAR);
/

-- Define a table of variable-length strings.
CREATE OR REPLACE TYPE card_deck_table
  AS TABLE OF VARCHAR2(17 CHAR);
/

DECLARE

  -- Define a counter to manage 1 to 52 cards in a deck.
  counter INTEGER := 0;

  -- Declare and initialize a varray of card suits.
  suits CARD_SUIT_VARRAY :=
    card_suit_varray('Clubs'
                    ,'Diamonds'
                    ,'Hearts'
                    ,'Spades');

  -- Declare and initialize a varray of card units.
  units CARD_UNIT_VARRAY :=
    card_unit_varray('Ace','Two','Three','Four'
                    ,'Five','Six','Seven','Eight'
                    ,'Nine','Ten','Jack','Queen'
                    ,'King');

  -- Declare and initialize a null nested table.
  deck CARD_DECK_TABLE := card_deck_table();

BEGIN

  -- Loop through the four suits of cards.
  FOR i IN 1..suits.COUNT LOOP

    -- Loop through the thirteen units of cards.
    FOR j IN 1..units.COUNT LOOP

      -- Increment counter.
      counter := counter + 1;

      -- Initialize row.
      deck.EXTEND;

      -- Assign a value to the element.
      deck(counter) := units(j)||' of '||suits(i);

    END LOOP;
```

```
  END LOOP;

  -- Print title.
  dbms_output.put_line('Deck of cards by suit.');
  dbms_output.put_line('-----------');

  -- Loop through the deck of cards.
  FOR i IN 1..counter LOOP

    -- Print the contents.
    dbms_output.put_line('['||deck(i)||']');

  END LOOP;

END;
/
```

The example program creates three object types. Two are varrays, which we covered in the prior section. The third is a nested table. While you can see that a deck of cards may be better defined as a varray, what if you are building a solution for the casinos in Nevada or Atlantic City? They may have more than one traditional deck of cards in their gaming deck of cards to discourage card counters.

The example program then uses an anonymous-block PL/SQL program to test the dynamic construction of the nested table. The anonymous-block program does the following:

- It defines and initializes a counter variable.

- It defines the suits variable as a card_suit_varray varray. Then, it initializes the suits variable with clubs, diamonds, hearts, and spades.

- It defines the units variable as a card_unit_varray varray. It then initializes the units variable with the unit values of the possible cards.

- It defines and initializes the card_deck_table as a null nested table collection.

- It uses a range for-loop to iterate through the suits variable. The upward range limit is established by using the Collection API COUNT method. It returns the number of elements that contain a null or data.

- It uses a nested range for-loop to iterate through the units variable. The nested loop manages the incrementing of the counter value. Then, it uses the Collection API EXTEND method to allocate space to the deck nested table variable, assigning values to the deck variable using the counter value as the index.

- It prints a title with the DBMS_OUTPUT utility.

- It uses a range for-loop and the DBMS_OUTPUT utility to print the newly assigned values. The upward range limit is set by the count method described previously.

The redacted output is shown here:

```
-- Available online as output from create_nestedtable4.sql

Deck of cards by suit.
-----------
[Ace of Clubs]
[Two of Clubs]
[Three of Clubs]
...
The remainder is redacted to conserve space.
...
[Jack of Spades]
[Queen of Spades]
[King of Spades]
```

You have developed skills using nested table collections as object types. The next section will use nested table collections and define tables that use them as column data types.

Defining and Using Nested Tables as Column Data Types in Tables

After creating a table with a column of a nested table data type, you need to know how to use it. Using it requires understanding DML access methods and how they work with nested tables. Nested tables, like varrays, present no unique conditions for deleting, since deletion is at the row level. However, there are substantive differences when it comes to using insert and update statements.

The differences are less than those encountered with varrays on updates. Nested tables provide a more intuitive access set for DML. Since the ERD represents street_address as a list, there is no need to redefine it. A varray or nested table is an implementation of a list.

While DML is more intuitive, you do lose some flexibility on database constraints. When you worked with varrays earlier in the chapter, you were able to define a collection column and set the constraint to disallow null values. This is a new feature in Oracle 10g. Varrays are now stored as inline structures, enabling a NOT NULL constraint. By contrast, nested tables as column values do not let you use a NOT NULL constraint. This is true when you define the table type with the default or override the default to disallow nulls. When you attempt to use a table type in a table definition and set the column constraint to NOT NULL, it will raise an ORA-02331 error.

NOTE
If you use the oerr tool to check an ORA-02331 error, it will tell you that it applies to varrays. This is no longer true.

You can test the limitation on database constraints easily. Create a nested table data type like the following:

-- Available online as part of create_addressbook3e.sql

```
CREATE OR REPLACE TYPE address_varray
  AS TABLE OF VARCHAR2(30 CHAR) NOT NULL;
/
```

Then, you can attempt to use it as a column data type in a table with the NOT NULL constraint. The create_addressbook3e.sql demonstrates this. You will see the following error raised if you run the script:

-- Available online as output from create_addressbook3e.sql

```
,street_address            ADDRESS_VARRAY       NOT NULL
                                                   *
ERROR at line 4:
ORA-02331: cannot create constraint on column of datatype
          Named Table Type
```

The table creation fails because the nested table type disallows using the NOT NULL constraint. Nested tables are not constrainable by definition. You should consider this when you use a nested table. You are storing a table that is only referenced through the parent table. Placing a NOT NULL column constraint is inconsistent with a nested table type.

A NOT NULL constraint on a nested table column is equivalent to mandating a row be inserted in the nested table before defining it. This is impossible. A NOT NULL constraint in this case acts like a database referential integrity constraint and is therefore disallowed. NOT NULL constraints for nested tables become application design considerations when inserting or updating rows.

After reading this section, you want to consider why you would use a varray in table definitions. You will see that nested tables provide a more natural access method to elements within DML update statements.

The create_addressbook3.sql script builds the environment for this section. You should run it before attempting to use any of the following scripts.

Like varrays covered earlier, insert statements have one type of access. It is an all-or-nothing approach to the data type. Insert statements allocate space necessary to the construction of the nested table. For example, in a nested table implementation of street_address, it is possible to insert one to any number of rows of data. When the insert is made to the row, an instance of the collection type is constructed with the number of rows chosen. As you see, the syntax to insert a nested table is a mirror to that used for a varray. The single exception is the name of the collection type used in the constructor.

-- Available online as part of nestedtable_dml1.sql

```
INSERT
INTO        addresses
VALUES
(21
,21
,address_table
  ('Office of Senator McCain'
  ,'450 West Paseo Redondo'
  ,'Suite 200')
,'Tucson'
,'AZ'
,'85701'
,'USA');
```

The example program inserts a full set of three rows into the nested table data type. It is important to note that in the values clause, the nested table data type name is used as the constructor name. The constructor uses the syntax previously presented with a list of comma-delimited actual parameters in a set of parentheses.

If you were to query the street_address column from the table, you would see a return set of the constructor with its actual parameters. This is illustrated by running a query like the following:

-- Available online as part of nestedtable_dml1.sql

```
SELECT    street_address
FROM      addresses;
```

The shortened output from the query is noted.

-- Available online as output from nestedtable_dml1.sql

```
STREET_ADDRESS
------------------------------
ADDRESS_TABLE('Office of Senator McCain', '450 West Paseo ...
```

This type of output is not very useful. It is also very different than what you might expect. Using data query language (DQL) to select a result from a nested table data type requires specialized syntax. Fortunately, unlike the varray you implemented by casting to a nested table, you can directly access nested tables in DQL.

The following example formats the output with SQL*Plus. It then selects the column values from the nested table one row at a time. A bit more intuitive than the varray DQL covered, it is still complex.

-- **Available online as part of nestedtable_dml1.sql**

```
-- Use SQL*Plus to format the output.
COL column_value FORMAT A30

-- Print a list of the varray elements.
SELECT    column_value
FROM      THE (SELECT    street_address
               FROM      addresses
               WHERE     address_id = 21);
```

The select statement does the following:

- The reserved word `column_value` is an access method for rows in a nested table. (As mention earlier, there is also a hidden column, `nested_table_id`, which is a foreign key that maps to the row in the parent table.)

- `THE` is a reserved word in SQL that enables a `column_value` to be selected from a query of a nested table.

The formatted output from the query is

-- **Available online as output from nestedtable_dml1.sql**

```
COLUMN_VALUE
---------------
Office of Senator McCain
450 West Paseo Redondo
Suite 200
```

The DQL to access the values in a nested table returns a row set. A problem with a row set is merging the row set with other data in SQL. Since other elements returned in a normal selection will have one occurrence per row, representing the

data is difficult. As you review the following query, it becomes clear that using SQL
to manage nested table returns is not effective:

```
-- Use SQL*Plus to format the output.
COL data FORMAT A30

SELECT    s.data
FROM      (SELECT    1 ordering
          ,          rownum roworder
          ,          individual_id
          ,          first_name
          ||          ' '
          ||          middle_initial
          ||          ' '
          ||          last_name data
          FROM       individuals i2
          UNION ALL
          SELECT     2 ordering
          ,          rownum roworder
          ,          individual_id
          ,          column_value data
          FROM       THE (SELECT    street_address
                         FROM       addresses)
          ,          addresses
          UNION ALL
          SELECT     3 ordering
          ,          rownum roworder
          ,          individual_id
          ,          city
          ||          ', '
          ||          state
          ||          ' '
          ||          postal_code data
          FROM       addresses a
          ORDER BY 1,2) s
,         individuals i
WHERE     s.individual_id = i.individual_id
AND       i.individual_id = 21;
```

The select statement does the following:

■   It returns the data column only for all rows that have an individual_id
    equal to 21.

■ It builds an inline table, sometimes called a run-time view. The inline table is three queries joined by the UNION ALL operator. The operator simply returns all rows from each of the joined queries, assuming there are no duplicates.

■ The inline table query would return in a random row order without an ORDER BY clause. Unfortunately, there is no natural data to use that will let you order the return values correctly. Each of the queries returns two pseudocolumns to enable the rows to be ordered. The first column is a numeric literal 1, 2, or 3, which is then used to group return sets. The second column is a numeric value derived by using the internal rownum value. The rownum value is assigned to each row returned from the query in the retrieval sequence. The rownum value preserves the ordering of the nested table.

■ The inline table individual_id return value is then joined to the rows returned from the individuals table.

The formatted output from the query is

-- Available online as output from nestedtable_dml1.sql

```
DATA
---------------
John   McCain
Office of Senator McCain
450 West Paseo Redondo
Suite 200
Tucson, AZ 85701
```

You see that SQL presents some limitations. PL/SQL can help you erase those limitations. You will build a function to return a single variable-length string with row breaks. If you need to review the details of building stored functions, please check Chapter 8. Likewise, you should check the Collection API later in this chapter for details on the count method. Then, you can use that to write an efficient DQL select statement.

The following function takes the row returns and creates a single variable-length string. You will find it a useful example, especially in the case of building mailing addresses:

-- Available online as output from nestedtable_dml1.sql

```
CREATE OR REPLACE FUNCTION many_to_one
   (street_address_in ADDRESS_TABLE)
RETURN VARCHAR2 IS
```

```
  -- Define a return variable and initial it.
  retval VARCHAR2(4000) := '';

BEGIN

  -- Loop from the beginning to end of the nested table.
  FOR i IN 1..street_address_in.COUNT LOOP

    -- Append the next value and a line break.
    retval := retval || street_address_in(i) || CHR(10);

  END LOOP;

  RETURN retval;

END many_to_one;
/
```

The stored function does the following:

- It takes a single formal parameter of a nested table. The nested table defined type is the one used throughout the example.

- It defines and initializes a variable-length string as return variable in the declaration section.

- It has a for-loop in the execution section that iterates through all the rows in the nested table passed into the function. In the for-loop it appends the value of all prior rows, the new row, and a line return.

- It returns a variable-length string after the for-loop.

SQL*Plus again formats the column. As you see, the query is much simpler than the one used previously:

-- **Available online as output from nestedtable_dml1.sql**

```
-- Use SQL*Plus to format the output.
COL address_label FORMAT A30

-- Print a list of the joined elements.
SELECT   i.first_name || ' '
||       i.middle_initial || ' '
||       i.last_name || CHR(10)
||       many_to_one(a.street_address)
||       city || ', '
||       state || ' '
```

```
  ||        postal_code address_label
FROM        addresses a
  ,         individuals i
WHERE       a.individual_id = i.individual_id
AND         i.individual_id = 21;
```

The select statement is shorter, easier to read, and more effective. The select statement does the following:

- It returns the data column only for all rows that have an `individual_id` equal to 21.

- It passes the nested table data type to a stored function that returns a variable string.

- It joins the primary key of the `individuals` table with the foreign key of the `addresses` table.

The formatted output from the query is

-- Available online as output from nestedtable_dml1.sql

```
ADDRESS_LABEL
---------------
John   McCain
Office of Senator McCain
450 West Paseo Redondo
Suite 200
Tucson, AZ 85701
```

As you have seen earlier in the chapter, PL/SQL is the only way to update varrays unless changing the entire content. This is not the case with nested tables. A key advantage of nested tables is that you can update individual row elements. These updates can be done directly in DML update statements.

You use the following example program to replace the entire content of the `street_address` nested table data type:

-- Available online as part of nestedtable_dml2.sql

```
-- Insert into address using the varray structure.
UPDATE    addresses
SET       street_address =
            address_table('Office of Senator McCain'
                         ,'2400 E. Arizona Biltmore Cir.'
                         ,'Suite 1150')
WHERE     address_id = 21;
```

The update statement assigns the value of a newly constructed `address_
table` collection type. It does so by constructing an instance of a nested table.
This is done through a construction process, where actual parameters are passed
inside parentheses and delimited by commas.

Using the same complex select statement to query the new data, you will see
the following output:

```
-- Available online as output from nestedtable_dml2.sql
```

```
COLUMN_VALUE
---------------
Office of Senator McCain
2400 E. Arizona Biltmore Cir.
Suite 1150
```

You can update a portion of a nested table column directly in SQL. Alternatively,
you may use two approaches in PL/SQL. This is an improvement over the lack of
direct update capability for the varray column.

The following program will update the first row in the `street_address`
nested table. It will add the senator's first name to the variable-length string:

```
-- Available online as part of nestedtable_dml3.sql
```

```
-- Update the column value directly in SQL.
UPDATE    THE (SELECT    street_address
              FROM       addresses
              WHERE      address_id = 21)
SET       column_value = 'Office of Senator John McCain'
WHERE     column_value = 'Office of Senator McCain';
```

The formatted output from the query is

```
-- Available online as output from nestedtable_dml3.sql
```

```
COLUMN_VALUE
---------------
Office of Senator John McCain
450 West Paseo Redondo
Suite 200
```

Alternatively, you can use PL/SQL to do the update. Two approaches you can
choose from in PL/SQL are

- A direct update of a row in the nested table

- An update of all the row contents for a nested table column

The update of all row contents is a mirror to the approach used earlier for varrays. You should check the example provided earlier in the chapter for that approach. Next you will see how to update a row in a nested table column directly. The example uses dynamic SQL and bind variables. Both are covered in Chapter 13.

-- **Available online as part of nestedtable_dml3.sql**

```
-- Anonymous block using PL/SQL nested table update.
DECLARE

  -- Define old and new values.
  new_value VARCHAR2(30 CHAR) :=
    'Office of Senator John McCain';
  old_value VARCHAR2(30 CHAR) :=
    'Office of Senator McCain';

  -- Build SQL statement to support bind variables.
  sql_statement VARCHAR2(100 CHAR)
    := 'UPDATE   THE (SELECT   street_address '
    || '                FROM      addresses '
    || '                WHERE     address_id = 21) '
    || 'SET      column_value = :1 '
    || 'WHERE    column_value = :2';

BEGIN

  -- Use dynamic SQL to run the update statement.
  EXECUTE IMMEDIATE sql_statement
  USING new_value, old_value;

END;
/
```

The PL/SQL program leverages bind variables and dynamic SQL to manage the update. You can see a more generic solution to this problem in Chapter 13. It will show you how to implement an API to hide the update syntax requirements from application developers. The PL/SQL program does the following:

■ It defines and declares a variable with the new data to put in the row of the nested table data type.

■ It defines and declares a variable with the old data to find the row in the nested table data type.

■ It defines a SQL update statement with two bind variables.

■ It executes a dynamic SQL execution of the update statement with the old and new data variables as bind variables.

NOTE
The bind variables are numerically numbered placeholders. Position-specific variables or strings reference them with the USING clause.

The formatted output from the query is the same as shown in the last example. It is not redisplayed to save space.

Updates can only be done for elements within a nested table. If you want to add an element to a nested table column value, you must use PL/SQL. The following program shows you how to add two rows of data.

The insert statement is the same except for type definition to the one you used in the varray update discussion. It inserts only one element into the `street_address` column, initializing only one element in the nested table collection for the row. The following example shows the insert statement:

```
-- Available online as part of nestedtable_dml4.sql

-- Insert into address using the varray structure.
INSERT
INTO      addresses
VALUES
(12
,12
,address_table('Office of Senator Kennedy')
,'Boston'
,'MA'
,'02203'
,'USA');
```

You can use the following solution to add the missing elements to the nested table collection column. You should note there is only one difference between a varray and nested table. That difference is the data type.

```
-- Available online as part of nestedtable_dml4.sql

DECLARE

  -- Define a record type for a row of the addresses table.
  TYPE address_type IS RECORD
  (address_id            INTEGER
```

```
    ,individual_id          INTEGER
    ,street_address         ADDRESS_TABLE
    ,city                   VARCHAR2(20 CHAR)
    ,state                  VARCHAR2(20 CHAR)
    ,postal_code            VARCHAR2(20 CHAR)
    ,country_code           VARCHAR2(10 CHAR));

  -- Define a variable of the addresses table record type.
  address               ADDRESS_TYPE;

  -- Define a cursor to return the %ROWTYPE value.
  CURSOR get_street_address
    (address_id_in        INTEGER) IS
    SELECT   *
    FROM     addresses
    WHERE    address_id = address_id_in;

BEGIN

  -- Open the cursor.
  OPEN  get_street_address(22);

  -- Fetch a into the record type variable.
  FETCH get_street_address
  INTO  address;

  -- Close the cursor.
  CLOSE get_street_address;

  -- Add element space.
  FOR i IN 2..3 LOOP
    address.street_address.EXTEND;
  END LOOP;

  -- Reset the first element of the varray type variable.
  address.street_address(2) := 'JFK Building';
  address.street_address(3) := 'Suite 2400';

  -- Update the varray column value.
  UPDATE    addresses
  SET       street_address = address.street_address
  WHERE     address_id = 22;

END;
/
```

The program does the following:

- It defines a record type that mirrors the `addresses` table.

- It defines a variable of the record type.

- It defines a cursor that takes a single formal parameter for the primary key of the `addresses` table.

- It opens a cursor, passing the required actual parameter.

- It fetches the `%ROWTYPE` value into the defined variable.

- It closes the open cursor.

- It uses a range for-loop and the Collection API to create space for two additional rows.

- It assigns values to the second and third elements in the nested table.

- It finally uses a DML update statement to replace the entire contents of the `street_address` nested table data type column.

You can see that the column now has three elements, using our nested table syntax again. The following output file shows the results:

```
-- Available online as output from varray_dml4.sql

COLUMN_VALUE
---------------
Office of Senator Kennedy
JFK Building
Suite 2400
```

You have now covered the features of nested tables in Oracle 10*g*. You have seen that nested tables are structured collection types. The advantages and disadvantages of nested tables have been covered and contrasted against varrays. Moreover, you will now know when and how to use this collection type.

Working with Associative Arrays

Associative arrays are single-dimensional structures of an Oracle 10*g* data type or a user-defined record/object type. As discussed at the beginning of the section, they were previously known as PL/SQL tables. This section focuses on single-dimensional structures of the associative array.

Associative arrays *cannot* be used in tables. They may be used only as programming structures. They can be accessed only in PL/SQL. They are like the other collection types and different than arrays in the traditional sense of programming languages such as Java, C, C++, and C#. They are close cousins to lists and maps. They do not have the capability of linked lists but may be made to act that way through a user-defined programming interface.

It is important to note some key issues presented by associative arrays. These issues drive a slightly different approach to illustrating their use. Associative arrays

- Do not require initialization and have no constructor syntax. They do not need to allocate space before assigning values, which eliminates using the Collection API EXTEND method.

- Can be indexed numerically up to and including Oracle 10*g*. In Oracle 10*g,* they can also use unique variable-length strings.

- Can use any integer as the index value, which means any negative, positive, or zero whole numbers.

- Are implicitly converted from equivalent %ROWTYPE, record type, and object type return values to associative array structures.

- Are the key to using the FORALL statement or BULK COLLECT clause, which enables bulk transfers from the database to a programming unit.

- Require special treatment when using a character string as an index value in any database using globalized settings, such as NLS_COMP or NLS_SORT initialization parameters.

You will start by seeing the expanded definition techniques provided in Oracle 10*g.* Then examine their principle uses as PL/SQL programming structures.

Defining and Using Associative Arrays as PL/SQL Program Constructs

The syntax to define an associative array in PL/SQL has two possibilities. One is

```
CREATE OR REPLACE TYPE type_name
  AS TABLE OF element_type [ NOT NULL ]
  INDEX BY [ PLS_INTEGER |
        BINARY_INTEGER |
        VARCHAR2(size) ];
```

The same issues around enabling or disabling null values in nested tables apply to associative arrays. As a rule, you should ensure that data in an array is not null. You can do that by enabling the constraint when defining an associative array or programmatically. It is a decision that you will need to make on a case-by-case basis.

You can use a negative, positive, or zero number as the index value for associative arrays. Both PLS_INTEGER and BINARY_INTEGER types are unconstrained types that map to call specifications in C/C++, C#, and Java in Oracle 10*g*.

You can use variable-length strings up to four thousand characters in length. The VARCHAR2 type supports the convention physical size or a size of CHAR for globalized implementation.

The other possible syntax to define an associate array is

```
CREATE OR REPLACE TYPE type_name
  AS TABLE OF element_type [ NOT NULL ]
  INDEX BY key_type;
```

The `key_type` alternative enables you to use VARCHAR2, STRING, or LONG data types. Both VARCHAR2 and STRING require a size definition. The LONG data type does not, because it is by definition a VARCHAR2(32760). You should refer to Chapter 16 for coverage of LONG data types.

As discussed, associative arrays do not require initialization and do not have a constructor syntax. This is a substantive difference between the other two collection types, varrays and nested tables. It is a tremendous advantage to using associative arrays in PL/SQL. This is especially true because the basic structure of associative arrays with an integer index has not changed much since their implementation in Oracle 7, release 7.3.

If you attempt to construct an associative array, you will raise a PLS-00222 exception. The following program attempts to construct an associative array:

-- **Available online as part of create_assocarray1.sql**

```
DECLARE

  -- Define an associative array of strings.
  TYPE card_table IS TABLE OF VARCHAR2(5 CHAR)
    INDEX BY BINARY_INTEGER;

  -- Declare and attempt to construct an associative array.
  cards CARD_TABLE := card_table('A','B','C');

BEGIN
  NULL;
END;
/
```

It will raise the following error messages:

-- **Available online as output from create_assocarray1.sql**

```
  cards CARD_TABLE := card_table('A','B','C');
                              *
ERROR at line 8:
ORA-06550: line 8, column 23:
```

```
PLS-00222: no function with name 'CARD_TABLE' exists in
          this scope
ORA-06550: line 8, column 9:
PL/SQL: Item ignored
```

The failure occurs because the INDEX BY clause has built an associative array, not a nested table. While a nested table type definition implicitly defines a constructor, an associative array does not.

In our previous discussion, the object constructor was qualified as a function. Other collection types, varrays and nested tables, are object types that implicitly define constructor functions. An associative array is a structure, not an object type. Therefore, it does not have an implicitly built constructor function and fails when you attempt to call the function.

Likewise, you cannot navigate an associative array until it contains elements. The following example program demonstrates the failure:

-- **Available online as part of create_assocarray2.sql**

```
DECLARE

  -- Define an associative array of strings.
  TYPE card_table IS TABLE OF VARCHAR2(5 CHAR)
    INDEX BY BINARY_INTEGER;

  -- Define an associative array variable.
  cards CARD_TABLE;

BEGIN

  -- Print an element of the cards associative array.
  DBMS_OUTPUT.PUT_LINE(cards(1));

END;
/
```

It will raise the following exception, which is quite different from those of other collection types. As qualified previously, you get an uninitialized collection error from varrays and nested tables. Associative arrays raise a no data found exception. The no data found error occurs because associative array elements are built through direct element assignment.

-- **Available online as output from create_assocarray2.sql**

```
DECLARE
*
ERROR at line 1:
```

```
ORA-01403: no data found
ORA-06512: at line 13
```

As a rule of thumb, you want to avoid the possibility of this error. The following program provides a mechanism to avoid encountering the error:

-- **Available online as part of create_assocarray3.sql**

```
DECLARE

  -- Define an associative array of strings.
  TYPE card_table IS TABLE OF VARCHAR2(5 CHAR)
    INDEX BY BINARY_INTEGER;

  -- Define an associative array variable.
  cards CARD_TABLE;

BEGIN

  IF cards.COUNT <> 0 THEN

    -- Print an element of the cards associative array.
    DBMS_OUTPUT.PUT_LINE(cards(1));

  ELSE

    -- Print an element of the cards associative array.
    DBMS_OUTPUT.PUT_LINE('The cards collection is empty.');

  END IF;

END;
/
```

The Collection API COUNT method returns a zero value under only two conditions:

- When a varray or nested table collection is initialized and no space is allocated to elements.
- When an associative array has no assigned elements.

Since the second condition is met, the program returns the message from the else statement. The output follows:

-- **Available online as output from create_assocarray3.sql**

```
The cards collection is empty.
```

The Collection API EXTEND method will fail to allocate space to an associative array. The following program illustrates the attempt:

-- Available online as part of create_assocarray4.sql

```
DECLARE

  -- Define an associative array of strings.
  TYPE card_table IS TABLE OF VARCHAR2(5 CHAR)
    INDEX BY BINARY_INTEGER;

  -- Define an associative array variable.
  cards CARD_TABLE;

BEGIN

  IF cards.COUNT <> 0 THEN

    -- Print an element of the cards associative array.
    DBMS_OUTPUT.PUT_LINE(cards(1));

  ELSE

    -- Allocate space like varray and nested tables do.
    cards.EXTEND;

  END IF;

END;
/
```

The attempt to extend an associative array raises the following error:

-- Available online as output from create_assocarray4.sql

```
    cards.EXTEND;
    *
ERROR at line 20:
ORA-06550: line 20, column 5:
PLS-00306: wrong number or types of arguments in call to
          'EXTEND'
ORA-06550: line 20, column 5:
PL/SQL: Statement ignored
```

The wrong number or types of arguments error is raised because the Collection API EXTEND method can only operate on varrays and nested tables. You see the type argument because an associative array is a structure, not an object type.

You have developed an appreciation of why associative arrays cannot be constructed like varrays and nested tables. You will now experiment with defining and initializing associative arrays.

Initializing Associative Arrays

As discussed, you can build associative arrays with a number index or a unique variable-length string. Number indexes must be integers, which are positive, negative, and zero numbers. Unique variable-length strings can be VARCHAR2, STRING, or LONG data types.

You see how to assign elements to a numerically indexed associative array in the following example:

```
-- Available online as part of create_assocarray5.sql

DECLARE

  -- Define a varray of twelve strings.
  TYPE months_varray IS VARRAY(12) OF STRING(9 CHAR);

  -- Define an associative array of strings.
  TYPE calendar_table IS TABLE OF VARCHAR2(9 CHAR)
    INDEX BY BINARY_INTEGER;

  -- Declare and construct a varray.
  month MONTHS_VARRAY :=
    months_varray('January','February','March'
                 ,'April','May','June'
                 ,'July','August','September'
                 ,'October','November','December');

  -- Declare an associative array variable.
  calendar CALENDAR_TABLE;

BEGIN

  -- Check if calendar has no elements.
  IF calendar.COUNT = 0 THEN

    -- Print a title
    DBMS_OUTPUT.PUT_LINE('Assignment loop:');
    DBMS_OUTPUT.PUT_LINE('--------');

    -- Loop through all the varray elements.
    FOR i IN month.FIRST..month.LAST LOOP
```

```
      -- Initialize a null associative array element.
      calendar(i) := '';

      -- Print an indexed element from the array.
      DBMS_OUTPUT.PUT_LINE(
        'Index ['||i||'] is ['||calendar(i)||']');

      -- Assign the numeric index valued varray element
      -- to an equal index valued array element.
      calendar(i) := month(i);

    END LOOP;

    -- Print a title
    DBMS_OUTPUT.PUT(CHR(10));
    DBMS_OUTPUT.PUT_LINE('Post-assignment loop:');
    DBMS_OUTPUT.PUT_LINE('-----------');

    -- Loop through all the associative array elements.
    FOR i IN calendar.FIRST..calendar.LAST LOOP

      -- Print an indexed element from the array.
      DBMS_OUTPUT.PUT_LINE(
        'Index ['||i||'] is ['||calendar(i)||']');

    END LOOP;

  END IF;

END;
/
```

The preceding example illustrates moving the contents of a varray to an associative array. In this example, both structures have a numeric index value.

- It defines a varray data type. The varray is named `months_varray`. It has a maximum size of twelve and a data type of string. The string is nine characters in length.

- It defines an associative array data type. The associative array is named `calendar_table`. It has no maximum size. The associative array uses a `VARCHAR2` data type. The `VARCHAR2` is nine characters in length. The associative array uses an integer as an index value.

- It declares and initializes a variable `month`. The variable is a varray data type, named `months_varray`. It is initialized as a twelve-element collection with month names as the values in each element.

- It checks that the associative array variable `calendar` has no elements. It checks for a zero value by comparing the Collection API COUNT method return.

- It uses a range for-loop to move from the first element to the last in the `month` varray. The range is established by using the Collection API FIRST and LAST methods.

- In the range for-loop, it assigns a null value using an index value equal to the `month` varray index. This is the only way to allocate space to an associative array. It effectively creates a numerically indexed null element.

- In the range for-loop, it assigns a value from the `month` varray to the `calendar` associative array. Using an index value equal to both the calendar and month collections, it effects the assignment. If the null assignment were skipped in the first loop, the assignment would do two things: the assignment would create an element with the equal numeric index value and then assign it the value held by the varray. Finally, it prints the assignment to the calendar associative array.

- It uses a range for-loop to move from the first element to the last in the `calendar` associative array. The range is established by using the Collection API FIRST and LAST methods.

- It prints the indexes and values from `calendar` associative array with the DBMS_OUTPUT utility.

Its output prints a line for each month for both collection types. The following is a shortened copy of the output:

```
-- Available online as output from create_assocarray5.sql
```

```
Assignment loop:
---------
Index [1] is []
Index [2] is []
...
Index [11] is []
Index [12] is []

Post-assignment loop:
-----------
Index [1] is [January]
Index [2] is [February]
...
Index [11] is [November]
Index [12] is [December]
```

If you decide, in Oracle 10*g*, to use a variable-length string as an index value, the process changes. The standard range for-loop works to assign values from the varray to the associative array. However, the same type of range for-loop will fail to read the associative array. The following example program shows you the failure:

-- **Available online as part of create_assocarray5e.sql**

```
DECLARE

  -- Define a varray of twelve strings.
  TYPE months_varray IS VARRAY(12) OF STRING(9 CHAR);

  -- Define an associative array of strings.
  TYPE calendar_table IS TABLE OF VARCHAR2(9 CHAR)
    INDEX BY VARCHAR2(9 CHAR);

  -- Declare and construct a varray.
  month MONTHS_VARRAY :=
    months_varray('January','February','March'
                 ,'April','May','June'
                 ,'July','August','September'
                 ,'October','November','December');

  -- Declare an associative array variable.
  calendar CALENDAR_TABLE;

BEGIN

  -- Check if calendar has no elements.
  IF calendar.COUNT = 0 THEN

    -- Print a title
    DBMS_OUTPUT.PUT_LINE('Assignment loop:');
    DBMS_OUTPUT.PUT_LINE('--------');

    -- Loop through all the varray elements.
    FOR i IN month.FIRST..month.LAST LOOP

      -- Assign the numeric index-valued varray element
      -- to an equal index-valued array element.
      calendar(month(i)) := i;

      -- Print an indexed element from the array.
      DBMS_OUTPUT.PUT_LINE(
        'Index ['||month(i)||'] is ['||i||']');

    END LOOP;
```

```
   -- Print a title
   DBMS_OUTPUT.PUT(CHR(10));
   DBMS_OUTPUT.PUT_LINE('Post-assignment loop:');
   DBMS_OUTPUT.PUT_LINE('-----------');

   -- Loop through all the associative array elements.
   FOR i IN calendar.FIRST..calendar.LAST LOOP

     -- Print an indexed element from the array.
     DBMS_OUTPUT.PUT_LINE(
       'Index ['||i||'] is ['||calendar(i)||']');

   END LOOP;

 END IF;

END;
/
```

The preceding example illustrates an attempt to navigate an associative array using string names as the index values in a range for-loop. There is one line that changes between the `create_assocarray5.sql` and `create_assocarray5e.sql` programs. The line follows:

create_assocarray5.sql	create_assocarray5e.sql
`-- Assign a numeric index.` `calendar(i) := ' ';`	`-- Assign a numeric index.` `Calendar(month(i)) := ' ';`

The initialization in this line works. However, the next range for-loop attempts to use the range loop counter as the index value for the associative array. When attempting to use a range for-loop with start and end positions set by the Collection API `FIRST` and `LAST` functions, it raises the following exception:

```
-- Available online as output from create_assocarray5e.sql

Assignment loop:
--------
Index [January] is [1]
Index [February] is [2]

Index [November] is [11]
Index [December] is [12]

Post-assignment loop:
-----------
```

```
DECLARE
 *
ERROR at line 1:
ORA-06502: PL/SQL: numeric or value error: character to
          number conversion error
ORA-06512: at line 48
```

The second range for-loop attempts to pass a non-numeric index value to the counter variable. The counter variable is `i` in the preceding program. A counter variable is defined as a `PLS_INTEGER`. Thus, the variable-length string index value cannot be cast to an integer because it is not an integer. Therefore, it raises an `ORA-06502` conversion error, as just shown. The same example worked previously because the counter variable was cast as a `VARCHAR2` when initializing members and cast back to an `INTEGER` when reading the associative array.

TIP
Associative arrays do not have a navigational syntax equivalent to their namesake in JavaScript. You cannot treat an associative array as a cursor by using a cursor for-loop structure.

This presents you with a problem. A non-numeric index value requires you to know where to start and how to increment. The Collection API `FIRST` and `NEXT` methods provide the tools. Details of the Collection API are covered later in the chapter if you want more on these methods now.

You can use the approach demonstrated in the following example program to solve the problem. In the second range for-loop, the logic to traverse a unique string index is provided:

-- **Available online as part of create_assocarray6.sql**

```
DECLARE

  -- Define variables to traverse an associative array that
  -- uses variable-length strings for index values.
  current VARCHAR2(9 CHAR);
  element INTEGER;

  -- Define a varray of twelve strings.
  TYPE months_varray IS VARRAY(12) OF STRING(9 CHAR);

  -- Define an associative array of strings.
  TYPE calendar_table IS TABLE OF VARCHAR2(9 CHAR)
    INDEX BY VARCHAR2(9 CHAR);
```

```
-- Declare and construct a varray.
month MONTHS_VARRAY :=
  months_varray('January','February','March'
               ,'April','May','June'
               ,'July','August','September'
               ,'October','November','December');

-- Declare an associative array variable.
calendar CALENDAR_TABLE;

BEGIN

-- Check if calendar has no elements.
IF calendar.COUNT = 0 THEN

  -- Print a title
  DBMS_OUTPUT.PUT_LINE('Assignment loop:');
  DBMS_OUTPUT.PUT_LINE('--------');

  -- Loop through all the varray elements.
  FOR i IN month.FIRST..month.LAST LOOP

    -- Assign the numeric index valued varray element
    -- to an equal index valued array element.
    calendar(month(i)) := TO_CHAR(i);

    -- Print an indexed element from the array.
    DBMS_OUTPUT.PUT_LINE(
      'Index ['||month(i)||'] is ['||i||']');

  END LOOP;

  -- Print a title
  DBMS_OUTPUT.PUT(CHR(10));
  DBMS_OUTPUT.PUT_LINE('Post-assignment loop:');
  DBMS_OUTPUT.PUT_LINE('-----------');

  -- Loop through all the associative array elements.
  FOR i IN 1..calendar.COUNT LOOP

    -- Check if the first element in the loop.
    IF i = 1 THEN

      -- Assign the first character index to a variable.
      current := calendar.FIRST;

      -- Use the derived index to find the next index.
      element := calendar(current);
```

```
      ELSE

        -- Check if next index value exists.
        IF calendar.NEXT(current) IS NOT NULL THEN

          -- Assign the character index to a variable.
          current := calendar.NEXT(current);

          -- Use the derived index to find the next index.
          element := calendar(current);

        ELSE

          -- Exit loop since last index value is read.
          EXIT;

        END IF;

      END IF;

      -- Print an indexed element from the array.
      DBMS_OUTPUT.PUT_LINE(
        'Index ['||current||'] is ['||element||']');

    END LOOP;

  END IF;

END;
/
```

The preceding example illustrates moving the contents of a varray with a numeric index to an associative array with a unique string index. Here's what the program is doing:

- It defines two variables to be used to manage navigation through the unique string indexed associative array. They are the current and element variables.

- It defines a varray data type. The varray is named `months_varray`. It has a maximum size of twelve and a data type of a string. The string is nine characters in length.

- It defines an associative array data type. The associative array is named `calendar_table`. It has no maximum size. The associative array uses a VARCHAR2 data type. The VARCHAR2 is nine characters in length. The associative array uses a unique string as an index value.

- It declares and initializes a variable month. The variable is a varray data type, named months_varray. It is initialized as a twelve-element collection with month names as the values in each element.

- It checks that the associative array variable calendar has no elements. It checks for a zero value by comparing the Collection API COUNT method return.

- It uses a range for-loop to move from the first element to the last in the month varray. The range is established by using the Collection API FIRST and LAST methods.

- In the range for-loop, it allocates and assigns a value from the month varray to the calendar associative array. The assignment moves the numeric index from the month varray to the element value in the associative array. Likewise, it uses the month varray data value as the index value for the calendar associative array. The integer is implicitly cast as a character and converted. Finally, it prints the assignment to the calendar associative array.

- It uses a range for-loop to move from the first element to the last in the calendar associative array. The range is established by using one as the lower range value and the Collection API COUNT methods for the upper range. This ensures an integer is returned to the for-loop counter variable.

- In the range for-loop, it uses a nested if-then-else statement to set and reset access indexes. Finding where to start is the first step. Then using the Collection API, you can step through the elements one by one.

The if statement checks whether or not the range for-loop counter is equal to 1. This finds our first record to start traversing the associative array.

If it is the first element in the range, you use the Collection API FIRST method to return the first unique string index value. It assigns the unique string index value to the current variable.

It then uses the current variable to find the data value and assign it to the element variable. At this point, it exits the if-then-else statement and prints the values, as described later.

On your second pass through the range for-loop, the if statement check will fail. It will then go to the else statement and encounter the nested if-then-else statement.

The if statement uses the Collection API NEXT to check whether there is another record in the associative array.

If there is another record in the associative array, it will use the `current` variable to find the next index value. Then, it assigns the value to replace the value in the `current` variable.

If there is another record in the associative array, it will process the nested else statement. At that point, it exits the range for-loop. This is the only exit from the range for-loop because the logic in the if-then-else statement prevents any other exit.

It prints the indexes and values from `calendar` associative array with the DBMS_OUTPUT utility.

The program generates the following output stream. Again, it has been edited to conserve space:

-- Available online as output from create_assocarray6.sql

```
Assignment loop:
--------
Index [January] is [1]
Index [February] is [2]

Index [November] is [11]
Index [December] is [12]

Post-assignment loop:
-----------
Index [April] is [4]
Index [August] is [8]
Index [December] is [12]
Index [February] is [2]
Index [January] is [1]
Index [July] is [7]
Index [June] is [6]
Index [March] is [3]
Index [May] is [5]
Index [November] is [11]
Index [October] is [10]
Index [September] is [9]
```

You can see that the population sequence of the associative array differs from how it can be traversed. The Collection API FIRST, NEXT, and PRIOR methods work from hash maps for the unique strings. Sorting is dependent on the NLS_COMP and NLS_SORT database parameters in globalized databases.

As a result of this sorting behavior, unique string index values present some interesting considerations. If you need to keep track of original ordering, you will need to use a record or object type that provides a pseudokey. The pseudokey can maintain your original ordering sequence.

TIP
If you are working in a globalized database, the NLS_COMP and NLS_SORT parameters may alter expected behavior of sorting. This is especially true when dealing with time stamps.

You have developed an appreciation of standard initialization methods for associative arrays. You have also explored key issues that you should avoid. Moreover, you have learned how to initialize and traverse associative arrays. You will now experiment with defining and initializing associative arrays as bulk collections.

Using Associative Arrays with BULK COLLECT and FORALL

Collections offer you many performance opportunities. They can be used in many places in your programs. In fact, a performance enhancement has been introduced in the Oracle 10g PL/SQL compiler. As covered in Chapter 8, the PL/SQL compiler translates your code into machine code before executing it. Oracle 10g now does the same thing but with a twist. The compiler dynamically rearranges your code during its conversion to machine code and optimizes its execution. This is done by default through the database PLSQL_OPTIMIZE_LEVEL initialization parameter, which is set to level two. If you want to disable the optimization, you can set PLSQL_OPTIMIZE_LEVEL to zero. At zero, the compiler does not rearrange your code.

Likewise, using BULK COLLECT and FORALL opens the door that eliminates row-level processing. BULK COLLECT allows you to retrieve sets of records that you can store in associative arrays or nested tables. FORALL enables you to send DML statements in batches. FORALL can insert, update, and delete data. These methods reduce the context switching between the PL/SQL and SQL engines. Without them, there would be too many parses and fetches.

You will remember that row-level processing leverages the %ROWTYPE or %TYPE. The former can map directly to record types. The BULK COLLECT enables a collection of %ROWTYPE or %TYPE values to be assigned as a set to an associative array or nested table. The FORALL provides a means to move the contents of an associative array or nested table into a database object.

Associative arrays and nested table collection types will work with BULK COLLECT and FORALL. A nested table requires construction as a null element collection. The BULK COLLECT will implicitly allocate space for you in the nested table. An associative array does not need construction, just a bulk assignment. Likewise, both associative arrays and nested tables can be the source structure for a FORALL SQL command.

You know either structure is possible as a solution. You should evaluate your needs and choose which is appropriate to your solution. You may find that associative arrays are generally a more natural fit to BULK COLLECT and FORALL operations.

You will want to retrieve data batches to improve the efficiency of your PL/SQL code. The efficiency comes from bulk binding. You can compare performance by trace file analysis. There are two files provided to support your trace file analysis. The bulk_collect1.sql program uses BULK COLLECT and FORALL operations against an associative array. The bulk_collect3.sql program, not displayed, uses a nonbulk approach to the insert and select statements. Both of the scripts have the necessary tuning commands remarked out. You can unremark them and run them.

If you generate and analyze trace information against both files, you will see the differences. While you will benefit from doing the exercise yourself, a quick comparative analysis is presented next. They contain comparative statistics on parse, execute, and fetch. Table 6-3 illustrates the impact on the insert statement, while Table 6-4 illustrates the impact on the select statement.

If you were wondering why the select statement executed and fetched 20,000 times instead of 10,000 times, it is the effect of the SORT BY operation. The reason 50,001 executes in the insert is not within the scope of this chapter. Moreover, the processing cost is too high.

The following bulk_collect1.sql example program demonstrates both FORALL and BULK COLLECT techniques with an associative array. As discussed, the nested table is found in bulk_collect2.sql. It is not displayed, since there is only one difference, and that difference has been covered previously in the nested table discussion.

Bulk Insert (bulk_collect1.sql)	**Nonbulk Insert** (bulk_collect3.sql)

INSERT INTO BULK_NUMBERS
VALUES
  (:B1)
	INSERT INTO BULK_NUMBERS
	VALUES
	  (:B1)

call count	call count
---- ---	---- ---
Parse 1	Parse 6
Execute 1	Execute 50001
Fetch 0	Fetch 0
---- ---	---- ---
total 2	total 50007

TABLE 6-3. *Bulk vs. Nonbulk Inserts*

Bulk Select	**Nonbulk Select**
(bulk_collect1.sql)	(bulk_collect3.sql)

SELECT NUMBER_ID
FROM
  BULK_NUMBERS ORDER BY 1
	SELECT NUMBER_ID
	FROM
	  BULK_NUMBERS
	  WHERE NUMBER_ID = :B1 ORDER BY 1

call count ---- --- Parse 1 Execute 1 Fetch 1 ---- --- total 3	call count ---- --- Parse 2 Execute 20000 Fetch 20000 ---- --- total 40002

TABLE 6-4.   *Bulk vs. Nonbulk Selects*

```
-- Available online as part of bulk_collect1.sql

-- Create a table for the example.
CREATE TABLE bulk_numbers
(number_id               NUMBER              NOT NULL
,CONSTRAINT number_id_pk  PRIMARY KEY (number_id));

-- Use a FORALL to move an associative array into a table.
DECLARE

  -- Define an associative array of integers.
  TYPE number_table IS TABLE OF bulk_numbers.number_id%TYPE
    INDEX BY BINARY_INTEGER;

  -- Define a variable of the associative array type.
  number_list NUMBER_TABLE;

BEGIN

  -- Loop from 1 to a million and increment array.
  FOR i IN 1..10000 LOOP

    -- Assign number value.
    number_list(i) := i;

  END LOOP;
```

```
-- Loop through all to do a bulk insert.
FORALL i IN 1..number_list.COUNT
   INSERT
   INTO      bulk_numbers
   VALUES   (number_list(i));

-- Commit records.
COMMIT;

END;
/

-- Use a BULK COLLECT to retrieve a table into an
-- associative array.
DECLARE

  -- Define an associative array of integers.
  TYPE number_table IS TABLE OF bulk_numbers.number_id%TYPE
    INDEX BY BINARY_INTEGER;

  -- Define a variable of the associative array type.
  number_list NUMBER_TABLE;

BEGIN

  -- Gather all rows in a bulk collect.
  SELECT   number_id
  BULK COLLECT
  INTO      number_list
  FROM      bulk_numbers
  ORDER BY 1;

  -- Print a title
  DBMS_OUTPUT.PUT_LINE('Bulk Collected:');
  DBMS_OUTPUT.PUT_LINE('--------');

  -- Loop through to print elements.
  FOR i IN number_list.FIRST..number_list.LAST LOOP

    -- Print only the first and last two.
    IF i <= 2 OR i >= 9999 THEN

      -- Print an indexed element from the array.
      DBMS_OUTPUT.PUT_LINE(
        'Number ['||number_list(i)||']');

    END IF;
```

```
    END LOOP;

END;
/
```

This program does three things:

- It defines a `bulk_numbers` table with a single column. The column uses an `INTEGER` data type.

- It defines an anonymous-block program that does these things:

    - It defines a `number_table` associative array of an `INTEGER` data type indexed by a `BINARY_INTEGER`.

    - It defines a `number_list` variable using the `number_table` associative array.

    - It uses a range for-loop to populate the `number_list` variable, which is done in the Oracle database SGA memory space.

    - It uses a `FORALL` statement to do a bulk insert into the `bulk_numbers` table.

    - It commits the work.

- It defines an anonymous-block program that does these things:

    - It defines an associative array of an `INTEGER` data type.

    - It defines a `number_list` variable using the `number_table` associative array.

    - It uses a select statement with a `BULK COLLECT` clause to return all rows into the `number_list` variable. It is important to note that the select statement is using an order by clause to ensure an ascending set of numbers. If the order by clause is omitted, you will not see the expected number sequence.

    - It then uses a range for-loop to print the first and last two rows returned into the `number_list` associative array.

Rendering a short output as follows:

-- Available online as output from bulk_collect1.sql

```
Bulk Collected:
--------
```

```
Number [1]
Number [2]
Number [9999]
Number [10000]
```

You should note that all the bulk collection example programs use the ORDER BY operation. There is a reason for this. If you do not order the elements, you will find that they may be retrieved by a hash value as opposed to their numerical order.

The following output is an unordered list from the table:

-- Available online as output from bulk_collect1.sql

```
Bulk Collected:
--------
Number [1721]
Number [1722]
Number [9142]
Number [9143]
```

You have now reviewed associative arrays. Added to the previously covered varrays and nested tables, you have worked with the three collection types in Oracle 10*g*. The collection types each have their respective strengths and weaknesses. You will judge which is appropriate to your programming problems.

While you have worked with some of the Collection API methods in the examples throughout the chapter, you have not formally covered them. Since working through the Collection API before the collections is tricky, you were introduced to the collections first. Unfortunately, you cannot demonstrate how to use collections without leveraging the Collection API. On balance, it is hoped that the choice of positioning works well for you.

Now, you will cover the Collection API.

Oracle 10*g* Collection API

Oracle 8*i* introduced the Collection API. The Collection API is provided to give simplified access to collections. These methods did simplify access before Oracle 10*g*. Unfortunately, they were not critical to master. The shift from Oracle 9*i* index-by tables to Oracle 10*g* associative arrays makes them critical for you to understand. You covered the reason working with associative arrays. The FIRST, LAST, NEXT, and PRIOR methods are the only way to navigate unique string indexes.

The Collection API methods are really not methods in a truly object-oriented sense. They are functions and procedures. Three, EXTEND, TRIM, and DELETE, are procedures. The rest are functions.

Table 6-5 summarizes the Oracle 10*g* Collection API.

Method	Description	Return Type	Collection(s) Supported
COUNT	The COUNT method returns the number of elements with space allocated in varrays and nested tables. The COUNT method returns the number of elements in associative arrays. COUNT can be smaller than LIMIT for varrays.	PLS_INTEGER	All
DELETE(n)	The DELETE method takes a single formal parameter that is overloaded. The formal parameter data types are PLS_INTEGER, VARCHAR2, and LONG. The formal parameter maps to a subscript for an element within the collection. It is a procedure and does not have a return type.	None	All
DELETE(n, m)	The DELETE method takes two formal parameters that are overloaded. The formal parameter data types are PLS_INTEGER, VARCHAR2, and LONG. The formal parameter maps to a minimum and maximum subscript. The parameters set an inclusive range of elements in the collection. It is a procedure and does not have a return type.	None	All
EXISTS(n)	The EXISTS method determines whether or not an element is found in a collection. It takes a single formal parameter that is overloaded. The parameter data types are PLS_INTEGER, VARCHAR2, and LONG. The formal parameter maps to a subscript value. If the collection is a null element structure, the EXISTS method will not raise a COLLECTION_IS_NULL exception.	TRUE orFALSE	All

TABLE 6-5. *The Oracle 10g Collection API*

Method	Description	Return Type	Collection(s) Supported
EXTEND	The EXTEND method allocates space for a new element in a collection. It is used to allocate space before adding a value to the collection. EXTEND will fail if it attempts to exceed the LIMIT of a varray.	None	Varray or nested table
EXTEND(n)	The EXTEND method allocates space for a number of new elements in a collection. It takes a single formal parameter. The parameter data type is a PLS_INTEGER. It is used to allocate space before adding a value to the collection. EXTEND will fail if it attempts to exceed the LIMIT of a varray.	None	Varray or nested table
EXTEND(n, i)	The EXTEND method allocates space for a number of new elements in a collection. It takes two formal parameters. The parameter data types are PLS_INTEGER. The first parameter is used to identify how many elements to add. The second references an existing element in the collection that will be replicated to the new elements. EXTEND will fail if it attempts to exceed the LIMIT of a varray.	None	Varray or nested table
FIRST	The FIRST method returns the lowest subscript value in a collection.	PLS_INTEGER, VARCHAR2, or LONG	All
LAST	The LAST method returns the highest subscript value in a collection.	PLS_INTEGER, VARCHAR2, or LONG	All

TABLE 6-5. *The Oracle 10g Collection API* (continued)

Method	Description	Return Type	Collection(s) Supported
LIMIT	The LIMIT method returns the highest allowed subscript value in a varray.	PLS_INTEGER	Varray
NEXT(n)	The NEXT method takes a single overloaded formal parameter. It accepts a parameter that can be a PLS_INTEGER, VARCHAR2, or LONG data type. The actual parameter must be a valid subscript in the collection. The NEXT method uses the subscript to find the next higher subscript in the collection. If there is no higher subscript value, NEXT returns a NULL.	PLS_INTEGER, VARCHAR2, or LONG	All
PRIOR(n)	The PRIOR method takes a single overloaded formal parameter. It accepts a parameter that can be a PLS_INTEGER, VARCHAR2, or LONG data type. The actual parameter must be a valid subscript in the collection. The PRIOR method uses the subscript to find the next lower subscript in the collection. If there is no lower subscript value, NEXT returns a NULL.	PLS_INTEGER, VARCHAR2, or LONG	All
TRIM	The TRIM method removes the highest subscripted value from a collection.	None	All
TRIM(n)	The TRIM method takes a single formal parameter. It accepts a PLS_INTEGER data type. The actual parameter must be an integer value less than the value returned by the COUNT method or it will raise an exception. It removes the number or elements passed as the actual parameter to the method.	None	All

TABLE 6-5. *The Oracle 10g Collection API* (continued)

You will examine each of the Collection API methods in example programs. It should be noted that only the EXISTS method will fail to raise an exception if the collection is empty.

There are five standard collection exceptions. They are described in Table 6-6.

You will examine each of the methods in alphabetical order. Some examples include multiple Collection API methods. Like the coverage of the collection types, it is hard to treat the Collection API methods in isolation.

Where a single example fully covers multiple methods, it will be cross-referenced. There are occasions where you may be forward referenced. Under each Collection API method, you will be referenced to appropriate example code.

Collection Exception	Raised By
COLLECTION_IS_NULL	An attempt to use a null collection.
NO_DATA_FOUND	An attempt to use a subscript that has been deleted or is a nonexistent unique string index value in an associative array.
SUBSCRIPT_BEYOND_COUNT	An attempt to use a numeric index value that is higher than the current maximum number value. This error applies only to varrays and nested tables. Associative arrays are not bound by the COUNT return value when adding new elements.
SUBSCRIPT_OUTSIDE_LIMIT	An attempt to use a numeric index value outside of the LIMIT return value. This error only applies to varrays and nested tables. The LIMIT value is defined one of two ways. Varrays set the maximum size, which becomes their limit value. Nested tables have no fixed maximum size, so the limit value is set by the space allocated by the EXTEND method.
VALUE_ERROR	An attempt is made to use a type that cannot be converted to a PLS_INTEGER, which is the data type for numeric subscripts.

TABLE 6-6. *Collection Exceptions*

COUNT Method

The COUNT method is really a function. It has no formal parameter list. It returns the number of elements in the array. The following example program illustrates that it returns a PLS_INTEGER value:

```
-- Available online as part of count.sql

DECLARE

  -- Define a nested table type of INTEGER.
  TYPE number_table IS TABLE OF INTEGER;

  -- Define a variable of the nested table type.
  number_list NUMBER_TABLE := number_table(1,2,3,4,5);

BEGIN

  -- Print a title.
  DBMS_OUTPUT.PUT_LINE('How many elements');
  DBMS_OUTPUT.PUT_LINE('---------');

  -- Print the list.
  DBMS_OUTPUT.PUT_LINE('Count ['||number_list.COUNT||']');

END;
/
```

The example program does the following:

- It defines a nested table type of an INTEGER data type.
- It defines a number_list variable that uses the nested table type.
- It prints a title using DBMS_OUTPUT utility.
- It prints the result of the Collection API COUNT method.

It generates the following output:

```
-- Available online as output from count.sql

How many elements
---------
Count [5]
```

DELETE Method

The DELETE method is really a procedure. It is an overloaded procedure. If the concept of overloading is new to you, please check Chapter 8.

It has one version that takes a single formal parameter. The parameter must be a valid subscript value in the collection. This version will remove the element with that subscript. It is illustrated in the EXISTS method example program.

The other version takes two formal parameters. Both parameters must be valid subscript values in the collection. This version deletes a continuous inclusive range of elements from a collection. The following example program illustrates a range delete from a collection:

```
-- Available online as part of delete.sql

DECLARE

  -- Define a nested table type of INTEGER.
  TYPE number_table IS TABLE OF INTEGER;

  -- Define a variable of the nested table type.
  number_list NUMBER_TABLE;

  -- Define a local procedure to check and print elements.
  PROCEDURE print_list
    (list_in NUMBER_TABLE) IS

  BEGIN

    -- Loop through the possible index values of the list.
    FOR i IN list_in.FIRST..list_in.LAST LOOP

      -- Check if the subscripted element is there.
      IF list_in.EXISTS(i) THEN

        -- Print the element.
        DBMS_OUTPUT.PUT_LINE('List ['||list_in(i)||']');

      END IF;

    END LOOP;

  END print_list;

BEGIN

  -- Check if a subscript element of one does not exists.
```

```
        IF NOT number_list.EXISTS(1) THEN

          -- Construct the collection.
          number_list := number_table(1,2,3,4,5);

        END IF;

        -- Print a title.
        DBMS_OUTPUT.PUT_LINE('Nested table before a deletion');
        DBMS_OUTPUT.PUT_LINE('---------------');

        -- Print the list.
        print_list(number_list);

        -- Delete an element.
        number_list.DELETE(2,4);

        -- Print a title.
        DBMS_OUTPUT.PUT_LINE(CHR(10)||
                             'Nested table after a deletion');
        DBMS_OUTPUT.PUT_LINE('---------------');

        -- Print the list.
        print_list(number_list);

END;
/
```

This example does the following:

- It defines a nested table type of an INTEGER data type.

- It defines a number_list variable that uses the nested table type.

    It defines a local procedure to manage printing the elements in the
    collection. The local procedure takes a single formal parameter of
    the defined nested table type. The print_list local procedure
    does the following:

    - It uses a numeric range for-loop to traverse the nested table. The
      Collection API FIRST and LAST methods establish the range.
      The FIRST method returns the lowest subscript index value. The
      LAST method returns the highest one. As a set, they cover a set of
      elements in a collection. This is true whether the collection is dense or
      sparse. In this example, the collection is dense and becomes sparse.

- It uses an if statement to evaluate whether or not there is an element that uses each numeric subscript value between the lowest and the highest. It does the evaluation by using the Collection API EXISTS method.

- It prints the element with the DBMS_OUTPUT utility if found.

- It uses an if statement to evaluate whether an element is using the subscript one. At this point, the collection is null element structure. Only the EXISTS method can be used at this point without raising an exception. Within the if statement, it initializes five elements, which are sequential. This is a dense collection at this point.

- It prints the list using the DBMS_OUTPUT utility.

- It deletes the element using a beginning subscript of two and an ending subscript of four.

- It prints the list using the DBMS_OUTPUT utility. (You will see the element missing in the output, which illustrates a sparse array.)

It generates the following output:

```
-- Available online as output from delete.sql
```

```
Nested table before a deletion
---------------
List [1]
List [2]
List [3]
List [4]
List [5]

Nested table after a deletion
---------------
List [1]
List [5]
```

EXISTS Method

The EXISTS method is really a function. It has only one formal parameter list that it supports. It takes a subscript value. The subscript may be a number or a unique string. The latter subscript index applies only to Oracle 10g associative arrays.

As mentioned, EXISTS is the *only* Collection API method that will not raise a COLLECTION_IS_NULL exception for a null element collection. Null element collections have two varieties. First, varrays and nested tables constructed with a null constructor. Second, associative arrays that have zero elements initialized.

The following program illustrates the EXISTS method. A portion of the program is redacted because it was used in a prior example program.

-- Available online as part of exists.sql

```
DECLARE

  -- Define a nested table type of INTEGER.
  TYPE number_table IS TABLE OF INTEGER;

  -- Define a variable of the nested table type.
  number_list NUMBER_TABLE;

  -- Define a local procedure to check and print elements.
  PROCEDURE print_list
    (list_in NUMBER_TABLE) IS

  BEGIN

    ... redacted for space ...

  END print_list;

BEGIN

  -- Check if a subscript element of one does not exists.
  IF NOT number_list.EXISTS(1) THEN

    -- Construct the collection.
    number_list := number_table(1,2,3,4,5);

  END IF;

  -- Print a title.
  DBMS_OUTPUT.PUT_LINE('Nested table before a deletion');
  DBMS_OUTPUT.PUT_LINE('---------------');

  -- Print the list.
  print_list(number_list);

  -- Delete an element.
  number_list.DELETE(2);

  -- Print a title.
```

```
       DBMS_OUTPUT.PUT_LINE(CHR(10)||
                           'Nested table after a deletion');
       DBMS_OUTPUT.PUT_LINE('---------------');

       -- Print the list.
       print_list(number_list);

    END;
    /
```

The example program does the following:

- It defines a nested table type of an INTEGER data type.

- It defines a number_list variable that uses the nested table type.

- It defines a local procedure to manage printing the elements in the collection. The local procedure takes a single formal parameter of the defined nested table type. The print_list local procedure is explained in the DELETE method example.

- It uses an if statement to evaluate whether an element is using the subscript one. At this point, the collection is null element structure. Only the EXISTS method can be used at this point without raising an exception. Within the if statement, it initializes five elements, which are sequential. This is a dense collection at this point.

- It prints the list using the DBMS_OUTPUT utility.

- It deletes the element using subscript two.

- It prints the list using the DBMS_OUTPUT utility. (You will see the element missing in the output, which illustrates a sparse array.)

It generates the following output:

```
-- Available online as output from exists.sql

Nested table before a deletion
---------------
List [1]
List [2]
List [3]
List [4]
List [5]

Nested table after a deletion
```

```
---------------
List [1]
List [3]
List [4]
List [5]
```

EXTEND Method

The EXTEND method is really a procedure. It is an overloaded procedure. If the concept of overloading is new to you, please check Chapter 8.

It has one version that takes no formal parameters. When used without formal parameter(s), EXTEND allocates space for a new element in a collection. However, if you attempt to EXTEND space beyond a LIMIT in a varray, it will raise an exception.

A second version takes a single formal parameter. The parameter must be a valid integer value. EXTEND with a single actual parameter will allocate space for that number of elements specified by the actual parameter. Like the version without a parameter, attempting to EXTEND space beyond a LIMIT in a varray will raise an exception. This method is illustrated in the following example.

The last version takes two formal parameters. Both parameters must be valid integers. The second must also be a valid subscript value in the collection. This version allocates element space equal to the first actual parameter. Then, it copies the contents of the referenced subscript found in the second actual parameter.

The following program illustrates the EXTEND method with one and two formal parameters. A portion of the program is redacted because it was used in a prior example program.

```
-- Available online as part of extend.sql

DECLARE

  -- Define a nested table type of INTEGER.
  TYPE number_table IS TABLE OF INTEGER;

  -- Define a variable of the nested table type.
  number_list NUMBER_TABLE := number_table(1,2);

  -- Define a local procedure to check and print elements.
  PROCEDURE print_list
    (list_in NUMBER_TABLE) IS

  BEGIN

    ... redacted for space ...

  END print_list;
```

```
BEGIN

  -- Print a title.
  DBMS_OUTPUT.PUT_LINE('Nested table before extension');
  DBMS_OUTPUT.PUT_LINE('---------------');

  -- Print the list.
  print_list(number_list);

  -- Allocate two null elements.
  number_list.EXTEND(2);

  -- Allocate three elements and copy element two.
  number_list.EXTEND(3,2);

  -- Print a title.
  DBMS_OUTPUT.PUT_LINE(CHR(10)||
                      'Nested table after extension');
  DBMS_OUTPUT.PUT_LINE('--------------');

  -- Print the list.
  print_list(number_list);

END;
/
```

The example program does the following:

- It defines a nested table type of an INTEGER data type.

- It defines a number_list variable that uses the nested table type.

- It defines a local procedure to manage printing the elements in the collection. The local procedure takes a single formal parameter of the defined nested table type. The print_list local procedure is explained in the DELETE method example.

- It uses an if statement to evaluate whether an element is using the subscript 1. At this point, the collection has null element structure. Only the EXISTS method can be used at this point without raising an exception. Within the if statement, it initializes five elements, which are sequential. This is a dense collection at this point.

- It prints the list using the DBMS_OUTPUT utility.

- It extends two null elements using EXTEND(2).

■ It extends space to three elements and copies the contents of the element in subscript 2.

■ It prints the list using the DBMS_OUTPUT utility. (You will see the element missing in the output, which illustrates a sparse array.)

It generates the following output:

```
-- Available online as output from extend.sql

Nested table before extension
---------------
List [1]
List [2]

Nested table after extension
--------------
List [1]
List [2]
List []
List []
List [2]
List [2]
List [2]
```

FIRST Method

The FIRST method is really a function. It returns the lowest subscript value used in a collection. If it is a numeric index, it returns a PLS_INTEGER. If it is an associative array, it returns a VARCHAR2 or LONG data type. You *cannot* use the FIRST method in a range for-loop when the index is non-numeric.

The FIRST method is illustrated in the example program for the DELETE method. That example uses a numeric index. The following example demonstrates the FIRST method with a non-numeric or unique string index. As discussed, non-numeric indexes in associative arrays are new in Oracle 10g functionality.

```
-- Available online as part of first.sql

DECLARE

  -- Define a nested table type of INTEGER.
  TYPE number_table IS TABLE OF INTEGER
    INDEX BY VARCHAR2(9 CHAR);

  -- Define a variable of the nested table type.
```

```
    number_list NUMBER_TABLE;

BEGIN

  -- Build three elements with unique string subscripts.
  number_list('One')  := 1;
  number_list('Two')  := 2;
  number_list('Nine') := 9;

  -- Print the first index and next.
  DBMS_OUTPUT.PUT_LINE(
    'FIRST Index ['||number_list.FIRST||']');
  DBMS_OUTPUT.PUT_LINE('NEXT Index ['
    ||number_list.NEXT(number_list.FIRST)||']');

  -- Print the last index and prior.
  DBMS_OUTPUT.PUT_LINE(CHR(10)||
    'LAST  Index ['||number_list.LAST||']');
  DBMS_OUTPUT.PUT_LINE('PRIOR Index ['
    ||number_list.PRIOR(number_list.LAST)||']');

END;
/
```

The example program does the following:

- It defines a nested table type of an INTEGER data type.

- It defines a number_list variable that uses the nested table type.

- It declares three elements with unique string index values and assigns them integer values.

- It prints the FIRST index value using the DBMS_OUTPUT utility.

- It prints the NEXT index value using the DBMS_OUTPUT utility.

- It prints the LAST index value using the DBMS_OUTPUT utility.

- It prints the PRIOR index value using the DBMS_OUTPUT utility.

If you raised your eyebrows at the output, you did not catch this earlier. When using a unique string as an index value, the ordering of values is based on the NLS environment. Therefore, you generate the following output, which is ordered alphabetically:

-- Available online as output from first.sql

```
FIRST Index [Nine]
NEXT  Index [One]

LAST  Index [Two]
PRIOR Index [One]
```

LAST Method

The LAST method is really a function. It returns the highest subscript value used in a collection. If it is a numeric index, it returns a PLS_INTEGER. If it is an associative array, it returns a VARCHAR2 or LONG data type. You *cannot* use the LAST method in a range for-loop when the index is non-numeric.

The LAST method is illustrated in the example program for the DELETE method. That example uses a numeric index. The example in the FIRST method also demonstrates the LAST method with a non-numeric or unique string index. As discussed, non-numeric indexes in associative arrays are new in Oracle 10*g* functionality.

LIMIT Method

The LIMIT method is really a function. It returns the highest possible subscript value used in a varray. It has no value for the other two collection types. It returns a PLS_INTEGER.

The example program that follows illustrates the LIMIT method:

```
-- Available online as part of limit.sql

DECLARE

  -- Define a varray type of INTEGER.
  TYPE number_varray IS VARRAY(5) OF INTEGER;

  -- Define a variable of the varray type.
  number_list NUMBER_VARRAY := number_varray(1,2,3);

  -- Define a local procedure to check and print elements.
  PROCEDURE print_list
    (list_in NUMBER_VARRAY) IS

BEGIN

  -- Loop through the possible index values of the list.
  FOR i IN list_in.FIRST..list_in.COUNT LOOP

    -- Print the element.
    DBMS_OUTPUT.PUT_LINE(
```

```
                       'List Index ['||i||'] '||
                       'List Value ['||list_in(i)||']');

            END LOOP;

        END print_list;

    BEGIN

        -- Print a title.
        DBMS_OUTPUT.PUT_LINE('Varray after initialization');
        DBMS_OUTPUT.PUT_LINE('--------------');

        -- Print the list.
        print_list(number_list);

        -- Extend null element to maximum limit.
        number_list.EXTEND(number_list.LIMIT - number_list.LAST);

        -- Print a title.
        DBMS_OUTPUT.PUT(CHR(10));
        DBMS_OUTPUT.PUT_LINE('Varray after extension');
        DBMS_OUTPUT.PUT_LINE('-----------');

        -- Print the list.
        print_list(number_list);

    END;
    /
```

The example program does the following:

- It defines a varray type of an INTEGER data type.

- It defines a number_list variable that uses the varray type.

- It defines a local procedure to manage printing the elements in the collection. The local procedure takes a single formal parameter of the defined nested table type. The print_list local procedure prints the index value and element contents.

- It prints a title using the DBMS_OUTPUT utility.

- It calls the local procedure to print the varray.

- It extends space for the difference between the COUNT and LIMIT methods, or the balance of available element space.

- It prints a title using the DBMS_OUTPUT utility.
- It calls the local procedure to print the varray.

It generates the following output:

-- Available online as output from limit.sql

```
Varray after initialization
---------------
List Index [1] List Value [1]
List Index [2] List Value [2]
List Index [3] List Value [3]

Varray after extension
-----------
List Index [1] List Value [1]
List Index [2] List Value [2]
List Index [3] List Value [3]
List Index [4] List Value []
List Index [5] List Value []
```

NEXT Method

The NEXT method is really a function. It returns the next subscript value used in a collection. If there is no higher subscript value, it returns a null. If it is a numeric index, it returns a PLS_INTEGER. If it is an associative array, it returns a VARCHAR2 or LONG data type.

The NEXT method is illustrated in the example program for the DELETE method. That example uses a numeric index. The example in the FIRST method also demonstrates the NEXT method with a non-numeric or unique string index. As discussed, non-numeric indexes in associative arrays are new in Oracle 10*g* functionality.

PRIOR Method

The PRIOR method is really a function. It returns the prior subscript value used in a collection. If there is no lower subscript value, it returns a null. If it is a numeric index, it returns a PLS_INTEGER. If it is an associative array, it returns a VARCHAR2 or LONG data type.

The PRIOR method is illustrated in the example program for the DELETE method. That example uses a numeric index. The example in the FIRST method also demonstrates the PRIOR method with a non-numeric or unique string index. As discussed, non-numeric indexes in associative arrays are new in Oracle 10*g* functionality.

TRIM Method

The TRIM method is really a procedure. It is an overloaded procedure. If the concept of overloading is new to you, please check Chapter 8.

It has one version that takes no formal parameters. When used without formal parameter(s), TRIM deallocates space for an element in a collection. However, if you attempt to TRIM space below zero elements, it will raise an exception.

The other version takes a single formal parameter. The parameter must be a valid integer value. TRIM with a single actual parameter will deallocate space for the number of elements specified by the actual parameter. Like the version without a parameter, attempting to TRIM space below zero elements will raise an exception.

The example program that follows illustrates the TRIM method:

```
-- Available online as part of trim.sql

DECLARE

  -- Define a varray type of INTEGER.
  TYPE number_varray IS VARRAY(5) OF INTEGER;

  -- Define a variable of the varray type.
  number_list NUMBER_VARRAY := number_varray(1,2,3,4,5);

  -- Define a local procedure to check and print elements.
  PROCEDURE print_list
    (list_in NUMBER_VARRAY) IS

  BEGIN

    ... redacted for space ...

  END print_list;

BEGIN

  -- Print a title.
  DBMS_OUTPUT.PUT_LINE('Varray after initialization');
  DBMS_OUTPUT.PUT_LINE('--------------');

  -- Print the list.
  print_list(number_list);

  -- Extend null element to maximum limit.
  number_list.TRIM;
```

```
-- Print a title.
DBMS_OUTPUT.PUT(CHR(10));
DBMS_OUTPUT.PUT_LINE(
  'Varray after a single element trim');
DBMS_OUTPUT.PUT_LINE(
  '----------------');

-- Print the list.
print_list(number_list);

-- Extend null element to maximum limit.
number_list.TRIM(3);

-- Print a title.
DBMS_OUTPUT.PUT(CHR(10));
DBMS_OUTPUT.PUT_LINE(
  'Varray after a three element trim');
DBMS_OUTPUT.PUT_LINE(
  '----------------');

-- Print the list.
print_list(number_list);

END;
/
```

The example program does the following:

- It defines a varray type of an INTEGER data type.

- It defines a number_list variable that uses the varray type.

- It defines a local procedure to manage printing the elements in the collection. The local procedure takes a single formal parameter of the defined nested table type. The print_list local procedure prints the index value and element contents. The full text for the print_list local procedure is found in the LIMIT method example program.

- It prints a title using the DBMS_OUTPUT utility.

- It calls the local procedure to print the varray.

- It uses the TRIM method to deallocate one element.

- It prints a title using the DBMS_OUTPUT utility.

- It calls the local procedure to print the varray.

- It uses the TRIM method to deallocate three elements.

■ It prints a title using the DBMS_OUTPUT utility.

■ It calls the local procedure to print the varray.

It generates the following output:

```
-- Available online as output from trim.sql

Varray after initialization
--------------
List Index [1] List Value [1]
List Index [2] List Value [2]
List Index [3] List Value [3]
List Index [4] List Value [4]
List Index [5] List Value [5]

Varray after a single element trim
-----------------
List Index [1] List Value [1]
List Index [2] List Value [2]
List Index [3] List Value [3]
List Index [4] List Value [4]

Varray after a three element trim
-----------------
List Index [1] List Value [1]
```

You have now gone through the complete Oracle 10g Collection API. It is time to summarize what you have covered in the chapter.

Summary

You have covered the definition and use of varrays, nested tables, and associative arrays, which are the Oracle 10g collection types. You have worked through examples in SQL DML and PL/SQL that use Oracle 10g collections. Finally, you worked through the details of the Collection API.

CHAPTER
7

Error Handling

ny well-written program must have the capability to handle errors
intelligently and recover from them if possible. PL/SQL implements
error handling with *exceptions* and *exception handlers*. Exceptions
can be associated with Oracle errors or with your own user-defined
errors. In this chapter, we will discuss the syntax of exceptions and
exception handlers, how exceptions are raised and handled, and the rules of
exception propagation. The chapter closes with guidelines on using exceptions.

What Is an Exception?

In Chapter 1 we discussed how PL/SQL is based on the Ada language. One of the
features of Ada that is incorporated into PL/SQL is the exception mechanism. By
using exceptions and exception handlers, you can make your PL/SQL programs
robust and able to deal with both unexpected and expected errors during execution.
PL/SQL exceptions are similar to Java exceptions. For example, Java exceptions are
thrown and caught in a manner like those in PL/SQL. Unlike Java exceptions,
however, PL/SQL exceptions are not objects and have no methods defined on them.

What kinds of errors can occur in a PL/SQL program? Errors can be classified as
described in Table 7-1. Exceptions are designed for run-time error handling, rather
than compile-time error handling. Errors that occur during the compilation phase
are detected by the PL/SQL engine and reported back to the user. The program
cannot handle these, since the program has not yet run. For example, consider
the following block:

```
DECLARE
   v_NumAuthors NUMBER;
BEGIN
  SELECT COUNT(*)
    INTO v_NumAuthors
    FROM aauthors;
END;
```

Error Type	Reported By	How Handled
Compile-time	PL/SQL compiler	Interactively: compiler reports errors, and you have to correct them.
Run-time	PL/SQL run-time engine	Programmatically: exceptions are raised and caught by exception handlers.

TABLE 7-1. *Types of PL/SQL Errors*

This will raise the compilation error

```
PLS-201: identifier 'AAUTHORS' must be declared
```

in Oracle8*i* and earlier, and the error

```
PL/SQL: ORA-00942: table or view does not exist
```

in Oracle9*i*R1 and higher because 'authors' is misspelled in the SELECT statement. Exceptions and exception handlers are the methods by which the program reacts and deals with run-time errors. Run-time errors include SQL errors such as

```
ORA-1: unique constraint violated
```

and procedural errors such as

```
ORA-06502: PL/SQL: numeric or value error
```

NOTE
PL/SQL has a facility known as dynamic SQL that allows you to create and run arbitrary SQL statements and PL/SQL blocks at run time. If you dynamically run a PL/SQL block or SQL statement that itself contains a compilation error, then this error will be raised at run time and can be caught by an exception handler. For more information on dynamic SQL, see Chapter 13.

When a run-time error occurs, an exception is *raised*. When this happens, control is passed to the exception handler, which is a separate section of the program. This separates the error handling from the rest of the program, which makes the logic of the program easier to understand. This also ensures that all errors will be trapped.

In a language that doesn't use the exception model for error handling (such as C), in order to ensure that your program can handle errors in all cases, you must explicitly insert error-handling code. For example,

```
int x = 1, y = 2, z = 3;
p(x);  /* Procedure call, passing x as an argument. */
if <an error occurred>
  handle_error(...);
y = 1 / z;
if <an error occurred>
  handle_error(...);
z = x + y;
if <an error occurred>
  handle_error(...);
```

Note that a check for errors must occur after each statement in the program. If you forget to insert the check, the program will not properly handle an error situation. In addition, the error handling can clutter up the program, making it difficult to understand the program's logic. Compare the preceding example to the similar example in PL/SQL:

```
DECLARE
  x NUMBER := 1;
  y NUMBER := 2;
  z NUMBER := 3;
BEGIN
  p(x);
  y := 1 / z;
  z := x + y;
EXCEPTION
  WHEN OTHERS THEN
    /* Handler to execute for all errors */
    handle_error(...);
END;
```

Note that the error handling is separated from the program logic. This solves both problems with the C example, namely:

- Program logic is easier to understand, since it is clearly visible.

- No matter which statement fails, the program will detect and handle the error. Note that program execution will not continue from the statement that raised the error, however. Instead, execution will continue to the exception handler, and then to any outer block.

Declaring Exceptions

Exceptions are declared in the declarative section of the block, raised in the executable section, and handled in the exception section. We will see how each of these is done in the following sections.

There are two types of exceptions: *user-defined* and *predefined*.

User-Defined Exceptions

A user-defined exception is an error that is defined by the programmer. The error that it signifies is not necessarily an Oracle error; it could be an error with the data, for example. Predefined exceptions, on the other hand, correspond to common SQL and PL/SQL errors.

User-defined exceptions are declared in the declarative section of a PL/SQL block. Just like variables, exceptions have a type (EXCEPTION) and a scope. For example,

```
DECLARE
  e_DuplicateAuthors EXCEPTION;
```

Here, e_DuplicateAuthors is an identifier that will be visible until the end of this block. Note that the scope of an exception is the same as the scope of any other variable or cursor in the same declarative section. See Chapter 3 for information on the scope and visibility rules for PL/SQL identifiers.

Predefined Exceptions

Oracle has predefined several exceptions that correspond to the most common Oracle errors. Like the predefined types (NUMBER, VARCHAR2, and so on), the identifiers for these exceptions are defined in package STANDARD. Because of this, they are already available to the program—it is not necessary to declare them in the declarative section like a user-defined exception. These predefined exceptions are described in Table 7-2.

NOTE
It is possible to associate user-defined exceptions with Oracle errors, as well. See the section "The EXCEPTION_INIT Pragma" later in this chapter for more information.

Oracle Error	Equivalent Exception	Description
ORA-0001	DUP_VAL_ON_INDEX	Unique constraint violated.
ORA-0051	TIMEOUT_ON_RESOURCE	Time-out occurred while waiting for resource.
ORA-1001	INVALID_CURSOR	Illegal cursor operation.
ORA-1012	NOT_LOGGED_ON	Not connected to Oracle.
ORA-1017	LOGIN_DENIED	Invalid user name/password.
ORA-1403	NO_DATA_FOUND	No data found.
ORA-1410	SYS_INVALID_ROWID	Conversion to a universal rowid failed.
ORA-1422	TOO_MANY_ROWS	A SELECT.INTO statement matches more than one row.
ORA-1476	ZERO_DIVIDE	Division by zero.
ORA-1722	INVALID_NUMBER	Conversion to a number failed; for example, '1A' is not valid.

TABLE 7-2. *Predefined Oracle Exceptions*

Oracle Error	Equivalent Exception	Description
ORA-1725	USERENV_COMMITSCN_ERROR[1]	Incorrect usage of the USERENV('COMMITSCN') function.
ORA-6500	STORAGE_ERROR	Internal PL/SQL error raised if PL/SQL runs out of memory.
ORA-6501	PROGRAM_ERROR	Internal PL/SQL error.
ORA-6502	VALUE_ERROR	Truncation, arithmetic, or conversion error.
ORA-6504	ROWTYPE_MISMATCH	Host cursor variable and PL/SQL cursor variable have incompatible row types.
ORA-6511	CURSOR_ALREADY_OPEN	Attempt to open a cursor that is already open.
ORA-6530	ACCESS_INTO_NULL	Attempt to assign values to the attributes of a NULL object.
ORA-6531	COLLECTION_IS_NULL	Attempt to apply collection methods other than EXISTS to a NULL PL/SQL table or varray.
ORA-6532	SUBSCRIPT_OUTSIDE_LIMIT	Reference to a nested table or varray index outside the declared range (such as –1).
ORA-6533	SUBSCRIPT_BEYOND_COUNT	Reference to a nested table or varray index higher than the number of elements in the collection.
ORA-6548	NO_DATA_NEEDED[1]	Caller of a pipelined function does not need more rows.
ORA-6592	CASE_NOT_FOUND[2]	No matching WHEN clause in a CASE statement is found.
ORA-30625	SELF_IS_NULL	Attempt to call a method on a null object instance.

[1]This exception is predefined in Oracle10*g*R1 and higher.
[2]This exception is predefined in Oracle9*i*R1 and higher.

TABLE 7-2. *Predefined Oracle Exceptions* (continued)

Raising Exceptions

When the error associated with an exception occurs, the exception is raised (just the way Java exceptions are thrown). User-defined exceptions are raised explicitly via the RAISE statement, while predefined exceptions (or user-defined exceptions associated with an Oracle error through the EXCEPTION_INIT pragma) are raised implicitly when their associated Oracle error occurs. If an Oracle error that is not associated with an exception occurs, an exception is also raised. This exception can be caught with an OTHERS handler (see the section "The OTHERS Exception Handler" later in this chapter for details). Predefined exceptions can be raised explicitly via the RAISE statement as well, if desired. Continuing the example started earlier, in the section "User-Defined Exceptions," we have this:

```
-- Available online as part of UserDefined.sql
DECLARE
   -- Exception to indicate an error condition
   e_DuplicateAuthors EXCEPTION;

   -- IDs for three authors
   v_Author1 books.author1%TYPE;
   v_Author2 books.author2%TYPE;
   v_Author3 books.author3%TYPE;
BEGIN
  /* Find the IDs for the 3 authors of 'Oracle9i DBA 101' */
  SELECT author1, author2, author3
    INTO v_Author1, v_Author2, v_Author3
    FROM books
    WHERE title = 'Oracle9i DBA 101';

  /* Ensure that there are no duplicates */
  IF (v_Author1 = v_Author2) OR (v_Author1 = v_Author3) OR
     (v_Author2 = v_Author3) THEN
     RAISE e_DuplicateAuthors;
  END IF;
END;
```

When an exception is raised, control immediately passes to the exception section of the block. If there is no exception section, the exception is propagated to the enclosing block (see the section "Exception Propagation" later in the chapter for more information). Once control passes to the exception handler, there is *no* way to return to the executable section of the block. This is illustrated in Figure 7-1.

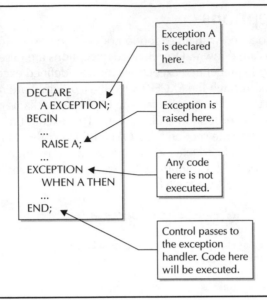

FIGURE 7-1. *Control passing to exception handler*

Predefined exceptions are automatically raised when the associated Oracle error occurs. For example, the following PL/SQL block will raise the DUP_VAL_ ON_INDEX exception:

```
-- Available online as DupValOnIndex.sql
BEGIN
  INSERT INTO authors (id, first_name, last_name)
    VALUES (20000, 'John', 'Smith');
  INSERT INTO authors (id, first_name, last_name)
    VALUES (20000, 'Susan', 'Ryan');
END;
```

The exception is raised because the ID column of the AUTHORS table is a primary key and therefore has a unique constraint defined on it. When the second INSERT statement attempts to insert 20000 into this column, the error

```
ORA-0001: unique constraint (<constraint name>) violated
```

is raised. This corresponds to the DUP_VAL_ON_INDEX exception.

Handling Exceptions

When an exception is raised, control passes to the exception section of the block, as we saw in Figure 7-1. The exception section consists of *handlers* for some or all of the exceptions. An exception handler contains the code that is executed when the error associated with the exception occurs, and the exception is raised. The syntax for the exception section is as follows:

EXCEPTION
  WHEN *exception_name* **THEN**
   sequence_of_statements1;
  WHEN *exception_name* **THEN**
   sequence_of_statements2;
[**WHEN** OTHERS **THEN**
   sequence_of_statements3;]
END;

Each exception handler consists of the WHEN clause and statements to execute when the exception is raised. The WHEN clause identifies which exception this handler is for. Continuing the example started earlier, we have

```
-- Available online as part of UserDefined.sql
DECLARE
    -- Exception to indicate an error condition
    e_DuplicateAuthors EXCEPTION;

    -- IDs for three authors
    v_Author1 books.author1%TYPE;
    v_Author2 books.author2%TYPE;
    v_Author3 books.author3%TYPE;
BEGIN
    /* Find the IDs for the 3 authors of 'Oracle9i DBA 101' */
    SELECT author1, author2, author3
      INTO v_Author1, v_Author2, v_Author3
      FROM books
      WHERE title = 'Oracle9i DBA 101';

    /* Ensure that there are no duplicates */
    IF (v_Author1 = v_Author2) OR (v_Author1 = v_Author3) OR
       (v_Author2 = v_Author3) THEN
        RAISE e_DuplicateAuthors;
    END IF;
EXCEPTION
    WHEN e_DuplicateAuthors THEN
        /* Handler which executes when there are duplicate authors for
           Oracle9i DBA 101. We will insert a log message recording
           what has happened. */
        INSERT INTO log_table (info)
          VALUES ('Oracle9i DBA 101 has duplicate authors');
END;
```

A single handler can also be executed for more than one exception. Simply list the exception names in the WHEN clause separated by the keyword OR:

```
EXCEPTION
    WHEN NO_DATA_FOUND OR TOO_MANY_ROWS THEN
        INSERT INTO log_table (info)
            VALUES ('A select error occurred.');
END;
```

NOTE
Unlike in Java, an exception section of a block can have handlers for exceptions that are not actually raised by the executable section. Likewise, it is not required that an exception handler be present for every possible exception that could be raised by the executable section. The PL/SQL compiler does not currently validate the exception section in this manner.

A given exception can be handled by at most one handler in an exception section. If there is more than one handler for an exception, the PL/SQL compiler will raise PLS-483, as shown by the following SQL*Plus session:

```
-- Available online as DuplicateHandlers.sql
SQL> DECLARE
  2      -- Declare 2 user defined exceptions
  3      e_Exception1 EXCEPTION;
  4      e_Exception2 EXCEPTION;
  5  BEGIN
  6      -- Raise just exception 1.
  7      RAISE e_Exception1;
  8  EXCEPTION
  9      WHEN e_Exception2 THEN
 10        INSERT INTO log_table (info)
 11          VALUES ('Handler 1 executed!');
 12      WHEN e_Exception1 THEN
 13        INSERT INTO log_table (info)
 14          VALUES ('Handler 3 executed!');
 15      WHEN e_Exception1 OR e_Exception2 THEN
 16        INSERT INTO log_table (info)
 17          VALUES ('Handler 4 executed!');
 18  END;
 19  /
    WHEN e_Exception1 OR e_Exception2 THEN
     *
ERROR at line 15:
ORA-06550: line 15, column 3:
```

```
PLS-00483: exception 'E_EXCEPTION2' may appear in at most one exception
          handler in this block
ORA-06550: line 0, column 0:
PL/SQL: Compilation unit analysis terminated
```

NOTE
It is impossible for an exception handler to be defined for more than one exception simultaneously; i.e.,

WHEN exception1 **AND** exception2

This will raise a compilation error.

The OTHERS Exception Handler

PL/SQL defines a special exception handler, known as OTHERS. This handler will execute for all raised exceptions that are not handled by any other WHEN clauses defined in the current exception section (similar to the generic Exception class in Java). It should always be the last handler in the block, so that all previous (and more specific) handlers will be scanned first. WHEN OTHERS will trap all exceptions, be they user-defined or predefined. It is good programming practice to have an OTHERS handler at the top level of your program (the outermost block) to ensure that no errors go undetected. If not, then the error will propagate out to the calling environment (see the section "Exception Propagation" for more details). In this case, the transaction will be rolled back by the server (see the section "Exceptions and Transactions" for details).

The next listing continues the previous example by adding an OTHERS handler:

```
-- Available online as part of UserDefined.sql
DECLARE
   -- Exception to indicate an error condition
   e_DuplicateAuthors EXCEPTION;

   -- IDs for three authors
   v_Author1 books.author1%TYPE;
   v_Author2 books.author2%TYPE;
   v_Author3 books.author3%TYPE;
BEGIN
   /* Find the IDs for the 3 authors of 'Oracle9i DBA 101' */
   SELECT author1, author2, author3
     INTO v_Author1, v_Author2, v_Author3
     FROM books
     WHERE title = 'Oracle9i DBA 101';

   /* Ensure that there are no duplicates */
   IF (v_Author1 = v_Author2) OR (v_Author1 = v_Author3) OR
      (v_Author2 = v_Author3) THEN
```

```
      RAISE e_DuplicateAuthors;
   END IF;
EXCEPTION
   WHEN e_DuplicateAuthors THEN
      /* Handler which executes when there are duplicate authors for
         Oracle9i DBA 101. We will insert a log message recording
         what has happened. */
      INSERT INTO log_table (info)
        VALUES ('Oracle9i DBA 101 has duplicate authors');
   WHEN OTHERS THEN
      /* Handler which executes for all other errors. */
      INSERT INTO log_table (info) VALUES ('Another error occurred');
END;
```

The OTHERS exception handler in this example simply records the fact that an error occurred. However, it doesn't record which error. We can determine which error raised the exception that is being handled by an OTHERS handler through the predefined functions SQLCODE and SQLERRM, described next.

TIP

In production code, do not write an exception handler like this one:

WHEN OTHERS THEN NULL;

Otherwise, it will silently trap any unexpected errors and not record the fact that they occurred. A good OTHERS handler will log the error and possibly provide additional information, for later analysis.

Examining the Error Stack

Although only one exception can be raised at a time, the actual error message text could contain several messages. For example, if an exception is raised from within a stored subprogram and propagated out (see the section "Exception Propagation" for details on this process), there will be ORA-6512 errors indicating the line where the exception was originally raised.

Inside an OTHERS handler, there are several ways of getting information about the error message stack, which we will see in the following sections.

SQLCODE and SQLERRM   PL/SQL provides error information via two built-in functions, SQLCODE and SQLERRM. SQLCODE returns the current error code, and SQLERRM returns the current error message text. For a user-defined exception, SQLCODE returns 1, and SQLERRM returns "User-defined Exception".

Here is the entire PL/SQL block that we have developed so far, with a complete OTHERS exception handler:

```
-- Available online as part of UserDefined.sql
DECLARE
   -- Exception to indicate an error condition
   e_DuplicateAuthors EXCEPTION;

   -- IDs for three authors
   v_Author1 books.author1%TYPE;
   v_Author2 books.author2%TYPE;
   v_Author3 books.author3%TYPE;

   -- Code and text of other run-time errors
   v_ErrorCode log_table.code%TYPE;
   v_ErrorText log_table.message%TYPE;
BEGIN
   /* Find the IDs for the 3 authors of 'Oracle9i DBA 101' */
   SELECT author1, author2, author3
     INTO v_Author1, v_Author2, v_Author3
     FROM books
     WHERE title = 'Oracle9i DBA 101';

   /* Ensure that there are no duplicates */
   IF (v_Author1 = v_Author2) OR (v_Author1 = v_Author3) OR
      (v_Author2 = v_Author3) THEN
      RAISE e_DuplicateAuthors;
   END IF;
EXCEPTION
   WHEN e_DuplicateAuthors THEN
      /* Handler which executes when there are duplicate authors for
         Oracle9i DBA 101. We will insert a log message recording
         what has happened. */
      INSERT INTO log_table (info)
        VALUES ('Oracle9i DBA 101 has duplicate authors');
   WHEN OTHERS THEN
      /* Handler which executes for all other errors. */
      v_ErrorCode := SQLCODE;
      -- Note the use of SUBSTR here.
      v_ErrorText := SUBSTR(SQLERRM, 1, 200);
      INSERT INTO log_table (code, message, info) VALUES
        (v_ErrorCode, v_ErrorText, 'Oracle error occurred');
END;
```

Each error message on the stack has a maximum of 512 characters, but there could be more than one message on the stack. In the preceding listing, v_ErrorText is only 200 characters (to match the message field of the log_table table). If the error message text is longer than 200 characters, the assignment

```
v_ErrorText := SQLERRM;
```

will itself raise the predefined exception VALUE_ERROR. To prevent this, we use the SUBSTR built-in function to ensure that at most 200 characters of the error message text are assigned to v_ErrorText.

Note that the values of SQLCODE and SQLERRM are assigned to local variables first; then these variables are used in a SQL statement. Because these functions are procedural, they cannot be used directly inside a SQL statement.

SQLERRM can also be called with a single number argument. In this case, it returns the text associated with the number. This argument should always be negative. If SQLERRM is called with zero, the message

```
ORA-0000: normal, successful completion
```

is returned. If SQLERRM is called with any positive value other than +100, messages such as

```
non-ORACLE Exception
```

are returned. SQLERRM(100) returns

```
ORA-1403: no data found
```

When called from an exception handler, SQLCODE will return a negative value indicating the Oracle error. The only exception to this is the error "ORA-1403: no data found," in which case SQLCODE returns +100. (100 corresponds to the ANSI specification for the NO DATA FOUND error.)

If SQLERRM (with no arguments) is called from the executable section of a block, it always returns

```
ORA-0000: normal, successful completion
```

and SQLCODE returns 0. All of these situations are shown in the following SQL*Plus session:

```
-- Available online as SQLERRM.sql
SQL> BEGIN
  2     DBMS_OUTPUT.PUT_LINE('SQLERRM(0): ' || SQLERRM(0));
  3     DBMS_OUTPUT.PUT_LINE('SQLERRM(100): ' || SQLERRM(100));
  4     DBMS_OUTPUT.PUT_LINE('SQLERRM(10): ' || SQLERRM(10));
  5     DBMS_OUTPUT.PUT_LINE('SQLERRM: ' || SQLERRM);
  6     DBMS_OUTPUT.PUT_LINE('SQLERRM(-1): ' || SQLERRM(-1));
```

```
  7    DBMS_OUTPUT.PUT_LINE('SQLERRM(-54): ' || SQLERRM(-54));
  8  END;
  9  /
SQLERRM(0): ORA-0000: normal, successful completion
SQLERRM(100): ORA-01403: no data found
SQLERRM(10):   -10: non-ORACLE exception
SQLERRM: ORA-0000: normal, successful completion
SQLERRM(-1): ORA-00001: unique constraint (.) violated
SQLERRM(-54): ORA-00054: resource busy and acquire with NOWAIT specified
PL/SQL procedure successfully completed.
```

TIP
*It is generally more useful to use SQLERRM with
no parameters, rather than passing a parameter
(such as SQLCODE). The version with no parameters
will return the complete error message, with any
substituted strings, such as the constraint name in
the case of the ORA-1 error in the previous example.*

DBMS_UTILITY.FORMAT_ERROR_STACK   The DBMS_UTILITY package provides
a function FORMAT_ERROR_STACK that returns the same information as SQLERRM,
also limited to 2000 bytes. We will discuss packages in Chapters 8 and 9. Since
FORMAT_ERROR_STACK is a packaged function, it can be used directly in a SQL
statement, so it does not have to be assigned to a local variable first like SQLERRM.
For example, we can rewrite the exception handling section of our example as follows:

```
-- Available online as part of UserDefined.sql
EXCEPTION
   WHEN e_DuplicateAuthors THEN
     /* Handler which executes when there are duplicate authors for
        Oracle9i DBA 101. We will insert a log message recording
        what has happened. */
     INSERT INTO log_table (into)
       VALUES ('Oracle9i DBA 101 has duplicate authors');
   WHEN OTHERS THEN
     INSERT INTO log_table (code, message, info) VALUES
       (NULL, SUBSTR(DBMS_UTILITY.FORMAT_ERROR_STACK, 1, 200),
       'Oracle error occurred');
END;
```

We still need to insert no more than the first 200 characters due to the size of message.

DBMS_UTILITY.FORMAT_ERROR_BACKTRACE   The FORMAT_ERROR_
BACKTRACE function is similar to FORMAT_ERROR_STACK, except that it is

not subject to the 2000-byte limit. It will return the complete error stack at the point the error was raised.

The EXCEPTION_INIT Pragma

You can associate a named exception with a particular Oracle error. This gives you the ability to trap this error specifically, rather than via an OTHERS handler. This is done via the EXCEPTION_INIT pragma. The EXCEPTION_INIT pragma is used as follows:

PRAGMA EXCEPTION_INIT (*exception_name, oracle_error_number*);

where *exception_name* is the name of an exception declared prior to the pragma, and *oracle_error_number* is the desired error code to be associated with this named exception. This pragma must be in the declarative section. The following example will raise the `e_MissingNull` user-defined exception if the "ORA-1400: mandatory NOT NULL column missing or NULL during insert" error is encountered at run time:

```
-- Available online as part of ExceptionInit.sql
SQL> DECLARE
  2    e_MissingNull EXCEPTION;
  3    PRAGMA EXCEPTION_INIT(e_MissingNull, -1400);
  4  BEGIN
  5    INSERT INTO authors (id) VALUES (NULL);
  6  EXCEPTION
  7    WHEN e_MissingNull then
  8      INSERT INTO log_table (info) VALUES ('ORA-1400 occurred');
  9  END;
 10  /

SQL> SELECT info FROM log_table;
INFO
-----------------------------------------------------------------
ORA-1400 occurred
```

Only one user-defined exception can be associated with an Oracle error with each occurrence of PRAGMA EXCEPTION_INIT. Inside the exception handler, SQLCODE and SQLERRM will return the code and message for the Oracle error that occurred, rather than "User-Defined Exception."

NOTE
The predefined exceptions described in Table 7-2 are associated with their corresponding Oracle errors with the EXCEPTION_INIT pragma as well, in package STANDARD.

Using RAISE_APPLICATION_ERROR

You can use the built-in function RAISE_APPLICATION_ERROR to create your own error messages, which can be more descriptive than named exceptions. User-defined errors are passed out of the block the same way as Oracle errors to the calling environment. The syntax of RAISE_APPLICATION_ERROR is

RAISE_APPLICATION_ERROR(*error_number*, *error_message*, [*keep_errors*]);

where *error_number* is a value between –20,000 and –20,999, *error_message* is the text associated with this error, and *keep_errors* is a Boolean value. The *error_message* parameter must be fewer than 512 characters. The Boolean parameter, *keep_errors*, is optional. If *keep_errors* is TRUE, the new error is added to the list of errors already raised (if one exists). If it is FALSE, which is the default, the new error will replace the current list of errors.

For example, the following procedure checks to ensure that the authors of a proposed new book are valid, and raises errors if they are not. Procedures are discussed in more detail starting in Chapter 8.

TIP
The constraints on the BOOKS table will not actually allow invalid entries (as checked by VerifyAuthors*) to be inserted. However,* VerifyAuthors *can be used to raise more user-friendly errors than constraint violations.*

```
-- Available online as part of VerifyAuthors.sql
/* Verifies that the authors passed in are valid for a book to be
   added to the inventory. Errors are raised in the following
situations:
        * author1 is null
        * any author does not exist in the authors table
        * there are author duplicates
   If the authors are valid, then the procedure completes without
   error. */
CREATE OR REPLACE PROCEDURE VerifyAuthors(
  p_Author1 IN books.author1%TYPE,
  p_Author2 IN books.author2%TYPE,
  p_Author3 IN books.author3%TYPE) AS

  v_AuthorCount NUMBER;
BEGIN
  /* First verify that each author is in the authors table */
  IF p_Author1 IS NULL THEN
    RAISE_APPLICATION_ERROR(-20000, 'Author1 cannot be null');
```

```
    ELSE
      SELECT COUNT(*)
        INTO v_AuthorCount
        FROM authors
        WHERE id = p_Author1;
      IF v_AuthorCount = 0 THEN
        RAISE_APPLICATION_ERROR(-20001,
          'Author1 ' || p_Author1 || ' does not exist');
      END IF;
    END IF;

    IF p_Author2 IS NOT NULL THEN
      SELECT COUNT(*)
        INTO v_AuthorCount
        FROM authors
        WHERE id = p_Author2;
      IF v_AuthorCount = 0 THEN
        RAISE_APPLICATION_ERROR(-20001,
          'Author2 ' || p_Author2 || ' does not exist');
      END IF;
    END IF;

    IF p_Author3 IS NOT NULL THEN
      SELECT COUNT(*)
        INTO v_AuthorCount
        FROM authors
        WHERE id = p_Author3;
      IF v_AuthorCount = 0 THEN
        RAISE_APPLICATION_ERROR(-20001,
          'Author3 ' || p_Author3 || ' does not exist');
      END IF;
    END IF;

    /* Now verify that there are no duplicate authors. */
    IF p_Author1 = p_Author2 THEN
      RAISE_APPLICATION_ERROR (-20002,
        'Author1 ' || p_Author1 || ' and author2 ' || p_Author2 ||
        ' are duplicates');
    ELSIF p_Author1 = p_Author3 THEN
      RAISE_APPLICATION_ERROR (-20002,
        'Author1 ' || p_Author1 || ' and author3 ' || p_Author3 ||
        ' are duplicates');
    ELSIF p_Author2 = p_Author3 THEN
      RAISE_APPLICATION_ERROR (-20002,
        'Author2 ' || p_Author2 || ' and author3 ' || p_Author3 ||
```

```
        ' are duplicates');
    END IF;
END VerifyAuthors;
```

The `VerifyAuthors` procedure uses RAISE_APPLICATION_ERROR in three different places. The first thing the procedure verifies is that `p_Author1` is not NULL, since all books must have at least one author. If it is NULL, then ORA-20000 is raised. It next verifies that, if they are specified, the author IDs exist in the `authors` table. If a given author ID does not exist (as verified by the SELECT COUNT(*) statement returning 0), then ORA-20001 is raised. Finally, the procedure verifies that there are no duplicate authors. If so, then ORA-20002 is raised. If all these tests pass, the procedure returns successfully with no errors.

`VerifyAuthors` also illustrates another useful feature of RAISE_APPLICATION_ ERROR. Because the program is in charge of creating the error message text, the error can include the actual data. For example, each one of the ORA-20002 calls includes the duplicate author IDs. Assuming that the tables are in their initial state (as created by `tables.sql`), the following SQL*Plus session illustrates the behavior of the `VerifyAuthors` procedure and the errors it raises:

```
-- Available online as part of VerifyAuthors.sql
SQL> -- The first three calls will raise errors
SQL> BEGIN VerifyAuthors(NULL, NULL, NULL); END;
  2  /
BEGIN VerifyAuthors(NULL, NULL, NULL); END;
*
ERROR at line 1:
ORA-20000: Author1 cannot be null
ORA-06512: at "EXAMPLE.VERIFYAUTHORS", line 10
ORA-06512: at line 1

SQL> BEGIN VerifyAuthors(30, 40, NULL); END;
  2  /
BEGIN VerifyAuthors(30, 40, NULL); END;
*
ERROR at line 1:
ORA-20001: Author2 40 does not exist
ORA-06512: at "EXAMPLE.VERIFYAUTHORS", line 28
ORA-06512: at line 1

SQL> BEGIN VerifyAuthors(30, 30, 1); END;
  2  /
BEGIN VerifyAuthors(30, 30, 1); END;
*
ERROR at line 1:
```

```
ORA-20002: Author1 30 and author2 30 are duplicates
ORA-06512: at "EXAMPLE.VERIFYAUTHORS", line 46
ORA-06512: at line 1

SQL> -- But these calls are successful
SQL> BEGIN VerifyAuthors(30, NULL, NULL); END;
  2  /
PL/SQL procedure successfully completed.
SQL> BEGIN VerifyAuthors(30, 14, 8); END;
  2  /
PL/SQL procedure successfully completed.
```

Compare the preceding output to the anonymous block that follows, which illustrates an anonymous block that simply raises the NO_DATA_FOUND exception:

 -- Available online as part of VerifyAuthors.sql
```
SQL> BEGIN
  2     RAISE NO_DATA_FOUND;
  3  END;
  4  /
BEGIN
*
ERROR at line 1:
ORA-01403: no data found
ORA-06512: at line 2
```

The format of both outputs is the same: an Oracle error number and text associated with it. Note that both also include an ORA-6512 statement indicating the line that caused the error. So RAISE_APPLICATION_ERROR can be used to return error conditions to the user in a manner consistent with other Oracle errors. This is very useful, because no special error handling is necessary for user-defined errors versus predefined ones.

TIP
Some Oracle components (such as Oracle Text) also use RAISE_APPLICATION_ERROR. So you may see ORA-20000 errors raised in other places, which could lead to error number duplication. You can use a unique prefix in your error text to distinguish your error messages from other products' messages.

Exception Propagation

Exceptions can occur in the declarative, executable, or the exception section of a PL/SQL block. We have seen in the previous section what happens when exceptions are raised in the executable portion of the block, and there is a handler for the exception. But what if there isn't a handler, or the exception is raised from a different section of the block? The process that governs this situation is known as *exception propagation.*

Exceptions Raised in the Executable Section

When an exception is raised in the executable section of a block, PL/SQL uses the following algorithm to determine which exception handler to invoke:

1. If the current block has a handler for the exception, execute it and complete the block successfully. Control then passes to the enclosing block.

2. If there is no handler for the current exception, propagate the exception by raising it in the enclosing block. Step 1 will then be executed for the enclosing block. If there is no enclosing block, then the exception will be propagated out to the calling environment, such as SQL*Plus.

Before we can examine this algorithm in detail, we need to define an *enclosing block.* A block can be embedded inside another block. In this case, the outer block encloses the inner block. For example,

```
DECLARE
  -- Begin outer block.
  ...
BEGIN
  ...
  DECLARE
    -- Begin inner block 1. This is embedded in the outer block.
  ...
  BEGIN
    ...
  END;
  ...
  BEGIN
    -- Begin inner block 2. This is also embedded in the outer block.
    -- Note that this block doesn't have a declarative part.
    ...
  END;
```

```
      ...
      -- End outer block.
   END;
```

In the preceding listing, inner blocks 1 and 2 are both enclosed by the outer block. Any unhandled exceptions in blocks 1 and 2 will be propagated to the outer block.

A procedure call will also create an enclosing block, as is illustrated in the following example:

```
   BEGIN
      -- Begin outer block.
      -- Call a procedure. This outer block will enclose the procedure.
      P(...);
   EXCEPTION
      WHEN OTHERS THEN
         -- Any exceptions raised by P will be caught here
   END;
```

If procedure P raises an unhandled exception, it will be propagated to the outer block, since it encloses the procedure.

Different cases for the exception propagation algorithm are illustrated in examples 1, 2, and 3 in the following sections.

Propagation Example 1

The example shown here illustrates application of rule 1. Exception A is raised and handled in the sub-block. Control then returns to the outer block.

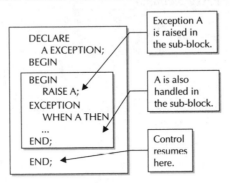

Propagation Example 2

In this example, rule 2 is applied for the sub-block. The exception B is propagated to the enclosing block, where rule 1 is applied. The enclosing block then completes successfully.

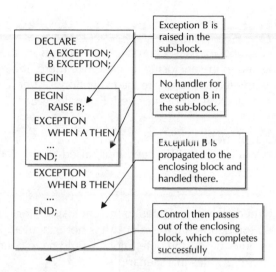

Propagation Example 3

Here, rule 2 is applied for the sub-block. The exception C is propagated to the enclosing block, where there is still no handler for it. Rule 2 is applied again, and the enclosing block completes unsuccessfully with an unhandled exception.

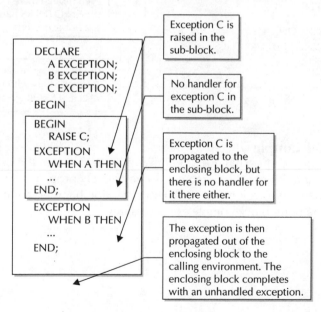

Exceptions Raised in the Declarative Section

If an assignment in the declarative section raises an exception, the exception is immediately propagated to the enclosing block. Once there, the rules given in the previous section are applied to propagate the exception further. Even if there is a handler in the current block, it is *not* executed. Examples 4 and 5 illustrate this.

Propagation Example 4

In this example, the VALUE_ERROR exception is raised by the declaration

```
v_Number NUMBER(3) := 'ABC';
```

This exception is immediately propagated to the enclosing block. Even though there is an OTHERS exception handler in this block, it is not executed. If this block had been enclosed in an outer block, the outer block would have been able to catch this exception. (Example 5 illustrates this scenario.)

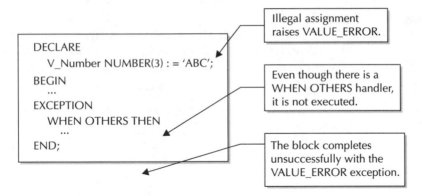

Propagation Example 5

Similar to example 4, the VALUE_ERROR exception is raised in the declarative section of the inner block. The exception is immediately propagated to the outer block. Since the outer block has an OTHERS exception handler, the exception is handled and the outer block completes successfully.

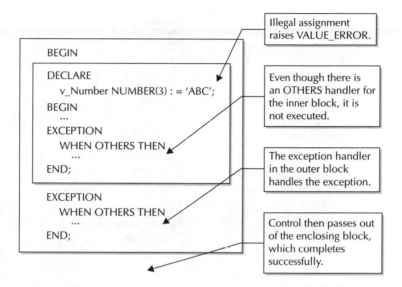

Illegal assignment raises VALUE_ERROR.

```
BEGIN
    DECLARE
        v_Number NUMBER(3) : = 'ABC';
    BEGIN
        ...
    EXCEPTION
        WHEN OTHERS THEN
            ...
    END;
EXCEPTION
    WHEN OTHERS THEN
        ...
END;
```

Even though there is an OTHERS handler for the inner block, it is not executed.

The exception handler in the outer block handles the exception.

Control then passes out of the enclosing block, which completes successfully.

Exceptions Raised in the Exception Section

Exceptions can also be raised while in an exception handler, either explicitly via the RAISE statement or implicitly via a run-time error. In either case, the exception is propagated immediately to the enclosing block, like exceptions that are raised in the declarative section. This is done because only one exception at a time can be "active" in the exception section. As soon as one is handled, another can be raised. But there cannot be more than one exception raised simultaneously. Examples 6, 7, and 8 illustrate this scenario.

Propagation Example 6

In this example, exception A is raised and then handled. But in the exception handler for A, exception B is raised. This exception is immediately propagated to the outer block, bypassing the handler for B. Similar to example 5, if this block had been enclosed in an outer block, this outer block could have caught exception B. (Example 7 illustrates the latter case.)

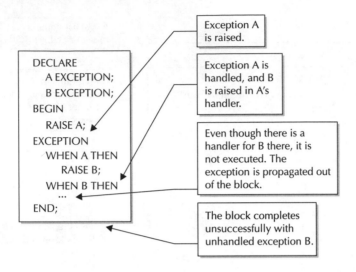

Propagation Example 7

Similar to example 6, exception B is raised in the handler for exception A. This exception is immediately propagated to the enclosing block, bypassing the inner handler for B. However, in example 7 we have an outer block that handles exception B and completes successfully.

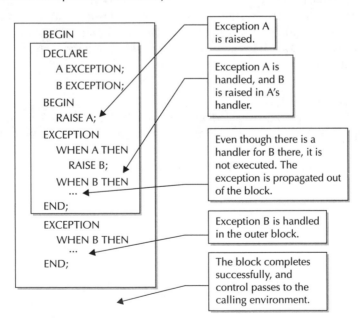

Propagation Example 8

As examples 6 and 7 illustrate, RAISE can be used to raise another exception inside a handler. In an exception handler, RAISE can also be used without an argument. If RAISE doesn't have an argument, the current exception is propagated to the enclosing block. This technique is useful for logging the error and/or doing any necessary cleanup because of it, and then notifying the enclosing block that it occurred. Example 8 illustrates this final scenario.

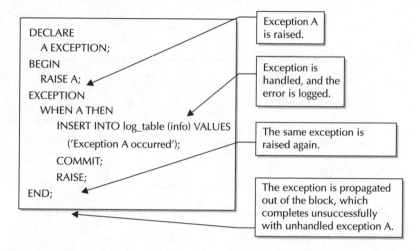

```
DECLARE
    A EXCEPTION;
BEGIN
    RAISE A;
EXCEPTION
    WHEN A THEN
        INSERT INTO log_table (info) VALUES
        ('Exception A occurred');
        COMMIT;
        RAISE;
END;
```

Exception A is raised.

Exception is handled, and the error is logged.

The same exception is raised again.

The exception is propagated out of the block, which completes unsuccessfully with unhandled exception A.

Note that there is a COMMIT after the INSERT statement in example 8. This ensures that the INSERT will be committed to the database, in case the transaction is rolled back. See Chapter 4 for more information about transactions.

TIP
Using a nontransactional logging technique such as the UTL_FILE package can avoid the need to commit a logging DML statement. This could also be accomplished though an autonomous transaction.

Exception Guidelines

This section contains guidelines and tips on how best to use exceptions in your programs. These guidelines include the scope of exceptions, how to avoid unhandled exceptions, how to identify which statement raised a given exception, and the relationship between exceptions and transactions. We will also discuss some coding styles related to exceptions. These guidelines should help you use exceptions more effectively in your own programs, and avoid some common pitfalls.

Scope of Exceptions

Exceptions are scoped just like variables. If a user-defined exception is propagated out of its scope, it can no longer be referenced by name. The next example illustrates this.

```
-- Available online as part of OutOfScope.sql
SQL> BEGIN
  2    DECLARE
  3      e_UserDefinedException EXCEPTION;
  4    BEGIN
  5      RAISE e_UserDefinedException;
  6    END;
  7  EXCEPTION
  8    /* e_UserDefinedException is out of scope here - can only be
  9       handled by an OTHERS handler */
 10    WHEN OTHERS THEN
 11      /* Just re-raise the exception, which will be propagated to the
 12         calling environment */
 13      RAISE;
 14  END;
 15  /
BEGIN
*
ERROR at line 1:
ORA-06510: PL/SQL: unhandled user-defined exception
ORA-06512: at line 13
```

In general, if a user-defined error is to be propagated out of a block, it is best to define the exception in a package so that it will still be visible outside the block, or to use RAISE_APPLICATION_ERROR instead. If we create a package called Globals and define e_UserDefinedException in this package, the exception will still be visible in the outer block. For example,

```
--Available online as part of OutOfScope.sql
CREATE OR REPLACE PACKAGE Globals AS
/* This package contains global declarations. Objects declared here
will
   be visible via qualified references for any other blocks or
procedures.
   Note that this package does not have a package body. */

  /* A user-defined exception. */
```

```
  e_UserDefinedException EXCEPTION;
END Globals;
```

Given package `Globals`, we can rewrite the preceding listing as

```
-- Available online as part of OutOfScope.sql
BEGIN
  BEGIN
    RAISE Globals.e_UserDefinedException;
  END;
EXCEPTION
  /* Since e_UserDefinedException is still visible, we can handle it
     explicitly */
  WHEN Globals.e_UserDefinedException THEN
    /* Just re-raise the exception, which will be propagated to the
       calling environment */
    RAISE;
END;
```

Package `Globals` can also be used for common PL/SQL tables, variables, and types, in addition to exceptions. See Chapters 8 and 9 for more information on packages.

Avoiding Unhandled Exceptions

It is good programming practice to avoid completing your program with an unhandled exception. This can be done via an OTHERS handler at the topmost level of your program. This handler may simply log the error and where it occurred. This way, you ensure that no error will go undetected. For example,

```
DECLARE
  v_ErrorNumber NUMBER;        -- Variable to hold the error number
  v_ErrorText VARCHAR2(200);   -- Variable to hold the error message text
BEGIN
  /* Normal PL/SQL processing */
  ...
EXCEPTION
  WHEN OTHERS THEN
    /* Log all exceptions so we complete successfully */
    v_ErrorNumber := SQLCODE;
    v_ErrorText := SUBSTR(SQLERRM, 1, 200);
    INSERT INTO log_table (code, message, info) VALUES
      (v_ErrorNumber, v_ErrorText, 'Oracle error occurred at ' ||
       TO_CHAR(SYSDATE, 'DD-MON-YY HH24:MI:SS'));
END;
```

DBMS_UTILITY.FORMAT_ERROR_BACKTRACE (available in 10*g*R1 and higher) could also be used in a top-level handler such as this, since it would record the original location of the exception.

Masking Location of the Error

Since the same exception section is examined for the entire block, it can be difficult to determine which SQL statement caused the error. Consider the following example:

```
BEGIN
   SELECT ...
   SELECT ...
   SELECT ...
EXCEPTION
   WHEN NO_DATA_FOUND THEN
      -- Which select statement raised the exception?
END;
```

There are two coding methods to solve this. The first is to increment a counter identifying the SQL statement:

```
DECLARE
   -- Variable to hold the select statement number
   v_SelectCounter NUMBER := 1;
BEGIN
   SELECT ...
   v_SelectCounter := 2;
   SELECT ...
   v_SelectCounter := 3;
   SELECT ...
EXCEPTION
   WHEN NO_DATA_FOUND THEN
      INSERT INTO log_table (info) VALUES ('No data found in select ' ||
        v_SelectCounter);
END;
```

The second method is to put each statement into its own sub-block:

```
BEGIN
   BEGIN
     SELECT ...
   EXCEPTION
     WHEN NO_DATA_FOUND THEN
        INSERT INTO log_table (info) VALUES ('No data found in select 1;);
   END;
   BEGIN
     SELECT ...
```

```
    EXCEPTION
      WHEN NO_DATA_FOUND THEN
        INSERT INTO log_table (info) VALUES ('No data found in select 2');
    END;
    BEGIN
      SELECT ...
    EXCEPTION
      WHEN NO_DATA_FOUND THEN
        INSERT INTO log_table (info) VALUES ('No data found in select 3');
    END;
  END;
```

TIP
*Again, DBMS_UTILITY.FORMAT_ERROR_
BACKTRACE (10g and higher) could be used to
determine the line at which the exception was
raised. This would require parsing the backtrace.*

Exceptions and Transactions

Raising an exception does not end a transaction, just as ending a block does
not end a transaction. However, if the top-level block exits with an unhandled
exception, which would be propagated to the calling environment, the transaction
will be rolled back automatically by the server. This is illustrated by the following
SQL*Plus session:

```
-- Available online as part of autoRollback.sql
SQL> BEGIN
  2      -- Insert a row into temp_table, and then raise an
  3      -- exception that will not be handled.
  4      INSERT INTO temp_table (char_col)
  5        VALUES ('This is my row!');
  6      RAISE VALUE_ERROR;
  7    END;
  8    /
BEGIN
*
ERROR at line 1:
ORA-06502: PL/SQL: numeric or value error
ORA-06512: at line 6

SQL>  -- The row is not present because the transaction has been rolled
SQL>  -- back.
SQL>  SELECT * FROM temp_table;
no rows selected
```

Exception Coding Styles

In the following sections we will discuss two issues regarding coding style of exceptions: when RAISE_APPLICATION_ERROR is appropriate versus RAISE, and how exceptions can be used as control statements.

RAISE_APPLICATION_ERROR vs. RAISE   A user-defined error condition can be indicated with both RAISE_APPLICATION_ERROR and RAISE of a user-defined exception. When is each appropriate? The differences between the two techniques are described here:

RAISE_APPLICATION_ERROR	**RAISE**
Allows you to supply your own error message text, which can contain application-specific data.	Does not allow for message text.
Exceptions cannot be caught by named handlers, only OTHERS.	Exceptions can be caught with named handlers, as long as the exception is within scope.

In general, I recommend using RAISE_APPLICATION_ERROR for errors that are designed to be seen by the end user. Specific error numbers and descriptive text are useful here. RAISE, on the other hand, is useful for errors that are designed to be handled programmatically. The UTL_FILE package (described in Appendix B) uses defined exceptions in this manner.

Using Exceptions as Control Statements   Because raising an exception will cause control to be passed immediately to the exception handling section of the block, a RAISE statement can be used as a control statement, similar to a GOTO. This can be useful, for example, if you have several deeply nested loops and need to exit from all of them.

Summary

In this chapter, we saw how PL/SQL programs can detect and react intelligently to run-time errors. The mechanism provided by PL/SQL to do this includes exceptions and exception handlers. We examined how exceptions are defined and how they correspond to either user-defined errors or predefined Oracle errors. We also discussed the rules for exception propagation, including exceptions raised in all parts of a PL/SQL block. The chapter concluded with guidelines on using exceptions.

CHAPTER
8

Creating Procedures, Functions, and Packages

s we saw in Chapter 3, there are two main kinds of PL/SQL blocks: anonymous and named. An *anonymous* block (beginning with either DECLARE or BEGIN) is compiled each time it is issued. It also is not stored in the database and cannot be called directly from other PL/SQL blocks. The constructs that we will look at in this and the next two chapters—procedures, functions, packages, and triggers—are all named blocks and thus do not have these restrictions. They can be stored in the database and run when appropriate. In this chapter, we will explore the syntax of creating procedures, functions, and packages. In Chapter 9, we will examine how to use them and some of their implications. Chapter 10 focuses on database triggers.

Procedures and Functions

PL/SQL procedures and functions behave very much like procedures and functions in other 3GLs (third-generation languages). They share many of the same properties. Collectively, procedures and functions are also known as *subprograms*. As an example, the following code creates a procedure in the database:

```
-- Available online as part of AddNewAuthor.sql
CREATE OR REPLACE PROCEDURE AddNewAuthor (
  p_ID authors.ID%TYPE,
  p_FirstName authors.first_name%TYPE,
  p_LastName authors.last_name%TYPE) AS
BEGIN
  -- Insert a new row into the authors table, using the supplied
  -- arguments for the column values.
  INSERT INTO authors (id, first_name, last name)
    VALUES (p_ID, p_FirstName, p_LastName);
END AddNewAuthor;
```

Once this procedure is created, we can call it from another PL/SQL block:

```
-- Available online as part of AddNewAuthor.sql
BEGIN
  AddNewAuthor(100, 'Zelda', 'Zudnik');
END;
```

This example illustrates several notable points:

- The `AddNewAuthor` procedure is created first with the CREATE OR REPLACE PROCEDURE statement. When a procedure is created, it is first compiled and then stored in the database in compiled form. This compiled code can then be run later from another PL/SQL block. (The source code for the procedure is also stored. See the section "Stored Subprograms and the Data Dictionary" in Chapter 9 for more information.)

- When the procedure is called, parameters can be passed. In the preceding example, the new author's ID and first and last names are passed to the procedure at run time. Inside the procedure, the parameter p_ID will have the value 100, p_FirstName will have the value 'Zelda', and p_LastName will have the value 'Zudnik', because these literals are passed to the procedure when it is called. The %TYPE declarations specify that the types of the parameters should match the authors table, just as they do for variable declarations.

- A procedure call is a PL/SQL statement by itself. It is not called as part of an expression. When a procedure is called, control passes to the first executable statement inside the procedure. When the procedure finishes, control resumes at the statement following the procedure call. In this regard, PL/SQL procedures behave the same as procedures in other 3GLs. Functions are called as part of an expression, as we will see later in this section.

- A procedure is a PL/SQL block, with a declarative section, an executable section, and an exception-handling section. As in an anonymous block, only the executable section is required. AddNewAuthor only has an executable section.

Subprogram Creation

Similar to other data dictionary objects, subprograms are created using the CREATE statement. Procedures are created with CREATE PROCEDURE, and functions are created with CREATE FUNCTION. We will examine the details of these statements in the following sections.

Creating a Procedure

The following railroad diagram illustrates the basic syntax for the CREATE OR REPLACE PROCEDURE statement:

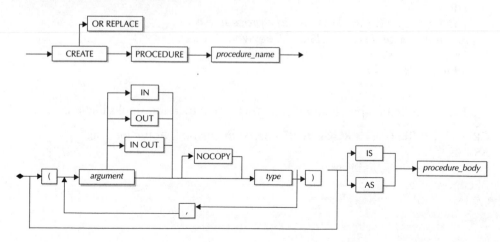

Procedure_name is the name of the procedure to be created, *argument* is the name of a procedure parameter, *type* is the type of the associated parameter, and *procedure_body* is a PL/SQL block that makes up the code of the procedure. See the section "Subprogram Parameters" later in this chapter for information on procedure and function parameters, and the meanings of the IN, OUT, IN OUT, and NOCOPY keywords. The argument list is optional. In this case, there are no parentheses either in the procedure declaration or in the procedure call. There are additional clauses for CREATE OR REPLACE PROCEDURE, which we will discuss later in this chapter.

In order to change the code of a procedure, the procedure must be dropped and then re-created. Since this is a common operation while the procedure is under development, the OR REPLACE keywords allow this to be done in one operation. If the procedure exists, it is dropped first, without a warning message. (To drop a procedure, use the DROP PROCEDURE command, described in the "Dropping Procedures and Functions" section later in this chapter.) If the procedure does not already exist, it is simply created. If the procedure exists and the OR REPLACE keywords are not present, the CREATE statement will return the Oracle error "ORA-955: Name is already used by an existing object."

As with other CREATE statements, creating a procedure is a DDL operation, so an implicit COMMIT is done both before and after the procedure is created. Either the IS or the AS keyword can be used—they are equivalent.

The Procedure Body   The body of a procedure is a PL/SQL block with declarative, executable, and exception sections. The declarative section is located between the IS or AS keyword and the BEGIN keyword. The executable section (the only one that is required) is located between the BEGIN and EXCEPTION keywords, or between the BEGIN and END keywords if there is no exception-handling section. The exception section, if present, is located between the EXCEPTION and END keywords.

TIP
There is no DECLARE keyword in a procedure or function declaration. The IS or AS keyword is used instead. This syntax originally comes from Ada, on which PL/SQL is based.

The structure of a procedure creation statement therefore looks like this:

CREATE OR REPLACE PROCEDURE *procedure_name* [*parameter_list*]
AS
  /* Declarative section is here */
BEGIN
  /* Executable section is here */

EXCEPTION
  /* Exception section is here */
END [*procedure_name*];

The procedure name can optionally be included after the final END statement in the procedure declaration. If there is an identifier after the END, it must match the name of the procedure.

TIP
It is good style to include the procedure name in the final END statement, because it makes the procedure easier to read, emphasizes the END that matches the CREATE statement, and enables the PL/SQL compiler to flag mismatched BEGIN-END pairs as early as possible.

Creating a Function

A function is very similar to a procedure. Both take parameters, which can be of any mode (parameters and modes are described later in this chapter in the section "Subprogram Parameters"). Both are different forms of PL/SQL blocks, with declarative, executable, and exception sections. Both can be stored in the database or declared within a block. However, a procedure call is a PL/SQL statement by itself, while a function call is called as part of an expression. For example, the following function returns TRUE if the specified book has three authors, and FALSE otherwise:

```
-- Available online as part of ThreeAuthors.sql
CREATE OR REPLACE FUNCTION ThreeAuthors(p_ISBN IN books.isbn%TYPE)
   RETURN BOOLEAN AS

  v_Author3 books.author3%TYPE;
BEGIN
  -- Select the third author for the supplied book into v_Author3.
  SELECT author3
    INTO v_Author3
    FROM books
    WHERE isbn = p_ISBN;

  -- If v_Author3 is NULL, that means that the book has less then 3
  -- authors, so we can return false.  Otherwise, return true.
  IF v_Author3 IS NULL THEN
    RETURN FALSE;
  ELSE
    RETURN TRUE;
  END IF;
END ThreeAuthors;
```

The `ThreeAuthors` function returns a Boolean value. The following SQL*Plus session shows how it can be called. Note that the function call is not a statement by itself—it is used as part of the IF statement inside the loop.

```
-- Available online as part of ThreeAuthors.sql
SQL> BEGIN
  2    FOR v_Rec IN (SELECT ISBN, title FROM books) LOOP
  3      IF ThreeAuthors(v_Rec.ISBN) THEN
  4        DBMS_OUTPUT.PUT_LINE('"' || v_Rec.title || '" has 3 authors');
  5      END IF;
  6    END LOOP;
  7  END;
  8  /
"Oracle DBA 101" has 3 authors
"Oracle Performance Tuning 101" has 3 authors
"Oracle9i: A Beginner's Guide" has 3 authors
"Oracle9i DBA 101" has 3 authors
"Oracle Database 10g A Beginner's Guide" has 3 authors
"Oracle E-Business Suite Financials Handbook" has 3 authors
"Oracle E-Business Suite Manufacturing & Supply Chain Management" has 3 authors
"Oracle Database 10g XML & SQL Design, Build, & Manage XML Applications in Java, C, C++,
& PL/SQL" has 3 authors
"Oracle PL/SQL Tips and Techniques" has 3 authors
PL/SQL procedure successfully completed.
```

Function Syntax   The syntax for creating a stored function is very similar to the syntax for a procedure. The following railroad diagram illustrates the syntax:

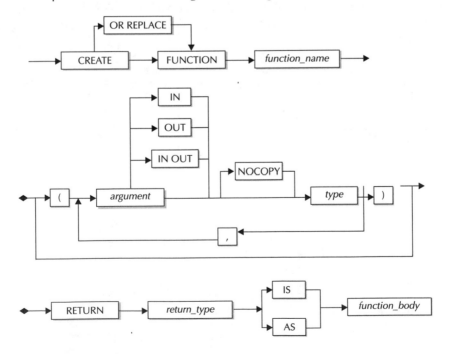

Function_name is the name of the function, *argument* and *type* are the same as for procedures, *return_type* is the type of value the function returns, and *function_ body* is a PL/SQL block containing the code for the function. The same rules apply for a function body as for a procedure body—for example, the function name can optionally appear after the final END.

As with procedures, the argument list is optional. In this case, there are no parentheses either in the function declaration or in the function call. However, the function return type is required, since the function call is part of an expression. The type of function is used to determine the type of the expression containing the function call.

The RETURN Statement   Inside the body of the function, the RETURN statement is used to return control to the calling environment with a value. The general syntax of the RETURN statement is

RETURN *expression*;

where *expression* is the value to be returned. When RETURN is executed, *expression* will be converted to the type specified in the RETURN clause of the function definition, if it is not already of that type. At this point, control immediately returns to the calling environment.

There can be more than one RETURN statement in a function, although only one of them will be executed. It is an error for a function to end without executing a RETURN. For example, the `ThreeAuthors` function that we examined in the previous section contained two RETURN statements. Which one is executed depends on whether or not the supplied book has three authors or not.

When used in a function, the RETURN statement must have an expression associated with it. RETURN can also be used in a procedure, however. In this case, it has no arguments, which causes control to pass back to the calling environment immediately. The current values of the formal parameters declared as OUT or IN OUT are passed back to the actual parameters, and execution continues from the statement following the procedure call. (See the section "Subprogram Parameters" later in this chapter for more information on parameters.)

Dropping Procedures and Functions

Just as a table can be dropped, procedures and functions can also be dropped. This removes the procedure or function from the data dictionary. The syntax for dropping a procedure is

DROP PROCEDURE *procedure_name*;

and the syntax for dropping a function is

DROP FUNCTION *function_name*;

where *procedure_name* is the name of an existing procedure, and *function_name* is the name of an existing function. For example, the following statement drops the AddNewAuthor procedure:

```
DROP PROCEDURE AddNewAuthor;
```

   If the object to be dropped is a function, you must use DROP FUNCTION, and if the object is a procedure, you must use DROP PROCEDURE. Like CREATE, DROP is a DDL command, so an implicit COMMIT is done both before and after the statement. If the subprogram does not exist, the DROP statement will raise the error "ORA-4043: Object does not exist."

Subprogram Parameters

As in other 3GLs, you can create procedures and functions that take parameters. These parameters can have different modes and may be passed by value or by reference. We will examine how to do this in the next few sections.

Parameter Modes

Given the AddNewAuthor procedure shown earlier, we can call this procedure from the following anonymous PL/SQL block:

```
-- Available online as callANA.sql
DECLARE
  -- Variables describing the new author
  v_NewFirstName authors.first_name%TYPE := 'Cynthia';
  v_NewLastName authors.last_name%TYPE := 'Camino';
  v_NewAuthorID authors.ID%TYPE := 100;
BEGIN
  -- Add Cynthia Camino to the database
AddNewAuthor(v_NewAuthorID, v_NewFirstName, v_NewLastName);
END;
```

The variables declared in the preceding block (v_NewAuthorID, v_NewFirstName, v_NewLastName) are passed as arguments to AddNewAuthor. In this context, they are known as *actual parameters,* while the parameters in the procedure declaration (p_ID, p_FirstName, p_LastName) are known as *formal parameters.* Actual parameters contain the values passed to the procedure when it is called, and they receive results from the procedure when it returns (depending on the mode). The values of the actual parameters are the ones that will be used in the procedure. The formal parameters are the placeholders for the values of the actual parameters. When the procedure is called, the formal parameters are assigned the values of the actual parameters. Inside the procedure, they are referred to by the formal parameters. When the procedure returns, the actual parameters are assigned the values of the formal parameters. These assignments follow the normal rules for PL/SQL assignment, including type conversion, if necessary.

Formal parameters can have three modes—IN, OUT, or IN OUT. (The NOCOPY modifier is described in the next section.) If the mode is not specified for a formal parameter, it defaults to IN. The differences between the modes are described in Table 8-1.

Mode	Description
IN	The value of the actual parameter is passed into the procedure when the procedure is invoked. Inside the procedure, the formal parameter acts like a PL/SQL constant—it is considered *read-only* and cannot be changed. When the procedure finishes and control returns to the calling environment, the actual parameter is not changed.
OUT	Any value the actual parameter has when the procedure is called is ignored. Inside the procedure, the formal parameter acts like an uninitialized PL/SQL variable and thus has a value of NULL. It can be read from and written to. When the procedure finishes and control returns to the calling environment, the contents of the formal parameter are assigned to the actual parameter. (This behavior can be altered by using the NOCOPY modifier—see the section "Passing Parameters by Value and by Reference" later in this chapter.)
IN OUT	This mode is a combination of IN and OUT. The value of the actual parameter is passed into the procedure when the procedure is invoked. Inside the procedure, the formal parameter acts like an initialized variable and can be read from and written to. When the procedure finishes and control returns to the calling environment, the contents of the formal parameter are assigned to the actual parameter (subject to NOCOPY, as for OUT).

TABLE 8-1.   *Parameter Modes*

Assigning Values to IN Parameters   Consider the following procedure, which takes a single IN parameter:

```
-- Available online as part of parameterModes.sql
CREATE OR REPLACE PROCEDURE ModeIn (
  p_InParameter IN NUMBER) AS

  v_LocalVariable NUMBER := 0;
BEGIN
  DBMS_OUTPUT.PUT('Inside ModeIn: ');
  IF (p_InParameter IS NULL) THEN
    DBMS_OUTPUT.PUT_LINE('p_InParameter is NULL');
  ELSE
    DBMS_OUTPUT.PUT_LINE('p_InParameter = ' || p_InParameter);
  END IF;

  /* Assign p_InParameter to v_LocalVariable. This is legal,
     since we are reading from an IN parameter and not writing
     to it. */
  v_LocalVariable := p_InParameter;

  DBMS_OUTPUT.PUT('At end of ModeIn: ');
  IF (p_InParameter IS NULL) THEN
    DBMS_OUTPUT.PUT_LINE('p_InParameter is NULL');
  ELSE
    DBMS_OUTPUT.PUT_LINE('p_InParameter = ' || p_InParameter);
  END IF;
END ModeIn;
```

The following SQL*Plus session illustrates a successful call to `ModeIn`:

```
-- Available online as part of parameterModes.sql
SQL> DECLARE
  2    v_In NUMBER := 1;
  3  BEGIN
  4    - Call ModeIn with a variable, which should remain unchanged.
  5    DBMS_OUTPUT.PUT_LINE('Before calling ModeIn, v_In = ' || v_In);
  6    ModeIn(v_In);
  7    DBMS_OUTPUT.PUT_LINE('After calling ModeIn, v_In = ' || v_In);
  8  END;
  9  /
Before calling ModeIn, v_In = 1
Inside ModeIn: p_InParameter = 1
At end of ModeIn: p_InParameter = 1
After calling ModeIn, v_In = 1
PL/SQL procedure successfully completed.
```

As expected, the value of `v_In` remains the same before, during, and after the procedure call.

Assigning Values to OUT Parameters   Now consider the following procedure, which takes a single OUT parameter:

```
-- Available online as part of parameterModes.sql
CREATE OR REPLACE PROCEDURE ModeOut (
  p_OutParameter OUT NUMBER) AS

  v_LocalVariable NUMBER := 0;
BEGIN
  DBMS_OUTPUT.PUT('Inside ModeOut: ');
  IF (p_OutParameter IS NULL) THEN
    DBMS_OUTPUT.PUT_LINE('p_OutParameter is NULL');
  ELSE
    DBMS_OUTPUT.PUT_LINE('p_OutParameter = ' || p_OutParameter);
  END IF;

  /* Assign 7 to p_OutParameter. This is legal, since we
     are writing to an OUT parameter. */
  p_OutParameter := 7;

  /* Assign p_OutParameter to v_LocalVariable. This is also legal,
   * since we are reading from an OUT parameter. */
  v_LocalVariable := p_OutParameter;

  DBMS_OUTPUT.PUT('At end of ModeOut: ');
  IF (p_OutParameter IS NULL) THEN
    DBMS_OUTPUT.PUT_LINE('p_OutParameter is NULL');
  ELSE
    DBMS_OUTPUT.PUT_LINE('p_OutParameter = ' || p_OutParameter);
  END IF;
END ModeOut;
```

The following SQL*Plus session illustrates a successful call to `ModeOut`:

```
-- Available online as part of parameterModes.sql
SQL> DECLARE
  2    v_Out NUMBER := 1;
  3  BEGIN
  4    - Call ModeOut with a variable, which should be modified.
  5    DBMS_OUTPUT.PUT_LINE('Before calling ModeOut, v_Out = ' || v_Out);
  6    ModeOut(v_Out);
  7    DBMS_OUTPUT.PUT_LINE('After calling ModeOut, v_Out = ' || v_Out);
  8  END;
```

```
  9  /
Before calling ModeOut, v_Out = 1
Inside ModeOut: p_OutParameter is NULL
At end of ModeOut: p_OutParameter = 7
After calling ModeOut, v_Out = 7
PL/SQL procedure successfully completed.
```

We can see two things from the preceding example—the formal parameter p_
OutParameter is NULL even though the actual parameter v_Out was initialized
to 1, and the final value of the formal parameter p_OutParameter is copied to
the actual parameter v_Out upon return from the procedure.

NOTE
*If the procedure raises an exception, the values of
IN OUT and OUT formal parameters are not copied
to their corresponding actual parameters (subject
to NOCOPY). See the section "Exceptions Raised
Inside Subprograms" later in this chapter.*

Assigning Values to IN OUT Parameters   Again, consider the following procedure,
which takes a single IN OUT parameter:

```
-- Available online as part of parameterModes.sql
CREATE OR REPLACE PROCEDURE ModeInOut (
  p_InOutParameter IN OUT NUMBER) IS

  v_LocalVariable  NUMBER := 0;
BEGIN
  DBMS_OUTPUT.PUT('Inside ModeInOut: ');
  IF (p_InOutParameter IS NULL) THEN
    DBMS_OUTPUT.PUT_LINE('p_InOutParameter is NULL');
  ELSE
    DBMS_OUTPUT.PUT_LINE('p_InOutParameter = ' || p_InOutParameter);
  END IF;

  /* Assign p_InOutParameter to v_LocalVariable. This is legal,
     since we are reading from an IN OUT parameter. */
  v_LocalVariable := p_InOutParameter;

  /* Assign 8 to p_InOutParameter. This is legal, since we
     are writing to an IN OUT parameter. */
  p_InOutParameter := 8;

  DBMS_OUTPUT.PUT('At end of ModeInOut: ');
  IF (p_InOutParameter IS NULL) THEN
```

```
      DBMS_OUTPUT.PUT_LINE('p_InOutParameter is NULL');
    ELSE
      DBMS_OUTPUT.PUT_LINE('p_InOutParameter = ' || p_InOutParameter);
    END IF;
END ModeInOut;
```

The following SQL*Plus session illustrates a successful call to `ModeInOut`:

```
-- Available online as part of parameterModes.sql
SQL> DECLARE
  2    v_InOut NUMBER := 1;
  3  BEGIN
  4    -- Call ModeInOut with a variable, which should be modified.
  5    DBMS_OUTPUT.PUT_LINE('Before calling ModeInOut, v_InOut = ' ||
  6                         v_InOut);
  7    ModeInOut(v_InOut);
  8    DBMS_OUTPUT.PUT_LINE('After calling ModeInOut, v_InOut = ' ||
  9                         v_InOut);
 10  END;
 11  /
Before calling ModeInOut, v_InOut = 1
Inside ModeInOut: p_InOutParameter = 1
At end of ModeInOut: p_InOutParameter = 8
After calling ModeInOut, v_InOut = 8
PL/SQL procedure successfully completed.
```

This differs from the output of `ModeOut` in one significant manner: the formal parameter `p_InOutParameter` is initialized with the value of the actual variable `v_InOut`. As with `ModeOut`, however, the final value of the formal parameter `p_InOutParameter` is copied to the actual parameter variable `v_InOut` upon return from the procedure.

Literals or Constants as Actual Parameters Because of this copying, the actual parameter that corresponds to an OUT or IN OUT formal parameter must be a variable; it cannot be a constant or expression. There must be a location where the returned value can be stored. The PL/SQL compiler will detect this situation and raise an error, as the following SQL*Plus session illustrates:

```
-- Available online as part of parameterModes.sql
SQL> BEGIN
  2    -- We cannot call ModeOut (or ModeInOut) with a constant, since
  3    -- the actual parameter must identify a storage location.
  4    ModeOut(3);
  5  END;
  6  /
  ModeOut(3);
```

```
              *
ERROR at line 4:
ORA-06550: line 4, column 11:
PLS-00363: expression '3' cannot be used as an assignment target
ORA-06550: line 4, column 3:
PL/SQL: Statement ignored
```

We can, however, use a constant actual parameter for a formal IN parameter without error:

```
-- Available online as part of parameterModes.sql
SQL> BEGIN
  2    -- We can call ModeIn with a constant, though.
  3    ModeIn(3);
  4  END;
  5  /
Inside ModeIn: p_InParameter = 3
At end of ModeIn: p_InParameter = 3
PL/SQL procedure successfully completed.
```

As expected, the formal parameter p_InParameter is unchanged throughout the execution of the procedure.

Modification of IN Parameters   In addition to checking the validity of OUT actual parameters as we saw in the previous section, the PL/SQL compiler will also check to ensure that an IN formal parameter is not modified, as the following SQL*Plus session shows:

```
-- Available online as part of parameterModes.sql
SQL> CREATE OR REPLACE PROCEDURE IllegalModeIn (
  2    p_InParameter IN NUMBER) AS
  3  BEGIN
  4    /* Assign 7 to p_InParameter. This is ILLEGAL, since we
  5       are writing to an IN parameter. */
  6    p_InParameter := 7;
  7  END IllegalModeIn;
  8  /
Warning: Procedure created with compilation errors.

SQL> show errors
Errors for PROCEDURE ILLEGALMODEIN:
LINE/COL ERROR
-------- ---------------------------------
6/3      PLS-00363: expression 'P_INPARAMETER' cannot be used as an
         assignment target
6/3      PL/SQL: Statement ignored
```

Constraints on Formal Parameters

When a procedure is called, the values of the actual parameters are passed in, and they are referred to using the formal parameters inside the procedure. The constraints on the variables are passed as well, as part of the parameter passing mechanism. In a procedure declaration, it is illegal to constrain CHAR and VARCHAR2 parameters with a length, or NUMBER parameters with a precision and/or scale, as the constraints will be taken from the actual parameters. For example, the following procedure declaration is illegal and will generate a compile error:

```
-- Available online as part of ParameterLength.sql
CREATE OR REPLACE PROCEDURE ParameterLength (
  p_Parameter1 IN OUT VARCHAR2(10),
  p_Parameter2 IN OUT NUMBER(3,1)) AS
BEGIN
  p_Parameter1 := 'abcdefghijklm'; - 15 characters in length
  p_Parameter2 := 12.3;
END ParameterLength;
```

The correct declaration for this procedure would be

```
-- Available online as part of ParameterLength.sql
CREATE OR REPLACE PROCEDURE ParameterLength (
  p_Parameter1 IN OUT VARCHAR2,
  p_Parameter2 IN OUT NUMBER) AS
BEGIN
  p_Parameter1 := 'abcdefghijklmno'; - 15 characters in length
  p_Parameter2 := 12.3;
END ParameterLength;
```

Given this example, what are the constraints on p_Parameter1 and p_Parameter2? They come from the actual parameters. If we call ParameterLength with

```
-- Available online as part of ParameterLength.sql
DECLARE
  v_Variable1 VARCHAR2(40);
  v_Variable2 NUMBER(7,3);
BEGIN
  ParameterLength(v_Variable1, v_Variable2);
END;
```

then p_Parameter1 will have a maximum length of 40 (coming from the actual parameter v_Variable1) and p_Parameter2 will have precision 7 and scale 3 (coming from the actual parameter v_Variable2). It is important to be aware of this. Consider the following block, which also calls ParameterLength:

```
-- Available online as part of ParameterLength.sql
DECLARE
  v_Variable1 VARCHAR2(10);
  v_Variable2 NUMBER(7,3);
BEGIN
  ParameterLength(v_Variable1, v_Variable2);
END;
```

The only difference between this block and the prior one is that v_Variable1, and hence p_Parameter1, has a length of 10 rather than 40. Since ParameterLength assigns a character string of length 15 to p_Parameter1 (and hence v_Variable1), there is not enough room in the string. This will result in the following Oracle errors when the procedure is called:

```
DECLARE
*
ERROR at line 1:
ORA-06502: PL/SQL: numeric or value error: character string buffer too small
ORA-06512: at "EXAMPLE.PARAMETERLENGTH", line 5
ORA-06512: at line 5
```

The source of the error is not in the procedure—it is in the code that calls the procedure. In addition, the ORA-6502 is a run-time error, not a compile error. Thus the block compiled successfully, and the error was actually raised when the procedure returned and the PL/SQL engine attempted to copy the actual value 'abcdefghijklmno' into the formal parameter.

TIP
In order to avoid errors such as ORA-6502, document any constraint requirements of the actual parameters when the procedure is created. This documentation could consist of comments stored with the procedure and include a description of what the procedure does in addition to any parameter definitions. Alternatively, you can use %TYPE to declare the formal parameters, as described in the next section.

%TYPE and Procedure Parameters   Although formal parameters cannot be declared with constraints, they can be constrained by using %TYPE. If a formal parameter is declared using %TYPE and the underlying type is constrained, the constraint will be on the formal parameter rather than the actual parameter. If we declare `ParameterLength` with

-- Available online as part of **ParameterLength.sql**

```
CREATE OR REPLACE PROCEDURE ParameterLength (
  p_Parameter1 IN OUT VARCHAR2,
  p_Parameter2 IN OUT books.copyright%TYPE) AS
BEGIN
  p_Parameter2 := 12345;
END ParameterLength;
```

`p_Parameter2` will be constrained with the precision of 3, because that is the precision of the `copyright` column. Even if we call `ParameterLength` with an actual parameter of enough precision, the formal precision is taken. Thus, the following example will generate the ORA-6502 error:

-- Available online as part of **ParameterLength.sql**

```
SQL> DECLARE
  2    v_Variable1 VARCHAR2(1);
  3    -- Declare v_Variable2 with no constraints
  4    v_Variable2 NUMBER;
  5  BEGIN
  6    -- Even though the actual parameter has room for 12345, the
  7    -- constraint on the formal parameter is taken and we get
  8    -- ORA-6502 on this procedure call.
  9    ParameterLength(v_Variable1, v_Variable2);
 10  END;
 11  /
DECLARE
*
ERROR at line 1:
ORA-06502: PL/SQL: numeric or value error: number precision too large
ORA-06512: at "EXAMPLE.PARAMETERLENGTH", line 5
ORA-06512: at line 9
```

NOTE
The text of the ORA-6502 error message was enhanced for Oracle8i. Prior to Oracle8i, the error is reported simply as "ORA-6502: PL/SQL numeric or value error", regardless of the actual cause of the error.

Exceptions Raised Inside Subprograms

If an error occurs inside a subprogram, an exception is raised. This exception may be user-defined or predefined. If the procedure has no exception handler for this error (or if an exception is raised from within an exception handler), control immediately passes out of the procedure to the calling environment, in accordance with the exception propagation rules (see Chapter 9 for more details). However, in this case, the values of OUT and IN OUT formal parameters are *not* returned to the actual parameters. The actual parameters will have the same values as they would have had if the procedure had not been called. For example, suppose we create the following procedure:

```
-- Available online as part of RaiseError.sql
/* Illustrates the behavior of unhandled exceptions and
 * OUT variables. If p_Raise is TRUE, then an unhandled
 * error is raised. If p_Raise is FALSE, the procedure
 * completes successfully.
 */
CREATE OR REPLACE PROCEDURE RaiseError (
  p_Raise IN BOOLEAN,
  p_ParameterA OUT NUMBER) AS
BEGIN
  p_ParameterA := 7;

  IF p_Raise THEN
    /* Even though we have assigned 7 to p_ParameterA, this
     * unhandled exception causes control to return immediately
     * without returning 7 to the actual parameter associated
     * with p_ParameterA.
     */
    RAISE DUP_VAL_ON_INDEX;
  ELSE
    -- Simply return with no error. This will return 7 to the
    -- actual parameter.
    RETURN;
  END IF;
END RaiseError;
```

If we call `RaiseError` with the following block:

```
-- Available online as part of RaiseError.sql
DECLARE
  v_Num NUMBER := 1;
BEGIN
  DBMS_OUTPUT.PUT_LINE('Value before first call: ' || v_Num);
  RaiseError(FALSE, v_Num);
```

```
DBMS_OUTPUT.PUT_LINE('Value after successful call: ' || v_Num);
DBMS_OUTPUT.PUT_LINE('');

v_Num := 2;
DBMS_OUTPUT.PUT_LINE('Value before second call: ' || v_Num);
RaiseError(TRUE, v_Num);
EXCEPTION
  WHEN OTHERS THEN
    DBMS_OUTPUT.PUT_LINE('Value after unsuccessful call: ' || v_Num);
END;
```

we get the following output:

```
Value before first call: 1
Value after successful call: 7

Value before second call: 2
Value after unsuccessful call: 2
```

Before the first call to RaiseError, v_Num contained 1. The first call was successful, and v_Num was assigned the value 7. The block then changed v_Num to 2 before the second call to RaiseError. This second call did not complete successfully, and v_Num was unchanged at 2 (rather than being changed to 7 again).

> **NOTE**
> *The semantics of exception handling change when an OUT or IN OUT parameter is declared with the NOCOPY hint. See the section "Exception Semantics with NOCOPY" later in this chapter for details.*

Passing Parameters by Reference and by Value

A subprogram parameter can be passed in one of two ways—by reference or by value. When a parameter is passed *by reference,* a pointer to the actual parameter is passed to the corresponding formal parameter. When a parameter is passed *by value,* on the other hand, it is copied from the actual parameter into the formal parameter. Passing by reference is generally faster, because it avoids the copy. This is especially true for collection parameters (tables and varrays, which we discussed in Chapter 6), due to their larger size. By default, PL/SQL will pass IN parameters by reference, and IN OUT and OUT parameters by value. This is done to preserve the exception semantics that we discussed in the previous section, and so that constraints on actual parameters can be verified. Prior to Oracle8i, there was no way to modify this behavior.

Using NOCOPY   Oracle8*i* includes a compiler hint known as NOCOPY. The syntax for declaring a parameter with this hint is

parameter_name [*mode*] NOCOPY *datatype*

where *parameter_name* is the name of the parameter, *mode* is the parameter mode (IN, OUT, or IN OUT), and *datatype* is the parameter datatype. If NOCOPY is present, the PL/SQL compiler will try to pass the parameter by reference, rather than by value. NOCOPY is a compiler hint, rather than a directive, so it will not always be taken (see the section "NOCOPY Restrictions" for details on when NOCOPY will be heeded). The following example illustrates the syntax of NOCOPY:

```
-- Available online as part of NoCopyTest.sql
CREATE OR REPLACE PROCEDURE NoCopyTest (
  p_InParameter     IN NUMBER,
  p_OutParameter    OUT NOCOPY VARCHAR2,
  p_InOutParameter IN OUT NOCOPY CHAR) IS
BEGIN
  NULL;
END NoCopyTest;
```

Using NOCOPY on an IN parameter will generate a compilation error, because IN parameters are always passed by reference and thus NOCOPY doesn't apply.

Exception Semantics with NOCOPY   When a parameter is passed by reference, any modifications to the formal parameter also modify the actual parameter, because both point to the same location. This means that if a procedure exits with an unhandled exception after the formal parameter has been changed, the original value of the actual parameter will be lost. Suppose we modify `RaiseError` to use NOCOPY, as follows:

```
-- Available online as part of NoCopyTest.sql
CREATE OR REPLACE PROCEDURE RaiseErrorNoCopy (
  p_Raise IN BOOLEAN,
  p_ParameterA OUT NOCOPY NUMBER) AS
BEGIN
  p_ParameterA := 7;
  IF p_Raise THEN
    RAISE DUP_VAL_ON_INDEX;
  ELSE
    RETURN;
  END IF;
END RaiseErrorCopy;
```

The only change is that `p_ParameterA` will now be passed by reference, rather than by value. Suppose we call `RaiseErrorNoCopy` with the following:

```
-- Available online as part of NoCopyTest.sql
  v_Num NUMBER := 1;
BEGIN
  DBMS_OUTPUT.PUT_LINE('Value before first call: ' || v_Num);
  RaiseErrorNoCopy(FALSE, v_Num);
  DBMS_OUTPUT.PUT_LINE('Value after successful call: ' || v_Num);
  DBMS_OUTPUT.PUT_LINE('');

  v_Num := 2;
  DBMS_OUTPUT.PUT_LINE('Value before second call: ' || v_Num);
  RaiseErrorNoCopy(TRUE, v_Num);
EXCEPTION
  WHEN OTHERS THEN
    DBMS_OUTPUT.PUT_LINE('Value after unsuccessful call: ' || v_Num);
END;
```

(This is the same block we saw earlier in the section "Exceptions Raised Inside Subprograms," except for calling `RaiseErrorNoCopy` instead of `RaiseError`.) The output of this block, however, is different now:

```
Value before first call: 1
Value after successful call: 7

Value before second call: 2
Value after unsuccessful call: 7
```

The actual parameter has been modified both times, even when the exception was raised.

NOCOPY Restrictions   In some cases, NOCOPY will be ignored, and the parameter will be passed by value. No error is generated in these cases. Remember that NOCOPY is a hint, and the compiler is not obligated to follow it. NOCOPY will be ignored in the following situations:

- The actual parameter is a member of an associative array. If the actual parameter is an entire array, however, this restriction does not apply.

- The actual parameter is constrained by a precision, scale, or NOT NULL constraint. This restriction does not apply to a character parameter constrained by a maximum length, though. The reason for this is that the PL/SQL compiler checks for constraint violations only when returning from a subprogram, when copying the value back from the formal parameter to the actual parameter. If there is a constraint violation, the original value of the actual parameter needs to be unchanged, which is impossible with NOCOPY.

- The actual and formal parameters are both records, and they were declared either implicitly as a loop control variable or using %ROWTYPE, and the constraints on the corresponding fields differ.

- Passing the actual parameter requires an implicit datatype conversion.

- The subprogram is involved in a remote procedure call (RPC). An RPC is a procedure call made over a database link to a remote server. Since the parameters must be transferred over the network, it is not possible to pass them by reference.

TIP
As the last point illustrates, if the subprogram is part of an RPC, NOCOPY will be ignored. If you modify an existing application to make some of the calls RPCs, rather than local calls, the exception semantics can change.

Benefits of NOCOPY   The primary advantage of NOCOPY is that it may increase performance. This is especially valuable when passing large PL/SQL arrays, as the following example illustrates:

```
-- Available online as CopyFast.sql
CREATE OR REPLACE PACKAGE CopyFast AS
  -- Associative array of books.
  TYPE BookArray IS
    TABLE OF books%ROWTYPE;

  -- Three procedures which take a parameter of BookArray, in
  -- different ways.  They each do nothing.
  PROCEDURE PassBooks1(p_Parameter IN BookArray);
  PROCEDURE PassBooks2(p_Parameter IN OUT BookArray);
  PROCEDURE PassBooks3(p_Parameter IN OUT NOCOPY BookArray);

  -- Test procedure.
  PROCEDURE Go;
END CopyFast;

CREATE OR REPLACE PACKAGE BODY CopyFast AS
  PROCEDURE PassBooks1(p_Parameter IN BookArray) IS
```

```
      BEGIN
        NULL;
      END PassBooks1;

      PROCEDURE PassBooks2(p_Parameter IN OUT BookArray) IS
      BEGIN
        NULL;
      END PassBooks2;

      PROCEDURE PassBooks3(p_Parameter IN OUT NOCOPY BookArray) IS
      BEGIN
        NULL;
      END PassBooks3;

      PROCEDURE Go IS
        v_BookArray BookArray := BookArray(NULL);
        v_Time1 NUMBER;
        v_Time2 NUMBER;
        v_Time3 NUMBER;
        v_Time4 NUMBER;
      BEGIN
        -- Fill up the array with 50,001 copies of a record.
        SELECT *
          INTO v_BookArray(1)
          FROM books
          WHERE ISBN = '72230665';
        v_BookArray.EXTEND(50000, 1);

        -- Call each version of PassBooks, and time them.
        -- DBMS_UTILITY.GET_TIME will return the current time, in
        -- hundredths of a second.
        v_Time1 := DBMS_UTILITY.GET_TIME;
        PassBooks1(v_BookArray);
        v_Time2 := DBMS_UTILITY.GET_TIME;
        PassBooks2(v_BookArray);
        v_Time3 := DBMS_UTILITY.GET_TIME;
        PassBooks3(v_BookArray);
        v_Time4 := DBMS_UTILITY.GET_TIME;

        -- Output the results.
        DBMS_OUTPUT.PUT_LINE('Time to pass IN: ' ||
                            TO_CHAR((v_Time2 - v_Time1) / 100));
        DBMS_OUTPUT.PUT_LINE('Time to pass IN OUT: ' ||
                            TO_CHAR((v_Time3 -   v_Time2) / 100));
        DBMS_OUTPUT.PUT_LINE('Time to pass IN OUT NOCOPY: ' ||
                            TO_CHAR((v_Time4 - v_Time3) / 100));
      END Go;
    END CopyFast;
```

NOTE
This example uses a package to group together related procedures. Packages are described in the section "Packages" later in this chapter. See also Chapter 6 for information on collections and how the EXTEND method is used, and Appendix B for information about DBMS_UTILITY.

Each of the `PassBooks` procedures does nothing—the procedures simply take a parameter that is an array of books. The parameter is 50,001 records, so it is reasonably large. The difference between the procedures is that `PassBooks1` takes the parameter as an IN, `PassBooks2` as an IN OUT, and `PassBooks3` as IN OUT NOCOPY. Thus, `PassBooks2` should pass the parameter by value and the other two by reference. We can see this by looking at the results of calling `CopyFast.Go`:

```
SQL> BEGIN
  2    CopyFast.Go;
  3  END;
  4  /
Time to pass IN: 0
Time to pass IN OUT: 1.27
Time to pass IN OUT NOCOPY: 0
PL/SQL procedure successfully completed.
```

Although the actual results may differ on your system, the time for passing the IN OUT parameter by value should be significantly more than passing the IN and IN OUT NOCOPY parameters by reference.

NOTE
Oracle10g has made changes to the PL/SQL optimizer, such that empty procedures may be optimized out. Thus, the time difference between the procedures may be less in Oracle10g and higher because the calls to the procedures have been removed. It is a good idea to test the performance impact of NOCOPY using your own system and data to determine realistic time savings.

Subprograms with No Parameters

If there are no parameters for a procedure, there are no parentheses in either the procedure declaration or the procedure call. This is also true for functions. The following example illustrates this:

```
-- Available online as noparams.sql
CREATE OR REPLACE PROCEDURE NoParamsP AS
BEGIN
  DBMS_OUTPUT.PUT_LINE('No Parameters!');
END NoParamsP;

CREATE OR REPLACE FUNCTION NoParamsF
  RETURN DATE AS
BEGIN
  RETURN SYSDATE;
END NoParamsF;

BEGIN
  NoParamsP;
  DBMS_OUTPUT.PUT_LINE('Calling NoParamsF on ' ||
    TO_CHAR(NoParamsF, 'DD-MON-YYYY'));
END;
```

NOTE
With the CALL syntax available with Oracle8i, the parentheses are optional. See the section "The CALL Statement" later in this chapter for details.

Positional and Named Notation

In all of the examples shown so far in this chapter, the actual arguments are associated with the formal arguments by position. Given a procedure declaration such as

```
-- Available online as part of CallMe.sql
CREATE OR REPLACE PROCEDURE CallMe(
  p_ParameterA VARCHAR2,
  p_ParameterB NUMBER,
  p_ParameterC BOOLEAN,
  p_ParameterD DATE) AS
BEGIN
  NULL;
END CallMe;
```

and a calling block such as

```
-- Available online as part of CallMe.sql
DECLARE
  v_Variable1 VARCHAR2(10);
  v_Variable2 NUMBER(7,6);
```

```
  v_Variable3 BOOLEAN;
  v_Variable4 DATE;
BEGIN
  CallMe(v_Variable1, v_Variable2, v_Variable3, v_Variable4);
END;
```

the actual parameters are associated with the formal parameters by position: v_
Variable1 is associated with p_ParameterA, v_Variable2 is associated
with p_ParameterB, and so on. This is known as *positional notation*. Positional
notation is more commonly used, and it is also the notation used in other 3GLs
such as C and Java.

Alternatively, we can call the procedure using *named notation*:

```
-- Available online as part of CallMe.sql
DECLARE
  v_Variable1 VARCHAR2(10);
  v_Variable2 NUMBER(7,6);
  v_Variable3 BOOLEAN;
  v_Variable4 DATE;
BEGIN
  CallMe(p_ParameterA => v_Variable1,
         p_ParameterB => v_Variable2,
         p_ParameterC => v_Variable3,
         p_ParameterD => v_Variable4);
END;
```

In named notation, the formal parameter and the actual parameter are both
included for each argument. This allows us to rearrange the order of the arguments,
if desired. For example, the following block also calls CallMe, with the same
arguments:

```
-- Available online as part of CallMe.sql
DECLARE
  v_Variable1 VARCHAR2(10);
  v_Variable2 NUMBER(7,6);
  v_Variable3 BOOLEAN;
  v_Variable4 DATE;
BEGIN
  CallMe(p_ParameterB => v_Variable2,
         p_ParameterC => v_Variable3,
         p_ParameterD => v_Variable4,
         p_ParameterA => v_Variable1);
END;
```

Positional and named notation can be mixed in the same call as well, if desired. The first arguments must be specified by position, and the remaining arguments can be specified by name. The following block illustrates this method:

```
-- Available online as part of CallMe.sql
DECLARE
  v_Variable1 VARCHAR2(10);
  v_Variable2 NUMBER(7,6);
  v_Variable3 BOOLEAN;
  v_Variable4 DATE;
BEGIN
  -- First 2 parameters passed by position, the second 2 are
  -- passed by name.
  CallMe(v_Variable1, v_Variable2,
         p_ParameterC => v_Variable3,
         p_ParameterD => v_Variable4);
END;
```

Named notation is another feature of PL/SQL that comes from Ada. When should you use positional notation, and when should you use named notation? Neither is more efficient than the other, so the only preference is one of style. Some of the style differences are illustrated in Table 8-2.

I generally use positional notation, as I prefer to write succinct code. It is important to use good names for the actual parameters, however. On the other hand, if the procedure takes a large number of arguments (more than ten is a good measure), named notation is desirable, because it is easier to match the formal and actual parameters. Procedures with this many arguments are fairly rare, however. Named notation is also useful for procedures with default arguments (see the next section for details).

TIP

The more parameters a procedure has, the more difficult it is to call and make sure that all of the required parameters are present. If you have a significant number of parameters that you would like to pass to or from a procedure, consider defining a record type with the parameters as fields within the record. Then you can use a single parameter of the record type. (Note that if the calling environment is not PL/SQL, you may not be able to bind a record type, however). PL/SQL has no explicit limit on the number of parameters.

Positional Notation	Named Notation
Relies more on good names for the actual parameters to illustrate what each is used for.	Clearly illustrates the association between the actual and formal parameters.
Names used for the formal and actual parameters are independent; one can be changed without modifying the other.	Can be more difficult to maintain because all calls to the procedure using named notation must be changed if the *names* of the formal parameters are changed.
Can be more difficult to maintain because all calls to the procedure using positional notation must be changed if the *order* of the formal parameters is changed.	The *order* used for the formal and actual parameters is independent; one can be changed without modifying the other.
More succinct than named notation.	Requires more coding, because both the formal and actual parameters are included in the procedure call. However, this additional coding serves to document the purpose of each actual parameter by explicitly including the associated formal parameter.
Parameters with default values must be at the end of the argument list.	Allows default values for formal parameters to be used, regardless of which parameter has the default.

TABLE 8-2. *Positional vs. Named Notation*

Parameter Default Values

As with variable declarations, the formal parameters to a procedure or function can have default values. If a parameter has a default value, it does not have to be passed from the calling environment. If it is passed, the value of the actual parameter will be used instead of the default. A default value for a parameter is included using the syntax

parameter_name [*mode*] [NOCOPY] *parameter_type*
  {:= | DEFAULT} *initial_value*

where *parameter_name* is the name of the formal parameter, *mode* is the parameter mode (IN, OUT, or IN OUT), *parameter_type* is the parameter type (either predefined or user-defined), and *initial_value* is the value to be assigned to the formal parameter by default. Either := or the DEFAULT keyword can be used. For example, consider the AddNewBook procedure:

```
-- Available online as part of AddNewBook.sql
CREATE OR REPLACE PROCEDURE AddNewBook(
  p_ISBN IN books.ISBN%TYPE,
  p_Category IN books.category%TYPE := 'Oracle Server',
  p_Title IN books.title%TYPE,
  p_NumPages IN books.num_pages%TYPE,
  p_Price IN books.price%TYPE,
  p_Copyright IN books.copyright%TYPE DEFAULT
TO_NUMBER(TO_CHAR(SYSDATE, 'YYYY')),
  p_Author1 IN books.author1%TYPE,
  p_Author2 IN books.author2%TYPE := NULL,
  p_Author3 IN books.author3%TYPE := NULL) AS

BEGIN
  -- Insert a new row into the table using the supplied
  -- parameters.
  INSERT INTO books (isbn, category, title, num_pages, price,
                     copyright, author1, author2, author3)
  VALUES (p_ISBN, p_Category, p_Title, p_NumPages, p_Price,
          p_Copyright, p_Author1, p_Author2, p_Author3);
END AddNewBook;
```

AddNewBook has four default parameters: p_Category, p_Copyright, p_Author2, and p_Author3. The default values for these parameters will be used if the formal parameter does not have an actual parameter associated with it in the procedure call. For example, we can avoid passing p_Author2 and p_Author3 with the following block:

```
-- Available online as part of AddNewBook.sql
BEGIN
  AddNewBook('0000000000', 'Oracle Basics', 'A Really Nifty Book',
             500, 34.99, 2004, 1);
END;
```

In this case, NULL will be used for both p_Author2 and p_Author3. We can also call AddNewBook with named notation:

```
-- Available online as part of AddNewBook.sql
BEGIN
  AddNewBook(p_ISBN => '0000000000',
             p_Category => 'Oracle Basics',
             p_Title => 'A Really Nifty Book',
             p_NumPages => 500,
```

```
                    p_Price => 34.99,
                    p_Copyright => 2004,
                    p_Author1 => 1);
END;
```

If positional notation is used, all parameters with default values that don't have an associated actual parameter must be at the end of the parameter list, as we saw in the first call to AddNewBook in the preceding example. If we wanted to use the default values for p_Category or p_Copyright, we would have to use named notation, as follows:

```
-- Available online as part of AddNewBook.sql
BEGIN
  AddNewBook(p_ISBN => '0000000000',
             p_Title => 'A Really Nifty Book',
             p_NumPages => 500,
             p_Price => 34.99,
             p_Author1 => 1);
END;
```

TIP
When using default values, make them the last parameters in the argument list if possible. This way, either positional or named notation can be used.

The CALL Statement

Oracle8*i* added a new SQL statement to call stored subprograms: the CALL statement, which can be used to call both PL/SQL and Java subprograms with a PL/SQL wrapper. It has the syntax given by the following railroad diagram:

Subprogram_name is a stand-alone or packaged subprogram. It can also be an object type method, and it can be at a remote database. The *argument_list* is a comma-separated list of arguments, and *host_variable* is a host variable used to retrieve the return value of functions. The following SQL*Plus session illustrates some legal and illegal uses of the CALL statement. This example uses the SQL*Plus VARIABLE command to declare a host variable; for more information on this command and other features of SQL*Plus, see the Oracle documentation.

```
-- Available online as calls.sql
SQL> CREATE OR REPLACE PROCEDURE CallProc1(p1 IN VARCHAR2 := NULL) AS
  2  BEGIN
  3    DBMS_OUTPUT.PUT_LINE('CallProc1 called with ' || p1);
  4  END CallProc1;
  5  /
Procedure created.

SQL> CREATE OR REPLACE PROCEDURE CallProc2(p1 IN OUT VARCHAR2) AS
  2  BEGIN
  3    DBMS_OUTPUT.PUT_LINE('CallProc2 called with ' || p1);
  4    p1 := p1 || ' returned!';
  5  END CallProc2;
  6  /
Procedure created.

SQL> CREATE OR REPLACE FUNCTION CallFunc(p1 IN VARCHAR2)
  2    RETURN VARCHAR2 AS
  3  BEGIN
  4    DBMS_OUTPUT.PUT_LINE('CallFunc called with ' || p1);
  5    RETURN p1;
  6  END CallFunc;
  7  /
Function created.

SQL> - Some valid calls direct from SQL.
SQL> CALL CallProc1('Hello!');
CallProc1 called with Hello!
Call completed.

SQL> CALL CallProc1();
CallProc1 called with
Call completed.

SQL> VARIABLE v_Output VARCHAR2(50);
SQL> CALL CallFunc('Hello!') INTO :v_Output;
CallFunc called with Hello!
Call completed.

SQL> PRINT v_Output
V_OUTPUT
-----------------------------------
Hello!

SQL> CALL CallProc2(:v_Output);
```

```
CallProc2 called with Hello!
Call completed.

SQL> PRINT v_Output
V_OUTPUT
-----------------------------------
Hello! returned!

SQL> - This is illegal
SQL> BEGIN
  2    CALL CallProc1();
  3  END;
  4  /
  CALL CallProc1();
       *
ERROR at line 2:
ORA-06550: line 2, column 8:
PLS-00103: Encountered the symbol "CALLPROC1" when expecting one of the
following:
:= . ( @ % ;
The symbol ":=" was substituted for "CALLPROC1" to continue.

SQL> - But these are legal
SQL> DECLARE
  2    v_Result VARCHAR2(50);
  3  BEGIN
  4    EXECUTE IMMEDIATE 'CALL CallProc1(''Hello from PL/SQL'')';
  5    EXECUTE IMMEDIATE
  6      'CALL CallFunc(''Hello from PL/SQL'') INTO :v_Result'
  7      USING OUT v_Result;
  8  END;
  9  /
CallProc1 called with Hello from PL/SQL
CallFunc called with Hello from PL/SQL
PL/SQL procedure successfully completed.
```

This example illustrates the following points:

- CALL is a SQL statement. It is not valid inside a PL/SQL block, but it is valid when executed using dynamic SQL, in this case, the EXECUTE IMMEDIATE statement. (Inside a PL/SQL block, you can call the subprogram using the PL/SQL syntax.) See Chapter 13 for more information about dynamic SQL.

- The parentheses are always required, even if the subprogram takes no arguments (or has default values for all the arguments).

- The INTO clause is used for the output variables of functions only. IN OUT or OUT parameters are specified as part of the *argument_list*.

Procedures vs. Functions

Procedures and functions share many of the same features:

- Both can return more than one value via OUT parameters.

- Both can have declarative, executable, and exception-handling sections.

- Both can accept default values.

- Both can be called using positional or named notation.

- Both can accept NOCOPY parameters.

So when is a function appropriate, and when is a procedure appropriate? It generally depends on how many values the subprogram is expected to return and how those values will be used. The rule of thumb is that if there is more than one return value, use a procedure. If there is only one return value, a function can be used. Although it is legal for a function to have OUT parameters (and thus return more than one value), it is generally considered poor programming style. Functions can also be called from within a SQL statement. (See Chapter 9 for more information.)

Packages

Another Ada feature incorporated in the design of PL/SQL is the *package*. A package is a PL/SQL construct that allows related objects to be stored together. A package has two separate parts: the specification and the body. Each of them is stored separately in the data dictionary. Unlike procedures and functions, which can be contained locally in a block or stored in the database, a package can only be stored; it cannot be local. Besides allowing related objects to be grouped together, packages are useful because they are less restrictive than stored subprograms with respect to dependencies. They also have performance advantages, which we will discuss later in the next chapter.

A package is essentially a named declarative section. Anything that can go in the declarative part of a block can go in a package. This includes procedures, functions, cursors, types, and variables. One advantage of putting these objects into a package is the ability to reference them from other PL/SQL blocks, so packages also provide global variables (within a single database session) for PL/SQL.

Package Specification

The *package specification* (also known as the *package header*) contains information about the contents of the package. However, it does not contain the code for any subprograms. Consider the following example:

```
-- Available online as part of InventoryOps.sql
CREATE OR REPLACE PACKAGE InventoryOps AS
```

```
-- Modifies the inventory data for the specified book.
PROCEDURE UpdateISBN(p_ISBN IN inventory.isbn%TYPE,
                     p_Status IN inventory.status%TYPE,
                     p_StatusDate IN inventory.status_date%TYPE,
                     p_Amount IN inventory.amount%TYPE);

-- Deletes the inventory data for the specified book.
PROCEDURE DeleteISBN(p_ISBN IN inventory.isbn%TYPE);

-- Exception raised by UpdateISBN or DeleteISBN when the specified
-- ISBN is not in the inventory table.
e_ISBNNotFound EXCEPTION;

TYPE t_ISBNTable IS TABLE OF inventory.isbn%TYPE
  INDEX BY BINARY_INTEGER;

-- Returns an array containing the books with the specified status.
PROCEDURE StatusList(p_Status IN inventory.status%TYPE,
                     p_Books OUT t_ISBNTable,
                     p_NumBooks OUT BINARY_INTEGER);
END InventoryOps;
```

InventoryOps contains three procedures, a type, and an exception. The general syntax for creating a package header is described by the following railroad diagram:

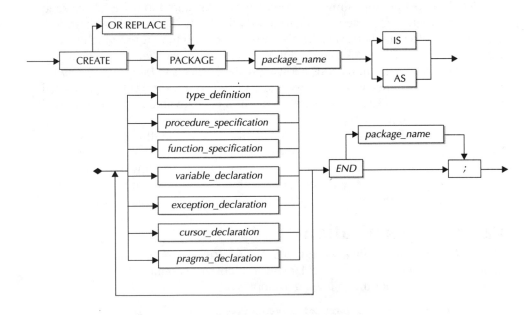

Package_name is the name of the package. The *elements* within the package (procedure and function specifications, variables, and so on) are the same as they would be in the declarative section of an anonymous block. The same syntax rules apply for a package header as for a declarative section, except for procedure and function declarations. These rules are as follows:

■ Package elements can appear in any order. However, as in a declarative section, an object must be declared before it is referenced. If a cursor contains a variable as part of the WHERE clause, for example, the variable must be declared before the cursor declaration.

■ All types of elements do not have to be present. A package can contain only procedure and function specifications, for example, without declaring any exceptions or types.

■ Any declarations for procedures and functions must be forward declarations. A *forward declaration* simply describes the subprogram and its arguments (if any); it does not include the code. This rule is different from the declarative section of a block, where both forward declarations and the actual code for procedures or functions may be found. The code that implements the package's procedures and functions is found in the package body.

Package Body

The *package body* is a separate data dictionary object from the package header. It cannot be successfully compiled unless the package header has already been successfully compiled. The body contains the code for the forward subprogram declarations in the package header. It can also contain additional declarations that are global to the package body but are not visible in the specification. The following example shows the package body for `InventoryOps`:

```
-- Available online as part of InventoryOps.sql
CREATE OR REPLACE PACKAGE BODY InventoryOps AS
  -- Modifies the inventory data for the specified book.
  PROCEDURE UpdateISBN(p_ISBN IN inventory.isbn%TYPE,
                       p_Status IN inventory.status%TYPE,
                       p_StatusDate IN inventory.status_date%TYPE,
                       p_Amount IN inventory.amount%TYPE) IS
  BEGIN
    UPDATE inventory
      SET status = p_Status, status_date = p_StatusDate, amount = p_Amount
      WHERE isbn = p_ISBN;

    -- Check for no books updated, and raise the exception.
    IF SQL%ROWCOUNT = 0 THEN
```

```
      RAISE e_ISBNNotFound;
    END IF;
END UpdateISBN;

-- Deletes the inventory data for the specified book.
PROCEDURE DeleteISBN(p_ISBN IN inventory.isbn%TYPE) IS
BEGIN
   DELETE FROM inventory
     WHERE isbn = p_ISBN;

   -- Check for no books deleted, and raise the exception.
   IF SQL%ROWCOUNT = 0 THEN
     RAISE e_ISBNNotFound;
   END IF;
END DeleteISBN;

-- Returns an array containing the books with the specified status.
PROCEDURE StatusList(p_Status IN inventory.status%TYPE,
                     p_Books OUT t_ISBNTable,
                     p_NumBooks OUT BINARY_INTEGER) IS
   v_ISBN inventory.isbn%TYPE;
   CURSOR c_Books IS
     SELECT isbn
       FROM inventory
       WHERE status = p_Status;

BEGIN
   /* p_NumBooks will be the array index. It will start at
    * 0, and be incremented each time through the fetch loop.
    * At the end of the loop, it will have the number of rows
    * fetched, and therefore the number of rows returned in
    * p_Books. */
   p_NumBooks := 0;
   OPEN c_Books;
   LOOP
     FETCH c_Books INTO v_ISBN;
     EXIT WHEN c_Books%NOTFOUND;

     p_NumBooks := p_NumBooks + 1;
     p_Books(p_NumBooks) := v_ISBN;
   END LOOP;
   CLOSE c_Books;
  END StatusList;
END InventoryOps;
```

The package body contains the code for the forward declarations in the package header and can also contain additional variables, cursors, types, or subprograms. Objects in the header that are not forward declarations (such as the e_ISBNNotFound exception) can be referenced directly in the package body.

The package body is optional. If the package header does not contain any procedures or functions (only variable declarations, cursors, types, and so on), the body does not have to be present. This technique is valuable for declaring global variables and types, because all objects in a package are visible outside the package. (Scope and visibility of packaged elements are discussed in the next section.)

Any forward declaration in the package header must be fleshed out in the package body. The specification for the procedure or function must be the same in both. This includes the name of the subprogram, the names of its parameters, and the modes of the parameters. For example, the following package header does not match the package body, because the body uses a different parameter list for `FunctionA`:

```
-- Available online as packageError.sql
CREATE OR REPLACE PACKAGE PackageA AS
   FUNCTION FunctionA(p_Parameter1 IN NUMBER,
                      p_Parameter2 IN DATE)
      RETURN VARCHAR2;
END PackageA;

CREATE OR REPLACE PACKAGE BODY PackageA AS
   FUNCTION FunctionA(p_Parameter1 IN CHAR)
      RETURN VARCHAR2;
END PackageA;
```

If we try to create `PackageA` as we did here, we get the following errors for the package body:

```
PLS-00328: A subprogram body must be defined for the forward
           declaration of FUNCTIONA.

PLS-00323: subprogram or cursor 'FUNCTIONA' is declared in a
           package specification and must be defined in the package
           body.
```

Packages and Scope

Any object declared in a package header is in scope and is visible outside the package, by qualifying the object with the package name. For example, we can call `InventoryOps.DeleteISBN` from the following PL/SQL block:

```
BEGIN
   InventoryOps.DeleteISBN('78824389');
END;
```

The procedure call is the same as it would be for a stand-alone procedure. The only difference is that it is prefixed by the package name. Packaged procedures can have default parameters, and they can be called using either positional or named notation, just like stand-alone stored procedures.

This also applies to user-defined types defined in the package. In order to call `StatusList`, for example, we need to declare a variable of type `InventoryOps.t_ISBNTable` (see Chapter 6 for more information on declaring and using PL/SQL collection types):

```
-- Available online as callSL.sql
DECLARE
  v_BooksInStock InventoryOps.t_ISBNTable;
  v_NumBooks BINARY_INTEGER;
BEGIN
  -- Fill the PL/SQL table with the ISBNs of the books which
  -- are in stock.
  InventoryOps.StatusList('IN STOCK', v_BooksInStock, v_NumBooks);

  -- And print them out.
  FOR v_LoopCounter IN 1..v_NumBooks LOOP
    DBMS_OUTPUT.PUT_LINE('ISBN ' || v_BooksInStock(v_LoopCounter) ||
                         ' is in stock');
  END LOOP;
END;
```

Inside the package body, objects in the header can be referenced without the package name. For example, the `UpdateISBN` and `DeleteISBN` procedures can reference the exception with simply `e_ISBNNotFound`, not `InventoryOps.e_ISBNNotFound`. The fully qualified name can be used if desired, however.

Scope of Objects in the Package Body

As currently written, `InventoryOps.UpdateISBN` and `InventoryOps.StatusList` do not validate the status that is passed in. We can do this by adding a procedure to the package body, as shown here:

```
-- Available online as part of InventoryOps2.sql
CREATE OR REPLACE PACKAGE BODY InventoryOps AS
  -- Validates the supplied status and raises an error if it is
  -- not IN STOCK, BACKORDERED, or FUTURE.
  PROCEDURE ValidateStatus(p_Status IN inventory.status%TYPE) IS
  BEGIN
    IF p_Status = 'IN STOCK' OR
       p_Status = 'BACKORDERED' OR
       p_Status = 'FUTURE' THEN
```

```
      RETURN;  - No error
   ELSE
     RAISE_APPLICATION_ERROR(20000,
        'Supplied status ' || p_Status || ' is not valid');
   END IF;
 END ValidateStatus;

-- Modifies the inventory data for the specified book.
 PROCEDURE UpdateISBN(p_ISBN IN inventory.isbn%TYPE,
                     p_Status IN inventory.status%TYPE,
                     p_StatusDate IN inventory.status_date%TYPE,
                     p_Amount IN inventory.amount%TYPE) IS
 BEGIN
  ValidateStatus(p_Status);
  UPDATE inventory
     SET status = p_Status, status_date = p_StatusDate, amount = p_Amount
     WHERE isbn = p_ISBN;

    -- Check for no books updated, and raise the exception.
    IF SQL%ROWCOUNT = 0 THEN
      RAISE e_ISBNNotFound;
    END IF;
 END UpdateISBN;

  ...

 -- Returns a PL/SQL table containing the books with the specified
 -- status.
 PROCEDURE StatusList(p_Status IN inventory.status%TYPE,
                     p_Books OUT t_ISBNTable,
                     p_NumBooks OUT BINARY_INTEGER) IS
   v_ISBN inventory.isbn%TYPE;
   CURSOR c_Books IS
     SELECT isbn
       FROM inventory
       WHERE status = p_Status;

 BEGIN
  ValidateStatus(p_Status);
    ...
 END StatusList;
END InventoryOps;
```

ValidateStatus is declared local to the package body. Its scope is therefore the package body itself. Consequently, it can be called from other procedures in the body (namely UpdateISBN and StatusList), but it is not visible from outside the body.

Overloading Packaged Subprograms

Inside a package, procedures and functions can be *overloaded*. This means that there is more than one procedure or function with the same name, but with different parameters. This is a very useful feature, because it allows the same operation to be applied to objects of different types. For example, suppose we want StatusList to return either an array of books, or an opened cursor selecting the books with the specified status. We could do this by modifying InventoryOps as follows:

```
-- Available online as part of overload.sql
CREATE OR REPLACE PACKAGE InventoryOps AS
  ...
  -- Returns an array containing the books with the specified status.
  PROCEDURE StatusList(p_Status IN inventory.status%TYPE,
                       p_Books OUT t_ISBNTable,
                       p_NumBooks OUT BINARY_INTEGER);


  TYPE c_ISBNCur IS REF CURSOR;

  -- Returns an opened cursor containing the books with the specified
  -- status.
  PROCEDURE StatusList(p_Status IN inventory.status%TYPE,
                       p_BookCur OUT c_ISBNCur);
END InventoryOps;

CREATE OR REPLACE PACKAGE BODY InventoryOps AS
  ...
  -- Returns an array containing the books with the specified status.
  PROCEDURE StatusList(p_Status IN inventory.status%TYPE,
                       p_Books OUT t_ISBNTable,
                       p_NumBooks OUT BINARY_INTEGER) IS
    v_ISBN inventory.isbn%TYPE;
    CURSOR c_Books IS
      SELECT isbn
        FROM inventory
        WHERE status = p_Status;

  BEGIN
    ValidateStatus(p_Status);

    /* p_NumBooks will be the array index. It will start at
     * 0, and be incremented each time through the fetch loop.
     * At the end of the loop, it will have the number of rows
     * fetched, and therefore the number of rows returned in
     * p_Books. */
    p_NumBooks := 0;
    OPEN c_Books;
```

```
    LOOP
      FETCH c_Books INTO v_ISBN;
      EXIT WHEN c_Books%NOTFOUND;

      p_NumBooks := p_NumBooks + 1;
      p_Books(p_NumBooks) := v_ISBN;
    END LOOP;
    CLOSE c_Books;
  END StatusList;


  -- Returns an opened cursor containing the books with the specified
  -- status.
  PROCEDURE StatusList(p_Status IN inventory.status%TYPE,
                       p_BookCur OUT c_ISBNCur) IS
  BEGIN
    ValidateStatus(p_Status);
    OPEN p_BookCur FOR
      SELECT isbn
        FROM inventory
        WHERE status = p_Status;
  END StatusList;
END InventoryOps;
```

The following SQL*Plus session illustrates both calls to InventoryOps.StatusList:

```
-- Available online as part of overload.sql
SQL> DECLARE
  2    v_BooksInStock InventoryOps.t_ISBNTable;
  3    v_NumBooks BINARY_INTEGER;
  4    v_BookCur InventoryOps.c_ISBNCur;
  5    v_ISBN inventory.isbn%TYPE;
  6  BEGIN
  7    DBMS_OUTPUT.PUT_LINE('First version of StatusList:');
  8    -- Fill the PL/SQL table with the ISBNs of the books which
  9    -- are backordered.
 10    InventoryOps.StatusList('BACKORDERED', v_BooksInStock, v_NumBooks);
 11
 12    -- And print them out.
 13    FOR v_LoopCounter IN 1..v_NumBooks LOOP
 14      DBMS_OUTPUT.PUT_LINE(' ISBN ' || v_BooksInStock(v_LoopCounter) ||
 15                         ' is backordered');
 16    END LOOP;
 17
 18    DBMS_OUTPUT.PUT_LINE('Second version of StatusList:');
 19    -- Get an opened cursor with the ISBNs of the books which are
 20    -- backordered.
 21    InventoryOps.StatusList('BACKORDERED', v_BookCur);
```

```
22
23    -- And print them out.
24    LOOP
25      FETCH v_BookCur INTO v_ISBN;
26      EXIT WHEN v_BookCur%NOTFOUND;
27      DBMS_OUTPUT.PUT_LINE(' ISBN ' || v_ISBN || ' is backordered');
28    END LOOP;
29    CLOSE v_BookCur;
30  END;
31  /
First version of StatusList:
ISBN 72121203   is backordered
ISBN 78824389   is backordered
Second version of StatusList:
ISBN 72121203   is backordered
ISBN 78824389   is backordered
PL/SQL procedure successfully completed.
```

Overloading can be a very useful technique when the same operation can be done on arguments of different types. Overloading is subject to several restrictions, however.

- You cannot overload two subprograms if their parameters differ only in name or mode. The following two procedures cannot be overloaded, for example:

  ```
  PROCEDURE OverloadMe(p_TheParameter IN NUMBER);
  PROCEDURE OverloadMe(p_TheParameter OUT NUMBER);
  ```

- You cannot overload two functions that differ only in their return type. For example, the following functions cannot be overloaded:

  ```
  FUNCTION OverloadMeToo RETURN DATE;
  FUNCTION OverloadMeToo RETURN NUMBER;
  ```

- The parameters of overloaded functions must differ by type family—you cannot overload on the same family. For example, since both CHAR and VARCHAR2 are in the same family, you can't overload the following procedures:

  ```
  PROCEDURE OverloadChar(p_TheParameter IN CHAR);
  PROCEDURE OverloadChar(p_TheParameter IN VARCHAR2);
  ```

- In Oracle10gR1, however, you can overload two subprograms if their parameters differ only in numeric datatype, such as BINARY_FLOAT vs. BINARY_DOUBLE. This is primarily useful for mathematical functions.

NOTE
The PL/SQL compiler will actually allow you to create a package that has subprograms that violate the preceding restrictions. However, the run-time engine will not be able to resolve the references and will always generate a "PLS-307: Too many declarations of 'subprogram' match this call" error.

Object Types and Overloading

Packaged subprograms can also be overloaded through use of user-defined object types. For example, suppose we create the following two object types:

```
-- Available online as part of objectOverload.sql
CREATE OR REPLACE TYPE t1 AS OBJECT (
  f NUMBER
);

CREATE OR REPLACE TYPE t2 AS OBJECT (
  f NUMBER
);
```

We can now create a package and package body that contains procedures that are overloaded in terms of the object type of their parameter:

```
-- Available online as part of objectOverload.sql
CREATE OR REPLACE PACKAGE Overload AS
  PROCEDURE Proc(p_Parameter1 IN t1);
  PROCEDURE Proc(p_Parameter1 IN t2);
END Overload;

CREATE OR REPLACE PACKAGE BODY Overload AS
  PROCEDURE Proc(p_Parameter1 IN t1) IS
  BEGIN
    DBMS_OUTPUT.PUT_LINE('Proc(t1): ' || p_Parameter1.f);
  END Proc;

  PROCEDURE Proc(p_Parameter1 IN t2) IS
  BEGIN
    DBMS_OUTPUT.PUT_LINE('Proc(t2): ' || p_Parameter1.f);
  END Proc;
END Overload;
```

As the following example shows, the correct procedure is called to correspond to the type of argument:

```
-- Available online as part of objectOverload.sql
SQL> DECLARE
  2     v_Obj1 t1 := t1(1);
  3     v_OBj2 t2 := t2(2);
  4  BEGIN
  5    Overload.Proc(v_Obj1);
  6    Overload.proc(v_Obj2);
  7  END;
  8  /
Proc(t1): 1
Proc(t2): 2
PL/SQL procedure successfully completed.
```

See Chapters 14 and 15 for more information on object types.

Package Initialization

The first time a packaged subprogram is called, or any reference to a packaged variable or type is made, the package is *instantiated.* This means that the package is read from disk into memory, and the compiled code of the called subprogram is run. At this point, memory is allocated for all variables defined in the package. Each session will have its own copy of packaged variables, ensuring that two sessions executing subprograms in the same package use different memory locations.

In many cases, initialization code needs to be run the first time the package is instantiated within a session. This can be done by adding an initialization section to the package body, after all other objects, with the syntax

CREATE OR REPLACE PACKAGE BODY *package_name* {IS | AS}

  ...

BEGIN
  initialization_code;
END [*package_name*];

where *package_name* is the name of the package, and *initialization_code* is the code to be run. For example, the following package implements a random number function:

```
-- Available online as Random.sql
CREATE OR REPLACE PACKAGE Random AS
  -- Random number generator.  Uses the same algorithm as the
  -- rand() function in C.

  -- Used to change the seed.  From a given seed, the same
  -- sequence of random numbers will be generated.
```

```
    PROCEDURE ChangeSeed(p_NewSeed IN NUMBER);

    -- Returns a random integer between 1 and 32767.
    FUNCTION Rand RETURN NUMBER;

    -- Same as Rand, but with a procedural interface.
    PROCEDURE GetRand(p_RandomNumber OUT NUMBER);

    -- Returns a random integer between 1 and p_MaxVal.
    FUNCTION RandMax(p_MaxVal IN NUMBER) RETURN NUMBER;

    -- Same as RandMax, but with a procedural interface.
    PROCEDURE GetRandMax(p_RandomNumber OUT NUMBER,
                         p_MaxVal IN NUMBER);
END Random;

CREATE OR REPLACE PACKAGE BODY Random AS

    /* Used for calculating the next number. */
    v_Multiplier   CONSTANT NUMBER := 22695477;
    v_Increment    CONSTANT NUMBER := 1;

    /* Seed used to generate random sequence. */
    v_Seed          number := 1;

    PROCEDURE ChangeSeed(p_NewSeed IN NUMBER) IS
    BEGIN
      v_Seed := p_NewSeed;
    END ChangeSeed;

    FUNCTION Rand RETURN NUMBER IS
    BEGIN
      v_Seed := MOD(v_Multiplier * v_Seed + v_Increment,
                   (2 ** 32));
      RETURN BITAND(v_Seed/(2 ** 16), 32767);
    END Rand;

    PROCEDURE GetRand(p_RandomNumber OUT NUMBER) IS
    BEGIN
      -- Simply call Rand and return the value.
      p_RandomNumber := Rand;
    END GetRand;

    FUNCTION RandMax(p_MaxVal IN NUMBER) RETURN NUMBER IS
    BEGIN
      RETURN MOD(Rand, p_MaxVal) + 1;
    END RandMax;
```

```
PROCEDURE GetRandMax(p_RandomNumber OUT NUMBER,
                     p_MaxVal IN NUMBER) IS
BEGIN
  -- Simply call RandMax and return the value.
  p_RandomNumber := RandMax(p_MaxVal);
END GetRandMax;

BEGIN
  /* Package initialization.  Initialize the seed to the current
     time in seconds. */
  ChangeSeed(TO_NUMBER(TO_CHAR(SYSDATE, 'SSSSS')));
END Random;
```

In order to retrieve a random number, you can simply call `Random.Rand`. The sequence of random numbers is controlled by the initial seed—the same sequence is generated for a given seed. Thus, in order to provide more random values, we need to initialize the seed to a different value each time the package is instantiated. To accomplish this, the `ChangeSeed` procedure is called from the package initialization section.

NOTE
Oracle includes a built-in package DBMS_RANDOM, which can also be used to provide random numbers. See Appendix B for more information on the built-in packages.

Summary

We have examined three types of named PL/SQL blocks in this chapter: procedures, functions, and packages. We discussed the syntax for creating each of these, paying particular attention to various types of parameter passing. In the next chapter, we will see more uses of procedures, functions, and packages. Chapter 9 will focus on types of subprograms, how they are stored in the data dictionary, and calling stored subprograms from SQL statements. In Chapter 10, we will cover a fourth type of named block: database triggers.

CHAPTER
9

Using Procedures, Functions, and Packages

I n the last chapter, we discussed the details of creating procedures, packages, and functions. In this chapter, we will look at some of their features, including the difference between stored and local subprograms, how stored subprograms interact with the data dictionary, and how to call stored subprograms from SQL statements. We will also examine some features of stored subprograms new in Oracle9*i* and Oracle10*g*. The examples we use are dependent on database tables found in `tables.sql`. We need to run `tables.sql` before testing the example files. We will examine triggers in Chapter 10.

Subprogram Locations

Subprograms and packages can be stored in the data dictionary, as all of the examples in the preceding chapter have shown. The subprogram is first created with the CREATE OR REPLACE command, and then it is called from another PL/SQL block. In addition to this, however, a subprogram can be defined within the declarative section of a block. In this case, it is known as a *local subprogram*. Packages must be stored in the data dictionary and cannot be local.

Stored Subprograms and the Data Dictionary

When a subprogram is created with CREATE OR REPLACE, it is stored in the data dictionary. In addition to the source text, the subprogram is stored in compiled form, which is known as *p-code*. The p-code has all of the references in the subprogram evaluated, and the source code is translated into a form that is easily readable by the PL/SQL engine. When the subprogram is called, the p-code is read from disk, if necessary, and executed. Once it is read from disk, the p-code is stored in the shared pool portion of the system global area (SGA), where multiple users can access it as needed. Like all of the contents of the shared pool, p-code is aged out of the shared pool according to a least recently used (LRU) algorithm.

P-code is analogous to the object code generated by other 3GL compilers, or to Java bytecodes that can be read by a Java run-time system. Since the p-code has the object references in the subprogram evaluated (this is a property of early binding, which we saw in Chapter 5), executing the p-code is a comparatively inexpensive operation.

NOTE
Beginning with Oracle9i, you may compile subprograms into native operating system code rather than p-code. See the section "Native Compilation" later in this chapter for more details.

Information about the subprogram is accessible through various data dictionary views. The USER_OBJECTS view contains information about all objects owned by the current user, including stored subprograms. This information includes when the object was created and last modified, the type of object (table, sequence, function, and so on), and the validity of the object. The USER_SOURCE view contains the original source code for the object. The USER_ERRORS view contains information about compile errors.

Consider the following simple procedure:

```
-- Available online as part of Simple.sql
CREATE OR REPLACE PROCEDURE Simple AS
  v_Counter NUMBER;
BEGIN
  v_Counter := 7;
END Simple;
/
```

After this procedure is created, USER_OBJECTS shows it as valid, and USER_SOURCE contains the source code for it. USER_ERRORS has no rows, because the procedure was compiled successfully. This is illustrated by the following SQL*Plus session.

```
-- Available online as part of Simple.sql
SELECT object_name, object_type, status
FROM user_objects
WHERE object_name = 'SIMPLE';
```

The output for the query is shown here:

```
OBJECT_NAME                    OBJECT_TYPE        STATUS
------------------ ---------- ----
SIMPLE                         PROCEDURE          VALID
```

You may see the source code by using this query:

```
SELECT text
FROM user_source
WHERE name = 'SIMPLE'
ORDER BY line;
```

The query returns the plain text for the stored object.

```
TEXT
--------------------------------
PROCEDURE Simple AS
```

```
   v_Counter NUMBER;
BEGIN
   v_Counter := 7;
END Simple;
```

A query of the USER_ERRORS table after compiling the procedure will select no rows.

```
SELECT line, position, text
FROM user_errors
WHERE name = 'SIMPLE'
ORDER BY sequence;
```

Suppose, however, we change the code of Simple so that it has a compile error (note the missing semicolon after the number 7), such as

```
-- Available online as part of Simple.sql
CREATE OR REPLACE PROCEDURE Simple AS
   v_Counter NUMBER;
BEGIN
   v_Counter := 7
END Simple;
/
```

and examine the same the USER_OBJECTS data dictionary view. We would see the source code missing the statement semicolon. Querying the USER_ERRORS view, we will see the following PLS-103 error by setting the SQL*Plus formatting parameters noted.

```
COL line FORMAT 999
COL position FORMAT 999
COL text FORMAT
SELECT line, position, text
FROM user_errors
WHERE name = 'SIMPLE'
ORDER BY sequence;
```

The query shows the following error message:

```
LINE POSITION TEXT
---- -------- ------------------------------
   5        1 PLS-00103: Encountered the symbol "END" when expecting one of
             the following:

             * & = - + ; < / > at in is mod remainder not rem
```

```
<an exponent (**)> <> or != or ~= >= <= <> and or like
between || multiset member SUBMULTISET_
The symbol ";" was substituted for "END" to continue.
```

TIP
In SQL*Plus, the SHOW ERRORS command queries USER_ERRORS for you and formats the output for readability. It will return information about errors for the last object that you created. You can use SHOW ERRORS after receiving the message "Warning: Procedure created with compilation errors." See Chapter 2 for more information on SQL*Plus. Other PL/SQL development tools have their own mechanisms for querying compilation errors such as these.

A stored subprogram that is invalid is still stored in the database. However, it cannot be called successfully until the error is fixed. If an invalid procedure is called, the PLS-905 error is returned. Next, we attempt to call the invalid stored procedure.

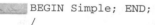
```
BEGIN Simple; END;
/
```

The attempted execution of an invalid stored object raises a PLS-905 error.

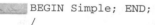
```
BEGIN Simple; END;
       *
ERROR at line 1:

ORA-06550: line 1, column 7:
PLS-00905: object EXAMPLE.SIMPLE is invalid
ORA-06550: line 1, column 7:
PL/SQL: Statement ignored
```

The data dictionary is discussed in more detail in Appendix C.

Local Subprograms

A local subprogram, declared in the declarative section of a PL/SQL block, is illustrated in the following example. If we have not run `tables.sql` at this point, the `localSub.sql` script will fail.

```
-- Available online as localSub.sql
SET SERVEROUTPUT ON SIZE 1000000
DECLARE
  CURSOR c_SomeAuthors IS
    SELECT first_name, last_name
    FROM authors
    WHERE last_name > 'L'
    ORDER BY last_name;

  v_FormattedName VARCHAR2(50);

  /* Function which will return the first and last name
     concatenated together, separated by a space. */
  FUNCTION FormatName(p_FirstName IN VARCHAR2,
                      p_LastName IN VARCHAR2)
  RETURN VARCHAR2 IS
  BEGIN
    RETURN p_FirstName || ' ' || p_LastName;
  END FormatName;

-- Begin main block.
BEGIN
  FOR v_AuthorRecord IN c_SomeAuthors LOOP
    v_FormattedName := FormatName(v_AuthorRecord.first_name,
                                  v_AuthorRecord.last_name);
    DBMS_OUTPUT.PUT_LINE(v_FormattedName);
  END LOOP;
END;
/
```

The anonymous PL/SQL block returns the following to the console:

```
Kevin Loney
Dan Natchek
Aaron Newman
Rich Niemic
Jason Price
Simon Russell
Sumit Sarin
Mark Scardina
Dirk Schepanek
Graham Seibert
Kenny Smith
Marlene Theriault
Joe Trezzo
Scott Urman
Gaja Vaidyanatha
```

```
Steve Vandivier
Rama Velpuri
James Viscusi
Jinyu Wang
PL/SQL procedure successfully completed.
```

The `FormatName` function is declared in the declarative section of the block. The function name is a PL/SQL identifier and thus follows the same scope and visibility rules as any other PL/SQL identifier. Specifically, it is visible only in the block in which it is declared. Its scope extends from the point of declaration until the end of the block. No other block can call `FormatName`, since it would not be visible from another block.

Local Subprograms as Part of Stored Subprograms

Local subprograms can also be declared as part of the declarative section of a stored subprogram, as the following example illustrates. In this case, `FormatName` can be called only from within `StoredProc`, since that is the limit of its scope.

```sql
-- Available online as part of localStored.sql
CREATE OR REPLACE PROCEDURE StoredProc AS
  /* Local declarations, which include a cursor, variable, and a
     function. */

  CURSOR c_SomeAuthors IS
    SELECT first_name, last_name
      FROM authors
      WHERE last_name > 'L'
      ORDER BY last_name;

  v_FormattedName VARCHAR2(50);

  /* Function which will return the first and last name
     concatenated together, separated by a space. */
  FUNCTION FormatName(p_FirstName IN VARCHAR2,
                      p_LastName IN VARCHAR2)
    RETURN VARCHAR2 IS
  BEGIN
    RETURN p_FirstName || ' ' || p_LastName;
  END FormatName;

-- Begin main block.
BEGIN
  FOR v_AuthorRecord IN c_SomeAuthors LOOP
    v_FormattedName := FormatName(v_AuthorRecord.first_name,
                                  v_AuthorRecord.last_name);
```

```
    DBMS_OUTPUT.PUT_LINE(v_FormattedName);
  END LOOP;
END StoredProc;
/
```

Given the preceding stored procedure, we can call it and receive the same output as for the previous anonymous block example, as follows:

```
-- Available online as part of localStored.sql
SET SERVEROUTPUT ON SIZE 1000000
BEGIN StoredProc; END;
/
```

The anonymous PL/SQL block returns the following to the console:

```
Kevin Loney
Dan Natchek
Aaron Newman
Rich Niemic
Jason Price
Simon Russell
Sumit Sarin
Mark Scardina
Dirk Schepanek
Graham Seibert
Kenny Smith
Marlene Theriault
Joe Trezzo
Scott Urman
Gaja Vaidyanatha
Steve Vandivier
Rama Velpuri
James Viscusi
Jinyu Wang
PL/SQL procedure successfully completed.
```

Location of Local Subprograms

Any local subprogram must be declared at the end of the declarative section. If we were to move `FormatName` above the declaration for `c_SomeAuthors`, as the following SQL*Plus session illustrates, we would get a compile error:

```
-- Available online as localError.sql
DECLARE
  /* Declare FormatName first. This will generate a compile
     error, since all other declarations have to be before
```

```
      any local subprograms. */
    FUNCTION FormatName(p_FirstName IN VARCHAR2,
                        p_LastName IN VARCHAR2)
    RETURN VARCHAR2 IS
    BEGIN
      RETURN p_FirstName || ' ' || p_LastName;
    END FormatName;

    CURSOR c_SomeAuthors IS
      SELECT first_name, last_name
      FROM authors
      WHERE last_name > 'L'
      ORDER BY last_name;

    v_FormattedName VARCHAR2(50);

  -- Begin main block.
  BEGIN
    FOR v_AuthorRecord IN c_SomeAuthors LOOP
      v_FormattedName := FormatName(v_AuthorRecord.first_name,
                                    v_AuthorRecord.last_name);
      DBMS_OUTPUT.PUT_LINE(v_FormattedName);
    END LOOP;
  END;
  /
```

The anonymous PL/SQL block fails because declarations follow the locally scoped `FormatName` function. When run, it will raise the following error:

```
  CURSOR c_SomeAuthors IS
  *
ERROR at line 12:
ORA-06550: line 12, column 3:
PLS-00103: Encountered the symbol "CURSOR" when expecting one of the following:
begin function package pragma procedure form
```

Forward Declarations

Since the names of local PL/SQL subprograms are identifiers, they must be declared before they are referenced. This is normally not a problem. However, in the case of mutually referential subprograms, this does present a difficulty. Consider the following example:

```
-- Available online as part of forwardDeclarations.sql
DECLARE
  v_TempVal BINARY_INTEGER := 5;
```

```
  -- Local procedure A. Note that the code of A calls procedure B.
  PROCEDURE A(p_Counter IN OUT BINARY_INTEGER) IS
    BEGIN
      DBMS_OUTPUT.PUT_LINE('A(' || p_Counter || ')');
        IF p_Counter > 0 THEN
          B(p_Counter);
          p_Counter := p_Counter - 1;
        END IF;
    END A;

  -- Local procedure B. Note that the code of B calls procedure A.
  PROCEDURE B(p_Counter IN OUT BINARY_INTEGER) IS
    BEGIN
      DBMS_OUTPUT.PUT_LINE('B(' || p_Counter || ')');
      p_Counter := p_Counter - 1;
      A(p_Counter);
END B;
BEGIN
  B(v_TempVal);
END;
/
```

The anonymous PL/SQL block fails because the A procedure does not have a forward reference to the B procedure. When run, it will raise the following error:

```
DECLARE
*
ERROR at line 1:
ORA-06550: line 9, column 7:
PLS-00313: 'B' not declared in this scope
ORA-06550: line 9, column 7:
PL/SQL: Statement ignored
```

The example fails to compile. Procedure A cannot call procedure B unless B is declared prior to A to resolve the reference to B. Likewise, procedure B calls procedure A, so A must be declared prior to B to resolve the reference to A. Both conditions cannot be true without a forward declaration. A forward declaration is a procedure name that may include formal parameters. It enables mutually referential procedures to exist. Forward declarations are also used in package specifications. The following example illustrates the technique:

```
-- Available online as part of forwardDeclarations.sql
SET SERVEROUTPUT ON SIZE 1000000
DECLARE
```

```
  v_TempVal BINARY_INTEGER := 5;

  -- Forward declaration of procedure B.
  PROCEDURE B(p_Counter IN OUT BINARY_INTEGER);

  PROCEDURE A(p_Counter IN OUT BINARY_INTEGER) IS
  BEGIN
    DBMS_OUTPUT.PUT_LINE('A(' || p_Counter || ')');
    IF p_Counter > 0 THEN
      B(p_Counter);
      p_Counter := p_Counter - 1;
    END IF;
  END A;

  PROCEDURE B(p_Counter IN OUT BINARY_INTEGER) IS
  BEGIN
    DBMS_OUTPUT.PUT_LINE('B(' || p_Counter || ')');
    p_Counter := p_Counter - 1;
    A(p_Counter);
  END B;
BEGIN
  B(v_TempVal);
END;
/
```

The output from the preceding block is shown here:

```
B(5)
A(4)
B(4)
A(3)
B(3)
A(2)
B(2)
A(1)
B(1)
A(0)
```

Overloading Local Subprograms

As we saw in Chapter 7, subprograms declared in packages can be overloaded.
This is also true for local subprograms, as the following example illustrates:

```
-- Available online as overloadedLocal.sql
SET SERVEROUTPUT ON SIZE 1000000
```

```
DECLARE
  -- Two overloaded local procedures
  PROCEDURE LocalProc(p_Parameter1 IN NUMBER) IS
  BEGIN
    DBMS_OUTPUT.PUT_LINE('In version 1, p_Parameter1 = ' ||
                         p_Parameter1);
  END LocalProc;

  PROCEDURE LocalProc(p_Parameter1 IN VARCHAR2) IS
  BEGIN
    DBMS_OUTPUT.PUT_LINE('In version 2, p_Parameter1 = ' ||
                         p_Parameter1);
  END LocalProc;
BEGIN
  -- Call version 1
  LocalProc(12345);

  -- And version 2
  LocalProc('abcdef');
END;
```

The output from the preceding example is

```
In version 1, p_Parameter1 = 12345
In version 2, p_Parameter1 = abcdef
```

Stored vs. Local Subprograms

Stored subprograms and local subprograms behave differently and have different
properties. When should each be used? We generally prefer to use stored
subprograms, and we will usually put them in a package. If you develop a
useful subprogram, it is likely that you will want to call it from more than one
block. In order to do this, the subprogram must be stored in the database. The
size and complexity benefits are also usually a factor. The only procedures and
functions that we declare local to a block tend to be short ones, which are called
from only one specific section of the program (their containing block). Local
subprograms of this sort are generally used to avoid code duplication within
a single block. This usage is similar to C macros. Table 9-1 summarizes the
differences between stored and local subprograms.

Stored Subprograms	Local Subprograms
The stored subprogram is stored in compiled p-code in the database; when the procedure is called, it does not have to be compiled.	The local subprogram is compiled as part of its containing block. If the containing block is anonymous and is run multiple times, the subprogram has to be compiled each time.
Stored subprograms can be called from any block submitted by a user who has EXECUTE privileges on the subprogram.	Local subprograms can be called only from the block containing the subprogram.
By keeping the subprogram code separate from the calling block, the calling block is shorter and easier to understand. The subprogram and calling block can also be maintained separately, if desired.	The subprogram and the calling block are one and the same, which can lead to confusion. If a change to the calling block is made, the subprogram will be recompiled as part of the recompilation of the containing block.
The compiled p-code can be pinned in the shared pool using the DBMS_SHARED_POOL.KEEP packaged procedure.* This can improve performance.	Local subprograms cannot be pinned in the shared pool by themselves.
Stand-alone stored subprograms cannot be overloaded, but packaged subprograms can be overloaded within the same package.	Local subprograms can be overloaded within the same block.

* The DBMS_SHARED_POOL package is discussed later in this chapter in the section "Pinning in the Shared Pool."

TABLE 9-1. *Stored vs. Local Subprograms*

Considerations of Stored Subprograms and Packages

Storing subprograms and packages as data dictionary objects has advantages. For example, it allows them to be shared among database users as needed. There are several implications of this, however. These include dependencies among stored objects, how package state is handled, and the privileges necessary to run stored subprograms and packages.

Subprogram Dependencies

When a stored procedure or function is compiled, all of the Oracle objects that it references are recorded in the data dictionary. The procedure is *dependent* on these objects. We have seen that a subprogram that has compile errors is marked as invalid in the data dictionary. A stored subprogram can also become invalid if a DDL operation is performed on one of its dependent objects. The best way to illustrate this is by example. The ThreeAuthors function (defined in Chapter 7) queries the books table. The dependencies of ThreeAuthors are illustrated in Figure 9-1. ThreeAuthors depends on only one object: books. The arrow in the figure indicates this.

Now if we create a procedure that calls ThreeAuthors, we can insert the results into temp_table. We need to ensure our environment contains the ThreeAuthors function. If it does not have the stored function, the following script will fail. We can add the ThreeAuthors function by running createThreeAuthors.sql script. This procedure is RecordThreeAuthors:

```
-- Available online as RecordThreeAuthors.sql
CREATE OR REPLACE PROCEDURE RecordThreeAuthors AS
  CURSOR c_Books IS
    SELECT *
      FROM books;
BEGIN
  FOR v_BookRecord in c_Books LOOP
    -- Record all the books which have three authors
    -- in temp_table.
    IF ThreeAuthors(v_BookRecord.ISBN) THEN
      INSERT INTO temp_table (char_col) VALUES
        (v_BookRecord.title || ' has three authors!');
    END IF;
  END LOOP;
END RecordThreeAuthors;
/
```

The arrows in Figure 9-2 illustrate the dependency information. RecordThreeAuthors depends both on ThreeAuthors and on temp_table. These are *direct* dependencies, because RecordThreeAuthors refers directly to both ThreeAuthors and temp_table. ThreeAuthors itself depends on books, so RecordThreeAuthors has an *indirect* dependency on books.

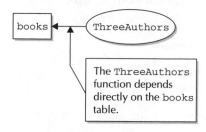

FIGURE 9-1. *ThreeAuthors dependencies*

If a DDL operation is performed on books, all objects that depend on books (directly or indirectly) are invalidated. Suppose we alter the books table in our example by adding an extra column:

```
ALTER TABLE authors
ADD (age NUMBER(2));
```

This will cause both ThreeAuthors and RecordThreeAuthors to become invalid, since they depend on authors. The following SQL statement will illustrate the status of these objects before we change a dependency:

```
-- Available online as part of automaticInvalidation.sql
SELECT object_name, status
FROM user_objects
WHERE object_name IN ('THREEAUTHORS', 'RECORDTHREEAUTHORS');
```

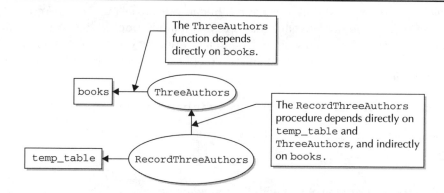

FIGURE 9-2. *RecordThreeAuthors dependencies*

The output shows both are valid in the database.

```
OBJECT_NAME              STATUS
----------  ----
RECORDTHREEAUTHORS       VALID
THREEAUTHORS             VALID
```

Modify the books table with the following DDL statement:

```
ALTER TABLE books MODIFY
(title VARCHAR2(150)  /* Increase size of title column */ );
Table altered.
```

Reselect the status of the object with this query:

```
SELECT object_name, status
FROM user_objects
WHERE object_name IN ('THREEAUTHORS', 'RECORDTHREEAUTHORS');
```

The output shows both are now invalid because of the change to the dependent object.

```
OBJECT_NAME              STATUS
----------  ----
RECORDTHREEAUTHORS       INVALID
THREEAUTHORS             INVALID
```

Automatic Recompilation

If a dependent object is invalidated, the PL/SQL engine will automatically attempt to recompile it the next time it is called. Because `RecordFullAuthors` and `ThreeAuthors` do not reference the `title` column in `books`, this recompilation will be successful. The following SQL continues from the preceding example. The call of the stored procedure automatically compiles it. This is often referred to as a lazy compile.

```
-- Available online as part of automaticInvalidation.sql
BEGIN
  RecordThreeAuthors;
END;
/
```

Reselect the status of the object with the following query:

```
SELECT object_name, status
FROM user_objects
WHERE object_name IN ('THREEAUTHORS', 'RECORDTHREEAUTHORS');
```

The output shows both are valid in the database.

```
OBJECT_NAME             STATUS
----------- ----
RECORDTHREEAUTHORS      VALID
THREEAUTHORS            VALID
```

CAUTION
The automatic recompilation can fail (especially if a table description is modified). In this case, the calling block will receive a compilation error. However, these errors will occur at run time, not compile time.

Packages and Dependencies

As the previous example showed, stored subprograms can be invalidated if their dependent objects are modified. The situation is different for packages, however. Consider the dependency picture for `InventoryOps` (which we saw in Chapter 7) in Figure 9-3. The package body depends on the `inventory` table and the package header. But, the package header does not depend on the package body or the inventory table. That is one advantage of packages—we can change the package body without having to change the header. Therefore, other objects that depend on the header won't have to be recompiled at all, since they never get invalidated. If

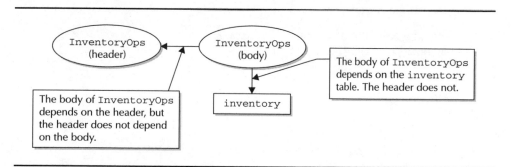

FIGURE 9-3. *InventoryOps dependencies*

the header is changed, this automatically invalidates the body. The body becomes invalid because it depends on the header.

NOTE
There are certain cases where a change in the package body necessitates a change in the header. For example, if the arguments to a procedure need to be changed, the header and body would have to be modified to match. The header would not have to be modified if the implementation of a body procedure were changed without affecting its declaration, however. Similarly, if you are using the signature dependency model (described in the next section, "How Invalidations Are Determined"), only changes to the signatures of objects in the package specification will invalidate the body. In addition, if you add an object to a package header (such as a cursor or variable), the body will be invalidated.

We can also see this behavior by creating a table and package that have no dependencies. We will call the independent package dependee. Then, we create a procedure with a dependency on the dependee package named depender.

```
-- Available online as dependencies.sql
CREATE TABLE simple_table (f1 NUMBER);

CREATE OR REPLACE PACKAGE Dependee AS
  PROCEDURE Example(p_Val IN NUMBER);
END Dependee;
/

CREATE OR REPLACE PACKAGE BODY Dependee AS
  PROCEDURE Example(p_Val IN NUMBER) IS
  BEGIN
    INSERT INTO simple_table VALUES (p_Val);
  END Example;
END Dependee;
/

CREATE OR REPLACE PROCEDURE Depender(p_Val IN NUMBER) AS
  BEGIN
    Dependee.Example(p_Val + 1);
  END Depender;
/
```

Querying the data dictionary, we can see if all the objects are created.

```
SELECT object_name, object_type, status
FROM user_objects
WHERE object_name IN ('DEPENDER', 'DEPENDEE','SIMPLE_TABLE');
```

The output shows all are valid in the database.

```
OBJECT_NAME                     OBJECT_TYPE    STATUS
--------------- ------- ----
SIMPLE_TABLE                    TABLE          VALID
DEPENDEE                        PACKAGE        VALID
DEPENDEE                        PACKAGE BODY   VALID
DEPENDER                        PROCEDURE      VALID
```

Change the package body with the following script:

```
CREATE OR REPLACE PACKAGE BODY Dependee AS
   PROCEDURE Example(p_Val IN NUMBER) IS
   BEGIN
     INSERT INTO simple_table VALUES (p_Val - 1);
   END Example;
END Dependee;
/
```

When we query the data dictionary, we see that all the objects are valid because we changed a package body, not the specification. The dependency is on the package name, the nested procedure name, and the formal parameter of the nested procedure. The specification provides these and has not been changed. The package body structure mirrors the specification and provides an implementation. The implementation may change without changing the structure of the package. Use the following query to check object status:

```
SELECT object_name, object_type, status
FROM user_objects
WHERE object_name IN ('DEPENDER', 'DEPENDEE','SIMPLE_TABLE');
```

The output shows all are valid in the database.

```
OBJECT_NAME                     OBJECT_TYPE    STATUS
--------------- ------- ----
SIMPLE_TABLE                    TABLE          VALID
DEPENDEE                        PACKAGE        VALID
DEPENDEE                        PACKAGE BODY   VALID
DEPENDER                        PROCEDURE      VALID
```

The package body provides the implementation, which has a dependency on a table. When we drop the table, it will invalidate only the package body. This is true because the package body contains the implementation that is dependent on the table. Use the following query to drop the table:

```
DROP TABLE simple_table;
```

Using our familiar query of the data dictionary, we can check the status of objects.

```
SELECT object_name, object_type, status
FROM user_objects
WHERE object_name IN ('DEPENDER', 'DEPENDEE','SIMPLE_TABLE');
```

The output shows that only the package body is invalid. The other objects are unaltered by the loss of the table from the data dictionary.

```
OBJECT_NAME                    OBJECT_TYPE    STATUS
---------------  -------  ----
DEPENDEE                       PACKAGE        VALID
DEPENDEE                       PACKAGE BODY   INVALID
DEPENDER                       PROCEDURE      VALID
```

> **NOTE**
> *The data dictionary views* user_dependencies,
> all_dependencies, *and* dba_dependencies
> *directly list the relationships between schema*
> *objects. For more information on these views,*
> *see Appendix C.*

Figure 9-4 shows the dependencies of the objects created by this script.

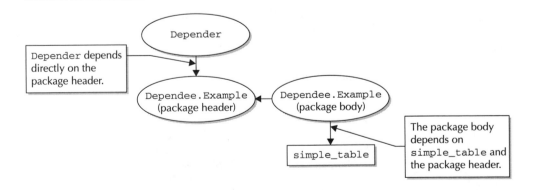

FIGURE 9-4. *More package dependencies*

How Invalidations Are Determined

When an object is altered, its dependent objects are invalidated, as we have seen. If all of the objects are in the same database, the dependent objects are invalidated as soon as the base object is altered. This can be done quickly, because the data dictionary tracks the dependencies. Suppose we create two procedures, P1 and P2, as illustrated in Figure 9-5. P1 depends on P2, which means that recompiling P2 will invalidate P1.

Create the P2 procedure before the P1 procedure because P1 depends on P2.

```
-- Available online as part of remoteDependencies.sql
CREATE OR REPLACE PROCEDURE P2 AS
BEGIN
  DBMS_OUTPUT.PUT_LINE('Inside P2!');
END P2;
/


CREATE OR REPLACE PROCEDURE P1 AS
BEGIN
  DBMS_OUTPUT.PUT_LINE('Inside P1!');
  P2;
END P1;
/
```

Using our familiar query of the data dictionary, we can check the status of objects.

```
SELECT object_name, object_type, status
FROM user_objects
WHERE object_name IN ('P1', 'P2');
```

The output returns confirmation that P1 and P2 are valid.

```
OBJECT_NAME                     OBJECT_TYPE     STATUS
--------------- -------- ----
P2                              PROCEDURE       VALID
P1                              PROCEDURE       VALID
```

Issue the alter command for the P2 procedure and the P1 procedure will immediately become invalid.

```
ALTER PROCEDURE P2 COMPILE;
```

Using our familiar query of the data dictionary, we see the invalidation.

```
SELECT object_name, object_type, status
FROM user_objects
WHERE object_name IN ('P1', 'P2');
```

The output returns confirmation that P1 is invalid while P2 is valid.

OBJECT_NAME	OBJECT_TYPE	STATUS
P2	PROCEDURE	**VALID**
P1	PROCEDURE	**INVALID**

Suppose, however, that P1 and P2 are in different databases, and P1 calls P2 over a database link. This situation is illustrated in Figure 9-6. In this case, recompiling P2 does not immediately invalidate P1.

There are some steps required to support the following example. Assuming you are using an Oracle user named USERA and the user has been granted the create database link responsibility, you must create a database link as USERA. We will walk through these steps in the example that follows.

Create a fixed-user database link that references USERA. You will need to replace the connect_string with the SERVICE_NAME value from in your listener.ora file. Also, the syntax assumes that the password for USERA is its own user name, which may not be the case in your database. If the password is the same, you should change it.

```
-- Available online as part of remoteDependencies.sql
CREATE DATABASE LINK loopback
CONNECT TO usera IDENTIFIED BY usera
USING 'connect_string';
```

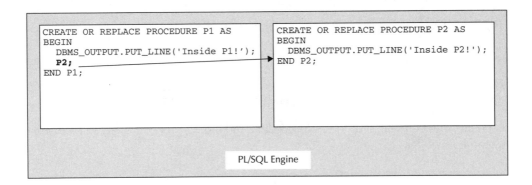

FIGURE 9-5. *P1 and P2 in the same database*

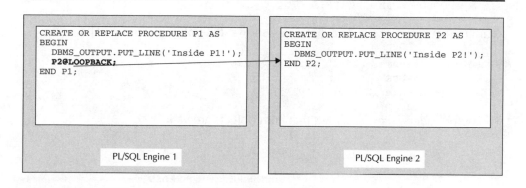

FIGURE 9-6. *P1 and P2 in different databases*

After creating the database link, run the statement that follows. It references the stored procedure resolved through the database link:

```
CREATE OR REPLACE PROCEDURE P1 AS
BEGIN
   DBMS_OUTPUT.PUT_LINE('Inside P1!');
   P2@loopback;
END P1;
/
```

Using our familiar query of the data dictionary, we see that both objects are valid.

```
SELECT object_name, object_type, status
FROM user_objects
WHERE object_name IN ('P1', 'P2');
```

The output will also show that both objects are valid.

```
OBJECT_NAME              OBJECT_TYPE     STATUS
---------------- -------- ----
P2                       PROCEDURE       VALID
P1                       PROCEDURE       VALID
```

When we recompile P2, P1 is not immediately invalidated because it is resolved through a database link.

```
ALTER PROCEDURE P2 COMPILE;
```

Our familiar query of the data dictionary shows that both objects are valid.

```
SELECT object_name, object_type, status
FROM user_objects
WHERE object_name IN ('P1', 'P2');
```

The output query likewise shows that both objects are valid.

```
OBJECT_NAME                     OBJECT_TYPE     STATUS
--------------- -------- ----
P2                              PROCEDURE       VALID
P1                              PROCEDURE       VALID
```

NOTE
In the preceding example, the database link is actually a loopback, which points to the same database. The observed behavior, however, is the same as if P1 and P2 were actually in separate databases. Using a loopback enables us to query the status of P1 and P2 in one SELECT statement.

Why is the behavior different in the remote case? The answer is that the data dictionary does not track remote dependencies. It would be too expensive to invalidate all the remote dependent objects, because they could be in different databases (that may or may not even be accessible at the time of the invalidation).

Instead, the validity of remote objects is checked at run time. When P1 is called, the remote data dictionary is queried to determine the status of P2 (if the remote database is inaccessible, an error is raised). P1 and P2 are compared to see if P1 needs to be recompiled. There are two different methods of comparison—the timestamp and signature methods.

NOTE
It is not necessary to have a database link to utilize run-time validity checking. If P1 were in a client-side PL/SQL engine (such as Oracle Forms), and P2 were in the server, the situation would be similar, and either the timestamp or signature method would be used. See Chapter 2 for more information about different PL/SQL execution environments.

Timestamp Model   With this model, the timestamps of the last modifications of the two objects are compared. The `last_ddl_time` column of `user_objects` contains this timestamp. If the base object has a newer timestamp than the dependent object, the dependent object will be recompiled. There are several issues with this model, however:

- The date comparison does not take the locations of the two PL/SQL engines into account. If they are in different time zones, the comparison may not be valid.

- Even if the two engines are in the same time zone, the timestamp model can result in unnecessary recompilations. In the preceding example, P2 was simply recompiled but was not actually changed. P1 does not really have to be recompiled, but because it has an older timestamp, it would be.

- Slightly more serious is when P1 is contained in a client-side PL/SQL engine, such as Oracle Forms. In this case, it may not be possible to recompile P1, because the source for it may not be included with the run-time version of Forms.

Signature Model   PL/SQL provides a different method for determining when remote dependent objects need to be recompiled, which resolves the issues with the timestamp model. This method is called the "signature model." When a procedure is created, a *signature* is stored in the data dictionary in addition to the p-code. The signature encodes the types and order of the parameters. With this model, the signature of P2 will change only when the parameters change. When P1 is compiled the first time, the signature of P2 is included (rather than the timestamp). Thus, P1 needs to be recompiled only when the signature of P2 changes.

In order to use the signature model, the parameter REMOTE_DEPENDENCIES_ MODE must be set to SIGNATURE. This is a parameter in the database initialization file. (The name and location of the initialization file, commonly called `init.ora`, varies depending on your system.) It can also be set interactively. There are three ways of setting this mode:

- Add the line REMOTE_DEPENDENCIES_MODE=SIGNATURE to the database initialization file. The next time the database is started, the mode will be set to SIGNATURE for all sessions.

- Issue the command

  ```
  ALTER SYSTEM SET REMOTE_DEPENDENCIES_MODE = SIGNATURE;
  ```

  This will affect the entire database (all sessions) from the time the statement is issued. You must have the ALTER SYSTEM system privilege to issue this command.

■ Issue the command

```
ALTER SESSION SET REMOTE_DEPENDENCIES_MODE = SIGNATURE;
```

This will affect only your session. Objects created after this point in the current session will use the signature method.

In all of these options, TIMESTAMP can be used instead of SIGNATURE to use the timestamp model. TIMESTAMP is the default. There are several things to be aware of when using the signature method:

■ Signatures don't get modified if the default values of formal parameters are changed. Suppose P2 has a default value for one of its parameters, and P1 is using this default value. If the default value in the specification for P2 is changed, P1 will not be recompiled by default. The old value for the default parameter will still be used until P1 is manually recompiled. This applies for IN parameters only.

■ If P1 is calling a packaged procedure P2, and a new overloaded version of P2 is added to the remote package, the signature is not changed. P1 will still use the old version (not the new overloaded one) until P1 is recompiled manually.

■ To manually recompile a procedure, use the command

```
ALTER PROCEDURE procedure_name COMPILE;
```

where *procedure_name* is the name of the procedure to be compiled. For functions, use

```
ALTER FUNCTION function_name COMPILE;
```

where *function_name* is the name of the function to be compiled. And for packages, use any of the following:

```
ALTER PACAKGE package_name COMPILE;
ALTER PACKAGE package_name COMPILE SPECIFICATION;
ALTER PACKAGE package_name COMPILE BODY;
```

where *package_name* is the name of the package. If SPECIFICATION is present, only the package header is compiled. If BODY is present, only the package body is compiled. If neither is present, both are compiled.

Package Run-Time State

When a package is first instantiated, the package code is read from disk into the shared pool. However, the run-time state of a package—namely, the packaged variables and cursors—arc kept in session memory. This means that each session has its own copy of the run-time state. It is initialized when the package is instantiated and remains until the session is closed, even if the package state is aged out of the shared pool. As we saw in Chapter 6, variables declared in a package header have global scope. They are visible for any PL/SQL block that has EXECUTE privilege for the package. Since the package state persists until the end of the session, variables in a package header can be used as global variables. The following example illustrates this:

```
-- Available online as PersistPkg.sql
CREATE OR REPLACE PACKAGE PersistPkg AS
  -- Type which holds an array of book ISBN's
  TYPE t_BookTable IS TABLE OF books.isbn%TYPE
    INDEX BY BINARY_INTEGER;

  -- Maximum number of rows to return each time.
  v_MaxRows NUMBER := 4;

  -- Returns up to v_MaxRows ISBN's
  PROCEDURE ReadBooks(p_BookTable OUT t_BookTable,
                      p_NumRows    OUT NUMBER);
END PersistPkg;
/

CREATE OR REPLACE PACKAGE BODY PersistPkg AS
  -- Query against books.  Since this is global to the package
  -- body, it will remain past a database call.
  CURSOR c_BasicBooks IS
    SELECT isbn
      FROM BOOKS
      WHERE category = 'Oracle Basics'
      ORDER BY title;

  PROCEDURE ReadBooks(p_BookTable OUT t_BookTable,
                      p_NumRows    OUT NUMBER) IS
    v_Done BOOLEAN := FALSE;
    v_NumRows NUMBER := 1;
  BEGIN
    IF NOT c_BasicBooks%ISOPEN THEN
      -- First open the cursor
      OPEN c_BasicBooks;
    END IF;

    -- Cursor is open, so we can fetch up to v_MaxRows
    WHILE NOT v_Done LOOP
      FETCH c_BasicBooks INTO p_BookTable(v_NumRows);
      IF c_BasicBooks%NOTFOUND THEN
```

```
      -- No more data, so we're finished.
      CLOSE c_BasicBooks;
      v_Done := TRUE;
    ELSE
      v_NumRows := v_NumRows + 1;
      IF v_NumRows > v_MaxRows THEN
        v_Done := TRUE;
      END IF;
    END IF;
  END LOOP;

  -- Return the actual number of rows fetched.
  p_NumRows := v_NumRows - 1;

  END ReadBooks;
END PersistPkg;
/
```

PersistPkg.ReadBooks will select from the c_BasicBooks cursor. Since this cursor is declared at the package level (not inside ReadBooks), it will remain past a call to ReadBooks. We can call PersistPkg.ReadBooks with the following block:

```
-- Available online as callPP.sql
DECLARE
  v_BookTable PersistPkg.t_BookTable;
  v_NumRows NUMBER := PersistPkg.v_MaxRows;
  v_Title books.title%TYPE;
BEGIN
  PersistPkg.ReadBooks(v_BookTable, v_NumRows);
  DBMS_OUTPUT.PUT_LINE(' Fetched ' || v_NumRows || ' rows:');
  FOR v_Count IN 1..v_NumRows LOOP
    SELECT title
      INTO v_Title
      FROM books
      WHERE isbn = v_BookTable(v_Count);
    DBMS_OUTPUT.PUT_LINE(v_Title);
  END LOOP;
END;
/
```

Use the testCallPP.sql script to generate the following output. Different data is returned because the cursor has remained open in between each call:

```
SQL> @testCallPP
Fetched 4 rows:
Oracle Backup & Recovery 101
Oracle DBA 101
Oracle Database 10g A Beginner's Guide
Oracle Enterprise Manager 101

PL/SQL procedure successfully completed.

Fetched 4 rows:
Oracle PL/SQL 101
Oracle Performance Tuning 101
Oracle8i: A Beginner's Guide
Oracle9i DBA 101

PL/SQL procedure successfully completed.

Fetched 1 rows:
Oracle9i: A Beginner's Guide

PL/SQL procedure successfully completed.
```

Serially Reusable Packages

PL/SQL lets you mark a package as serially reusable. The run-time state of a *serially reusable* package will last only for each database call, rather than for the entire session. A serially reusable package has the syntax

PRAGMA SERIALLY_REUSABLE;

in the package header (and also the package body, if present). If we modify `PersistPkg` to include this pragma, the output changes. Here is the modified package:

```
-- Available online as PersistPkg2.sql
CREATE OR REPLACE PACKAGE PersistPkg AS
  PRAGMA SERIALLY_REUSABLE;

  TYPE t_BookTable IS TABLE OF books.isbn%TYPE
    INDEX BY BINARY_INTEGER;

  -- Maximum number of rows to return each time.
  v_MaxRows NUMBER := 4;

  -- Returns up to v_MaxRows ISBN's
```

```
     PROCEDURE ReadBooks(p_BookTable OUT t_BookTable,
                         p_NumRows    OUT NUMBER);
END PersistPkg;
/

CREATE OR REPLACE PACKAGE BODY PersistPkg AS
  PRAGMA SERIALLY_REUSABLE;

  -- Query against books.  Even though this is global to the
  -- package body, it will be reset after each database call,
  -- because the package is now serially reusable.
  CURSOR c_BasicBooks IS
    SELECT isbn
      FROM BOOKS
      WHERE category = 'Oracle Basics'
      ORDER BY title;
  ...
END PersistPkg;
/
```

The output from running the serially reusable version of `PersistPkg` appears next. You can rerun the `testCallPP.sql` script to generate the output on your system.

```
Fetched 4 rows:
Oracle DBA 101
Oracle PL/SQL 101
Oracle Performance Tuning 101
Oracle8i: A Beginner's Guide

PL/SQL procedure successfully completed.

Fetched 4 rows:
Oracle DBA 101
Oracle PL/SQL 101
Oracle Performance Tuning 101
Oracle8i: A Beginner's Guide

PL/SQL procedure successfully completed.
```

Note the difference in behavior between the two versions—the non–serially reusable version will maintain the state of the cursor over database calls, while the serially reusable version resets the state (and thus the output) each time. The differences between serially reusable and non–serially reusable packages are summarized in the following table. Serially reusable packages can save memory, at the expense of the package state being reset after each call.

Serially Reusable Packages	Non–Serially Reusable Packages
Run-time state is kept in shared memory and is freed after every database call.	Run-time state is kept in process memory and lasts for the life of the database session.
The maximum memory used is proportional to the number of concurrent users of the package.	The maximum memory used is proportional to the number of concurrently logged-on users, which is typically much higher.

Dependencies of Package Run-Time State

In addition to dependencies between stored objects, dependencies can exist between package state and anonymous blocks. For example, consider the following package:

```
-- Available online as anonymousDependencies.sql
CREATE OR REPLACE PACKAGE SimplePkg AS
  v_GlobalVar NUMBER := 1;
  PROCEDURE UpdateVar;
END SimplePkg;
/

CREATE OR REPLACE PACKAGE BODY SimplePkg AS
  PROCEDURE UpdateVar IS
  BEGIN
    v_GlobalVar := 7;
  END UpdateVar;
END SimplePkg;
/
```

SimplePkg contains a package global—v_GlobalVar. Suppose we create SimplePkg from one database session. Then, in a second session, we call SimplePkg.UpdateVar with the following block:

```
BEGIN
  SimplePkg.UpdateVar;
END;
/
```

Back in the first session, we run the anonymousDependencies.sql creation script that drops and re-creates SimplePkg. Returning to session 2, we run the same anonymous block and get the following error. If we re-created the package without a change to the package specification, we would not encounter an error, because the package would not be recompiled. The error happens only when there is a change to the package specification in the data dictionary. Dropping and re-creating the package or modifying the package forces a recompile in the data dictionary. It generates this error:

```
BEGIN
 *
ERROR at line 1:
ORA-04068: existing state of packages has been discarded
ORA-04061: existing state of package "USERA.SIMPLEPKG" has been invalidated
ORA-04065: not executed, altered or dropped package "USERA.SIMPLEPKG"
ORA-06508: PL/SQL: could not find program unit being called
ORA-06512: at line 2
```

What has happened here? The dependency picture for this situation is shown in Figure 9-7. The anonymous block depends on `SimplePkg`, in the same sense that we have seen earlier. This is a compile-time dependency, in that it is determined when the anonymous block is first compiled. However, there is also a run-time dependency in the SimplePkg. SimplePkg contains a package variable. Each session has its own copy of packaged variables. Thus, when `SimplePkg` is recompiled the run-time dependency is followed, which invalidates the block and raises the ORA-4068 error.

Run-time dependencies exist only on a package state. This includes variables and cursors declared in a package. If the package had no global variables, the second execution of the anonymous block would have succeeded.

Privileges and Stored Subprograms

Stored subprograms and packages are objects in the data dictionary, and as such a particular database user, or schema, owns them. Other users can access these objects if they are granted the correct privileges on them. Privileges and roles also come into play when creating a stored object, with regard to the access available inside the subprogram.

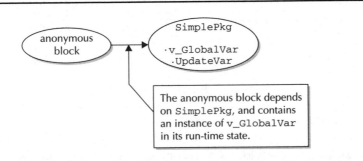

FIGURE 9-7. *Package global dependencies*

EXECUTE Privilege

In order to allow access to a table, the SELECT, INSERT, UPDATE, and DELETE object privileges are used. The GRANT statement gives these privileges to a database user or a role. For stored subprograms and packages, the relevant privilege is EXECUTE. Consider the RecordThreeAuthors procedure, which we examined earlier in this chapter:

```
-- Available online as part of execute.sql
CREATE OR REPLACE PROCEDURE RecordThreeAuthors AS
  CURSOR c_Books IS
    SELECT *
      FROM books;
BEGIN
  FOR v_BookRecord in c_Books LOOP
    -- Record all the books which have three authors
    -- in temp_table.
    IF ThreeAuthors(v_BookRecord.ISBN) THEN
      INSERT INTO temp_table (char_col) VALUES
        (v_BookRecord.title || ' has three authors!');
    END IF;
  END LOOP;
END RecordThreeAuthors;
/
```

> **NOTE**
> *The online example* execute.sql *will first create the users* UserA *and* UserB *and then create the necessary objects for the examples in this section. You may have to modify the password used for the DBA account in order to get the example to work on your system. You can see the output from running* execute.sql *in* execute.out, *also available online. The* execute.sql *file creates the* books *table with only two rows.*

Suppose the UserA user owns the objects RecordThreeAuthors depends on (the ThreeAuthors function and books and temp_table tables). Likewise, UserA owns RecordThreeAuthors. If we grant the EXECUTE privilege on RecordThreeAuthors to another database user, say UserB, with

```
-- Available online as part of execute.sql
GRANT EXECUTE ON RecordThreeAuthors TO UserB;
```

then UserB can execute RecordFullAuthors with the following block. Note that dot notation is used to indicate the schema:

```
BEGIN
   UserA.RecordThreeAuthors;
END;
/
```

In this scenario, UserA owns all of the database objects. This situation is illustrated in Figure 9-8. The dotted line signifies the GRANT statement from UserA to UserB, while the solid lines signify object dependencies. After executing the preceding block, the results will be inserted into UserA.temp_table.

Now suppose that UserB has another table, also called temp_table, as illustrated in Figure 9-9. If UserB calls UserA.RecordThreeAuthors (by executing the anonymous block just shown), which table gets modified? The table in UserA does. By default, a subprogram executes under the privilege set of its owner. Even though UserB is calling RecordThreeAuthors, RecordThreeAuthors is owned by UserA. Thus, the identifier temp_table will evaluate to the table belonging to UserA, *not* UserB.

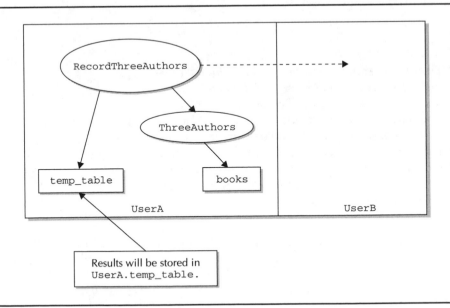

FIGURE 9-8. *Database objects owned by UserA*

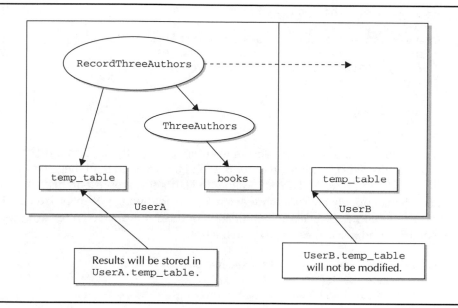

FIGURE 9-9. *temp_table owned by UserB and UserA*

NOTE
*It is possible to specify that a procedure should
execute under the privilege set of its owner, or of
its caller. See the section "Invoker's vs. Definer's
Rights" later in this chapter for details.*

Stored Subprograms and Roles

Let's modify the situation in Figure 9-9 slightly. Suppose UserA does not own
temp_table or RecordThreeAuthors, and these are owned by UserB.
Furthermore, suppose we have modified RecordThreeAuthors to explicitly refer
to the objects in UserA. This is illustrated by the following listing and Figure 9-10.

```
-- Available online as part of execute.sql
CREATE OR REPLACE PROCEDURE RecordThreeAuthors AS
  CURSOR c_Books IS
    SELECT *
      FROM UserA.books;
BEGIN
  FOR v_BookRecord in c_Books LOOP
```

```
      -- Record all the books which have three authors
      -- in temp_table.
      IF UserA.ThreeAuthors(v_BookRecord.ISBN) THEN
         INSERT INTO temp_table (char_col) VALUES
            (v_BookRecord.title || ' has three authors!');
      END IF;
   END LOOP;
END RecordThreeAuthors;
/
```

In order for `RecordThreeAuthors` to compile correctly, `UserA` must have granted the SELECT privilege on `books` and the EXECUTE privilege on `ThreeAuthors` to `UserB`. The dotted lines in Figure 9-10 represent this. The grant must be done explicitly and *not* through a role. The following GRANTs, executed by `UserA`, would allow a successful compilation of `UserB.RecordThreeAuthors`; they can be found in `recreateRTA.sql` script.

```
-- Available online as part of execute.sql
GRANT SELECT ON books TO UserB;
GRANT EXECUTE ON ThreeAuthors TO UserB;
```

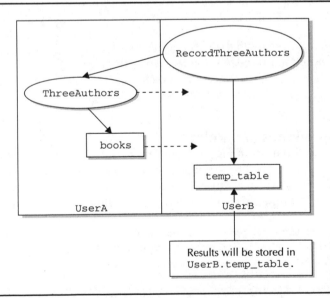

FIGURE 9-10.   *RecordThreeAuthors owned by UserB*

A GRANT done through an intermediate role, as in

```
-- Available online as part of execute.sql
CREATE ROLE UserA_Role;
GRANT SELECT ON classes TO UserA_Role;
GRANT EXECUTE ON AlmostFull TO UserA_Role;
GRANT UserA_Role to UserB;
```

will *not* work. The role is illustrated in Figure 9-11.

So we can clarify the rule in the previous section as this: A subprogram executes under the privileges that have been granted explicitly to its owner, not via a role.

If the grants had been done via a role, we would have received ORA-942 and PLS-201 errors when we tried to compile RecordThreeAuthors:

```
SQL> show errors
Errors for PROCEDURE RECORDTHREEAUTHORS:

LINE/COL ERROR
---- -------------------------------
3/5      PL/SQL: SQL Statement ignored
4/18     PL/SQL: ORA-00942: table or view does not exist
9/5      PL/SQL: Statement ignored
9/8      PLS-00201: identifier 'USERA.THREEAUTHORS' must be declared
```

This rule also applies for triggers and packages, which are stored in the database as well. Essentially, by default, the only objects available inside a stored procedure, function, package, or trigger are the ones owned by the owner of the subprogram, or explicitly granted to the owner.

Why is this? To explain this restriction, we need to examine binding. PL/SQL uses early binding—references are evaluated when a subprogram is compiled, not when it is run. GRANT and REVOKE are both DDL statements. They take effect immediately, and the new privileges are recorded in the data dictionary. All database sessions will see the new privilege set. However, this is not necessarily true for roles. A role can be granted to a user, and that user can then choose to disable the role with the SET ROLE command. The distinction is that SET ROLE applies to one database session only, while GRANT and REVOKE apply to all sessions. A role can be disabled in one session but enabled in other sessions.

In order to allow privileges granted via a role to be used inside stored subprograms and triggers, the privileges would have to be checked every time the procedure is run. The privileges are checked as part of the binding process. But early binding means that the privileges are checked at compile time, not run time. In order to maintain early binding, all roles are disabled inside stored procedures, functions, packages, and triggers.

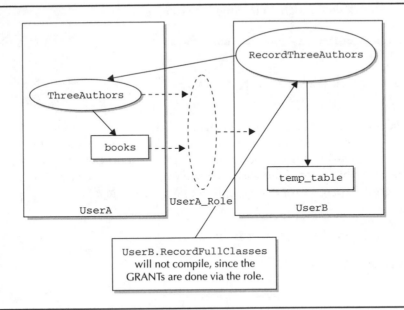

FIGURE 9-11. *GRANTs done via a role*

Invoker's vs. Definer's Rights

Consider the situation that we examined earlier in this chapter in the section "EXECUTE Privilege," and illustrated earlier in Figure 9-9. In this situation, both UserA and UserB own a copy of temp_table, and RecordThreeAuthors, since UserA owns it, inserts into UserA.temp_table. As we saw in the previous sections, unqualified external references within RecordThreeAuthors are resolved under the privilege set of its owner, or definer. Thus, RecordThreeAuthors is known as a *definer's rights* procedure.

Oracle8*i* introduced a different kind of external reference resolution. In an *invoker's rights* subprogram, external references are resolved under the privilege set of the caller, or invoker, not the owner. Using the AUTHID clause creates an invoker's rights routine. It is valid for stand-alone subprograms, package specifications, and object type specifications (see Chapters 14–16 for information about object types) only.

Individual subprograms within a package must be all invoker's or definer's, not a mix. The syntax of AUTHID is given here:

CREATE [OR REPLACE] FUNCTION *function_name*
  [*parameter_list*] RETURN *return_type*
  [AUTHID {CURRENT_USER | DEFINER}] {IS | AS}
  function_body;

CREATE [OR REPLACE] PROCEDURE *procedure_name*
  [*parameter_list*]
  [AUTHID {CURRENT_USER | DEFINER}] {IS | AS}
  function_body;

CREATE [OR REPLACE] PACKAGE *package_spec_name*
  [AUTHID {CURRENT_USER | DEFINER}] {IS | AS}
  package_spec;

If CURRENT_USER is specified in the AUTHID clause, the object will have invoker's rights. If DEFINER is specified, then the object will have definer's rights. The default if the AUTHID clause is not present is definer's rights.

For example, the following version of RecordThreeAuthors is an invoker's rights procedure:

```
-- Available online as part of invokers.sql
CREATE OR REPLACE PROCEDURE RecordThreeAuthors
  AUTHID CURRENT_USER AS
  CURSOR c_Books IS
    SELECT *
      FROM UserA.books;
BEGIN
  FOR v_BookRecord in c_Books LOOP
    -- Record all the books which have three authors
    -- in temp_table.
    IF UserA.ThreeAuthors(v_BookRecord.ISBN) THEN
      INSERT INTO temp_table (char_col) VALUES
        (v_BookRecord.title || ' has three authors!');
    END IF;
  END LOOP;
END RecordThreeAuthors;
/
```

NOTE
The online example invokers.sql *will first create the users* UserA *and* UserB *and then create the necessary objects for the examples in this section. You may have to modify the password used for the DBA account in order to get the example to work on your system. You can see the output from running* invokers.sql *in* invokers.out, *also available online. The* invokers.sql *file creates the* books *table with only two rows.*

This version of RecordThreeAuthors explicitly references UserA.books and UserA.ThreeAuthors. The only unqualified reference is temp_table.

Thus, if UserB executes RecordThreeAuthors, the insert will be done in UserB.temp_table. If UserA executes it, the insert will be done in UserA.temp_table. The logic is illustrated in Figure 9-12.

Before doing this example, you may elect to run execute.sql from a privileged user like SYS or SYSTEM. With a clean environment, connect to the database using UserA. Execute the following anonymous block, which may be copied from the invokers.sql script. Doing so, there is an assumption that we have run createThreeAuthors.sql and RecordThreeAuthors.sql. If those scripts have not been run, we should run them now. Alternatively, we may run invokers.sql to rebuild the environment.

```
BEGIN
  RecordThreeAuthors;
  COMMIT;
END;
/
```

Query the UserA.TEMP_TABLE to confirm the insert, as shown here:

```
SELECT * FROM temp_table;
```

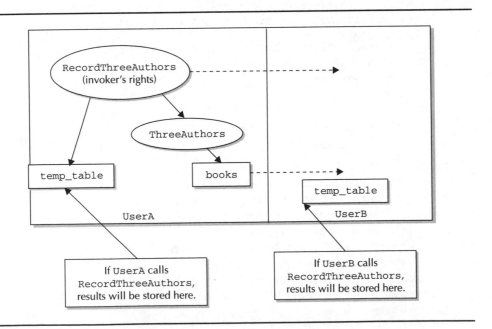

FIGURE 9-12. *Invoker's Rights* RecordThreeAuthors

The output will show two rows if the environment was refreshed by running
`invokers.sql` before you started this section.

```
   NUM_COL CHAR_COL
----- ------------------------------
         Oracle DBA 101 has three authors!
         Oracle DBA 101 has three authors!
```

As `UserB`, grant execute system privileges to `UserB` for `RecordThreeAuthors`
procedure.

```
GRANT SELECT ON books TO userb;
GRANT EXECUTE ON ThreeAuthors TO userb;
Connect to UserB and create the temp_table illustrated below.
-- Available online as part of create_temp_table.sql
CREATE TABLE temp_table
  (num_col     NUMBER
  ,char_col    VARCHAR2(60));
```

Execute the following anonymous block, which may be copied from the
`invokers.sql` script.

```
-- Available online as part of invokeRTA.sql
BEGIN
  UserA.RecordThreeAuthors;
  COMMIT;
END;
/
```

Query the `temp_table` from `UserB` and you will find the following three rows:

```
   NUM_COL CHAR_COL
----- ------------------------------
         Oracle DBA 101 has three authors!
         Oracle DBA 101 has three authors!
         Oracle DBA 101 has three authors!
```

Resolution with Invoker's Rights   In an invoker's rights routine, external references
in SQL statements will be resolved using the caller's privilege set. However,
references in PL/SQL statements (such as assignments or procedure calls) are still
resolved under the owner's privilege set. This is why, back in Figure 9-12, GRANTs
need be done only on `RecordThreeAuthors` and the `books` table. Since the

call to `ThreeAuthors` is a PL/SQL reference, it will always be done under `UserA`'s privilege set, and thus it does not need to be GRANTed to `UserB`.

However, suppose that the GRANT on `books` was not done. In this case, `UserA` can successfully compile and run the procedure, because all of the SQL objects are accessible from `UserA`'s privilege set. But `UserB` will receive an ORA-942 error upon calling `RecordThreeAuthors`. Before attempting this example, let's clean up any grants that may lead to an erroneous result. We should connect as SYSTEM before attempting a revocation of system privileges. Revoking SELECT system privileges from both `UserB` and the `UserA_Role` will ensure the example works.

```
REVOKE SELECT ON books FROM usera_role;
REVOKE SELECT ON books FROM userb;
```

Execute the following anonymous block, which may be copied from the `invokers.sql` script.

```
-- Available online as part of invokeRTA.sql
BEGIN
  UserA.RecordThreeAuthors;
END;
/
```

The output will produce the following error stack:

```
BEGIN
*
ERROR at line 1:
ORA-00942: table or view does not exist
ORA-06512: at "USERA.RECORDTHREEAUTHORS", line 4
ORA-06512: at "USERA.RECORDTHREEAUTHORS", line 7
ORA-06512: at line 2
```

Figure 9-13 shows the relationship between the package owner and non-package owner schemas:

NOTE
The error received here is ORA-942 and not PLS-201. It is a database compilation error, but we receive it at run time.

Roles and Invoker's Rights   Suppose the GRANT on classes was done via a role, and not directly. Recall from the situation earlier in Figure 9-11 that definer's rights procedures must have all privileges GRANTed explicitly. For invoker's rights routines, however, this is not the case. Because the resolution of external references

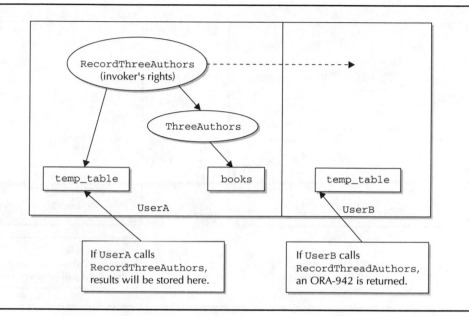

FIGURE 9-13. *Revoked SELECT on books*

for invoker's rights routines is done at run time, the current privilege set is available. This implies that privileges GRANTed via a role to the caller will be accessible. This is why we revoked rights from UserB and the UserA_Role.

NOTE
References that are resolved at the time of procedure compilation must still be GRANTed directly. Only those references that are resolved at run time can be GRANTed via a role. This also implies that the SET ROLE command (if executed through dynamic SQL) can be used with run-time references.

Figure 9-14 shows the role relationship between the owning and calling schemas.

Triggers, Views, and Invoker's Rights   A database trigger will always be executed with definer's rights and will execute under the privilege set of the schema that owns the triggering table. This is also true for a PL/SQL function that is called from a view. In this case, the function will execute under the privilege set of the view's owner.

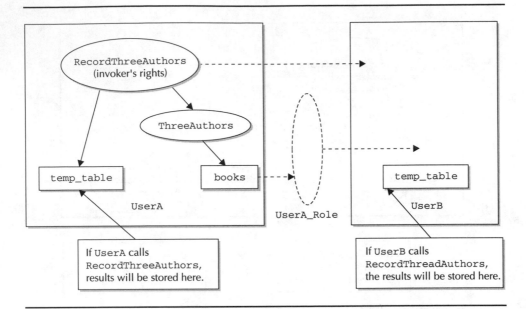

FIGURE 9-14. *Roles and Invoker's Rights*

Stored Functions and SQL Statements

In general, because calls to subprograms are procedural, they cannot be called from SQL statements. However, if a stand-alone or packaged function meets certain restrictions, it can be called during execution of a SQL statement. There are two different methods of using stored functions in SQL statements: single valued and multiple valued.

Single-Valued Functions

For the single-value case, a user-defined function is called the same way as built-in functions such as TO_CHAR, UPPER, or ADD_MONTHS. To be used in this manner, the function must return a single scalar value, as opposed to a collection.

Restrictions

Depending on where and how a user-defined function is used, it must meet the following restrictions:

- Any function called from a SELECT statement cannot modify any database tables.

- A function called by a DML statement (INSERT, UPDATE, or DELETE) cannot query or modify any tables affected by the statement. It can reference other tables, however.

- In order for a DML statement containing a function to be parallelized, the function must not modify any database tables.

- A function called by a query or a DML statement must not execute any transaction control statements (COMMIT, ROLLBACK), session control statements (ALTER SESSION, SET ROLE), or system control statements (ALTER SYSTEM). This implies that it cannot execute any DDL statements (CREATE, DROP) because they issue an implicit COMMIT.

- Any procedures and functions called by the top-level function must meet the same restrictions as the top-level function for it to be callable.

- The function has to be stored in the database, either stand-alone or as part of a package. It must not be local to another block.

- The function can take only IN parameters, no IN OUT or OUT.

- The formal parameters must use only database types, not PL/SQL types such as BOOLEAN or RECORD. These types can be user defined, if they are defined with a schema-level CREATE TYPE statement.

- The return type of the function must also be a database type or defined with a schema-level CREATE TYPE statement.

As an example, the `FullName` function meets all of the preceding restrictions. Given an author ID, it returns the first and last names concatenated. We should run it from the `usera` schema.

```
-- Available online as part of SQLFunctions.sql
CREATE OR REPLACE FUNCTION FullName (
  p_AuthorID  authors.ID%TYPE)
  RETURN VARCHAR2 IS

  v_Result  VARCHAR2(100);
BEGIN
  SELECT first_name || ' ' || last_name
    INTO v_Result
    FROM authors
    WHERE ID = p_AuthorID;

  RETURN v_Result;
END FullName;
/
```

We can use `FullName` as part of the select list in a query, as well as in DML statements, as shown next. The `FullName` function can be used in SQL queries because it meets all the restrictions.

```
-- Available online as part of SQLFunction.sql
SELECT FullName(ID) full_name
FROM authors
WHERE ID < 10
ORDER BY full_name;
```

The output lists the first nine rows in the `authors` table by concatenating the `first_name` column, a white space, and the `last_name` column.

```
FULL_NAME
-----------------------------------
Gaja Vaidyanatha
Ian Abramson
James Viscusi
John Kostelac
Kirtikumar Deshpande
Marlene Theriault
Michael Abbey
Michael Corey
Rachel Carmichael

9 rows selected.
```

We can use the `FullName` function in DML statements like the one that follows in the anonymous PL/SQL block:

```
DECLARE
   CURSOR c_IDs IS
     SELECT ID FROM authors WHERE ID BETWEEN 10 AND 20;
BEGIN
  FOR v_Rec IN c_IDs LOOP
    INSERT INTO temp_table (num_col, char_col)
    VALUES (v_Rec.ID, FullName(v_Rec.ID));
  END LOOP;
END;
/
```

A query against the `temp_table` will show that the tenth through twentieth records have been concatenated and inserted into the table.

```
SELECT *
FROM temp_table
ORDER BY num_col;
```

This is the output for the query:

```
    NUM_COL CHAR_COL
----- ------------------------------
        10 Kenny Smith
        11 Stephan Haisley
        12 Lars Bo
        13 Dirk Schepanek
        14 Christopher Allen
        15 David James
        16 Graham Seibert
        17 Simon Russell
        18 Bastin Gerald
        19 Nigel King
        20 Dan Natchek

11 rows selected.
```

The restrictions are checked when the SQL statement containing the function is executed. For example, if we modify `FullName` to insert into `temp_table`, it will no longer be callable from a query. This is illustrated by this modification:

```
-- Available online as part of SQLFunction.sql
CREATE OR REPLACE FUNCTION FullName (p_AuthorID  authors.ID%TYPE)
  RETURN VARCHAR2 IS

  v_Result  VARCHAR2(100);
BEGIN
  SELECT first_name || ' ' || last_name
  INTO v_Result
  FROM authors
  WHERE ID = p_AuthorID;

  INSERT INTO temp_table (num_col, char_col)
  VALUES (p_AuthorID, 'called by FullName!');

  RETURN v_Result;
END FullName;
/
```

Rerunning the query used before will generate an error while both objects are valid.

```
SELECT FullName(ID) full_name
FROM authors
WHERE ID < 10
ORDER BY full_name;
```

It raises an ORA-14551 error, which tells us that the function cannot perform a DML operation when included in a selection predicate.

```
SELECT FullName(ID) full_name
       *
ERROR at line 1:
ORA-14551: cannot perform a DML operation inside a query
ORA-06512: at "EXAMPLE.FULLNAME", line 12
```

Default Parameters

When calling a function from a procedural statement, you can use the default values for formal parameters, if they are present. When calling a function from a SQL statement, however, all parameters must be specified. Furthermore, you have to use positional notation and not named notation. The following call to FullName is illegal:

```
SELECT FullName(p_AuthorID => 37) FROM dual;
```

When we attempt this, we get the following error:

```
SELECT FullName(p_AuthorID => 37) FROM dual
                           *
ERROR at line 1:
ORA-00907: missing right parenthesis
```

Purity Levels and RESTRICT_REFERENCES

If a function does not meet the restrictions for being called from a SQL statement, an error (such as ORA-14551) is raised at run time when the function is actually called. It is possible, however, for the PL/SQL compiler to determine if the restrictions are met at compile time, and raise an error then if they are not. This is done through purity levels. A *purity level* defines what kinds of data structures the function reads or modifies. The available levels are listed in Table 9-2.

We can redefine the rules for calling functions in terms of the purity levels. For example, a function called from a query must have at least the WNDS purity level, since it cannot modify any database tables.

Purity Level	Meaning	Description
WNDS	Writes no database state	The function does not modify any database tables (using DML statements).
RNDS	Reads no database state	The function does not read any database tables (using the SELECT statement).
WNPS	Writes no package state	The function does not modify any packaged variables (no packaged variables are used on the left side of an assignment or in a FETCH statement).
RNPS	Reads no package state	The function does not examine any packaged variables (no packaged variables appear on the right side of an assignment or as part of a procedural or SQL expression).

TABLE 9-2.   *Function Purity Levels*

In order for the compiler to check the purity level of a given function, you use the RESTRICT_REFERENCES pragma. This pragma is defined with the syntax

PRAGMA RESTRICT_REFERENCES(*subprogram_or_package_name*,
  [WNDS] [, WNPS] [, RNDS] [, RNPS] [TRUST] [DEFAULT]);

where *subprogram_or_package_name* is the name of a package, or a packaged subprogram. The purity levels can be specified in any order. The pragma goes in the package header, with the specification for the function. For example, we can add pragma statements to the `InventoryOps` package, which we first saw in Chapter 7:

```
-- Available online as part of RestrictReferences.sql
CREATE OR REPLACE PACKAGE InventoryOps AS
  -- Modifies the inventory data for the specified book.
  PROCEDURE UpdateISBN(p_ISBN IN inventory.isbn%TYPE,
                       p_Status IN inventory.status%TYPE,
                       p_StatusDate IN inventory.status_date%TYPE,
                       p_Amount IN inventory.amount%TYPE);
  PRAGMA RESTRICT_REFERENCES(UpdateISBN, RNPS, WNPS);

  -- Deletes the inventory data for the specified book.
  PROCEDURE DeleteISBN(p_ISBN IN inventory.isbn%TYPE);
  PRAGMA RESTRICT_REFERENCES(DeleteISBN, RNPS, WNPS);

  -- Exception raised by UpdateISBN or DeleteISBN when the specified
```

```
      -- ISBN is not in the inventory table.
      e_ISBNNotFound EXCEPTION;

      TYPE t_ISBNTable IS TABLE OF inventory.isbn%TYPE
        INDEX BY BINARY_INTEGER;

      -- Returns a PL/SQL table containing the books with the specified
      -- status.
      PROCEDURE StatusList(p_Status IN inventory.status%TYPE,
                           p_Books OUT t_ISBNTable,
                           p_NumBooks OUT BINARY_INTEGER);
      PRAGMA RESTRICT_REFERENCES(StatusList, RNPS, WNPS, WNDS);


    END InventoryOps;
    /
```

Rationale for RESTRICT_REFERENCES   Since the PL/SQL engine will raise an error if a given function (or procedure called from a function) does not meet the requirements for being called from SQL, why use this pragma? It serves as a form of documentation for the function, as well as ensuring that it will be callable from SQL. Any modifications to the function that violate the pragma will be raised at compile time. For example, if we modify InventoryOps.StatusList to insert into temp_table, this will violate the pragma and we will get an error:

```
    -- Available online as part of RestrictReferences.sql
    CREATE OR REPLACE PACKAGE BODY InventoryOps AS
      ...
      -- Returns a PL/SQL table containing the books with the specified
      -- status.
      PROCEDURE StatusList(p_Status IN inventory.status%TYPE,
                           p_Books OUT t_ISBNTable,
                           p_NumBooks OUT BINARY_INTEGER) IS
        v_ISBN inventory.isbn%TYPE;
        CURSOR c_Books IS
          SELECT isbn
          FROM inventory
          WHERE status = p_Status;

      BEGIN
        INSERT INTO temp_table (char_col)
        VALUES ('Hello from StatusList!');

        /* p_NumBooks will be the table index. It will start at
         * 0, and be incremented each time through the fetch loop.
         * At the end of the loop, it will have the number of rows
```

```
      * fetched, and therefore the number of rows returned in
      * p_Books. */
     p_NumBooks := 0;
     OPEN c_Books;
     LOOP
       FETCH c_Books INTO v_ISBN;
       EXIT WHEN c_Books%NOTFOUND;

       p_NumBooks := p_NumBooks + 1;
       p_Books(p_NumBooks) := v_ISBN;
     END LOOP;
     CLOSE c_Books;
   END StatusList;
END InventoryOps;
/
```

The pragma violation will raise a PLS-452 compilation error due to the insert DML within the StatusList procedure.

```
LINE/COL ERROR
---- --------------------------------
32/3    PLS-00452: Subprogram 'STATUSLIST' violates its associated pragma
```

TIP
Before Oracle8i, the PL/SQL engine could verify the purity levels of stand-alone functions at run time, but packaged functions only at compile time. This was the original reason for the RESTRICT_REFERENCES pragma.

Initialization Section   The code in the initialization section of a package can have a purity level as well. The first time any function in the package is called, the initialization section is run. Consequently, a packaged function is only as pure as the initialization section of the containing package. The purity level for a package is guaranteed with RESTRICT_REFERENCES. This is done by referencing the package name rather than a function name:

```
CREATE OR REPLACE PACKAGE InventoryOps AS
   PRAGMA RESTRICT_REFERENCES (InventoryOps, WNDS);
   ...
END InventoryOps;
/
```

DEFAULT Keyword   If no RESTRICT_REFERENCES pragma is associated with a given packaged function, it will not have any purity level asserted. However, you can change the default purity level for a package. The DEFAULT keyword is used instead of the subprogram name in the pragma:

PRAGMA RESTRICT_REFERENCES(DEFAULT,
 WNDS [, WNPS] [, RNDS] [, RNPS]);

Any subsequent subprograms in the package must comply with the purity levels specified. For example, consider the DefaultPragma package:

```
-- Available online as DefaultPragma.sql
CREATE OR REPLACE PACKAGE DefaultPragma AS
  FUNCTION F1 RETURN NUMBER;
  PRAGMA RESTRICT_REFERENCES(F1, RNDS, RNPS);

  PRAGMA RESTRICT_REFERENCES(DEFAULT, WNDS, WNPS, RNDS, RNPS);
  FUNCTION F2 RETURN NUMBER;

  FUNCTION F3 RETURN NUMBER;
END DefaultPragma;
/

CREATE OR REPLACE PACKAGE BODY DefaultPragma AS
  FUNCTION F1 RETURN NUMBER IS
  BEGIN
    INSERT INTO temp_table (num_col, char_col)
      VALUES (1, 'F1!');
    RETURN 1;
  END F1;

  FUNCTION F2 RETURN NUMBER IS
  BEGIN
    RETURN 2;
  END F2;

  -- This function violates the default pragma.
  FUNCTION F3 RETURN NUMBER IS
  BEGIN
    INSERT INTO temp_table (num_col, char_col)
      VALUES (1, 'F3!');
    RETURN 3;
  END F3;
END DefaultPragma;
/
```

The default pragma (which asserts all four purity levels) will be applied to both `F2` and `F3`. Since `F3` INSERTs into `temp_table`, it violates the pragma. Compiling the preceding package will return the following errors:

```
LINE/COL ERROR
---- --------------------------------
15/3     PLS-00452: Subprogram 'F3' violates its associated pragma
```

TRUST Keyword   Although RESTRICT_REFERENCES is no longer required (and in fact cannot be used for external routines), code written prior to Oracle8*i* may use it. The pragma can also be used for documentation, as we discussed in the previous section. Thus, you may want to call a function that does not have the pragma from one that is declared pure. To aid this, Oracle provides an additional keyword that can be used in the pragma, in addition to or instead of the purity levels—TRUST.

If the TRUST keyword is present, the restrictions listed in the pragma are not enforced. Rather, they are trusted to be true. This allows you to write new code that does not use RESTRICT_REFERENCES, and call the new code from functions that are declared pure. For example, consider the following package:

```
-- Available online as TrustPkg.sql
CREATE OR REPLACE PACKAGE TrustPkg AS
  FUNCTION ToUpper (p_a VARCHAR2) RETURN VARCHAR2 IS
    LANGUAGE JAVA
    NAME 'Test.Uppercase(char[]) return char[]';
    PRAGMA RESTRICT_REFERENCES(ToUpper, WNDS, TRUST);

  PROCEDURE Demo(p_in IN VARCHAR2, p_out OUT VARCHAR2);
  PRAGMA RESTRICT_REFERENCES(Demo, WNDS);
END TrustPkg;
/

CREATE OR REPLACE PACKAGE BODY TrustPkg AS
  PROCEDURE Demo(p_in IN VARCHAR2, p_out OUT VARCHAR2) IS
  BEGIN
    p_out := ToUpper(p_in);
  END Demo;
END TrustPkg;
/
```

`TrustPkg.ToUpper` is an external routine—the body of the function is actually written in Java, and will return its input parameter in all uppercase. Since the body is not in PL/SQL, the TRUST keyword is necessary for the pragma. Then, because `ToUpper` is trusted to have the WNDS purity, we can call `ToUpper` from `Demo`.

> **NOTE**
> *Although* `TrustPkg` *can be compiled without having the Java stored procedure present, it cannot be run without first creating* `Test.Uppercase`.

Overloaded Functions   RESTRICT_REFERENCES can appear anywhere in the package specification, after the function declaration. It can apply to only one function definition, however. For overloaded functions, the pragma applies to the nearest definition prior to the pragma. In the following example, each pragma applies to the version of TestFunc just prior to it:

```
-- Available online as part of OverloadRestrictReferences.sql
CREATE OR REPLACE PACKAGE Overload AS
  FUNCTION TestFunc(p_Parameter1 IN NUMBER)
    RETURN VARCHAR2;
  PRAGMA RESTRICT_REFERENCES(TestFunc, WNDS, RNDS, WNPS, RNPS);

  FUNCTION TestFunc(p_ParameterA IN VARCHAR2,
                    p_ParameterB IN DATE)
    RETURN VARCHAR2;
  PRAGMA RESTRICT_REFERENCES(TestFunc, WNDS, RNDS, WNPS, RNPS);
END Overload;
/

CREATE OR REPLACE PACKAGE BODY Overload AS
  FUNCTION TestFunc(p_Parameter1 IN NUMBER)
    RETURN VARCHAR2 IS
  BEGIN
    RETURN 'Version 1';
  END TestFunc;

  FUNCTION TestFunc(p_ParameterA IN VARCHAR2,
                    p_ParameterB IN DATE)
    RETURN VARCHAR2 IS
  BEGIN
    RETURN 'Version 2';
  END TestFunc;
END Overload;
/
```

A query against `Overload.TestFunc` with a number signature demonstrates one of the overloaded functions.

```
-- Available online as part of Overload.sql
SELECT Overload.TestFunc(1) FROM dual;
```

The output shows that number signature overloaded function is successful.

```
OVERLOAD.TESTFUNC(1)
----------------------------
Version 1
```

A query against `Overload.TestFunc` with a variable-length string and date signature demonstrates the other overloaded function.

```
SELECT Overload.TestFunc('abc', SYSDATE) FROM dual;
```

The output shows that variable-length string and date signature overloaded function is successful.

```
OVERLOAD.TESTFUNC('ABC',SYSDATE)
----------------------------
Version 2
```

TIP
*We generally prefer to code the RESTRICT_
REFERENCES pragma immediately after
each function so that it is clear to which
version it applies.*

Multiple-Valued Functions

As we have seen in the previous section, a single-valued function returns a
scalar value. A multiple-valued function, or *table function,* on the other hand,
returns a collection of values. With the TABLE SQL operator, this collection can
itself be used as a relational table in a SQL query. For example, consider the
`SomeBooks` function:

```
-- Available online as part of TableFunctions.sql
CREATE TYPE BookType AS OBJECT
(isbn  CHAR(10)
,title VARCHAR2(100));
/

CREATE TYPE BookTypes AS TABLE OF BookType;
/

CREATE OR REPLACE FUNCTION SomeBooks(p_Category IN books.category%TYPE)
```

```
    RETURN BookTypes AS

    v_ResultSet BookTypes := BookTypes();

    CURSOR c_SomeBooks IS
      SELECT isbn, title
        FROM books
        WHERE category = p_Category;

BEGIN
  FOR v_Rec IN c_SomeBooks LOOP

    v_ResultSet.EXTEND;
    v_ResultSet(v_ResultSet.LAST) := BookType(v_Rec.isbn, v_Rec.title);

  END LOOP;

  RETURN v_ResultSet;
END SomeBooks;
/
```

SomeBooks returns a table of BookType, which itself is an object type consisting of two fields, isbn and title. (See Chapter 6 for more information on collections and Chapters 14–16 for more information about object types.) We can call SomeBooks from SQL, since it does not violate any of the restrictions we saw in the previous sections:

```
-- Available online as part of TableFunctions.sql
SELECT SomeBooks('Oracle Basics') FROM dual;
```

The output shows that a table of BookType is returned.

```
SOMEBOOKS('ORACLEBASICS')(ISBN, TITLE)
----------------------------------------
BOOKTYPES(BOOKTYPE('72121203  ', 'Oracle DBA 101'), BOOKTYPE('72122048  ', 'Orac
le8i: A Beginner''s Guide'), BOOKTYPE('0072131454', 'Oracle Performance Tuning 1
01'), BOOKTYPE('007212606X', 'Oracle PL/SQL 101')))
```

NOTE
The preceding output indicates that the return value of the function is itself a collection of records. This is the SQL*Plus formatting for such a return type.

We can now go one step further and use the SQL TABLE operator. This operator takes a collection as input, and returns the same data in a form that can be directly queried by a SELECT statement. For example,

```
-- Available online as part of TableFunctions.sql
SELECT *
FROM TABLE(SomeBooks('Oracle Basics'));
```

The output shows the record structure of the table of `BookType`.

```
ISBN        TITLE
-----  --------------------
72121203    Oracle DBA 101
72122048    Oracle8i: A Beginner's Guide
0072131454 Oracle Performance Tuning 101
007212606X Oracle PL/SQL 101
```

Although this example is somewhat contrived, it illustrates how the TABLE operator works. The function that generates the result set can use any arbitrary logic to create it, which may or may not include querying tables. This is especially useful for functions that are computationally expensive, since it provides an easy method of iterating through the results using straight SQL.

Deterministic Table Functions

If the function will always return the same output given the same input, we can use the DETERMINISTIC keyword in the function definition. This allows Oracle to internally cache the values of the function for use in repeated queries using TABLE, which can improve performance. DETERMINISTIC is found after the return type, before IS or AS, as the following example illustrates:

```
-- Available online as part of TableFunctions.sql
CREATE OR REPLACE FUNCTION SomeBooks(p_Category IN books.category%TYPE)
  RETURN BookTypes DETERMINISTIC AS

  v_ResultSet BookTypes := BookTypes();

  CURSOR c_SomeBooks IS
    SELECT isbn, title
      FROM books
      WHERE category = p_Category;

BEGIN
```

```
FOR v_Rec IN c_SomeBooks LOOP

   v_ResultSet.EXTEND;
   v_ResultSet(v_ResultSet.LAST) := BookType(v_Rec.isbn, v_Rec.title);
END LOOP;

   RETURN v_ResultSet;
END SomeBooks;
/
```

NOTE
Oracle does not actually verify that the function is truly deterministic. Thus, you should use it only for functions that you know to be deterministic.

Pipelined Table Functions

In many cases, it will take time for a table function to compute the entire result set. However, this must be done before any further processing of the TABLE operator. If the rows in the result set can be determined individually, however, then you can use a pipelined table function. A *pipelined* function is identified by the PIPELINED keyword before IS or AS. (The DETERMINISTIC keyword may be present as well.) Furthermore, a pipelined function uses the PIPE ROW statement to return an individual row. PIPE ROW is defined as

PIPE ROW (*row_type*)

where *row_type* is a single row in the result set. RETURN is used to signal the end of processing. For example, consider the following types and function:

```
-- Available online as part of OracleErrors.sql
CREATE OR REPLACE TYPE OracleError AS OBJECT (
  ErrNumber INTEGER,
  Message VARCHAR2(4000));
/

CREATE OR REPLACE TYPE OracleErrors AS TABLE OF OracleError;
/
```

Create the function with the DETERMINISTIC keyword because the function will always return the same output.

```
CREATE OR REPLACE FUNCTION OracleErrorTable
   RETURN OracleErrors DETERMINISTIC PIPELINED
AS
   v_Low PLS_INTEGER := -65535;
   v_High PLS_INTEGER := 100;
```

```
    v_Message VARCHAR2(4000);
BEGIN
  FOR i IN v_Low..v_High LOOP
    -- Get the message for the given error number
    v_Message := SQLERRM(i);

    -- If it is legal, then output it.
    IF v_Message != ' -' || TO_CHAR(i) || ': non-ORACLE exception '
    AND v_Message != 'ORA' || TO_CHAR(i, '00000') || ': Message ' ||
        TO_CHAR(-i) || ' not found;  product=RDBMS; facility=ORA'
    THEN
      PIPE ROW(OracleError(i, v_Message));
    END IF;
  END LOOP;
  RETURN;
END;
/
```

`OracleErrorTable` will return a collection of `OracleError` objects, each of which will represent the code and text for a particular error message. Because of the PIPE ROW, each row will be returned as soon as it is created. We can now create a view using the TABLE operator, as follows:

```
-- Available online as part of OracleErrors.sql
CREATE OR REPLACE VIEW all_oracle_errors
  AS SELECT * FROM TABLE(OracleErrorTable());
```

Query the view for the minimum and maximum numbers and the count of errors.

```
SELECT MIN(errnumber), MAX(errnumber), COUNT(*)
FROM all_oracle_errors;
```

```
MIN(ERRNUMBER) MAX(ERRNUMBER)   COUNT(*)
------- ------- -----
        -43016           100        14427
```

Native Compilation

Similar to Java bytecode, p-code is first generated by the PL/SQL engine, which interprets the PL/SQL program code and creates p-code. This is a very portable design, in that the same PL/SQL code can be run in different databases, possibly on different platforms. However, because it is interpreted, it is not as fast as compiled object code. Object code is machine level instructions specific to an operating system platform.

In Oracle9*i*, you can choose to have PL/SQL compiled to native code. This will create a shared library, which is then run by the Oracle shadow process. In order to use this feature, you must have a C compiler installed on your system, as the PL/SQL compiler will generate C code that is then compiled into the native library.

For details on how to do this, see the Oracle documentation.

Pinning in the Shared Pool

The *shared pool* is the portion of the SGA that contains, among other things, the p-code of compiled subprograms as they are run. The first time a stored subprogram is called, the p-code is loaded from disk into the shared pool. Once the object is no longer referenced, it is free to be aged out. Objects are aged out of the shared pool using an LRU (least recently used) algorithm. See *Oracle Concepts* for more information on the shared pool and how it works.

The DBMS_SHARED_POOL package allows you to pin objects in the shared pool. When an object is *pinned,* it will never be aged out until you request it, no matter how full the pool gets or how often the object is accessed. This can improve performance, as it takes time to reload a package from disk. Pinning an object also helps minimize fragmentation of the shared pool. DBMS_SHARED_POOL has four procedures: DBMS_SHARED_POOL.KEEP, DBMS_SHARED_POOL.UNKEEP, DBMS_SHARED_POOL.SIZES, and DBMS_SHARED_POOL.ABORTED_REQUEST_THRESHOLD.

KEEP

The DBMS_SHARED_POOL.KEEP procedure is used to pin objects in the pool. Packages, triggers, sequences, object types, Java objects (Oracle8*i* and higher), and SQL statements can be pinned. KEEP is defined with the syntax

```
PROCEDURE KEEP(name VARCHAR2,
              flag CHAR DEFAULT 'P');
```

The parameters are described in Table 9-3. Once an object has been kept, it will not be removed until the database is shut down or the DBMS_SHARED_POOL.UNKEEP procedure is used. Note that DBMS_SHARED_POOL.KEEP does not load the package into the shared pool immediately; rather, it will be pinned the first time it is subsequently loaded.

UNKEEP

UNKEEP is the only way to remove a kept object from the shared pool, without restarting the database. Kept objects are never aged out automatically. UNKEEP is defined with the syntax.

PROCEDURE UNKEEP(*name* VARCHAR2,
                            flag CHAR DEFAULT 'P');

The arguments are the same as for KEEP. If the specified object does not already exist in the shared pool, an error is raised.

SIZES

SIZES will echo the contents of the shared pool to the screen. It is defined with the syntax

PROCEDURE SIZES(*minsize* NUMBER);

Objects with a size greater than *minsize* will be returned. SIZES uses DBMS_OUTPUT to return the data, so be sure to use "set serveroutput on" in SQL*Plus or Server Manager before calling the procedure.

ABORTED_REQUEST_THRESHOLD

When the database determines that there is not enough memory in the shared pool to satisfy a given request, it will begin aging objects out until there is enough

Parameter	Type	Description
name	VARCHAR2	Name of the object. This can be an object name or the identifier associated with a SQL statement. The SQL identifier is the concatenation of the `address` and `hash_value` fields in the `v$sqlarea` view (by default, selectable only by SYS) and is returned by the SIZES procedure.
flag	CHAR	Determines the type of the object. The values for *flag* have the following meanings: P Package, function, or procedure Q Sequence R Trigger T Object type (Oracle8 and higher) JS Java source (Oracle8*i* and higher) JC Java class (Oracle8*i* and higher) JR Java resource (Oracle8*i* and higher) JD Java shared data (Oracle8*i* and higher) C SQL cursor

TABLE 9-3.   *DBMS_SHARED_POOL.KEEP Parameters*

memory. If enough objects are aged out, this can have a performance impact on other database sessions. The ABORTED_REQUEST_THRESHOLD can be used to remedy this. It is defined with the syntax

PROCEDURE ABORTED_REQUEST_THRESHOLD(*threshold_size* NUMBER);

Once this procedure is called, Oracle will not start aging objects from the pool unless at least *threshold_size* bytes is needed.

The PL/SQL Wrapper

Oracle applications often consist of multiple subprograms and packages. In many cases, the source code for these applications is proprietary, and the authors do not want the details to be visible. However, they still have to be installed at a customer site. In order to accomplish this, Oracle provides the PL/SQL wrapper. The wrapper is an operating system utility that takes a SQL source file as input, containing CREATE OR REPLACE statements for subprograms or packages. The output is another SQL source file with CREATE OR REPLACE statements, but with the source code obfuscated so that it is not human-readable. It is, however, still readable to the system, and the file can be loaded into the database with SQL*Plus just like the original files.

TIP
The Oracle supplied packages (such as DBMS_ SHARED_POOL, which we examined in the previous section) are all shipped in wrapped form. The package headers are in clear text, while the package bodies are wrapped. This is a good model to adopt for your own code, since the package header source provides documentation for the packages.

Summary

We have continued our discussion of three types of named PL/SQL blocks in this chapter—procedures, functions, and packages. This included the differences between local and stored subprograms, and how dependencies among stored subprograms work. We also discussed how to call stored subprograms from SQL statements. We closed the chapter with a discussion of the DBMS_SHARED_POOL package. In the next chapter, we will cover a fourth type of named PL/SQL block: database triggers.

CHAPTER
10

Database Triggers

he fourth type of named PL/SQL block is the trigger. Triggers share many of the same characteristics as subprograms (which we have examined in the previous two chapters), but they have significant differences both in how they are created and how they are called. In this chapter, we will examine how to create different types of triggers and discuss some possible applications.

Types of Triggers

Triggers are similar to procedures or functions in that they are named PL/SQL blocks with declarative, executable, and exception handling sections. Like packages and object types (which we will discuss in Chapters 14–16), triggers must be stored as stand-alone objects in the database and cannot be local to a block or package. As we have seen in the past two chapters, a procedure is executed explicitly from another block via a procedure call, which can also pass arguments. On the other hand, a trigger is executed implicitly whenever the triggering event happens, and a trigger doesn't accept arguments. The act of executing a trigger is known as *firing* the trigger. The triggering event can be a DML (INSERT, UPDATE, or DELETE) operation on a database table or certain kinds of views; or a system event, such as database startup or shutdown, and certain kinds of DDL operations. We will discuss the triggering events in detail later in this chapter.

Triggers can be used for many things, including the following:

- Maintaining complex integrity constraints not possible through declarative constraints enabled at table creation

- Auditing information in a table by recording the changes made and who made them

- Automatically signaling other programs that action needs to take place when changes are made to a table

- Publishing information about various events in a publish-subscribe environment

There are three main kinds of triggers: DML, instead-of, and system triggers. In the following sections, we will introduce each kind. We will offer more details later in the section "Creating Triggers."

NOTE
Oracle allows triggers to be written in either PL/SQL or other languages that can be called as external routines. See the section "Trigger Bodies" later in this chapter for more information (as well as Chapter 12 for more information on external routines in general).

DML Triggers

A *DML trigger* is fired by a DML statement, and the type of statement determines the type of DML trigger. DML triggers can be defined for INSERT, UPDATE, or DELETE operations. They can be fired before or after the operation on a row. DML triggers can act on all rows or only some rows. They act on a subset of rows when they are defined as statement-level triggers. The difference is a statement-level trigger uses a WHEN clause to evaluate where a specific type of change is occurring. By putting the condition in a WHEN clause, it eliminates running the trigger unless the condition is met.

As an example, suppose we want to track statistics about different categories, including the number of books in the database and the average price in each category. We are going to store these results in the `category_stats` table:

```
-- Available online as part of tables.sql
CREATE TABLE category_stats (
  category       VARCHAR2(20),
  total_books    NUMBER,
  average_price  NUMBER
);
```

In order to keep `category_stats` up-to-date, we can create a trigger on `books` that will update `category_stats` every time `books` is modified. The `UpdateCategoryStats` trigger, shown next, does this. After any DML operation on `books`, the trigger will execute. The body of the trigger queries `books` and updates `category_stats` with the current statistics.

```
-- Available online as UpdateCategoryStats.sql
CREATE OR REPLACE TRIGGER UpdateCategoryStats
  /* Keeps the category_stats table up-to-date with changes made
     to the books table. */
```

```
    AFTER INSERT OR DELETE OR UPDATE ON books
DECLARE
   CURSOR c_Statistics IS
     SELECT category,
            COUNT(*) total_books,
            AVG(price) average_price
     FROM books
     GROUP BY category;
BEGIN
   /* First delete from category_stats.  This will clear the
      statistics, and is necessary to account for the deletion
      of all books in a given category */
   DELETE FROM category_stats;

   /* Now loop through each category, and insert the appropriate row into
      category_stats. */
   FOR v_StatsRecord in c_Statistics LOOP
     INSERT INTO category_stats (category, total_books, average_price)
       VALUES (v_StatsRecord.category, v_StatsRecord.total_books,
               v_StatsRecord.average_price);
   END LOOP;
END UpdateCategoryStats;
/
```

A statement trigger can be fired for more than one type of triggering statement. For example, `UpdateCategoryStats` is fired on INSERT, UPDATE, and DELETE statements. The triggering event specifies one or more of the DML operations that should fire the trigger.

Instead-of Triggers

Instead-of triggers can be defined on views (either relational or object) only. Unlike a DML trigger, which executes in addition to the DML operation, an instead-of trigger will execute instead of the DML statement that fired it. Instead-of triggers must be row level. For example, consider the `books_authors` view:

```
-- Available online as part of insteadOf1.sql
CREATE OR REPLACE VIEW books_authors AS
  SELECT b.isbn, b.title, a.first_name, a.last_name
    FROM books b, authors a
   WHERE b.author1 = a.id
      OR b.author2 = a.id
      OR b.author3 = a.id;
```

It is illegal to INSERT into this view directly, because it is a join of two tables and the INSERT requires that both underlying tables be modified, as the following SQL*Plus session shows:

-- **Available online as part of insteadOf1.sql**
```
INSERT INTO books_authors (isbn, title, first_name, last_name)
VALUES ('72230665', 'Oracle Database 10g PL/SQL Programming','Joe', 'Blow');
```

The output illustrates the insert failure to the view:

```
INSERT INTO books_authors (isbn, title, first_name, last_name)
                          *
ERROR at line 1:
ORA-01779: cannot modify a column which maps to a non key-preserved table
```

However, we can create an instead-of trigger that does the correct thing for an
INSERT, namely to update the underlying tables:

-- **Available online as part of insteadOf2.sql**
```
CREATE OR REPLACE TRIGGER InsertBooksAuthors
  INSTEAD OF INSERT ON books_authors
DECLARE

  v_Book books%ROWTYPE;
  v_AuthorID authors.id%TYPE;
BEGIN
  -- Figure out the ID of the new author
  BEGIN
    SELECT id
      INTO v_AuthorID
      FROM authors
      WHERE first_name = :new.first_name
        AND last_name = :new.last_name;
  EXCEPTION
    WHEN NO_DATA_FOUND THEN
      -- No author found, create a new one
      INSERT INTO authors (id, first_name, last_name)
        VALUES (author_sequence.NEXTVAL, :new.first_name, :new.last_name)
        RETURNING ID INTO v_AuthorID;
  END;

  SELECT *
    INTO v_Book
    FROM books
    WHERE isbn = :new.isbn;

  -- Figure out whether the book already has 1 or 2 authors, and update
  -- accordingly
  IF v_Book.author2 IS NULL THEN
    UPDATE books
      SET author2 = v_AuthorID
      WHERE isbn = :new.isbn;
```

```
    ELSE
      UPDATE books
        SET author3 = v_AuthorID
        WHERE isbn = :new.isbn;
    END IF;
END InsertBooksAuthors;
/
```

With the `InsertBooksAuthors` trigger in place, the INSERT statement succeeds and does the correct thing.

> **NOTE**
> *As currently written, `InsertBooksAuthors` does not have any error checking. We will rectify this later in this chapter in the section "Creating Instead-of Triggers."*

System Triggers

A *system trigger* fires when a system event, such as database startup or shutdown, occurs, rather than on a DML operation on a table. A system trigger can also be fired on DDL operations, such as table creation. For example, suppose we want to record whenever a data dictionary object is created. We can do this by creating a table, as follows:

```
-- Available online as part of LogCreations.sql
CREATE TABLE ddl_creations (
  user_id       VARCHAR2(30),
  object_type   VARCHAR2(20),
  object_name   VARCHAR2(30),
  object_owner  VARCHAR2(30),
  creation_date DATE);
```

Once this table is available, we can create a system trigger to record the relevant information. The `LogCreations` trigger does just that—after every CREATE operation on the current schema, it records information about the object just created in `ddl_creations`.

```
-- Available online as part of LogCreations.sql
CREATE OR REPLACE TRIGGER LogCreations
  AFTER CREATE ON SCHEMA
BEGIN
  INSERT INTO ddl_creations (user_id, object_type, object_name,
                             object_owner, creation_date)
```

```
       VALUES (USER, ORA_DICT_OBJ_TYPE, ORA_DICT_OBJ_NAME,
              ORA_DICT_OBJ_OWNER, SYSDATE);
END LogCreations;
/
```

Creating Triggers

Regardless of the type, all triggers are created using the same syntax. The general
syntax for creating a trigger is

CREATE [OR REPLACE] TRIGGER *trigger_name*
  {BEFORE | AFTER | INSTEAD OF} *triggering_event*
[*referencing_clause*]
  [WHEN *trigger_condition*]
  [FOR EACH ROW]
  trigger_body;

where *trigger_name* is the name of the trigger, *triggering_event* specifies the event
that fires the trigger (possibly including a specific table or view), and *trigger_body*
is the main code for the trigger. The *referencing_clause* is used to refer to the data in
the row currently being modified by a different name. The *trigger_condition* in the
WHEN clause, if present, is evaluated first, and the body of the trigger is executed
only when this condition evaluates to TRUE. We will see more examples of different
kinds of triggers in the following sections.

NOTE
*The trigger body cannot exceed 32K. If you have a
trigger that exceeds this size, you can reduce it by
moving some of the code to separately compiled
packages or stored procedures, and calling these
from the trigger body. It is generally a good idea
to keep trigger bodies small, because of the
frequency with which they execute.*

The trigger body is a PL/SQL block, which must contain at least an executable
section. Like any other block, the declarative and exception handling sections are
optional. If there is a declarative section, however, the *trigger_body* must begin with
the DECLARE keyword. This is different from a subprogram, where the DECLARE
keyword is not present.

Creating DML Triggers

A DML trigger is fired on an INSERT, UPDATE, or DELETE operation on a database
table. It can be fired either before or after the statement executes and can be fired

once per affected row, or once per statement. The combination of these factors determines the type of the trigger. There are a total of 28 possible types: (3 statements + 4 combination statements) × 2 timing × 2 levels. For example, all of the following are valid DML trigger types:

- Before UPDATE statement level

- After INSERT row level

- Before DELETE row level

Table 10-1 summarizes the various options. A trigger can also be fired for more than one kind of DML statement on a given table—INSERT and UPDATE, for example. Any code in the trigger will be executed along with the triggering statement itself, as part of the same transaction.

A table can have any number of triggers defined on it, including more than one of a given DML type. For example, you can define two after DELETE statement-level triggers. All triggers of the same type will fire sequentially. (For more information on the order of trigger firing, see the following section.)

The triggering event for a DML trigger specifies the name of the table (and column) on which the trigger will fire. A trigger can also fire on a column of a nested table. See Chapter 6 for more information on nested tables.

Category	Values	Comments
Statement	INSERT, DELETE, or UPDATE	Defines which kind of DML statement causes the trigger to fire.
Timing	BEFORE or AFTER	Defines whether the trigger fires before or after the statement is executed.
Level	Row or statement	If the trigger is a row-level trigger, it fires once for each row affected by the triggering statement. If the trigger is a statement-level trigger, it fires once, either before or after the statement. A row-level trigger is identified by the FOR EACH ROW clause in the trigger definition.

TABLE 10-1. *Types of DML Triggers*

Order of DML Trigger Firing

Triggers are fired as the DML statement is executed. The algorithm for executing a DML statement is given here:

1. Execute the before statement-level triggers, if present.

2. For each row affected by the statement:

   ■ Execute the before row-level triggers, if present.

   ■ Execute the statement itself.

   ■ Execute the after row-level triggers, if present.

3. Execute the after statement-level triggers, if present.

To illustrate this, suppose we create all four kinds of UPDATE triggers on the books table—before and after, statement and row levels. We will also create three before-row triggers and two after-statement triggers, as follows:

```
-- Available online as part of firingOrder.sql
CREATE SEQUENCE trig_seq
  START WITH 1
  INCREMENT BY 1;

CREATE OR REPLACE PACKAGE TrigPackage AS
  -- Global counter for use in the triggers
  v_Counter NUMBER;
END TrigPackage;
/

CREATE OR REPLACE TRIGGER BooksBStatement
  BEFORE UPDATE ON books
BEGIN
  -- Reset the counter first.
  TrigPackage.v_Counter := 0;

  INSERT INTO temp_table (num_col, char_col)
    VALUES (trig_seq.NEXTVAL,
      'Before Statement: counter = ' || TrigPackage.v_Counter);

  -- And now increment it for the next trigger.
  TrigPackage.v_Counter := TrigPackage.v_Counter + 1;
END BooksBStatement;
/
```

```
CREATE OR REPLACE TRIGGER BooksAStatement1
  AFTER UPDATE ON books
BEGIN
  INSERT INTO temp_table (num_col, char_col)
    VALUES (trig_seq.NEXTVAL,
      'After Statement 1: counter = ' || TrigPackage.v_Counter);

  -- Increment for the next trigger.
  TrigPackage.v_Counter := TrigPackage.v_Counter + 1;
END BooksAStatement1;
/

CREATE OR REPLACE TRIGGER BooksAStatement2
  AFTER UPDATE ON books
BEGIN
  INSERT INTO temp_table (num_col, char_col)
    VALUES (trig_seq.NEXTVAL,
      'After Statement 2: counter = ' || TrigPackage.v_Counter);

  -- Increment for the next trigger.
  TrigPackage.v_Counter := TrigPackage.v_Counter + 1;
END BooksAStatement2;
/

CREATE OR REPLACE TRIGGER BooksBRow1
  BEFORE UPDATE ON books
  FOR EACH ROW
BEGIN
  INSERT INTO temp_table (num_col, char_col)
    VALUES (trig_seq.NEXTVAL,
      'Before Row 1: counter = ' || TrigPackage.v_Counter);

  -- Increment for the next trigger.
  TrigPackage.v_Counter := TrigPackage.v_Counter + 1;
END BooksBRow1;
/

CREATE OR REPLACE TRIGGER BooksBRow2
  BEFORE UPDATE ON books
  FOR EACH ROW
BEGIN
  INSERT INTO temp_table (num_col, char_col)
    VALUES (trig_seq.NEXTVAL,
      'Before Row 2: counter = ' || TrigPackage.v_Counter);

  -- Increment for the next trigger.
```

```
    TrigPackage.v_Counter := TrigPackage.v_Counter + 1;
END BooksBRow2;
/

CREATE OR REPLACE TRIGGER BooksBRow3
  BEFORE UPDATE ON books
  FOR EACH ROW
BEGIN
  INSERT INTO temp_table (num_col, char_col)
    VALUES (trig_seq.NEXTVAL,
      'Before Row 3: counter = ' || TrigPackage.v_Counter);

  -- Increment for the next trigger.
  TrigPackage.v_Counter := TrigPackage.v_Counter + 1;
END BooksBRow3;
/

CREATE OR REPLACE TRIGGER BooksARow
  AFTER UPDATE ON books
  FOR EACH ROW
BEGIN
  INSERT INTO temp_table (num_col, char_col)
    VALUES (trig_seq.NEXTVAL,
      'After Row: counter - ' || TrigPackage.v_Counter);

  -- Increment for the next trigger.
  TrigPackage.v_Counter := TrigPackage.v_Counter + 1;
END BooksARow;
/
```

Suppose we now issue the following UPDATE statement:

```
-- Available online as part of firingOrder.sql
UPDATE books
  SET category = category
  WHERE category = 'Oracle Ebusiness';
```

This statement affects three rows. The before and after statement-level triggers are each executed once, and the before and after row-level triggers are each executed three times. We can use the following query to select from temp_table:

```
-- Available online as part of firingOrder.sql
SELECT *
FROM temp_table
ORDER BY num_col;
```

We will see the following output:

```
NUM_COL CHAR_COL
----- ----------------------
      1 Before Statement: counter = 0
      2 Before Row 3: counter = 1
      3 Before Row 2: counter = 2
      4 Before Row 1: counter = 3
      5 After Row: counter = 4
      6 Before Row 3: counter = 5
      7 Before Row 2: counter = 6
      8 Before Row 1: counter = 7
      9 After Row: counter = 8
     10 Before Row 3: counter = 9
     11 Before Row 2: counter = 10
     12 Before Row 1: counter = 11
     13 After Row: counter = 12
     14 After Statement 2: counter = 13
     15 After Statement 1: counter = 14
```

As each trigger is fired, it will see the changes made by the earlier triggers, as well as any database changes made by the statement so far. This can be seen by the counter value printed by each trigger. (See Chapter 9 for more information about using packaged variables.)

The order in which triggers of the same type are fired is not defined. As in the preceding example, each trigger will see changes made by earlier triggers. If the order is important, combine all of the operations into one trigger.

NOTE
When you create a snapshot log for a table, Oracle will automatically create an after-row trigger for the table, that will update the log after every DML statement. You should be aware of this if you need to create an additional after-row trigger on that table. There are also additional restrictions on triggers and snapshots (known as materialized views in Oracle9i). For more information, check the Oracle Database Advanced Replication documentation.

Correlation Identifiers in Row-Level Triggers
A row-level trigger fires once per row processed by the triggering statement. Inside the trigger, you can access the data in the row that is currently being processed.

This is accomplished through two correlation identifiers—:old and :new. A *correlation identifier* is a special kind of PL/SQL bind variable. The colon in front of each indicates that they are bind variables, in the sense of host variables used in embedded PL/SQL, and indicates that they are not regular PL/SQL variables. The PL/SQL compiler will treat them as records of type

triggering_table%ROWTYPE

where *triggering_table* is the table for which the trigger is defined. Thus, a reference such as

:new.*field*

will be valid only if *field* is a field in the triggering table. The meanings of :old and :new are described in Table 10-2. Although syntactically they are treated as records, in reality they are not (this is discussed later in the section "Pseudorecords"); :old and :new are also known as *pseudorecords* for this reason.

NOTE
The :old *identifier is undefined for INSERT statements, and* :new *is undefined for DELETE statements. The PL/SQL compiler will not generate an error if you use* :old *in an INSERT or* :new *in a DELETE, but the field values of both will be NULL.*

Oracle defines one additional correlation identifier—:parent. If the trigger is defined on a nested table, :old and :new refer to the rows in the nested table, while :parent refers to the current row of the parent table. For more information, see the Oracle documentation.

Triggering Statement	:old	:new
INSERT	Undefined—all fields are NULL	Values that will be inserted when the statement is complete
UPDATE	Original values for the row before the update	New values that will be updated when the statement is complete
DELETE	Original values before the row is deleted	Undefined—all fields are NULL

TABLE 10-2. *The* :old *and* :new *Correlation Identifier*

Using :old and :new   The GenerateAuthorID trigger, shown next, uses :new. It is a before-INSERT trigger, and its purpose is to fill in the ID field of authors with a value generated from the author_sequence sequence.

```
-- Available online as part of GenerateAuthorID.sql
CREATE OR REPLACE TRIGGER GenerateAuthorID
  BEFORE INSERT OR UPDATE ON authors
  FOR EACH ROW
BEGIN
  /* Fill in the ID field of authors with the next value from
     author_sequence. Since ID is a column in authors, :new.ID
     is a valid reference. */
  SELECT author_sequence.NEXTVAL
    INTO :new.ID
    FROM dual;
END GenerateAuthorID;
/
```

GenerateAuthorID actually modifies the value of :new.ID. This is one of the useful features of :new—when the statement is actually executed, whatever values are in :new will be used. With GenerateAuthorID, we can issue an INSERT statement such as

```
-- Available online as part of GenerateAuthorID.sql
INSERT INTO authors (first_name, last_name)
  VALUES ('Lolita', 'Lazarus');
```

without generating an error. Even though we haven't specified a value for the primary-key column ID (which is required), the trigger will supply it. In fact, if we do specify a value for ID, it will be ignored, since the trigger changes it. If we issue

```
-- Available online as part of GenerateAuthorID.sql
INSERT INTO authors (ID, first_name, last_name)
  VALUES (-7, 'Zelda', 'Zoom');
```

the ID column will be populated from author_sequence.NEXTVAL, rather than containing –7.

As a result of this, you cannot change :new in an after row-level trigger, because the statement has already been processed. In general, :new is modified only in a before row-level trigger, and :old is never modified, only read from.

The :new and :old records are valid only inside row-level triggers. If you try to reference either inside a statement-level trigger, you will get a compile error. Since a statement-level trigger executes once—even if many rows are processed by the statement— :old and :new have no meaning. Which row would they refer to?

Pseudorecords   Although :new and :old are syntactically treated as records of *triggering_table*%ROWTYPE, in reality they are not. As a result, operations that would normally be valid on records are not valid for :new and :old. For example, they cannot be assigned as entire records. Only the individual fields within them may be assigned. The following example illustrates this:

```
-- Available online as pseudoRecords.sql
CREATE OR REPLACE TRIGGER TempDelete
  BEFORE DELETE ON temp_table
  FOR EACH ROW
DECLARE
  v_TempRec temp_table%ROWTYPE;
BEGIN
  /* This is not a legal assignment, since :old is not truly
     a record. */
  v_TempRec := :old;
  /* We can accomplish the same thing, however, by assigning
     the fields individually. */
  v_TempRec.char_col := :old.char_col;
  v_TempRec.num_col := :old.num_col;
END TempDelete;
/
```

In addition, :old and :new cannot be passed to procedures or functions that take arguments of *triggering_table*%ROWTYPE. The pseudoRecords.sql script will fail due to this behavior with the following error message:

```
LINE/COL ERROR
---- --------------------------------
6/16    PLS-00049: bad bind variable 'OLD'
```

REFERENCING Clause   If you choose, you can use the REFERENCING clause to specify a different name for :old and :new. This clause is found after the triggering event, before the WHEN clause, with syntax

REFERENCING [OLD AS *old_name*] [NEW AS *new_name*]

In the trigger body, you can use :*old_name* and :*new_name* instead of :old and :new. Note that the correlation identifiers do *not* have colons within the REFERENCING clause. What follows is an alternate version of the GenerateAuthorID trigger, which uses REFERENCING to refer to :new as :new_author:

```
-- Available online as part of GenerateStudentID.sql
CREATE OR REPLACE TRIGGER GenerateAuthorID
  BEFORE INSERT OR UPDATE ON authors
```

```
    REFERENCING new AS new_author
    FOR EACH ROW
BEGIN
   /* Fill in the ID field of authors with the next value from
      author_sequence. Since ID is a column in authors, :new.ID
      is a valid reference. */
   SELECT author_sequence.NEXTVAL
     INTO :new_author.ID
     FROM dual;
END GenerateAuthorID;
/
```

The WHEN Clause

The WHEN clause is valid only for row-level triggers. If present, the trigger body will be executed only for those rows that meet the condition specified by the WHEN clause. The WHEN clause looks like

WHEN *trigger_condition*

where *trigger_condition* is a Boolean expression. It will be evaluated for each row. The :new and :old records can be referenced inside *trigger_condition* as well, but as with REFERENCING, the colon is *not* used there. The colon is valid only in the trigger body. For example, the body of the CheckPrice trigger is executed only if the price of a given book is more than $49.99:

```
-- Available online as part of CheckPrice1.sql
CREATE OR REPLACE TRIGGER CheckPrice
  BEFORE INSERT OR UPDATE OF price ON books
  FOR EACH ROW
  WHEN (new.price > 49.99) BEGIN
  /* Trigger body goes here. */
  NULL;
END;
/
```

CheckPrice could also be written as follows:

```
CREATE OR REPLACE TRIGGER CheckPrice
   BEFORE INSERT OR UPDATE OF price ON books
   FOR EACH ROW
BEGIN
   IF :new.price > 49.99 THEN
     /* Trigger body goes here. */
     NULL;
   END IF;
END;
/
```

Trigger Predicates: INSERTING, UPDATING, and DELETING

The `UpdateCategoryStats` trigger earlier in this chapter is an INSERT, UPDATE, and DELETE trigger. Inside a trigger of this type (which will fire for different kinds of DML statements) there are three Boolean functions that you can use to determine what the operation is. These predicates are INSERTING, UPDATING, and DELETING. Their behavior is described in the following table:

Predicate	Behavior
INSERTING	TRUE if the triggering statement is an INSERT; FALSE otherwise
UPDATING	TRUE if the triggering statement is an UPDATE; FALSE otherwise
DELETING	TRUE if the triggering statement is a DELETE; FALSE otherwise

NOTE
There are additional functions that can be called from within a trigger body, similar to trigger predicates. See the section "Event Attribute Functions" later in this chapter for more details.

The `LogInventoryChanges` trigger uses these predicates to record all changes made to the `inventory` table. In addition to the change, it records the user who makes the change. The records are kept in the `inventory_audit` table, which looks like this:

```
- Available online as part of logInventoryChanges1.sql
CREATE TABLE inventory_audit (
  change_type      CHAR(1) NOT NULL,
  changed_by       VARCHAR2(8) NOT NULL,
  timestamp        DATE NOT NULL,
  old_isbn         CHAR(10),
  new_isbn         CHAR(10),
  old_status       VARCHAR2(25),
  new_status       VARCHAR2(25),
  old_status_date  DATE,
  new_status_date  DATE,
  old_amount       NUMBER,
  new_amount       NUMBER
);
```

`LogInventoryChanges` is created with

```
-- Available online as part of logInventoryChanges1.sql
CREATE OR REPLACE TRIGGER LogInventoryChanges
  BEFORE INSERT OR DELETE OR UPDATE ON inventory
  FOR EACH ROW
DECLARE
  v_ChangeType CHAR(1);
BEGIN
  /* Use 'I' for an INSERT, 'D' for DELETE, and 'U' for UPDATE. */
  IF INSERTING THEN
    v_ChangeType := 'I';
  ELSIF UPDATING THEN
    v_ChangeType := 'U';
  ELSE
    v_ChangeType := 'D';
  END IF;

  /* Record all the changes made to inventory in
     inventory_audit. Use SYSDATE to generate the timestamp, and
     USER to return the userid of the current user. */
  INSERT INTO inventory_audit
    (change_type, changed_by, timestamp,
     old_isbn, old_status, old_status_date, old_amount,
     new_isbn, new_status, new_status_date, new_amount)
  VALUES
    (v_ChangeType, USER, SYSDATE,
     :old.isbn, :old.status, :old.status_date, :old.amount,
     :new.isbn, :new.status, :new.status_date, :new.amount);
END LogInventoryChanges;
/
```

The following update statement will update two rows and illustrate the behavior of
LogInventoryChanges:

```
-- Available online as part of logInventoryChanges2.sql
UPDATE inventory
SET amount = 2000
WHERE isbn IN ('72223049', '72223855');
```

We can query the Inventory_Audit table to see the trigger working.

```
SELECT change_type, old_amount, new_amount FROM inventory_audit;
```

The output from the query is shown here:

```
C OLD_AMOUNT NEW_AMOUNT
- ----- -----
```

```
U      1,000     2,000
U      1,000     2,000
```

Triggers are commonly used for auditing, as in `LogInventoryChanges`. While auditing at the level of `LogInventoryChanges` is available as part of the database, triggers allow for more customized and flexible recording. `LogInventoryChanges` could be modified, for example, to record changes made by only certain people. It could also check to see if users have permission to make changes and raise an error (with RAISE_APPLICATION_ERROR) if they don't.

Creating Instead-of Triggers

Unlike DML triggers, which fire in addition to the INSERT, UPDATE, or DELETE operation (either before or after them), instead-of triggers (as their name implies) fire instead of and replace a DML operation. Also, instead-of triggers can be defined only on views, while DML triggers are defined on tables. Instead-of triggers are used in two cases:

- To allow a view that would otherwise not be modifiable to be modified

- To modify the columns of a nested table column in a view

We will discuss the first case in this section. For more information on nested tables, see Chapter 6.

Modifiable vs. Nonmodifiable Views

A *modifiable view* is one against which you can issue a DML statement. In general, a view is modifiable if it does not contain any of the following:

- Set operators (UNION, UNION ALL, MINUS)

- Aggregate functions (SUM, AVG, etc.)

- GROUP BY, CONNECT BY, or START WITH clauses

- The DISTINCT operator

- Joins

There are, however, some views that contain joins that are modifiable. In general, a join view is modifiable if the DML operation on it modifies only one base table at a time, and if the DML statement meets the conditions in Table 10-3. (For more information on modifiable vs. nonmodifiable join views, see *Oracle Database*

DML Operation	Permitted if
INSERT	The statement does not refer, implicitly or explicitly, to the columns of a non-key-preserved table.
UPDATE	The updated columns map to columns of a key-preserved table.
DELETE	There is exactly one key-preserved table in the join.

TABLE 10-3. *Modifiable Join Views*

Concepts documentation.) If a view is nonmodifiable, you can write an instead-of trigger on it that does the correct thing, thus allowing it to be modified. An instead-of trigger can also be written on a modifiable view, if additional processing is required.

Table 10-3 refers to key-preserved tables. A table is *key-preserved* if, after a join with another table, the keys in the original table are also keys in the resultant join. For more details on key-preserved tables, see the Oracle Database *Application Developer's Guide – Fundamentals.*

Instead-of Example

Consider the `books_authors` view that we saw earlier in this chapter:

```
-- Available online as part of insteadOf1.sql
CREATE OR REPLACE VIEW books_authors AS
  SELECT b.isbn, b.title, a.first_name, a.last_name
    FROM books b, authors a
    WHERE b.author1 = a.id
       OR b.author2 = a.id
       OR b.author3 = a.id;
```

As we saw earlier, it is illegal to INSERT into this view. It is also illegal to UPDATE or DELETE from the view. This is true partially because it is possible to define different behavior for each of the DML operations on the view. Suppose, however, that they have the following meanings:

Operation	Meaning
INSERT	Update the row containing the book to include the supplied author. This will result in an update of either `author2` or `author3`. If the author does not exist, add it to the `authors` table first using `author_sequence` to generate the author ID.

Operation	Meaning
UPDATE	Same as the INSERT case, except that if the author is changing `author1`, `author2`, or `author3` could be modified.
DELETE	Update the row containing the book to remove the supplied author. This could result in an update of any of the authors columns.
All	For all operations, allow only changes to the `first_name` and `last_name` fields of `books_authors`. Changes to `isbn` or `title` should be done on the base table.

The `InsteadBooksAuthors` trigger, shown next, enforces the preceding rules and allows DML operations to be performed correctly against `books_authors`. This is a more complete version of the `InsertBooksAuthors` trigger that we saw in the introductory sections of this chapter, and it also includes error handling. Note that some of the error handling is taken care of by the constraints on the `books` table itself, rather than within the trigger.

```
-- Available online as part of InsteadBooksAuthors.sql
CREATE OR REPLACE TRIGGER InsteadBooksAuthors
  INSTEAD OF INSERT OR UPDATE OR DELETE ON books_authors
  FOR EACH ROW
DECLARE

  v_Book books%ROWTYPE;
  v_NewAuthorID authors.ID%TYPE;
  v_OldAuthorID authors.ID%TYPE;

  -- Local function which returns the ID of the new authors.
  -- If the first and last names do not exist in authors
  -- then a new ID is generated from author_sequence.
  FUNCTION getID(p_FirstName IN authors.first_name%TYPE,
                 p_LastName IN authors.last_name%TYPE)
    RETURN authors.ID%TYPE IS
    v_AuthorID authors.ID%TYPE;
  BEGIN
    -- Make sure that first and last name are both specified
    IF p_FirstName IS NULL or p_LastName IS NULL THEN
      RAISE_APPLICATION_ERROR(-20004,
        'Both first and last name must be specified');
    END IF;

    -- Use a nested block to trap the NO_DATA_FOUND exception
```

```
   BEGIN
     SELECT id
       INTO v_AuthorID
       FROM authors
       WHERE first_name = p_FirstName
         AND last_name = p_LastName;
   EXCEPTION
     WHEN NO_DATA_FOUND THEN
       - No author found, create a new one
       INSERT INTO authors (id, first_name, last_name)
         VALUES (author_sequence.NEXTVAL, p_FirstName, p_LastName)
           RETURNING ID INTO v_AuthorID;
   END;

     -- Now v_AuthorID contains the correct ID and we can return it.
     RETURN v_AuthorID;
   END getID;

-- Local function which returns the row identified by either
-- ISBN or title.
FUNCTION getBook(p_ISBN IN books.ISBN%TYPE,
                 p_Title IN books.title%TYPE)
   RETURN books%ROWTYPE IS

   v_Book books%ROWTYPE;
BEGIN
   -- Ensure that at least one of isbn or title is supplied
   IF p_ISBN IS NULL AND p_Title IS NULL THEN
     RAISE_APPLICATION_ERROR(-20001,
       'Either ISBN or title must be specified');
   ELSIF p_ISBN IS NOT NULL AND p_Title IS NOT NULL THEN
     -- Both specified, so use both title and ISBN in query
     SELECT *
       INTO v_Book
       FROM books
       WHERE isbn = p_ISBN
         AND title = p_Title;
   ELSE
     -- Only one specified, so use either title or ISBN in query
     SELECT *
       INTO v_Book
       FROM books
       WHERE isbn = p_ISBN
         OR title = p_Title;
   END IF;
```

```
    RETURN v_Book;
  EXCEPTION
    WHEN NO_DATA_FOUND THEN
      RAISE_APPLICATION_ERROR(-20002,
        'Could not find book with supplied ISBN/title');
    WHEN TOO_MANY_ROWS THEN
      RAISE_APPLICATION_ERROR(-20003,
        'ISBN/title must match a single book');
  END getBook;


BEGIN  /* Start of main trigger body */
  IF INSERTING THEN
    -- Get the book and author info
    v_Book := getBook(:new.ISBN, :new.title);
    v_NewAuthorID := getID(:new.first_name, :new.last_name);

    -- Ensure there are no duplicates
    IF v_Book.author1 = v_NewAuthorID OR
       v_Book.author2 = v_NewAuthorID THEN
      RAISE_APPLICATION_ERROR(-20006,
        'Cannot have duplicate authors');
    END IF;

    -- Figure out whether the book already has 1 or 2 authors, and
    -- update accordingly
    IF v_Book.author2 IS NULL THEN
      UPDATE books
        SET author2 = v_NewAuthorID
        WHERE ISBN = v_Book.ISBN;
    ELSIF v_Book.author3 IS NULL THEN
      UPDATE books
        SET author3 = v_NewAuthorID
        WHERE ISBN = v_Book.ISBN;
    ELSE
      -- Too many authors, cannot insert
      RAISE_APPLICATION_ERROR(-20005,
        v_Book.title || ' already has 3 authors');
    END IF;

  ELSIF UPDATING THEN
    -- First check to ensure that the ISBN or title fields are not
    -- modified.
    IF (:new.ISBN != :old.ISBN OR
                   :new.title != :old.title) THEN
      RAISE_APPLICATION_ERROR(-20007,
```

```
              'Cannot modify ISBN or title in books_authors');
       END IF;

       -- Get the book and author info
       v_Book := getBook(:new.ISBN, :new.title);
       v_NewAuthorID := getID(:new.first_name, :new.last_name);
       v_OldAuthorID := getID(:old.first_name, :old.last_name);

       -- Figure out which of author1, author2, or author3 to modify
       -- and update accordingly
       IF v_Book.author1 = v_OldAuthorID THEN
         UPDATE books
           SET author1 = v_NewAuthorID
           WHERE ISBN = v_Book.ISBN;
       ELSIF v_Book.author2 = v_OldAuthorID THEN
         UPDATE books
           SET author2 = v_NewAuthorID
           WHERE ISBN = v_Book.ISBN;
       ELSE
         UPDATE BOOKS
           SET author3 = v_NewAuthorID
           WHERE ISBN = v_Book.ISBN;
       END IF;
     ELSE
       -- Get the book and author info
       v_Book := getBook(:old.ISBN, :old.title);
       v_OldAuthorID := getID(:old.first_name, :old.last_name);

       -- Figure out which of author1, author2, or author3 to modify
       -- and update accordingly.  Note that if this results in
       -- all authors being removed from the table the NOT NULL
       -- constraint on author1 will raise an error.
       IF v_Book.author1 = v_OldAuthorID THEN
         -- Set author1 = author2, author2 = author3
         v_Book.Author1 := v_Book.Author2;
         v_Book.Author2 := v_Book.Author3;
       ELSIF v_Book.author2 = v_OldAuthorID THEN
         -- Set author2 = author 3
         v_Book.Author2 := v_Book.Author3;
       ELSE
         -- Clear author3
         v_Book.Author3 := NULL;
       END IF;
       UPDATE BOOKS
         SET author1 = v_Book.Author1,
             author2 = v_Book.Author2,
             author3 = v_Book.Author3
           WHERE ISBN = v_Book.ISBN;
```

```
    END IF;
END InsteadBooksAuthors;
/
```

NOTE
The FOR EACH ROW clause is optional for an instead-of trigger. All instead-of triggers are row level, whether or not the clause is present.

InsteadBooksAuthors uses trigger predicates to determine the DML operation being performed, and to take the appropriate action. Figure 10-1 contains the original contents for books, authors, and books_authors for ISBN 72223855, *Oracle 9i New Features*. Suppose we then issue the following INSERT statement:

```
-- Available online as part of InsteadBooksAuthors.sql
INSERT INTO books_authors(ISBN, title, first_name, last_name)
   VALUES ('72223855', 'Oracle 9i New Features', 'Esther', 'Elegant');
```

The trigger causes books to be updated to reflect the new author, and a new row to be inserted into authors. (The author ID for Esther Elegant may be different, depending on the value of author_sequence.) Figure 10-2 illustrates the situation that occurs after the INSERT. Now, suppose we issue the following UPDATE statement:

```
-- Available online as part of InsteadBooksAuthors.sql
UPDATE books_authors
   SET first_name = 'Rose', last_name = 'Riznit'
   WHERE ISBN = '72223855'
   AND last_name = 'Elegant';
```

books

ISBN	Title	Author1	Author2	Author3
72223855	Oracle 9i New Features	38		

authors

ID	First_Name	Last_Name
38	Robert	Freeman

books_authors

ISBN	Title	First_Name	Last_Name
72223855	Oracle 9i New Features	Robert	Freeman

FIGURE 10-1. *Original Contents of books, authors, and books_authors for ISBN 72223855*

books

ISBN	Title	Author1	Author2	Author3
72223855	Oracle 9i New Features	38	1000	

authors

ID	First_Name	Last_Name
38	Robert	Freeman
1000	Esther	Elegant

books_authors

ISBN	Title	First_Name	Last_Name
72223855	Oracle 9i New Features	Esther	Elegant
72223855	Oracle 9i New Features	Robert	Freeman

FIGURE 10-2. *Contents after INSERT*

Figure 10-3 illustrates the situation after the UPDATE. The books table has been updated again, and one more row is inserted into authors. Finally, suppose we issue the following DELETE statement:

```
-- Available online as part of InsteadBooksAuthors.sql
DELETE FROM books_authors
  WHERE ISBN = '72223855'
  AND last_name = 'Riznit';
```

The books table is now back to where it was originally, along with books_authors. But we still have the two additional rows in authors, as shown in Figure 10-4.

ISBN	Title	Author1	Author2	Author3
72223855	Oracle 9i New Features	38	1001	

ID	First_Name	Last_Name
38	Robert	Freeman
1000	Esther	Elegant
1001	Rose	Riznit

ISBN	Title	First_Name	Last_Name
72223855	Oracle 9i New Features	Rose	Riznit
72223855	Oracle 9i New Features	Robert	Freeman

FIGURE 10-3. *Contents after UPDATE*

books				
ISBN	**Title**	**Author1**	**Author2**	**Author3**
72223855	Oracle 9i New Features	38		

authors		
ID	**First_Name**	**Last_Name**
38	Robert	Freeman
1000	Esther	Elegant
1001	Rose	Riznit

books_authors			
ISBN	**Title**	**First_Name**	**Last_Name**
72223855	Oracle 9i New Features	Robert	Freeman

FIGURE 10-4. *Contents after DELETE*

Creating System Triggers

As we have seen in the previous sections, both DML and instead-of triggers fire on (or instead of) DML events, namely INSERT, UPDATE, or DELETE statements. System triggers, on the other hand, fire on two different kinds of events: DDL or database. *DDL events* include CREATE, ALTER, or DROP statements, while *database events* include startup/shutdown of the server, logon/logoff of a user, and a server error. The syntax for creating a system trigger is as follows:

CREATE [OR REPLACE] TRIGGER [*schema.*]*trigger_name*
 {BEFORE | AFTER}
 {*ddl_event_list* | *database_event_list*}
 ON {DATABASE | [*schema.*]SCHEMA}
 [*when_clause*]
 trigger_body;

where *ddl_event_list* is one or more DDL events (separated by the OR keyword), and *database_event_list* is one or more database events (separated by the OR keyword).

Table 10-4 describes the DDL and database events, along with their allowed timings (BEFORE or AFTER). You cannot create an instead-of system trigger.

NOTE
You must have the ADMINISTER DATABASE TRIGGER system privilege in order to create a system trigger. See the section "Trigger Privileges" later in this chapter for more information.

Event	Timings Allowed	Description
STARTUP	AFTER	Fired when an instance is started up.
SHUTDOWN	BEFORE	Fired when an instance is shut down. This event may not fire if the database is shut down abnormally (as in a shutdown abort).
SERVERERROR	AFTER	Fired whenever an error occurs.
LOGON	AFTER	Fired after a user has successfully connected to the database.
LOGOFF	BEFORE	Fired at the start of a user logoff.
CREATE	BEFORE, AFTER	Fired before or after a schema object is created.
DROP	BEFORE, AFTER	Fired before or after a schema object is dropped.
ALTER	BEFORE, AFTER	Fired before or after a schema object is altered.
TRUNCATE	BEFORE, AFTER	Fired before or after a TRUNCATE statement is issued.
DDL	BEFORE, AFTER	Fired before or after most DDL statements are issued. This event will not fire for ALTER DATABASE, CREATE CONTROLFILE, or CREATE DATABASE statement, nor will it fire for DDL issued through a procedural interface, such as AQ.
ANALYZE	BEFORE, AFTER	Fired before or after an ANALYZE STATEMENT is issued.
ASSOCIATE STATISTICS	BEFORE, AFTER	Fired before or after an ASSOCIATE STATISTICS statement is issued.
DISASSOCIATE STATISTICS	BEFORE, AFTER	Fired before or after a DISASSOCIATE STATISTICS statement is issued.
AUDIT	BEFORE, AFTER	Fired before or after an AUDIT statement is issued.
NOAUDIT	BEFORE, AFTER	Fired before or after a NOAUDIT statement is issued.
COMMENT	BEFORE, AFTER	Fired before or after a COMMENT statement is issued
GRANT	BEFORE, AFTER	Fired before or after a GRANT statement is issued.
REVOKE	BEFORE, AFTER	Fired before or after a REVOKE statement is issued.

TABLE 10-4. *System DDL and Database Events*

Event	Timings Allowed	Description
RENAME	BEFORE, AFTER	Fired before or after a RENAME statement is issued.
SUSPEND*	AFTER	Fired after a SQL statement is suspended due to an out of space condition. In this case, the trigger can correct the situation, so the statement can be reissued.

*This event is available with Oracle9*i* and higher.

TABLE 10-4. *System DDL and Database Events* (continued)

Database vs. Schema Triggers

A system trigger can be defined at the database level or a schema level. A database-level trigger will fire whenever the triggering event occurs, while a schema-level trigger will fire only when the triggering event occurs for the specified schema. The DATABASE and SCHEMA keywords determine the level for a given system trigger. If the schema is not specified with the SCHEMA keyword, it defaults to the schema that owns the trigger. For example, suppose we create the following trigger while connected as `UserA`:

NOTE
These examples require that `UserA`, `UserB`, and `Example` exist in the database. Please run `createUser.sql` if they are not present before running `DatabaseSchema1.sql`. See `DatabaseSchema1.sql` for more details. Also, you need to run the `DatabaseSchema1.sql` script as the system user or a user with the DBA role privileges. It creates the `example` user and grants necessary system privileges.

```
-- Available online as part of DatabaseSchema1.sql
CREATE OR REPLACE TRIGGER LogUserAConnects
  AFTER LOGON ON SCHEMA
BEGIN
  INSERT INTO example.temp_table
    VALUES (1, 'LogUserAConnects fired!');
END LogUserAConnects;
/
```

LogUserAConnects will record in `temp_table` whenever UserA connects to the database. We can do likewise for UserB by creating the following while connected as UserB:

```
-- Available online as part of DatabaseSchema.sql
CREATE OR REPLACE TRIGGER LogUserBConnects
  AFTER LOGON ON SCHEMA
BEGIN
  INSERT INTO example.temp_table
    VALUES (2, 'LogUserBConnects fired!');
END LogUserBConnects;
/
```

Finally, we can create the following trigger while connected as example. LogAllConnects will record all connects to the database, because it is a database-level trigger.

```
-- Available online as part of DatabaseSchema1.sql
CREATE OR REPLACE TRIGGER LogAllConnects
  AFTER LOGON ON DATABASE
BEGIN
  INSERT INTO example.temp_table
    VALUES (3, 'LogAllConnects fired!');
END LogAllConnects;
/
```

We can now connect to the database as UserA, UserB, and Example and see the effects of the different triggers. The after-logon trigger to the schema fires first, followed by the after-logon trigger to the database.

```
-- Available online as part of DatabaseSchema1.sql
connect UserA/UserA
connect UserB/UserB
connect example/example
```

A SQL*Plus formatted query against the temporary table enables us to see the sequence of fired triggers.

```
COL num_col FORMAT 9
COL char_col FORMAT A50
SELECT * FROM temp_table;
```

The UserA schema trigger is the first record in the table, followed by the after-logon to the database trigger. The third and fourth entries mirror the behavior for UserB.

The `Example` user does not have a schema-level trigger. The connection to that schema fires only the after–logon to the database trigger.

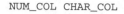

```
NUM_COL CHAR_COL
----- -------------------------------
    1 LogUserAConnects fired!
    3 LogAllConnects fired!
    2 LogUserBConnects fired!
    3 LogAllConnects fired!
    3 LogAllConnects fired!
```

`LogAllConnects` has fired three times (once for all three connections), while `LogUserAConnects` and `LogUserBConnects` have fired only once, as expected.

NOTE
STARTUP and SHUTDOWN triggers are relevant only at the database level. It is not illegal to create them at the schema level, but they will not fire.

Event Attribute Functions

Within a system trigger, several event attribute functions are available. Similar to the trigger predicates (INSERTING, UPDATING, and DELETING), they allow a trigger body to get information about the triggering event. Although it is legal to call these functions from other PL/SQL blocks (not necessarily in a system trigger body), they will not always return a valid result. The event attribute functions are described in Table 10-5.

The `LogCreations` trigger, which we saw at the beginning of this chapter, uses some of the attribute functions. Unlike trigger predicates, event attribute functions are stand-alone PL/SQL functions. They have public synonyms defined for them, and they begin with ORA_.

Before running this section, we should connect to the example schema.

```
-- Available online as part of LogCreations.sql
CREATE OR REPLACE TRIGGER LogCreations
  AFTER CREATE ON SCHEMA
BEGIN
  INSERT INTO ddl_creations (user_id, object_type, object_name,
                             object_owner, creation_date)
    VALUES (USER, ORA_DICT_OBJ_TYPE, ORA_DICT_OBJ_NAME,
            ORA_DICT_OBJ_OWNER, SYSDATE);
END LogCreations;
/
```

TIP
Prior to Oracle8i, the event attribute functions, in addition to having different names, were owned by SYS and did not have synonyms defined for them. Consequently, they had to be prefixed by SYS in order to be resolved. Although this syntax is still legal, you should use the current syntax.

Use the describe command in SQL*Plus to view the ORA_DICT_OBJ_NAME_LIST argument list, type, and mode.

```
FUNCTION ora_dict_obj_name_list RETURNS BINARY_INTEGER
 Argument Name                   Type                    In/Out Default?
 --------------- ------------ --- ----
 OBJECT_LIST                     DBMS_STANDARD           OUT
 /
```

Some of the attribute functions (such as ORA_DICT_OBJ_NAME_LIST) have OUT parameters of type ORA_NAME_LIST_T. This type is defined as follows:

```
TYPE ORA_NAME_LIST_T IS TABLE OF VARCHAR2(64);
```

as part of package STANDARD. The OUT parameters are described in Table 10-5.

Attribute Function	Return Type	System Events Applicable For	Description
ORA_CLIENT_IP_ADDRESS	VARCHAR2	LOGON	Returns the IP address of the client for a database logon. If the protocol is not TCP/IP, then this function is not valid.
ORA_DATABASE_NAME	VARCHAR2(50)	All events	Returns the name of the database.
ORA_DES_ENCRYPTED_PASSWORD	VARCHAR2	ALTER	For ALTER USER events, returns the DES-encrypted password of the user.

TABLE 10-5. *Event Attribute Functions*

Attribute Function	Return Type	System Events Applicable For	Description
ORA_DICT_OBJ_ NAME	VARCHAR2(30)	ALTER, ANALYZE, ASSOCIATE STATISTICS, COMMENT, CREATE, DDL, DISASSOCIATE STATISTICS, DROP, GRANT, RENAME, REVOKE, TRUNCATE	Returns the name of the dictionary object on which a DDL operation occurred.
ORA_DICT_OBJ_ NAME_LIST(name_ list OUT ORA_ NAME_LIST_T)	BINARY_ INTEGER	ASSOCIATE STATISTICS, DISASSOCIATE STATISTICS	The name_list will contain a list of object names being modified by the event. The return value is the size of the array.
ORA_DICT_OBJ_ OWNER	VARCHAR2(30)	ALTER, ANALYZE, ASSOCIATE STATISTICS, COMMENT, CREATE, DDL, DISASSOCIATE STATISTICS, DROP, GRANT, RENAME, REVOKE, TRUNCATE	Returns the owner of the dictionary object on which a DDL operation occurred.
ORA_DICT_OBJ_ OWNER_ LIST(name_list OUT ORA_NAME_ LIST_T)	BINARY_ INTEGER	ASSOCIATE STATISTICS, DISASSOCIATE STATISTICS	The name_list will contain a list of the owners of objects being modified by the event. The return value is the size of the array.

TABLE 10-5. *Event Attribute Functions* (continued)

Attribute Function	Return Type	System Events Applicable For	Description
ORA_DICT_OBJ_ TYPE	VARCHAR2(20)	ALTER, ANALYZE, ASSOCIATE STATISTICS, COMMENT, CREATE, DDL, DISASSOCIATE STATISTICS, DROP, GRANT, RENAME, REVOKE, TRUNCATE	Returns the type of the dictionary object on which a DDL operation occurred.
ORA_ GRANTEE(*user_list* OUT ORA_NAME_ LIST_T)	BINARY_ INTEGER	GRANT	The *user_list* will contain the grantees for a GRANT statement. The return value is the size of the array.
ORA_INSTANCE_ NUM	NUMBER	All events	Returns the instance number.
ORA_IS_ALTER_ COLUMN(*column_ name* IN VARCHAR2)	BOOLEAN	ALTER	For ALTER TABLE events, returns true if *column_name* is being altered.
ORA_IS_ CREATING_ NESTED_TABLE	BOOLEAN	CREATE	Returns true if the current event is creating a nested table.
ORA_IS_DROP_ COLUMN(*column_ name* IN VARCHAR2)	BOOLEAN	DROP	Returns true if *column_name* is being dropped.
ORA_IS_ SERVERERROR(*error _num* IN BINARY_ INTEGER)	BOOLEAN	SERVERERROR, SUSPEND	Returns true if *error_num* is on the error stack.
ORA_LOGIN_USER	VARCHAR2(30)	All events	Returns the login user name.

TABLE 10-5. *Event Attribute Functions* (continued)

Attribute Function	Return Type	System Events Applicable For	Description
ORA_PARTITION_POS[*]	BINARY_INTEGER	CREATE	For a CREATE TABLE statement, returns the position within the text where a PARTITION clause could be inserted.
ORA_PRIVILEGE_LIST(*privilege_list* OUT ORA_NAME_LIST_T)	BINARY_INTEGER	GRANT, REVOKE	The *privilege_list* will contain the privileges being granted or revoked. The return value is the size of the array.
ORA_REVOKEE(*user_list* OUT ORA_NAME_LIST_T)	BINARY_INTEGER	REVOKE	The *user_list* will contain the revokees for a REVOKE statement. The return value is the size of the array.
ORA_SERVER_ERROR(*position* IN BINARY_INTEGER)	NUMBER	SERVERERROR	Returns the error number at the given position in the error stack. The top of the stack is position 1.
ORA_SERVER_ERROR_DEPTH[*]	BINARY_INTEGER	SERVERERROR	Returns the total number of errors on the error stack.
ORA_SERVER_ERROR_MSG(*position* IN BINARY_INTEGER)[*]	VARCHAR2	SERVERERROR	Returns the error message at the given position in the error stack. The top of the stack is position 1.
ORA_SERVER_ERROR_NUM_PARAMS(*position* IN BINARY_INTEGER)[*]	BINARY_INTEGER	SERVERERROR	Returns the number of parameters for the error message at the given position. A parameter is inserted into an error message using a format string like "%s" or "%d" in the error message text. The top of the stack is position 1.
ORA_SERVER_ERROR_PARAM(*position* IN BINARY_INTEGER), *param* IN BINARY_INTEGER)[*]	VARCHAR2	SERVERERROR	Returns the value substituted for the given parameter (1 is the first parameter) at the given position in the error stack. The top of the stack is position 1.

TABLE 10-5. *Event Attribute Functions* (continued)

Attribute Function	Return Type	System Events Applicable For	Description
ORA_SQL_TEXT(*sql_ text* OUT ORA_ NAME_LIST_T*	BINARY_ INTEGER	All events	Returns the text of the triggering statement. If the statement is long, it is broken up into multiple elements, with the return value specifying the size of the array.
ORA_SYSEVENT	VARCHAR2	All events	Name of the system event firing the trigger.
ORA_WITH_ GRANT_OPTION	BOOLEAN	GRANT	Returns true if privileges are being granted with the grant option.
SPACE_ERROR_ INFO(*error_number* OUT NUMBER, *error_type* OUT VARCHAR2, *object_ owner* OUT VARCHAR2, *table_ space_name* OUT VARCHAR2, *object_ name* OUT VARCHAR2, *sub_ object_name* OUT VARCHAR2)*	BOOLEAN	SERVERERROR, SUSPEND	Returns true if the error is related to an out-of-space condition, and the out parameters are filled in with information about the object causing the error.

*This function is available with Oracle9*i*R1 and higher.

TABLE 10-5. *Event Attribute Functions* (continued)

System Triggers and Transactions

Depending on the triggering event, the transactional behavior of a system trigger varies. A system trigger will either fire as a separate transaction that is committed upon successful completion of the trigger, or it will fire as part of the current user transaction. STARTUP, SHUTDOWN, SERVERERROR, and LOGON triggers all fire as separate transactions, while LOGOFF and DDL triggers fire as part of the current transaction.

It is important to note, however, that the work done by the trigger will generally be committed regardless. In the case of a DDL trigger, the current transaction (namely, the CREATE, ALTER, or DROP statement) is automatically committed, which commits the work in the trigger. The work in a LOGOFF trigger will also be committed as part of the final transaction in the session.

NOTE
Because system triggers are generally committed anyway, declaring them as autonomous will not have any effect.

System Triggers and the WHEN Clause
Just like DML triggers, system triggers can use the WHEN clause to specify a condition on the trigger firing. However, there are restrictions on the types of conditions that can be specified for each type of system trigger, namely

- STARTUP and SHUTDOWN triggers cannot have any conditions.

- SERVERERROR triggers can use the ERRNO test to check for a specific error only.

- LOGON and LOGOFF triggers can check the user ID or user name with the USERID or USERNAME tests.

- DDL triggers can check the type and name of the object being modified, and can check the user ID or user name.

Other Trigger Issues

In this section, we will discuss some remaining issues about triggers. These include the namespace for trigger names, various restrictions on using triggers, and different kinds of trigger bodies. The section closes with a discussion of the privileges related to triggers.

Trigger Names
The namespace for trigger names is different from that of other subprograms. A *namespace* is the set of legal identifiers available for use as the names of an object. Procedures, packages, and tables all share the same namespace. This means that, within one database schema, all objects in the same namespace must have unique names. For example, it is illegal to give the same name to a procedure and a package.

Triggers, however, exist in a separate namespace. This means that a trigger can have the same name as a table or procedure. Within one schema, however, a given name can be used for only one trigger. For example, we can create a trigger called inventory on the inventory table, but it is illegal to create a procedure also called `inventory`. The following needs to be tested within the `UserA` account because of the dependency on the `inventory` table created in it. Alternatively, you may run the `tables.sql` script into another schema to test it.

 `-- Available online as samename.sql`
```
CREATE OR REPLACE TRIGGER inventory
   BEFORE INSERT ON inventory
BEGIN
   INSERT INTO temp_table (char_col)
   VALUES ('Trigger fired!');
END inventory;
/
```

If we attempt to create a procedure called `inventory` after creating the trigger with the same name, it will fail because it attempts to occupy the same namespace.

`-- Available online as samename.sql`
```
CREATE OR REPLACE PROCEDURE inventory AS
BEGIN
   INSERT INTO temp_table (char_col)
   VALUES ('Procedure called!');
END inventory;
/
```

The attempt to create the procedure will raise the following error:

```
CREATE OR REPLACE PROCEDURE inventory AS
*
ERROR at line 1:
ORA-00955: name is already used by an existing object
```

TIP
Although it is possible to use the same name for a trigger and a table, we don't recommend it. It is better to give each trigger a unique name that identifies its function as well as the table on which it is defined, or to prefix triggers with a common sequence of characters (such as TRG_).

Restrictions on Triggers
The body of a trigger is a PL/SQL block or CALL statement (see the next section for details on using CALL). Any statement that is legal in a PL/SQL block is legal in a trigger body, subject to the following restrictions:

- A trigger may not issue any transaction control statements—COMMIT, ROLLBACK, SAVEPOINT, or SET TRANSACTION. The PL/SQL compiler will allow a trigger to be created that contains one of these statements, but you will receive an error when the trigger is fired. This is because it is fired as part of the execution of the triggering statement and is in the same transaction as the triggering statement. When the triggering statement is committed or rolled back, the work in the trigger is committed or rolled back as well. (You can create a trigger that executes as an autonomous transaction, in which case the work in the trigger can be committed or rolled back independent of the state of the triggering statement. See Chapter 4 for more information about autonomous transactions.)

- Likewise, any procedures or functions that are called by the trigger body cannot issue any transaction control statements (unless they are also declared as autonomous).

- The trigger body cannot declare any LONG or LONG RAW variables. Also, :new and :old cannot refer to a LONG or LONG RAW column in the table for which the trigger is defined.

- Code in a trigger body may reference and use LOB (Large OBject) columns, but it may not modify the values of the columns. This is also true for object columns.

There are also restrictions on which tables a trigger body may access. Depending on the type of trigger and the constraints on the tables, tables may be mutating. This situation is discussed in detail in the section "Mutating Tables" later in this chapter.

Trigger Bodies

Prior to Oracle8*i*, trigger bodies had to be PL/SQL blocks. In Oracle8*i* and higher, however, a trigger body can consist of a CALL statement instead. The procedure that is called can be a PL/SQL stored subprogram, or it can be a wrapper for a C or Java routine. This allows you to create triggers where the functional code is written in Java. For example, suppose we want to record connects and disconnects to the database, in the following table found in the `UserA` schema:

```
-- Available online as part of tables.sql
CREATE TABLE connect_audit (
  user_name   VARCHAR2(30),
  operation   VARCHAR2(30),
  timestamp   DATE);
```

We can use the following package to record connects and disconnects:

```
-- Available online as LogPkg1.sql
CREATE OR REPLACE PACKAGE LogPkg AS
  PROCEDURE LogConnect(p_UserID IN VARCHAR2);
  PROCEDURE LogDisconnect(p_UserID IN VARCHAR2);
END LogPkg;
/

CREATE OR REPLACE PACKAGE BODY LogPkg AS
  PROCEDURE LogConnect(p_UserID IN VARCHAR2) IS
  BEGIN
    INSERT INTO connect_audit (user_name, operation, timestamp)
      VALUES (p_USerID, 'CONNECT', SYSDATE);
  END LogConnect;

  PROCEDURE LogDisconnect(p_UserID IN VARCHAR2) IS
  BEGIN
    INSERT INTO connect_audit (user_name, operation, timestamp)
      VALUES (p_USerID, 'DISCONNECT', SYSDATE);
  END LogDisconnect;
END LogPkg;
/
```

Both `LogPkg.LogConnect` and `LogPkg.LogDisconnect` take a username as an argument and insert a row into `connect_audit`. Finally, we can call them from LOGON and LOGOFF triggers, as follows:

```
-- Available online as LogConnects.sql
CREATE OR REPLACE TRIGGER LogConnects
  AFTER LOGON ON DATABASE
  CALL LogPkg.LogConnect(SYS.LOGIN_USER)
/

CREATE OR REPLACE TRIGGER LogDisconnects
  BEFORE LOGOFF ON DATABASE
  CALL LogPkg.LogDisconnect(SYS.LOGIN_USER)
/
```

NOTE
Since LogConnects and LogDisconnects are system triggers on the database (as opposed to a schema), you must have the ADMINISTER DATABASE TRIGGER system privilege to create them.

The trigger body for both `LogConnects` and `LogDisconnects` is simply a CALL statement, which indicates the procedure to be executed. The current user is passed as the only argument. In the preceding example, the target of the CALL is a standard PL/SQL packaged procedure. However, it could be a wrapper for a C or Java external routine. For example, suppose we load the following Java class into the database and test it.

Before we attempt to load the Java program into the database, we need to ensure that we have our environment set up correctly. We need to ensure that our CLASSPATH environment variable is set up. This is done a bit differently in Windows and in Unix. Both syntaxes are noted here. If the `classes12.zip` Java archive is in the CLASSPATH, then we may not need to set it.

UNIX

```
# echo $CLASSPATH
```

Windows

```
C:> echo %CLASSPATH%
```

If the CLASSPATH environment variable does not contain `classes12.zip` and a reference to our present working directory, we must add them to the classpath. Java archives may have several extension types, but the most common are `*.jar` and `*.zip`. These files are treated like directories. When you place them in the CLASSPATH environment variable, you need to treat them as directories. The present working directory will be required when you execute a loadjava command to the database. If a CLASSPATH variable exists, you should prepend it to the `classes12.zip` file.

UNIX

```
# export set CLASSPATH=$ORACLE_HOME/jdbc/lib/classes12.zip:.
```

Windows

```
C:> set CLASSPATH=%ORACLE_HOME%/jdbc/lib/classes12.zip;.
```

Copy the `Logger.java` file that follows from the web site or type it in your working directory and compile the file. The syntax is the same whether on Unix or Windows. This will create a Thick Java client program that must be executed from the server where the Oracle database resides. This limitation is due to the library dependencies external to the Oracle JDBC implementation.

```
javac Logger.java
```

This will generate a Java byte file, named `Logger.class`. We will load that into the database with the loadjava utility and the following syntax. This will load the Java byte code into the database for the `Example` schema.

```
loadjava -r -f -o -user example/example Logger.class
```

```java
// Available online as Logger.java
import java.sql.*;
import oracle.jdbc.driver.*;

public class Logger {
  public static void LogConnect(String userID)
    throws SQLException {
    // Get default JDBC connection
    Connection conn = new OracleDriver().defaultConnection();

    String insertString = "INSERT INTO connect_audit " +
                          "(user_name, operation, timestamp) " +
                          "VALUES (?, 'CONNECT', SYSDATE)";

    // Prepare and execute a statement that does the insert
    PreparedStatement insertStatement =
      conn.prepareStatement(insertString);
    insertStatement.setString(1, userID);
    insertStatement.execute();
  }

  public static void LogDisconnect(String userID)
    throws SQLException {
    // Get default JDBC connection
    Connection conn = new OracleDriver().defaultConnection();

    String insertString =
      "INSERT INTO connect_audit (user_name, operation, timestamp)" +
      "  VALUES (?, 'DISCONNECT', SYSDATE)";

    // Prepare and execute a statement that does the insert
    PreparedStatement insertStatement =
      conn.prepareStatement(insertString);
    insertStatement.setString(1, userID);
    insertStatement.execute();
  }
}
```

We create the PL/SQL LogPkg package as a wrapper for the Java class we have created.

```sql
-- Available online as LogPkg2.sql
CREATE OR REPLACE PACKAGE LogPkg AS
  PROCEDURE LogConnect(p_UserID IN VARCHAR2);
```

```
      PROCEDURE LogDisconnect(p_UserID IN VARCHAR2);
END LogPkg;
/

CREATE OR REPLACE PACKAGE BODY LogPkg AS
   PROCEDURE LogConnect(p_UserID IN VARCHAR2) IS
      LANGUAGE JAVA
      NAME 'Logger.LogConnect(java.lang.String)';

   PROCEDURE LogDisconnect(p_UserID IN VARCHAR2) IS
      LANGUAGE JAVA
      NAME 'Logger.LogDisconnect(java.lang.String)';
END LogPkg;
/
```

Before testing the wrappers, we will need to create a copy of the connect_audit
table in the Example schema. If we fail to do so, we will get an uncaught Java error
and an ORA-00942 error when we attempt to test the PL/SQL wrappers.

-- Available online as part of createConnectAudit.sql
```
CREATE TABLE connect_audit (
   user_name   VARCHAR2(30),
   operation   VARCHAR2(30),
   timestamp   DATE);
```

We can build an anonymous block PL/SQL program to test connection and
disconnection. They would be defined as follows:

-- Available online as testLogPkg.sql
```
DECLARE
   v_string VARCHAR2(80) := 'USERA';
BEGIN
   logpkg.logconnect(v_string);
END;
/

DECLARE
   v_string VARCHAR2(80) := 'USERA';
BEGIN
   logpkg.logdisconnect(v_string);
END;
/
```

We can see the results of our test by querying the connect_audit table. Likewise, we
can use the same triggers to achieve the desired effect. See Chapter 12 for more
information about external routines.

NOTE
Trigger predicates such as INSERTING, UPDATING, and DELETING, and the :old and :new correlation identifiers (and :parent), can be used only if the trigger body is a complete PL/SQL block and not a CALL statement.

Trigger Privileges

There are five system privileges that apply to triggers, which are described in Table 10-6. In addition to these, the owner of a trigger must have the necessary object privileges on the objects referenced by the trigger. Since a trigger is a compiled object, these privileges must be granted directly and not through a role (triggers are defined with definers rights only).

Triggers and the Data Dictionary

Similar to stored subprograms, certain data dictionary views contain information about triggers and their status. These views are updated whenever a trigger is created or dropped.

System Privilege	Description
CREATE TRIGGER	Allows the grantee to create a trigger in his or her own schema.
CREATE ANY TRIGGER	Allows the grantee to create triggers in any schema except SYS. It is not recommended to create triggers on data dictionary tables.
ALTER ANY TRIGGER	Allows the grantee to enable, disable, or compile database triggers in any schema except SYS. Note that if the grantee does not have CREATE ANY TRIGGER, he or she cannot change trigger code.
DROP ANY TRIGGER	Allows the grantee to drop database triggers in any schema except SYS.
ADMINISTER DATABASE TRIGGER	Allows the grantee to create or alter a system trigger on the database (as opposed to the current schema). The grantee must also have either CREATE TRIGGER or CREATE ANY TRIGGER.

TABLE 10-6. *System Privileges Related to Triggers*

Data Dictionary Views

When a trigger is created, its source code is stored in the data dictionary view
`user_triggers`. This view includes the trigger body, WHEN clause, triggering
table, and the trigger type. For example, the following formatted query returns
information about `UpdateMajorStats` after running `GenerateAuthorID.sql`
script in the `UserA` schema:

```
COL table_name FORMAT A10
COL triggering_event FORMAT A20
SELECT trigger_type, table_name, triggering_event
FROM user_triggers
WHERE trigger_name = 'GENERATEAUTHORID';
```

We will see the trigger type, the table name, and the triggering event in the output
from the query.

```
TRIGGER_TYPE      TABLE_NAME  TRIGGERING_EVENT
--------      -----  --------
BEFORE EACH ROW   AUTHORS     INSERT OR UPDATE
```

The `user_triggers` view contains information about the triggers owned by
the current user. There are also two additional views: `all_triggers` contains
information about the triggers that are accessible to the current user (but might be
owned by a different user), and `dba_triggers` contains information about all
triggers in the database.

Dropping and Disabling Triggers

Like procedures and packages, triggers can be dropped. The command to do this
has the syntax

DROP TRIGGER *triggername*;

where *triggername* is the name of the trigger to be dropped. This permanently
removes the trigger from the data dictionary. As in subprograms, the OR REPLACE
clause can be specified in the trigger CREATE statement. In this case, the trigger is
dropped first, if it already exists.

Unlike procedures and packages, however, a trigger can be disabled without
dropping it. When a trigger is disabled, it still exists in the data dictionary but is
never fired. To disable a trigger, use the ALTER TRIGGER statement:

ALTER TRIGGER *triggername* {DISABLE | ENABLE};

where *triggername* is the name of the trigger. All triggers are enabled by default
when they are created. ALTER TRIGGER can disable and then reenable any trigger.
For example, the following code disables and then reenables `UpdateMajorStats`:

```
ALTER TRIGGER GenerateAuthorID DISABLE;

ALTER TRIGGER GenerateAuthorID ENABLE;
```

All triggers for a particular table can be enabled or disabled using the ALTER TABLE command as well, by adding the ENABLE ALL TRIGGERS or the DISABLE ALL TRIGGERS clause. For example:

```
ALTER TABLE authors ENABLE ALL TRIGGERS;

ALTER TABLE authors DISABLE ALL TRIGGERS;
```

The `status` column of `user_triggers` contains either 'ENABLED' or 'DISABLED,' indicating the current status of a trigger. Disabling a trigger does not remove it from the data dictionary, as dropping it would do. We can use the following query to check the status:

```
SELECT trigger_name, status
FROM user_triggers
WHERE trigger_name = 'trigger_name';
```

Trigger P-Code

When a package or subprogram is stored in the data dictionary, the compiled p-code is stored in addition to the source code for the object. This is also true for triggers. This means that triggers can be called without recompilation, and that dependency information is stored. Thus they can be automatically invalidated in the same manner as packages and subprograms. When a trigger is invalidated, it will be recompiled the next time it is fired.

Mutating Tables

There are restrictions on the tables and columns that a trigger body may access. In order to define these restrictions, it is necessary to understand mutating and constraining tables. A *mutating table* is a table that is currently being modified by a DML statement. For a trigger, this is the table on which the trigger is defined. Tables that may need to be updated as a result of DELETE CASCADE referential integrity constraints are also mutating. (For more information on referential integrity constraints, see the *Oracle Application Developer Guide— Fundamentals*.) A *constraining table* is a table that might need to be read from for a referential integrity constraint. To illustrate these definitions, consider the `students`, `classes` and `registered_students` tables. The `students` and `classes` tables have no dependencies, but the `registered_students` table has two foreign key dependencies. One dependency is on the primary key of the `students` table, and the other is on the primary key of the `classes` table. These ensure referential integrity at the database level but carry a processing overhead. You may run all these example scripts by using the `createObjects.sql` script.

```
-- Available online as part of createStudents.sql
CREATE TABLE students (
   id                       NUMBER(5)     NOT NULL,
   current_credits          NUMBER(2),
   major                    VARCHAR2(20),
   last_name                VARCHAR2(20) NOT NULL,
   first_name               VARCHAR2(20) NOT NULL,
   middle_initial           VARCHAR2(1)   NOT NULL,
   CONSTRAINT students_pk    PRIMARY KEY (id));

-- Available online as part of createClasses.sql
CREATE TABLE classes (
   department               CHAR(3)       NOT NULL,
   course                   NUMBER(3)     NOT NULL,
   current_students         NUMBER(3)     NOT NULL,
   num_credits              NUMBER(1)     NOT NULL,
   name                     VARCHAR2(30) NOT NULL,
   CONSTRAINT classes_pk PRIMARY KEY (department,course));

-- Available online as part of createRegisteredStudents.sql
CREATE TABLE registered_students (
   student_id               NUMBER(5)     NOT NULL,
   department               CHAR(3)       NOT NULL,
   course                   NUMBER(3)     NOT NULL,
   grade                    CHAR(1),
   CONSTRAINT rs_grade
     CHECK (grade IN ('A', 'B', 'C', 'D', 'F')),
   CONSTRAINT rs_student_id
     FOREIGN KEY (student_id) REFERENCES students (id),
   CONSTRAINT rs_department_course
     FOREIGN KEY (department, course)
     REFERENCES classes (department, course));
```

Registered_students has two declarative referential integrity constraints. As such, both students and classes are constraining tables for registered_students. Because of the constraints, classes and students may need to be modified and/or queried by the DML statement. Also, registered_students itself is mutating during execution of a DML statement against it.

SQL statements in a trigger body may not

■ Read from or modify any mutating table of the triggering statement. This includes the triggering table itself.

■ Read from or modify the primary-, unique-, or foreign-key columns of a constraining table of the triggering table. They may, however, modify the other columns if desired.

These restrictions apply to all row-level triggers. They apply for statement triggers only when the statement trigger would be fired as a result of a DELETE CASCADE operation.

NOTE
If an INSERT statement affects only one row, the before- and after-row triggers for that row do not treat the triggering table as mutating. This is the only case where a row-level trigger may read from or modify the triggering table. Statements such as INSERT INTO table SELECT . . . *always treat the triggering table as mutating, even if the subquery returns only one row.*

As an example, consider the `CascadeRSInserts` trigger, shown next. Even though it modifies both `students` and `classes`, it is legal because the columns in `students` and `classes` that are modified are not key columns. In the next section, we will examine an illegal trigger.

```
-- Available online as cascadeRSInsert.sql
CREATE OR REPLACE TRIGGER CascadeRSInserts
  /* Keep the registered_students, students, and classes
     tables in synch when an INSERT is done to registered_students. */
  BEFORE INSERT ON registered_students
  FOR EACH ROW
DECLARE
  v_Credits classes.num_credits%TYPE;
BEGIN
  -- Determine the number of credits for this class.
  SELECT num_credits
    INTO v_Credits
    FROM classes
    WHERE department = :new.department
    AND course = :new.course;

  -- Modify the current credits for this student.
  UPDATE students
    SET current_credits = current_credits + v_Credits
    WHERE ID = :new.student_id;

  -- Add one to the number of students in the class.
  UPDATE classes
    SET current_students = current_students + 1
    WHERE department - :new.department
```

```
      AND course = :new.course;
END CascadeRSInserts;
/
```

Mutating Table Example

Suppose we want to limit the number of students in each major to five. We could accomplish this with a before INSERT or UPDATE row-level trigger on `students`, given here:

```
-- Available online as part of limitMajors.sql
CREATE OR REPLACE TRIGGER LimitMajors
  /* Limits the number of students in each major to 5.
     If this limit is exceeded, an error is raised through
     raise_application_error. */
  BEFORE INSERT OR UPDATE OF major ON students
  FOR EACH ROW
DECLARE
  v_MaxStudents CONSTANT NUMBER := 5;
  v_CurrentStudents NUMBER;
BEGIN
  -- Determine the current number of students in this
  -- major.
  SELECT COUNT(*)
    INTO v_CurrentStudents
    FROM students
    WHERE major = :new.major;

  -- If there isn't room, raise an error.
  IF v_CurrentStudents + 1 > v_MaxStudents THEN
    RAISE_APPLICATION_ERROR(-20000,
      'Too many students in major ' || :new.major);
  END IF;
END LimitMajors;
/
```

At first glance, this trigger seems to accomplish the desired result. However, if we attempt to update `students`, it will fire the LimitMajor trigger. We will need to populate the tables with data before testing the update statement. This can be done by running `insertAcademicRecords.sql` or rerunning `createObjects.sql`.

```
-- Available online as part of limitMajors.sql
UPDATE students
SET major = 'History'
WHERE id = 1;
```

The LimitMajor trigger will raise the following exception.

```
UPDATE students
       *
ERROR at line 1:
ORA-04091: table USERA.STUDENTS is mutating, trigger/function may not
see it
ORA-06512: at "USERA.LIMITMAJORS", line 7
ORA-04088: error during execution of trigger 'USERA.LIMITMAJORS'
```

The ORA-4091 error results because `LimitMajors` queries its own triggering table, which is mutating. ORA-4091 is raised when the trigger is fired, not when it is created.

Workaround for the Mutating Table Error

`Students` is mutating only for a row-level trigger. This means that we cannot query it in a row-level trigger, but we can in a statement-level trigger. However, we cannot simply make `LimitMajors` into a statement trigger, since we need to use the value of `:new.major` in the trigger body. The solution for this is to create two triggers—one row level and the other statement level. In the row-level trigger, we record the value of `:new.major`, but we don't query `students`. The query is done in the statement-level trigger and uses the value recorded in the row trigger.

How do we record this value? One way is to use a PL/SQL table inside a package. This way, we can save multiple values per update. Also, each session gets its own instantiation of packaged variables, so we don't have to worry about simultaneous updates by different sessions. This solution is implemented with the `student_data` package and the `RLimitMajors` and `SLimitMajors` triggers:

```
-- Available online as part of createNonMutating.sql
CREATE OR REPLACE PACKAGE StudentData AS
  TYPE t_Majors IS TABLE OF students.major%TYPE
    INDEX BY BINARY_INTEGER;
  TYPE t_IDs IS TABLE OF students.ID%TYPE
    INDEX BY BINARY_INTEGER;

  v_StudentMajors t_Majors;
  v_StudentIDs    t_IDs;
  v_NumEntries    BINARY_INTEGER := 0;
END StudentData;
/

CREATE OR REPLACE TRIGGER RLimitMajors
  BEFORE INSERT OR UPDATE OF major ON students
  FOR EACH ROW
BEGIN
```

```
    /* Record the new data in StudentData. We don't make any
       changes to students, to avoid the ORA-4091 error. */
    StudentData.v_NumEntries := StudentData.v_NumEntries + 1;
    StudentData.v_StudentMajors(StudentData.v_NumEntries) :=
      :new.major;
    StudentData.v_StudentIDs(StudentData.v_NumEntries) := :new.id;
END RLimitMajors;
/


CREATE OR REPLACE TRIGGER SLimitMajors
  AFTER INSERT OR UPDATE OF major ON students
DECLARE
  v_MaxStudents      CONSTANT NUMBER := 2;
  v_CurrentStudents  NUMBER;
  v_StudentID        students.ID%TYPE;
  v_Major            students.major%TYPE;
BEGIN
  /* Loop through each student inserted or updated, and verify
     that we are still within the limit. */
  FOR v_LoopIndex IN 1..StudentData.v_NumEntries LOOP
    v_StudentID := StudentData.v_StudentIDs(v_LoopIndex);
    v_Major := StudentData.v_StudentMajors(v_LoopIndex);

    -- Determine the current number of students in this major.
    SELECT COUNT(*)
      INTO v_CurrentStudents
      FROM students
      WHERE major = v_Major;

    -- If there isn't room, raise an error.
    IF v_CurrentStudents > v_MaxStudents THEN
      RAISE_APPLICATION_ERROR(-20000,
        'Too many students for major ' || v_Major ||
        ' because of student ' || v_StudentID);
    END IF;
  END LOOP;

  -- Reset the counter so the next execution will use new data.
  StudentData.v_NumEntries := 0;
END SlimitMajors;
/
```

NOTE
*Be sure to drop the incorrect LimitMajors
trigger before running the preceding script.*

We can now test this series of triggers by updating `students` until we have too many history majors. This can be done by using the `testNonMutating.sql` script or typing the following update statement:

```
-- Available online as part of testNonMutating.sql
UPDATE students
SET major = 'History'
WHERE id IN (1,2,3);
```

The limit on majors is set at two in the SlimitMajors trigger. The update statement attempts to put three history majors in the system. It fails with this error message:

```
UPDATE students
       *
ERROR at line 1:
ORA- 20000: Too many students for major History because of student 2
ORA-06512: at "USERA.SLIMITMAJORS", line 21
ORA-04088: error during execution of trigger 'USERA.SLIMITMAJORS'
```

This is the desired behavior. This technique can be applied to occurrences of ORA-4091 when a row-level trigger reads from or modifies a mutating table. Instead of doing the illegal processing in the row-level trigger, we defer the processing to an after statement-level trigger, where it is legal. The packaged PL/SQL tables are used to store the rows that were changed.

There are several things to note about this technique:

- The PL/SQL tables are contained in a package so that they will be visible to both the row-level trigger and the statement-level trigger. The only way to ensure that variables are global is to put them in a package.

- A counter variable, `StudentData.v_NumEntries`, is used. This is initialized to zero when the package is created. It is incremented by the row-level trigger. The statement-level trigger references it and then resets it to zero after processing. This is necessary so that the next UPDATE statement issued by this session will have the correct value.

- The check in `SLimitMajors` for the maximum number of students had to be changed slightly. Since this is now an after-statement trigger, `v_CurrentStudents` will hold the number of students in the major after the insert or update, not before. Thus the check for `v_CurrentStudents + 1`, which we did in `LimitMajors`, is replaced by `v_CurrentStudents`.

■ A database table could have been used instead of PL/SQL tables. We don't recommend this technique, because simultaneous sessions issuing an UPDATE would interfere with each other (in Oracle8*i* and higher you could use a temporary table, however). Packaged PL/SQL tables are unique among sessions, which avoids the problem.

Summary

As we have seen, triggers are a valuable addition to PL/SQL and Oracle. They can be used to enforce data constraints that are much more complex than normal referential integrity constraints, as well as implement the correct behavior for complex views. Event attribute functions can be used for system triggers to determine all kinds of information about the triggering event and the situation that caused it. In the next section, we will begin our discussion of the built-in packages with intersession communication.

PART
II

Advanced PL/
SQL Features

CHAPTER
11

Intersession
Communication

ntersession communication is the ability to communicate between different user connections. Sessions are individual work areas. Sessions begin when you connect and end when you disconnect from the Oracle 10*g* database. You have several approaches that enable you to communicate between sessions. The `DBMS_PIPE` and `DBMS_ALERT` built-in utilities are the focus of the chapter.

You will cover topics as follows. The chapter assumes you read it sequentially. It also assumes you have read the preceding ten chapters. If you feel comfortable with an area, please feel free to move to the section of interest. However, the chapter assumes you have mastery of earlier sections.

- Introducing intersession communication

- `DBMS_PIPE` built-in package

- `DBMS_ALERT` built-in package

Introducing Intersession Communication

Intersession communication is the ability to communicate between different user connections. When users connect to the database, they establish sessions. The duration of a session starts at connection and ends at disconnection. During the session users are in full control of their resources. Resources are anything that they own directly or have access permissions to perform, for example, using DQL, DML, or PL/SQL execution against resources.

You can communicate between sessions in Oracle 10*g* using several approaches. They each have pluses and minuses. Two types involve permanent or semipermanent objects in the database. The other two types involve SGA memory segments, called *named pipes.* A synopsis of methods follows.

Requiring Permanent or Semipermanent Structures

Permanent or semipermanent structures enable you to do the following:

- You can leverage the Advanced Queuing facility introduced in Oracle 8 with the DBMS_AQADM and DBMS_AQ packages. These involve setting up advanced queuing for each of the participants. Then, you use messages to exchange information between the sessions. This technology underpins Oracle's implementation of workflow applications.

- You can use tables, grants, and synonyms to exchange data between sessions. The solution is simple but subject to transaction control limitations. Transaction control limits mean that a transaction must complete and commit permanently the change to the database. The solution more or less involves implementing triggers to restrict DML operations based on other table values.

Not Requiring Permanent or Semipermanent Structures

Here you can do the following:

- You can use the DBMS_PIPE built-in package. DBMS_PIPE uses dynamic memory structures in the SGA called pipes. They are very similar to Unix pipes. Pipes may be local, private, or publicly accessible. They act as first-in and last-out (FIFO) queues. Transaction control issues do not bind them. You can use pipes to send and receive data between sessions asynchronously.

- You can use the DBMS_ALERT built-in package. DBMS_ALERT also uses a memory structure in the SGA. While the structure is not formally referred to as a pipe, it works as a public pipe. These are likewise similar to Unix pipes. They are publicly accessible pipes or FIFO queues. These pipes are populated on event triggers and subject to transaction control limits. The alert pipes communicate between sessions asynchronously at the conclusion of an event. Events are anything that you can build a trigger against, like a DML or system action (check Chapter 10 for more on triggers). Unlike DBMS_PIPE, the DBMS_ALERT built-in package works on a publish-and-subscribe paradigm. It publishes notifications. Then it enables subscribers to register their interest in the alert and receive the alert notifications.

You should understand when and where to use these approaches. As a rule of thumb, you do not want to use permanent or semipermanent structures to exchange information when they can be avoided. Using these types of structures incurs file access, which can slow your application down. Intersession communication should be done in memory where possible.

Both DBMS_PIPE and DBMS_ALERT work in memory. They do not have permanent or semipermanent structures in the database. The structures are designed to support intersession communication. Pipes can be defined to support intersession communication two ways: Pipes can support communication between two or more sessions of a single user. Alternatively, they can support communication between two or more users. Alerts also supports two or more sessions of a single user.

DBMS_ALERT works best as an asynchronous transaction control mechanism. The DBMS_ALERT notifies subscribers of an event. The subscribers can then take action on events. DBMS_ALERT implements a publish-and-subscribe paradigm. When you use a publish-and-subscribe process, polling daemons are simplified or eliminated. Polling daemons run as background processes. They consume varying resources, depending on how you implement them. If you eliminate polling daemons, you reduce resource demands on the database and physical machine.

DBMS_PIPE can help you mimic POSIX-compliant threads. Such threads provide structures that you may use as C/C++ mutex variables. Likewise, they are ideal for passing information to external processes that may monitor or control system resources. For example, DBMS_PIPE can:

- Enable you to use *local pipes* to control a single program's execution.

- Enable you to use *private pipes* to control concurrent programs run by the single user.

- Enable you to use *public pipes* to control concurrent programs run by multiple users.

The DBMS_PIPE Built-in Package

In Oracle 10g, DBMS_PIPE is a privileged package owned by the SYS user. You or your DBA must grant EXECUTE permission on the DBMS_PIPE package to the PLSQL user as well as to another user you may choose—some of the examples and exercises in this chapter require two users to carry out. The second user may be one used before in the book, like USERA/USERB, or another of your choosing. That user also requires EXECUTE permission on the DBMS_PIPE package.

TIP
You or your DBA should probably grant execute permission with the grant option to SYSTEM. Then, the SYSTEM user should grant execute permission to the PLSQL user manually. Alternatively, you can run the create_user.sql *script.*

Introducing the DBMS_PIPE Package

The architecture of DBMS_PIPE is key to understanding its use. You need to understand three perspectives presented by DBMS_PIPE. The perspectives are represented by access privileges. Also, the structures used to temporarily store the data are memory structures in the PGA or the SGA.

DBMS_PIPE has session local, user private, and public pipe variations. It is possible that using multiple types in the same session can cause problems. Typically, the problems relate to inadvertent destruction of the session local pipe contents. The session local pipe acts as a private buffer. Unfortunately, the same private buffer serves as the access to and from user private and public pipes. The private buffer is a PGA pipe and is inaccessible by named reference externally to the session. Private and public pipes are SGA structures.

You will now examine each of the access methods. Local pipes are first. The local pipe is only a buffer. The buffer can contain only one element. You write a variable-length string to the local buffer. Then you may read the string from the buffer. If the element is not read locally or forwarded to a named private or public pipe before the next write, the original value is lost. Figure 11-1 depicts a local pipe read-and-write operation. Forwarding the element will be covered later.

Having mastered the local read-and-write buffer, you will examine a private user pipe read-and-write operation. Private user pipes are accessible to all sessions of the user who created the pipe. Before writing to the private pipe, the data must be written to the local buffer. Then, you send the contents of the local buffer to the private pipe. The contents of the private pipe can then be read to a local session buffer. The local session buffer can then be read and assigned to a variable. Figure 11-2 illustrates a private user pipe.

Figure 11-2 shows that there are one or two sessions when using a private user pipe. It is possible that the same user session creating a private pipe can write and read to it. As discussed, the local pipe is a buffer that contains only one value. A private pipe may contain any number of values in a FIFO queue. Therefore, a session that needs to write a series of data values may write to and read from a private pipe.

Alternatively, the same user can have two or more sessions and share the FIFO queue. This scenario presents some interesting issues because any session created by the user who owns the queue can write to or read from it. There is no way to track which session wrote to the pipe unless you tokenize the variable-length string.

Tokenizing a variable-length string means that you build a string that contains a delimiter and substrings. The delimiter separates substrings. You can tokenize a string by using a comma, for instance. The first value before the comma can contain

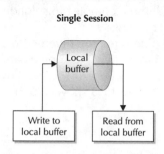

FIGURE 11-1. *Session local buffer read-and-write operation*

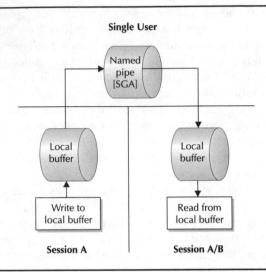

FIGURE 11-2. *Private pipe read-and-write operation*

a string that identifies the originating, or writing, session. The next delimited string can contain the destination, or reading, session. The last substring can contain the value substring or a series of delimited substrings.

In the tokenized string scenario, it is possible for the wrong session to read a message. If you implement this architecture, you will need to ensure the code puts the message back into the queue. Unfortunately, it will be out of sequence. This behavior is a natural consequence of FIFO queues. When using FIFO queues, you should not depend solely on sequencing of data. As an alternative, you can use a tokenized message. A *tokenized message* is a series of delimited substrings that are sequential. You can get much more complex in solutions, but that belongs in another book.

The premise of a private pipe is not too different from that of a public pipe. In fact, all the activity described in a private user pipe can be done in a public pipe. A public pipe is also the default pipe created. You must override the default behavior to create a private user pipe. Figure 11-3 shows a public pipe.

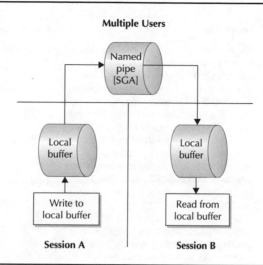

FIGURE 11-3. *Public pipe read-and-write operation*

Moreover, public pipes are designed for sharing between two users. Figure 11-3 depicts two sessions, which would occur for multiple users sharing a public pipe. All read and write operations mirror the previously described behaviors.

You should now have a high-level view of what DBMS_PIPE uses as memory structures. This architectural view will be important as we cover the procedures and functions of the DBMS_PIPE built-in.

Defining the DBMS_PIPE Package

The DBMS_PIPE package contains procedures and functions. Typically, procedures would be limited to PL/SQL execution and functions enabled for SQL and PL/SQL. The CREATE_PIPE function has limited utility in SQL because the PRIVATE formal parameter is a Boolean data type, and Boolean data types cannot be used in SQL. Since the default value for the PRIVATE formal parameter is true, you must use PL/SQL to create a public pipe.

Table 11-1 describes the DBMS_PIPE package.

Having defined the DBMS_PIPE package, you will work with DBMS_PIPE in the next section.

Function or Procedure	Description	Return Type	SQL Access
CREATE_PIPE	The CREATE_PIPE function takes three formal parameters: PIPENAME is positionally the first and is a mandatory parameter. It is defined as a VARCHAR2 data type. Its maximum size should be 128 bytes. You should not use ORA$ as a preface to any of your pipes because those are reserved by Oracle Corporation for their own use. MAXPIPESIZE is positionally the second and an optional formal parameter. It has an INTEGER data type. The default value is 8192. PRIVATE is positionally the third and an optional parameter. It has a BOOLEAN data type. The default value is TRUE, which maps to a default private pipe. If a privileged user calls the CREATE_PIPE function and the pipe already exists, it will not alter the existing pipe. It will return a zero value. The zero value indicates successful completion, but in this case nothing was created; it was ignored. You may attempt to re-create a public pipe as another user. It will appear to work but in reality the command is ignored. If you lack permission to create the object, you raise an ORA-23322 exception.	INTEGER	Limited
NEXT_ITEM_TYPE	The NEXT_ITEM_TYPE function takes no formal parameters. It reads the contents of the local pipe or buffer. It returns an INTEGER that maps to the following: 0: An empty buffer. 6: A NUMBER data type. 9: A VARCHAR2 data type. 11: A ROWID data type. 12: A DATE data type. 23: A RAW data type. If you empty the local buffer, you will raise an ORA-06556 exception when attempting to secure a return value.	INTEGER	Yes

TABLE 11-1.   *The DBMS_PIPE Package*

Function or Procedure	Description	Return Type	SQL Access
PACK_MESSAGE	The PACK_MESSAGE procedure takes a single formal parameter. The parameter can be a DATE, NCHAR, NUMBER, or VARCHAR2 data type. PACK_MESSAGE takes the value of the actual parameter and puts it into the local pipe or buffer.	None	No
PACK_MESSAGE_RAW	The PACK_MESSAGE_RAW procedure takes a single formal parameter. The parameter is a RAW data type. PACK_MESSAGE_RAW takes the value of the actual parameter and puts it into the local pipe or buffer.	None	No
PACK_MESSAGE_ ROWID	The PACK_MESSAGE_ROWID procedure takes a single formal parameter. The parameter is a ROWID data type. PACK_MESSAGE_ROWID takes the value of the actual parameter and puts it into the local pipe or buffer.	None	No
PURGE	The PURGE procedure takes a single formal parameter. The parameter is a VARCHAR2 data type and must be a valid private or public pipe name.	None	No
RECEIVE_MESSAGE	The RECEIVE_MESSAGE function takes one or two formal parameters. The first positional parameter is a VARCHAR2 data type and must be a valid private or public pipe name. The second positional and optional parameter is an INTEGER data type. Unless you can allow your program to hang for 1000 days, you should override this value to a suitably lower count in seconds. It reads the contents of the named pipe and transfers it to the local buffer. It returns an INTEGER that maps to the following: 0: Successful completion. 1: A timeout without a reply. 2: A pipe message too large for the buffer, which should never happen. 3: An interrupt of some kind. If you lack permission to access the pipe, you raise an ORA-23322 exception. The error means you cannot receive from that pipe.	INTEGER	Yes

TABLE 11-1. *The DBMS_PIPE Package* (continued)

Function or Procedure	Description	Return Type	SQL Access
REMOVE_PIPE	The REMOVE_PIPE function takes one formal parameter. It is a VARCHAR2 data type and must be a valid private or public pipe name. It returns an INTEGER that maps to the following: 0: Successful completion. If you lack permission to remove the object, you raise an ORA-23322 exception. If the user who created the named pipe is not known, the DBA has one of two choices. The DBA can shut down and restart the instance to get rid of the conflicting named pipe. Alternatively, as SYSDBA, you can remove the offending named pipe.	INTEGER	Yes
RESET_BUFFER	The RESET_BUFFER procedure takes no formal parameter. It removes the contents of the local buffer.	None	No
SEND_MESSAGE	The SEND_MESSAGE function takes one to three formal parameters. The first positional parameter is a VARCHAR2 data type and must be a valid private or public pipe name. The second positional and optional parameter is an INTEGER data type. Unless you can allow your program to hang for 1000 days, you should override this value to a suitably lower count in seconds. The third positional and optional parameter is an INTEGER representing the total size of all messages placed in the pipe. This number *must* be *equal to* or *less than* the value used when creating the named pipe. It writes the contents of the local buffer to the named pipe. It returns an INTEGER that maps to the following: 0: Successful completion. 1: A timeout without a reply. 2: A pipe message too large for the buffer, which should never happen. 3: An interrupt of some kind. If you lack permission to access the pipe, you raise an ORA-23322 exception. The error means you cannot write to that pipe.	INTEGER	Yes

TABLE 11-1. *The DBMS_PIPE Package* (continued)

Function or Procedure	Description	Return Type	SQL Access
UNIQUE_SESSION_NAME	The UNIQUE_SESSION_NAME function takes no formal parameter. It returns a VARCHAR2 string that represents the current session.	VARCHAR2	Yes
UNPACK_MESSAGE	The UNPACK_MESSAGE procedure takes a single formal parameter. The parameter can be a DATE, NCHAR, NUMBER, or VARCHAR2 data type. UNPACK_MESSAGE takes the value from the local pipe or buffer and returns it as the OUT mode value of the actual parameter.	None	No
UNPACK_MESSAGE_RAW	The UNPACK_MESSAGE_RAW procedure takes a single formal parameter. The parameter must be a RAW data type. UNPACK_MESSAGE_RAW takes the value from the local pipe or buffer and returns it as the OUT mode value of the actual parameter.	None	No
UNPACK_MESSAGE_ROWID	The UNPACK_MESSAGE_ROWID procedure takes a single formal parameter. The parameter must be a ROWID data type. UNPACK_MESSAGE_ROWID takes the value from the local pipe or buffer and returns it as the OUT mode value of the actual parameter.	None	No

TABLE 11-1.   *The DBMS_PIPE Package* (continued)

Working with the DBMS_PIPE Package

In this section, you will work with the following:

- Sending to and receiving from the local pipe or buffer
- Creating pipes
- Reading and writing from pipes
- Putting a wrapper around DBMS_PIPE

These topics will help prepare you to use DBMS_PIPE successfully. The topics also should prepare you to experiment with the package.

If you do not have a PLSQL account with the correct permissions, you can run the `create_user.sql` script to build one.

Sending to and Receiving from the Local Pipe or Buffer

The local buffer is very important. You can write programs that will return an anomalous result if you do not understand how to use the local buffer. Only the session that writes to the local buffer can access the local buffer.

The following program shows how to write to the local buffer:

```
-- Available online as part of write_local.sql

DECLARE

  -- Define variables for functions and procedures.
  message    VARCHAR2(30 CHAR);
  success    INTEGER;

BEGIN

  -- Assign the unique session name to message.
  message := DBMS_PIPE.UNIQUE_SESSION_NAME;

  -- Reset the local private pipe.
  DBMS_PIPE.RESET_BUFFER;

  -- Write a message to the local private pipe.
  DBMS_PIPE.PACK_MESSAGE(message);

  -- Write what was written to the pipe.
  DBMS_OUTPUT.PUT_LINE('Written to pipe ['||message||']');

END;
/
```

The sample program does the following:

- It defines and declares a variable `message` using a `VARCHAR2` data type.

- It defines and declares a variable `success` using an `INTEGER` data type.

- It assigns to the `message` variable the return value of the unique session name.

- It resets the local buffer to ensure it is empty.

- It packs or sends the `message` variable to the local buffer.

- It uses `DBMS_OUTPUT` to print a message to console.

This has placed a value in your local buffer. The following program will let you read and print the contents of the pipe to the console. As with previous PL/SQL programs, this uses the DBMS_OUTPUT utility to print the data. The SERVEROUTPUT parameter should be enabled in SQL*Plus to see the output.

```
-- Available online as part of read_local.sql

DECLARE

    -- Define variables for functions and procedures.
    message    VARCHAR2(30 CHAR);
    success    INTEGER;

BEGIN

    -- Read a message from the local private pipe.
    DBMS_PIPE.UNPACK_MESSAGE(message);

    -- Print the contents of the message.
    DBMS_OUTPUT.PUT_LINE('Message ['||message||']');

END;
/
```

The sample program does the following:

■ It defines and declares a variable message using a VARCHAR2 data type.

■ It defines and declares a variable success using an INTEGER data type.

■ It assigns to the message variable the OUT mode value of the DBMS_PIPE.UNPACK_MESSAGE procedure.

■ It uses DBMS_OUTPUT to print the output to console.

You have learned how to write to and read from the local buffer. If you attempted to receive the contents from a named pipe in this session between writing to and reading from the local buffer, you would raise a pipe is empty exception.

The following SQL query reads the contents of a nonexistent named pipe. What it really does is attempt to transfer the contents of a nonexistent named pipe to the local buffer. If you insert the following SQL statement between the write_local.sql and read_local.sql programs, it will return a 1.

A 1 indicates the pipe is empty. When the RECEIVE_MESSAGE function returns any value, it has done one of two things: it has returned the contents of a named pipe or a null into the local buffer.

-- Available online as part of read_local_error.sql

```
SELECT    DBMS_PIPE.RECEIVE_MESSAGE('NOWHERE',0)
FROM      dual;
```

You can test this behavior by running the `read_local_error.sql` script. The script will produce the following output error messages:

-- Available online as output from read_local_error.sql

```
DECLARE
*
ERROR at line 1:
ORA-06556: the pipe is empty, cannot fulfill the
           unpack_message request
ORA-06512: at "SYS.DBMS_PIPE", line 78
ORA-06512: at line 10
```

You have seen that sequencing of commands is critical to having something in the local buffer. Also, you have seen that a call to the RECEIVE_MESSAGE function will fail but write a null to the local buffer.

You will now learn how to create named pipes.

Creating Pipes

As discussed, there are two types of named pipes. One is a private named pipe; the other is a public named pipe. The former is the default type for named pipes.

You will learn how to build a named private pipe and public pipe. You should ensure you run this as the PLSQL user, since the pipe name is hard-coded. The following example demonstrates creating a private pipe:

-- Available online as part of create_pipe1.sql

```
DECLARE

  -- Define and declare variables.
  message_pipe VARCHAR2(30) := 'PLSQL$MESSAGE_INBOX';
  message_size INTEGER       := 20000;

  -- Function output variable.
  retval INTEGER;

BEGIN
```

```
  -- Define a private pipe.
  retval := DBMS_PIPE.CREATE_PIPE(message_pipe
                                 ,message_size);

  -- Print the retval status.
  IF (retval = 0) THEN
    DBMS_OUTPUT.PUT_LINE('MESSAGE_INBOX pipe is created.');
  END IF;

EXCEPTION

  -- Raise generic exception.
  WHEN others THEN
    DBMS_OUTPUT.PUT_LINE(SQLERRM);
    RETURN;

END;
/
```

The sample program does the following:

■ It defines and declares a variable `message_pipe` using a VARCHAR2 data type.

■ It defines and declares a variable `message_size` using an INTEGER data type.

■ It defines and declares a variable `retval` using an INTEGER data type.

■ It assigns to the `retval` variable the return value from the DBMS_PIPE.CREATE_PIPE function. The creation uses only two actual parameters. By default, the third parameter is true. Therefore, it creates a private pipe.

■ It evaluates if the `retval` value is zero and prints a success message by using the DBMS_OUTPUT utility.

■ It handles all exceptions and prints the SQL error message raised by using the DBMS_OUTPUT utility.

Unfortunately, there is no convenient way to display defined pipes. If you connect as another user (like USERA) and attempt to run the create_pipe1.sql script, it will raise two errors. The attempt to use DBMS_PIPE.REMOVE_PIPE will result in an untrapped error. This is the default error message:

-- Available online as output from create_pipe1.sql

```
DECLARE
*
```

```
ERROR at line 1:
ORA-23322: Privilege error accessing pipe
ORA-06512: at "SYS.DBMS_SYS_ERROR", line 86
ORA-06512: at "SYS.DBMS_PIPE", line 130
ORA-06512: at line 4
```

The attempt to create a named pipe owned by the PLSQL user will raise SQLERRM only. It does so because it is managed in the exception handler. It raises the following exception:

-- **Available online as output from create_pipe1.sql**

```
ORA-23322: Privilege error accessing pipe
```

You have learned that the user who created the private named pipes is the only one who can alter them. Any other user will receive a privilege error when attempting to remove or re-create a private named pipe. You will now see the differences between creating private and publicly accessible pipes.

The following example should be run as the PLSQL user. It shows you how to create a public pipe:

-- **Available online as part of create_pipe2.sql**

```
-- An anonymous block program to delete a pipe.
DECLARE

  -- Define and declare a variable by removing a pipe.
  retval INTEGER :=
    DBMS_PIPE.REMOVE_PIPE('PLSQL$MESSAGE_INBOX');

BEGIN

 NULL;

END;
/

-- An anonymous block program to create a pipe.
DECLARE

  -- Define and declare variables.
  message_pipe VARCHAR2(30) := 'PLSQL$MESSAGE_INBOX';
  message_size INTEGER      := 20000;
  message_flag BOOLEAN      := TRUE;

  -- Function output variable.
```

```
   retval INTEGER;

BEGIN

  -- Define a public pipe.
  retval := DBMS_PIPE.CREATE_PIPE(message_pipe
                                 ,message_size
                                 ,message_flag);

  -- Print the retval status.
  IF (retval = 0) THEN
    DBMS_OUTPUT.PUT_LINE('MESSAGE_INBOX pipe is created.');
  END IF;

EXCEPTION

  -- Raise generic exception.
  WHEN others THEN
    DBMS_OUTPUT.PUT_LINE(SQLERRM);
    RETURN;

END;
/
```

The sample program does the following:

- It defines a `retval` variable of `INTEGER` type and declares it as the return value of `DBMS_PIPE.REMOVE_PIPE` function. This is how you remove an existing pipe. If you fail to remove a named pipe before trying to create a variation using the same name, it will raise an `ORA-23322` error. There is unfortunately no equivalent to the SQL create or replace command syntax for database objects in the `DBMS_PIPE` package.

- It defines and declares a variable `message_pipe` using a `VARCHAR2` data type.

- It defines and declares a variable `message_size` using an `INTEGER` data type.

- It defines and declares a variable `retval` using an `INTEGER` data type.

- It assigns to the `retval` variable the return value from the `DBMS_PIPE.CREATE_PIPE` function. The creation is only using all three actual parameters. It overrides the private default value, and the pipe created is a public pipe.

- It evaluates if the `retval` value is zero and prints a success message by using the `DBMS_OUTPUT` utility.

- It handles all exceptions and prints the SQL error message raised by using the `DBMS_OUTPUT` utility.

The next test assumes you have run `create_pipe2.sql` as the `PLSQL` user. If you connect as `USERA`, you will find that you can rerun the `create_pipe2.sql` statement without raising an exception.

It appears that the public pipe is re-created under a new user because no exception was raised. This is not the case. A zero, or success, is returned when the public pipe already exists with the same signature. (A *signature* is a collection of formal parameter(s) that define a function, method, or procedure.)

The lack of a raised exception is misleading. Unfortunately, that's the way `DBMS_PIPE.CREATE_PIPE` works when the same signature is used. You can test the lack of a privilege error by running `create_pipe1.sql` in the `PLSQL` schema and then running `create_pipe2.sql` in another user's schema.

It will raise the following exception:

```
ORA-23322: Privilege error accessing pipe
```

If you attempt to run `create_pipe1.sql` in the `USERA` schema, you will raise an exception. The reason it now returns a privilege exception is straightforward. `USERA` is attempting to modify the signature for the pipe, making it private when it is public. `USERA` cannot override the pipe created in that name because it is not the user who created it.

While it would have taken too much space in the book, a `create_pipe3.sql` script can be found on the web site. It has all the appropriate error trapping and good coding practices. You should take a look at how it works. Much of the anonymous block logic is migrated into the `DBMS_PIPE` wrapper discussed later in this chapter.

You have learned how to create private and public pipes. You have also seen that the privileges error can sometimes be suppressed. The next section will show how to read from and write to named pipes.

Writing to and Reading from Pipes

Private and public pipes are written to and read from in the same way. You write data by placing it in the local buffer and sending it to the named pipe. Then, you read data by the inverse process. You receive data from a named pipe into the local buffer and then read data from the local buffer.

You will examine two programs. One will write data to a named pipe. The other will read from a named pipe. You should use the `PLSQL` schema to write and read the data. However, you can read the data from any other user that has the execute privilege on `DBMS_PIPE`, provided you last ran `create_pipe2.sql` in the `PLSQL` schema, which builds a public pipe.

The following program writes to a named pipe:

-- **Available online as part of write_pipe.sql**

```
DECLARE

  -- Define line return to separate pipe writes.
  line_return VARCHAR2(1) := CHR(10);

  -- Define a return value
  flag        INTEGER;

BEGIN

  -- Purge pipe content.
  dbms_pipe.purge('PLSQL$MESSAGE_INBOX');

  -- Print input title.
  DBMS_OUTPUT.PUT_LINE('Input Message to Pipe');
  DBMS_OUTPUT.PUT_LINE('--------------------');

  -- Use a range for-loop to send three messages.
  FOR i IN 1..3 LOOP

    -- Print the input line.
    DBMS_OUTPUT.PUT_LINE('Message ['||i||']');

    -- Put a message in the local buffer.
    DBMS_PIPE.PACK_MESSAGE(
      'Message ['||i||']'||line_return);

    -- Send message, success is a zero return value.
    flag := DBMS_PIPE.SEND_MESSAGE('PLSQL$MESSAGE_INBOX');

  END LOOP;

  -- Print message based on flag status.
  IF (flag = 0) THEN
    DBMS_OUTPUT.PUT_LINE(
      'Message sent to PLSQL$MESSAGE_INBOX.');
  END IF;

END;
/
```

The sample program does the following:

■ It defines and declares a variable line_return using a VARCHAR2 data type.

- It defines `flag` as an `INTEGER` variable to receive the execution code from the `SEND_MESSAGE` function.

- It uses the `DBMS_PIPE.PURGE` procedure to remove any existing contents from the named pipe.

- It uses `DBMS_OUTPUT` utility to print a title.

- Using a range for-loop, the program does the following:

  - It uses `DBMS_OUTPUT` to print each line that will be sent as a message.

  - It uses `DBMS_PIPE.PACK_MESSAGE` to put the actual parameter into the local buffer.

  - It uses `DBMS_PIPE.SEND_MESSAGE` to move the contents of the local buffer to the named pipe.

- It evaluates if the `flag` value is zero and prints a success message by using the `DBMS_OUTPUT` utility.

The program outputs this:

```
-- Available online as output from write_pipe.sql

Input Message to Pipe
--------------------
Message [1]
Message [2]
Message [3]
Message sent to PLSQL$MESSAGE_INBOX.
```

You can read the data from the named pipe by inverting the write process. The process is demonstrated in the following program:

```
-- Available online as part of read_pipe.sql

DECLARE

  -- Define message variable.
  line_return VARCHAR2(1)     := CHR(10);
  message     VARCHAR2(4000);
  output      VARCHAR2(4000);

  -- Define a return value
  flag        INTEGER;

BEGIN
```

```
  -- Reset the local buffer.
  DBMS_PIPE.RESET_BUFFER;

  -- Print input title.
  DBMS_OUTPUT.PUT(line_return);
  DBMS_OUTPUT.PUT_LINE('Output Message from Pipe');
  DBMS_OUTPUT.PUT_LINE('------------------------');

  -- Use range for-loop to receive and read three messages.
  FOR i IN 1..3 LOOP

    -- Receive message, success is a zero return value.
    flag :=
      DBMS_PIPE.RECEIVE_MESSAGE('PLSQL$MESSAGE_INBOX',0);

    -- Read message from local buffer.
    DBMS_PIPE.UNPACK_MESSAGE(message);

    -- Append message to output variable.
    output := output || message;

  END LOOP;

  -- Print message based on flag status.
  IF (flag = 0) THEN

    -- Print the output variable.
    DBMS_OUTPUT.PUT(output);

    -- Print confirmation message.
    DBMS_OUTPUT.PUT_LINE(
      'Message received from PLSQL$MESSAGE_INBOX.');

  END IF;

END;
/
```

The sample program does the following:

- It defines and declares a variable line_return using a VARCHAR2 data type.
- It defines message as a VARCHAR2 variable.
- It defines output as a VARCHAR2 variable.

- It defines `flag` as an `INTEGER` variable to receive the execution code from the `RECEIVE_MESSAGE` function.

- It uses `DBMS_OUTPUT` utility to print a title.

- Using a range for-loop, the program does the following:

  - It does *not* use the DBMS_PIPE.PURGE procedure to remove any existing contents from the named pipe. If it did so, it would not retrieve any data.

  - It does use the DBMS_PIPE.RESET_BUFFER procedure to clear the local buffer. While unnecessary when nothing is done with the buffer contents before retrieving from a named pipe, this procedure can cause erroneous data to be retrieved from the local buffer. It is a good programming practice to use it before reading from a named pipe.

  - It uses DBMS_PIPE.RECEIVE_MESSAGE to move the contents from the named pipe to the local buffer. It uses a second parameter of zero. This forces an immediate read on the pipe. Unless you override the time-out of 1000 days, your program could hang on an empty pipe instead of returning an error message.

  - It uses DBMS_PIPE.UNPACK_MESSAGE to put the contents of the local buffer into the actual parameter.

  - It appends to the output variable by assigning it to itself and the message value.

  - It evaluates if the flag value is zero. Then, it prints the contents of the output variable and a success message by using the DBMS_OUTPUT utility.

The program outputs this:

```
-- Available online as output from write_pipe.sql

Output Message from Pipe
------------------------
Message [1]
Message [2]
Message [3]
Message received from PLSQL$MESSAGE_INBOX.
```

You should notice that the output from the pipe is ordered the same as when it was written. This is a property of a FIFO queue. As you learned earlier in the chapter, all pipes are FIFO queues.

You have learned how to create private and public pipes. Moreover, you can now write to and read from pipes. The `PACK_MESSAGE_RAW`, `PACK_MESSAGE_ROWID`, `UNPACK_MESSAGE_RAW`, and `UNPACK_MESSAGE_ROWID` procedures are not covered because they work like the PACK_MESSAGE and UNPACK_MESSAGE procedures. Two other commands have not been covered in earlier examples: the NEXT_ITEM_TYPE and UNIQUE_SESSION_NAME function will be covered in the next example.

The NEXT_ITEM_TYPE and UNIQUE_SESSION_NAME functions are covered in the following example program:

```
-- Available online as part of next_item_type.sql

DECLARE

  -- Define session.
  session     VARCHAR2(30) :=
    DBMS_PIPE.UNIQUE_SESSION_NAME;

  -- Define line return to separate pipe writes.
  line_return VARCHAR2(1) := CHR(10);
  message     VARCHAR2(4000);
  output      VARCHAR2(4000);

  -- Define a return values.
  flag        INTEGER;
  code        INTEGER;

  -- Define and declare input variables.
  message1    INTEGER     := 1776;
  message2    DATE        := TO_DATE('04-JUL-1776');
  message3    VARCHAR2(30 CHAR) := 'John Adams';

  -- Define output variables.
  message11   INTEGER;
  message12   DATE;
  message13   VARCHAR2(30 CHAR);

BEGIN

  -- Purge pipe content.
  DBMS_PIPE.PURGE('PLSQL$MESSAGE_INBOX');

  -- Print input title.
  DBMS_OUTPUT.PUT_LINE('Input Message to Pipe');
  DBMS_OUTPUT.PUT_LINE('Session: ['||session||']');
  DBMS_OUTPUT.PUT_LINE('-------------------------------');

  -- Do the following for message1, message2, and message3:
  -- 1. Print the input line.
  -- 2. Use the procedure to put a message in local buffer
  --    of a specific data type.
```

```
-- 3. Send message, success is a zero return value.

-- Process message1.
DBMS_OUTPUT.PUT_LINE(message1||'[NUMBER]');
DBMS_PIPE.PACK_MESSAGE(message1);
flag := DBMS_PIPE.SEND_MESSAGE('PLSQL$MESSAGE_INBOX');

-- Process message2.
DBMS_OUTPUT.PUT_LINE(message2||'[DATE]');
DBMS_PIPE.PACK_MESSAGE(message2);
flag := DBMS_PIPE.SEND_MESSAGE('PLSQL$MESSAGE_INBOX');

-- Process message3.
DBMS_OUTPUT.PUT_LINE(message3||'[VARCHAR2]');
DBMS_PIPE.PACK_MESSAGE(message3);
flag := DBMS_PIPE.SEND_MESSAGE('PLSQL$MESSAGE_INBOX');

-- Print message based on flag status.
IF (flag = 0) THEN
  DBMS_OUTPUT.PUT_LINE(
    'Message sent to PLSQL$MESSAGE_INBOX.');
END IF;

-- Print input title.
DBMS_OUTPUT.PUT(line_return);
DBMS_OUTPUT.PUT_LINE('Output Message from Pipe');
DBMS_OUTPUT.PUT_LINE('Session: ['||session||']');
DBMS_OUTPUT.PUT_LINE('--------------------------------');

-- Use range for-loop to receive and read three messages.
FOR i IN 1..3 LOOP

  -- Reset the local buffer.
  DBMS_PIPE.RESET_BUFFER;

  -- Receive message, success is a zero return value.
  flag :=
    DBMS_PIPE.RECEIVE_MESSAGE('PLSQL$MESSAGE_INBOX',0);

  -- Get the item type from the buffer contents.
  code := DBMS_PIPE.NEXT_ITEM_TYPE;

  -- Use case statement to return string.
  CASE code

    -- When buffer contents is a NUMBER.
    WHEN 6 THEN
```

```
      -- Unpack into a NUMBER variable type.
      DBMS_PIPE.UNPACK_MESSAGE(message11);
      output := output || message11
               ||'[NUMBER]'||line_return;

    -- When buffer contents is a VARCHAR2.
    WHEN 9 THEN

      -- Unpack into a VARCHAR2 variable type.
      DBMS_PIPE.UNPACK_MESSAGE(message13);
      output := output || message13
               ||'[VARCHAR2]'||line_return;

    -- When buffer contents is a DATE.
    WHEN 12 THEN

      -- Unpack into a DATE variable type.
      DBMS_PIPE.UNPACK_MESSAGE(message12);
      output := output || message12
               ||'[DATE]'||line_return;

  END CASE;

END LOOP;

-- Print message based on flag status.
IF (flag = 0) THEN

  -- Print the output variable.
  DBMS_OUTPUT.PUT(output);

  -- Print confirmation message.
  DBMS_OUTPUT.PUT_LINE(
    'Message received from PLSQL$MESSAGE_INBOX.');

END IF;

END;
/
```

The sample program does the following:

- It defines and declares a variable `session` using a `VARCHAR2` data type. It is assigned the value from the `DBMS_PIPE.UNIQUE_SESSION_NAME` function.

■ It defines and declares a variable `line_return` using a VARCHAR2 data type.

■ It defines `message` as a VARCHAR2 variable.

■ It defines `output` as a VARCHAR2 variable.

■ It defines a `flag` and `code` function return assignment targets that are INTEGER data types.

■ It defines and declares three input message variables: `message1`, `message2`, and `message3`. They are INTEGER, DATE, and VARCHAR2 data types, respectively.

■ It defines three output message variables: `message11`, `message12`, and `message13`. Like the input message variables, these are INTEGER, DATE, and VARCHAR2 data types, respectively.

■ It uses the DBMS_PIPE.PURGE procedure to remove any existing contents from the named pipe.

■ It uses DBMS_OUTPUT utility to print an input title.

■ For each of the three input data types:

   ■ It uses DBMS_OUTPUT utility to print the input message.

   ■ It uses DBMS_PIPE.PACK_MESSAGE to put the message into the local buffer.

   ■ It uses DBMS_PIPE.SEND_MESSAGE to transfer the local buffer contents to the named pipe.

■ It evaluates if the flag value is zero. Then, it prints the contents of the output variable and a success message by using the DBMS_OUTPUT utility.

■ It uses DBMS_OUTPUT utility to print an input title.

■ Using a range for-loop, the program does the following:

   ■ It uses DBMS_PIPE.RESET_BUFFER to clean the local buffer.

   ■ It uses DBMS_PIPE.RECEIVE_MESSAGE to move the contents from the named pipe to the local buffer. It uses a second parameter of zero. This forces an immediate read on the pipe. Unless you override the time-out of 1000 days, your program could hang on an empty pipe instead of returning an error message.

   ■ It assigns a code value from DBMS_PIPE.NEXT_ITEM_TYPE that identifies the data type of the local buffer.

■ It uses a case statement to evaluate the data type before using the DBMS_PIPE.UNPACK_MESSAGE utility. The case statement manages retrieval by data type. The DBMS_PIPE.UNPACK_MESSAGE is an overloaded procedure that returns a DATE, NUMBER, or VARCHAR2 data type variable. The DBMS_PIPE.NEXT_ITEM_TYPE enables you to pass into and manage different data types through a common pipe. You should check the definition of the DBMS_PIPE utility presented earlier in the chapter to review the data type to INTEGER return values.

■ It appends to the output variable by assigning it to itself and the message value.

■ It evaluates if the flag value is zero. Then, it prints the contents of the output variable and a success message by using the DBMS_OUTPUT utility.

The following is the output from next_item_type.sql script. It shows the data type in square brackets to the right of the value sent in and received from the pipe.

 -- Available online as output from next_item_type.sql

```
Input Message to Pipe
Session: [ORA$PIPE$00F2AFC20001]
---------------------------------
1776[NUMBER]
04-JUL-76[DATE]
John Adams[VARCHAR2]
Message sent to PLSQL$MESSAGE_INBOX.

Output Message from Pipe
Session: [ORA$PIPE$00F2AFC20001]
---------------------------------
1776[NUMBER]
04-JUL-76[DATE]
John Adams[VARCHAR2]
Message received from PLSQL$MESSAGE_INBOX.
```

TIP
The DBMS_PIPE.PACK_MESSAGE and DBMS_PIPE.UNPACK_MESSAGE procedures are overloaded. They can use DATE, NUMBER, and VARCHAR2 data types. You must ensure you evaluate data types before reading them from the local buffer when you use more than VARCHAR2 data types.

The preceding program has highlighted how you manage DATE, NUMBER, and VARCHAR2 into and out of database pipes. The DBMS_PIPE.NEXT_ITEM_TYPE function provides the tool to read out different data types.

You will now see how some of the complexity of DBMS_PIPE can be hidden from your users.

Putting a Wrapper Around DBMS_PIPE

You probably noticed that working with DBMS_PIPE is a bit tedious. Much of the problem is because of the awkward mix of functions and procedures. Functions require return variables, and procedures, the UNPACK_MESSAGE procedure, for instance, require active actual parameter values.

Access to these can be simplified by writing a PL/SQL stored procedure that wraps (a fancy word for hides the complexity) of the DBMS_PIPE package. The following package provides a wrapper to exchange messages between all users on the system. The package builds two pipes for any user by using the create_pipe3.sql script mentioned earlier in the chapter. These pipes are named USER$MESSAGE_INBOX and USER$MESSAGE_OUTBOX, respectively.

The package specification creates two functions: SEND_MESSAGE and RECEIVE_MESSAGE. These wrap the complexity of the DBMS_PIPE package.

The package body implements the two published functions and creates a local function GET_USER. It returns the user name for the current session. This eliminates any formal parameters for the RECEIVE_MESSAGE function.

The MESSENGER package provides the ability to send and receive messages in SQL or PL/SQL. It manages only VARCHAR2 data types. The MESSENGER package provides a glimpse into building components based on the DBMS_PIPE package. The following contains the package specification and body:

```
-- Available online as part of create_messenger.sql

-- Create package specification.
CREATE OR REPLACE PACKAGE messenger IS

  -- Define function specification.
  FUNCTION send_message
    (user_name      VARCHAR2
    ,message        VARCHAR2
    ,message_box    VARCHAR2 DEFAULT 'MESSAGE_INBOX')
    RETURN INTEGER;

  -- Define function specification.
  FUNCTION receive_message
    RETURN VARCHAR2;

END messenger;
```

```
/

-- Create package body.
CREATE OR REPLACE PACKAGE BODY messenger IS

  -- Define local package function to return user name.
  FUNCTION get_user
    RETURN VARCHAR2 IS

  BEGIN

    -- Use a cursor for-loop to get user name.
    FOR i IN (SELECT user FROM dual) LOOP

      -- Return the user.
      return i.user;

    END LOOP;

  END get_user;

  -- Implement package function defined in specification.
  FUNCTION send_message
    (user_name      VARCHAR2
    ,message        VARCHAR2
    ,message_box    VARCHAR2 DEFAULT 'MESSAGE_INBOX')
    RETURN INTEGER IS

    -- Define variable for target mailbox.
    message_pipe    VARCHAR2(100 CHAR);

  BEGIN

    -- Purge local pipe content.
    DBMS_PIPE.RESET_BUFFER;

    -- Declare the target outbox for a message.
    message_pipe := UPPER(user_name) || '$'
                 || UPPER(message_box);

    -- Put a message in the local buffer.
    DBMS_PIPE.PACK_MESSAGE(message);

    -- Send message, success is a zero return value.
    IF (DBMS_PIPE.send_message(message_pipe) = 0) THEN

      -- Message sent, so return 0.
      RETURN 0;
```

```
   ELSE

     -- Message not sent, so return 1.
     RETURN 1;

   END IF;

END send_message;

-- Implement package function defined in specification.
FUNCTION receive_message
  RETURN VARCHAR2 IS

  -- Define variable for target mailbox.
  message          VARCHAR2(4000 CHAR) :=  NULL;
  message_box      VARCHAR2(100 CHAR);
  inbox            VARCHAR2(14 CHAR) := 'MESSAGE_INBOX';
  timeout          INTEGER := 0;
  return_code      INTEGER;

BEGIN

  -- Purge local pipe content.
  DBMS_PIPE.RESET_BUFFER;

  -- Declare the target outbox for a message.
  message_box := get_user || '$' || inbox;

  -- Put a message in the local buffer.
  return_code :=
    DBMS_PIPE.receive_message(message_box,timeout);

  -- Evaluate and process return code.
  CASE return_code
    WHEN 0 THEN

      -- Read the message into a variable.
      DBMS_PIPE.UNPACK_MESSAGE(message);

    WHEN 1 THEN

      message := 'The message pipe is empty.';

    WHEN 2 THEN

      message :=
        'The message is too large for variable.';

    WHEN 3 THEN
```

```
        message :=
            'An interrupt occurred, contact the DBA.';

    END CASE;

    -- Return the message.
    RETURN message;

  END receive_message;

END messenger;
/
```

As a rule, programs are explained in text. For a package like this, a text description is unproductive. You can see the package lets you exchange messages with other users, provided they have execute privileges to the wrapper MESSENGER package or a separate copy in their user source code.

The specification for the package follows:

```
-- Available as the output from the SQL*Plus DESCRIBE.

FUNCTION RECEIVE_MESSAGE RETURNS VARCHAR2
FUNCTION SEND_MESSAGE RETURNS NUMBER(38)
 Argument Name      Type                        In/Out Default?
 ---------------    ----------------------      ------ --------

 USER_NAME          VARCHAR2                     IN
 MESSAGE            VARCHAR2                     IN
 MESSAGE_BOX        VARCHAR2                     IN     DEFAULT
```

The following program illustrates sending and receiving a message using the wrapper MESSENGER package:

```
-- Available online as part of use_messenger.sql

DECLARE

  -- Define local package function to return user name.
  FUNCTION get_user
    RETURN VARCHAR2 IS

  BEGIN

    -- Use a cursor for-loop to get user name.
    FOR i IN (SELECT user FROM dual) LOOP

      -- Return the user.
      return i.user;
```

```
      END LOOP;

  END get_user;

BEGIN

  -- Send a message.
  IF (MESSENGER.SEND_MESSAGE(get_user,'Hello World!') = 0)
  THEN

    -- Receive and print message.
    DBMS_OUTPUT.PUT_LINE(MESSENGER.RECEIVE_MESSAGE);

  END IF;

END;
/
```

The sample program does the following:

- It implements the same `get_user` local function as used in the `MESSENGER` package. By doing so, this program will succeed in your environment whether you are using the `PLSQL` user or another user.

- It uses an if-then-else statement to successfully send of a message.

- It uses `DBMS_OUTPUT` to print the message sent and received.

You can use this package or create your own to experiment with `DBMS_PIPE`. You have now covered the `DBMS_PIPE` package and a key feature—intersession messaging. You will now learn about `DBMS_ALERT`.

DBMS_ALERT Built-in Package

`DBMS_ALERT` is the second intersession communication tool provided by Oracle 10*g*. It builds on the behavior of `DBMS_PIPE` and leverages the `DBMS_PIPE` package.

Introducing the DBMS_ALERT Package

`DBMS_ALERT` is an asynchronous transaction control mechanism. It publishes an event. Other users become subscribers by registering their interest in the named alert. `DBMS_ALERT` implements a publish-and-subscribe paradigm.

As mentioned at the beginning of the chapter, a publish-and-subscribe process eliminates polling daemons. Polling daemons run as background processes. They loop until they find an event. The event triggers the polling daemon to signal, spawn another program activity, or terminate. There are three components to polling daemons: One is the monitoring loop. Another is the signal processing detection. Finally, there is the activity or termination logic triggered by receiving a signal.

If you eliminate polling daemons, you can reduce resource demands on the database and physical machine. Unfortunately, there are good business reasons for using polling daemons. DBMS_ALERT provides a means of automating the monitoring loop and signal processing detection components. DBMS_ALERT implements public pipes through using the DBMS_PIPE package.

DBMS_ALERT also uses the DBMS_PIPE memory structure in the SGA. While the structure is not formally referred to as a pipe, it works as a public pipe through DBMS_PIPE. As discussed earlier in the chapter, they are publicly accessible pipes or FIFO queues similar to Unix pipes. These pipes are populated on event triggers and subject to transaction control limits. Moreover, alert pipes communicate between sessions asynchronously after a transaction occurs. DBMS_ALERT extends DBMS_PIPE by implementing a publish-and-subscribe paradigm. It publishes notifications. Then it enables subscribers to register to receive event notifications.

Defining the DBMS_ALERT Package

The DBMS_ALERT package contains *only* procedures. Procedures are limited to PL/SQL execution. The DBMS_ALERT procedures support only VARCHAR2 data type pipes. Like the MESSENGER package provided earlier in the chapter, DBMS_ALERT is a wrapper package to the DBMS_PIPE package. There is one exception. DBMS_ALERT maintains a new memory structure that enables the publish-and-subscribe process. That memory structure contains a list of pipes and those who are interested in their receipt.

Table 11-2 describes the DBMS_ALERT package.

Procedure	Description
REGISTER	The REGISTER procedure takes a single formal parameter, NAME, which accepts a valid SIGNAL name. Unfortunately, if you attempt to register for a signal name that does not exist, no exception will be raised.
	Use REGISTER to subscribe to an alert. You may use it to subscribe to a number of alerts. You should keep a list of subscribed alerts. There is no tool to check what you have registered an interest in.

TABLE 11-2. *The DBMS_ALERT Package*

Procedure	Description
REMOVE	The REMOVE procedure takes a single formal parameter, NAME, which accepts a valid SIGNAL name. Unfortunately, if you attempt to remove a signal name that does not exist, no exception will be raised. Use REMOVE to unsubscribe from an alert. You may use it to unsubscribe from a number of alerts. You should keep a list of subscribed alerts. There is no tool to check what you have registered an interest in.
REMOVEALL	The REMOVEALL procedure takes no formal parameter. Use REMOVEALL to unsubscribe from all alerts. You may use it to unsubscribe from all previously subscribed alert lists. This eliminates the need to keep a list of subscribed alerts.
SET_DEFAULTS	The SET_DEFAULTS procedure takes a single formal parameter, SENSITIVITY, which accepts a valid INTEGER. It sets the polling frequency for the DBMS_ALERT package. The default SENSITIVITY value is five seconds.
SIGNAL	The SIGNAL procedure takes two formal parameters, the NAME and MESSAGE parameters. The NAME parameter accepts a valid SIGNAL name. A SIGNAL name must be no longer than 30 characters. The MESSAGE parameter accepts a valid VARCHAR2 name. The MESSAGE VARCHAR2 size is limited to 1800 bytes or less. This presents potential issues using Unicode character sets. You should not use ORA$ as a preface to any of your alerts, because those are reserved by Oracle Corporation for their own use. You should keep a list of signaled alerts. Since there is no tool to check what you have signaled, it may help you clean up your environment without bouncing the instance.

TABLE 11-2. *The DBMS_ALERT Package* (continued)

Procedure	Description
WAITONE	The WAITONE procedure takes four formal parameters. They are covered here: NAME is positionally the first and a mandatory parameter. It is defined as a VARCHAR2 data type. The formal parameter NAME accepts a valid SIGNAL name. MESSAGE is positionally the second and a mandatory formal parameter. It is an OUT mode parameter and as such is the output for a value from the procedure. It has a VARCHAR2 data type and a maximum size of 1800 bytes. STATUS is positionally the third and a mandatory formal parameter. It is an OUT mode parameter and as such is the output for a value from the procedure. It has an INTEGER data type. It returns a zero or a one as possible values. A zero means that it was successful. A one means that the program timed out before an alert was signaled. TIMEOUT is positionally the fourth and an optional formal parameter. It is an IN mode parameter and sets the length of time allowed to check for the alert. When using the WAITONE procedure, you need to ensure that the variable is equal to or larger than the actual message sent. If you size the variable too small, you will not receive the message. Since DBMS_ALERT uses DBMS_LOCK, you should ensure that you do not attempt to override an existing lock. If you do, you will receive a status four from DBMS_LOCK.

TABLE 11-2.   *The DBMS_ALERT Package* (continued)

Procedure	Description
WAITANY	The WAITANY procedure takes four formal parameters. They are covered here:
	NAME is positionally the first and a mandatory parameter. It is defined as a VARCHAR2 data type. The formal parameter NAME accepts a valid SIGNAL name.
	MESSAGE is positionally the second and a mandatory formal parameter. It is an OUT mode parameter and as such is the output for a value from the procedure. It has a VARCHAR2 data type and a maximum size of 1800 bytes.
	STATUS is positionally the third and a mandatory formal parameter. It is an OUT mode parameter and as such is the output for a value from the procedure. It has an INTEGER data type. It returns a zero or a one as possible values. A zero means that it was successful. A one means that the program timed out before an alert was signaled.
	TIMEOUT is positionally the fourth and an optional formal parameter. It is an IN mode parameter and sets the length of time allowed to check for the alert.
	When using the WAITANY procedure, you need to ensure that the variable is equal to or larger than the actual message sent. If you size the variable too small, you will not receive the message.
	Since DBMS_ALERT uses DBMS_LOCK, you should ensure that you do not attempt to override an existing lock. If you do, you will receive a status four from DBMS_LOCK.

TABLE 11-2. *The DBMS_ALERT Package* (continued)

You have reviewed the idea, utility, and specifics of the DBMS_ALERT package. In the next section, you will see how DBMS_ALERT works.

Working with the DBMS_ALERT Package

In this section, you will work with the following:

- Building a trigger to signal an alert
- Registering interest in an alert

- Waiting on an alert

- Triggering an alert

- Analyzing the impact of transaction-based alerts

These topics will help prepare you to use DBMS_ALERT successfully. The topics also should prepare you to experiment with the package. Before running any of these scripts, you should run create_messages_table.sql. It will build necessary database tables to support the examples.

Building a Trigger to Signal an Alert

These topics will help prepare you to use DBMS_ALERT successfully. The topics also should prepare you to experiment with the package. Before running any of these scripts, you should run create_messages_table.sql. It will build necessary database tables to support the examples.

The following row-level trigger allows you to see how to capture inserts, updates, and deletes from a table. As you work with the trigger and DBMS_ALERT, you will find there are some design issues to consider. This trigger is our signaling device. Any call to DBMS_ALERT.SIGNAL should be found in a database trigger. If it is not in a trigger, you are leveraging DBMS_ALERT in an unintended way.

-- **Available online as part of create_signal_trigger.sql**

```
CREATE OR REPLACE TRIGGER signal_messages
AFTER
INSERT OR UPDATE OR DELETE
OF message_id
  ,message_source
  ,message_destination
  ,message
ON messages
FOR EACH ROW

BEGIN

  -- Check if no row previously existed - an insert.
  IF :old.message_id IS NULL THEN

    -- Signal Event.
    DBMS_ALERT.SIGNAL(
      'EVENT_MESSAGE_QUEUE'
      ,:new.message_source||':Insert');

    -- Insert alert message.
```

```
     INSERT
     INTO      messages_alerts
     VALUES    (:new.message_source||':Insert');

  -- Check if no row will exist after DML - a delete.
  ELSIF :new.message_id IS NULL THEN

     -- Signal Event.
     DBMS_ALERT.SIGNAL(
       'EVENT_MESSAGE_QUEUE'
       ,:old.message_source||':Delete');

     -- Insert alert message.
     INSERT
     INTO      messages_alerts
     VALUES    (:old.message_source||':Delete');

  -- This handles update DMLs.
  ELSE

     -- Check if message source is updated.
     IF :new.message_source IS NULL THEN

        -- Signal Event.
        DBMS_ALERT.SIGNAL(
          'EVENT_MESSAGE_QUEUE'
          ,:new.message_source||':Update#1');

        -- Insert alert message.
        INSERT
        INTO      messages_alerts
        VALUES    (:new.message_source||'Update#1');

     -- A column other than message source is updated.
     ELSE

        -- Signal Event.
        DBMS_ALERT.SIGNAL(
          'EVENT_MESSAGE_QUEUE'
          ,:old.message_source||':Update#2');

        -- Insert alert message.
        INSERT
        INTO      messages_alerts
        VALUES    (:old.message_source||':Update#2');

     END IF;
```

```
    END IF;

END;
/
```

The sample trigger does the following:

- It creates a row-level trigger on the messages table. The trigger will fire after an insert, update, or delete from the messages table.

- It checks if the :old.message_id does not exist. This condition is met whenever a new row is inserted into the target table. If this condition is met, it uses DBMS_ALERT to signal an alert to EVENT_MESSAGE_QUEUE and insert a matching message into the messages_alert table.

- It checks if the :new.message_id does not exist. This condition is met whenever a row is deleted from the target table. If this condition is met, it uses DBMS_ALERT to signal an alert to EVENT_MESSAGE_QUEUE and insert a matching message into the messages_alert table.

- The all other category, or ELSE, handles updates. There are two types of updates that the trigger is interested in capturing. One is an update that changes the message_source. The other is any updates that change something other than the message_source. Within the ELSE clause, it does the following:

  - It checks if the :new.message_source does not exist. This condition is met whenever an update to the row does not change the message_source. If this condition is met, it uses DBMS_ALERT to signal an alert to EVENT_MESSAGE_QUEUE and insert a matching message into the messages_alert table.

  - It uses the ELSE clause to process any change to the message_source column. If this condition is met, it uses DBMS_ALERT to signal an alert to EVENT_MESSAGE_QUEUE and insert a matching message into the messages_alert table.

You have built your signaling device. It will publish the message. The next section will examine how you subscribe to see the published message.

Registering Interest in an Alert

When you register your interest in an alert, you are subscribing to an alert. You register within the scope of a session. This means that each session that is interested in a published alert must subscribe.

The following example program subscribes to a named alert:

-- Available online as part of register_interest.sql

```
BEGIN

  -- Register interest in an alert.
  DBMS_ALERT.REGISTER('EVENT_MESSAGE_QUEUE');

END;
/
```

The sample program registers interest in the EVENT_MESSAGE_QUEUE alert. You have now registered interest in the EVENT_MESSAGE_QUEUE alert. Alternatively, you have subscribed to the alert. Every time the alert fires after an insert, update, or delete, you will receive a message if you are waiting to handle its receipt.

Waiting on an ALERT

After you have registered your interest in an alert, you may or may not receive an alert. Part of a publish-and-subscribe paradigm requires you to wait to receive a message. It is very much like a baseball pitcher's and catcher's relationship. If the catcher is not there and the pitcher throws the ball, the ball will not be caught.

In the following program, you will learn to catch the ball. The program shows you how to wait on a single alert. You should also note that the SENSITIVITY, or polling rate, discussed earlier is the default. The default is checking every five seconds.

-- Available online as part of waitone.sql

```
DECLARE

  -- Define OUT mode variables required from WAITONE.
  message        VARCHAR2(30 CHAR);
  status         INTEGER;

BEGIN

  -- Register interest in an alert.
  DBMS_ALERT.WAITONE('EVENT_MESSAGE_QUEUE'
                    ,message
                    ,status
                    ,30);

  IF (STATUS <> 0) THEN
```

```
         -- Print an error message.
         DBMS_OUTPUT.PUT_LINE('A timeout has happened.');

      ELSE

         -- Print title.
         DBMS_OUTPUT.PUT_LINE('Alert Messages Received');
         DBMS_OUTPUT.PUT_LINE('-----------------------');

         -- Print alert message received.
         DBMS_OUTPUT.PUT_LINE(message);

      END IF;

   END;
   /
```

The sample program does the following:

■ It defines a `message` variable of `VARCHAR2` data type.

■ It defines a `status` variable of `INTEGER` data type.

■ It uses `DBMS_ALERT.WAITONE` procedure to create a polling loop for 30 seconds. Given a five-second default interval, the polling loop will run six times before ending.

■ It uses an if-then-else statement to check if the status was due to a time-out. A time-out occurs when no alert was received. If the time-out does not occur before an alert is received, it will print the alert.

You should run this without doing anything to trigger the alert. It will show you a time-out message:

-- Available online as output from waitone.sql

```
A timeout has happened.
```

You have worked through subscribing to an alert. Unfortunately, there was no alert signaled before the scheduled time-out. The next section will show you how to trigger events.

Triggering an Alert
After you have built a trigger and registered interest in another session where you are waiting for a signaled alert, you can trigger the alert. That means you need two

sessions connected to the PLSQL user to do this. In one session, you need to start the waitone.sql script discussed previously. In the other session, you need to run the following program before the thirty seconds has expired. If thirty seconds is too short a time, then you should modify waitone.sql to allow yourself more time.

The following program will trigger an alert:

-- Available online as part of trigger_alerts1.sql

```
-- Insert a new row.
INSERT
INTO      messages
VALUES (4,'PLSQL','USERA','Insert, Shazaam.');

-- Upgrade a row.
UPDATE    messages
SET       message = 'Update, Shazaam.'
WHERE     message_id = 2;

-- Delete a row.
DELETE    messages
WHERE     message_id = 3;

-- Commit the changes.
COMMIT;
```

The preceding program inserted, updated, and deleted rows from the messages table. After making all three changes, it committed the changes.

The waitone.sql script will now return the following formatted output:

-- Available online as output from waitone.sql

```
Alert Messages Received
-----------------------
PLSQL:Delete


MESSAGE
------------------------------
PLSQL:Insert
PLSQL:Update#2
PLSQL:Delete
```

You can see the benefit of doing the INSERT statement within the signal_ messages trigger. It sends the messages and inserts a duplicate into a table. The commit for the external transaction commits the writes to the messages_alerts table. As you can see, there are three messages, but the DBMS_ALERT subscription returned only the last one. The other two messages were lost. This is why the output for alert messages received shows only the last DML change made.

In the next section, you will analyze why you lost two messages with DBMS_ ALERT. You may already have guessed the answer. If so, you have two choices at this point. You can skip the next section or confirm your analysis.

Analyzing the Impact of Transaction-Based Alerts

The general answer is that the polling loop returns immediately the alert message. In the preceding script, the commit occurs only once at the end of the program. Actually, three messages were sent by DBMS_ALERT.SIGNAL. The second message overwrote the value of the first, and the third, the value of the second. The third value was actually the only value published because it was the last value signaled before the commit.

DBMS_ALERT operates much like DBMS_PIPE. Individual signals are stuffed into a private pipe that acts like a local buffer. Imitating a local buffer, the private pipe can contain only one signal value. Therefore, only the last private pipe value is signaled to the subscribers.

The following program will trigger three alerts:

-- **Available online as part of trigger_alerts2.sql**

```
-- Insert a new row.
INSERT
INTO      messages
VALUES (4,'PLSQL','USERA','Insert, Shazaam.');

-- Commit the change.
COMMIT;

-- Upgrade a row.
UPDATE    messages
SET       message = 'Update, Shazaam.'
WHERE     message_id = 2;

-- Commit the change.
COMMIT;

-- Delete a row.
DELETE    messages
WHERE     message_id = 3;

-- Commit the change.
COMMIT;
```

The preceding program inserted, updated, and deleted rows from the messages table. It committed each change before making another.

You can now rerun the `waitone.sql` program in one session and `trigger_alerts2.sql` in another. The `waitone.sql` script will generate the following results:

```
-- Available online as output from waitone.sql

Alert Messages Received
-----------------------
PLSQL:Insert

MESSAGE
------------------------------
PLSQL:Insert
PLSQL:Update#2
PLSQL:Delete
```

As you can see, only the first signaled message is received by the polling program `waitone.sql`. The reason is that the polling program is a simple illustration of how you catch the signal. The commit terminates the transaction. Termination of the transaction triggers the signaling of the alert.

The presentation has laid a foundation for you. More elegant solutions can be developed. You develop them by nesting the polling logic into signal management programming logic.

Summary

You have covered both mechanisms for accomplishing intersession communication, DBMS_ALERT and DBMS_PIPE. The DBMS_PIPE package gives you more freedom of latitude but requires more programming management, while the DBMS_ALERT package is very limited in scope because of how it is linked to transaction processing.

The chapter has provided coverage of both utilities. You should be able to leverage the material to rapidly build intersession communication solutions.

CHAPTER
12

External Routines

xternal routines are delivered in Oracle 10g through external procedures. They enable the database to communicate with external applications through PL/SQL. While it is nontrivial to configure the database to support them, external procedures provide a critical feature.

You will cover topics as follows. The chapter assumes you read it sequentially. It also assumes you have read the preceding eleven chapters. If you feel comfortable with an area, please feel free to move to the section of interest. However, the chapter assumes you have mastery of earlier sections.

- Introducing external procedures

- Working with external procedures

A new script, `create_user.sql`, is provided for use with this chapter. You will need to run it to work through the examples in the chapter.

Introducing External Procedures

External routines provide the ability to communicate between the database and external programs written in C, C++, COBOL, FORTRAN, PL/1, Visual Basic, and Java. There is one caveat; the language must be callable from C. While the surgeon general has not provided a warning, other languages can present different challenges than PL/SQL. The chapter will focus on implementations of C and Java libraries as external routines.

Development teams may want to isolate programming logic from the database. External routines are the natural solution. They are ideal for computation-intensive programs, providing an interface between external data sources and the database. Unlike stand-alone Oracle Pro*C programs, they are callable from PL/SQL.

You will work with a C shared library and a Java class library in this chapter. The C and Java examples have been made as small and narrow in scope as possible to conserve space while you focus on PL/SQL programming.

External routines leverage Oracle Net Services transport layer. You will need to work through a number of architectural and configuration issues to run the basic samples. It is helpful if you have some formal background in C or Java, but it is not necessary. This chapter is important because PL/SQL programmers can be expected to explain the process to C and Java programmers. You will also write the PL/SQL library definitions, which become the gateways to these libraries. These are often called PL/SQL wrappers.

NOTE
The documentation for this chapter is spread far and wide. The key configuration references are Chapter 8 in the Database Application Developer's Guide – Fundamentals, Chapter 5 in the Heterogeneous Connectivity Administrator's Guide, and Chapter 13 in the Net Services Administrator's Guide.

You will now work with implementing external procedures.

Working with External Procedures

As discussed, external procedures enable you to communicate through PL/SQL with external programs. The external programs can call back to an Oracle database using the Oracle Call Interface (OCI). They can also communicate with external databases such as Sybase, IBM DB2, and Microsoft SQL Server. External procedures are ideal to work with external applications. External applications can use other databases or file systems as data repositories. Moreover, any combination of these is supported.

You will now learn about the architecture for external procedures. Then you will learn the setup issues for Oracle Networking and the heterogeneous service agent. When you have learned how to configure your environment, you will then work with building and accessing C and Java libraries from PL/SQL.

Defining the `extproc` Architecture

Oracle built an extensible architecture for external procedures. It is flexible to support any programming language that is callable by the C programming language. For example, you can call a C++ program using the `extern` command in C. However, callbacks into the database by the external programming languages are limited to those supported by OCI. OCI supports C, C++, COBOL, FORTRAN, PL/1, Visual Basic, and Java.

Whatever programming language you choose to implement must support building a shared library. Likewise, the platform must support shared libraries. Shared libraries, also called dynamic link libraries (DLLs), are code modules that can be leveraged by your program. Java shared libraries are called libunits. When you access shared libraries from PL/SQL, the libraries are loaded dynamically at run time as external procedures. By default, each remote procedure call uses a discrete and dedicated `extproc` agent to access the shared library. Alternatively, you can configure a multithreaded agent through the Oracle Heterogeneous Services. If you do so, you can share the `extproc` agent among any number of database sessions.

External procedures use the PL/SQL library definition to exchange data between the PL/SQL run-time engine and shared libraries. The PL/SQL library definition acts as a wrapper to the shared library. It defines the external call specification and maps PL/SQL data types to native language equivalents. The map between data types is used to translate data types when exchanging information. Figure 12-1 illustrates the external procedure architecture.

A call to a PL/SQL wrapper translates types. Then, the wrapper sends a signal across Oracle Net Services. Oracle Net Services receives the signal and spawns or forks an `extproc` agent process. It is the `extproc` agent that accesses the shared library. The `extproc` agent forks a Remote Procedure Call (RPC) to the shared library. The shared library result is returned to the `extproc` agent by the RPC. The `extproc` agent then returns the result to the PL/SQL wrapper. Next, the PL/SQL wrapper receives and translates the data types from the local language to the native PL/SQL data types. Ultimately, the PL/SQL wrapper returns the value to the calling PL/SQL program.

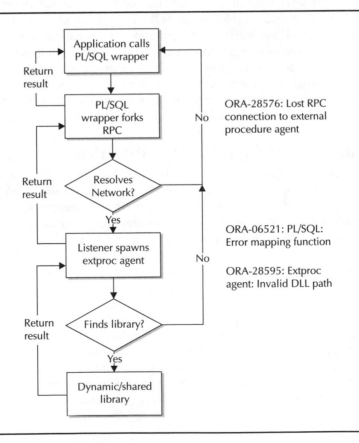

FIGURE 12-1. *External procedure architecture*

As you can see from Figure 12-1, there are two potential failure points to dynamic execution. The decision diamonds in the process flow chart qualify potential failure points. Both failure points are linked to the listener. The second failure point can also be missing libraries in the defined locations.

One failure point exists when a separate `extproc` agent listener is not configured or incorrectly configured. The other failure point arises in two possible cases. One case is when the `extproc` listener fails to resolve the connection. Another case is when a physical shared library is not found where defined in the PL/SQL library definition.

Configuring the heterogeneous multithreaded agent is complex. However, it enables you to share a single `extproc` agent among multiple database sessions. Benefits of this implementation are a reduction in resources required to dynamically fork `extproc` agents. The default behavior of external procedures is to fork a new `extproc` agent for each external procedure call. The default works but consumes too many resources too frequently. When you have many sessions using external libraries, you should use a multithreaded `extproc` agent. Figure 12-2 looks at how a multithreaded `extproc` agent works.

As shown in the diagram, multiple database sessions can connect through the heterogeneous multithreaded `extproc` agent, which fits into the `extproc` agent niche in Figure 12-1. Once the signal arrives at the agent, the monitor thread puts

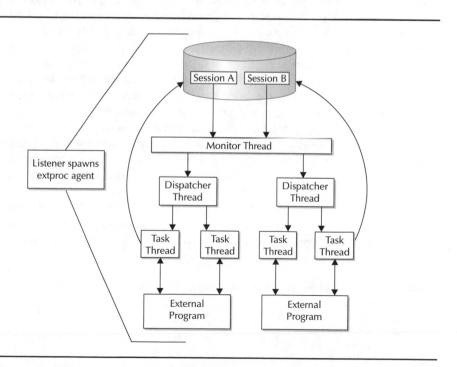

FIGURE 12-2.   *Multithreaded agent architecture*

the connection into a FIFO queue. The monitor thread maintains load-balancing information; using that information, the monitor thread passes the connection to the first available dispatcher thread, which puts the request into another FIFO queue. Task threads read the dispatcher FIFO queues and process requests. Each task thread sends the result back to the requesting session. You will cover more about the multithreaded agent later in this chapter.

You have developed an understanding of the basic architecture of external procedures. The next section will show you how to set up and configure Oracle Net Services to support external procedures.

Defining `extproc` Oracle Net Services Configuration

External procedures use Oracle Net Services to fork or link signals to the `extproc` agent. As discussed, the `extproc` agent can be the default stand-alone unit or a multithreaded `extproc` agent. Unfortunately, configuring your `listener.ora` and `tnsnames.ora` files is a manual process.

The standard listener built by the Net Configuration Assistant on installation does not provide a complete `extproc` agent listener. Net Configuration Assistant likewise does not provide an automated way to create an `extproc` agent listener. The standard listener includes an `extproc` handler service in the standard listener. This is not adequate for implementing the `extproc` agent. You must set up an exclusive listener for external procedures.

As a PL/SQL developer, configuring Oracle Net Services may not be something you do often. It is also possible your DBA may be unfamiliar with the nuances required to support `extproc` agents. This section provides the steps required to configure Oracle Net Services to support `extproc` agents.

The `listener.ora` file can be found in one of two locations. It can be found in the directory pointed to by the `$TNS_ADMIN` environment variable. Alternatively, the default location is in the `$ORACLE_HOME/network/admin` directory. The standard `listener.ora file` contains two entries: one is the `LISTENER` and the other is the `SID_LIST_LISTENER`.

The `LISTENER` describes an address list or set of address lists. Addresses consist of a protocol definition and a key value, or else a protocol definition, a host name, and a port number. The Oracle 10*g* standard fresh install `LISTENER` entry in the `listener.ora` file follows:

```
-- Available online as listener1.ora
LISTENER =
  (DESCRIPTION_LIST =
    (DESCRIPTION =
      (ADDRESS_LIST =
        (ADDRESS = (PROTOCOL = IPC)
                   (KEY = EXTPROC)
```

```
        )
      )
      (ADDRESS_LIST =
        (ADDRESS = (PROTOCOL = TCP)
                   (HOST = <host_name>.<domain_name>)
                   (PORT = 1521)
        )
      )
    )
  )
```

The standard `listener.ora` file has a problem supporting the `extproc` agent. The problem is that the listener has two `ADDRESS_LIST` parameters using different protocols. The first listens for Internal Procedure Calls (IPCs). The second listens for TCP messages, like RPCs. This is the principal reason why a separate listener is required for `extproc` IPC calls.

The `SID_LIST_LISTENER`, the second entry in the standard `listener.ora` file, contains the `SID` description. The Oracle 10*g* standard `SID_DESC` is defined by the `SID_NAME`, `ORACLE_HOME`, and `PROGRAM` parameter definitions. The `SID_NAME` parameter is defined as `PLSExtProc`, which is used as the `extproc` identifier. The `ORACLE_HOME` parameter defines the Oracle home directory. Finally, the `PROGRAM` parameter defines the `extproc` agent as the program. The Oracle 10*g* standard `SID_LIST_LISTENER` entry in the `listener.ora` file follows:

```
-- Available online as listener1.ora
SID_LIST_LISTENER =
  (SID_LIST =
    (SID_DESC =
      (SID_NAME = PLSExtProc)
      (ORACLE_HOME = <oracle_home_directory)
      (PROGRAM = extproc)
    )
  )
```

The standard `SID_LIST_LISTENER` is another mix of two purposes in one definition. The `SID_NAME` and `PROGRAM` parameters are there to support the `extproc` agent signals. The `ORACLE_HOME` parameter is provided for both the TCP listener and `extproc` IPC services. These two services run under a single standard listener, although they really are suited to separate listeners. The clincher is that external procedures require their own listener.

NOTE
Oracle provides the preceding caveat for the extproc *listener in Chapter 8 of the Oracle Database Application Developer's Guide – Fundamentals.*

The standard `listener.ora` file works in tandem with the standard
`tnsnames.ora` file. The `listener.ora` and `tnsnames.ora` files are used by
Oracle Net Services. The standard `tnsnames.ora` file provides two service names.
One is CODE, which maps to the standard listener to the database. The other is
EXTPROC_CONNECTION_DATA, which maps to the `extproc` agent. The following
is an example of the standard `tnsnames.ora` file:

```
-- Available online as part of tnsnames1.ora
CODE =
  (DESCRIPTION =
    (ADDRESS = (PROTOCOL = TCP)
               (HOST = <host_name>.<domain_name>)
               (PORT = 1521)
    )
    (CONNECT_DATA =
      (SERVER = DEDICATED)
      (SERVICE_NAME = <database_sid>)
    )
  )

EXTPROC_CONNECTION_DATA =
  (DESCRIPTION =
    (ADDRESS_LIST =
      (ADDRESS = (PROTOCOL = IPC)
                 (KEY = EXTPROC)
      )
    )
    (CONNECT_DATA =
      (SID = PLSExtProc)
      (PRESENTATION = RO)
    )
  )
```

The `tnsnames.ora` service names provide connection aliases that enable
users and programs to connect to the listener. They resolve requests for connections
by matching the `tnsnames.ora` ADDRESS parameter to the address in a running
listener. Then they use the CONNECTION_DATA parameters to connect a database
or agent. The `extproc` agent is not the only agent supported by Oracle 10*g*. You
can define any number of heterogeneous servers that enable communication
between Oracle and other databases.

On any case-insensitive system, these files resolve `extproc` across Oracle
Net Services. They fail on a case-sensitive system. The KEY parameter in the
`listener.ora` file is lowercase, while the KEY value in the `tnsnames.ora` is
uppercase. The two will fail to resolve. You can see if your system contains the
error by using the `tnsping` utility.

For example, run `tnsping` with the following:

```
$ tnsping EXTPROC_CONNECTION_DATA
```

If you get the following, everything is correctly configured:

```
TNS Ping Utility for Linux: Version 10.1.0.2.0 - Production on 07-JUL-2004
Copyright (c) 1997, 2003, Oracle.  All rights reserved.
Used parameter files:
/u02/oracle/10g/10.1.0/network/admin/sqlnet.ora
Used TNSNAMES adapter to resolve the alias
Attempting to contact (DESCRIPTION = (ADDRESS_LIST = (ADDRESS = (PROTOCOL =
IPC)(KEY = extproc))) (CONNECT_DATA = (SID = PLSExtProc) (PRESENTATION = RO)))
OK (0 msec)
```

If you get a TNS-12541 error when using `tnsping`, the likelihood is that there is a mismatch between the `ADDRESS` parameter values in the `listener.ora` and `tnsnames.ora` files.

Before you are introduced to working files, you need to learn about the `PROGRAM` and `ENV` parameters in `listener.ora` files. The `PROGRAM` parameter must specify a valid executable in the `$ORACLE_HOME/bin` directory. The program can access only libraries found in the `$ORACLE_HOME/lib` directory by default. You can change the default by doing any of the following:

- Define `EXTPROC_DLLS` to enable loading of shared libraries. You have three choices for using `EXTPROC_DLLS`. They are shown in Table 12-1.

- Define the `$LD_LIBRARY_PATH` for the `extproc` agent.

- Define the `$PATH` for the `extproc` agent.

- Define the `$APL_ENV_FILE` to specify a set of environment variables for the external `extproc` agent.

Syntax	Description	Security Level
`DLL:DLL`	Allows the `extproc` agent to load any of the specified shared libraries located in the `$ORACLE_HOME/lib` directory.	Medium
`ONLY:DLL:DLL`	Allows `extproc` to run any entered DLLs from specified directories.	High (Recommended)
`ANY`	Allows `extproc` to load any DLL. It disables DLL checking.	Low

TABLE 12-1.   *Options for EXTPROC_DLLS*

The following `listener.ora` file separates the two listeners. It also defines an external library that you will work with later in the chapter. You can use it as an example to build your own `listener.ora` file.

```
-- Available online as part of listener2.ora
LISTENER =
  (DESCRIPTION_LIST =
    (DESCRIPTION =
      (ADDRESS_LIST =
        (ADDRESS = (PROTOCOL = TCP)
                   (HOST = <host_name>.<domain_name>)
                   (PORT = 1521)
        )
      )
    )
  )

SID_LIST_LISTENER =
  (SID_LIST =
    (SID_DESC =
      (SID_NAME = <database_name>)
      (ORACLE_HOME = <oracle_home_directory>)
    )
  )

CALLOUT_LISTENER =
  (DESCRIPTION_LIST =
    (DESCRIPTION =
      (ADDRESS_LIST =
        (ADDRESS = (PROTOCOL = IPC)
                   (KEY = extproc)
        )
      )
    )
  )

SID_LIST_CALLOUT_LISTENER =
  (SID_LIST =
    (SID_DESC =
      (SID_NAME = PLSExtProc)
      (ORACLE_HOME = <oracle_home_directory>)
      (PROGRAM = extproc)
      (ENV = "EXTPROC_DLLS=ONLY:
              <oracle_home_directory>/customlib/writestr1.so
             ,LD_LIBRARY_PATH=<oracle_home_directory>/lib")
    )
  )
```

The sample `listener.ora` file delivers the following:

■ It has a standard `LISTENER` TCP listener on port 1521. You should note that the IPC `ADDRESS` information has been removed from the standard listener. The name of the standard listener is `LISTENER`.

■ It has a standard `SID_LIST_LISTENER`. You should notice that the `SID_NAME` parameter value is no longer `PLSExtProc`, which was used for the extproc agent. It uses the database name. You should also notice that the `PROGRAM` parameter and value are no longer in the `SID_LIST_LISTENER`.

■ It has an `extproc` `CALLOUT_LISTENER` ICP listener using a `KEY` value of `extproc` (all lowercase). Basically, the second address was removed from the standard listener and put in a separate listener.

■ It has an `extproc` `SID_LIST_CALLOUT_LISTENER`. You should notice that the `SID_NAME` parameter has a value of `PLSExtProc`, which should map to a case-sensitive equivalent `SID` parameter value in the `CONNECT_DATA` `tnsnames.ora` service name. Also, the `PROGRAM` parameter is there with a new `ENV` parameter. The `ENV` parameter provides the recommended security implementation that allows access to only a specified library and the `LD_LIBRARY_PATH` for the external procedure.

The new `listener.ora` requires a new `tnsnames.ora` file. The following file works with the new `listener.ora` previously covered:

```
-- Available online as part of tnsnames2.ora
CODE =
  (DESCRIPTION =
    (ADDRESS = (PROTOCOL = TCP)
               (HOST = <host_name>.<domain_name>)
               (PORT = 1521)
    )
    (CONNECT_DATA =
      (SERVER = DEDICATED)
      (SERVICE_NAME = CODE)
    )
  )

EXTPROC_CONNECTION_DATA =
  (DESCRIPTION =
    (ADDRESS_LIST =
      (ADDRESS = (PROTOCOL = IPC)
                 (KEY = extproc)
      )
    )
```

```
(CONNECT_DATA =
  (SID = PLSExtProc)
  (PRESENTATION = RO)
 )
)
```

The sample `tnsnames.ora` file delivers the following:

- It has a `CODE` alias that uses an `ADDRESS` pointing to the database and a `CONNECT_DATA` parameter supporting a dedicated connection. These components are defined as follows:

  - The `ADDRESS` contains three parameters. `PROTOCOL` has a value of TCP. `HOST` has a value of the host name and domain name. `PORT` has a value for the listening port number.

  - The `CONNECT_DATA` parameter contains two parameters. `SERVER` has a value that is dedicated, which means a dedicated server connection. `SERVICE_NAME` has a value equal to the `ORACLE_SID` value.

- It has an `EXTPROC_CONNECTION_DATA` alias that uses a single `ADDRESS` to an IPC and `CONNECT_DATA` to the `extproc` SID. These components are defined as follows:

  - The `ADDRESS` points to an IPC `PROTOCOL` using a `KEY` value. The `KEY` value is known as the listener key. You need to know that the choice of using `extproc` is arbitrary. The listener key can be any string, provided it is equally defined in both the `listener.ora` and `tnsnames.ora` files.

  - The `CONNECT_DATA` parameter supports a `SID` value of `PLSExtProc`. The `SID` points to the `extproc` SID value. Like the listener key, it is an arbitrary string token. The only limitation is that what you define in the `listener.ora` should resolve through the `tnsnames.ora` file. `PLSExtProc` was used as the `extproc` SID because it happens to be the Oracle default value.

You now have working `listener.ora` and `tnsnames.ora` files. You will need to shut down the listener services, copy the files into the new locations, and restart the listener. The following are the steps to take to replace the listener, by platform.

Microsoft Windows

- As the Oracle user, source your environment, navigate to your system services and shut down the Oracle listener.

- Copy the original `listener.ora` and `tnsnames.ora` files in the `%ORACLE_HOME%\network\admin` directory to `listener.ora.orig` and `tnsnames.ora.orig`.

- Copy the new `listener2.ora` and `tnsnames2.ora` files into the `%ORACLE_HOME%\network\admin` directory and rename them as `listener.ora` and `tnsnames.ora`, respectively.

- As the Oracle user, source your environment, navigate to your system services, and start up the Oracle listener. In Windows, you will need to rebuild the original service and build a new service for the second listener.

- Verify that you have two listener processes running by using the Task Manager. You will find the running services under the Processes tab.

Unix

- As the Oracle user, source your environment and shut down the Oracle listener. You can use the following on a generic demonstration database:

  ```
  $ lsnrctl stop LISTENER
  ```

- Copy the original `listener.ora` and `tnsnames.ora` files in the `$ORACLE_HOME/network/admin` directory to `listener.ora.orig` and `tnsnames.ora.orig`.

- Copy the new `listener2.ora` and `tnsnames2.ora` files into the `$ORACLE_HOME/network/admin` directory and rename them as `listener.ora` and `tnsnames.ora`, respectively.

- As the Oracle user, source your environment and start up the Oracle listener and `extproc` agent listener. You can use the following syntax, based on a generic demonstration database:

  ```
  $ lsnrctl start LISTENER
  $ lsnrctl start CALLOUT_LISTENER
  ```

- Verify that you have two listener processes running by using the ps utility, as shown:

  ```
  $ ps -ef | grep -v grep | grep tnslsnr
  ```

At this point, you should have a `LISTENER` for the database and a `CALLOUT_LISTENER` for the `extproc` agent. You should also have a background process running for the `extproc` agent. In Microsoft Windows, you can check with the Task Manager for an `extprocPLSExtProc` process. In Unix, you can use the `ps` utility to find it.

Assuming you have successfully started the two listeners, you need to confirm whether or not it can communicate to the `extproc` agent. There are two steps to validating whether or not it is working. After sourcing your environment files, you should first use the `tnsping` utility as you did earlier in the chapter to test the network connection. You will use the EXTPROC_CONNECTION_DATA alias to check connectivity. Run tnsping with the following:

```
$ tnsping EXTPROC_CONNECTION_DATA
```

If you get the following, everything is correctly configured:

```
TNS Ping Utility for Linux: Version 10.1.0.2.0 - Production on 07-JUL-2004
Copyright (c) 1997, 2003, Oracle.  All rights reserved.
Used parameter files:
/u02/oracle/10g/10.1.0/network/admin/sqlnet.ora
```

If you get a TNS-12541 error when using tnsping, the likelihood is that there is a mismatch between the ADDRESS parameter values in the listener.ora and tnsnames.ora files. Please check if there is a typo in either the listener.ora or tnsnames.ora file. You must resolve any TNS-12541 error before continuing with the examples in the chapter.

Assuming you have successfully used the tnsping utility, the second step is to attempt to connect to the extproc agent TNS alias. Use this to attempt to connect to the extproc agent TNS alias:

```
$ sqlplus plsql/plsql@EXTPROC_CONNECTION_DATA
```

It should always fail. You should get the following output:

```
SQL*Plus: Release 10.1.0.2.0 - Production on Thu Jul 8 16:15:50 2004
Copyright (c) 1982, 2004, Oracle.  All rights reserved.
ERROR:
ORA-28547: connection to server failed, probable Net8 admin error
```

This is the correct behavior. It is actually telling you that the SQL*Plus connection is rejected by the extproc agent. For this message to be returned, the connection had to be begun and rejected as not supported.

You have now learned how to configure your listener to support the extproc agent. The next section will demonstrate an alternative to spawning a dedicated extproc agent for each database session.

Defining the Multithreaded External Procedure Agent

As discussed in the review of architecture, configuring the heterogeneous multithreaded agent is complex. However, it enables you to share a single extproc agent among multiple database sessions. Implementing a multithreaded external procedure agent reduces resources required to dynamically fork extproc agents.

The default behavior of external procedures is to fork a new `extproc` agent for each external procedure call. This default works but consumes too many resources too frequently. When you have many sessions using external libraries, you should use a multithreaded `extproc` agent. This section will show you how to configure and use the mutlithreaded `extproc` agent.

Before you begin to learn how to configure the multithreaded external procedure agent, there are three things to note about it:

- The external library must be thread-safe.

- The agent process, the database server, and the listener process must be on the same host.

- The agent process must run from the same database instance that issues the external procedure call.

When using the multithreaded external procedure agent, you must start the agent separately from the database. The multithreaded external procedure agent is an implementation of Oracle Heterogeneous Connectivity Services. The `agtctl` executable to start and manage sessions is the Agent Control utility. You will find it in the $ORACLE_HOME/hs directory.

If you attempt to use this tool without setting either the $AGTCTL_ADMIN or $TNS_ADMIN environment variable, you will generate the following error message:

```
$ agtctl

AGTCTL: Release 10.1.0.2.0 - Production on Wed Jul 7 07:57:24 2004

Copyright (c) 1982, 2004, Oracle.  All rights reserved.

ORA-28591: agent control utility: unable to access parameter file
ORA-28591: agent control utility: unable to access parameter file
```

It is recommended that you set the $AGTCTL_ADMIN environment variable to point to the $ORACLE_HOME/hs/admin directory. Any environment variables configured in the ENV parameter within your `extproc` listener must be in the sourced environment of the Oracle user when running `agtctl`.

The `agtctl` utility has two interfaces. One is the single-line command mode, and the other is the `agtctl` shell mode. There is no GUI interface to the `agtctl` utility. There is no text configuration file for this utility. It maintains parameter values in the $ORACLE_HOME/hs/admin/initagt.dat control file, which is a binary file maintained by the `agtctl` utility. Before you run the `agtctl` utility, the file will not exist. Table 12-2 provides a synopsis of the command structure.

There are six initialization parameters. All have default behaviors that can be overridden by using the `agtctl set` command. Table 12-3 provides the initialization parameters and their default values and descriptions.

Command Syntax	Description
delete *agent_sid*	Deletes an `agent_sid` entry.
Exit	Exits the `agtctl` file.
Help	Displays available commands.
set *parameter_name* *parameter_value*	Sets a configuration parameter.
Show *parameter_name*	Shows a parameters value.
shutdown *agent_sid*	Shuts down an *agent_sid* multithreaded agent.
startup *agent_sid*	Starts an *agent_sid* multithreaded agent.
unset *parameter_name* *parameter_value*	Unsets a configuration parameter.

TABLE 12-2.   *Commands for the agtctl Utility*

Parameter	Default Value	Description
Listener_address	(ADDRESS_LIST = (ADDRESS = (PROTOCOL = IPC) (KEY = PNPKEY)) (ADDRESS = (PROTOCOL = IPC) (KEY= <oracle_sid>) (ADDRESS = (PROTOCOL = TCP) (HOST = 127.0.0.1) (PORT = 1521)))	Address list for the agent controller listener. The <oracle_sid> value is the <service_name> parameter in the `tnsnames.ora` entry for the database.
max_dispatchers	1	Maximum number of dispatchers.
max_sessions	5	Maximum number of sessions.
max_task_threads	2	Maximum number of threads.
shutdown_address	(ADDRESS_LIST = (ADDRESS = (PROTOCOL = IPC) (KEY = extproc)))	Address on which `agtctl` listens for shutdown instruction.
tcp_dispatchers	0	Number of dispatchers listening on TCP. All other dispatchers listen on IPC.

TABLE 12-3.   *Initialization Parameters for the agtctl Utility*

You will now configure the `extproc` multithreaded agent using the `agtctl` shell mode. The following steps will enable one hundred sessions and four dispatchers before starting the `extproc` multithreaded agent:

```
AGTCTL> set agent_sid CALLOUT_LISTENER
AGTCTL> set max_dispatchers 4
AGTCTL> set max_sessions 100
AGTCTL> show max_dispatchers
4
AGTCTL> show max_sessions
100
AGTCTL> startup extproc
```

In Unix, you can use the ps utility to see the multithreaded external procedure agent. The task manager in Microsoft Windows will also let you see the process. Here is the Unix command:

```
$ ps -ef | grep -v grep | grep extprocCALLOUT
```

The output from this command is

```
oracle    4635    1  0 18:41 ?   00:00:01 extprocCALLOUT_LISTENER -mt
```

You can now shut down the multithreaded external procedure agent by using the shutdown command. Shutdown without an argument acts like a shutdown of the database, which means it allows transactions in progress to complete. Shutdown immediate will cause in-progress external procedure calls to abort. This is the immediate command:

```
AGTCTL> shutdown immediate
```

When you start the `extproc` multithreaded agent, all new external procedure calls will route through the multithreaded agent. However, any calls previously started with dynamic stand-alone `extproc` agents will continue to completion.

When you shut down the `extproc` multithreaded agent, all previously started external procedure calls will complete unless you specify immediate. After the shutdown command, no new calls will be accepted by the multithreaded external procedure monitoring thread. Dynamic `extproc` agents will be spawned for any new external procedure calls.

You have now learned how to start, configure, and stop the multithreaded external procedure agent. You have seen how you can seamlessly move between dedicated dynamic `extproc` sessions and a background multithreaded agent. The next section will demonstrate how you create an external C shared library.

Working with a C Shared Library

As discussed when you covered the `extproc` architecture, Oracle built an extensible architecture for external procedures. It is flexible to support any programming language that is callable by the C programming language. For example, you can call a C++ program using the `extern` command in C. You could call another C program from the shared library. It could then call back into the database. The second C program would use embedded SQL to access data. Using embedded SQL requires use of the Oracle Pro*C precompiler and the Oracle Call Interface (OCI). Both the Pro*C precompiler and OCI tools require a solid working knowledge of C or C++.

Defining the C Shared Library

You will now define a simple C shared library. You will use the following C program as a dynamic link library (DLL) or shared library. The structure of this program has been chosen to avoid having to introduce you to the extensive details of Oracle Pro*C precompiler and OCI functionality. You will need to have a C compiler installed on your platform to compile this example.

Compiling a C program has several nuances. A C compiler does several things. It preprocesses the source code by breaking it down into tokens while validating syntax. Then, it compiles the program into assembly programming code and uses an assembler to create object code. After creating the object code, the compiler then links other object code into the program to create a stand-alone program unit.

The following program includes standard library header files but does not link libraries:

```
-- Available online as part of writestr1.c
/* Include standard IO. */
#include <stdio.h>

/* Declare a writestr function. */
void writestr(char *path, char *message)
{
  /* Declare a FILE variable. */
  FILE *file_name;

  /* Open the File. */
  file_name = fopen(path,"w");

  /* Write to file the message received. */
  fprintf(file_name,"%s\n",message);

  /* Close the file. */
  fclose(file_name);

}
```

The program does the following:

- It includes the stdio.h file, which is called a header file. stdio.h contains the definitions required to do basic operations in C programs. The #include <stdio.h> statement tells the C precompiler to include the contents of /usr/include/stdio.h file in the program.

- It declares a writestr function. The function takes two arguments. The arguments are single-dimensional character arrays, which are what PL/SQL programmers see as strings. Strings map to PL/SQL VARCHAR2 data types.

- It declares a FILE variable type.

- It assigns the FILE returned by the fopen() function to the FILE variable file_name.

- It uses the fprintf() function to write a string to the opened file.

- It uses the fclose() function to close the open file.

It should be noted that the writestr1.c program does not have a main() function. A main() function is required for a stand-alone C program. This program can be used only as a DLL or shared library.

If you attempt a generic compilation of a library file that lacks a main() function, it will raise an error. For example, if writestr1.c were a stand-alone program, you would compile it into object code like this:

```
$ cc -o writestr.o writestr1.c
```

This will raise an error because there is no main() function in the program. The error message follows:

```
/usr/lib/gcc-lib/i386-redhat-linux7/2.96/../../../crt1.o(.text+0x18): In function
`_start':
: undefined reference to `main'
collect2: ld returned 1 exit status
```

It is assumed that you have a C or C++ Development IDE if you are working on the Microsoft Windows platform. Since each IDE works a bit differently, you will have to understand how to use your IDE to compile the program as a DLL.

If you are working on Unix, you live in the command-line world. The following examples illustrate the two methods for creating a C shared library in Unix. The first example will work on the Sun Microsystems C compiler. The second example is the most common approach and supported on Linux.

Unix C Compiler that supports the –G option

```
cc -G -o writestr1.so writestr1.c
```

Unix C Compiler that supports the –shared option

```
cc -shared -o writestr1.so writestr1.c
- OR -
gcc -shared -o writestr1.so writestr1.c
```

TIP
If you are using IBM AIX and the IBM C compiler, you need to ensure that you have a symbolic link named cc *that points to* xlc. *The IBM C compiler will attempt to include proprietary libraries that are not referenced in the sample program. It will not attempt to include those libraries if the calling executable is* cc.

You should now have a C shared library. Now, you or your DBA should create a customer library directory off your $ORACLE_HOME. Please name it *customlib* if you want to be consistent with the examples in this chapter. You should ensure the permissions for the directory is read, write, and execute for owner and read and execute for group and user.

If you are not the DBA but a member of the DBA group, copying the file and executing it will work. If are not in the DBA group, please have your DBA change the group ownership of the file to the DBA group. It will not prevent you from executing the shared library, but it is a check-in mechanism. Any files not in the DBA group would be considered development or stage program units.

You have now created a C DLL or shared library and positioned it where a database external procedure can call it. Next, you will define the PL/SQL library definition and wrapper.

Defining and Calling the PL/SQL Library Wrapper
You have configured your network; learned how to start, configure, and shut down a multithreaded and stand-alone `extproc` agent; and created a C DLL or shared library. Now you need to define a PL/SQL library definition and wrapper so that you can pass information from the database to your C program.

PL/SQL Library Definition

The first step is to define the external library in the database. You do this after you have decided where to place your library. $ORACLE_HOME/customlib is used for the C external procedure example. As discussed, using a custom library requires configuration of the EXTPROC_DLLS value in the ENV parameter. The ENV parameter is found in the listener.ora file. Alternatively, you can put your libraries in the $ORACLE_HOME/bin or $ORACLE_HOME/lib directories and not configure the EXTPROC_DLLS value. If you have customized where you place your libraries, please synchronize the directory path for the library with your listener.ora file.

The generalized format to create a PL/SQL library is

```
CREATE [OR REPLACE] LIBRARY <library_name> AS | IS
'<file_specification>'
AGENT '<agent_dblink>';
/
```

The create_library1.sql and create_library2.sql files use Dynamic Native SQL (DNS) to build the library creation DLL. This was done to simplify your submission of a directory path. The command is provided in the comments section for the programs and noted in the following:

```
-- Available online as part of create_library1.sql
CREATE OR REPLACE LIBRARY library_write_string AS
'<oracle_home_directory>/<custom_library>/<file_name>.<file_ext>';
/
```

The PL/SQL library role defines the name of the library and the physical location where the library will be found. There is no validation of whether or not the file is physically located where you have specified. The library name is the access point for your PL/SQL wrapper. You will now learn about the PL/SQL library wrapper.

PL/SQL Library Wrapper

The principal role of the PL/SQL library wrapper is to define an interface between the database and the external procedure. The interface defines how the formal parameters map between PL/SQL and C data types. It also defines any context and the location of the external procedure or library. When you create a PL/SQL library wrapper, there is no check whether or not the shared library is in the directory. You need to have a management process to ensure check-in and version control.

Oracle provides additional derived types to support OCI. The table columns show the source of the types. The table also shows you the default conversion type. Table 12-4 maps PL/SQL and C data types:

PL/SQL	Native C	Oracle	Default
BINARY_INTEGER BOOLEAN PLS_INTEGER	[UNSIGNED] CHAR [UNSIGNED] SHORT [UNSIGNED] INT [UNSIGNED] LONG	SB1, SB2, SB4 UB1, UB2, UB4 SIZE_T	INT
NATURAL NATURALN POSITIVE POSITIVEN SIGNTYPE	[UNSIGNED] CHAR [UNSIGNED] SHORT [UNSIGNED] INT [UNSIGNED] LONG	SB1, SB2, SB4 UB1, UB2, UB4 SIZE_T	[UNSIGNED] INT
FLOAT REAL	FLOAT		FLOAT
DOUBLE PRECISION	DOUBLE		DOUBLE
CHAR CHARACTER LONG NCHAR NVARCHAR2 ROWID VARCHAR VARCHAR2		STRING OCISTRING	STRING
LONG RAW RAW		RAW OCIRAW	RAW
BFILE BLOB CLOB NCLOB		OCILOBLOCATOR	OCILOBLOCATOR
NUMBER DEC DECIMAL INT INTEGER NUMERIC SMALLINT		OCINUMBER	OCINUMBER
DATE		OCIDATE	OCIDATE
TIMESTAMP TIMESTAMP WITH TIME ZONE TIMESTAMP WITH LOCAL TIME ZONE		OCIDATETIME	OCIDATETIME

TABLE 12-4. *Mapping PL/SQL Data Types to C*

PL/SQL	Native C	Oracle	Default
INTERVAL DAY TO SECOND INTERVAL YEAR TO MONTH		OCIINTERVAL	OCIINTERVAL
Composite Object Types: ADTs		dvoid	Dvoid
Composite Object Types: Collections (VARRAYS, NESTED TABLES)		OCICOLL	OCICOLL

TABLE 12-4. *Mapping PL/SQL Data Types to C* (continued)

In your small example, data types are converted only from PL/SQL to C, but the library definition supports bidirectional conversions. The bidirectional support is independent of the external shared library. Whether the external C library returns data or not, the PL/SQL library wrapper has defined it as bidirectional.

There are some differences beyond mapping between PL/SQL and C data types. They are qualified here:

- A variable can be NULL in PL/SQL, but there is no equivalent of a null value in C. When a variable can be NULL, you must use another variable to notify that a variable is null or not. This second variable is known as an indicator. You use OCI_IND_NULL and OCI_IND_NOTNULL to check whether the indicator variable is null or not. The indicator value is passed by value unless you override that behavior and pass by reference. An advanced consideration for an indicator variable is that it can have a type descriptor object (TDO) for composite objects and collections.

- Both C and PL/SQL need to know the length of character strings when they are exchanged. This is problematic because there is no standard means of determining the length of RAW or STRING parameter types. You can use the LENGTH or MAXLEN functions to determine the length of a formal parameter. It is important to note that LENGTH is passed into the external procedure by value when the mode is IN. It is passed by reference when using mode OUT.

- CHARSETID and CHARSETFORM are subject to globalization complexity if the extproc agent database is running in a different database. The calling database NLS_LANG and NLS_CHAR values are the expected values for the extproc agent. If this is not the case for the extproc agent, you need to use the OCI attribute names to set these for the program. The OCI attributes are OCI_ATTR_CHARSET_ID and OCI_ATTR_CHARSET_FORM. Both CHARSETID and CHARSETFORM are passed by value for IN mode and by reference for OUT mode.

The generalized format for creating a C library wrapper procedure is noted here:

```
CREATE [OR REPLACE] PROCEDURE name [parameter_list]
AS EXTERNAL
LIBRARY_NAME library_name
NAME "external_library_name"
AGENT IN [parameter_list]
WITH CONTEXT
PARAMETER [parameter_list];
```

It is important to note that the external_library_name is case sensitive when the operating system supports case sensitivity. Even while working on Microsoft Windows, you should always treat it as case sensitive. Good PL/SQL coding habits can make your life simpler when you change work environments.

When you define the parameter lists for a PL/SQL wrapper, positional order is not important. The PL/SQL wrapper relates them by name.

Objects present a unique case with the normally implicit SELF. In PL/SQL, you do not have to manage an object type's SELF member function, because it is implicitly managed. The problem is that the SELF reference is a parameter in the formal parameter list. The external C program requires the PL/SQL external procedure wrapper to define a complete formal parameter list. This means that it must formally define SELF. You pass an object to an external procedure by using the WITH CONTEXT clause when you define the object type. The following example illustrates defining an external object type:

```
CREATE OR REPLACE TYPE BODY object_library_sample AS
MEMBER FUNCTION get_tea_temperature
RETURN NUMBER
AS LANGUAGE C
NAME "tea_temp"
WITH CONTEXT
PARAMETERS
( CONTEXT
, SELF
, SELF INDICATOR STRUCT
, SELF TDO
, RETURN INDICATOR);
END;
/
```

Another rule applies to passing variables by reference to an external procedure. You must append the BY REFERENCE phrase to all variables passed by reference.

The AGENT IN clause allows run-time identification of the external agent program. This is an advanced feature. It is useful when you have more than one external agent running or configured. An example that would benefit from this type of PL/SQL wrapper is an environment with multiple external applications. Making the external agent a dynamic component gives you more flexibility. You can then use stored objects to make dynamic calls to different external application libraries.

You are now ready to create your PL/SQL external procedure wrapper. The sample program to build the PL/SQL wrapper follows:

-- **Available online as part of create_library1.sql**
```
CREATE OR REPLACE PROCEDURE write_string
  (path        VARCHAR2
  ,message     VARCHAR2) AS EXTERNAL
LIBRARY library_write_string
NAME "writestr"
PARAMETERS
  (path        STRING
  ,message     STRING);
/
```

The PL/SQL external procedure wrapper does the following:

- It creates an external procedure wrapper named `write_string`. This creates a data dictionary entry for a procedure named `write_string`.

- It accepts two variables of a `VARCHAR2` data type.

- It names the library `library_write_string`. This creates a data dictionary entry for a library named `library_write_string`.

- It qualifies the name of the external procedure without the `*.so` suffix (or on Microsoft Windows platforms, a `*.dll`). The suffix is automatically postpended. If it were included in the definition of the `NAME` value, the extproc agent would look for `writestr1.so.so` and fail.

- It passes the `VARCHAR2` data types as `STRING` data types to the external library.

You have learned how to define and configure a PL/SQL wrapper. Previously, you learned how to do all network plumbing, library coding, and agent configuration. It is now time to see if it was done correctly.

If you are working in Unix, use the online file. However, if you are working in Microsoft Windows, change the first argument to the `write_string` procedure. It should change from "`/tmp/file.txt`" to "`C:\TEMP\FILE.TXT`". You can now execute the external procedure by invoking the PL/SQL wrapper, as shown in the following code:

-- **Available online as part of create_library1.sql**
```
BEGIN

  -- Call the external procedure.
  write_string('/tmp/file.txt','Hello World!');

END;
/
```

When the procedure completes successfully, you can then open the file in the Unix /tmp or Microsoft Windows C:\TEMP directory. Rerunning the program will create a new file of the same name and rewrite the same string. If the file is in the /tmp or C:\TEMP directory, only the file's date stamp will appear to change.

There are some restrictions when working with external procedures. The restrictions are these:

- You should not use global variables, because they are not thread safe.

- You should not use external static variables, because they are not thread safe.

- You can use this feature only on platforms that support DLLs or shared libraries.

- You can use only programming languages callable from the C programming language.

- You must use objects when you want to pass cursor or record variables to an external procedure.

- You cannot use a DB_LINK in the LIBRARY section of a PL/SQL wrapper declaration.

- You can pass a maximum of 128 parameters. If you have float or double data types, they count for two parameters.

You have completed everything required to configure and set up a C DLL or shared library. If everything worked, please accept our congratulations. However, if something failed, you can go straight to the troubleshooting section. In that section, you will troubleshoot the most common problems.

Alternatively, it is time to look at creating Java external procedures.

Working with a Java Shared Library

As discussed when you covered the `extproc` architecture, Oracle built an extensible architecture for external procedures. It is flexible enough to support any programming language that is callable by the C programming language.

Oracle directly supports Java as part of the database. Java libraries do not use the `extproc` agent because they are natively part of the Oracle database. This simplifies much but does restrict some activities. Those restricted activities make the case for using the `extproc` agent and external C or C callable libraries.

Java has a few advantages over C:

- Java understands SQL types. It avoids the tedious data type mapping when using C.

- Java is loaded into the Oracle database. It avoids the file management issues and listener `ENV` parameter processes because it does not use the `extproc` agent.

- Java is natively thread safe. It does not require you to deal with the threading nuances provided you avoid static variables.

- Java does not require management of memory addresses. Memory addresses are called pointers in C/C++.

NOTE
Java static variables are considered class-level variables, which means they are built at compile time, not run time. There can be only one copy of a class variable in a Java Virtual Machine (JVM), provided there is only one Java class loader. Unfortunately, within the context of the Oracle JVM, there can be more than one Java class loader. Therefore, if you plan on using a Java class for an external procedure, avoid using static variables.

Java has a few disadvantages relative to C:

- Java uses the Java pool in the SGA for processing, whereas C external procedures use their own memory space. Effectively, C external programs lower the memory consumption of the SGA, while Java increases the load on the SGA.

- Java is not as fast as C because native Java byte code needs to be interpreted by the JVM.

- Java has restricted access to files. This protects the integrity of the database. The DBMS_JAVA package provides a means to define read and write access for Java library programs.

- PL/SQL wrapper functions that use Java libraries impose a limit on method definitions. All Java class methods accessed by PL/SQL wrapper functions must be static. Therefore, Java libraries that support PL/SQL wrapper functions are *not* thread safe.

You will now define a simple Java library.

Defining the Java Library
Java is an interpreted language, as opposed to a compiled language like C. C compilation results in a file of object code, which is machine code or binary instructions. Java compilation results in a Java byte stream. The JVM interprets the byte stream and executes the run-time object code. JVMs are platform specific, while byte streams are generic. This is why Java class files are portable across platforms.

Compiling a Java program does several things. It preprocesses the source code by breaking it down into tokens while validating syntax. Then, it compiles the program into Java byte code and writes a Java `.class` file. Java `.class` files are positionally dependent at run time on any included libraries.

The following program includes a standard I/O library. This will enable the database to access a physical file external to the instance. You do not define permission to Java file access in the `initSID.ora` parameter file. You must use the `DBMS_JAVA` package to grant permission from the `SYSTEM` account. The grant has already been done if you ran the online `create_user.sql` script for this chapter. The following shows the command required to grant read-only access to the `/tmp/file.txt` file:

```
-- Available online as part of create_user.sql
-- Grant Java permissions to file IO against a file.
   DBMS_JAVA.GRANT_PERMISSION('PLSQL'
                             ,'SYS:java.io.FilePermission'
                             ,'/tmp/file.txt'
                             ,'read');
```

Much as when using the C external procedure, you will first need to define the Java library. At a minimum, you will need to configure your Java environment. If you are using a Java IDE, it is assumed you know how to compile Java source code into class files. Only the command-line steps are covered in here.

Unlike the example in Chapter 10, the Java program will not interact with the database through SQL. That means you do not need to include the class files to support SQL. Therefore, you do not need to set your `$CLASSPATH`. For reference, the Oracle SQL class files are found in `$ORACLE_HOME/jdbc/lib/classes12.zip`.

Assuming you have access to the Java SDK, you will need to download the following program and compile it to Java byte code:

```
-- Available online as part of ReadFile1.java
// Class imports.
import java.io.*;

// Class defintion.
public class ReadFile1
{
   // Define readString() method with String input.
   public static String readString(String s)
   {
     // Call the readString() method with File input.
     return readFileString(new File(s));
   }

   // Define readFileString() method with File input.
   private static String readFileString(File file)
```

```java
{
  // Define a int to read the file.
  int c;

  // Define a String to return the text.
  String s = new String();

  // Define a FileReader.
  FileReader inFile;

  // Use a try-catch block because FileReader requires it.
  try
  {
    // Assign the file.
    inFile = new FileReader(file);

    // Read a character at a time.
    while ((c = inFile.read()) != -1)
    {
      // Append a character to the string.
      s += (char) c;

    } // End of while loop.

  } // End of try block.
  catch (IOException e)
  {
    // Return the error.
    return e.getMessage();

  } // End of catch block.

  // Return the string.
  return s;

} // End of readFileString() method.

// Define the main() method.
public static void main(String[] args)
{
  // Define the file name.
  String file = new String("/tmp/file.txt");

  // Output the string.
  System.out.println(ReadFile1.readString(file));

} // End of main() method.

} // End of ReadFile class.
```

The program does the following:

- It includes the `java.io.*`, which is the contents of the Java I/O package. The Java I/O package is used to read and write to files.

- It defines a `ReadFile1` class. Class names must exactly match the filename. If they do not match, you cannot compile them.

- It defines a static `readString()` method. The method takes a Java String variable and returns the same data type. Internally, it returns the output from the `readFileString()` method. To call the `readFileString()` method, it must construct an instance of the Java `File` class.

- It defines a static `readFileString()` method. The method takes a Java File variable and returns a Java String variable. Internally, it does the following:

  - It declares a variable `c`, using an integer data type.

  - It declares and instantiates a null Java String variable.

  - It declares a Java `FileReader` variable. `FileReader` is one of the streams implemented in Java. Streams in C are typically limited to `STDIN`, `STDOUT`, and `STDERR`, but Java has over thirty stream types. It will allow you to manage opening the file for reading.

  - It uses a try-catch block to read the file because the FileReader may raise an exception. In Java, if you work with a class library that can raise an exception, you must access it within a try-catch block. It is similar to a `BEGIN` and `EXCEPTION` concept in PL/SQL programming.

  - It assigns the `FileReader` variable to the file referenced by the `File` formal parameter to the method. In the example, that is the `/tmp/file.txt` file.

  - It use a while loop to read all the characters in the file. Within the while loop, it casts the integer reads to a character and appends them to the local String variable, `s`. If an error is encountered, it returns the error message instead of the file contents.

  - It uses a static `main()` method. This method is only for testing external to the database. The `main()` method becomes inaccessible once the class is loaded into the database.

Once you have downloaded the file and compiled it, you need to load it into the database. You can do so with the Oracle `loadjava` utility. The following `loadjava` command will make the Java class available in the `PLSQL` schema:

```
$ loadjava -r -f -o -user plsql/plsql ReadFile1.class
```

You have now completed the library Java library definition. You will now define and call the PL/SQL library wrapper to the Java library.

Defining and Calling the PL/SQL Library Wrapper

Writing the PL/SQL library wrapper to a Java module is called *publishing* the Java library. Since you used a C external procedure, you will define a Java library function. There are a couple reasons for doing so. First, Java libraries must use static methods when they are published as PL/SQL functions. Second, it gives you an opportunity to see how arguments for Java libraries are limited.

When you use Java, only arrays support a pass by reference semantic. A pass by reference semantic means that the memory address is passed by the PL/SQL run-time engine to the Java library. After the Java library updates the array and completes processing, it will return control to the PL/SQL run-time engine. PL/SQL knows the address and can access any changed data values. If you want to move data into and out of a Java library, you must do one of two things:

- You define a function and manage the return type of the function. The downside to a function is that it is not thread safe because you must use static method definitions.

- You define a procedure and use an array in OUT mode. The array option requires including the `classes12.zip` file and using an `oracle.sql.ARRAY[]` data type. `oracle.sql.ARRAY[]` is a nested table collection with a numeric index value.

Java libraries and PL/SQL have a mapping relationship like C. Table 12-5 qualifies the mapping.

SQL Data Types	Java Class Data Types
CHAR	oracle.sql.CHAR
LONG	java.lang.String
VARCHAR2	java.lang.Byte
	java.lang.Short
	java.lang.Integer
	java.lang.Long
	java.lang.Float
	java.lang.Double
	java.lang.BigDecimal
	java.sql.Date
	java.sql.Time
	java.sql.Timestamp
	byte
	short
	int
	long
	float
	double

TABLE 12-5. *SQL and Java Data Types*

SQL Data Types	Java Class Data Types
DATE	oracle.sql.DATE java.lang.String java.sql.Date java.sql.Time java.sql.Timestamp
NUMBER	oracle.sql.NUMBER java.lang.Byte java.lang.Short java.lang.Integer java.lang.Long java.lang.Float java.lang.Double java.lang.BigDecimal byte short int long float double
OPAQUE	oracle.sql.OPAQUE
RAW LONG RAW	oracle.sql.RAW byte[]
ROWID	oracle.sql.CHAR oracle.sql.ROWID java.lang.String
BFILE	oracle.sql.BFILE
BLOB	oracle.sql.BLOB oracle.jdbc.Blob (JDK 1.1.x)
CLOB NCLOB	oracle.sql.CLOB oracle.jdbc.Clob (JDK 1.1.x)
OBJECT Object types	oracle.sql.STRUCT java.sql.Struct (JDK 1.1.x) java.sql.SQLData oracle.sql.ORAData
REF Reference types	oracle.sql.REF java.sql.Ref (JDK 1.1.x) oracle.sql.ORAData
TABLE VARRAY Nested table & types VARRAY types	oracle.sql.ARRAY java.sql.Array (JDK 1.1.x) oracle.sql.ORAData
Any of the preceding SQL types	oracle.sql.CustomDatum oracle.sql.Datum

TABLE 12-5. *SQL and Java Data Types* (continued)

Most of the types are straightforward. The LONG and LONG RAW data types are limited to 32K. The oracle.sql.Datum is an abstract class. This means that it becomes whatever SQL type is passed to it.

You can publish your Java function by using the following wrapper:

```
-- Available online as part of create_javalib1.sql
CREATE OR REPLACE FUNCTION read_string
  (file IN VARCHAR2)
  RETURN VARCHAR2 IS
  LANGUAGE JAVA
  NAME 'ReadFile.readString(java.lang.String) return String';
/
```

The PL/SQL Java library wrapper publishes the Java class. It is important to point out that you must define the formal parameter with the fully qualified path. If you attempt to use String and not java.lang.String, it will compile successfully but fail at run time. The following program can test success or failure:

```
-- Available online as part of call_javawrapper.sql
SELECT    read_string('/tmp/file.txt')
FROM      dual;
```

It will return the following output from the /tmp/file.txt file if you modify the input formal parameter as described previously, that is, if you change the java.lang.String to String.

```
-- Available as output from call_javawrapper.sql
FROM      dual
          *
ERROR at line 2:
ORA-29531: no method readString in class ReadFile
```

You have now defined a Java library and published the Java class file. Next, you will take a look at troubleshooting the extproc agent and external procedures.

Troubleshooting the Shared Library

This is the section where you try to find out why something is not working. Hopefully, we have put most of the explanation in the chapter already. This section will cover some known errors and their fixes.

External procedures typically fail because of two issues. One is the configuration of the listener, shared library, or environment. That is why you went through all the components and how they fit together. Another is when the definition of the external program differs from the PL/SQL wrapper. This typically happens when data types are incorrectly mapped. Each class of problem is described in the two subsections that follow.

Configuration of the Listener or Environment

There are four general problems with network connectivity. They are noted here with the typical error messages and explanations.

Listener ENV Parameter Is Incorrect

As discussed in the `extproc` Oracle Net Services configuration, the following error will be raised when the `ENV` variable is incorrectly configured:

```
BEGIN
*
ERROR at line 1:
ORA-06520: PL/SQL: Error loading external library
ORA-06522: /u02/oracle/10g/10.1.0/lib/writestr1.so: cannot open shared object
file: No such file or directory
ORA-06512: at "PLSQL.WRITE_STRING", line 1
ORA-06512: at line 4
```

If you receive this error, you have experienced one of two types of failures. One is that the library is not in the directory you have designated, is named differently, or is case sensitive. Another is that you have made an error in configuring the `ENV` parameter in your `listener.ora` file.

File Path Problem

If the file path is not in the directory you have designated in the `ENV` value, correcting the file path should resolve the problem. If the file path is missing a component or is not consistent in case with the PL/SQL wrapper `NAME` parameter value or `EXTPROC_DLLS` value, synchronizing all three entries will fix it.

   If the file path is in the directory and all three locations mentioned are matched in spelling and case, the problem is in the listener `ENV` variable. Two areas can cause the problem: a bad `EXTPROC_DLLS` or a bad `LD_LIBRARY_PATH` entry. There is a third potential error: the `APL_ENV_FILE` value. This third error is typically a problem only when you have positioned the `extproc` agent in another Oracle home.

EXTPROC_DLLS Value Problem

You need to check the `ENV` variable in `CALLOUT_LISTENER`. The general rule is that you should have an entry for `EXTPROC_DLLS` and `LD_LIBRARY_PATH` in the `ENV` value. `EXTPROC_DLLS` should specify an equal sign, the word `ONLY`, a colon and the shared libraries you want to use or a list of shared libraries separated by a colon. Alternatively, you can choose to leave out the `ONLY` qualifier and provide a shared library or list of shared libraries separated by a colon. If you leave the `ONLY` qualifier out, you have not restricted the IPC listener to only those libraries. It is recommended by Oracle that you use `ONLY` to narrow the privileges of the listener.

You also need to check whether the shared libraries have a fully qualified path statement, the filename, and the file extension. Likewise, the LD_LIBRARY_PATH should at a minimum specify the fully qualified path to the $ORACLE_HOME/lib directory. If your libraries require other libraries, you would use the LD_LIBRARY_PATH reference. When you have more than the one library in the LD_LIBRARY_PATH, you use a set of fully qualified path statements separated by a colon.

If you would like to see this error, you can do the following:

■ Rename the shared library path in the PL/SQL wrapper. You would do this by rerunning the create_library1.sql script with an incorrect path statement.

■ Rerun the anonymous block PL/SQL call to the write_string procedure.

NOTE
If you do this test, do not forget to fix everything before you move on to the rest of the chapter.

The extproc Listener Is Incorrectly Configured or Not Running

As discussed in the extproc Oracle Net Services configuration, the following error will be raised when the extproc listener is not running or misconfigured.

```
BEGIN
*
ERROR at line 1:
ORA-28576: lost RPC connection to external procedure agent
ORA-06512: at "PLSQL.WRITE_STRING", line 1
ORA-06512: at line 4
```

If you receive this error, the extproc listener is not running or the KEY parameters in listener.ora and in tnsnames.ora fails to agree. You need to verify the setup of your listener.ora and tnsnames.ora files. The method to do so is described in an earlier section of this chapter, "Defining extproc Oracle Net Services Configuration."

If you would like to see this error, you can do the following:

■ Shut down the CALLOUT_LISTENER.

■ Alter the KEY parameter value in the listener.ora file so that it no longer agrees with the tnsnames.ora file.

■ Start up the CALLOUT_LISTENER.

■ Rerun the anonymous-block PL/SQL call to the write_string procedure.

NOTE
*If you do this test, do not forget to fix everything
before you move on to the rest of the chapter.*

There Is No Separate `extproc` Listener

As discussed in connection with the `extproc` Oracle Net Services configuration, the following error will be raised when three conditions are met:

- The correct environment is defined in the `extproc` listener.

- There is no separate `extproc` listener.

- The `extproc` agent is attempting to access the `DLL` or shared library in any directory other than `$ORACLE_HOME/bin` or `$ORACLE_HOME/lib`.

```
BEGIN
*
ERROR at line 1:
ORA-28595: Extproc agent : Invalid DLL Path
ORA-06522: h§n¶h§n¶
```

If you receive this error, these three conditions are met, since you have configured a perfect `ENV` variable in the standard single `LISTENER`. You now need to do one of two things. You can migrate the `extproc` agent listener to a separate listener. This is described in the section "Defining `extproc` Oracle Net Services Configuration."

Alternatively, you can abandon the custom library directory and put the external libraries in the `$ORACLE_HOME/lib` directory.

If you would like to see this error, you can do the following:

- Shut down the `CALLOUT_LISTENER`.

- Using the online `listener1.ora` and `tnsnames2.ora` files, replace your `listener.ora` and `tnsnames.ora`, respectively. Do not forget to configure these files. You need to provide full path statements that match your system for them to work. Do not forget to make a copy of your modified files so that you can restore them.

- Start up the `CALLOUT_LISTENER`.

- Rerun the anonymous block PL/SQL call to the `write_string` procedure.

NOTE
*If you do this test, do not forget to fix everything
before you move on to the rest of the chapter.*

PL/SQL Wrapper Defined NAME Value Is Incorrect

As discussed in the defining and calling the PL/SQL library wrapper, the following error will be raised when the NAME variable is incorrectly entered:

```
BEGIN
*
ERROR at line 1:
ORA-06521: PL/SQL: Error mapping function
ORA-06522: /u02/oracle/10g/10.1.0/lib/libagtsh.so: undefined symbol:
writestr1.so
ORA-06512: at "PLSQL.WRITE_STRING", line 1
ORA-06512: at line 3
```

If you receive this error, you need to check the NAME variable in the PL/SQL external library definition. The ORA-06522 error returns the filename of the object that cannot be found. It is unclear from the error if it was looking for the writestr1.so file in the $ORACLE_HOME/lib directory. Actually, it first looked in the designated custom library directory, then in the $ORACLE_HOME/lib directory. It could not find the writestr1.so.so file. Defining the NAME parameter of the external procedure with the filename and suffix can cause the problem. It should always be only the filename. The extproc agent implicitly appends .so or .DLL, depending on the platform.

> **NOTE**
> *The extproc agent always searches the ENV defined directories first and the $ORACLE_HOME/lib last. Anytime the DLL or shared library name fails to match the value in the PL/SQL library definition, the ORA-06522 will return the $ORACLE_HOME/lib directory.*

If you encounter this error and verify everything is working, shut down your extproc listener. Use the ps utility to find the running extprocPLSExtProc agent. If it is running after you shut down the listener, it should not be running. Use the kill utility to end it. Then restart your extproc listener. This eliminates the conflict with the preserved state in the extproc agent.

If you would like to see this error, you can do the following:

- Rename the writestr.so shared library file.

- Rerun the anonymous block PL/SQL call to the write_string procedure.

> **NOTE**
> *If you do this test, do not forget to fix everything before you move on to the rest of the chapter.*

The `LD_LIBRARY_PATH` should at a minimum specify the fully qualified path to the `$ORACLE_HOME/lib` directory. If you use the default location for your shared library, you can exclude it.

Configuration of the Shared Library or PL/SQL Library Wrapper

As you built the shared external library file and PL/SQL wrapper, you probably noticed that the formal parameter types mapped correctly. When they do not map correctly, you will lose the RPC connection and generate the following error message:

```
BEGIN
*
ERROR at line 1:
ORA-28576: lost RPC connection to external procedure agent
ORA-06512: at "PLSQL.WRITE_STRING", line 1
ORA-06512: at line 4
```

If you receive this error, the PL/SQL library is defining a mapping relationship that cannot be implicitly caste. This error is raised when you try to fork an external library with actual parameters that do not implicitly caste to the formal parameters of the library.

NOTE
Actually, implicit casting is a big nightmare. If you run into an implicit caste, you will not get an error during the call to the external procedure. You will likely get bad data from your program, and it may take a while to sort out why. Ensuring the external library types match the definition in the PL/SQL wrapper is a configuration management issue. You will save yourself countless hours of frustration and lost productivity if you create a check-in process that ensures external library definitions agree with PL/SQL library definitions.

If you would like to see this error, you can do the following:

- Create a `writestr2.so` shared library from the online `writestr2.c` file.

- Shut down the `CALLOUT_LISTENER`.

■ Use the online `listener3.ora` and `tnsnames3.ora` files to replace your `listener.ora` and `tnsnames.ora` files, respectively. Do not forget to configure these files. You need to provide full path statements that match your system for them to work.

■ Start up the `CALLOUT_LISTENER`.

■ Run the online `create_library2.sql` file to build the PL/SQL external procedure wrapper.

■ Rerun the anonymous block PL/SQL call to the `write_string` procedure.

NOTE
If you do this test, do not forget to fix everything before you move on to the rest of the chapter.

You have now completed the troubleshooting section. It is time to summarize what you have done in the chapter.

Summary

You have learned what external procedures do and how to configure the Oracle Net Services to support them. You have worked through defining and calling `extproc` and native Java libraries. Then, you learned how to troubleshoot the most common problems.

CHAPTER
13

Dynamic SQL

ynamic SQL delivered in Oracle 9*i* provides a replacement for most of the functionality delivered in the Oracle DBMS_SQL built in. It is a powerful technology that lets you do many things that were more difficult when using DBMS_SQL. This chapter will cover both utilities and provide you with comparative examples.
You will cover topics as follows. The chapter assumes you read it sequentially. It also assumes you have read the preceding twelve chapters. If you feel comfortable with an area, please feel free to move to the section of interest. However, the chapter assumes you have mastery of earlier sections.

- Introducing dynamic SQL

- Working with Native Dynamic SQL (NDS)

There is a new `create_user.sql` script with this chapter. Before you run the `create_user.sql` script from the SYSTEM account or an account with the DBA role, you need to grant privileges from the SYS user. The following grant from the SYS user is required to use the DBMS_SQL package successfully in the chapter exercises:

```
-- Not available in an online file.
GRANT EXECUTE ON dbms_sys_sql TO SYSTEM WITH GRANT OPTION;
GRANT EXECUTE ON dbms_sql TO SYSTEM WITH GRANT OPTION;
```

After you have granted privileges on the SYS.DBMS_SYS_SQL and SYS.DBMS_SQL packages to the SYSTEM user, you can run the `create_user.sql` script to rebuild the PLSQL user. If you fail to run the script, you will raise the following exception:

```
DECLARE
*
ERROR at line 1:
ORA-01031: insufficient privileges
ORA-06512: at "SYS.DBMS_SYS_SQL", line 906
ORA-06512: at "SYS.DBMS_SQL", line 39
ORA-06512: at "PLSQL.DBMS_SQL_TUTORIAL", line 92
ORA-06512: at line 15
```

If you have other objects that you do not want to lose from the PLSQL user account, you can manually execute the following grants from the SYSTEM user in lieu of running `create_user.sql`:

```
-- Not available in an online file.
GRANT EXECUTE ON sys.dbms_sys_sql TO PLSQL;
```

```
GRANT EXECUTE ON dbms_sql TO PLSQL;
GRANT CREATE TABLE TO PLSQL;
GRANT CREATE SEQUENCE TO PLSQL;
```

You will need to run `create_user.sql` or manually execute the grants to work through the examples in the chapter. There are also two key packages that support this chapter. They are `dbms_sql.sql` and `nds_sql.sql`, and they build the `DBMS_SQL_TUTORIAL` and `NDS_TUTORIAL` packages, respectively. You should run these after the `create_user.sql` script to support the examples in the chapter.

Introducing Dynamic SQL

Dynamic SQL is the ability to build and run SQL statements on the fly. Prior to DBMS_SQL, you needed to know the columns and tables of any DQL or DML statement. When you reference and store known columns and tables in a SQL statement, that statement is called a static SQL statement.

There are three benefits of static SQL statements:

- When you compile or test them, you know immediately whether or not all supporting database objects are present. If the dependent objects are not there, the SQL will immediately fail.

- When you compile or test them, you know immediately whether or not all grants, privileges, and synonyms have been defined properly. If the dependencies are not there, the SQL fails and complains of missing objects.

- When you use static SQL, you can tune it for optimal performance. This is a critical benefit when high-volume activity is involved.

While some programmers would say these benefits indicate you should always use static SQL, it is not always possible. Moreover, there is another approach to problems. That other approach teaches you to write robust, reusable, and dynamic algorithmic solutions. This is an object-oriented philosophy. In a nutshell, dynamic SQL enables you to write elegant PL/SQL code that is polymorphic whether or not you use the object types provided by Oracle.

Polymorphism is the ability for your program to do two things: One is to discern from actual parameters what it should do. The other is to enable it to take different actions based on the actual parameters. PL/SQL can deliver polymorphism with static SQL statements, but it makes the programs much larger.

For example, you can use a multilevel if-then-else or case statement to evaluate what the program should do. Then, you can hard-code each of the static SQL statements in the appropriate block of the if-then-else or case statement. Dynamic

SQL reduces what you need in those if-then-else blocks, since you can build run-time SQL statements.

Here are other benefits of dynamic SQL:

■ You can include DDL statements within your PL/SQL programs.

■ You can write code that adjusts to table redefinitions.

■ You can enable stored programs to support various user inputs.

On balance, you will use dynamic SQL to solve programming problems. The key choices with Oracle 10*g* are when to use NDS over DBMS_SQL. While you should make your own judgment, Oracle 10*g* NDS delivers performance superior to DBMS_SQL.

NDS provides flexibility and simpler syntax than the DBMS_SQL built-in. NDS also provides a direct solution to working with collection and object types. Unfortunately, there is one exception to that rule. NDS does not support dynamic SQL where you do not know the number, name, or data types of arguments in advance. You will need to use DBMS_SQL for those occasions.

You will cover both DBMS_SQL and NDS for two reasons. There are millions of DBMS_SQL lines of code in the Oracle community, and you will need to understand how that code works. NDS is the future strategy and direction of dynamic SQL for the Oracle database. Using comparative analysis will help build and reinforce learning of these two technologies. You will learn NDS first and then DBMS_SQL.

Working with Native Dynamic SQL

Native Dynamic SQL has become well known under the acronym of NDS. It is a powerful tool for running dynamic SQL against the Oracle 10*g* database. NDS runs faster than DBMS_SQL. It is the future vision for dynamic SQL in the Oracle database.

NDS delivers three dynamic SQL functionalities to your PL/SQL programs:

■ Dynamic DDL and DML without bind variables

■ Dynamic DML with a known list of bind variables

■ Dynamic DQL

You will cover each of these dynamic SQL functionalities in sequence. As you work through these examples, collection and object types will be leveraged. If you need to check out object types, please refer to Chapters 14–16. There will be some forward referencing to the DBMS_SQL built-in as you work through this section. The following are advantages of NDS over DBMS_SQL:

■ It performs faster than DBMS_SQL.

■ It has syntax that mirrors the standard static SQL statements. Many programmers find its syntax easier than using the DBMS_SQL built-in.

■ It can fetch directly into PL/SQL record types, while DBMS_SQL cannot.

■ It supports all PL/SQL data types supported by static SQL statements. These include user-defined types, user-defined objects, and reference cursors. DBMS_SQL does not support user-defined types.

EXECUTE IMMEDIATE provides the syntax to parse (prepare a statement) and execute dynamic SQL. It takes a single argument, which is a string containing a SQL statement. The string is a VARCHAR2 data type. SQL statements have a single semicolon that is equivalent to the "/" or execute command. When preparing a SQL statement, you should not include the semicolon in the string.

The semicolon must be included when you put an anonymous-block PL/SQL program into the string argument. PL/SQL requires the terminating semicolon to end its block definition and a "/" to execute the program. The EXECUTE IMMEDIATE command appends an execution signal to the statement string. That is why a SQL statement does not require it and why an anonymous-block PL/SQL program unit does. Table 13-1 summarizes the available clauses to the EXECUTE IMMEDIATE command.

NDS also supports bulk processing. As discussed in the Chapter 6, bulk processing enables you to work with moving collections into and out of the database. Bulk processing with NDS has a set of different semantics. There are three commands, two additional clauses, and one cursor attribute to support bulk processing:

■ The BULK FETCH statement

■ The BULK EXECUTE IMMEDIATE statement

■ The FORALL statement

■ The COLLECT INTO clause

■ The RETURNING INTO clause

■ The %BULK_ROWCOUNT cursor attribute

The NDS_TUTORIAL package is provided online as a test repository of procedures. Example procedures will be used to demonstrate NDS techniques.

NDS Clause	Mode	Description
INTO	OUT	The INTO clause specifies variable targets only for single-row return statements. There must be a value defined in the INTO clause for each column returned by the query. It is positionally specific to the column order in the query.
RETURNING <variable> INTO <bind_variable	IN OUT	The RETURNING INTO clause provides a means to alter the positional return values and assign them to specific target variables. Like the INTO clause, it must retrieve only one row.
USING	IN OUT	The USING clause enables both IN and OUT modes unless you have also used RETURNING INTO clause. If you use both clauses, the USING clause is restricted to an IN-only mode.

TABLE 13-1.   *Clauses Available to the EXECUTE IMMEDIATE Command*

Working with DDL and DML Without Bind Variables

If you have taken a moment to refer to some of the online scripts, you will have found that we use NDS frequently to ensure the integrity of the scripts. We do not, however, use the DBMS_SQL built-in. The reason is that NDS is simpler to use and less dependent on database privileges. Like those privileges you set up to ensure, you could work through the DBMS_SQL built-in exercises.

The simplest approach to using dynamic SQL is the place you will start. Building and executing dynamic DDL and DML SQL statements has two approaches. One approach uses concatenation of static text and variables into strings that are assigned to a VARCHAR2 statement variable. The other approach is to use bind variables that are substituted at run time.

This section will cover concatenation approaches. The next section will cover bind variable approaches. There is no magic to the statement variable name, but by convention it is widely used. The variable name statement seems to enhance the readability of native dynamic SQL and DBMS_SQL programs.

The following procedure is taken from the NDS_TUTORIAL package. It demonstrates NDS using concatenation to do a DDL sequence creation statement:

-- **Available online as part of nds_sql.sql**

```
PROCEDURE create_sequence
  ( sequence_name              IN      VARCHAR2) IS

  -- Define local variable.
  statement                 VARCHAR2(2000);

  -- Define local function to find a sequence.
  FUNCTION verify_not_sequence
    ( sequence_name_in         IN      VARCHAR2)
  RETURN BOOLEAN IS

    -- Defines default return value.
    retval                  BOOLEAN := TRUE;

    -- Cursor returns a single row when finding a sequence.
    CURSOR find_sequence IS
      SELECT    null
      FROM      user_objects
      WHERE     object_name = sequence_name_in;

  BEGIN

    -- Sets the Boolean when it finds a sequence.
    FOR i IN find_sequence LOOP
      retval := FALSE;
    END LOOP;

    -- Return Boolean state.
    RETURN retval;

  END verify_not_sequence;

BEGIN

  -- If sequence does not exist create it.
  IF verify_not_sequence(sequence_name) = TRUE THEN

    -- Build dynamic SQL statement.
    statement := 'CREATE SEQUENCE '||sequence_name||CHR(10)
              || '  INCREMENT BY    1'            ||CHR(10)
              || '  START WITH      1'            ||CHR(10)
              || '  CACHE          20'            ||CHR(10)
              || '  ORDER';

    -- Use NDS to run the statement.
```

```
      EXECUTE IMMEDIATE statement;

      -- Print successful output message.
      dbms_output.put_line(
        '-> nds_tutorial.create_sequence');

      -- Print output break.
      dbms_output.put_line(sline);

      -- Print sequence created.
      dbms_output.put_line(
        'Created Sequence <'||sequence_name||'>');

    ELSE

      -- Print module name output message.
      dbms_output.put_line(
        '-> nds_tutorial.create_sequence');

      -- Print output line break.
      dbms_output.put_line(sline);

      -- Print output message.
      dbms_output.put_line(
        'Sequence <'||sequence_name||'> already exists');

    END IF;

END create_sequence;
```

The procedure does the following:

- It defines a procedure that takes a single formal parameter of `sequence_name`.

- It defines a local `statement` variable. The `statement` variable is used as the argument to an `EXECUTE IMMEDIATE` NDS call.

- It defines a local `verify_not_sequence` function. The function takes a sequence name and checks whether it exists.

- An if-then-else statement uses the `verify_not_sequence` function to check if a sequence exists. It does the following if false:

    - It assigns a concatenated static string with the actual parameter `sequence_name`.

■ It uses EXECUTE IMMEDIATE with an argument of the statement variable, which runs the NDS statement.

■ It prints a success message to the console.

If the function returns true, the sequence does not exist, and it prints a failure message to the console.

In the NDS_TUTORIAL package, there is a mirror to this create_sequence procedure in the drop_sequence procedure. It is a mirror in its approach to dropping a sequence with an NDS statement. Please check the online file to examine the drop_sequence procedure. Both of these illustrate using concatenation to build a DDL statement and execute it as an NDS statement.

The following anonymous-block program calls the create_sequence, increment_sequence, and drop_sequence procedures:

```
-- Available online as part of nds_sql_01.sql
DECLARE

  -- Define local variables.
  value_in          VARCHAR2(30) := 'TESTING_S1';
  value_out         NUMBER;

BEGIN

  -- Break output stream.
  dbms_output.put_line(nds_tutorial.dline);

  -- Test create sequence.
  nds_tutorial.create_sequence(value_in);

  -- Break output stream.
  dbms_output.put_line(nds_tutorial.dline);

  -- Use for loop to increment sequence three times.
  FOR i IN 1..3 LOOP

    -- Increment sequence.
    nds_tutorial.increment_sequence(value_in,value_out);

    -- Break output stream.
    dbms_output.put_line(nds_tutorial.sline);

  END LOOP;

  -- Break output stream.
```

```
      dbms_output.put_line(nds_tutorial.dline);

      -- Drop the sequence.
      nds_tutorial.drop_sequence(value_in);

      -- Break output stream.
      dbms_output.put_line(nds_tutorial.dline);

END;
/
```

The program does the following:

- It defines two local variables, assigning the first a TESTING_S1 value. The second is used later in the program as an output variable.

- It prints a double line break.

- It prints the results of nds_tutorial.create_sequence.

- It prints a double line break.

- It uses a for-loop to call the increment_sequence procedure three times and prints a line break.

- It prints a double line break.

- It calls the drop_sequence procedure.

- It prints a double line break.

The program produces the following output:

```
-- Available as output from online nds_sql_01.sql
=========================================================
-> nds_tutorial.create_sequence
------------------------------
Created Sequence <TESTING_S1>
=========================================================
-> nds_tutorial.increment_sequence
------------------------------
Sequence <TESTING_S1> Value <1>
------------------------------
-> nds_tutorial.increment_sequence
------------------------------
Sequence <TESTING_S1> Value <2>
------------------------------
-> nds_tutorial.increment_sequence
```

```
------------------------------
Sequence <TESTING_S1> Value <3>
------------------------------

============================================================
-> nds_tutorial.drop_sequence
------------------------------
Dropped Sequence <TESTING_S1>
============================================================
```

A DML without bind variables works more or less the same way. You define formal parameters and concatenate them into a VARCHAR2 string. Then, you use the VARCHAR2 string as the argument to the EXECUTE IMMEDIATE command.

DDL commands work well with the concatenation method because of the variable mode. Using NDS, all DDL commands take only IN-mode variables. Some DML commands work well using NDS concatenation in statement strings. The following insert_into_table procedure from the nds_tutorial package illustrates a DML insert using concatenation:

```
-- Available online as part of nds_sql.sql
  -- Procedure demonstrates a DML without bind variables.
  PROCEDURE insert_into_table
    ( table_name                IN      VARCHAR2
    , table_column_value1       IN      NUMBER
    , table_column_value2       IN      VARCHAR2
    , table_column_value3       IN      VARCHAR2) IS

    -- Define local variables.
    statement                   VARCHAR2(2000);

    -- Define a local function to ensure table does exist.
    FUNCTION verify_table
      ( object_name_in          IN      VARCHAR2)
    RETURN BOOLEAN IS

      -- Defines default return value.
      retval                    BOOLEAN := FALSE;

      -- Cursor returns a single row when finding a table.
      CURSOR find_object IS
        SELECT   null
        FROM     user_objects
        WHERE    object_name = object_name_in;

    BEGIN

      -- The for-loop sets the Boolean when a table is found.
```

```
      FOR i IN find_object LOOP
        retval := TRUE;
      END LOOP;

      -- Return Boolean state.
      RETURN retval;

    END verify_table;

BEGIN

  -- If table exists insert into it.
  IF verify_table(table_name) = TRUE THEN

    -- Build dynamic SQL statement.
    statement := 'INSERT '
              || 'INTO '||table_name||' '
              || 'VALUES ('
              || ''''||table_column_value1||''','
              || ''''||table_column_value2||''','
              || ''''||table_column_value3||''')';

    -- Execute the NDS statement.
    EXECUTE IMMEDIATE statement;

    -- Commit the records.
    commit;

    -- Print module name output message.
    dbms_output.put_line(
      '-> nds_tutorial.insert_into_table');

    -- Print line break.
    dbms_output.put_line(sline);

    -- Print data output.
    dbms_output.put_line(
      'Value inserted <'||table_column_value1||'>');
    dbms_output.put_line(
      'Value inserted <'||table_column_value2||'>');
    dbms_output.put_line(
      'Value inserted <'||table_column_value3||'>');

  ELSE

    -- Print module name output message.
    dbms_output.put_line(
      '-> nds_tutorial.insert_into_table');
```

```
   -- Print line break.
   dbms_output.put_line(sline);

   -- Print error output message.
   dbms_output.put_line(
      'Object <'||table_name||'> does not exist');

   END IF;

END insert_into_table;
```

The procedure does the following:

- It defines a procedure that takes four formal parameters.

- It defines a local `statement` variable. The `statement` variable is used as the argument to an EXECUTE IMMEDIATE NDS call.

- It defines a local `verify_table` function. The function takes a table name and checks whether it exists.

- An if-then-else statement uses the `verify_table` function to check if a table exists. It does the following if false:

  - It assigns a concatenated static string with the actual parameter `table_name`.

  - It uses EXECUTE IMMEDIATE with an argument of the `statement` variable, which runs the NDS statement.

  - It prints a success message to the console.

If the function returns true, the table exists, and it prints a failure message to the console.

The `nds_sql_02.sql` test script demonstrates the `insert_into_table` procedure. It contains three program units. The first program unit is an anonymous-block PL/SQL program that calls two procedures, `create_table` and `insert_into_table`. The second program unit is a SELECT statement that queries the `test_messages` table. Last is another anonymous-block PL/SQL program that uses the `single_row_return` procedure and then the `drop_table` procedure.

If you have more than a single row in the `test_messages` table, the `nds_sql_02.sql` script will raise an error. You can get the error if you ran the `nds_sql_03.sql` script before running this script. If so, the program will raise the following error:

```
BEGIN
*
```

```
ERROR at line 1:
ORA-01422: exact fetch returns more than requested number of rows
ORA-06512: at "PLSQL.NDS_TUTORIAL", line 739
ORA-06512: at line 7
```

There are also four bind variables declared in the nds_sql_02.sql script. The bind variables allow the two anonymous PL/SQL block programs to share variable values in the same session. You should refer to Chapter 3 if you need a quick update on bind variables. The following script tests the insert_into_table procedure:

```
-- Available online as part of nds_sql_02.sql
DECLARE

  -- Define local variables.
  table_name_in          VARCHAR2(30)  := 'TEST_MESSAGES';
  table_definition_in    VARCHAR2(2000);
  column_name1           VARCHAR2(30)  := 'TEST_MESSAGE_ID';
  column_name2           VARCHAR2(30)  := 'MESSAGE_SENT';
  column_name3           VARCHAR2(30)  := 'REVIEWED_BY';
  table_column_value1    NUMBER        := '1';
  table_column_value2    VARCHAR2(20)  := 'Hello World';
  table_column_value3    VARCHAR2(30)  := USER;

BEGIN

  -- Assign table name to bind variable.
  :table_name := table_name_in;
  :column_name1 := column_name1;
  :column_name2 := column_name2;
  :column_name3 := column_name3;

  -- Initialize table definition.
  table_definition_in := '( test_message_id NUMBER'        ||CHR(10)
                      || ', message_sent    VARCHAR2(20)'||CHR(10)
                      || ', reviewed_by     VARCHAR2(30))';

  -- Print line break.
  dbms_output.put_line(nds_tutorial.dline);

  -- Create the table.
  nds_tutorial.create_table(table_name_in,table_definition_in);

  -- Print line break.
  dbms_output.put_line(nds_tutorial.dline);
```

```
-- Insert into the table.
nds_tutorial.insert_into_table( table_name_in
                               , table_column_value1
                               , table_column_value2
                               , table_column_value3);

-- Print line break.
dbms_output.put_line(nds_tutorial.dline);

END;
/
```

The program does the following:

- ■ It defines local variables.

- ■ It assigns the four local variables to session-level bind variables. These are the values for the table and column names that will be inserted into the table.

- ■ It builds an insert statement and assigns it to a variable.

- ■ It calls the `nds_tutorial.create_table` procedure that uses NDS to dynamically build the table.

- ■ It prints a line break to the output stream.

- ■ It calls the `nds_tutorial.insert_into_table` procedure that uses NDS to dynamically insert into the table.

- ■ It prints a line break to the output stream.

A query against the table shows that the row has been inserted by returning the following:

```
-- Available online as output from dns_sql_02.sql
    Test
Message
    ID # Message Sent         Reviewed By
---- ---------- ---------------
       1 Hello World          PLSQL
```

You have now covered how to use NDS to process DDL and DML statements. These have worked without using bind variables. The next section will illustrate several approaches to DML statements that use bind variables.

Working with DML and a Known List of Bind Variables

Bind variables are very powerful devices, as you learned in Chapter 3. You also got a chance to see how they can support moving data between two anonymous-block PL/SQL programs in the prior section. Briefly, bind variables exist within the context of the session, not a program unit. As long as the session does not unset the bind variable, it is available.

When NDS executes a statement, it does so within the context of the user session and behaves like a Unix subshell. Bind variables provide the means of exchanging information between your programs. For example, consider the program that executes an NDS call as the shell environment and the spawned NDS statement as the subshell. Bind variables act as targets that you pass data to. This is called passing by value. In other cases, bind variables are passed by address. This is called passing by reference. If the mode is IN for a bind variable, the data is passed by value. If the mode is OUT for a bind variable, the data is passed by reference.

You will now work with another procedure from the `nds_tutorial` package. The `inserts_into_table` procedure is a clone of the `insert_into_table` procedure. The `statement` variable has changed to include bind variables. As a result of the addition of bind variables in the `statement` variable, the `USING` clause is added. The following procedure demonstrates using bind variables:

```
-- Available online as part of nds_sql.sql
PROCEDURE inserts_into_table
  ( table_name            IN      VARCHAR2
  , table_column_value1   IN      NUMBER
  , table_column_value2   IN      VARCHAR2
  , table_column_value3   IN      VARCHAR2) IS

  -- Define local variables.
  statement               VARCHAR2(2000);

  -- Define a local function to ensure table does exist.
  FUNCTION verify_table
    ( object_name_in      IN      VARCHAR2)
  RETURN BOOLEAN IS

    -- Defines default return value.
    retval                BOOLEAN := FALSE;

    -- Cursor returns a single row when finding a table.
    CURSOR find_object IS
      SELECT    null
```

```
       FROM      user_objects
       WHERE     object_name = object_name_in;

  BEGIN

    -- The for-loop sets the Boolean when a table is found.
    FOR i IN find_object LOOP
      retval := TRUE;
    END LOOP;

    -- Return Boolean state.
    RETURN retval;

  END verify_table;

BEGIN

  -- If table exists insert into it.
  IF verify_table(table_name) = TRUE THEN

    -- Build dynamic SQL statement.
    statement := 'INSERT '
               || 'INTO '||table_name||' '
               || 'VALUES (:col_one, :col_two, :col_three)';

    -- Execute the NDS statement.
    EXECUTE IMMEDIATE statement
      USING table_column_value1
      ,     table_column_value2
      ,     table_column_value3;

    -- Commit the records.
    commit;

    -- Print module name output message.
    dbms_output.put_line(
      '-> nds_tutorial.insert_into_table');

    -- Print line break.
    dbms_output.put_line(sline);

    -- Print data output.
    dbms_output.put_line(
      'Value inserted <'||table_column_value1||'>');
    dbms_output.put_line(
      'Value inserted <'||table_column_value2||'>');
```

```
      dbms_output.put_line(
        'Value inserted <'||table_column_value3||'>');

   ELSE

      -- Print module name output message.
      dbms_output.put_line(
        '-> nds_tutorial.insert_into_table');

      -- Print line break.
      dbms_output.put_line(sline);

      -- Print error output message.
      dbms_output.put_line(
        'Object <'||table_name||'> does not exist');

   END IF;

END inserts_into_table;
```

The procedure does the following:

- It defines a procedure that takes four formal parameters.

- It defines a local `statement` variable. The `statement` variable is used as the argument to an `EXECUTE IMMEDIATE` NDS call.

- It defines a local `verify_table` function. The function takes a table name and checks whether it exists.

- An if-then-else statement uses the `verify_table` function to check if a table exists. It does the following if true:

  - It assigns a concatenated static string with the actual parameter `table_name` and three bind variables. The bind variables `:col_one`, `:col_two`, and `:col_three` are placeholders. They map positionally to the variables in the `USING` clause.

  - It uses `EXECUTE IMMEDIATE` with an argument of the `statement` variable, which runs the NDS statement. It also has a `USING` clause followed by three of the formal parameters to the procedure.

  - It prints a success message to the console.

If the function returns false, the table does not exist, and it prints a failure message to the console.

The program to test the `insert_bind_table` procedure is a clone of the one used to test the `insert_into_table` procedure. The only difference is the name of the procedure. Please refer back to the example provided from `nds_sql_02.sql`. Likewise, it produces the same output, which is not repeated here.

You will now see how to select a collection using NDS, bind variables, and a bulk collection operation.

Working with DQL

You will work with selecting a row from the database using NDS, bind variables, and a bulk collection operation. There are two details you need to know to use bulk processing within NDS:

- NDS can only work with database types. This means that if you want to return a collection, you must define the collection type in the database.

- NDS can use bulk collections only from within an anonymous-block PL/SQL program.

NOTE
DBMS_SQL does not support user-defined types.

For example, for this chapter you will need to define the following types:

```
-- Available online as part of create_types.sql
CREATE OR REPLACE TYPE varchar2_table1 IS
VARRAY(100) OF VARCHAR2(1);
/

-- Create a Varray of number.
CREATE OR REPLACE TYPE card_number_varray IS
VARRAY(100) OF NUMBER;
/

-- Create a Varray of twenty-character string.
CREATE OR REPLACE TYPE card_name_varray IS
VARRAY(100) OF VARCHAR2(2000);
/

-- Create a Varray of thirty-character string.
CREATE OR REPLACE TYPE card_suit_varray IS
VARRAY(100) OF VARCHAR2(2000);
/
```

TIP
While the examples use varrays, you probably should consider using nested tables. They are better solutions for NDS because they are not upward-bound array structures. As you know, the number of rows from a query or transactional processing insert, update, or delete is unknown until run time.

You will see in the next sample procedure how the varray data type is used. The second detail is that you must encapsulate bulk processing within anonymous-block PL/SQL units. If you rewrite the NDS `statement` in the `multiple_row_return` procedure as follows, it will fail:

```
-- Build dynamic SQL statement.
statement := 'SELECT ''A'' '
          || 'BULK COLLECT INTO :col_val '
          || 'FROM DUAL';
```

While the package will successfully compile, at run time you will see it fail. You can use the following anonymous block to test it:

```
BEGIN nds_tutorial.multiple_row_return; END;
/
```

Attempting this, you will raise the following error:

```
BEGIN nds_tutorial.multiple_row_return; END;
*
ERROR at line 1:
ORA-03001: unimplemented feature
ORA-06512: at "PLSQL.NDS_TUTORIAL", line 631
ORA-06512: at line 1
```

If you inspect the `nds_tutorial` package, you will find the `multiple_row_return` procedure is overloaded. You will first test the form of the procedure that takes no parameters and returns only a single row. The `multiple_row_return` procedure without parameters lets you work through the basic syntax.

The `multiple_row_return` procedure is listed here:

```
-- Available online as part of nds_sql.sql
PROCEDURE multiple_row_return IS

  -- Define local variables.
  statement                  VARCHAR2(2000);
```

```
    value_out                    VARCHAR2_TABLE2;

BEGIN

  -- Build dynamic SQL statement.
  statement := 'BEGIN '
            || 'SELECT ''A'' '
            || 'BULK COLLECT INTO :col_val '
            || 'FROM DUAL;'
            || 'END;';

  -- Use Bulk NDS to query a static string.
    EXECUTE IMMEDIATE statement
      USING OUT value_out;

    -- Print module name message.
    dbms_output.put_line(
      '-> nds_tutorial.multiple_row_return');

    -- Print line break.
    dbms_output.put_line(sline);

  -- Use a range loop to read the values.
  FOR i IN 1..value_out.COUNT LOOP

    -- Print output message.
    dbms_output.put_line(
      'Value from COLUMN_VALUE <'||value_out(i)||'>');

  END LOOP;

END multiple_row_return;
```

The procedure does the following:

- It defines two local variables. One is for the NDS statement value, and the other is for the output string from the NDS statement.

- It builds the NDS statement with an anonymous-block PL/SQL program. This uses a BULK COLLECT INTO statement. The bulk collect assigns the result to the :col_val bind variable.

- It executes the NDS statement value and the USING clause to receive the value from the NDS statement execution.

- It prints an output title and a line break.

■ It uses a for-loop to print the returned values, which in this case will always be one returned value.

The following enables you to test the `multiple_row_return` procedure:

```
-- Available online as part of nds_sql_02.sql
BEGIN

  -- Print line break.
  dbms_output.put_line(nds_tutorial.dline);

  -- Run dynamic DQL against table.
  nds_tutorial.single_row_return(:table_name
                                ,:column_name1
                                ,:column_name2
                                ,:column_name3);

  -- Print line break.
  dbms_output.put_line(nds_tutorial.dline);

  -- Drop table.
  nds_tutorial.drop_table(:table_name);

  -- Print line break.
  dbms_output.put_line(nds_tutorial.dline);

END;
/
```

The program does the following:

■ It prints a line break.

■ It calls the `nds_tutorial.multiple_row_return` procedure with bind variables set in an earlier program unit. You should check the online script to see how the bind variables work.

■ It prints a line break.

■ It calls the `nds_tutorial.drop_table` procedure with a bind variable set in an earlier program unit. You should check the online script to see how the bind variables work.

■ It prints a line break.

It will generate the following output:

```
-- Available online as output from dns_sql_02.sql
=============================================================
-> nds_tutorial.single_row_return
-------------------------------
Value from COLUMN_VALUE <1>
Value from COLUMN_VALUE <Hello World>
Value from COLUMN_VALUE <PLSQL>
=============================================================
=============================================================
-> nds_tutorial.drop_table
-------------------------------
Dropped Table <TEST_MESSAGES>
=============================================================
```

The first example returned only a single row because there was only one row. You saw how the mechanics of the BULK COLLECT worked in NDS. The following nds_sql_03.sql example provides another example, returning multiple columns into varray data types.

The procedure does the following:

```
-- Available online as part of nds_sql.sql
   -- Procedure demonstrates multiple row with columns DQL.
   PROCEDURE multiple_row_return
     ( table_name     VARCHAR2
     , column_name1   VARCHAR2
     , column_name2   VARCHAR2
     , column_name3   VARCHAR2 ) IS

     -- Define local Native Dynamic SQL variables.
     statement                VARCHAR2(2000);
     cvalue_out1              CARD_NAME_VARRAY;
     cvalue_out2              CARD_SUIT_VARRAY;
     nvalue_out               CARD_NUMBER_VARRAY;

   BEGIN

     -- Build dynamic SQL statement.
     statement := 'BEGIN '
               || 'SELECT '
               ||  column_name1 ||','
               ||  column_name2 ||','
               ||  column_name3 ||' '
               || 'BULK COLLECT INTO :col1, :col2, :col3 '
               || 'FROM '|| table_name ||';'
               || 'END;';

     -- Execute native dynamic SQL.
```

```
EXECUTE IMMEDIATE statement
  USING OUT nvalue_out, OUT cvalue_out1, cvalue_out2;

  -- Print module name message.
  dbms_output.put_line('-> nds_tutorial.multiple_row_return');

  -- Print line break.
  dbms_output.put_line(sline);

  FOR i IN 1..nvalue_out.COUNT LOOP

    -- Print data output.
    dbms_output.put_line(
      'Value from ['||column_name1||'] '||
      'is: ['||nvalue_out(i)||']');
    dbms_output.put_line(
      'Value from ['||column_name1||'] '||
      'is: ['||SUBSTR(cvalue_out1(i),1,20)||']');
    dbms_output.put_line(
      'Value from ['||column_name1||'] '||
      'is: ['||SUBSTR(cvalue_out2(i),1,30)||']');

  END LOOP;

END multiple_row_return;
```

The procedure does the following:

- It defines two local variables. One is for the NDS statement value, and the other is for the output string from the NDS statement.

- It builds the NDS statement with an anonymous-block PL/SQL program. This uses a BULK COLLECT INTO statement. The bulk collect assigns the result to :col1, :col2, and :col3 bind variables.

- It executes the NDS statement value and the USING clause to receive the value from the NDS statement execution. Each variable in the USING clause has an OUT mode specified. The OUT mode must be specified because the default mode is IN. If the default mode is used, you will raise an ORA-06536 error.

- It prints an output title and line break.

- It uses a for-loop to print the returned values, which in this case will always be one returned value.

You can test it with the following program:

-- Available online as part of nds_sql_03.sql
```
BEGIN

    -- Print line break.
    dbms_output.put_line(nds_tutorial.dline);

    -- Run dynamic DQL against table.
    nds_tutorial.multiple_row_return(:table_name
                                    ,:column_name1
                                    ,:column_name2
                                    ,:column_name3);

    -- Print line break.
    dbms_output.put_line(nds_tutorial.dline);

    -- Print line break.
    dbms_output.put_line(nds_tutorial.dline);

    -- Drop table.
    nds_tutorial.drop_table(:table_name);

    -- Print line break.
    dbms_output.put_line(nds_tutorial.dline);

END;
/
```

It provides the following output:

-- Available online as output from nds_sql_03.sql
```
============================================================
-> nds_tutorial.multiple_row_return
-------------------------------
Value from [TEST_MESSAGE_ID] is: [1]
Value from [TEST_MESSAGE_ID] is: [Hello World!]
Value from [TEST_MESSAGE_ID] is: [PLSQL]
Value from [TEST_MESSAGE_ID] is: [2]
Value from [TEST_MESSAGE_ID] is: [Hello Universe!]
Value from [TEST_MESSAGE_ID] is: [PLSQL]
============================================================
```

You should note that the OUT mode is specified for each BULK COLLECT target variable. If you fail to designate the mode for each of the variables, you will raise an exception. For example, you can use nds_sqle.sql to create another version of the `nds_tutorial` package. It will remove the OUT mode from one of the variables in the `multiple_row_return` procedure, raising the following exception when you run `nds_sql_03.sql`:

```
-- Available online as output from nds_sql_03.sql
BEGIN
*
ERROR at line 1:
ORA-06536: IN bind variable bound to an OUT position
ORA-06512: at "PLSQL.NDS_TUTORIAL", line 684
ORA-06512: at line 7
```

NDS does not manage NULL values. *You* must manage NULL values. The following provides you with a working example:

```
-- Available online as part of nds_null.sql
DECLARE

  -- Declare a variable and do not initialize it.
  null_value    VARCHAR2(1);

BEGIN

  -- Use NDS to select nothing into a bind variable.
  EXECUTE IMMEDIATE 'BEGIN SELECT null INTO :out FROM DUAL; END;'
  USING OUT null_value;

  -- Print the output message.
  dbms_output.put_line('Null is ['||null_value||']');

END;
/
```

The program does three things:

- It declares a variable but does not initialize it.
- It executes native dynamic SQL against a PL/SQL block.
- It prints the output message.

If you remove the PL/SQL block delimiters, you will raise the following exception:

```
DECLARE
*
ERROR at line 1:
```

```
ORA-00911: invalid character
ORA-06512: at line 7
```

You have now covered NDS. You have found it is a powerful facility with a few quirks related to bulk processing. You will now work with the DBMS_SQL built-in.

Working with the Oracle DBMS_SQL Built-in Package

Oracle introduced the DBMS_SQL built-in package in Oracle 7. It provided a means to store object code in the database that would dynamically build SQL statements, and it innovated a solution around the object validation phase of PL/SQL compilation. Prior to DBMS_SQL, you could not store a SQL statement unless the table existed with the same definition.

DBMS_SQL was enhanced to facilitate collections in Oracle 8*i*. It has grown to a considerable size. The built-in provides a number of overloaded procedures. If you were to do run a describe command on the DBMS_SQL package, you would find a copy of each of these overloaded procedures for the types listed. Table 13-2 lists the DBMS_SQL procedures, with types of scalar and nested table variables in the types column.

DBMS_SQL still has a major feature that is not delivered in NDS. It does not need to know beforehand the number and types of arguments it will receive and process. This feature is available because of two procedures, DESCRIBE_COLUMNS and DESCRIBE_COLUMNS2.

Like the NDS approach, DBMS_SQL supports string concatenation and bind variables. If you need a refresh on bind variables, please check Chapter 3.

Unlike NDS, the DBMS_SQL package requires explicit grants. For example, you have to grant execute permission on DBMS_SYS_SQL to the SYSTEM account with GRANT OPTION from the SYSDBA account. Another security caveat of the DBMS_SQL package is that some privileges must be directly granted as opposed to being provisioned by roles. If there is a missing privilege, you will raise the following exception:

```
ORA-01031: insufficient privileges
```

Both the dns_tutorial and the dbms_sql_tutorial are designed to have the same procedure specifications. However, the internals of each procedure are different. You will now work through DBMS_SQL examples with and without bind variables. You will also cover how to use DQL using DBMS_SQL.

Function or Procedure	Formal Parameters	Formal Data Types	Mode	Types
BIND_ARRAY	C	NUMBER(38)	IN	BINARY FILE LOB
	NAME	NAME	IN	BINARY_FLOAT
	\<Table Name>	\<Nested Table>	IN	BINARY_DOUBLE
				BLOB
				CLOB
				DATE
				INTERVAL YEAR TO MONTH
				INTERVAL DAY TO SECOND
				NUMBER
				ROWID
				TIME
				TIME W/TIME ZONE
				TIMESTAMP
				TIMESTAMP W/TIME ZONE
				VARCHAR2(2000)
BIND_ARRAY	C	NUMBER(38)	IN	BINARY FILE LOB
	NAME	NAME	IN	BINARY_FLOAT
	\<Table Name>	\<Nested Table>	IN	BINARY_DOUBLE
	INDEX1	NUMBER(38)	IN	BLOB
	INDEX2	NUMBER(38)	IN	CLOB
				DATE
				INTERVAL YEAR TO MONTH
				INTERVAL DAY TO SECOND
				NUMBER
				ROWID
				TIME
				TIME W/TIME ZONE
				TIMESTAMP
				TIMESTAMP W/TIME ZONE
				VARCHAR2(2000)

TABLE 13-2. *DBMS_SQL Procedures*

Function or Procedure	Formal Parameters	Formal Data Types	Mode	Types
BIND_VALUE	C NAME VALUE	NUMBER(38) VARCHAR2 <Types>	IN IN IN	BINARY FILE LOB BINARY_FLOAT BINARY_DOUBLE BLOB CHAR CLOB DATE INTERVAL YEAR TO MONTH INTERVAL DAY TO SECOND NUMBER RAW ROWID TIME TIME W/TIME ZONE TIMESTAMP TIMESTAMP W/TIME ZONE VARCHAR2(2000)
BIND_VALUE	C NAME VALUE OUT_VALUE_SIZE	NUMBER(38) NAME <Nested Table> NUMBER(38)	IN IN IN IN	CHAR NUMBER RAW VARCHAR2
CLOSE_CURSOR	C	NUMBER(38)	IN/OUT	
COLUMN_VALUE	C POSITION VALUE	NUMBER(38) NUMBER(38) <Type>	IN IN OUT	BINARY FILE LOB BINARY_FLOAT BINARY_DOUBLE BLOB CLOB DATE INTERVAL YEAR TO MONTH INTERVAL DAY TO SECOND NUMBER ROWID TIME TIME W/TIME ZONE TIMESTAMP TIMESTAMP W/TIME ZONE VARCHAR2

TABLE 13-2. *DBMS_SQL Procedures* (continued)

Function or Procedure	Formal Parameters	Formal Data Types	Mode	Types
COLUMN_VALUE	C	NUMBER(38)	IN	BINARY FILE LOB
	NAME	NUMBER(38)	IN	BINARY_FLOAT
	\<Table Name>	\<Nested Type>	IN	BINARY_DOUBLE
				BLOB
				CLOB
				DATE
				INTERVAL YEAR TO MONTH
				INTERVAL DAY TO SECOND
				NUMBER
				ROWID
				TIME
				TIME W/TIME ZONE
				TIMESTAMP
				TIMESTAMP W/TIME ZONE
				VARCHAR2
COLUMN_VALUE	C	NUMBER(38)	IN	DATE
	NAME	NUMBER(38)	IN	NUMBER
	VALUE	\<Type>	OUT	VARCHAR2
	COLUMN_ERROR	NUMBER	OUT	
	ACTUAL_LENGTH	NUMBER(38)	OUT	
COLUMN_VALUE_CHAR	C	NUMBER(38)	IN	CHAR
	POSITION	NUMBER(38)	IN	
	VALUE	\<Type>	OUT	
COLUMN_VALUE_CHAR	C	NUMBER(38)	IN	CHAR
	POSITION	NUMBER(38)	IN	
	VALUE	\<Type>	OUT	
	COLUMN_ERROR	NUMBER	OUT	
	ACTUAL_LENGTH	NUMBER(38)	OUT	
COLUMN_VALUE_LONG	C	NUMBER(38)	IN	LONG
	POSITION	NUMBER(38)	IN	
	OFFSET	NUMBER(38)	IN	
	VALUE	NUMBER(38)	IN	
	VALUE_LENGTH	VARCHAR2	OUT	
	ACTUAL_LENGTH	NUMBER(38)	OUT	

TABLE 13-2. *DBMS_SQL Procedures* (continued)

Function or Procedure	Formal Parameters	Formal Data Types	Mode	Types
COLUMN_ VALUE_RAW	C POSITION VALUE	NUMBER(38) NUMBER(38) NUMBER	IN IN OUT	RAW
COLUMN_ VALUE_RAW	C POSITION VALUE COLUMN_ ERROR ACTUAL_ LENGTH	NUMBER(38) NUMBER(38) NUMBER NUMBER NUMBER(38)	IN IN OUT OUT OUT	RAW
COLUMN_ VALUE_ROWID	C POSITION VALUE	NUMBER(38) NUMBER(38) NUMBER	IN IN OUT	ROWID
COLUMN_ VALUE_ROWID	C POSITION VALUE COLUMN_ ERROR ACTUAL_ LENGTH	NUMBER(38) NUMBER(38) NUMBER NUMBER NUMBER(38)	IN IN OUT OUT OUT	ROWID
DEFINE_ ARRAY	C POSITION \<Table Name> COLUMN_ ERROR LOWER_ BOUND	NUMBER(38) NUMBER(38) \<Nested Table> NUMBER(38) NUMBER(38)	IN IN IN IN IN	BINARY FILE LOB BINARY_FLOAT BINARY_DOUBLE BLOB CLOB DATE INTERVAL YEAR TO MONTH INTERVAL DAY TO SECOND NUMBER ROWID TIME TIME W/TIME ZONE TIMESTAMP TIMESTAMP W/TIME ZONE VARCHAR2

TABLE 13-2. *DBMS_SQL Procedures* (continued)

Function or Procedure	Formal Parameters	Formal Data Types	Mode	Types
DEFINE_ COLUMN	C POSITION COLUMN	NUMBER(38) NUMBER(38) \<Type>	IN IN IN	BINARY FILE LOB BINARY_FLOAT BINARY_DOUBLE BLOB CLOB DATE INTERVAL YEAR TO MONTH INTERVAL DAY TO SECOND NUMBER ROWID TIME TIME W/TIME ZONE TIMESTAMP TIMESTAMP W/TIME ZONE VARCHAR2
DEFINE_ VALUE_CHAR	C POSITION COLUMN COLUMN_ SIZE	NUMBER(38) NUMBER(38) CHAR NUMBER(38)	IN IN IN IN	CHAR
DEFINE_ VALUE_LONG	C POSITION	NUMBER(38) NUMBER(38)	IN IN	LONG
DEFINE_ VALUE_RAW	C POSITION COLUMN COLUMN_ SIZE	NUMBER(38) NUMBER(38) RAW NUMBER(38)	IN IN IN IN	RAW
DEFINE_ VALUE_ROWID	C POSITION COLUMN	NUMBER(38) NUMBER(38) ROWID	IN IN IN	ROWID

TABLE 13-2. *DBMS_SQL Procedures* (continued)

Function or Procedure	Formal Parameters	Formal Data Types	Mode	Types
DESCRIBE_ COLUMNS	C COL_CNT DESC_T	NUMBER(38) NUMBER(38) <Nested Table>	IN OUT OUT	BINARY FILE LOB BINARY_FLOAT BINARY_DOUBLE BLOB CLOB DATE INTERVAL YEAR TO MONTH INTERVAL DAY TO SECOND NUMBER ROWID TIME TIME W/TIME ZONE TIMESTAMP TIMESTAMP W/TIME ZONE VARCHAR2
DESCRIBE_ COLUMNS2	C COL_CNT DESC_T	NUMBER(38) NUMBER(38) <Nested Table>	IN OUT OUT	BINARY FILE LOB BINARY_FLOAT BINARY_DOUBLE BLOB CLOB DATE INTERVAL YEAR TO MONTH INTERVAL DAY TO SECOND NUMBER ROWID TIME TIME W/TIME ZONE TIMESTAMP TIMESTAMP W/TIME ZONE VARCHAR2

TABLE 13-2. *DBMS_SQL Procedures* (continued)

Function or Procedure	Formal Parameters	Formal Data Types	Mode	Types
EXECUTE	C	NUMBER(38)	IN	RETURNS INTEGER
EXECUTE_ AND_FETCH	C EXACT	NUMBER(38) BOOLEAN	IN IN	RETURNS INTEGER
FETCH_ROWS	C	NUMBER(38)	IN	RETURNS INTEGER
IS_OPEN	C	NUMBER(38)	IN	RETURNS INTEGER
LAST_ERROR_ POSITION				RETURNS INTEGER
LAST_ROW_ COUNT				RETURNS INTEGER
LAST_ROW_ID				RETURNS INTEGER
LAST_SQL_ FUNCTION_ CODE				RETURNS INTEGER
OPEN_CURSOR				RETURNS INTEGER
PARSE	C STATEMENT LANGUAGE_ FLAG	NUMBER(38) VARCHAR2 NUMBER(38)	IN IN IN	VARCHAR2
PARSE	C STATEMENT LB UB LFFLG LANGUAGE_ FLAG	NUMBER(38) <Nested Table> NUMBER(38) NUMBER(38) BOOLEAN NUMBER(38)	IN IN IN IN IN IN	VARCHAR2(256) VARCHAR2(32767)

TABLE 13-2. *DBMS_SQL Procedures* (continued)

Function or Procedure	Formal Parameters	Formal Data Types	Mode	Types
VARIABLE_ VALUE	C NAME VALUE	NUMBER(38) VARCHAR2 <Type>	IN IN IN	BINARY FILE LOB BINARY_FLOAT BINARY_DOUBLE BLOB CHAR CLOB DATE INTERVAL YEAR TO MONTH INTERVAL DAY TO SECOND NUMBER RAW ROWID TIME TIME W/TIME ZONE TIMESTAMP TIMESTAMP W/TIME ZONE VARCHAR2
VARIABLE_ VALUE	C NAME VALUE	NUMBER(38) VARCHAR2 <Type>	IN IN IN	BINARY FILE LOB BINARY_FLOAT BINARY_DOUBLE BLOB CLOB DATE INTERVAL YEAR TO MONTH INTERVAL DAY TO SECOND NUMBER RAW ROWID TIME TIME W/TIME ZONE TIMESTAMP TIMESTAMP W/TIME ZONE VARCHAR2(2000)

TABLE 13-2. *DBMS_SQL Procedures* (continued)

Working with DDL and DML Without Bind Variables

DBMS_SQL supports string concatenation much like NDS. The key difference is that a number of additional steps are required to implement a simple procedure. You will now work with an alternative to the earlier nds_sql.create_sequence procedure. The following dbms_sql.create_sequence procedure should look familiar:

```
-- Available online as part of dbms_sql.sql
PROCEDURE create_sequence
  ( sequence_name          IN      VARCHAR2) IS

  -- Define local DBMS_SQL variables.
  c               INTEGER := dbms_sql.open_cursor;
  fdbk            INTEGER;
  statement       VARCHAR2(2000);

  -- Define a local function to find sequence.
  FUNCTION verify_not_sequence
    ( sequence_name_in     IN      VARCHAR2)
  RETURN BOOLEAN IS

    -- Defines default return value.
    retval                 BOOLEAN := TRUE;

    -- Cursor returns a single row when finding a sequence.
    CURSOR find_sequence IS
      SELECT   null
      FROM     user_objects
      WHERE    object_name = sequence_name_in;

  BEGIN

    -- Sets the Boolean when a sequence is found.
    FOR i IN find_sequence LOOP
      retval := FALSE;
    END LOOP;

    -- Return Boolean state.
    RETURN retval;

  END verify_not_sequence;
```

```
BEGIN

   -- If sequence does not exist create it.
   IF verify_not_sequence(sequence_name) = TRUE THEN

      -- Build dynamic SQL statement.
      statement := 'CREATE SEQUENCE '||sequence_name||CHR(10)
                || '   INCREMENT BY   1'            ||CHR(10)
                || '   START WITH     1'            ||CHR(10)
                || '   CACHE          20'           ||CHR(10)
                || '   ORDER';

      -- Parse and execute the statement.
      dbms_sql.parse(c,statement,dbms_sql.native);
      fdbk := dbms_sql.execute(c);

      -- Close the open cursor.
      dbms_sql.close_cursor(c);

      -- Print module name message.
      dbms_output.put_line(
        '-> dbms_sql_tutorial.create_sequence');

      -- Print line break.
      dbms_output.put_line(sline);

      -- Print the output message.
      dbms_output.put_line(
        'Created Sequence <'||sequence_name||'>');

   ELSE

      -- Print module name message.
      dbms_output.put_line(
        '-> dbms_sql_tutorial.create_sequence');

      -- Print line break.
      dbms_output.put_line(sline);

      -- Print the output message.
      dbms_output.put_line(
        'Sequence <'||sequence_name||'> already exists');

   END IF;

END create_sequence;
```

The procedure does the following:

- It defines a procedure that takes a single formal parameter of `sequence_name`.

- It defines a local `statement` variable. The `statement` variable is used as the argument to a `DBMS_SQL.PARSE` procedure call.

- It defines two variables required for DBMS_SQL. One is `fdbk`, or the feedback variable, and the other is `c`, or the cursor variable.

- It defines a local `verify_not_sequence` function. The function takes a sequence name and checks whether it exists.

- An if-then-else statement uses the `verify_not_sequence` function to check if a sequence does not exist. It does the following if true:

  - It assigns a concatenated static string with the actual parameter `sequence_name`.

  - It uses `DBMS_SQL.PARSE` with three arguments. The first is `c`, which is the cursor number. Second is the `statement` variable, which is the DDL or DML statement. Third is the type of DBMS_SQL environment constant.

  - It uses `DBMS_SQL.EXECUTE` with the cursor number to run the DDL or DML statement.

  - It uses `DBMS_SQL.CLOSE_CURSOR` to close the open cursor.

  - It prints a module name.

  - It prints a line break.

  - It prints the success message with the sequence name.

If the function returns false, the sequence exists, and it prints a failure message to the console.

You can use the following to test the `dbms_tutorial.create_sequence` procedure:

```
-- Available online as part of dbms_sql_01.sql
DECLARE

  -- Define local variables.
  value_in          VARCHAR2(30) := 'TESTING_S1';
  value_out         NUMBER;

BEGIN
```

```
-- Break output stream.
dbms_output.put_line(dbms_sql_tutorial.dline);

-- Test create sequence.
dbms_sql_tutorial.create_sequence(value_in);

-- Break output stream.
dbms_output.put_line(dbms_sql_tutorial.dline);

-- Loop six times.
FOR i IN 1..3 LOOP

  -- Test increment_sequence procedure.
  dbms_sql_tutorial.increment_sequence(value_in,value_out);

END LOOP;

-- Print line break.
dbms_output.put_line(dbms_sql_tutorial.dline);

-- Drop the sequence.
dbms_sql_tutorial.drop_sequence(value_in);

-- Print line break.
dbms_output.put_line(dbms_sql_tutorial.dline);

END;
/
```

The program does the following:

- It defines two local variables, assigning the first a TESTING_S1 value. The second is used later in the program as an output variable.

- It prints a double line break.

- It prints the results of dbms_sql_tutorial.create_sequence.

- It prints a double line break.

- It uses a for-loop to call the increment_sequence procedure three times and print a line break.

- It prints a double line break.

- It calls the drop_sequence procedure.

- It prints a double line break.

It generates the following output:

```
-- Available online as output from dbms_sql_01.sql
=========================================================
-> dbms_sql_tutorial.create_sequence
----------------------------
Created Sequence <TESTING_S1>
=========================================================
Sequence <TESTING_S1> Value <1>
Sequence <TESTING_S1> Value <2>
Sequence <TESTING_S1> Value <3>
=========================================================
-> dbms_sql_tutorial.drop_sequence
----------------------------
Dropped Sequence <TESTING_S1>
=========================================================
```

As you can see, NDS and DBMS_SQL perform much the same. Unfortunately, there is a lot more syntax to manage with DBMS_SQL. Now you will see a comparative version of a bulk insert using DBMS_SQL.

Working with DML and a Known List of Bind Variables

Oracle 8*i* introduced additional procedures to the DBMS_SQL package. These enabled programmers to do bulk collections. They are limited in Oracle 10*g* to associative arrays that are indexed by BINARY_INTEGER values. As discussed previously, DBMS_SQL has no support for user-defined types.

There are four poorly documented errors that can occur when using DBMS_SQL. They are qualified in Table 13-3.

Error Message	Description
ORA-06502: PL/SQL: numeric or value error	An explicit size is required for CHAR, RAW, and VARCHAR2 variables. The overloaded procedure has an output size variable in the fourth position that you need to use.
PLS-00049: bad bind variable	A bad bind variable message means the identifier is outside of the expected SQL data type, like a NUMBER or VARCHAR2 string. When this happens, the bind variable is treated as an undefined session-level variable.

TABLE 13-3. *Errors That Can Occur When Using DBMS_SQL*

Error Message	Description
ORA-00928: missing SELECT keyword	This can occur on an insert statement when you put bind variables into the INTO clause for column names.
ORA-01006: bind variable does not exist	This can happen when you have quote marks around VARCHAR2 bind variables; you may raise the "bind variable does not exist" error. If you need to use that syntax, you can encapsulate the DML in a PLSQL wrapper.

TABLE 13-3. *Errors That Can Occur When Using DBMS_SQL* (continued)

A single row return and table insert can be done with dbms_sql_02.sql. The following DML procedure with bind variables illustrates a bulk insert:

```
-- Available online as part of dbms_sql.sql
PROCEDURE inserts_into_table
  ( table_name               IN      VARCHAR2
  , table_column_values1     IN      DBMS_SQL.NUMBER_TABLE
  , table_column_values2     IN      DBMS_SQL.VARCHAR2_TABLE
  , table_column_values3     IN      DBMS_SQL.VARCHAR2_TABLE) IS

  -- Define local DBMS_SQL variables.
  c                          INTEGER := dbms_sql.open_cursor;
  fdbk                       INTEGER;
  statement                  VARCHAR2(2000);

  -- Define a local function to ensure table does exist.
  FUNCTION verify_table
    ( object_name_in         IN      VARCHAR2)
  RETURN BOOLEAN IS

    -- Defines default return value.
    retval                   BOOLEAN := FALSE;

    -- Cursor returns a single row when finding a table.
    CURSOR find_object IS
      SELECT   null
      FROM     user_objects
      WHERE    object_name = object_name_in;

  BEGIN

    -- The for-loop sets the Boolean when a table is found.
```

```
      FOR i IN find_object LOOP
        retval := TRUE;
      END LOOP;

      -- Return Boolean state.
      RETURN retval;

   END verify_table;

BEGIN

   -- If table exists insert into it.
   IF verify_table(table_name) = TRUE THEN

      -- Build dynamic SQL statement.
      statement := 'INSERT '
                || 'INTO '||table_name||' '
                || '( card_number '
                || ', card_name '
                || ', card_suit)'
                || 'VALUES '
                || '( :card_number'
                || ', :card_name'
                || ', :card_suit)';

      -- Parse the statement.
      dbms_sql.parse(c,statement,dbms_sql.native);

      -- Bind each bind variable.
      dbms_sql.bind_array(c,'card_number',table_column_values1);
      dbms_sql.bind_array(c,'card_name',table_column_values2);
      dbms_sql.bind_array(c,'card_suit',table_column_values3);

      -- Execute the dynamic statement.
      fdbk := dbms_sql.execute(c);

      -- Print the number of rows inserted.
      dbms_output.put_line('Inserted ['||fdbk||'].');

      -- Close the open cursor.
      dbms_sql.close_cursor(c);

      -- Commit the records.
      commit;

      -- Print module name message.
      dbms_output.put_line('-> dbms_sql_tutorial.inserts_into_table');
```

```
-- Print line break.
dbms_output.put_line(sline);

-- Use a for-loop to print values.
FOR i IN 1..table_column_values1.COUNT LOOP

  -- Print output message.
  dbms_output.put_line(
    'Value inserted <'||table_column_values1(i)||'>');
  dbms_output.put_line(
    'Value inserted <'||table_column_values2(i)||'>');
  dbms_output.put_line(
    'Value inserted <'||table_column_values3(i)||'>');

END LOOP;

ELSE

  -- Print module name message.
  dbms_output.put_line(
    '-> dbms_sql_tutorial.inserts_into_table');

  -- Print line break.
  dbms_output.put_line(sline);

  -- Print output message.
  dbms_output.put_line(
    'Object <'||table_name||'> does not exist');

END IF;

END inserts_into_table;
```

The procedure does the following:

■ It defines a procedure that takes four formal parameters. One is a VARCHAR2 used to map to the table name. The other three are variable types defined in the DBMS_SQL package.

■ It defines a local statement variable. The statement variable is used as the argument to a DBMS_SQL.PARSE procedure call.

■ It defines two variables required for DBMS_SQL. One is fdbk, or the feedback variable, and the other is c, or the cursor variable.

■ It defines a local verify_table function. The function takes a table name and checks whether it exists.

■ An if-then-else statement uses the `verify_table` function to check if a table exists. It does the following if true:

   ■ It assigns a concatenated static string with the actual parameter `sequence_name`.

   ■ It uses `DBMS_SQL.PARSE` with three arguments. The first is `c`, which is the cursor number. Second is the `statement` variable, which is the DDL or DML statement. Third is the type of DBMS_SQL environment constant.

   ■ It uses `DBMS_SQL.BIND_ARRAY` to bind the Oracle 10g associative arrays to the internal bind variables.

   ■ It uses `DBMS_SQL.EXECUTE` with the cursor number to run the DDL or DML statement.

   ■ It prints the number of rows captured by the `fdbk` (feedback) integer.

   ■ It uses `DBMS_SQL.CLOSE_CURSOR` to close the open cursor.

   ■ It prints a module name.

   ■ It prints a line break.

   ■ It uses a for-loop to print the success message with the row values retrieved.

If the function returns false, the table does exist, and it prints a failure message to the console.

Unfortunately, to test this bulk insert requires a long test script. You can test it by using the following:

```
-- Available online as part of dbms_sql_03.sql
-- Set bind variable to pass table name.
VARIABLE table_name    VARCHAR2(30)
VARIABLE column_name1 VARCHAR2(30)
VARIABLE column_name2 VARCHAR2(30)
VARIABLE column_name3 VARCHAR2(30)

DECLARE

  -- Define a nested tables.
  TYPE card_number_table IS TABLE OF NUMBER
                              INDEX BY BINARY_INTEGER;
  TYPE card_name_table   IS TABLE OF VARCHAR2(2000)
                              INDEX BY BINARY_INTEGER;
  TYPE card_suit_table   IS TABLE OF VARCHAR2(2000)
```

```
                       INDEX BY BINARY_INTEGER;

  -- Declare and initialize a nested table with three rows.
  card_numbers CARD_NUMBER_TABLE;
  card_names   CARD_NAME_TABLE;
  card_suits   CARD_SUIT_TABLE;

  -- Define local variables.
  column_name1          VARCHAR2(30)  := 'CARD_NUMBER';
  column_name2          VARCHAR2(30)  := 'CARD_NAME';
  column_name3          VARCHAR2(30)  := 'CARD_SUIT';
  table_name_in         VARCHAR2(30)     := 'CARD_DECK';
  table_definition_in   VARCHAR2(2000);
  table_column_value1   DBMS_SQL.NUMBER_TABLE;
  table_column_value2   DBMS_SQL.VARCHAR2_TABLE;
  table_column_value3   DBMS_SQL.VARCHAR2_TABLE;

BEGIN

  -- Assign table name to bind variable.
  :table_name    := table_name_in;
  :column_name1 := column_name1;
  :column_name2 := column_name2;
  :column_name3 := column_name3;

  -- Initialize the card numbers;
  FOR i IN 1..13 LOOP
    card_numbers(i) := i;
  END LOOP;

  -- Initialize the care names.
  card_names(1)   := 'Ace';
  card_names(2)   := 'Two';
  card_names(3)   := 'Three';
  card_names(4)   := 'Four';
  card_names(5)   := 'Five';
  card_names(6)   := 'Six';
  card_names(7)   := 'Seven';
  card_names(8)   := 'Eight';
  card_names(9)   := 'Nine';
  card_names(10) := 'Ten';
  card_names(11) := 'Jack';
  card_names(12) := 'Queen';
  card_names(13) := 'King';

  -- Initialize the card suits.
  card_suits(1)   := 'Spades';
  card_suits(2)   := 'Hearts';
```

```
  card_suits(3)   := 'Diamonds';
  card_suits(4)   := 'Clubs';
  card_suits(5)   := 'Spades';
  card_suits(6)   := 'Hearts';
  card_suits(7)   := 'Diamonds';
  card_suits(8)   := 'Clubs';
  card_suits(9)   := 'Spades';
  card_suits(10)  := 'Hearts';
  card_suits(11)  := 'Diamonds';
  card_suits(12)  := 'Clubs';
  card_suits(13)  := 'Spades';

  -- Assign card numbers in a for-loop.
  FOR i IN CARD_NUMBERS.FIRST..CARD_NUMBERS.LAST LOOP
    table_column_value1(i) := card_numbers(i);
  END LOOP;

  -- Assign card names in a for-loop.
  FOR i IN CARD_NAMES.FIRST..CARD_NAMES.LAST LOOP
    table_column_value2(i) := card_names(i);
  END LOOP;

  -- Assign card names in a for-loop.
  FOR i IN CARD_SUITS.FIRST..CARD_SUITS.LAST LOOP
    table_column_value3(i) := card_suits(i);
  END LOOP;

  -- Initialize table definition.
  table_definition_in := '('||column_name1||' NUMBER'            ||CHR(10)
                       || ','||column_name2||' VARCHAR2(2000)'||CHR(10)
                       || ','||column_name3||' VARCHAR2(2000))';

  -- Print the output.
  dbms_output.put_line(dbms_sql_tutorial.dline);
  dbms_sql_tutorial.create_table(table_name_in,table_definition_in);

  -- Insert into the table.
  dbms_output.put_line(dbms_sql_tutorial.dline);
  dbms_sql_tutorial.inserts_into_table( table_name_in
                                      , table_column_value1
                                      , table_column_value2
                                      , table_column_value3);
  dbms_output.put_line(dbms_sql_tutorial.dline);

END;
/

-- Set SQL*Plus environment formatting.
```

```
COL c1     FORMAT 999       HEADING "Test|Message|ID #"
COL c2     FORMAT A20       HEADING "Message Sent"
COL c3     FORMAT A30       HEADING "Reviewed By"

-- Select from the dynamically created table.
SELECT     card_number c1
,          card_name c2
,          card_suit c3
FROM       card_deck;

-- Use DBMS_SQL_TUTORIAL to drop the table.
BEGIN

  -- Run dynamic DQL against table.
  dbms_output.put_line(dbms_sql_tutorial.dline);
  dbms_sql_tutorial.multiple_row_return(:table_name
                                       ,:column_name1
                                       ,:column_name2
                                       ,:column_name3);
  dbms_output.put_line(dbms_sql_tutorial.dline);

  -- Drop table.
  dbms_output.put_line(dbms_sql_tutorial.dline);
  dbms_sql_tutorial.drop_table(:table_name);
  dbms_output.put_line(dbms_sql_tutorial.dline);

END;
/
```

The test program does the following:

- It defines four bind variables to share values across multiple program units in a session.

- It defines three associative arrays that are indexed by a BINARY_INTEGER.

- It defines local variables. These include a variable for the table name and variables for column names. Three variables for column inputs use DBMS_ SQL data types.

- It assigns the table and column names to the session-level bind variables.

- It uses a for-loop to populate the associative array of numbers.

- It manually assigns thirteen values to both of the VARCHAR2 associative arrays.

- It uses three for-loops to assign the associative array values to the DBMS_ SQL.NUMBER_TABLE and two DBMS_SQL.VARCHAR2_TABLE data types.

■ It assigns the table definition.

■ It prints a line break.

■ It creates a table by calling the `dbms_sql_tutorial.create_table` procedure.

■ It prints a line break.

■ It calls the `dbms_sql_tutorial.inserts_into_table` procedure and does a bulk insert into the table.

■ It prints a line break.

■ It runs a SQL command to print the contents of the table to the console.

■ It prints a line break.

■ It calls the `dbms_sql_tutorial.multiple_row_returns` procedure. The process of the `multiple_row_returns` procedure will be covered in the next section.

■ It prints a line break.

The shortened output looks like this:

```
-- Available online as output from dbms_sql_03.sql
============================================================
-> dbms_sql_tutorial.create_table
-----------------------------
Created Table <CARD_DECK>
============================================================
Inserted [13].
-> dbms_sql_tutorial.inserts_into_table
-----------------------------
Value inserted <1>
Value inserted <Ace>
Value inserted <Spades>
... shortened ...
Value inserted <13>
Value inserted <King>
Value inserted <Spades>
============================================================
    1 Ace                    Spades
... shortened ...
   13 King                   Spades
============================================================
-> dbms_sql_tutorial.multiple_row_return
-----------------------------
```

```
Value from [CARD_NUMBER] is: [1]
Value from [CARD_NUMBER] is: [Ace]
Value from [CARD_NUMBER] is: [Spades]
-> dbms_sql_tutorial.multiple_row_return
-------------------------------
... shortened ...
-------------------------------
Value from [CARD_NUMBER] is: [13]
Value from [CARD_NUMBER] is: [King]
Value from [CARD_NUMBER] is: [Spades]
===========================================================
===========================================================
        -> dbms_sql_tutorial.drop_table
-------------------------------
Dropped Table <CARD_DECK>
===========================================================
```

You have now seen how DBMS_SQL supports the same activity as NDS for bulk processing. It has substantially more complex syntax than NDS. In the next section, you will see the complexity of DQL using DBMS_SQL.

Working with DQL

The DBMS_SQL built-in supports DQL, but you rarely see it used. The rarity is probably related to its complexity.

TIP
The DBMS_SQL.DEFINE_COLUMN procedure presents a surprise if you are not careful. CHAR, RAW, and VARCHAR2 columns must specify a size argument. Failure to provide a size value will raise the following error:

```
PLS-00307: too many declarations of 'DEFINE_COLUMN' match this call
```

The following DQL procedure with bind variables illustrates a bulk collect:

```
-- Available online as part of dbms_sql.sql
PROCEDURE multiple_row_return
  ( table_name     VARCHAR2
  , column_name1   VARCHAR2
  , column_name2   VARCHAR2
  , column_name3   VARCHAR2 )IS

  - Define local DBMS_SQL variables.
  c                         INTEGER := dbms_sql.open_cursor;
```

```
        fdbk                        INTEGER;
        statement                   VARCHAR2(2000);
        cvalue_out1                 VARCHAR2(2000);
        cvalue_out2                 VARCHAR2(2000);
        nvalue_out                  NUMBER;

    BEGIN

        -- Build dynamic SQL statement.
        statement := 'SELECT '
                  ||    column_name1 ||','
                  ||    column_name2 ||','
                  ||    column_name3 ||' '
                  || 'FROM '|| table_name;

        -- Parse dynamic SQL statement.
        dbms_sql.parse(c,statement,dbms_sql.native);


        -- Define the column mapping to the value_out variable.
        dbms_sql.define_column(c,1,nvalue_out);
        dbms_sql.define_column(c,2,cvalue_out1,2000);
        dbms_sql.define_column(c,3,cvalue_out2,2000);

        -- Execute dynamic SQL statement.
        fdbk := dbms_sql.execute(c);

        -- Use a loop to read all rows.
        LOOP

          -- Exit when no more rows to fetch.
          EXIT WHEN dbms_sql.fetch_rows(c) = 0;

          -- Copy the contents of column #1 to the value_out variable.
          dbms_sql.column_value(c,1,nvalue_out);
          dbms_sql.column_value(c,2,cvalue_out1);
          dbms_sql.column_value(c,3,cvalue_out2);

          -- Print module name.
          dbms_output.put_line(
            '-> dbms_sql_tutorial.multiple_row_return');

          -- Print line break.
          dbms_output.put_line(sline);

          -- Print output message.
          dbms_output.put_line(
```

```
        'Value from ['||column_name1||'] '||
        'is: ['||nvalue_out||']');
    dbms_output.put_line(
        'Value from ['||column_name1||'] '||
        'is: ['||SUBSTR(cvalue_out1,1,5)||']');
    dbms_output.put_line(
        'Value from ['||column_name1||'] '||
        'is: ['||SUBSTR(cvalue_out2,1,8)||']');

  END LOOP;

  -- Close the open cursor.
  dbms_sql.close_cursor(c);

END multiple_row_return;
```

The procedure does the following:

- It defines five local variables. Three are for the DBMS_SQL statement, and three are to capture the output of the query.

- It builds the DBMS_SQL statement.

- It parses the `statement` value.

- It uses the `DBMS_SQL.DEFINE_COLUMN` procedure to map column values returned by the select statement to assignment target variables. The target variables are `nvalue_out`, `cvalue_out1`, and `cvalue_out2`.

- It executes the cursor.

- It uses a simple loop to read until `DBMS_SQL.FETCH_ROWS` returns a zero value. The zero value indicates that there are no more rows to read.

- It uses `DBMS_SQL.COLUMN_VALUE` to assign the columns of a row to the defined columns.

- It prints a module name.

- It prints a line break.

- It prints the columns of data.

- It closes the open cursor.

The `dbms_sql_03.sql` script tests the `multiple_row_return` procedure's functionality. It was reviewed in the preceding section, on DBMS_SQL DMLs. Please refer back to the prior section to review it.

You have now covered the DBMS_SQL DQL utility. It is time to summarize the chapter.

Summary

You have learned about the concepts of dynamic SQL, exploring features and approaches in Native Dynamic SQL (NDS) and DBMS_SQL. The presentation drew clear contrasts in coding approaches between the two techniques.

NDS is the simpler form and the future direction for dynamic SQL. DBMS_SQL is the standard for dynamic SQL and supports the dynamic marshaling of column descriptions. You should have gained an ability to read, understand, and use both dynamic SQL approaches.

CHAPTER
14

Introduction to Objects

upport for object-oriented programming (OOP) in PL/SQL began in version 8. Since then, enhancements including inheritance, attribute chaining, type evolution, and user-defined constructor methods have caught the eye of OOP enthusiasts and provided programmers with an alternative to traditional PL/SQL development. In this chapter, we introduce you to Oracle's OOP implementation in PL/SQL, describe enhancements in 9*i* and 10*g*, and discuss benefits and drawbacks of moving your application development to objects.

Introduction to Object-Oriented Programming

Mention object-oriented programming languages and Java and C++ generally come to mind. They have the greatest following in the OOP world and are known for their capability to simplify complex applications using a modular design. Object-oriented languages are designed to model real-world objects rather than focusing on their data sources. A non-OO programmer may be wondering what all the fuss is about. Well, imagine being able to model your application just like your business. Code can be easily reused by different parts of your application, and base objects you define can pass their features, or attributes, to related subobjects or subtypes.

In the publishing world, for example, there are authors, editors, bookstores, and a publisher all working together to release a book to market. Authors submit chapters to editors, and they accept or return chapters to the author for changes. Once these changes are accepted, the publisher releases the book. Bookstores determine books they wish to carry, track inventory and sales, and stock their shelves.

NOTE
Unless otherwise noted, the base release for this chapter is Oracle 9iR1, since this is where most of the complex object features were added.

Data and Procedural Abstraction

OOP takes the model we described and uses it directly in the application. The Object layer is used in application design instead of the lower-level data structures. Figure 14-1 illustrates the difference between the Object layer and the underlying data structures for a bookstore. Inventory, music, books, hard cover books, and soft cover books are all types of objects—abstract representations of the real-world objects.

The Object layer implements both data and procedural abstraction. The data is manipulated through object methods rather than directly by SQL, reducing the complexity of application development and maintenance.

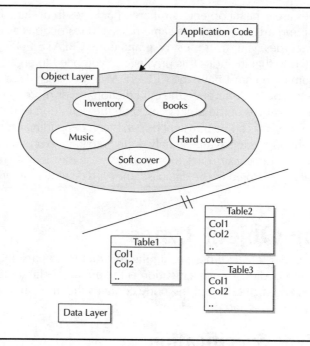

FIGURE 14-1.   *Object diagram*

Object Type Overview

An *object type* is the definition, or template, of an object, and not the object itself. Java and C++ programmers—when you hear object types, think classes! Object types, like classes, consist of attributes and methods. Attributes describe the object. A bookstore, for example, has a name, square footage, date opened, etc. Methods are the procedures and functions that represent the actions or behavior of the object.

Bookstore	
Attributes	Name Address SqFootage DateOpened Status
Methods	Increase_Inventory Change_Name Change_Status Change_SqFootage Change_Address

Object types are schema objects, similar to packages in design. They are owned by their creator and are subject to the same rules and restrictions as other objects. To create object types, your user must be granted the CREATE TYPE privilege or the RESOURCE role that includes this privilege. If you need to create object types in another schema, you must have the CREATE ANY TYPE privilege. As with other database objects, you can reference the data dictionary for more information.

At run time, instances of the object based on the definition of the object type are created. The objects can be transient or persistent, depending on how they were created. Transient objects are available only during program execution and are deleted when the program is done. Examples in this chapter are transient. Persistent objects, on the other hand, are stored in the database; they are dealt with in greater detail in Chapter 15.

Creating Object Types

As mentioned earlier, object types are similar in structure to packages. They have specifications and bodies. The specification is the public declaration of the object type's attributes and methods, and the body contains the implementation of the methods using functions and procedures.

Object Type Specification

The *specification* contains the attributes and forward declarations of the methods. Just as with packages, the specification is public, so attributes and method declarations are visible to the outside world. If a user has EXECUTE privileges on an object type, that user can modify the attributes of that type.

To create an object type specification, use the CREATE TYPE .. AS OBJECT statement using the following syntax:

```
CREATE [OR REPLACE] TYPE [schema.]type_name
 [AUTHID {CURRENT_USER|DEFINER} ] AS OBJECT (
 attribute1 datatype,
 [attribute2 datatype,]
 [method1]
 [method2]);
/
```

AUTHID indicates that the methods will be executed using the privilege set of the CURRENT_USER or DEFINER as defined at creation time. CURRENT_USER is the user calling the method, and DEFINER is the owner.

Let's take a look at a bookstore example. Our bookstore carries all kinds of inventory, including books, music, magazines, etc. With this wide variety of items, an object type created for inventory can handle only a few attributes in order to remain a generic inventory object. The areas in common among these different types of objects are the number of items in stock, the reorder status, and the price of the item. We include these three attributes of inventory, along with the unique `item_id`, in our specification. See the following definition of the *inventory_obj* object type specification:

```
-- Available online as part of Inheritance.sql
CREATE OR REPLACE TYPE inventory_obj AS OBJECT (
    item_id         NUMBER(10),
    num_in_stock    NUMBER(10),
    reorder_status  VARCHAR2(20),
    price           NUMBER(10,2),
...
);
/
```

Attributes

Attribute declarations are similar to variable declarations. There are a few restrictions, however:

- Attributes *must* be listed prior to methods. Including methods before all attributes are listed results in the following exception:

  ```
  PLS-00311: the declaration of "OBJECT_NAME" is incomplete or malformed
  ```

- The datatype can be any database datatype except for ROWID, UROWID, LONG, LONG RAW, NCHAR, NCLOB, NVARCHAR2, any PL/SQL-specific type, or types defined inside a PL/SQL package. You *can* use any other built-in or user-defined datatype, or else another Object Type.

- Types available only in PL/SQL but not in the database are not allowed. These include BINARY_INTEGER, BOOLEAN, PLS_INTEGER, RECORD, and REF CURSOR.

- A NOT NULL constraint cannot be used, though a similar result can be obtained by using database triggers on instances of the object.

- At least one attribute *must* be listed.

- A DEFAULT value cannot be used.

One more restriction, but one with a caveat: %TYPE and %ROWTYPE cannot be applied directly to an attribute or object type. You can, however, apply them to an attribute of an object instance. How are these different? See the following example:

```
-- Available online as part of TypeAttribute.sql
-- This example works fine. %TYPE is applied
-- to the variable, not the object type directly.
DECLARE
```

```
      v_discount_price    discount_price_obj;
      v_price             v_discount_price.price%TYPE;
BEGIN
   NULL;
END;
/
PL/SQL procedure successfully completed.

-- This example throws an exception. %TYPE is applied
-- directly to the object type.
DECLARE
   v_price              discount_price_obj.price%TYPE;
BEGIN
   NULL;
END;
/
ORA-06550: line 3, column 22:
PLS-00206: %TYPE must be applied to a variable, column, field or attribute,
  not to "DISCOUNT_PRICE_OBJ.PRICE"
```

Complex Object Types   Complex object types can include another object type as
the datatype of an attribute. In our `inventory_obj` example we see the attribute
price has a datatype of number. For bookstore1, however, we want to discount the
price. We can accomplish this by nesting object types. The following example adds
a `discount_price_obj` and recreates the `inventory_obj` object type to
modify the price attribute's datatype:

```
-- Available online as part of ComplexObj.sql
CREATE OR REPLACE TYPE discount_price_obj AS OBJECT (
   discount_rate   NUMBER(10,4),
   price           NUMBER(10,2),

   MEMBER FUNCTION discount_price RETURN NUMBER)
INSTANTIABLE
FINAL;
/
```

Now recreate the `inventory_obj`, specifying `discount_price_obj` as
the datatype.

```
-- Available online as part of ComplexObj.sql
CREATE OR REPLACE TYPE inventory_obj AS OBJECT (
   item_id        NUMBER(10),
   num_in_stock   NUMBER(10),
   reorder_status VARCHAR2(20),
   price          DISCOUNT_PRICE_OBJ);
/
```

This method of nesting object types allows us to make complex object types from
other very basic types.

Character Semantics   The `inventory_obj.reorder_status` attribute has a string datatype of VARCHAR2(20). The precision of 20 is not a problem as long as we are working with single-byte characters, but if we support multibyte characters, this can become an issue. UTF-8 encoding supports characters up to three bytes if using supplementary characters, they take four bytes), so it is possible that a precision of 20 can support only six characters.

Oracle 9*i* and 10*g* provide a method of handling this issue, called character semantics. With a slight change in syntax, precision is based on number of characters, regardless of byte size. See the change in bold:

```
-- Available online as part of Inheritance.sql
CREATE OR REPLACE TYPE inventory_obj AS OBJECT (
    item_id         NUMBER(10),
    num_in_stock    NUMBER(10),
    reorder_status  VARCHAR2(20 CHAR),
    price           DISCOUNT_PRICE_OBJ,
...
);
/
```

Adding `CHAR` guarantees, regardless of the number of bytes, that 20 characters can be assigned to the attribute.

NOTE
For more information on globalization in Oracle, see the globalization support guide at http://otn.oracle.com. For more information on Unicode, see www.unicode.org.

Methods

Methods are either functions or procedures that are declared in the specification after attributes. Where attributes describe an object, methods act on them. If you recall our syntax diagram for creating the specification, the method list is separated by commas and uses the MEMBER, CONSTRUCTOR, or STATIC keywords. MAP or ORDER can be added to the MEMBER method for additional functionality. For functions, return type datatypes are under the same restrictions listed for attributes earlier in the chapter. Here is the extended syntax for method declaration:

[STATIC | MEMBER] PROCEDURE *procedure_spec,*
[STATIC | MEMBER | CONSTRUCTOR] FUNCTION *function_spec,*
[MAP | ORDER] MEMBER FUNCTION *function_spec,*
pragma_declaration

This declaration is not too different from the package specification. The STATIC, CONSTRUCTOR, and MEMBER keywords are the main difference. MAP and ORDER are used to determine the sort order for this object type. They are covered later in the chapter, in the section "MAP and ORDER Methods."

MEMBER Method   *Member* methods, though similar to packaged subprograms, are called differently. Each instantiation of a given object must reference the object instance it is to operate upon. Like procedures in a package, methods can be called with either positional or named notation, and the parameters can have default values. They can also be overloaded on the type and number of arguments, as we will see later.

Here we examine our member declaration to the discount_price_obj object specification:

```
-- Available online as part of MemberMethod.sql
CREATE OR REPLACE TYPE discount_price_obj AS OBJECT (
    discount_rate   NUMBER(10,4),
    price           NUMBER(10,2),

    MEMBER FUNCTION discount_price RETURN NUMBER)
INSTANTIABLE
FINAL;
/
```

The discount_price function can reference the attributes of the object type when we create the body.

Member methods are invoked against instances of the object, not the object type. To invoke the MEMBER method, use the following syntax:

instance_expression.method_name()

For example, to use the discount_price method in the discount_price_obj object we created, call it as follows:

```
SET SERVEROUTPUT ON SIZE 1000000
DECLARE
    v_price DISCOUNT_PRICE_OBJ := discount_price_obj(.1, 75.00);
    v_value NUMBER(10);
BEGIN
    v_value := v_price.discount_price;   -- invokes the discount_price method
    DBMS_OUTPUT.PUT_LINE('v_value ['||v_value||']');
END;
/
```

In this example, v_price is the *instance_expression,* and discount_price is the *method_name.*

STATIC Method   *Static* methods are independent of the object instance and cannot refer to the attributes of the object in the object type body. They were very useful before

9*i* Release 2, as they allowed us to "fake" a user-defined constructor method. Here we modify the `discount_price_obj` object type to include a static method:

```
-- Available online as part of StaticMethod.sql
CREATE OR REPLACE TYPE discount_price_obj AS OBJECT (
   discount_rate   NUMBER(10,4),
   price           NUMBER(10,2),

   STATIC FUNCTION new_price (
      i_price IN NUMBER,
      i_discount_rate IN NUMBER DEFAULT .1) RETURN NUMBER)
INSTANTIABLE
FINAL;
/
```

In this implementation we provide a default value for `i_discount_rate`. Notice that we have the same attributes in this case as the `object_type` itself.

To invoked the static method, we use the object type itself, rather than an instance of it, using the syntax

object_type_name.method_name

This `discount_rate_obj` example uses this syntax:

```
-- Note - only the price is passed. We have a default discount rate.
SET SERVEROUTPUT ON SIZE 1000000
exec DBMS_OUTPUT.PUT_LINE(discount_price_obj.new_price(75));
```

CONSTRUCTOR Method   So far we have seen only explicitly declared member and static methods that use procedures and functions to operate on the attributes. *Constructor* methods, on the other hand, have historically been system-defined functions that return an initialized object and take as arguments the values for the object's attributes. For every object type, Oracle predefines a constructor with the same name and attributes as the type.

Beginning with Oracle 9*i* Release 2, though, user-defined types are available that allow you to override the system-defined method or add additional constructor methods. Here is an example of a constructor method in the `discount_price_obj` object type:

```
-- Available online as part of ConstructorMethod.sql
CREATE OR REPLACE TYPE discount_price_obj AS OBJECT (
   discount_rate   NUMBER(10,4),
   price           NUMBER(10,2),
   CONSTRUCTOR FUNCTION discount_price_obj (
      price NUMBER)
   RETURN SELF AS RESULT)
```

```
INSTANTIABLE
FINAL;
/
```

In this case, the user-defined constructor method is the same as the object type, but it has only one attribute, where the object type specification lists two. We are overloading using the constructor method. In cases where the `discount_rate` is different from the default of 10 percent, we can specify it in our call, and the system-defined constructor is used. If the default of 10 percent is okay, simply pass the value for the price and the user-defined constructor method is used. If we had the object type and constructor with the same name and the same number of attributes, then the constructor would actually override the system-defined constructor.

TIP
Remember, you do not need to explicitly define your own constructor. Every object type has one implicitly created for it. It is a good practice to explicitly create it, however. Doing so provides the ability to add default attribute values, modify the default attribute list, and use overloading.

Declaring and Initializing Objects

Through our examples, we have seen cases of both declaring and initializing objects. Just like any other PL/SQL variable, an object is declared simply by placing it syntactically after its type in the declarative section of the block. For example,

```
DECLARE
    v_price DISCOUNT_PRICE_OBJ;
...
```

In this case, `v_price` is an instance of object type `discount_price_obj`. Since we did not use the constructor, the object has been initialized to NULL. Since the object is NULL, any reference to one of its attributes will result in an exception being thrown. For example, the following anonymous block raises an error because of the null:

```
SET SERVEROUTPUT ON SIZE 1000000
DECLARE
    v_price DISCOUNT_PRICE_OBJ;
BEGIN
    v_price.price := 75;
    dbms_output.PUT_LINE(v_price.price);
END;
/
```

The raised error is shown here:

```
ERROR at line 1:
ORA-06530: Reference to uninitialized composite
ORA-06512: at line 4
```

The solution to this is to initialize the object. We do this using the constructor method we just discussed. As mentioned in the last section, *every* object type has a constructor method. We can fix the preceding anonymous block by doing the following:

```
SET SERVEROUTPUT ON SIZE 1000000
DECLARE
    v_price DISCOUNT_PRICE_OBJ := discount_price_obj(null, null);
BEGIN
    v_price.price := 75;
    dbms_output.PUT_LINE(v_price.price);
END;
/
75
```

Now that the object has been initialized, we can reference it in the body of the block without the exception.

Object Type Body

The body of the object type is similar to that of a package. Where the specification is made up of attributes and declarations of methods, only method bodies are in the object type body. If an object type specification contains only attributes, then there is *no* need for the object type body.

To create an object type body, use the following syntax:

```
CREATE [OR REPLACE] TYPE BODY [schema.]type_name {IS | AS}
[STATIC | MEMBER] PROCEDURE procedure_body
  [STATIC | MEMBER | CONSTRUCTOR] FUNCTION function_body
  [MAP | ORDER] MEMBER function_body
END;
```

where *procedure_body* and *function_body* are the implementation of methods defined in the type specification, just like subprograms defined in a package body. Let's take a look at a simple example. Here is the body of the discount_price_obj object type:

```
-- Available online as part of Inheritance.sql
CREATE OR REPLACE TYPE BODY discount_price_obj AS
    MEMBER FUNCTION discount_price RETURN NUMBER
    IS
    BEGIN
```

```
      RETURN (price * (1-discount_rate));
   END discount_price;
END;
/
```

The `discount_price_obj` specification includes two attributes and a declaration of one method, a function called `discount_price`. The object body `discount_price_obj` defines how the `discount_price` method acts upon the data structure. In this case, the return value is a calculation of the discounted price and statement of savings based on the discount provided.

We can test out our object type with an anonymous block that passes in two values for the attributes:

```
SET SERVEROUTPUT ON SIZE 1000000
DECLARE
   v_price DISCOUNT_PRICE_OBJ := discount_price_obj(.1, 75.00);
BEGIN
   DBMS_OUTPUT.PUT_LINE(v_price.discount_price);
END;
/
```

```
67.5
```

Here we provided a 10 percent discount on a base price of $75, and the resulting price is 67.5. Our object works.

Although the package body and object type body may seem nearly identical, there are some key differences to remember:

- Initial values in an object type are set using the constructor. Packages can contain an initialization section.

- Packages are a type of schema object that group together related declarations. Object types are actually PL/SQL types. Variables, for example, can be declared of a particular object type.

- The name of the object type body does not appear after the final END. Names appear only after the END for the methods.

- Private declarations are allowed in package bodies. Object type bodies can contain only member and constructor subprograms.

SELF Parameter
The keyword SELF simply refers to the current object instance. Similar to the Java *this* keyword, it can be used to refer to the entire object or to a method or attribute of the current object.

SELF is automatically declared as the first parameter of a MEMBER method and defaults to IN for MEMBER functions and IN OUT for MEMBER procedures, if not stated explicitly. SELF cannot be declared as an OUT parameter and must be the same datatype as the original object.

For the `discount_price_obj` example, we did not have to include the SELF keyword, since references to the attributes use the current object by default. We also did not explicitly declare SELF as an IN parameter to the method, yet our next example illustrates that we can reference its attributes to represent the object that was instantiated. In the following example, `SELF.price` relates to the price attribute of the current object, and `SELF.discount_rate` is the `discount_rate` of the current object.

```
-- Available online as part of MemberMethod.sql
CREATE OR REPLACE TYPE BODY discount_price_obj AS
   MEMBER FUNCTION discount_price RETURN NUMBER
   IS
   BEGIN
      RETURN (SELF.price * (1-SELF.discount_rate));
   END discount_price;
END;
/
```

While the preceding example used SELF as an optional keyword, user-defined constructor methods *must* use RETURN SELF AS RESULT in the return clause.

```
-- Available online as part of ConstructorMethod.sql
CREATE OR REPLACE TYPE BODY discount_price_obj AS
   CONSTRUCTOR FUNCTION discount_price_obj (price NUMBER)
   RETURN SELF AS RESULT
   AS
   BEGIN
      self.price := price * .9;
      RETURN;
   END discount_price_obj;
END;
/
```

Attempting to use anything but SELF in the return yields the following exception:

```
PLS-00659: constructor method must return SELF AS RESULT
```

SELF is also required if you wish to pass the current object instance, or a reference to it, as an argument to another procedure or method, or if a method is called from another method in an object type.

Static methods cannot use the SELF keyword. As we discussed earlier, static methods do not have a current object—they operate independent of it and actually fail if there is an attempt to reference an attribute from the object type in the method body. This being the case, use of SELF would be pointless.

MAP and ORDER Methods

Our object type specification and body syntax includes two more types of MEMBER methods: MAP and ORDER. Oracle built-in types have an implicit ordering sequence for the data they represent. NUMBER, for example, allows you to determine if one value is greater than the other. Object types have no implicit ordering associated with them, so these two methods are introduced to help us in ordering and comparison of the instantiated objects. MAP and ORDER methods not only allow comparisons between objects, but they can be used to sort objects stored in the database, as will be shown in Chapter 15.

Before diving into each one individually, here are some rules that apply to both methods:

- Only one MAP or ORDER method is allowed per object.

- Both MAP and ORDER cannot be defined in the same object.

- MAP and ORDER allow for comparison between objects in procedural code. If they are not used, an exception is thrown. Tests for equality can be done in SQL, however, since the comparison simply compares all of the attributes (more on this in Chapter 15).

The following example compares discount prices from `discount_price_obj`, which does not use MAP or ORDER methods. It demonstrates the error you get when comparing object instances without using MAP or ORDER methods:

```
SET SERVEROUTPUT ON SIZE 1000000
DECLARE
    v_price1 DISCOUNT_PRICE_OBJ := discount_price_obj(.1, 75);
    v_price2 DISCOUNT_PRICE_OBJ := discount_price_obj(.2, 75);
BEGIN
    IF v_price1 = v_price2 THEN
        DBMS_OUTPUT.PUT_LINE(
            v_price1.discount_price
            ||' equals '
            ||v_price2.discount_price);
    ELSE
        DBMS_OUTPUT.PUT_LINE(
            v_price2.discount_price
            ||' Does not equal '
```

```
      ||v_price2.discount_price);
   END IF;
END;
/
```

The anonymous block returns the following exception:

```
   IF v_price1 = v_price2 THEN
             *
ERROR at line 5:
ORA-06550: line 5, column 16:
PLS-00526: A MAP or ORDER function is required for comparing objects in
PL/SQL.
```

MAP Method   When Oracle needs to compare two objects (Boolean comparison) or compare objects using GROUP BY, ORDER BY, or DISTINCT clauses, it can call the MAP function to convert the object to a type that can be sorted. MAP is more efficient than ORDER when working with large groups of objects because it converts the entire set of objects to a simpler type (operating as a hash function), which is then sorted. MAP allows only the SELF parameter and returns a scalar type of DATE, NUMBER, VARCHAR2, CHAR, or REAL.

Let's take a look at an example using the MAP method. Returning to our bookstore example, the bookstore inventory contains objects of type book. Here we create a new object type specification and include a MAP method that returns the isbn from the object:

```
-- Available online as part of MapMethod.sql
CREATE OR REPLACE TYPE book_obj AS OBJECT (
   isbn          CHAR(10),
   title      VARCHAR2(100),
   num_pages NUMBER,
   MAP MEMBER FUNCTION return_isbn RETURN CHAR
);
/
```

The object type body simply returns the SELF.isbn, or the isbn of the current object.

```
-- Available online as part of MapMethod.sql
CREATE OR REPLACE TYPE BODY book_obj AS
 MAP MEMBER FUNCTION return_isbn RETURN CHAR IS
   BEGIN
      RETURN SELF.isbn;
   END return_isbn;
END;
/
```

Now we are able to compare two objects by isbn:

```
-- Available online as part of MapMethod.sql
SET SERVEROUTPUT ON SIZE 1000000
DECLARE
    v_book1 BOOK_OBJ := book_obj('72121203', 'Oracle DBA 101', 563);
    v_book2 BOOK_OBJ := book_obj('72122048',
                                 'Oracle 8i: A Beginner''s Guide', 765);
BEGIN
    IF v_book1 < v_book2 THEN
        DBMS_OUTPUT.PUT_LINE(v_book1.title
                             ||' < '
                             ||v_book2.title);
    ELSIF v_book1 = v_book2 THEN
        DBMS_OUTPUT.PUT_LINE(v_book1.title
                             ||' = '
                             ||v_book2.title);
    ELSE
        DBMS_OUTPUT.PUT_LINE(v_book1.title
                             ||' > '
                             ||v_book2.title);
    END IF;
END;
/
```

The anonymous block returns the following:

```
Oracle DBA 101 < Oracle 8i: A Beginner's Guide
PL/SQL procedure successfully completed.
```

NOTE
When using object type inheritance (see the later section "Object Type Inheritance"), you can include map methods in subtypes, but only if the top-level base type also has one.

ORDER Method   An ORDER method is similar to the MAP method in function, though execution is a bit different. It takes as an argument one parameter of the object type and must return a NUMBER.

We see the difference in implementation by recreating the book object type. The comparison accomplishes the same thing, but notice the difference in object type bodies between the ORDER method example and the MAP method example:

```
-- Available online as part of OrderMethod.sql
CREATE OR REPLACE TYPE book_obj AS OBJECT (
    isbn         CHAR(10),
```

```
   title      VARCHAR2(100),
   num_pages NUMBER,
   ORDER MEMBER FUNCTION compare_book (i_isbn IN BOOK_OBJ)
     RETURN NUMBER
);
/
```

Now to recreate the body:

-- **Available online as part of OrderMethod.sql**
```
CREATE OR REPLACE TYPE BODY book_obj AS
  ORDER MEMBER FUNCTION compare_book (i_isbn IN BOOK_OBJ)
    RETURN NUMBER IS
  BEGIN
      IF i_isbn.isbn < SELF.isbn THEN
        RETURN 1;
      ELSIF i_isbn.isbn > SELF.isbn THEN
        RETURN -1;
      ELSE
        RETURN 0;
      END IF;
  END compare_book;
END;
/
```

The anonymous block remains the same:

-- **Available online as part of OrderMethod.sql**
```
DECLARE
   v_book1 BOOK_OBJ := book_obj('72121203', 'Oracle DBA 101', 563);
   v_book2 BOOK_OBJ := book_obj('72122048',
                              'Oracle 8i: A Beginner''s Guide', 765);
BEGIN
   IF v_book1 < v_book2 THEN
      dbms_output.PUT_LINE(v_book1.title
                          ||' < '
                          ||v_book2.title);
   ELSIF v_book1 = v_book2 THEN
      dbms_output.PUT_LINE(v_book1.title
                          ||' = '
                          ||v_book2.title);
   ELSE
      dbms_output.PUT_LINE(v_book1.title
                          ||' > '
                          ||v_book2.title);
   END IF;
END;
/
```

The anonymous block returns the following:

```
Oracle DBA 101 < Oracle 8i: A Beginner's Guide
PL/SQL procedure successfully completed.
```

> **NOTE**
> *Order methods must be in the top-level object type*
> *when working with object type inheritance (see*
> *the next section, "Object Type Inheritance"), and*
> *accordingly, subtypes cannot override the method.*

Object Type Inheritance

Inheritance refers to the ability of one object type to take attributes and methods from a parent, or base, object type as their own. Inheritance was one of the major breakthroughs in PL/SQL's OOP implementation in Oracle 9*i*.

In the "Object Types" section, we learned that an object type is made up of attributes, which define an object, and methods, which act upon the object. Object type inheritance allows us to create a base object type, or parent, whose attributes and methods can be inherited by another object type. We can then create a subtype, or child, to either use the inherited attributes and methods or overwrite them with its own.

In our bookstore example, inheritance allows us to create a fairly generic object to model inventory. Our inventory_obj object provides an item ID, in-stock/out-of-stock tracking, reorder status, and price. These four attributes are generic to all items contained in the store. We do not want to repeat all four of these attributes in each of the object types for book and music objects.

This is where object type inheritance can help. We can create an inventory object type as a base type (parent) and then create subtypes (children) for books and music. We do not have to code the attributes and methods from the inventory object into all of the subobjects. They will automatically inherit them and have the ability to use them. What's more, the subtypes automatically pick up any changes to the base type.

Figure 14-2 is a model of the bookstore using object type inheritance. It lays out the object model, including subtypes and inherited attributes and methods.

If needed, we can add even more complexity to Figure 14-2 by adding subtypes to book_obj for hard cover and soft cover books. Each level of the inheritance tree adds detail to the Base object type or overrides something from its parent. All subtypes in the tree are related, however, to a common object type called the supertype, which is the topmost object type in the tree.

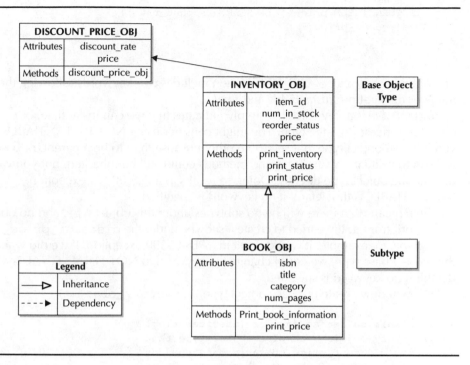

FIGURE 14-2. *Object type inheritance model*

There are a number of steps to build our application. We'll walk through each one, explaining syntax along the way.

```
-- Available online as part of Inheritance.sql
CREATE OR REPLACE TYPE discount_price_obj AS OBJECT (
   discount_rate   NUMBER(10,4),
   price           NUMBER(10,2),

   MEMBER FUNCTION discount_price RETURN NUMBER)
INSTANTIABLE
FINAL;
/

CREATE OR REPLACE TYPE BODY discount_price_obj AS
   MEMBER FUNCTION discount_price RETURN NUMBER
   IS
   BEGIN
```

```
        RETURN (SELF.price * (1-SELF.discount_rate));
    END discount_price;
END;
/
```

The `discount_price_obj` specification includes two keywords following the member declaration: *instantiable* and *final*.

Instantiable is a keyword that simply indicates that we can instantiate, or create object instances, from the type. You might consider using NOT INSTANTIABLE if you have an object type that serves no other purpose than to be a parent, or base, type. In that situation, attributes and methods could still be inherited, but you would not call the object type directly. Doing so results in a PLS-00713 exception. INSTANTIABLE is the default if no keyword is specified.

Final means that there will be no subtypes under this object type, and no objects will inherit from it. If we tried to create a subtype under the `discount_price_obj` object type, for example, it would result in a PLS-00590 exception. If we did want this to be a base type, we could change the keyword to NOT FINAL. FINAL is the default if no keyword is specified.

We will now create our base object type, `inventory_obj`:

```
-- Available online as part of Inheritance.sql
-- inventory_obj is a complex object type that
--    uses discount_price_obj as a datatype for
--    the price attribute. We also create it to
--    be a base object type that can be instantiated.

-- inventory_obj specification
CREATE OR REPLACE TYPE inventory_obj AS OBJECT (
    item_id           NUMBER (10),
    num_in_stock      NUMBER (10),
    reorder_status    VARCHAR2 (20 CHAR),
    price             NUMBER,
    CONSTRUCTOR FUNCTION inventory_obj (
        item_id        IN    NUMBER,
        num_in_stock   IN    NUMBER,
        price          IN    NUMBER
    )
        RETURN SELF AS RESULT,
    MEMBER PROCEDURE print_inventory,
    MEMBER PROCEDURE print_status,
    MEMBER PROCEDURE print_price
)
INSTANTIABLE NOT FINAL;
/
```

We specify the `inventory_obj` object type as NOT FINAL so that we can add subtypes under it. We also overloaded the constructor method by adding a constructor function. Here is the body:

```
-- Available online as part of Inheritance.sql
CREATE OR REPLACE TYPE BODY inventory_obj
AS
    CONSTRUCTOR FUNCTION inventory_obj (
        item_id        IN    NUMBER,
        num_in_stock   IN    NUMBER,
        price          IN    NUMBER
    )
        RETURN SELF AS RESULT
    IS
    BEGIN
        SELF.item_id := item_id;
        SELF.num_in_stock := num_in_stock;
        SELF.price := price;
        RETURN;
    END;
    MEMBER PROCEDURE print_inventory
    IS
    BEGIN
        DBMS_OUTPUT.PUT_LINE ('INVENTORY FOR BOOKSTORE1');
        DBMS_OUTPUT.PUT_LINE ('=========================');
        DBMS_OUTPUT.PUT_LINE (   'Item number '
                              || SELF.item_id
                              || ' has '
                              || SELF.num_in_stock
                              || ' in stock'
                             );
    END print_inventory;
    MEMBER PROCEDURE print_status
    IS
        v_status   VARCHAR2 (20);
    BEGIN
        IF SELF.num_in_stock > 0
        THEN
            v_status := 'IN STOCK';
        ELSE
            v_status := 'OUT OF STOCK';
        END IF;
        DBMS_OUTPUT.PUT_LINE ('INVENTORY STATUS FOR BOOKSTORE1');
        DBMS_OUTPUT.PUT_LINE ('================================');
        DBMS_OUTPUT.PUT_LINE ('Item number '
                           || SELF.item_id
```

```
                        || ' is '
                        || v_status
                    );
    END print_status;
    MEMBER PROCEDURE print_price
    IS
        -- Notice that the print_price method calls another object,
        -- using SELF and the price attribute to pass the value
        -- required for the other object type's constructor.

v_discount_price    discount_price_obj
:= discount_price_obj (SELF.price);
BEGIN
        DBMS_OUTPUT.PUT_LINE ('BOOKSTORE1 PRICES');
        DBMS_OUTPUT.PUT_LINE ('=================');
        DBMS_OUTPUT.PUT_LINE ('Item number '
                        || SELF.item_id);
        DBMS_OUTPUT.PUT_LINE ('Retail cost: '
                        || SELF.price
                        || ' US dollars');
        DBMS_OUTPUT.PUT_LINE (   'OUR LOW - LOW - LOW DISCOUNT PRICE: '
                        || v_discount_price.price
                        || ' US dollars'
                    );
    END print_price;
END;
/
```

Use the following anonymous block to test our object:

```
-- Available online as part of Inheritance.sql
SET SERVEROUTPUT ON SIZE 1000000
DECLARE
    v_prices    INVENTORY_OBJ := inventory_obj (3124, 15, 39.99);
BEGIN
    v_prices.print_inventory;
    DBMS_OUTPUT.PUT_LINE ('   ');
    v_prices.print_status;
    DBMS_OUTPUT.PUT_LINE ('   ');
    v_prices.print_price;
END;
/
```

The anonymous block results in the following:

```
INVENTORY FOR BOOKSTORE1
========================
Item number 3124 has 15 in stock
```

```
INVENTORY STATUS FOR BOOKSTORE1
================================
Item number 3124 is IN STOCK

BOOKSTORE1 PRICES
=================
Item number 3124
Retail cost: 39.99 US dollars
OUR LOW - LOW - LOW DISCOUNT PRICE: 35.99 US DOLLARS

PL/SQL procedure successfully completed.
```

Our base object includes four attributes and four methods (one *constructor* and three *members*). The book subtype creation includes additional attributes for isbn, title, category, and number of pages. We also create additional methods, as well as override the `print_price` method (our low, low, low prices for books don't apply).

-- **Available online as part of Inheritance.sql**
-- book_obj is a subtype of inventory_obj

```
CREATE OR REPLACE TYPE book_obj
UNDER inventory_obj (
    isbn        CHAR (10 CHAR),
    CATEGORY    VARCHAR2 (20 CHAR),
    title       VARCHAR2 (100 CHAR),
    num_pages   NUMBER,
CONSTRUCTOR FUNCTION book_obj (
item_id         NUMBER,
num_in_stock    NUMBER,
price           NUMBER,
isbn            CHAR,
title           VARCHAR2,
num_pages       NUMBER
)
RETURN SELF AS RESULT,
    MEMBER PROCEDURE print_book_information,
    OVERRIDING MEMBER PROCEDURE print_price
)
INSTANTIABLE FINAL;
/
```

We highlighted a few keywords in bold in the last example. A typical specification includes the keywords AS OBJECT. In our example, that is replaced by UNDER, along with the object that serves as its base type. The keyword OVERRIDING with the `print_price` method causes the subtype's method to take precedence over the base type's method of the same name. Book_obj is also FINAL, meaning that no subtypes can be created under it.

Base types and subtypes have a "one-to-many" relationship. Inventory_obj can have many subtypes associated with it, but a subtype can be associated with only a single base type. If we think of inheritance in the context of the family and genetics, parents are the base type and children are subtypes. Attributes (genes) are passed from parent to child, not the other way around. Object types can chain together as well, creating multiple levels of inheritance, just as children inherit attributes from grandparents through their parents.

We can see the attributes of both base type and subtype by doing a describe on the book_obj specification.

```
SQL> desc book_obj

book_obj extends OBJECTS_USER.INVENTORY_OBJ
 Name                                      Null?    Type
 ---------------------------------------- -------- ----------------------
 ITEM_ID                                            NUMBER(10)
 NUM_IN_STOCK                                       NUMBER(10)
 REORDER_STATUS                                     VARCHAR2(20 CHAR)
 PRICE                                              NUMBER(10,2)
 ISBN                                               CHAR(10 CHAR)
 CATEGORY                                           VARCHAR2(20 CHAR)
 TITLE                                              VARCHAR2(100 CHAR)
 NUM_PAGES                                          NUMBER
 MEMBER PROCEDURE PRINT_INVENTORY
 MEMBER PROCEDURE PRINT_STATUS

METHOD
------
 FINAL CONSTRUCTOR FUNCTION BOOK_OBJ RETURNS SELF AS RESULT
 Argument Name                     Type                     In/Out Default?
 -------------------------------- ----------------------- ------ --------
 ITEM_ID                           NUMBER                   IN
 NUM_IN_STOCK                      NUMBER                   IN
 PRICE                             NUMBER                   IN
 ISBN                              CHAR                     IN
 TITLE                             VARCHAR2                 IN
 NUM_PAGES                         NUMBER                   IN
 MEMBER PROCEDURE PRINT_BOOK_INFORMATION
 MEMBER PROCEDURE PRINT_PRICE
```

The default constructor would include all of the attributes listed here. We want the ability to use a subset of those, so we created a user-defined constructor method. The book_obj constructor method includes some attributes from inventory_obj and some from book_obj. Here is the body for book_obj:

```
-- Available online as part of Inheritance.sql
CREATE OR REPLACE TYPE BODY book_obj
IS
    CONSTRUCTOR FUNCTION book_obj (
        item_id         NUMBER,
        num_in_stock    NUMBER,
        price           NUMBER,
        isbn            CHAR,
        title           VARCHAR2,
        num_pages       NUMBER
    )
        RETURN SELF AS RESULT
    IS
    BEGIN
        SELF.item_id := item_id;
        SELF.num_in_stock := num_in_stock;
        SELF.price := price;
        SELF.isbn := isbn;
        SELF.title := title;
        SELF.num_pages := num_pages;
        RETURN;
    END book_obj;
    MEMBER PROCEDURE print_book_information
    IS
    BEGIN
        DBMS_OUTPUT.PUT_LINE ('BOOK INFORMATION');
        DBMS_OUTPUT.PUT_LINE ('================');
        DBMS_OUTPUT.PUT_LINE ('Title: '
                            || SELF.title);
        DBMS_OUTPUT.PUT_LINE ('# Pages: '
                            || SELF.num_pages);
        DBMS_OUTPUT.PUT_LINE ('# In Stock: '
                            || SELF.num_in_stock);
    END print_book_information;
    OVERRIDING MEMBER PROCEDURE print_price
    IS
    BEGIN
        DBMS_OUTPUT.PUT_LINE ('BOOKSTORE1 PRICES');
        DBMS_OUTPUT.PUT_LINE ('=================');
        DBMS_OUTPUT.PUT_LINE ('Title: '
                            || SELF.title);
        DBMS_OUTPUT.PUT_LINE ('Always low price of: '
                            || SELF.price);
    END print_price;
END;
/
```

We can test how the inheritance and method overriding works with the following:

```
-- Available online as part of Inheritance.sql
SET SERVEROUTPUT ON SIZE 1000000
DECLARE
    v_book BOOK_OBJ := book_obj (
                3124, 15, 39.99, '72121203', 'Oracle DBA 101', 563);
BEGIN
    v_book.print_book_information;
    DBMS_OUTPUT.PUT_LINE ('   ');
    v_book.print_price;
END;
/
```

The anonymous block returns the following result:

```
Book Information
================
Title: Oracle DBA 101
# Pages: 563
# In Stock: 15

BOOKSTORE1 PRICES
=================
Title: Oracle DBA 101
Always low price of: 39.99
```

> **NOTE**
> *If we were to alter the* book_obj *object type to be NOT FINAL and create a new subtype beneath it, would the* print_price *method from* book_obj *or* inventory_obj *be inherited? The method for* book_obj *would be inherited because it is closer to the new subtype in the hierarchy and overrode the base type.*

Dynamic Method Dispatch

Overloading has been a heavily used feature of PL/SQL for years. For those unfamiliar with it, the basic premise is that if you have two functions in a package with the same name, but different parameter lists, Oracle is able to determine which function is appropriate given the number and type of arguments provided. This is sometimes referred to as *static polymorphism*—the ability for a program to determine which method to execute when more than one have the same name, and to do so at compile time.

Object type inheritance provides a different kind of overloading capability—
dynamic method dispatch, sometimes called *dynamic polymorphism* or *run-time
polymorphism.* Here, the decision of which method to run is not made until the
code is actually executed. Inheritance includes methods, but rules of OVERRIDING
and FINAL that can apply to methods mean that the decision cannot be made solely
on number of parameters. There is an order of precedence in the hierarchy, where
the object type closest to you that meets the requirements is chosen.

Let's take a look at an example:

```
-- Available online as part of DynamicDispatch.sql
CREATE OR REPLACE TYPE abbrev_inventory_obj AS OBJECT (
    item_id    NUMBER (10),
    price      NUMBER (10, 2),
    MEMBER PROCEDURE print_price
)
NOT FINAL INSTANTIABLE;
/

CREATE OR REPLACE TYPE BODY abbrev_inventory_obj
AS
    MEMBER PROCEDURE print_price
    IS
        v_price    NUMBER := SELF.price * .80;
    BEGIN
        DBMS_OUTPUT.PUT_LINE ('Wholesale Cost: ' || v_price);
    END print_price;
END;
/

CREATE OR REPLACE TYPE abbrev_book_obj
UNDER abbrev_inventory_obj (
    isbn    VARCHAR2 (50),
    OVERRIDING MEMBER PROCEDURE print_price
)
FINAL INSTANTIABLE;
/

CREATE OR REPLACE TYPE BODY abbrev_book_obj
AS
    OVERRIDING MEMBER PROCEDURE print_price
    IS
    BEGIN
        DBMS_OUTPUT.PUT_LINE ('Retail Cost: ' || SELF.price);
    END print_price;
END;
/
```

Abbrev_book_obj is a subtype of abbrev_inventory_obj, and the print_price method is in both. The print_price method in the subtype overrides the base type. The following example illustrates dynamic method dispatch under these circumstances:

```
-- Available online as part of DynamicDispatch.sql
SET SERVEROUTPUT ON SIZE 1000000
DECLARE
    v_wholesale    ABBREV_INVENTORY_OBJ
                          := abbrev_inventory_obj (22, 54.95);
    v_retail       ABBREV_BOOK_OBJ
                          := abbrev_book_obj (22, 54.95, 23022843);
BEGIN
    DBMS_OUTPUT.PUT_LINE ('SUBTYPE EXECUTION - FULL PRICE');
    DBMS_OUTPUT.PUT_LINE ('==============================');
    v_retail.print_price;
    DBMS_OUTPUT.PUT_LINE ('     ');
    DBMS_OUTPUT.PUT_LINE ('BASE TYPE EXECUTION - REDUCED PRICE');
    DBMS_OUTPUT.PUT_LINE ('==================================');
    v_wholesale.print_price;
    DBMS_OUTPUT.PUT_LINE ('     ');
    DBMS_OUTPUT.PUT_LINE ('EXAMPLE OF DYNAMIC DISPATCH');
    DBMS_OUTPUT.PUT_LINE ('SUBTYPE METHOD RUN WHEN BASE TYPE IS EXECUTED');
    DBMS_OUTPUT.PUT_LINE ('=============================================');
    v_wholesale := v_retail;
    v_wholesale.print_price;
END;
/
```

The anonymous block returns the following:

```
SUBTYPE EXECUTION - FULL PRICE
==============================
Retail Cost: 54.95

BASE TYPE EXECUTION - REDUCED PRICE
==================================
Wholesale Cost: 43.96

EXAMPLE OF DYNAMIC DISPATCH
SUBTYPE METHOD RUN WHEN BASE TYPE IS EXECUTED
=============================================
Retail Cost: 54.95

PL/SQL procedure successfully completed.
```

The abbrev_inventory_obj object type was executed for the last price, but the results are from abbrev_book_obj.

Attribute Chaining

We saw a small example of attribute chaining when discussing complex object types. If you recall, we set the datatype of one attribute to be another object type. We can access the attributes of that object type and any other object type in the chain. Let's look at an example:

```
-- Available online as part of AttributeChain.sql
CREATE OR REPLACE TYPE address_obj AS OBJECT (
    address1    VARCHAR2 (30 CHAR),
    address2    VARCHAR2 (30 CHAR),
    city        VARCHAR2 (30 CHAR),
    state       CHAR (2 CHAR)
)
INSTANTIABLE FINAL;
/

CREATE OR REPLACE TYPE person_obj AS OBJECT (
    first_name    VARCHAR2 (20),
    last_name     VARCHAR2 (20)
)
INSTANTIABLE FINAL;
/
```

Address_obj and person_obj are at one end of the chain. After our section on inheritance, the keyword FINAL should make more sense. There can be no subtypes under these, so we are not looking at inheritance at all. Here we create our first object type that uses the object types as attribute datatypes:

```
-- Available online as part of AttributeChain.sql
CREATE OR REPLACE TYPE contact_obj AS OBJECT (
    NAME       PERSON_OBJ,
    address    ADDRESS_OBJ,
    phone      NUMBER (10)
)
INSTANTIABLE FINAL;
/
```

The contact_obj object type includes three attributes, the first two of which have other object types as their datatypes. Again, this is marked as FINAL. You will also notice that there is *no* body associated with any of the first three object types. There are no methods, only attributes, so the body is not necessary.

Let's take a look at the fourth and final object type specification and body that pulls this together:

```
-- Available online as part of AttributeChain.sql
-- Specification
```

```
CREATE OR REPLACE TYPE publisher_obj AS OBJECT (
   pub_name          VARCHAR2 (30),
   contact_info      CONTACT_OBJ,
   MEMBER PROCEDURE show_contact
)
INSTANTIABLE FINAL;
/
```

```
 1 CREATE OR REPLACE TYPE BODY publisher_obj
 2  AS
 3     MEMBER PROCEDURE show_contact
 4     IS
 5     BEGIN
 6        DBMS_OUTPUT.PUT_LINE ('CONTACT INFORMATION');
 7        DBMS_OUTPUT.PUT_LINE ('====================');
 8        DBMS_OUTPUT.PUT_LINE (SELF.pub_name);
 9        DBMS_OUTPUT.PUT_LINE (   SELF.contact_info.NAME.first_name
10                              || ' '
11                              || SELF.contact_info.NAME.last_name
12                              );
13        DBMS_OUTPUT.PUT_LINE (SELF.contact_info.address.address1);
14        DBMS_OUTPUT.PUT_LINE (SELF.contact_info.address.city);
15        DBMS_OUTPUT.PUT_LINE (SELF.contact_info.address.state);
16        DBMS_OUTPUT.PUT_LINE (SELF.contact_info.phone);
17        RETURN;
18     END show_contact;
19  END;
20  /
```

NOTE
*We included the line numbers for illustration
purposes only.*

Let's take a look at what is happening:

- The `contact_info` datatype is the `contact_obj` object type.

- The `contact_obj` object type has two attributes, name and address,
  whose datatypes are other object types.

- All of the contact information we need is contained in the attributes of
  these four object types. Attributes are referenced by name and can use
  the keyword SELF to reference the current instance of the object, but
  when the attribute is from another object type, we cannot reference the
  attribute directly.

- We are not working with inherited attributes, so the only way to get the information in the current object instance is to follow the chain of attributes back to the end of the chain.

- Line 8 starts us off with one of `publisher_obj`'s attributes. Using SELF is sufficient.

- Line 9 requires a large chain of attributes to pull in `first_name` (SELF `.contact_info.name.first_name`). The remaining lines use a similar structure, all going to the last attribute in the chain to get the required value. Notice that only attributes are referenced in this string, not their object types. This is because the object types are already known from their declaration in the specification. For example, if we know `contact_info` has a datatype of `contact_obj`, we know we need to look in `contact_obj` to find the next attribute listed in the chain. See Figure 14-3 for a more detailed look at this.

The only thing left to do is test it. The following block instantiates all four object types and then uses the `show_contact` method from `publisher_obj` object type to pull it all together:

```
-- Available online as part of AttributeChain.sql
DECLARE
   v_person      PERSON_OBJ    := person_obj ('Ron', 'Hardman');
   v_address     ADDRESS_OBJ   := address_obj ('123 Ora Way',
                                    NULL,
                                    'Colorado Springs',
                                    'CO');
```

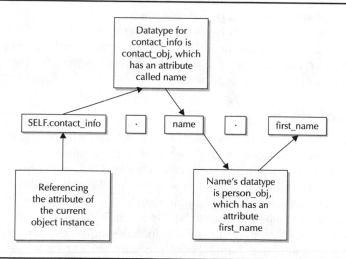

FIGURE 14-3. *Attribute chaining diagram*

```
    v_contact      CONTACT_OBJ   := contact_obj (
                                          v_person, -- variable declared above
                                          v_address, -- variable declared above
                                          5555555555);
    v_publisher    PUBLISHER_OBJ := publisher_obj ('Oracle Press',
                                          v_contact); -- variable declared above
BEGIN
    v_publisher.show_contact;
END;
/
```

The anonymous block returns the following:

```
CONTACT INFORMATION
====================
Oracle Press
Ron Hardman
123 Ora Way
Colorado Springs
CO
5555555555
```

Making Changes

It is inevitable. No application is perfect upon creation (at least according to users), and none can escape evolving requirements and user needs. The concept of object types—subtypes, object tables, and object views (more on these in Chapter 15), attribute chaining, etc.—likely sends shivers down the spines of all those responsible for application maintenance and design changes.

Oracle made altering object types much easier in 9*i* and 10*g* with the introduction of type evolution. In addition, object types are schema objects, so information about them can be obtained from the data dictionary. They are also created and maintained using SQL.

Type Evolution

Type evolution refers to any modification of an object type and, in turn, its dependents. This became extremely important in 9*i*, when object type inheritance was introduced. A change to attributes of a base type needs to be reflected in subtypes that inherit the attributes and methods. The full scope of type evolution's impact will be clear in Chapter 15, when we look at persistent objects.

The following examples include inheritance, attribute chaining, and overloading of the constructor method in a subtype that includes attributes from the base type that are part of the attribute chain. The `music_obj` object type is the base type. Both composer and artist attributes have the `music_person_obj` object type as the datatype. The `cd_obj` is a subtype under `music_obj` and has a constructor method defined that includes attributes from the base type.

```
-- Available online in TypeEvolution.sql
-- Specification only - provides first and last name
-- as part of an attribute chain.
CREATE OR REPLACE TYPE music_person_obj AS OBJECT (
    first_name    VARCHAR2 (50 CHAR),
    last_name     VARCHAR2 (50 CHAR)
)
FINAL INSTANTIABLE;
/


-- Also specification only as there are no
-- methods. This is the base type for our example.
CREATE OR REPLACE TYPE music_obj AS OBJECT (
    style       VARCHAR2 (50 CHAR),
    composer    music_person_obj,
    artist      music_person_obj
)
NOT FINAL INSTANTIABLE;
/


-- subtype under music_obj. Note the constructor
-- method. Both spec and body created.
CREATE OR REPLACE TYPE cd_obj
UNDER music_obj (
    title           VARCHAR2 (50 CHAR),
    date_released   DATE,
    CONSTRUCTOR FUNCTION cd_obj (
        artist          music_person_obj,
        title           VARCHAR2,
        date_released   DATE
    )
        RETURN SELF AS RESULT,
    MEMBER PROCEDURE show_cd
)
FINAL INSTANTIABLE;
/

CREATE OR REPLACE TYPE BODY cd_obj
AS
    CONSTRUCTOR FUNCTION cd_obj (
        artist          music_person_obj,
        title           VARCHAR2,
        date_released   DATE
    )
```

```
      RETURN SELF AS RESULT
   IS
   BEGIN
      SELF.artist := artist;
      SELF.title := title;
      SELF.date_released := date_released;
      RETURN;
   END cd_obj;
   MEMBER PROCEDURE show_cd
   IS
   BEGIN
      DBMS_OUTPUT.PUT_LINE ('MUSIC TITLES IN BOOKSTORE1');
      DBMS_OUTPUT.PUT_LINE ('==========================');
      DBMS_OUTPUT.PUT_LINE ('TITLE: ' || SELF.title);
      DBMS_OUTPUT.PUT_LINE (   'ARTIST: '
                            || SELF.artist.first_name
                            || ' '
                            || SELF.artist.last_name
                           );
      DBMS_OUTPUT.PUT_LINE ('DATE RELEASED: ' || SELF.date_released);
   END show_cd;
END;
/
```

Let's run a quick test to make sure everything works.

```
DECLARE
   v_person   MUSIC_PERSON_OBJ := music_person_obj ('Chuck', 'Soulful');
   v_cd       CD_OBJ     := cd_obj (v_person, 'GMAN Blues', '01-JUN-1995');
BEGIN
   v_cd.show_cd;
END;
/
```

The anonymous block produces the following output:

```
MUSIC TITLES IN BOOKSTORE1
==========================
TITLE: GMAN Blues
ARTIST: Chuck Soulful
DATE RELEASED: 01-JUN-95
```

One more verification—let's do a describe on the cd_obj object type so that we have something to compare against.

```
SQL> desc cd_obj
 cd_obj extends SCHEMA.MUSIC_OBJ
 Name                                      Null?    Type
```

```
---------------------------------------------- -------- ----------------------
STYLE                                                   VARCHAR2(50 CHAR)
COMPOSER                                                MUSIC_PERSON_OBJ
ARTIST                                                  MUSIC_PERSON_OBJ
TITLE                                                   VARCHAR2(50 CHAR)
DATE_RELEASED                                           DATE

METHOD
------
FINAL CONSTRUCTOR FUNCTION CD_OBJ RETURNS SELF AS RESULT
Argument Name                      Type                    In/Out Default?
---------------------------------- ----------------------- ------ --------
ARTIST                             MUSIC_PERSON_OBJ        IN
TITLE                              VARCHAR2                IN
DATE_RELEASED                      DATE                    IN
MEMBER PROCEDURE SHOW_CD
```

Altering and Dropping Types

The ALTER TYPE statement is used to modify and recompile object types. The syntax is as follows:

ALTER TYPE *type_name* COMPILE [SPECIFICATION | BODY];

If *specification* or *body* keywords are not used, both specification and body are compiled. The compile is done using the current definition according to the data dictionary, the same way any other schema object is compiled.

We can also alter the object to change its structure. If we want to add a subtitle for the cd_obj object type, we can just make the modification using the ALTER TYPE command:

```
-- Modify the cd_obj attributes to include a subtitle
ALTER TYPE cd_obj
ADD ATTRIBUTE subtitle VARCHAR2(50 CHAR);

Type altered.
```

To verify the change, describe the cd_obj object type:

```
SQL> desc cd_obj
ERROR:
ORA-22337: the type of accessed object has been evolved
```

We get this exception because we did a describe of the object type before altering it, without having disconnected in the meantime. The type was loaded to our client cache, and unless we reconnect, the client cache is not cleared. If we had not described the object type prior to altering it, or had cleared our session by logging out, we would not receive this error. At the time of this writing, there is no mechanism for flushing the client cache without disconnecting your session.

```
SQL> conn schema/oracle
Connected.
SQL> desc cd_obj
 cd_obj extends SCHEMA.MUSIC_OBJ
 Name                                       Null?     Type
 ------------------------------------------ --------  --------------------
 STYLE                                                VARCHAR2(50 CHAR)
 COMPOSER                                             MUSIC_PERSON_OBJ
 ARTIST                                               MUSIC_PERSON_OBJ
 TITLE                                                VARCHAR2(50 CHAR)
 DATE_RELEASED                                        DATE
 SUBTITLE                                             VARCHAR2(50 CHAR)
```

Subtitle has been added. This tested only the alter command, though; it didn't test type evolution based on dependencies. For that, we need to modify the base type.

Let's change the artist attribute to VARCHAR2(50 CHAR). We can't alter the attribute in this case. We will need to drop and recreate it. Note that the artist attribute is in the base type and is part of the user-defined constructor method of the cd_obj object type.

```
-- Drop and recreate artist attribute

alter type music_obj
drop attribute artist cascade;

Type altered.

-- Reconnect in SQL*Plus if needed
-- The attribute is no longer present for cd_obj

SQL> desc cd_obj
 Name                                       Null?     Type
 ------------------------------------------ --------  --------------------
 STYLE                                                VARCHAR2(50 CHAR)
 COMPOSER                                             MUSIC_PERSON_OBJ
 TITLE                                                VARCHAR2(50 CHAR)
 DATE_RELEASED                                        DATE
 SUBTITLE                                             VARCHAR2(50 CHAR)

-- Add the artist attribute back in with a VARCHAR2 datatype
ALTER TYPE music_obj
ADD ATTRIBUTE artist VARCHAR2(50 CHAR) CASCADE;

SQL> desc cd_obj
 Name                                       Null?     Type
 ------------------------------------------ --------  --------------------
 STYLE                                                VARCHAR2(50 CHAR)
 COMPOSER                                             MUSIC_PERSON_OBJ
```

ARTIST	VARCHAR2(50 CHAR)
TITLE	VARCHAR2(50 CHAR)
DATE_RELEASED	DATE
SUBTITLE	VARCHAR2(50 CHAR)

Artist is back on the list of inherited attributes, and the datatype is now VARCHAR2. Although Oracle did a wonderful job on type evolution here, we are still responsible for our own code. Our cd_obj body references first and last names of artists, and it is marked as invalid until we can fix it and recompile.

Not only can we alter the type to add, modify, and delete attributes, but we can also maintain the methods in the object type. We did not specify a user-defined constructor method in the music_obj object type. In fact, there is no object body at all, since there were no methods declared. To add a method to the object type specification, type

```
ALTER TYPE music_obj ADD CONSTRUCTOR FUNCTION music_obj (
style VARCHAR2,
artist MUSIC_PERSON_OBJ)
RETURN SELF AS RESULT CASCADE;

Type altered.

-- A description of music_obj shows the new method
SQL> DESC music_obj
 music_obj is NOT FINAL
 Name                                             Null?    Type
 ------------------------------------------------ -------- --------------------
 STYLE                                                     VARCHAR2(50 CHAR)
 COMPOSER                                                  MUSIC_PERSON_OBJ
 ARTIST                                                    MUSIC_PERSON_OBJ
 METHOD
 ------
 FINAL CONSTRUCTOR FUNCTION MUSIC_OBJ RETURNS SELF AS RESULT
 Argument Name                   Type                     In/Out Default?
 ------------------------------- ------------------------ ------ --------
 STYLE                           VARCHAR2                 IN
 ARTIST                          MUSIC_PERSON_OBJ         IN
```

We don't have an object type body to implement the constructor method. If we do not want to keep it, we can use the drop command:

```
ALTER TYPE music_obj
DROP CONSTRUCTOR FUNCTION music_obj (
style varchar2,
artist music_person_obj)
RETURN SELF AS RESULT CASCADE;
```

NOTE
It is not required that you provide the entire method syntax when altering the object type, but it is good practice.

To drop an object type, we use the DROP TYPE command. This can be made more specific to the object type body by using DROP TYPE BODY. To test this, we can drop the `music_person_obj` object type:

```
SQL> DROP TYPE music_person_obj;
drop type music_person_obj
     *
ERROR at line 1:
ORA-02303: cannot drop or replace a type with type or table dependents
```

This fails because `music_person_obj` is used as the datatype for two `music_obj` attributes. We can add the FORCE keyword to make the drop ignore the dependencies.

```
SQL> DROP TYPE music_person_obj FORCE;

Type dropped.
```

Using FORCE allows the drop to succeed, but the remaining objects are marked as invalid. Should we recreate the `music_person_obj` object, we must recompile the invalid objects. In the next chapter (Chapter 15) we will also explore the VALIDATE keyword, and its usefulness when working with object tables.

Summary

In this chapter we reviewed object-oriented programming (OOP) concepts, discussed Oracle's implementation of OOP in PL/SQL, and tested features such as inheritance, type evolution, and attribute chaining. In the next chapter we continue our discussion of objects, but we shift to persistent objects in the database.

CHAPTER
15

Objects in the
Database

I n Chapter 14 we discussed object-oriented programming and introduced object types and object instances. The focus of the chapter was on transient objects, or objects that exist only in the context of program execution. In this chapter we extend the objects discussion to persistent objects, or objects that exist after program execution, such as object tables and object views. You will also learn how to use DML and built-in functions with objects, and explore type evolution with persistent objects.

> **NOTE**
> *If you are unfamiliar with object type creation, inheritance, type evolution, and differences between transience and persistence, it is highly recommended that you read Chapter 14 before reading this chapter.*

Introduction to Objects in the Database

Chapter 14 introduced you to object-oriented programming (OOP) and Oracle's implementation of it in PL/SQL. Inheritance and dynamic dispatch, while fairly new to PL/SQL, are standard features of other OOP languages like C++ and Java. So why choose PL/SQL for your OOP needs? PL/SQL objects can be stored in the database and created, maintained, and accessed using SQL and PL/SQL, providing persistence to objects.

Persistence, or the ability to store objects in the database rather than memory, provides a way for an object to exist outside the context of a single program's execution. Object types are still at the heart of the design, but the implementation extends to object tables, object views, and built-in functions to help us use and manage the objects.

Figure 15-1 shows how we can model a bookstore using objects. We have created only transient objects to this point. Let's take a look at how we can create persistent objects from this model in the database.

> **NOTE**
> *Unless otherwise noted, the base release for this chapter is Oracle 9iR1, since this is where most of the complex object features were added.*

Object Tables

Object tables are created from object types and match the definitions of the object type attributes. Object tables contain object rows. Each row in the object table is an instance of the object, and the table contains only columns matching the attributes of the object type it is created from.

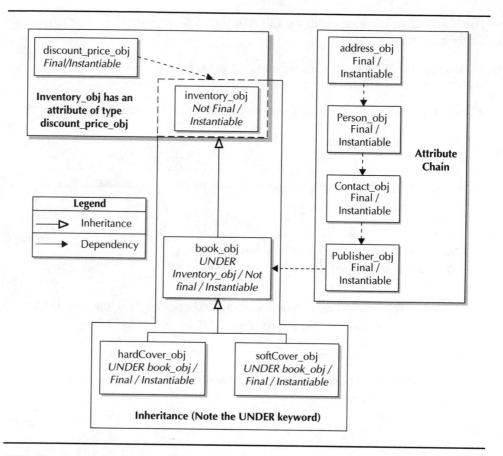

FIGURE 15-1. *Bookstore object model*

Creating Object Tables

We create object tables using the CREATE TABLE...OF statement. The object table takes the attributes of the object type as its columns. If an attribute `discount_rate` in the `discount_price_obj` object type has a datatype of NUMBER (10, 4), then the table created from it has a column named `discount_rate` and a datatype of NUMBER (10, 4). See the following example:

```
-- Available online as part of ObjectTable.sql
CREATE OR REPLACE TYPE discount_price_obj AS OBJECT (
      discount_rate     NUMBER (10, 4),
      price             NUMBER (10, 2),
      CONSTRUCTOR FUNCTION discount_price_obj (price NUMBER)
          RETURN SELF AS RESULT
   )
   INSTANTIABLE FINAL;
/
```

The object table is created with the CREATE TABLE *table_name* OF *object_type_name* statement.

```
-- Available online as part of ObjectTable.sql
CREATE TABLE discount_price_tbl OF discount_price_obj;
```

A describe of the table shows us the same definition as `discount_price_obj`:

```
DESC discount_price_tbl
 Name                                      Null?     Type
 ----------------------------------------- --------  -------------
 DISCOUNT_RATE                                       NUMBER(10,4)
 PRICE                                               NUMBER(10,2)
```

> **NOTE**
> *The object table is based on the system-defined constructor rather than the user-defined constructor.*

The object table and object type it was created from are tied together. Let's attempt to drop the `discount_price_obj` example we just created.

```
DROP TYPE discount_price_obj;
```

If you attempt to drop the type without first invalidating or dropping the table, you will receive the following error:

```
drop type discount_price_obj
     *
ERROR at line 1:
ORA-02303: cannot drop or replace a type with type or table dependents
```

Any modifications to the table must be done through the type. The following example attempts to alter `discount_price_tbl` to add a column:

```
ALTER TABLE discount_price_tbl
   ADD col1 VARCHAR2(200 CHAR);
```

This generates the following error:

```
ADD col1 VARCHAR2(200 CHAR)
      *
ERROR at line 2:
ORA-22856: cannot add columns to object tables
```

NOTE
If you are unfamiliar with the use of CHAR with a string datatype, refer to the "Character Semantics" section of Chapter 14.

We will discuss persistent object maintenance and type evolution at greater length later in this chapter, under the heading "Maintaining Persistent Objects."

Inheritance and Attribute Chaining

Creating object tables is straightforward when the object type is not very complex. Adding inheritance and attribute chaining throws a bit of a wrinkle into our nice, neat object table example, though.

Chapter 14 introduced the concept of attribute chaining, which provides a way to link object types to attributes of other object types. If contact information is a composite structure made up of name, address, and phone number, and the address is made up of multiple attributes as well, we can "chain" the list of attributes together and present them as a composite in our `publisher_obj.contact_info` attribute. Refer back to Figure 15-1 for a diagram of the following example:

```
-- Available online as part of AttributeChain.sql
CREATE OR REPLACE TYPE address_obj AS OBJECT (
        address1    VARCHAR2 (30 CHAR),
        address2    VARCHAR2 (30 CHAR),
        city        VARCHAR2 (30 CHAR),
        state       CHAR (2 CHAR)
    )
    INSTANTIABLE FINAL;
/


CREATE OR REPLACE TYPE person_obj AS OBJECT (
        first_name  VARCHAR2 (20 CHAR),
        last_name   VARCHAR2 (20 CHAR)
    )
    INSTANTIABLE FINAL;
/
```

`Address_obj` and `person_obj` are at the end of the chain and have no dependencies. `Contact_obj`, created next, uses `address_obj` and `person_obj` for two of its attribute types.

```
-- Available online as part of AttributeChain.sql
CREATE OR REPLACE TYPE contact_obj AS OBJECT (
        name        PERSON_OBJ,
        address     ADDRESS_OBJ,
```

```
        phone        NUMBER (10)
    )
    INSTANTIABLE FINAL;
/
```

Finally, `publisher_obj` is created to use `contact_obj` for one of its datatypes.

```
-- Available online as part of AttributeChain.sql
CREATE OR REPLACE TYPE publisher_obj AS OBJECT (
        pub_name          VARCHAR2 (30),
        contact_info     CONTACT_OBJ,
        MEMBER PROCEDURE show_contact
    )
    INSTANTIABLE FINAL;
/
```

Base the object table on the `publisher_obj` object type.

```
CREATE TABLE publisher_tbl OF publisher_obj;
```

The table `publisher_tbl` should now have the same structure as the object type `publisher_obj` that it is based on. A describe of both `publisher_obj` and `publisher_tbl` show the same structure:

```
SQL> desc publisher_obj
 Name                                      Null?     Type
 ---------------------------------------- --------  ------------
 PUB_NAME                                            VARCHAR2(30)
 CONTACT_INFO                                        CONTACT_OBJ
 MEMBER PROCEDURE SHOW_CONTACT

SQL> desc publisher_tbl
 Name                                      Null?     Type
 ---------------------------------------- --------  ------------
 PUB_NAME                                            VARCHAR2(30)
 CONTACT_INFO                                        CONTACT_OBJ
```

Our new object table is a mirror of our object type including the attribute chain. In this case, `contact_info` has a datatype of `contact_obj`.

Inheritance provides an object type hierarchy where subtypes inherit attributes and methods from their parents, all the way up to the supertype. Figure 15-1 shows our inheritance model that is used in the following example:

```
-- Available online as part of Inheritance.sql
CREATE OR REPLACE TYPE inventory_obj AS OBJECT (
        item_id           NUMBER (10),
        num_in_stock      NUMBER (10),
        reorder_status    VARCHAR2 (20 CHAR),
        price             NUMBER (10, 2),
```

```
        CONSTRUCTOR FUNCTION inventory_obj (
            item_id        IN    NUMBER,
            num_in_stock   IN    NUMBER,
            price          IN    NUMBER
        )
            RETURN SELF AS RESULT,
        MEMBER PROCEDURE print_inventory,
        MEMBER PROCEDURE print_status,
        MEMBER PROCEDURE print_price
    )
    INSTANTIABLE NOT FINAL;
/

CREATE OR REPLACE TYPE book_obj
    UNDER inventory_obj (
        isbn         CHAR (10 CHAR),
        CATEGORY     VARCHAR2 (20 CHAR),
        title        VARCHAR2 (100 CHAR),
        num_pages    NUMBER,
        publisher    PUBLISHER_OBJ,
        CONSTRUCTOR FUNCTION book_obj (
            item_id        NUMBER,
            num_in_stock   NUMBER,
            price          NUMBER,
            isbn           CHAR,
            title          VARCHAR2,
            num_pages      NUMBER
        )
            RETURN SELF AS RESULT,
        MEMBER PROCEDURE print_book_information,
        OVERRIDING MEMBER PROCEDURE print_price
    )
    INSTANTIABLE NOT FINAL;
/

CREATE OR REPLACE TYPE hard_cover_obj
    UNDER book_obj (
        distribution_date   DATE,
        OVERRIDING MEMBER PROCEDURE print_price
    )
    INSTANTIABLE FINAL;
/

CREATE OR REPLACE TYPE soft_cover_obj
    UNDER book_obj (
        distribution_date   DATE,
        OVERRIDING MEMBER PROCEDURE print_price
    )
    INSTANTIABLE FINAL;
/
```

Now we can create an object table for `soft_cover_obj`.

```
SQL> create table soft_cover_tbl of soft_cover_obj;
```

A describe of the `soft_cover_tbl` shows all attributes included in the hierarchy:

```
SQL> desc soft_cover_tbl
 Name                          Type
 --------------------------    ------------------
 ITEM_ID                       NUMBER(10)
 NUM_IN_STOCK                  NUMBER(10)
 REORDER_STATUS                VARCHAR2(20 CHAR)
 PRICE                         NUMBER(10,2)
 ISBN                          CHAR(10 CHAR)
 CATEGORY                      VARCHAR2(20 CHAR)
 TITLE                         VARCHAR2(100 CHAR)
 NUM_PAGES                     NUMBER
 PUBLISHER                     PUBLISHER_OBJ -- Part of Attribute Chain
 DISTRIBUTION_DATE             DATE
```

Describing Object Tables

Describing the object tables using default settings does not provide a complete picture of our table, as the attributes included in `publisher_obj` were not included in our describe of `soft_cover_obj`. The SET DESC(RIBE) command can provide a more complete picture of our object table. The syntax is as follows:

SET DESCRIBE [DEPTH {1|n|ALL}]
  [LINENUM {ON|OFF}] [INDENT {ON|OFF}]

Let's set the depth to all and linenum on so that we can view the hierarchy:

```
SQL> SET DESC DEPTH ALL LINENUM ON
SQL> DESC soft_cover_tbl
          Name                             Null?    Type
          --------------------------    --------    --------------------
     1    ITEM_ID                                    NUMBER(10)
     2    NUM_IN_STOCK                               NUMBER(10)
     3    REORDER_STATUS                             VARCHAR2(20 CHAR)
     4    PRICE                                      NUMBER(10,2)
     5    ISBN                                       CHAR(10 CHAR)
     6    CATEGORY                                   VARCHAR2(20 CHAR)
     7    TITLE                                      VARCHAR2(100 CHAR)
     8    NUM_PAGES                                  NUMBER
     9    PUBLISHER                                  PUBLISHER_OBJ
    10  9   PUB_NAME                                 VARCHAR2(30)
    11  9   CONTACT_INFO                             CONTACT_OBJ
    12 11     NAME                                   PERSON_OBJ
```

```
13    12        FIRST_NAME              VARCHAR2(20)
14    12        LAST_NAME               VARCHAR2(20)
15    11      ADDRESS                   ADDRESS_OBJ
16    15        ADDRESS1                VARCHAR2(30 CHAR)
17    15        ADDRESS2                VARCHAR2(30 CHAR)
18    15        CITY                    VARCHAR2(30 CHAR)
19    15        STATE                   CHAR(2 CHAR)
20    11      PHONE                     NUMBER(10)
MEMBER PROCEDURE SHOW_CONTACT
21            DISTRIBUTION_DATE         DATE
```

This provides a little better view of our object! It allows us to see the complete object table, and shows the hierarchy with line numbers and indentation.

NOTE
For expanded coverage on this topic, refer to Jason Price, Oracle 10g SQL (McGraw-Hill/Osborne, 2004), or visit http://otn.oracle.com and view the online SQL*Plus documentation.

Object Identifiers

Relational tables have unique identifiers called *rowid's* that are system generated. Similarly, object tables have unique identifiers that are system generated called *object identifiers,* or *OIDs*. Each *row object* receives an OID that is guaranteed unique and allows a *reference* to the object instance, or row object, in your program. Read more on object references in the section "Accessing Persistent Objects Using SQL and PL/SQL."

OIDs are created only for object tables and object views (discussed later in this chapter) and are not available for use with transient objects and object columns (also discussed later). Once an OID is assigned to an object, it is forever with that object. Oracle allows for a whopping 2^{128} OIDs to avoid problems of objects "stepping" on each other during operations such as export/import. If I export objects and then import them again, the OID stays with that object.

Oracle does allow us to override the system generated OID with our primary key at object table creation if we wish. See the following example:

```
CREATE TABLE soft_cover_tbl
  OF soft_cover_obj
  (CONSTRAINT soft_cover_tbl_p PRIMARY KEY (item_id))
  OBJECT IDENTIFIER IS PRIMARY KEY;
```

Notice line 4—the OID is now based on the primary key, and the hidden column SYS_NC_OID$ in soft_cover_tbl can be used similar to rowid.

Synonyms

We can create synonyms for our object tables just as we can for relational tables. Consider the following example:

```
CREATE OR REPLACE SYNONYM soft_cover_syn
  FOR objects_user.soft_cover_tbl;
```

While synonyms are created using the same syntax regardless of the type of table, access to the data is still restricted according to the rules of the underlying table.

Column Objects

Column objects are created as part of a relational or object table by setting the datatype of a column as an object type. In our examples for object tables, the `soft_cover_tbl` table is an object table but also contains object columns. The `publisher` column was of type `publisher_obj`.

One of the main differences between column objects and object tables is the latter's ability to reference object instances using OID's. There are no OIDs assigned to column objects. The object instance is part of the relational record that has a rowid assigned.

Creating Column Objects

We can create a relational table similar in structure to the `inventory_obj` object type, but not based on it. As part of the relational table, we will create the price column with a `discount_price_obj` object type.

```
-- Available online as part of ColObj.sql
CREATE TABLE inventory_tbl (
      item_id            NUMBER (10) PRIMARY KEY,
      num_in_stock       NUMBER (10),
      reorder_status     VARCHAR2 (20 CHAR),
      price              DISCOUNT_PRICE_OBJ)
/
```

By doing a describe of the table using our SET DESC settings discussed earlier, we can see the structure of the `inventory_tbl` table:

```
SQL> desc inventory_tbl
           Name                            Null?      Type
           ------------------------------- --------   -------------------
      --
      1       ITEM_ID                      NOT NULL   NUMBER(10)
      2       NUM_IN_STOCK                            NUMBER(10)
      3       REORDER_STATUS                          VARCHAR2(20 CHAR)
      4       PRICE                                   DISCOUNT_PRICE_OBJ
      5   4   DISCOUNT_RATE                           NUMBER(10,4)
      6   4   PRICE                                   NUMBER(10,2)
```

```
METHOD
------
 FINAL CONSTRUCTOR FUNCTION DISCOUNT_PRICE_OBJ RETURNS SELF AS RESULT
 Argument Name                        Type                    In/Out Default?
 ------------------------------       ----------------------  ------ --------
 PRICE                                NUMBER                  IN
```

Our relational table has a `price` column that looks similar to a nested table and also has access to the `discount_price_obj.price` method.

While object tables are tied to their object type and do not allow alteration of the table directly, tables containing column objects have no such restriction. If we wish to add a column to the table, we do so with a normal ALTER TABLE statement.

```
SQL> ALTER TABLE inventory_tbl
  2  ADD backordered CHAR(1);

Table altered.
```

Object Views

Object views allow us to use object features with relational structures. This is especially handy when changing an application to use OO features over time. It is also useful for extending relational applications to use OO features where modification of the original source is not possible.

Creating Basic Object Views

To create an object view, we must create a type whose attributes match the underlying column names in the table(s). The following example re-creates the specification of the `discount_price_obj` and `inventory_obj` object types. Notice that while the attributes in the `inventory_obj` specification match those in the `inventory_tbl` relational table, the column `num_in_stock` is not included in the object type definition.

```
-- Available online as part of ObjectView.sql
CREATE OR REPLACE TYPE discount_price_obj AS OBJECT (
      discount_rate    NUMBER (10, 4),
      price            NUMBER (10, 2),
      MEMBER FUNCTION discount_price
          RETURN NUMBER
   )
   INSTANTIABLE FINAL;
   /


CREATE OR REPLACE TYPE BODY discount_price_obj
   AS
      MEMBER FUNCTION discount_price
          RETURN NUMBER
      IS
```

```
        BEGIN
            RETURN (SELF.price * (1 - SELF.discount_rate));
        END discount_price;
    END;
/

CREATE OR REPLACE TYPE inventory_obj AS OBJECT (
        item_id            NUMBER (10),
        reorder_status     VARCHAR2 (20 CHAR),
        price              DISCOUNT_PRICE_OBJ,
        MEMBER PROCEDURE print_inventory,
        MEMBER PROCEDURE print_status,
        MEMBER PROCEDURE print_price
    )
    INSTANTIABLE NOT FINAL;
/
```

Now that we have the object type specification created, we can base the object view on it. We must decide the type of OID we want to use with the CREATE VIEW statement. Object views are created with an OID that is either based on the primary key of the underlying table or is system generated. The object identifiers provide the same ability as an OID on an object table to support object references. Let's look at an example that creates the view using the `item_id` column for the OID.

```
-- Available online as part of ObjectView.sql
CREATE VIEW inventory_vie
    OF inventory_obj
    WITH OBJECT IDENTIFIER (item_id)
AS
    SELECT i.item_id, i.num_in_stock, i.reorder_status,
           i.price
    FROM   inventory_tbl i
/
```

A describe of the `inventory_tbl` table shows the following structure:

```
SET DESC DEPTH ALL LINENUM ON

-- Describe of the TABLE
DESC inventory_tbl
            Name                             Null?     Type
            ------------------------------   --------  -------------------
    -

    1       ITEM_ID                          NOT NULL  NUMBER(10)
    2       NUM_IN_STOCK                               NUMBER(10)
    3       REORDER_STATUS                             VARCHAR2(20 CHAR)
    4       PRICE                                      DISCOUNT_PRICE_OBJ
```

```
5     4    DISCOUNT_RATE                        NUMBER(10,4)
6     4    PRICE                                NUMBER(10,2)

METHOD
------
  MEMBER FUNCTION DISCOUNT_PRICE RETURNS NUMBER
```

Now, compare the table's structure to that of the `inventory_vie` view.

```
desc inventory_vie
           Name                                 Null?     Type
           ------------------------------ --------  ------------------
   1       ITEM_ID                                   NUMBER(10)
   2       REORDER_STATUS                            VARCHAR2(20 CHAR)
   3       PRICE                                     DISCOUNT_PRICE_OBJ
   4    3  DISCOUNT_RATE                             NUMBER(10,4)
   5    3  PRICE                                     NUMBER(10,2)

METHOD
------
  MEMBER FUNCTION DISCOUNT_PRICE RETURNS NUMBER
```

Here we see the view is nearly identical to the table, including access to the member function `discount_price`. The difference between the two is that the `num_in_stock` attribute is no longer visible.

In the "Objects View" subsection of "Accessing Persistent Objects Using SQL and PL/SQL," we will use this view to retrieve data from the `inventory_tbl` table, and introduce a method of inserting records into object views using INSTEAD OF triggers.

Accessing Persistent Objects Using SQL and PL/SQL

At the beginning of this chapter we pointed out that PL/SQL objects can be stored in the database and created, maintained, and accessed using SQL and PL/SQL. As such, DML operations against objects are transactional and subject to the same read-consistency and undo rules as any other DML operation. In this section we discuss various methods of using SQL and PL/SQL to access persistent objects.

Object Tables

Let's start by looking at a very basic example using INSERT, UPDATE, DELETE, and SELECT against an object table. Our `discount_price_obj` object type has two columns, both with NUMBER datatypes. In the following example, we create the discount_price_tbl table from the discount_price_obj type:

-- Available online as part of objectTable.sql

```
CREATE OR REPLACE TYPE discount_price_obj AS OBJECT (
    discount_rate    NUMBER (10, 4),
    price            NUMBER (10, 2),
    MEMBER FUNCTION discount_price
        RETURN NUMBER
    )
    INSTANTIABLE FINAL;
/

CREATE OR REPLACE TYPE BODY discount_price_obj
    AS
        MEMBER FUNCTION discount_price
            RETURN NUMBER
        IS
        BEGIN
            RETURN (SELF.price * (1 - SELF.discount_rate));
        END discount_price;
    END;
/

CREATE TABLE discount_price_tbl OF discount_price_obj;
```

The following block performs DML as if the object table were a standard relational table:

-- Available online as part of ObjectTable.sql

```
SET SERVEROUTPUT ON SIZE 1000000
DECLARE
    v_DiscountRate     discount_price_tbl.discount_rate%TYPE;
    v_OriginalPrice    discount_price_tbl.price%TYPE;
    v_DiscountPrice    discount_price_tbl.price%TYPE;
  BEGIN
    -- INSERT a new row into the discount_price_tbl table
    INSERT INTO discount_price_tbl
        VALUES (.1, 54.95);

    -- UPDATE the record, changing the discount rate
    UPDATE discount_price_tbl
      SET discount_rate = .15
    WHERE discount_rate = .1;

    -- SELECT and print the values to the screen
    SELECT discount_rate, price, price - (discount_rate * price)
      INTO v_DiscountRate, v_OriginalPrice, v_DiscountPrice
      FROM discount_price_tbl
```

```
        WHERE rownum < 2;

    DBMS_OUTPUT.PUT_LINE ('Original Price: ' || v_OriginalPrice);
    DBMS_OUTPUT.PUT_LINE (    'Discount Rate Applied: '
                        || v_DiscountRate * 100
                        || '%'
                      );
    DBMS_OUTPUT.PUT_LINE ('Our LOW, LOW price: ' || v_DiscountPrice);

    -- DELETE the row we added
    DELETE FROM discount_price_tbl;
  END;
/
```

This anonymous block returns the following:

```
Original Price: 54.95
Discount Rate Applied: 15%
Our LOW, LOW price: 46.71
```

Our `discount_price_obj` method called `discount_price` is for retrieval, so we will need to seed the table prior to calling the method.

```
-- Available online as part of ObjectTable.sql
DELETE FROM discount_price_tbl;
INSERT INTO discount_price_tbl VALUES (.1, 54.95);
INSERT INTO discount_price_tbl VALUES (.1, 39.95);
INSERT INTO discount_price_tbl VALUES (.15, 42.95);
INSERT INTO discount_price_tbl VALUES (.2, 65.95);
INSERT INTO discount_price_tbl VALUES (.1, 52.95);
commit;
```

This simple select shows how we call the `discount_price` method:

```
-- Available online as part of ObjectTable.sql
SELECT d.price "Original Price", d.discount_price() "Our Price"
  FROM discount_price_tbl d;
```

This select results in the following:

```
Original Price  Our Price
--------------  ----------
        54.95     49.455
        39.95     35.955
        42.95    36.5075
        65.95      52.76
        52.95     47.655

5 rows selected.
```

Notice the call to the `discount_price` method. We created our table from the `discount_price_obj` object type that contains the `discount_price` method. In our select statement, the call to the `discount_price` method uses the table alias, not the object type name! If we had simply created the table as a normal relational table, this would not be possible.

The table alias in this case is the correlation identifier, and it must be used to access methods and/or attributes of the object table. The correlation identifier will become of even greater importance in our discussion of object references in the next section.

Carrying this one step further, let's create a table based on the `inventory_obj` object type specification. Where the `discount_price_obj` object type specification included attributes with standard Oracle datatypes, the `inventory_obj` object type is a complex object that uses another object type as a datatype.

```
-- Available online as part of objectTable.sql
CREATE OR REPLACE TYPE inventory_obj AS OBJECT (
        item_id          NUMBER (10),
        num_in_stock     NUMBER (10),
        reorder_status   VARCHAR2 (20 CHAR),
        price            DISCOUNT_PRICE_OBJ,
        MEMBER PROCEDURE print_inventory,
        MEMBER PROCEDURE print_status,
        MEMBER PROCEDURE print_price
    )
    INSTANTIABLE NOT FINAL;
/

CREATE TABLE inventory_tbl OF inventory_obj;
```

Now describe the table to examine the structure.

```
DESC inventory_tbl
          Name                                Null?     Type
          -------------------------------- --------  ------------------
    1     ITEM_ID                                     NUMBER(10)
    2     NUM_IN_STOCK                                NUMBER(10)
    3     REORDER_STATUS                              VARCHAR2(20 CHAR)
    4     PRICE                                       DISCOUNT_PRICE_OBJ
    5   4    DISCOUNT_RATE                            NUMBER(10,4)
    6   4    PRICE                                    NUMBER(10,2)
METHOD
------
  MEMBER FUNCTION DISCOUNT_PRICE RETURNS NUMBER
```

The price column has `discount_price_obj` as its datatype, just like the `inventory_obj` object type specification. Adding data is a bit more complex now. Here we attempt a basic insert:

```
INSERT INTO inventory_tbl
        VALUES (1, 10, 'IN STOCK', 54.95);
```

The insert returns the following error:

```
        VALUES (1, 10, 'IN STOCK', 54.95)
                                    *
ERROR at line 2:
ORA-00932: inconsistent datatypes: expected UDT got NUMBER
```

To complete the insert, we must first create an instance of the type by using a constructor method. A *constructor* is a function that returns an initialized object and takes as arguments the values for the object's attributes. For every object type, Oracle predefines a constructor with the same name as the type. Here is our insert using the `discount_price_obj` constructor:

```
-- Available online as part of objectTable.sql
INSERT INTO inventory_tbl
        VALUES (1, 10, 'IN STOCK', discount_price_obj (.1, 75));
```

The insert is now successful.

Accessing Column Objects

As we discussed earlier in the chapter, column objects are created in a relational or object table when the type of a column is set to another object type. As you saw in the "Object Tables" section, most DML operations work without modification when operating on a basic object table. Column objects add some complexity but also a number of additional benefits. Let's drop and re-create the `inventory_tbl` table as a relational table, still keeping the same structure:

```
-- Available online as part of ColObj.sql
CREATE TABLE inventory_tbl (
    item_id NUMBER(10) PRIMARY KEY,
    num_in_stock NUMBER(10),
    reorder_status VARCHAR2(20 CHAR),
    price DISCOUNT_PRICE_OBJ)
/
```

We saw how to perform an insert into this table in the object table section:

```
-- Available online as part of ColObj.sql
INSERT INTO inventory_tbl
        VALUES (1, 10, 'IN STOCK', discount_price_obj (.1, 75));
```

Describing the table shows the attribute chain for the price column, as well as the method we have access to through the `discount_price_obj` object type:

```
desc inventory_tbl
  Name                                         Null?     Type
  ------------------------------------------ --------  ----------------------
      1        ITEM_ID                       NOT NULL  NUMBER(10)
      2        NUM_IN_STOCK                            NUMBER(10)
      3        REORDER_STATUS                          VARCHAR2(20 CHAR)
      4        PRICE                                   DISCOUNT_PRICE_OBJ
      5     4    DISCOUNT_RATE                         NUMBER(10,4)
      6     4    PRICE                                 NUMBER(10,2)
 METHOD
 ------
  MEMBER FUNCTION DISCOUNT_PRICE RETURNS NUMBER
```

A SELECT from our table results in the following:

```
COL reorder_status FORMAT A15
COL price FORMAT A30
SELECT *
FROM inventory_tbl;

ITEM_ID NUM_IN_STOCK REORDER_STATUS     PRICE(DISCOUNT_RATE, PRICE)
---------- ------------ ---------------   ----------------------------------
         1           10 IN STOCK          DISCOUNT_PRICE_OBJ(.1, 75)
```

The value stored in the column object includes the name of the object type. We can make reference to both attributes and methods of the `discount_price_obj` object type, as is demonstrated in the following example:

```
-- Available online as part of ColObj.sql
SET SERVEROUTPUT ON SIZE 1000000
DECLARE
     v_Price    DISCOUNT_PRICE_OBJ;
  BEGIN
  -- Update attribute of the price object
     SELECT price
       INTO v_Price
       FROM inventory_tbl
      WHERE item_id = 1;

     DBMS_OUTPUT.PUT_LINE (' ');
     DBMS_OUTPUT.PUT_LINE ('Price BEFORE update: '
                           || v_Price.discount_price);
     v_Price.discount_rate := .2;

     UPDATE inventory_tbl
        SET price = v_Price;
```

```
      DBMS_OUTPUT.PUT_LINE (' ');
      DBMS_OUTPUT.PUT_LINE ('Price AFTER update: '
                            || v_Price.discount_price);
      ROLLBACK;
   END;
/
```

This block produces the following result:

```
Price BEFORE update: 67.5
Price AFTER update: 60
```

In this block we referenced both attributes and methods in the discount_ price_obj object type. If we attempt this in SQL, there is a slight difference in that we must use the correlation ID.

```
-- Available online as part of ColObj.sql
SELECT i.price.price, i.price.discount_rate
  FROM inventory_tbl i;
```

The select returns

```
PRICE.PRICE PRICE.DISCOUNT_RATE
----------- -------------------
         75                  .1
```

This SELECT returns attribute values only. If we want to access the methods via SQL, we use dot notation as well but include the parameter list in the call.

```
-- Available online as part of ColObj.sql
SELECT i.price.discount_price()
  FROM inventory_tbl i;
```

This select returns the following:

```
I.PRICE.DISCOUNT_PRICE()
-----------------------
                   67.5
```

The parameter list in this case is take care of by the column object itself, so we use () in the call.

Accessing Object Views

Object views present relational data in an object-oriented way. Earlier in the chapter we re-created the table inventory_tbl as a relational table with an object column, and then we created an object view of the structure. We will extend this example here, showing how to access the attributes and methods of the object column through the view rather than the table.

Retrieving Rows

The following example creates the object view on the relational table:

```
-- Available online as part of ObjectView.sql
CREATE VIEW inventory_vie
    OF inventory_obj
    WITH OBJECT IDENTIFIER (item_id)
  AS
    SELECT i.item_id OID, i.reorder_status, i.price
      FROM inventory_tbl I
/
```

Now, to seed records in the `inventory_tbl` table:

```
INSERT INTO inventory_tbl
    VALUES (1, 10, 'IN STOCK', discount_price_obj (.1, 75));
INSERT INTO inventory_tbl
    VALUES (2, 13, 'IN STOCK', discount_price_obj (.1, 54.95));
INSERT INTO inventory_tbl
    VALUES (3, 24, 'IN STOCK', discount_price_obj (.15, 43.95));
INSERT INTO inventory_tbl
    VALUES (4, 13, 'IN STOCK', discount_price_obj (.1, 60));
INSERT INTO inventory_tbl
    VALUES (5, 5, 'IN STOCK', discount_price_obj (.20, 42.95));
```

The methods of selecting data from the object views and from the object tables are nearly identical. One difference, as you may have noticed, is that the view definition is missing the `num_in_stock` column. This column is present in the `inventory_tbl` table. Just as with standard views, you can access columns or attributes present in the view only when selecting from the view.

The following SELECT accesses the object view, retrieving attributes from the column object, and uses the `discount_price` method from the column object:

```
-- Available online as part of ObjectView.sql
SELECT i.item_id, i.price.price, i.price.discount_rate,
       i.price.discount_price ()
  FROM inventory_vie I
/
```

This returns the following result:

```
  ITEM_ID PRICE.PRICE PRICE.DISCOUNT_RATE I.PRICE.DISCOUNT_PRICE()
---------- ----------- ------------------- ------------------------
        1          75                  .1                     67.5
        2       54.95                  .1                   49.455
        3       43.95                 .15                  37.3575
        4          60                  .1                       54
        5       42.95                  .2                    34.36
        6       64.95                 .15                  55.2075
```

Inserting and Updating

Although direct inserting and updating of object views is not supported, we can create an INSTEAD OF trigger to facilitate this for us. Here we create a trigger that performs an insert into the `inventory_tbl` table whenever an insert is performed against the view:

```
-- Available online as part of ObjectView.sql
CREATE OR REPLACE TRIGGER inventory_trg
    INSTEAD OF INSERT ON inventory_vie
    FOR EACH ROW
    BEGIN
    INSERT INTO inventory_tbl
        VALUES (:NEW.item_id, NULL, :NEW.reorder_status, :NEW.price);
    END;
/
```

We test this by performing an insert into the `inventory_vie` view.

```
INSERT INTO inventory_vie
    VALUES (7, 'ON ORDER', discount_price_obj(.15, 68.95));
```

```
1 row created.
```

We can verify the row was inserted into the `inventory_tbl` table with a simple select:

```
-- Available online as part of ObjectView.sql
SELECT *
  FROM inventory_tbl
 WHERE item_id = 7;
```

This returns the following:

```
   ITEM_ID NUM_IN_STOCK REORDER_STATUS  PRICE(DISCOUNT_RATE, PRICE)
---------- ------------ --------------- -------------------------------
--
         7              ON ORDER        DISCOUNT_PRICE_OBJ(.15, 68.95)
```

Object Related Functions and Operators

Earlier in the chapter we discussed the object identifier (OID) and some of its uses with object tables and object views. Object references are pointers to the rows of our object tables and views; they are possible because of the OID. The reference, or REF, stores the OID and the table ID, allowing us to retrieve and navigate object rows based on the REF value. Oracle provides additional capabilities using functions such as TREAT, VALUE, and SYS_TYPEID. We will review these functions and more in this section.

REF

You can think of a REF value simply as a pointer to an object instance in an object table or object view. The syntax for REF is as follows:

REF(*co_id*)

where *co_id* is the correlation identifier for the object table or object view being accessed. The following simple example retrieves an object reference for a row object in the `inventory_tbl` table with an `item_id` attribute of 1:

```
SELECT REF(i)
  FROM inventory_tbl i
 WHERE item_id = 1;
```

The REF value for `item_id` 1 is returned.

```
REF(I)
---------------------------------------------------------------------------------
00002802094BB784FE506643A0B0C48386C259A337E03E98B727144068BAD3219746127480018000FF0000
```

Let's use the `inventory_obj` object type and the `inventory_tbl` object table to test out the REF function further. In this block we declare a variable to reference an object. The syntax for declaring an object reference in a declarative section or table definition is

variable_or_column_name REF *object_type*;

where *variable_or_column_name* is the name of the object reference, and *object_type* is the object type. See the following example for the implementation:

```
-- Available online as part of RefObj.sql
DELETE FROM inventory_tbl;
INSERT INTO inventory_tbl (item_id, num_in_stock, reorder_status, price)
    VALUES (1, 10, 'IN STOCK', discount_price_obj (.1, 75));
INSERT INTO inventory_tbl (item_id, num_in_stock, reorder_status, price)
    VALUES (2, 2, 'ON ORDER', discount_price_obj (.1, 54.95));
INSERT INTO inventory_tbl (item_id, num_in_stock, reorder_status, price)
    VALUES (3, 24, 'IN STOCK', discount_price_obj (.1, 63.95));
COMMIT ;
```

The following block sets a variable as a REF of `inventory_obj`, retrieves the REF value of an item, and then uses that REF value in the remainder of the block to *reference* the row object:

```
-- Available online as part of RefObj.sql
DECLARE
        v_InventoryRef      REF INVENTORY_OBJ;
        v_ItemID            NUMBER (10);
        v_ReorderStatus   VARCHAR2 (20 CHAR);
```

```
BEGIN
   SELECT REF (i)
     INTO v_InventoryRef
     FROM inventory_tbl i
    WHERE reorder_status = 'ON ORDER';

   SELECT i.item_id, i.reorder_status
     INTO v_ItemID, v_ReorderStatus
     FROM inventory_tbl I
    WHERE REF (i) = v_InventoryRef;

   DBMS_OUTPUT.PUT_LINE (    'Item ID '
                         || v_ItemID
                         || ' is '
                         || v_ReorderStatus
                        );
END;
/
```

Executing the block returns the following:

```
Item ID 2 is ON ORDER
```

As the results show, we were able to use the REF value as the pointer to the row we needed.

NOTE
Though the object reference, or REF, is a logical pointer, it is a static binary value that can be stored in a physical table if you wish.

Forward Type Declaration
What happens if I am creating a specification that references another object type, but that other type does not yet exist? This can be problematic, especially if I do not yet know how I want the other object type structured. The inventory_obj object type that follows references discount_price_obj:

```
-- Available online as part of ForwardDeclaration.sql
CREATE OR REPLACE TYPE inventory_obj AS OBJECT (
    item_id         NUMBER(10),
    num_in_stock    NUMBER(10),
    reorder_status VARCHAR2(20),
    price          REF   DISCOUNT_PRICE_OBJ);
/
PLS-00201: identifier 'DISCOUNT_PRICE_OBJ' must be declared
```

Running this without first specifying `discount_price_obj` results in the exception just shown. To solve this problem, we can use a forward type:

```
CREATE OR REPLACE TYPE discount_price_obj;
/
```

This simple type allows `inventory_obj` to be created successfully even though there is no definition for `discount_price_obj`.

```
CREATE OR REPLACE TYPE inventory_obj AS OBJECT (
     item_id         NUMBER(10),
     num_in_stock    NUMBER(10),
     reorder_status  VARCHAR2(20),
     price           REF    discount_price_obj);
/
```

DEREF

DEREF returns the object instance that the REF value points to. This is more easily explained with a simple example. In this case, DEREF is passed the REF value for the correlation ID of the `inventory_tbl`:

```
SELECT DEREF(REF(i))
  FROM inventory_tbl i
 WHERE item_id = 1;
```

The object instance associated with the REF value of `item_id` 1 is returned:

```
DEREF(REF(I))(ITEM_ID, NUM_IN_STOCK, REORDER_STATUS, PRICE(DISCOUNT_RA
------------------------------------------------------------------
INVENTORY_OBJ(1, 10, 'IN STOCK', DISCOUNT_PRICE_OBJ(.1, 75))
```

IS DANGLING

REFs that point to nothing are considered dangling. The following example illustrates how this is possible:

```
-- Available online as part of IsDangling.sql
SET SERVEROUTPUT ON SIZE 1000000
DECLARE
     v_InventoryRef     REF INVENTORY_OBJ;
     v_ItemID           NUMBER (10);
     v_ReorderStatus    VARCHAR2 (20 CHAR);
     v_Status           VARCHAR2 (20 CHAR);
  BEGIN
    SELECT REF (i)
      INTO v_InventoryRef
      FROM inventory_tbl i
```

```
        WHERE reorder_status = 'ON ORDER';

    DELETE FROM inventory_tbl I
         WHERE REF (i) = v_InventoryRef;

    SELECT 'I''M DANGLING'
      INTO v_Status
      FROM DUAL
     WHERE v_InventoryRef IS DANGLING;

    DBMS_OUTPUT.PUT_LINE (v_Status);
  END;
/
```

In this block we retrieved a REF value for an item into a variable, then deleted that item. We were able to test the REF value then by using a SELECT...FROM that includes the IS DANGLING test. The where clause evaluates to true, so the following is returned:

```
I'M DANGLING
```

TREAT
The TREAT function does verification at run time to see if a base type can be treated as one of its subtypes. In our example (illustrated earlier in the chapter in Figure 15-1), we see an inventory_obj object type with book_obj as its subtype. Inventory_obj may have music_obj as its subtype as well, so not all object instances of inventory_obj are guaranteed to be books. TREAT allows us to use methods, or access attributes, of a subtype if the object instance is of that subtype. We use the following syntax:

TREAT (*object_instance*|*REF* AS *subtype*) [. *attribute*|*method*]

Object_instance, in the case of our example, is an instance of inventory_obj. The *REF* value can also be used when working with object tables and object views to point to the instance. *Subtype* is under the base type whose instance is evaluated, and is part of the same inheritance hierarchy. *Attribute* and *method* are from the subtype.

   In our DEREF example we can see the stored object instance in the inventory_tbl table is of type inventory_obj. Inventory_obj includes subtypes of book_obj and music_obj, so with a slight modification to our insert statement, we can make records of each of these types:

TIP
You may choose to run cleanSchema.sql prior to running treat.sql, as some of the base objects change in the treat.sql example.

```
-- Available online as part of Treat.sql
CREATE OR REPLACE TYPE inventory_obj AS OBJECT (
        item_id           NUMBER (10),
        num_in_stock      NUMBER (10),
        reorder_status    VARCHAR2 (20 CHAR),
        price             NUMBER(10,2),
        CONSTRUCTOR FUNCTION inventory_obj (
          item_id          IN    NUMBER,
          num_in_stock     IN    NUMBER,
          price            IN    NUMBER
      )
        RETURN SELF AS RESULT,
      MEMBER PROCEDURE print_inventory,
      MEMBER PROCEDURE print_status,
      MEMBER PROCEDURE print_price
    )
    INSTANTIABLE NOT FINAL;
/
```

Now create the object table based on `inventory_obj`:

```
CREATE TABLE inventory_tbl OF inventory_obj;
```

We can insert records into our `inventory_tbl` table as follows:

```
-- Available online as part of Treat.sql
INSERT INTO inventory_tbl
        VALUES (music_obj (1,
                           10,
                           'IN STOCK',
                           11.99,
                           'Hip-Hop',
                           music_person_obj ('George', 'Instructor'),
                           music_person_obj ('George', 'Instructor')
                           ));

INSERT INTO inventory_tbl
        VALUES (book_obj (2,
                          13,
                          'IN STOCK',
                          54.95,
                          '72121203',
                          'TECHNICAL',
                          'Oracle DBA 101',
                          563,
                          publisher_obj ('Oracle Press',
                                    contact_obj (person_obj ('Susan',
                                                        Publisher'
```

```
                                                                   ),
                                           address_obj ('123 Street',
                                                        'Suite 2',
                                                        'My City',
                                                        'CO'
                                                        ),
                                               '5555555555'
                                           )
                                )
                    ));
```

NOTE
Notice the amount of nesting in the last insert. This is the result of attribute chaining and the amount of detail that is included in a single object instance.

Now when we perform a select against the `inventory_tbl` table, we can see both rows and the subtypes associated with them.

```
SELECT SYS_NC_ROWINFO$
    FROM inventory_tbl;

SYS_NC_ROWINFO$(ITEM_ID, NUM_IN_STOCK, REORDER_STATUS, PRICE)
---------------------------------------------------------------------
MUSIC_OBJ(1, 10, 'IN STOCK', 11.99, 'Hip-Hop', MUSIC_PERSON_OBJ('George',
'Instructor'), MUSIC_PERSON_OBJ('George', 'Instructor'))

BOOK_OBJ(2, 13, 'IN STOCK', 54.95, '72121203  ', 'TECHNICAL', 'Oracle DBA 101',
563, PUBLISHER_OBJ('Oracle Press', CONTACT_OBJ(PERSON_OBJ('Susan', 'Publisher'),
ADDRESS_OBJ('123 Street', 'Suite 2', 'My City', 'CO'), 5555555555)))
```

The two records, stored in the same object table, contain totally different information outside of the four initial attributes of the supertype.

NOTE
SYS_NC_ROWINFO$ is a hidden column in object tables that can be used in select statements to retrieve complete row objects.

Now we can use the TREAT function. As part of the TREAT function, we specify the subtype. In the following example, we use the `book_obj` object type:

```
SELECT TREAT(VALUE(i) AS book_obj)
    FROM inventory_tbl i;
```

This select returns the following:

```
TREAT(VALUE(I)ASBOOK_OBJ)(ITEM_ID, NUM_IN_STOCK, REORDER_STATUS, PRICE, ISBN,
CATEGORY, TITLE, NUM_P
--------------------------------------------------------------------------

BOOK_OBJ(2, 13, 'IN STOCK', 54.95, '72121203   ', 'TECHNICAL', 'Oracle DBA 101',
563, PUBLISHER_OBJ('Oracle Press', CONTACT_OBJ(PERSON_OBJ('Susan', 'Publisher'),
ADDRESS_OBJ('123 Street', 'Suite 2', 'My City', 'CO'), 5555555555)))

2 rows selected.
```

We can rerun the select, replacing book_obj with music_obj.

```
SQL> SELECT TREAT(VALUE(i) AS music_obj)
  2  FROM inventory_tbl i;
```

This select returns the following:

```
TREAT(VALUE(I)ASMUSIC_OBJ)(ITEM_ID, NUM_IN_STOCK, REORDER_STATUS, PRICE, STYLE,
COMPOSER(FIRST_NAME
--------------------------------------------------------------------------
MUSIC_OBJ(1, 10, 'IN STOCK', 11.99, 'Hip-Hop', MUSIC_PERSON_OBJ('George',
'Instructor'), MUSIC_PERSON_OBJ('George', 'Instructor'))

2 rows selected.
```

Notice that there are two rows selected in each case. The decision of which row(s) to return with a value is made at run time. NULL is always returned when the record in the table does not match the subtype specified.

We can also TREAT the REF value so that only REF values are returned that match the specified subtype. See the following example:

```
SELECT TREAT(REF(i) AS REF book_obj)
     FROM inventory_tbl i;
```

This select returns the following:

```
TREAT(REF(I)ASREFBOOK_OBJ)
----------------------------------------------------------------------------------
00002802097656A76CF1524CE4A26CDC19D05FBAF577F1D1ED4A304B62ADF6CFED98EC2699018000FF0001

2 rows selected.
```

VALUE

The VALUE function takes as input the correlation ID and returns the object instances from the object table or object view. Syntax for VALUE is

VALUE(*co_id*)[. *attribute*|*method*]

where *co_id* is the correlation identifier for the object table or object view being accessed. The following simple select returns all object instances from the `inventory_obj` object table:

```
SELECT VALUE(i)
    FROM inventory_tbl i;
```

This select returns the following:

```
VALUE(I)(ITEM_ID, NUM_IN_STOCK, REORDER_STATUS, PRICE)
--------------------------------------------------------------------------
MUSIC_OBJ(1, 10, 'IN STOCK', 11.99, 'Hip-Hop', MUSIC_PERSON_OBJ('George',
'Instructor'), MUSIC_PERSON_OBJ('George', 'Instructor'))

BOOK_OBJ(2, 13, 'IN STOCK', 54.95, '72121203   ', 'TECHNICAL', 'Oracle DBA 101',
563, PUBLISHER_OBJ('Oracle Press', CONTACT_OBJ(PERSON_OBJ('Susan', 'Publisher'),
ADDRESS_OBJ('123 Street', 'Suite 2', 'My City', 'CO'), 5555555555)))

2 rows selected.
```

We can use dot notation to extract only the attributes we want to see. The following example retrieves the `item_id` and price attributes:

```
SELECT VALUE(i).item_id, VALUE(i).price
    FROM inventory_tbl i;
```

The select returns the following:

```
VALUE(I).ITEM_ID VALUE(I).PRICE
---------------- --------------
               1          11.99
               2          54.95
```

Methods can also be used with the same dot notation.

IS OF

IS OF is a predicate used to determine whether a value or variable is of a particular type. The following example is the same as one of our VALUE examples, except in the WHERE clause:

```
SELECT VALUE(i)
   FROM inventory_tbl I
   WHERE VALUE(i) IS OF (book_obj);
```

The select returns the following:

```
VALUE(I)(ITEM_ID, NUM_IN_STOCK, REORDER_STATUS, PRICE)
---------------------------------------------------------------------------
BOOK_OBJ(2, 13, 'IN STOCK', 54.95, '72121203   ', 'TECHNICAL', 'Oracle DBA 101',
563, PUBLISHER_OBJ('Oracle Press', CONTACT_OBJ(PERSON_OBJ('Susan', 'Publisher'),
ADDRESS_OBJ('123 Street', 'Suite 2', 'My City', 'CO'), 5555555555)))
```

In this case, IS OF checks to see whether the object instances are of the type specified. If we had objects of a subtype of book_obj, such as soft_cover_obj, those values would have been returned as well.

Oracle provides the ONLY keyword to restrict the return result to only those values related directly to the stated type. The following statement modifies the last example to use the ONLY keyword:

```
SELECT VALUE(i)
    FROM inventory_tbl I
    WHERE VALUE(i) IS OF (ONLY book_obj);
```

We can use IS OF in a PL/SQL block, as is demonstrated in the next example:

```
SET SERVEROUTPUT ON SIZE 1000000
DECLARE
    v_inventory   INVENTORY_OBJ;
  BEGIN
    SELECT VALUE (i)
      INTO v_Inventory
      FROM inventory_tbl i
     WHERE VALUE (i).item_id = 1;

    IF v_Inventory IS OF (book_obj)
    THEN
        DBMS_OUTPUT.PUT_LINE (   'Item ID '
                              || v_Inventory.item_id
                              || ' is of type BOOK_OBJ'
                            );
    ELSIF v_inventory IS OF (music_obj)
    THEN
        DBMS_OUTPUT.PUT_LINE (   'Item ID '
                              || v_Inventory.item_id
                              || ' is of type MUSIC_OBJ'
                            );
    END IF;
  END;
/
```

Execution of the block returns the following:

```
Item ID 1 is of type MUSIC_OBJ
```

SYS_TYPEID

The `SYS_TYPEID` function returns the typeid of the object instance. The following example illustrates this:

```
SELECT VALUE(i).item_id, SYS_TYPEID(VALUE(i))
    FROM inventory_tbl i;
```

The results of the select are as follows:

```
VALUE(I).ITEM_ID SYS_TYPEID(VALUE(I))
---------------- --------------------------------
               1 03
               2 02
```

The function takes the object instance as its argument, hence the VALUE function's use in the last example. Another way to get the same information is to select from the SYS_NC_TYPEID$ hidden column.

```
SELECT VALUE(i).item_id, SYS_NC_TYPEID$
   FROM inventory_tbl i;
```

The select returns the following:

```
VALUE(I).ITEM_ID SYS_NC_TYPEID$
---------------- --------------------------------
               1 03
               2 02
```

UTL_REF

The `UTL_REF` package performs various actions against an object instance given a *reference* to it. The six procedures included in the package perform tasks such as retrieving an object instance, locking an object, updating an object, and more. Table 15-1 lists the six procedures and explains what each can do.

Procedure	Arguments	Description
SELECT_OBJECT	*ref_in* IN *var_out* OUT	Retrieves an object from an object table, given a reference to it
SELECT_OBJECT_WITH_CR	*ref_in* IN *var_out* OUT	Retrieves an object from an object table, given a reference to it, and makes a copy of the object
LOCK_OBJECT	*ref_in* IN	Locks an object from an object table, given a reference to it

TABLE 15-1. *UTL_REF Built-In Package*

Procedure	Arguments	Description
LOCK_OBJECT	*ref_in* IN *var_out* OUT	Locks an object from an object table, given a reference to it, and retrieves it
UPDATE_OBJECT	*ref_in* IN *var_out* OUT	Updates an object in an object table, given a reference to it
DELETE_OBJECT	*ref_in* IN	Deletes an object from an object table, given a reference to it

TABLE 15-1. *UTL_REF Built-In Package* (continued)

The following example demonstrates the SELECT_OBJECT and DELETE_OBJECT procedures:

```
-- Available online as part of UtlRef.sql
-- Must be run as part of UtlRef
SET SERVEROUTPUT ON 1000000
DECLARE
   CURSOR c_inventory
   IS
      SELECT REF (i)
        FROM inventory_tbl i
       WHERE VALUE (i) IS OF (book_obj);

   v_InventoryRef    REF INVENTORY_OBJ;
   v_Inventory       INVENTORY_OBJ;
   v_Status          VARCHAR2 (200 CHAR);
   v_Book            BOOK_OBJ;
BEGIN
-- Delete one of the records in the inventory_tbl table
   SELECT REF (i)
     INTO v_InventoryRef
     FROM inventory_tbl i
    WHERE item_id = 2;

   UTL_REF.DELETE_OBJECT (v_InventoryRef);
   DBMS_OUTPUT.PUT_LINE ('    ');
   DBMS_OUTPUT.PUT_LINE ('DELETE_OBJECT');
   DBMS_OUTPUT.PUT_LINE ('=============');

   -- Verify that the row was deleted
   SELECT    'The row was deleted with DELETE_OBJECT and '
          || 'my REF is DANGLING!  I will rollback so we can continue.'
```

```
    INTO v_Status
    FROM DUAL
  WHERE v_InventoryRef IS DANGLING;

  DBMS_OUTPUT.PUT_LINE (v_status);
  DBMS_OUTPUT.PUT_LINE ('      ');
  ROLLBACK;
  DBMS_OUTPUT.PUT_LINE ('SELECT_OBJECT');
  DBMS_OUTPUT.PUT_LINE ('=============');
  DBMS_OUTPUT.PUT_LINE
     ('Use the SELECT_OBJECT procedure to return the object instance, ');
  DBMS_OUTPUT.PUT_LINE
     ('then use TREAT on the inventory object to allow access to the ');
  DBMS_OUTPUT.PUT_LINE ('print_book_information method of the subtype.');
  DBMS_OUTPUT.PUT_LINE ('      ');

  -- Retrieve the object instance using the ref we retrieved earlier
  UTL_REF.SELECT_OBJECT (v_InventoryRef, v_Inventory);

  SELECT TREAT (v_Inventory AS book_obj)
    INTO v_Book
    FROM DUAL;
  v_Book.print_book_information;
END;
/
```

Maintaining Persistent Objects

Object maintenance became much easier in 9*i* with the introduction of type evolution. This is especially important when object tables, object columns, object views, and inheritance create very complex structures. The ability to cascade changes through dependent objects removes the need to track down and re-create all objects because of one small change.

Type Evolution

In Chapter 14 we discussed type evolution as it applied to transient objects. I'm sure by now you appreciate its features more after seeing the implementation of persistent objects. In the following example we create object types showing inheritance, an object table, and an object view. We can then alter one of the object types to change the underlying structures.

TIP
You may choose to run `cleanSchema.sql` *prior to running* `objMaintain.sql`, *as some of the objects change in the* `objMaintain.sql` *example.*

```
-- Available online as part of ObjMaintain.sql
CREATE OR REPLACE TYPE inventory_obj AS OBJECT (
        item_id             NUMBER (10),
        num_in_stock        NUMBER (10),
        reorder_status      VARCHAR2 (20 CHAR),
        price               NUMBER (10, 2),
        CONSTRUCTOR FUNCTION inventory_obj (
            item_id         IN    NUMBER,
            num_in_stock    IN    NUMBER,
            price           IN    NUMBER
        )
            RETURN SELF AS RESULT,
        MEMBER PROCEDURE print_inventory,
        MEMBER PROCEDURE print_status,
        MEMBER PROCEDURE print_price
    )
    INSTANTIABLE NOT FINAL;
/

CREATE OR REPLACE TYPE book_obj
    UNDER inventory_obj (
        isbn        CHAR (10 CHAR),
        CATEGORY    VARCHAR2 (20 CHAR),
        title       VARCHAR2 (100 CHAR),
        num_pages   NUMBER,
        publisher   PUBLISHER_OBJ,
        CONSTRUCTOR FUNCTION book_obj (
            item_id         NUMBER,
            num_in_stock    NUMBER,
            price           NUMBER,
            isbn            CHAR,
            title           VARCHAR2,
            num_pages       NUMBER
        )
            RETURN SELF AS RESULT,
        MEMBER PROCEDURE print_book_information,
        OVERRIDING MEMBER PROCEDURE print_price
    )
    INSTANTIABLE NOT FINAL;
/
```

The object type specifications are created, so we can create the object table:

```
CREATE TABLE book_tbl OF book_obj;
```

Finally, we create the view:

```
CREATE VIEW book_vie
      OF book_obj
      WITH OBJECT IDENTIFIER (item_id)
   AS
      SELECT item_id, num_in_stock, reorder_status,
             price, isbn, CATEGORY, title,
             num_pages, publisher
         FROM book_tbl;
```

In this example, we have a supertype `inventory_obj`, with a subtype `book_obj`. A table was created from `book_obj`, and an object view was created from `book_obj` with a select of `book_tbl`.

NOTE
For the sake of space, the inserts that are included in the `objMaintain.sql` script are omitted from the preceding example. If you are using the examples, the insert statements are part of the `objMaintain.sql` script.

Let's test out type evolution by adding an attribute to the supertype `inventory_obj`.

```
ALTER TYPE inventory_obj
   ADD ATTRIBUTE location VARCHAR2(100 CHAR);
```

This statement returns the following:

```
ALTER TYPE inventory_obj
*
ERROR at line 1:
ORA-22312: must specify either CASCADE or INVALIDATE option
```

Oracle recognized the dependencies on this type and throws an exception. Let's try it again, specifying CASCADE.

```
ALTER TYPE inventory_obj
   ADD ATTRIBUTE location VARCHAR2(100 CHAR) CASCADE;
```

This time the alter statement will work. Now that we have successfully altered the type, let's check the definition of the subtype, object table, and object view.

```
desc book_obj
```

A describe after altering the type may result in the following exception:

```
ERROR:
ORA-22337: the type of accessed object has been evolved
```

The exception we get here is expected and was discussed in Chapter 14. You may or may not get this exception. If you did a describe prior to altering the type, then you will likely get this exception. It is simply stating that the client cache has an older copy, and you need to disconnect and reconnect your session to clear the cache.

```
desc book_tbl
           Name                           Null?    Type
           ------------------------ -------- ------------
      1    ITEM_ID                           NUMBER(10)
      2    NUM_IN_STOCK                      NUMBER(10)
      3    REORDER_STATUS                    VARCHAR2(20 CHAR)
      4    PRICE                             NUMBER(10,2)
 ...
     21    LOCATION                          VARCHAR2(100 CHAR)
```

The describe of the `book_tbl` table shows that it picked up the new attribute.

```
desc book_vie
ERROR:
ORA-24372: invalid object for describe
```

The view is the only problem, as it is marked as invalid. Let's verify this in the data dictionary.

```
SELECT object_name, status
   FROM user_objects
   WHERE object_name = 'BOOK_VIE'
```

This select statement returns the following:

```
OBJECT_NAME                  STATUS
-------------------------- -------
BOOK_VIE                     INVALID
```

The reason can be seen on the describe of the `book_obj` object type that the view is based on—remember to clear your client cache by reconnecting:

```
desc book_obj
  book_obj extends OBJECTS_USER.INVENTORY_OBJ
  book_obj is NOT FINAL
```

```
        Name                              Null?     Type
        ------------------------------    --------  --------------------
1       ITEM_ID                                     NUMBER(10)
2       NUM_IN_STOCK                                NUMBER(10)
3       REORDER_STATUS                              VARCHAR2(20 CHAR)
4       PRICE                                       NUMBER(10,2)
5       LOCATION                                    VARCHAR2(100 CHAR)
...
```

So the addition of the location attribute cascaded to the `book_obj` object type, making the view invalid due to a column mismatch. To fix the view, we will need to re-create it.

Summary

In Chapter 14 and the present chapter, we discussed transient and persistent objects and demonstrated many of their key features. Chapter 14 discussed transient objects, inheritance, and attribute chaining. This chapter focused on persistent objects and using those objects in SQL and PL/SQL. In the next chapter we discuss Large Objects (LOBs) in Oracle.

CHAPTER
16

Large Objects

ARCHAR2 and CHAR datatypes are great for storing small amounts of data, but what if you need to store large amounts of data such as chapters of a book, an image of the book cover, or the complete book in PDF format? Oracle provides LOB (Large OBject) datatypes to work with these kinds of data. In this chapter we look at the different kinds of LOBs, ways to manipulate them using SQL and PL/SQL, the DBMS_LOB package, and performance considerations when working with LOBs, including the use of Oracle Text.

Introduction to Large Objects

First introduced in Oracle 8, *large objects,* or LOBs, provide a means to store, manipulate, and retrieve large amounts of text and binary data. Prior to Oracle 8, LONG and LONG RAW datatypes were used for these purposes, but the use of LONG and LONG RAW datatypes have a number of restrictions:

- A table can have only one LONG or LONG RAW column.

- Storage is limited to 2GB.

- SQL access to the values stored in a LONG or LONG RAW column is an all-or-nothing proposition. There is no ability to retrieve or manipulate just a portion of the data using SQL.

LONG and LONG RAW types are still available, but Oracle recommends converting to LOBs because they solve many of the problems just noted. They provide the following benefits to the application developer:

- Depending on the block size of the database, they can store from 8 to 128 terabytes in a single column in Oracle 10*g*R1 (4GB in all prior releases).

- DML can be used on all, or just a portion of, the data stored in a LOB column.

- More than one LOB column can be created in a single table.

- Advanced features such as Oracle interMedia text in 8*i,* and Oracle Text in 9*i* and 10*g* can index LOB columns, providing full-text information retrieval on the LOB contents.

- LOB data can be stored in the database, or on a file system that can be accessed by the database.

Now, you may be wondering, as we did, where the LOB size limit of 8 to 128 terabytes came from. It seems that some of the size limitations in Oracle are drawn from a hat, or are a developer's lucky number. Not so here.

The terabyte LOB limits are set by the formula (4G – 1) * DB_BLOCK_SIZE. The Oracle block size (specified by the DB_BLOCK_SIZE parameter) can range from 2K to 32K. In my case, my DB_BLOCK_SIZE is set to 8K, so my limit is 4G * 8K = 32 terabytes (just under actually, since we ignored the "'–1" in the formula for simplicity).

The storage capabilities should not be surprising given some of the other size-related enhancements to Oracle 10*g*. For example, an Oracle database can store 8 exabytes (8 million terabytes), and large datafiles support up to 4 terabytes in a single file. Honestly, we can't think of anything to store in a LOB column beyond 40G or so, but it is nice to know the extra space is there should we ever need it!

Features Comparison

Chances are, you are not running just one version of the database in your company. To avoid version differences catching you by surprise, Table 16-1 contains a list of LOB-related features, and the releases where they are available.

NOTE
This is a summary list of features. For a complete list of LOB features available for your specific release, visit the Oracle Technology Network (OTN) documentation web site at http://otn.oracle.com/ documentation/index.html.

Types of LOBs

A LOB is not a datatype itself. It is a classification of datatypes that handle large objects. There are four LOB datatypes that are divided into two distinct categories: *internal LOBs* and *external LOBs.* Both internal and external LOBs have *LOB locators* and *LOB values,* but they manage them in different ways. Internal LOBs, or LOBs whose data is stored and managed in the database, include BLOB, CLOB, and NCLOB types. There is one external LOB called BFILE whose data is stored and managed outside the database.

LOB Locators

Before diving headfirst into internal and external LOBs, we need to discuss *LOB locators.* Each LOB, regardless of type, has a LOB locator. When you insert an internal LOB value that is greater than 4K, it is not stored directly in the table. External

Feature	8i	9iR1	9iR2	10gR1
Manipulate data piecewise using DML	X	X	X	X
LOB storage—internal and external to the database	X	X	X	X
Indexing using interMedia Text and Oracle Text supported	X	X	X	X
Client-side access to the DBMS_LOB package		X	X	X
SQL operators and functions supported		X	X	X
Implicit conversion between VARCHAR2 and CLOB		X	X	X
C++ API added—Oracle C++ Cal Interface (OCCI)		X	X	X
Limited support for execution of DML in parallel			X	X
LOB columns can be created in locally managed tablespaces			X	X
Full support LOBs in partitioned index-organized tables (IOT)				X
Implicit conversion between CLOB and NCLOB				X
Support for regular expressions				X
Allows 8 to 128 terabytes storage depending on system configuration				X

TABLE 16-1. *LOB Features*

LOBs are never stored directly in the table. Instead a locator, or reference, to the actual physical storage location is what gets inserted. Oracle uses this LOB locator to retrieve the correct LOB value when it is needed.

NOTE
LOB values can be stored in-row in a table. If they are stored out-of-row, additional structures are created. See the sections "LOB Structure" as well as "Internal LOB Storage," "External LOB Storage," and "Temporary LOB Storage" later in this chapter for a much more detailed discussion on how and where LOB values are stored.

Internal LOBs

An internal LOB, or a LOB whose storage is managed by the database, is stored either as part of a table, or in the database tablespace with a *LOB locator* stored in the table. An internal LOB instance has both a *LOB value* and a *LOB locator.* The locator in this case points to the location to the LOB value stored within the database.

Internal LOB instances that are stored in a table are considered *persistent.* They can be used by multiple transactions and applications that access the data, and are not terminated with the session. The default tablespace is used to store the LOB value unless another tablespace is specified. Standard SQL rules such as two-phase commit apply, and the data is treated with regard to backup/recovery operations as any other datatype.

Internal LOBs can also be *temporary,* where the LOB instance exists only in the context of the current session or application. In this case, the temporary tablespace is used to store the LOB value. If you insert the instance into a table, it becomes *persistent.* Otherwise, the LOB instance is deleted when you *free* the instance, or your session ends. You can *free* the instance using the DBMS_LOB built-in package discussed later in this chapter.

Regardless of whether the LOB instance is persistent or temporary, Oracle copies both the *LOB locator* and the *LOB value* during DML operations. This is referred to as *copy semantics,* since both locator and value are stored and managed within the database.

BLOB   A *binary large object,* or BLOB, can store binary objects such as images, video, or audio files. You can also store files like PDF or Word documents in their original form. Since BLOBs are *internal,* they are stored and managed in the database.

CLOB   *Character large object,* or CLOBs, are typically used to store large amounts of text. Characters are stored in the database character encoding as specified by the parameter NLS_CHARACTERSET.

NCLOB   *National character Set large objects,* or NCLOBs, also store text, but they do so using the National Character Set of the database. The national character set is determined by the parameter NLS_NCHAR_CHARACTERSET.

External LOBs

External LOBs are stored and managed outside of the database by the operating system. Since file management is under the control of the operating system, we are limited in what we can do with them within the database. Oracle cannot guarantee read-consistency of the file, and backup/recovery operations must explicitly include the External LOB operating system files—they are not included by default.

When inserting external LOBs, Oracle copies only the LOB locator, since the LOB value is external to the database. This is referred to as *reference semantics,* since only the reference, or locator, is copied.

BFILE   Oracle provides one datatype called BFILE, or *binary file,* to handle external LOBs. A pointer to the file is stored in the database, but all management of the file itself is under the control of the operating system. The file can be stored in any operating system directory that allows Oracle to access it, including CDs and other servers on your network.

Unlike when using the other LOB types, we are limited to read-only access to the files. Any changes to the files, aside from modifying the location, require a direct change to the file via the operating system.

Other Types That Are Stored as LOBs

Yes, we know we said there were two categories of LOBs—internal and external. We have a special category, however, that encompasses user-defined types and some newer Oracle datatypes. A VARRAY, or variable-size array, can be stored as a LOB under certain circumstances, and the XMLType datatype is stored as a CLOB in 9*i*R1.

VARRAY   As discussed earlier in the book, a VARRAY is a predefined composite datatype. If your VARRAY is less than 4K, it is stored in a table. A VARRAY is stored as a LOB if the declared size is greater than 4K, or if the ...STORE AS LOB... syntax is added to the VARRAY declaration. The ability to store a VARRAY as a LOB was first introduced in Oracle 9*i*R1.

The following example creates three object type specifications as VARRAYs of varying sizes and creates a table with the storage clause specified for one of the columns.

NOTE
The `CreateLobUser.sql` *script has been provided to create the LOB_USER schema. Use this schema for all examples.*

```
-- Available online as VarrayLob.sql
CREATE or REPLACE TYPE varray_table_obj
   AS VARRAY(3964) OF VARCHAR2(10);
/
CREATE OR REPLACE TYPE varray_lob_obj
   AS VARRAY(4001) OF VARCHAR2(10);
/
```

```
CREATE OR REPLACE TYPE varray_lob2_obj
   AS VARRAY(3964) OF VARCHAR2(10);
/
CREATE TABLE varray_lob (
   column1    varray_table_obj,
   column2    varray_lob_obj,
   column3    varray_lob2_obj)
   VARRAY column3 STORE AS LOB column3_seg;
```

In this example, VARRAY_LOB.COLUMN1 is the only column not stored as a LOB.
Notice that the object type definition for VARRAY_TABLE_OBJ does not exceed
the 4K limit, and the VARRAY STORE AS... clause is not specified for that column.
COLUMN2 and COLUMN3 are both stored as LOBs, though. COLUMN2 exceeds 4K,
and COLUMN3 is included in the STORE AS LOB... clause at table creation.

XMLType   The XMLType datatype was first introduced in Oracle 9*i*R1. The following
table creation sets a column datatype to XMLType:

```
CREATE TABLE XMLType_table (
   COLUMN1    XMLTYPE);
```

The data stored in column1 is stored as a CLOB. Accordingly, you can specify
storage attributes similar to other LOBs, including specifying a separate tablespace
to store your XML data. To add a storage clause for an XMLType column, use the
XMLTYPE... STORE AS syntax as follows:

XMLTYPE COLUMN *column_name*
STORE AS CLOB [*lob_segment_name*]
[(TABLESPACE *tablespace*
 {ENABLE|DISABLE} STORAGE IN ROW
 STORAGE *storage_clause*
 CHUNK int
 PCTVERSION int)

NOTE
*Each of the storage options noted here is
explained in the section titled "LOB Storage."*

LOB Structure

Earlier we discussed LOB locators. They point to the location of the LOB values. To
get a little more detail on the internal structure of a LOB, we can look at a block
dump. Figure 16-1 provides an illustration of what we see when a LOB value is
stored outside the table.

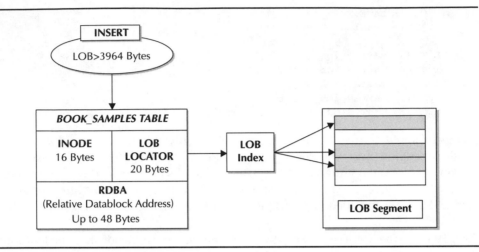

FIGURE 16-1. *Out-of-row LOB*

So, on closer examination, we are not just dealing with LOB locators and LOB values. In reality, we have LOB locators, LOB inodes, LOB indexes, and LOB segments, along with additional control information.

For a table that stores LOBs, a segment and an index are created by default for each LOB column. When we need to work with the LOB, the locator, index, and segment are needed. Figure 16-1 shows that the locator are 20 bytes. If you do a block dump, you will see that ten bytes of this are actually a LOB ID (the other ten bytes are miscellaneous information related to the LOB). The LOB ID is passed to the LOB index, which in turn has a listing of all of the blocks in the LOB segment that are used to store the LOB value. The LOB index is essentially a map that allows us to piece our out-of-row LOB together.

NOTE
More on chunks and storage options in the next section, "Internal LOB Storage."

Internal LOB Storage

Why should the PL/SQL programmer care about how LOBs are created and stored?

- DML and DDL operations involving LOBs are tied to LOB locators and LOB values. Failing to understand how LOB values are stored and accessed will result in inefficient code.

■ You can better determine which LOB type is appropriate, and under what circumstances they should be used, if there is a clear understanding of how the data is stored and retrieved.

■ When working with software development on Oracle, interaction and communication between the Developer and the DBA is critical. PL/SQL developers who can communicate storage requirements are worth their weight in gold to the DBA responsible for the environment.

Let's start our discussion regarding LOB storage by looking at how to create a table with LOBs columns. Table creation can include separate storage clauses for each LOB column. If no storage options are specified, the LOBs are created in the table's tablespace. To specify different storage options, use the following syntax in your create table statement:

CREATE TABLE *table_name* (
lob_column l*ob_datatype*
) LOB (*lob_column*,..) STORE AS [*lob_segment_name*]
[(TABLESPACE *tablespace*
  {ENABLE|DISABLE} STORAGE IN ROW
  STORAGE *storage_clause*
  CHUNK int
  PCTVERSION int
  CACHE
  CACHE READS [[NO]LOGGING]
  NOCACHE [[NO]LOGGING])
/

Next we create a sample table that includes all four LOB types. Note the storage information that follows the create table statement:

```
-- Available online as part of CreateLobTables.sql
CREATE TABLE book_samples (
    book_sample_id    NUMBER (10) PRIMARY KEY,
    isbn              CHAR(10 CHAR),
    description       CLOB,
    nls_description   NCLOB,
    book_cover        BLOB,
    chapter_title     VARCHAR2(30 CHAR),
    chapter           BFILE
)    LOB (book_cover)
     STORE AS blob_seg( TABLESPACE blob_ts
                CHUNK 16384
                PCTVERSION 0
                NOCACHE
                NOLOGGING
```

```
                    DISABLE STORAGE IN ROW)
LOB (description, nls_description)
   STORE AS ( TABLESPACE clob_ts
              CHUNK 16384
              PCTVERSION 10
              NOCACHE
              LOGGING
              ENABLE STORAGE IN ROW);
```

Let's review each of these options in more detail.

LOB (lob_column,...) STORE AS

We split our storage up in our example. The BLOB column has one set of storage options, and CLOB and NCLOB have another. Now, we have ourselves an interesting dilemma with the optional *LOB segment* name. The first LOB listing includes a LOB segment name, but the second does not. This is because a LOB segment name has a restriction related to the LOB column list. If we were to add an optional LOB segment name to the second LOB clause, we would get the following exception:

```
ORA-22855: optional name for LOB storage segment incorrectly specified
```

We can still specify storage names for these other two columns, but we must have a LOB clause for each column rather than a comma-separated list. For our example we will allow the system to name the LOB segment names for the last clause, just as it is displayed here.

Tablespace

If you will be storing large LOB values, it may be a good idea, for performance reasons, to store them in a tablespace separate from the tables. In our example, the CLOB and NCLOB values are stored in the CLOB_TS tablespace. The BLOB values are stored in the BLOB_TS tablespace.

TIP
There is no rule about when you should break your CLOB storage to separate tablespaces. It all depends on your usage and implementation. If you are considering splitting your LOBs to separate tablespaces, speak to your DBA first, and review a Statspack report (8i through 10gR1), or ADDM output (10g only). They can tell you whether the activity on your tablespace warrants a move.

Chunk

LOB I/O is done in chunks. By default, a single chunk is equal to a single block, but this can be overwritten using the CHUNK storage option. It is recommended that the CHUNK value be a multiple of the block size.

For performance reasons, do not use the default size for CHUNK. Larger chunks provide the ability to read multiple blocks at a time. Keep in mind that if you specify INITIAL and NEXT storage options, you should make them larger than the chunk size.

PCTVersion

PCTVERSION indicates the percent of total LOB blocks that can contain old LOB data. When a LOB value is changed, the old LOB blocks are not purged immediately. They are kept until the PCTVERSION threshold is met, and then Oracle begins reusing the old blocks. The default is 10 percent.

Retention

Where PCTVERSION is related to space for old LOB data, the RETENTION parameter is related to the amount of time the old data is kept. If RETENTION is specified at table creation, the time set for the database parameter UNDO_RETENTION is used for the LOB RETENTION as well.

NOTE
*PCTVERSION and RETENTION cannot
be specified at the same time.*

Cache | NoCache | CacheReads

The database buffer cache is an area of memory in the database SGA. Caching data in the buffer cache generally improves performance for subsequent operations against it by avoiding trips to disk. This is not always the case with LOBs, however. The following table shows three settings and provides descriptions of each.

CACHE	LOB blocks are read into the buffer cache for read and write operations.
NOCACHE	LOB blocks are not read into the buffer cache. NOCACHE is the default setting.
CACHEREADS	LOB blocks are read into the buffer cache for read operations only.

As noted, NOCACHE is the default setting if not included as a storage option. Only use the CACHE setting when accessing the LOBs often.

Logging | NoLogging

This parameter determines whether redo is generated for inserts into the LOB column. NOLOGGING is best reserved for large loads, as it decreases the overhead. For normal operations, LOGGING is recommended.

Enable | Disable Storage In Row

ENABLE STORAGE IN ROW, which is the default setting, says that if the LOB value is less than 4K (including control information), store it inline. In the case of our book_cover column, we have elected to DISABLE STORAGE IN ROW. This means that regardless of the size of the BLOB, it will not be stored inline.

This is all performance related. If a LOB can be stored inline, the LOB locator is still used to find the LOB value. The benefit is that if the LOB value is less than 4K, the value can be retrieved without added overhead of going to disk again for the value. It has already been read into the buffer cache with the rest of the row.

Now that we have our table created, let's try altering it to change the BLOB column to allow inline storage.

```
ALTER TABLE book_samples
    MODIFY (book_cover BLOB) LOB (book_cover)
        STORE AS (ENABLE STORAGE IN ROW);

    MODIFY (book_cover BLOB) LOB (book_cover)
           *
ERROR at line 2:
ORA-22858: invalid alteration of datatype
```

As you can see, this is an illegal operation. Once we set the inline storage for a column, we cannot change it without dropping and recreating the table. This makes perfect sense, of course. If we used a table for a period of time and then modified where the LOB values are stored, new records would use inline storage for a column, while old records would not.

External LOB Storage

BFILEs do not store their values in the database at all, so the storage options are completely different from internal LOBs. An OS directory is created to hold the files on the operating system, and a named directory is created in Oracle to point to that location as follows:

```
CREATE DIRECTORY book_samples_loc AS '/home/oracle/';
```

As with every operation in Oracle, permission is required to create directories. You must have the CREATE DIRECTORY privilege or the DBA role to create the directory in SQL*Plus, as well as READ privileges on the directory to work with the contents stored there.

TIP
*Make sure your user has OS privileges on the
specified file path. Oracle does not verify your
file path when you create the directory. In fact, we
are able to create the directory in the preceding
example (Unix file path) in our Windows
environment without error. Just try using it!*

At table creation, no additional storage options are required for the BFILE
column. Twenty bytes are still allocated in the row for the LOB locator, and
some additional space is needed for the directory path to the stored image.

If you wish to see the directories that are created in your instance, query
the DBA_DIRECTORIES or ALL_DIRECTORIES views.

```
select * from dba_directories;
```

Here you will find the directory just created:

```
OWNER                           DIRECTORY_NAME
--------------- ----------
DIRECTORY_PATH
-------------------------
SYS                             BOOK_SAMPLES_LOC
/home/oracle/
```

Should we need to drop a directory, we can use the DROP DIRECTORY command
as follows:

```
DROP DIRECTORY book_samples_loc;
```

Temporary LOB Storage

Temporary LOBs are just that, temporary. The LOB instance is stored in a temporary
tablespace and only exists in the context of the current session. As soon as the
session is terminated, the temporary space used for the LOB instance is freed.

A temporary LOB can be created explicitly as part of the application design,
or behind the scenes as support for SQL and PL/SQL operations. When the LOB is
created explicitly using PL/SQL, the CACHE parameter can improve performance
substantially. Setting the CACHE parameter to *true* allows the LOB to pass through
the buffer cache. If it is set to false, all reads and writes are to disk only. More on
temporary LOB creation in the section titled "DBMS_LOB" later in this chapter.

Oracle provides a view called V$TEMPORARY_LOBS that shows information on temporary LOBs and the sessions that hold them. You can use this to monitor and maintain temporary LOB usage in the instance.

Migrating from LONGs to LOBs

Hopefully you have enough information at this point to decide whether you will migrate your current environment from using LONGs to LOBs. We definitely recommend it for all of the reasons listed earlier.

Migration from LONG to LOB is a fairly simple operation. We can use either the ALTER TABLE command or the TO_LOB operator. In this example, we create a table containing a column of type LONG:

```
-- Available online as part of LongToLob.sql
CREATE TABLE long_to_lob (
    id NUMBER,
    text LONG);

INSERT INTO long_to_lob (id, text)
VALUES (1, 'Change the column from LONG to CLOB');

COMMIT;
```

We now have a table with one row that includes a column of type LONG, as the following describe shows:

```
DESC long_to_lob
Name                             Type
---------------------- ---
 ID                               NUMBER
 TEXT                             LONG
```

We can alter the table to make the column a CLOB.

```
-- Available online as part of LongToLob.sql
ALTER TABLE long_to_lob
MODIFY text CLOB;
```

To verify the change, let's do a DESCRIBE on the LONG_TO_LOB table.

```
DESC long_to_lob
 Name                             Type
---------------------- ----
 ID                               NUMBER
 TEXT                             CLOB
```

The conversion was successful. Had our column been a LONG RAW type, we would have used the same command, but BLOB would have been the datatype to convert to.

LOBs and SQL

In this section we put what we learned about LOB locators and LOB structure and storage to use. We discuss how to manipulate LOB values using SQL.

SQL for Internal Persistent LOBs

Internal persistent LOBs differ from external LOBs in their support for SQL operations. Using SQL, we can insert, update, and delete internal LOBs. Many SQL features/functions such as regular expressions and character functions now support LOBs. SQL does not yet support piecewise manipulation of LOBs. To modify a portion of a LOB value, we must use PL/SQL with DBMS_LOB, or one of the other supported interfaces. DBMS_LOB is covered later in this chapter, in the section titled "LOBs and PL/SQL."

LOB Initialization

LOB initialization is done during insert or update operations. LOBs either are NULL, are empty with only a LOB locator, or contain both LOB locator and LOB value. As you will see in the INSERT and UPDATE sections, we can initialize LOBs using a built-in function that leaves the LOB empty with only a locator, or by inserting/updating it with a small amount of data.

Initialization is especially critical when we get to our discussion later in the chapter on the PL/SQL API called DBMS_LOB. External APIs, such as DBMS_LOB, require a LOB locator. Although it is possible to set a LOB column to NULL, APIs such as DBMS_LOB require a LOB instance to work with, and you cannot get a LOB instance without a locator.

Insert

We can initialize a LOB column during inserts either by including a value less than 3964 bytes in the insert statement so that the LOB is in-row or by using EMPTY_BLOB() or EMPTY_CLOB() at run time.

Let's look at the following insert statement into the BOOK_SAMPLES table:

```
-- Available online as part of LobInsert.sql
CREATE DIRECTORY book_samples_loc AS 'C:\files';

INSERT INTO book_samples (
    book_sample_id,
```

```
      isbn,
      description,
      nls_description,
      book_cover,
      chapter)
    VALUES (
      1,
      '72230665',
      'The essential reference for PL/SQL has been revised and
       expanded, featuring all new examples throughout based on
       the new Oracle Database 10g, plus all the book's code
       and expanded topics are included on the website for download.',
      EMPTY_CLOB(),
      EMPTY_BLOB(),
      BFILENAME('BOOK_SAMPLES_LOC', '72230665.jpg'));

commit;
```

The CLOB value is less than 3964 bytes, so we initialized the LOB just with the insert. On INSERT, a locator is automatically created pointing to the inline value. For our NCLOB column called NLS_DESCRIPTON, we initialized the column with function EMPTY_CLOB(). This function creates a locator in the row. Aside from the locator, it is empty—no other values exist—yet it is not NULL. Take a look at the following example:

```
SELECT LENGTH(nls_description)
  FROM book_samples;

LENGTH(NLS_DESCRIPTION)
------------
                      0
```

So, there is nothing in the column, but at the same time it is not NULL.

```
SELECT COUNT(rowid)
  FROM book_samples
  WHERE nls_description IS NULL;

COUNT(ROWID)
------
           0
```

Notice in our insert into BOOK_SAMPLES that we used EMPTY_BLOB() to do the same thing for our BLOB column. The BFILE simply uses BFILENAME() and includes the directory and filename. More on this appears in the section titled "External LOB – BFILE."

TIP
If you anticipate having to initialize your LOB columns with EMPTY_CLOB() or EMPTY_BLOB(), do it at table creation time! Simply put a DEFAULT EMPTY_CLOB() next to your column definition.

Update

Updates operate similar to inserts. We can use EMPTY_CLOB() or EMPTY_BLOB() in the update statement to initialize the LOB, or include a small amount of text that creates the locator automatically.

In the following example, we build off of our earlier insert example and update the description column to be empty:

```
-- Available online as part of LobUpdate.sql
UPDATE book_samples
   SET description = EMPTY_CLOB()
   WHERE description IS NOT NULL;

COMMIT;
```

The column containing the book's description that included text is now *empty* (not NULL).

```
SELECT LENGTH(description)
   FROM book_samples;

LENGTH(DESCRIPTION)
-----------
               0
```

Updates work the same for BLOBs, CLOBs, and NCLOBs.

Delete

There is nothing fancy about deleting internal persistent LOBs. Just as with any other datatype, the entire row is deleted, including the LOB locator and LOB value if stored inline. Out-of-row LOBs also have their segment and index freed.

Select

If you are new to LOBs, SELECT statements will likely be a source of frustration initially. We'll try and ease the pain a bit by answering a few of the most frequently asked questions.

CLOB and NCLOB   Retrieving character data using a select statement is fairly straightforward—when selecting small amounts of data, that is. If the CLOB|NCLOB values are 80 bytes or less, the full value is returned to the UI using basic SQL syntax.

NOTE
*The value of LONG is 80 in my environment, but yours may be different, depending on your session settings. To find out how many bytes will be returned when selecting CLOB|NCLOB values type **show long** at the SQL prompt.*

This is nothing new if you have worked with the LONG datatype before, but we'll take a quick look at it in case you are not familiar with it. The following example performs an insert back into the BOOK_SAMPLES table and then performs a simple select:

```
-- Available online as part of LobInsert.sql
INSERT INTO book_samples (
    book_sample_id,
    isbn,
    description,
    nls_description,
    book_cover,
    chapter)
 VALUES (
    1,
    '72230665',
    'The essential reference for PL/SQL has been revised and
     expanded, featuring all new examples throughout based
     on the new Oracle Database 10g, plus all the book's code
     and expanded topics are included on the website for download.',
    EMPTY_CLOB(),
    EMPTY_BLOB(),
    BFILENAME('BOOK_SAMPLES_LOC', '72230665.jpg'));

commit;

SELECT description
FROM book_samples;

DESCRIPTION
----------------------------------------
```

```
The essential reference for PL/SQL has been revised and expanded,
featuring all
```

The value returned to the UI was in fact truncated to 80 bytes. Now, let's set LONG to a value greater than 80 and redo the select.

```
-- Available online as part of LobInsert.sql
SET LONG 64000
SELECT description
  FROM book_samples;


DESCRIPTION
---------------------------------------
The essential reference for PL/SQL has been revised and expanded,
featuring all new examples throughout based on the new Oracle
Database 10g, plus all the book's code and expanded topics are
included on the website for download.
```

Much better! Our CLOB|NCLOB information is easily retrieved.

BLOB   BLOBs react totally different when it comes to selects. In fact, you *can't* select BLOBs at all using SQL*Plus. It makes sense, really. I don't know about you, but binary data displayed in a text window doesn't mean much to me. If you try to select a BLOB you will get the following:

```
SELECT book_cover
  FROM book_samples;
SP2-0678: Column or attribute type can not be displayed by SQL*Plus
```

More on retrieving BLOBs appears in the later section titled "LOBs and PL/SQL."

External LOB – BFILE

Inserts and updates are done using the SQL function BFILENAME. The function takes the directory name and the filename as arguments. The LOB locator and physical location of the file are stored in the row, but the file itself is on the operating system. Figure 16-2 illustrates this. Deletes remove the LOB locator and file location from the database table, but the file itself must be removed from the OS through the OS file utilities like Windows Explorer or the *rm* command in Unix.

There is very little else we can do with external LOBs using SQL. Since the value is actually stored external to the database, we are unable to select the LOB value using SQL*Plus. We'll see how to work with BFILES in the next section.

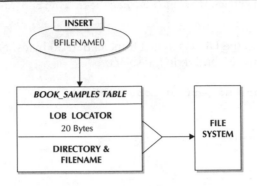

FIGURE 16-2. *External LOB*

LOBs and PL/SQL

Oracle provides a number of APIs in different programming environments that can work with LOBs. Supported environments include

- C++ (OCCI & PRO*C)
- OCI
- COBOL
- Visual Basic
- .NET Framework
- Java (JDBC)
- PL/SQL

These interfaces provide much more flexibility when working with LOBs. We noted in the "LOBs and SQL" section that piecewise manipulation of LOBs was not possible with SQL alone. As we will see in this section, PL/SQL provides support for piecewise data manipulation, as well as greater support for External LOBs.

DBMS_LOB

The PL/SQL API is a package called DBMS_LOB. Table 16-2 lists procedures and functions available as part of the API.

Name	Type	Description
APPEND	PROCEDURE	Overloaded procedure that appends one LOB instance to another instance, provided the LOBs already exist and are the same type. Available for CLOBs and BLOBs.
CLOSE	PROCEDURE	Overloaded procedure available for BLOB, CLOB, and BFILE operations to close the instance. Closing the LOB is required if you have opened it.
COMPARE	FUNCTION	Overloaded function to compare LOBs of the same type. It is available for BLOBs, CLOBs, and BFILEs. It is possible to compare either all or a part of the LOBs.
CONVERTTOBLOB	PROCEDURE	Converts character to binary. It takes a source CLOB as input and returns the destination BLOB.
CONVERTTOCLOB	PROCEDURE	This is the opposite of CONVERTTOBLOB. It takes a source BLOB as input and returns the destination CLOB.
COPY	PROCEDURE	Overloaded procedure to copy one LOB to another. It is possible to copy all or part of the LOB. The LOBs must be of the same type.
CREATETEMPORARY	PROCEDURE	Overloaded procedure to explicitly create a temporary LOB.
ERASE	PROCEDURE	Overloaded procedure that erases part of a LOB as determined by the offset passed to the procedure.
FILECLOSE	PROCEDURE	Procedure available for BFILE operations only. It closes the specified BFILE. Oracle now recommends CLOSE be used instead.
FILECLOSEALL	PROCEDURE	BFILE procedure only. It closes all open BFILEs and is the only procedure or function that takes no arguments.
FILEEXISTS	FUNCTION	BFILE function only. This function tests to see whether the BFILE is present on the file system.
FILEGETNAME	PROCEDURE	Procedure to retrieve the directory and filename of a BFILE with only the LOB locator passed in.

TABLE 16-2. *DBMS_LOB*

Name	Type	Description
FILEISOPEN	FUNCTION	This BFILE function tests to see if the file is already open.
FILEOPEN	PROCEDURE	Procedure to open BFILEs. Oracle recommends that new development use OPEN instead.
FREETEMPORARY	PROCEDURE	Overloaded procedure to free temporary LOBs. Although temporary LOBs exist only in the scope of the application, or as long as your session is connected, use this procedure to explicitly free the resources.
GETCHUNKSIZE	FUNCTION	Overloaded function that returns the actual space used in the LOB chunk for the LOB value.
GETLENGTH	FUNCTION	Overloaded function that returns the length of the LOB.
GET_STORAGE_LIMIT	FUNCTION	The 10g LOB storage limitation is between 8 and 128 terabytes. This function returns the storage limit for your configuration. This is a 10g function only!
INSTR	FUNCTION	Overloaded function that tests for patterns. You provide the LOB locator and pattern to search for, and this function determines whether it exists in the LOB.
ISOPEN	FUNCTION	Overloaded function that determines whether the LOB instance is open or not.
ISTEMPORARY	FUNCTION	Overloaded function tests to see if a LOB is temporary or not.
LOADBLOBFROMFILE	PROCEDURE	First introduced in Oracle 9iR2, this procedure loads binary data from a BFILE into a BLOB column. An offset can be specified to load only a portion of the file.
LOADCLOBFROMFILE	PROCEDURE	The procedure was added in Oracle 9iR2; it loads character data from a file to CLOB or NCLOB columns. It can also perform character set conversion on load. An offset can be specified to load only a portion of the file.

TABLE 16-2. *DBMS_LOB* (continued)

Name	Type	Description
LOADFROMFILE	PROCEDURE	Loads data from a BFILE to CLOB, NCLOB, and BLOB columns. An offset can be specified to load only a portion of the file. It is recommended that LOADBLOBFROMFILE or LOADCLOBFROMFILE be used, depending on the type of data being loaded.
OPEN	PROCEDURE	Overloaded procedure that opens a LOB instance.
READ	PROCEDURE	Overloaded procedure that retrieves a specified *amount* of data into the buffer beginning at a stated *position*.
SUBSTR	FUNCTION	Overloaded function that reads a part of a LOB beginning at a specified offset.
TRIM	PROCEDURE	Overloaded procedure that trims a LOB value to the size specified.
WRITE	PROCEDURE	Overloaded procedure that writes the buffer to a LOB.
WRITEAPPEND	PROCEDURE	Overloaded procedure that appends the buffer contents to a LOB.

TABLE 16-2. *DBMS_LOB* (continued)

All of the procedures and functions listed in Table 16-2, except FILECLOSEALL, take the LOB locator as input. The reason FILECLOSEALL does not require a locator is that it impacts all files, not just one individually.

The following sections provide expanded coverage of many procedures and functions in Table 16-2. While we cannot cover all of them, we focus on those not covered well in the online Oracle documentation, and we provide some hints to help you avoid problems in your implementation. Basic procedures and functions (such as OPEN and CLOSE) will not have their own headings but are used throughout the other examples.

NOTE
If you wish to run the examples shown in the following sections, you can find the complete examples (that include the table creation and seed data) on the web site in this chapter's directory.

APPEND

Append takes source and destination LOB locators and appends the source LOB instance to the destination LOB instance. The procedure is overloaded and works for BLOBs, CLOBs, and NCLOBs. You cannot append a CLOB to a BLOB. The procedure definition is as follows in Oracle 10g:

```
PROCEDURE APPEND
   Argument Name                    Type            In/Out Default?
   --------------- ------------ --- ----
   DEST_LOB                         BLOB            IN/OUT
   SRC_LOB                          BLOB            IN
PROCEDURE APPEND
   Argument Name                    Type            In/Out Default?
   --------------- ------------ --- ----
   DEST_LOB                         CLOB            IN/OUT
   SRC_LOB                          CLOB            IN
```

To demonstrate the APPEND functionality, let's start by creating a procedure that does the bulk of the work for us. The following procedure appends one NCLOB to another NCLOB:

```
-- Available online as part of NclobAppend.sql
CREATE OR REPLACE PROCEDURE LOBAPPEND (
    io_lob_source IN OUT NCLOB,
    io_lob_destination IN OUT NCLOB)
AS
BEGIN
    DBMS_LOB.OPEN(io_lob_source, DBMS_LOB.LOB_READONLY);
    DBMS_LOB.OPEN(io_lob_destination, DBMS_LOB.LOB_READWRITE);

    DBMS_LOB.APPEND(io_lob_destination, io_lob_source);
EXCEPTION
    WHEN OTHERS
      THEN
        DBMS_OUTPUT.PUT_LINE('Append failed!');
END;
/
```

NOTE
See if you can spot the mistake in this block. We will reveal the problem at the end of this section.

The procedure itself is fairly straightforward. It takes source and destination LOB locators as arguments and appends the source to the destination. For our example, we have two tables with one row in each. Our destination `table.column` was initialized using `EMPTY_CLOB()`. Recall that this gives us our locator so that we can use it with the LOB APIs (DBMS_LOB, for example).

```
-- Available online as part of NclobAppend.sql
SET SERVEROUTPUT ON
DECLARE
    v_source_lob_loc NCLOB;
    v_destination_lob_loc NCLOB;
    v_combined_lob NCLOB;
BEGIN
    SELECT nls_description
    INTO v_source_lob_loc
    FROM book_samples_nls
    FOR UPDATE;

    SELECT nls_description
    INTO v_destination_lob_loc
    FROM book_samples
    FOR UPDATE;

    LOBAPPEND(v_source_lob_loc, v_destination_lob_loc);

    SELECT nls_description
    INTO v_combined_lob
    from book_samples;

    DBMS_OUTPUT.PUT_LINE(SUBSTR(v_combined_lob, 1, 150));
    DBMS_OUTPUT.PUT_LINE(SUBSTR(v_combined_lob, 151, 300));
EXCEPTION
    WHEN OTHERS
    THEN
      DBMS_OUTPUT.PUT_LINE('OOPS!');
      DBMS_OUTPUT.PUT_LINE(SQLERRM);
END;
/
```

Notice how our SELECT statements that retrieve the LOB locator include a FOR UPDATE clause. If you do not do this, the LOBAPPEND procedure will throw the following error:

```
ORA-22292: Cannot open a LOB in read-write mode without a transaction
```

We mentioned earlier that there was a problem with the LOBAPPEND procedure we created. The LOBs were never closed! What happens when you don't close your LOBs? Here we try dropping the `book_samples_loc` directory:

```
DROP DIRECTORY book_samples_loc;
*
ERROR at line 1:
ORA-22297: warning: Open LOBs exist at transaction commit time
```

Always close your LOBs!

COMPARE

There are three varieties of the COMPARE function that deal with CLOBs/NCLOBs, BLOBs, and BFILEs. The function takes LOB_1 and LOB_2 as input, and the LOB instances are compared to see whether they are identical. If 0 is returned, then the LOBs are the same. If 1 is returned, then they are different.

The DBMS_LOB spec shows the following definition for the COMPARE function for CLOBs in Oracle 10*g*R1:

```
FUNCTION COMPARE RETURNS NUMBER(38)
 Argument Name              Type              In/Out Default?
 ---------------  ------------  --- ----
 LOB_1                        CLOB                IN
 LOB_2                        CLOB                IN
 AMOUNT                       NUMBER(38)          IN      DEFAULT
 OFFSET_1                     NUMBER(38)          IN      DEFAULT
 OFFSET_2                     NUMBER(38)          IN      DEFAULT
```

The other two functions by the same name are identical, with the exception of the datatypes for LOB_1 and LOB_2. Also, the argument names for BFILEs are FILE_1 and FILE_2.

The following example compares two CLOB columns. We compare the full text of the column, though we could compare a partial value if we needed to. This procedure takes the locator values for the LOBs we wish to compare as arguments. The call to the COMPARE function also takes the buffer size (we use the max of 32K) and the offset values (we will compare the entire CLOB) as arguments.

```
-- Available online as part of ClobCompare.sql
CREATE OR REPLACE PROCEDURE CLOB_COMPARE (
    v_lob1 IN OUT CLOB,
    v_lob2 IN OUT CLOB)
AS
    v_compare PLS_INTEGER := 0;
BEGIN
    DBMS_LOB.OPEN(v_lob1, DBMS_LOB.LOB_READONLY);
```

```
      DBMS_LOB.OPEN(v_lob2, DBMS_LOB.LOB_READONLY);

      v_compare := DBMS_LOB.COMPARE(v_lob1,v_lob2, 32764, 1, 1);

      DBMS_OUTPUT.PUT_LINE('The value returned by COMPARE is: '||v_compare);

      IF v_compare = 0
      THEN
         DBMS_OUTPUT.PUT_LINE('=====================');
         DBMS_OUTPUT.PUT_LINE('The LOBs are the same');
         DBMS_OUTPUT.PUT_LINE('=====================');
      ELSE
         DBMS_OUTPUT.PUT_LINE('=====================');
         DBMS_OUTPUT.PUT_LINE('The LOBs are different');
         DBMS_OUTPUT.PUT_LINE('=====================');
      END IF;

      DBMS_LOB.CLOSE(v_lob1);
      DBMS_LOB.CLOSE(v_lob2);
EXCEPTION
   WHEN OTHERS
   THEN
      DBMS_OUTPUT.PUT_LINE(SQLERRM);
END;
/
```

COMPARE returns 0 if the LOBs are the same and 1 if they are different. We can test our procedure with the following anonymous block:

```
-- Available online as part of ClobCompare.sql
SET SERVEROUTPUT ON
DECLARE
   v_lob1 CLOB;
   v_lob2 CLOB;
   v_lob3 CLOB;
BEGIN
   SELECT description
   INTO v_lob1
   FROM book_samples
   WHERE book_sample_id = 1;

   SELECT description
   INTO v_lob2
   FROM book_samples
   WHERE book_sample_id = 2;

   SELECT description
```

```
      INTO v_lob3
      FROM book_samples
      WHERE book_sample_id = 3;

      DBMS_OUTPUT.PUT_LINE('Test comparison of different values');
      DBMS_OUTPUT.PUT_LINE('===================================');
      CLOB_COMPARE(v_lob1, v_lob2);

      DBMS_OUTPUT.PUT_LINE('Test comparison of identical values');
      DBMS_OUTPUT.PUT_LINE('===================================');
      CLOB_COMPARE(v_lob1, v_lob3);

EXCEPTION
   WHEN OTHERS
   THEN
      DBMS_OUTPUT.PUT_LINE('I''m Broken!');
      DBMS_OUTPUT.PUT_LINE(SQLERRM);
END;
/
```

This returns the following result:

```
Test comparison of different values
===================================
The value returned by the COMPARE function is: 1
The LOBs are different

Test comparison of identical values
===================================
The value returned by the COMPARE function is: 0
The LOBs are the same
```

Our implementation using COMPARE worked nicely. Remember, if you wish to compare only a portion of the LOB, simply specify the offset.

CONVERTTOBLOB/CONVERTTOCLOB

CONVERTTOBLOB converts CLOBs to BLOBs. CONVERTTOCLOB does the reverse. The convert procedures are defined as follows in Oracle 10*g*R1:

```
PROCEDURE CONVERTTOBLOB
 Argument Name                  Type                    In/Out Default?
 --------------- ------------ --- ----
 DEST_LOB                       BLOB                    IN/OUT
 SRC_CLOB                       CLOB                    IN
 AMOUNT                         NUMBER(38)              IN
 DEST_OFFSET                    NUMBER(38)              IN/OUT
```

SRC_OFFSET	NUMBER(38)	IN/OUT
BLOB_CSID	NUMBER	IN
LANG_CONTEXT	NUMBER(38)	IN/OUT
WARNING	NUMBER(38)	OUT

PROCEDURE CONVERTTOCLOB

Argument Name	Type	In/Out Default?
DEST_LOB	CLOB	IN/OUT
SRC_BLOB	BLOB	IN
AMOUNT	NUMBER(38)	IN
DEST_OFFSET	NUMBER(38)	IN/OUT
SRC_OFFSET	NUMBER(38)	IN/OUT
BLOB_CSID	NUMBER	IN
LANG_CONTEXT	NUMBER(38)	IN/OUT
WARNING	NUMBER(38)	OUT

The following procedure can either convert from a CLOB column to a BLOB or convert a BLOB to a CLOB. We will leave the line numbers in for reference later:

```
-- Available online as part of Convert.sql
SQL> CREATE OR REPLACE PROCEDURE CONVERT_ME (
  2       v_blob_or_clob IN NUMBER,
  3       v_blob IN OUT BLOB,
  4       v_clob IN OUT CLOB,
  5       v_amount IN OUT NUMBER,
  6       v_blob_offset IN OUT NUMBER,
  7       v_clob_offset IN OUT NUMBER,
  8       v_lang_context IN OUT NUMBER,
  9       v_warning OUT NUMBER)
 10  AS
 11  BEGIN
 12
 13      DBMS_LOB.OPEN(v_blob, DBMS_LOB.LOB_READWRITE);
 14      DBMS_LOB.OPEN(v_clob, DBMS_LOB.LOB_READWRITE);
 15
 16      IF v_blob_or_clob = 0
 17      THEN
 18      DBMS_LOB.CONVERTTOBLOB(v_blob,
 19                             v_clob,
 20                             v_amount,
 21                             v_blob_offset,
 22                             v_clob_offset,
 23                             1,
 24                             v_lang_context,
 25                             v_warning);
 26      ELSE
```

```
27        DBMS_LOB.CONVERTTOCLOB(v_clob,
28                               v_blob,
29                               v_amount,
30                               v_clob_offset,
31                               v_blob_offset,
32                               1,
33                               v_lang_context,
34                               v_warning);
35     END IF;
36
37     DBMS_LOB.CLOSE(v_blob);
38     DBMS_LOB.CLOSE(v_clob);
39
40  EXCEPTION
41     WHEN OTHERS
42     THEN
43        DBMS_OUTPUT.PUT_LINE('The conver_me procedure is broken ...');
44        DBMS_OUTPUT.PUT_LINE(SQLERRM);
45  END;
46  /
```

Let's start with lines 13 and 14. We are opening the LOBs with READWRITE. If we were simply going to convert from CLOB to BLOB, or do the reverse, one could be READWRITE, and the other READONLY. In this case, however, we are supporting both operations in the same procedure, so both types of LOBs may be written to. Alternatively, we could push the OPEN operation inside the IF – THEN statement.

Line 16 begins our IF – THEN section. If we pass a value of zero, the CONVERTTOBLOB procedure is called; ELSE the CONVERTTOCLOB procedure is used.

Our test block converts a CLOB to a BLOB, copies the BLOB from record 1 to record 2, and then converts the BLOB back to a CLOB and displays the end result:

```
-- Available online as part of Convert.sql
DECLARE
   v_clob_or_blob NUMBER;
   v_blob_locator BLOB;
   v_clob_locator CLOB;
   v_blob_offset NUMBER;
   v_clob_offset NUMBER;
   v_lang_context NUMBER := DBMS_LOB.DEFAULT_LANG_CTX;
   v_warning NUMBER;
   v_string_length NUMBER(10);
   v_source_locator BLOB;
   v_destination_locator BLOB;
   v_amount PLS_INTEGER;
```

```
      v_string CLOB;
BEGIN

      -- CONVERT CLOB TO BLOB
      SELECT description
      INTO v_clob_locator
      FROM book_samples
      WHERE book_sample_id = 1
      FOR UPDATE;

      SELECT misc
      INTO v_blob_locator
      FROM book_samples
      WHERE book_sample_id = 1
      FOR UPDATE;

      v_string_length := DBMS_LOB.GETLENGTH(v_blob_locator);
      v_amount := DBMS_LOB.GETLENGTH(v_clob_locator);

      DBMS_OUTPUT.PUT_LINE(
          'The initial length of the BLOB is: '||v_string_length);

          v_clob_or_blob := 0; - Convert clob to blob
          v_clob_offset := 1;
          v_blob_offset := 1;

          CONVERT_ME(v_clob_or_blob,
                  v_blob_locator,
                  v_clob_locator,
                  v_amount,
                  v_blob_offset,
                  v_clob_offset,
                  v_lang_context,
                  v_warning);

      v_string_length := DBMS_LOB.GETLENGTH(v_blob_locator);

      DBMS_OUTPUT.PUT_LINE(
          'The length of the BLOB post-conversion is: '||v_string_length);

      -- COPY BLOB FOR ONE ROW TO BLOB IN ANOTHER
      v_source_locator := v_blob_locator;

      SELECT misc
      INTO v_destination_locator
      FROM book_samples
      WHERE book_sample_id = 2
      FOR UPDATE;
```

```
DBMS_LOB.COPY(v_destination_locator, v_source_locator, 32768, 1, 1);

v_string_length := DBMS_LOB.GETLENGTH(v_destination_locator);

DBMS_OUTPUT.PUT_LINE(
   'The length of the BLOB post-copy is: '||v_string_length);

-- COPY BLOB FOR RECORD 2 BACK TO A CLOB
SELECT description
INTO v_clob_locator
FROM book_samples
WHERE book_sample_id = 2
FOR UPDATE;

SELECT misc
INTO v_blob_locator
FROM book_samples
WHERE book_sample_id = 2
FOR UPDATE;

v_string_length := DBMS_LOB.GETLENGTH(v_clob_locator);
v_amount := DBMS_LOB.GETLENGTH(v_blob_locator);

DBMS_OUTPUT.PUT_LINE(
   'The initial length of the CLOB (record 2) is: '||v_string_length);

    v_clob_or_blob := 1; - Convert blob to clob
    v_clob_offset := 1;
    v_blob_offset := 1;

    CONVERT_ME(v_clob_or_blob,
            v_blob_locator,
            v_clob_locator,
            v_amount,
            v_clob_offset,
            v_blob_offset,
            v_lang_context,
            v_warning);

v_string_length := DBMS_LOB.GETLENGTH(v_clob_locator);

SELECT description
INTO v_string
FROM book_samples
WHERE book_sample_id = 2;
```

```
    DBMS_OUTPUT.PUT_LINE(
        'The length of the CLOB post-conversion is: '||v_string_length);

    DBMS_OUTPUT.PUT_LINE('==================');
    DBMS_OUTPUT.PUT_LINE('The converted CLOB');
    DBMS_OUTPUT.PUT_LINE('==================');
    DBMS_OUTPUT.PUT_LINE(SUBSTR(v_string,1,150));
    DBMS_OUTPUT.PUT_LINE(SUBSTR(v_string,151,300));

EXCEPTION
    WHEN OTHERS
    THEN
        DBMS_OUTPUT.PUT_LINE('I''M BROKEN ... FIX ME!');
        DBMS_OUTPUT.PUT_LINE(SQLERRM);
END;
/
```

This results in the following:

```
The initial length of the BLOB is: 0
The length of the BLOB post-conversion is: 228
The length of the BLOB post-copy is: 228
The initial length of the CLOB (record 2) is: 0
The length of the CLOB post-conversion is: 228

The converted CLOB
==================
The essential reference for PL/SQL has been revised and
expanded, featuring all new examples throughout based on
the new Oracle Database 10g, plus all the book's code
and expanded topics are included on the website for download.
```

A couple of observations about this example:

- Once again, our select statement required a FOR UPDATE clause. Any time we need to write to a LOB column, we must specify FOR UPDATE. An exception will be raised otherwise.

- When testing the compare function, we set the AMOUNT to 32K. Doing so in this case would have resulted in the following exception on conversion of the BLOB to CLOB:

  ```
  ORA-22993: specified input amount is greater than actual source amount
  ```

  Instead, we set the AMOUNT (assigned to V_AMOUNT) to the exact size of the value by using the GETLENGTH function.

■ We had to re-initialize our CLOB and BLOB offset variables (`v_clob_offset` and `v_blob_offset`) back to 1 after calling CONVERTTOBLOB. If this is skipped, CONVERTTOCLOB will fail with the following:

```
ORA-22994: source offset is beyond the end of the source LOB
```

The reason for the error? The `SRC_OFFSET` and `DEST_OFFSET` parameters are IN OUT. When we call CONVERTTOBLOB, the `SRC_OFFSET` and `DEST_OFFSET` return the length of the LOB instance plus 1, or 229 in this case. To pass this to CONVERTTOCLOB does not work, as an offset of 229 exceeds the total length of the BLOB, causing the ORA-22994 exception.

BFILE – FILEEXISTS

This function tests whether a file exists by the name specified in the insert statement. We begin with a `BOOK_SAMPLES` table that contains the following row:

```
-- Available online as part of BfileFileExists.sql
INSERT INTO book_samples (
   book_sample_id,
   isbn,
   description,
   nls_description,
   misc,
   bfile_description)
VALUES (
   1,
   '72230665',
   EMPTY_CLOB(),
   EMPTY_CLOB(),
   EMPTY_BLOB(),
   BFILENAME('BOOK_SAMPLES_LOC', 'bfile_example.pdf'));

COMMIT;
```

The CHECK_FILE procedure uses the `DBMS_LOB.FILEEXISTS` function to see if our BFILE is where we said it should be. If it returns a value of 0, the file does not exist. If 1 is returned, the file exists where we said it would be.

```
-- Available online as part of BfileFileExists.sql
CREATE OR REPLACE PROCEDURE CHECK_FILE (
   v_bfile IN BFILE)
AS
   v_exists PLS_INTEGER :- 0;
BEGIN
   v_exists := DBMS_LOB.FILEEXISTS(v_bfile);

   IF v_exists = 0
```

```
       THEN
          DBMS_OUTPUT.PUT_LINE ('The file does not exists in the directory specified.');
          DBMS_OUTPUT.PUT_LINE ('  Check to be sure the directory exists, and the file');
          DBMS_OUTPUT.PUT_LINE ('  name is valid.');
       ELSE
          DBMS_OUTPUT.PUT_LINE ('The file exists and the directory valid!');
       END IF;
EXCEPTION
   WHEN OTHERS
   THEN
       DBMS_OUTPUT.PUT_LINE(SQLERRM);
END;
/
```

We call this procedure with the following block:

```
-- Available online as part of BfileFileExists.sql
DECLARE
   v_bfile BFILE;
BEGIN
   SELECT bfile_description
   INTO v_bfile
   FROM book_samples
   WHERE book_sample_id = 1;

   CHECK_FILE(v_bfile);
END;
/
```

In this instance (since we have the `bfile_example.pdf` saved to our C:\files directory), the test is successful.

```
The file exists and the directory valid!
```

Please refer to the INSERT statement shown earlier. Notice that the directory name we provided is in quotes and is in uppercase. Remember, when a string is in quotes, it is literal and case sensitive. If you select from the DBA_DIRECTORIES data dictionary view, even though we created the directory with the name in lowercase, it is stored in all capital letters for the data dictionary.

Here we insert another record, but this time we include our directory name in lowercase:

```
INSERT INTO book_samples (
      book_sample_id,
      isbn,
      description,
      nls_description,
      misc,
      bfile_description)
```

```
   VALUES (
     2,
     '72230665',
     EMPTY_CLOB(),
     EMPTY_CLOB(),
     EMPTY_BLOB(),
     BFILENAME('book_samples_loc', 'bfile_example2.pdf'));

COMMIT;
```

Now, we can test it again.

```
DECLARE
    v_bfile BFILE;
BEGIN
    SELECT bfile_description
    INTO v_bfile
    FROM book_samples
    WHERE book_sample_id = 2;

    CHECK_FILE(v_bfile);
END;
/
```

This throws an exception:

```
ORA-22285: non-existent directory or file for FILEEXISTS operation
```

'book_samples_loc' does not equal 'BOOK_SAMPLES_LOC'.

BFILE – FILEOPEN/OPEN

Oracle recommends that OPEN be used instead of FILEOPEN. OPEN can be used for all LOB types. When used with a BFILE, its definition is as follows:

```
PROCEDURE OPEN
   Argument Name                       Type                  In/Out Default?
   --------------- ------------ --- ----
   FILE_LOC                            BINARY FILE LOB       IN/OUT
   OPEN_MODE                           BINARY_INTEGER        IN      DEFAULT
```

We are required to pass the `file_loc`, or LOB locator, to the procedure. When working with BFILES, the OPEN_MODE parameter is optional. It is required with other types of LOBs. `Open_mode` can be set to DBMS_LOB.LOB_READONLY or DBMS_LOB.LOB_READWRITE.

BFILE – FILEISOPEN/ISOPEN

ISOPEN should be used in place of FILEISOPEN when possible. ISOPEN is more flexible, since it can test to see if CLOBs, NCLOBs, and BLOBs are open, not just BFILEs.

The CHECK_STATUS procedure that follows uses the ISOPEN function to determine whether a BFILE is open:

```
-- Available online as part of BfileIsOpen.sql
CREATE OR REPLACE PROCEDURE CHECK_STATUS (
    v_bfile IN BFILE)
AS
    v_isopen PLS_INTEGER := 0;
BEGIN
    v_isopen := DBMS_LOB.ISOPEN(v_bfile);

    IF v_isopen = 0
    THEN
        DBMS_OUTPUT.PUT_LINE ('The file is not open. You must open the');
        DBMS_OUTPUT.PUT_LINE ('  file before working with it.');
    ELSE
        DBMS_OUTPUT.PUT_LINE ('The file is open already.');
    END IF;
EXCEPTION
    WHEN OTHERS
    THEN
        DBMS_OUTPUT.PUT_LINE (SQLERRM);
END;
/
```

The following block passes the BFILE LOB locator to the CHECK_STATUS procedure without opening the BFILE:

```
-- Available online as part of BfileIsOpen.sql
DECLARE
    v_bfile BFILE;
BEGIN
    SELECT bfile_description
    INTO v_bfile
    FROM book_samples
    WHERE book_sample_id = 1;

    CHECK_STATUS(v_bfile);
END;
/
```

This returns the following result:

```
The file is not open. You must open the
file before working with it.
```

We can test this again, but this time we open the BFILE prior to calling CHECK_
STATUS:

```
-- Available online as part of BfileIsOpen.sql
DECLARE
    v_bfile BFILE;
BEGIN
    SELECT bfile_description
    INTO v_bfile
    FROM book_samples
    WHERE book_sample_id = 1;

    DBMS_LOB.OPEN(v_bfile);
    CHECK_STATUS(v_bfile);
END;
/
```

Our result changes to reflect the open file.

```
The file is open already.
```

BFILE – FILECLOSE/CLOSE/FILECLOSEALL

FILECLOSE and CLOSE both close one BFILE at a time, while FILECLOSEALL closes all open BFILEs. It is recommended by Oracle that CLOSE be used rather than FILECLOSE for all new development. CLOSE can be used with all LOB types, not just BFILEs.

We will once again emphasize the importance of closing all LOBs when they have been opened. In addition to certain operations failing when we forget/neglect to close our LOBs (like our attempted drop of a directory in the earlier section "APPEND"), there is a limit to the number of BFILEs that can be open at a given time. Taking care to close LOBs when we are done with them ensures that we do not run into the limit unnecessarily.

NOTE
SESSION_MAX_OPEN_FILES is the parameter that determines the number of BFILEs that can be open at any one time.

The CLOSE_FILE procedure we create next opens a BFILE in the BOOK_
SAMPLES table, verifies it is open, closes it again, and then verifies it is closed:

```
-- Available online as part of BfileClose.sql
CREATE OR REPLACE PROCEDURE CLOSE_FILE (
    v_bfile IN OUT BFILE)
AS
    v_isopen PLS_INTEGER := 0;
BEGIN

    DBMS_OUTPUT.PUT_LINE('Test to see if the file is open');
    DBMS_OUTPUT.PUT_LINE('=================================');
    DBMS_LOB.OPEN(v_bfile);
    v_isopen := DBMS_LOB.ISOPEN(v_bfile);

    IF v_isopen = 0
    THEN
        DBMS_OUTPUT.PUT_LINE ('The file is closed.');
    ELSE
        DBMS_OUTPUT.PUT_LINE ('The file is open.');
    END IF;

    DBMS_OUTPUT.PUT_LINE ('=================================');
    DBMS_OUTPUT.PUT_LINE ('Test to see if the file is closed');
    DBMS_OUTPUT.PUT_LINE('=================================');

    DBMS_LOB.CLOSE(v_bfile);

    v_isopen := DBMS_LOB.ISOPEN(v_bfile);

    IF v_isopen = 0
    THEN
        DBMS_OUTPUT.PUT_LINE ('The file is closed.');
    ELSE
        DBMS_OUTPUT.PUT_LINE ('The file is open.');
    END IF;
EXCEPTION
    WHEN OTHERS
    THEN
        DBMS_OUTPUT.PUT_LINE (SQLERRM);
END;
/
```

To test it, we can use the following anonymous block:

```
-- Available online as part of BfileClose.sql
DECLARE
```

```
    v_bfile BFILE;
BEGIN
    SELECT bfile_description
    INTO v_bfile
    FROM book_samples
    WHERE book_sample_id = 1;

    CLOSE_FILE(v_bfile);
END;
/
```

So, we were able to close a single file with the CLOSE procedure, but what about large numbers of BFILEs? CLOSE and FILECLOSE require a LOB locator to work. FILECLOSEALL does not, and it operates on all open BFILEs at once. Let's look at an example:

```
-- Available online as part of BfileCloseAll.sql
SET SERVEROUTPUT ON

CREATE OR REPLACE PROCEDURE CLOSE_ALL_FILES
AS
    v_isopen PLS_INTEGER := 0;
    v_counter PLS_INTEGER := 0;
    v_bfile BFILE;

    CURSOR cur_bfile IS
    SELECT bfile_description
    FROM book_samples;
BEGIN

    DBMS_OUTPUT.PUT_LINE('Open all BFILEs in the table');
    DBMS_OUTPUT.PUT_LINE('=============================');

    OPEN cur_bfile;

    LOOP
    FETCH cur_bfile INTO v_bfile;
    EXIT WHEN cur_bfile%NOTFOUND;
       BEGIN
          v_counter := v_counter + 1;

          DBMS_LOB.OPEN(v_bfile);
          v_isopen := DBMS_LOB.ISOPEN(v_bfile);

          IF v_isopen = 0
```

```
              THEN
                  DBMS_OUTPUT.PUT_LINE ('File number '||v_counter||' is closed.');
              ELSE
                  DBMS_OUTPUT.PUT_LINE ('File number '||v_counter||' is open.');
              END IF;
          END;
      END LOOP;
      CLOSE cur_bfile;

      DBMS_OUTPUT.PUT_LINE('=====================');
      DBMS_OUTPUT.PUT_LINE('Close all open BFILEs');
      DBMS_OUTPUT.PUT_LINE('=====================');
      DBMS_LOB.FILECLOSEALL();
      DBMS_OUTPUT.PUT_LINE('          DONE          ');
      DBMS_OUTPUT.PUT_LINE('=====================');

      DBMS_OUTPUT.PUT_LINE('Test to verify all BFILEs were closed');
      DBMS_OUTPUT.PUT_LINE('=====================================');

      OPEN cur_bfile;

      LOOP
      FETCH cur_bfile INTO v_bfile;
      EXIT WHEN cur_bfile%NOTFOUND;
          BEGIN
             v_counter := v_counter + 1;

             v_isopen := DBMS_LOB.ISOPEN(v_bfile);

             IF v_isopen = 0
             THEN
                 DBMS_OUTPUT.PUT_LINE ('File number '||v_counter||' is closed.');
             ELSE
                 DBMS_OUTPUT.PUT_LINE ('File number '||v_counter||' is open.');
             END IF;
          END;
      END LOOP;
      CLOSE cur_bfile;

EXCEPTION
   WHEN OTHERS
   THEN
       DBMS_OUTPUT.PUT_LINE (SQLERRM);
END;
/
```

Executing this procedure, we can see that our call to DBMS_LOB.FILECLOSEALL caused all open BFILEs to close:

```
-- Available online as part of BfileCloseAll.sql
EXEC close_all_files()

Open all BFILEs in the table
============================
File number 1 is open
File number 2 is open

Close all open BFILEs
=====================
DONE

Test to verify all BFILEs were closed
=====================================
File number 1 is closed
File number 2 is closed
```

DBMS_LOB.FILECLOSEALL caused all open LOBs to close.

LOADFROMFILE/LOADCLOBFROMFILE/LOADBLOBFROMFILE

These procedures allow us to load file contents to CLOB and BLOB columns. It is recommended that LOADCLOBFROMFILE and LOADBLOBFROMFILE be used for their specific datatypes rather than using the generic overloaded LOADFROMFILE.

LOADFROMFILE has the following definition in Oracle 10g:

```
PROCEDURE LOADFROMFILE
 Argument Name              Type                  In/Out Default?
 --------------- ------------ --- ----
 DEST_LOB                   BLOB                  IN/OUT
 SRC_LOB                    BINARY FILE LOB       IN
 AMOUNT                     NUMBER(38)            IN
 DEST_OFFSET                NUMBER(38)            IN      DEFAULT
 SRC_OFFSET                 NUMBER(38)            IN      DEFAULT
```

The CLOB version of the procedure is identical, except for the DEST_LOB datatype. We also specify the amount, or LOB size, and the offset values for both source and destination. Remember, the source is the BFILE and the destination is the CLOB/BLOB column.

The following example uses our bfile_example.pdf and bfile_example.txt files as the source. We load our destination CLOB and BLOB columns using the LOADFROMFILE procedure:

```
-- Available online as part of LoadFromFile.sql
DECLARE
    v_dest_blob BLOB;
    v_dest_clob CLOB;
    v_source_locator1 BFILE := BFILENAME('BOOK_SAMPLES_LOC',
        'bfile_example.pdf');
    v_source_locator2 BFILE := BFILENAME('BOOK_SAMPLES_LOC',
        'bfile_example.txt');

BEGIN
    -- Empty the description and misc columns
    UPDATE book_samples
    SET description = EMPTY_CLOB(),
        misc = EMPTY_BLOB()
    WHERE book_sample_id = 1;

    -- Retrieve the locators for the two destination columns
    SELECT description, misc
    INTO v_dest_clob, v_dest_blob
    FROM book_samples
    WHERE book_sample_id = 1
    FOR UPDATE;

    -- Open the BFILEs and destination LOBs
    DBMS_LOB.OPEN(v_source_locator1, DBMS_LOB.LOB_READONLY);
    DBMS_LOB.OPEN(v_source_locator2, DBMS_LOB.LOB_READONLY);
    DBMS_LOB.OPEN(v_dest_blob, DBMS_LOB.LOB_READWRITE);
    DBMS_LOB.OPEN(v_dest_clob, DBMS_LOB.LOB_READWRITE);

    DBMS_OUTPUT.PUT_LINE('Length of the BLOB file is: '
        ||DBMS_LOB.GETLENGTH(v_source_locator1));
    DBMS_OUTPUT.PUT_LINE('Length of the CLOB file is: '
        ||DBMS_LOB.GETLENGTH(v_source_locator2));
    DBMS_OUTPUT.PUT_LINE('Size of BLOB pre-load: '
        ||DBMS_LOB.GETLENGTH(v_dest_blob));
    DBMS_OUTPUT.PUT_LINE('Size of CLOB pre-load: '
        ||DBMS_LOB.GETLENGTH(v_dest_clob));

    -- Load the destination columns from the source
    DBMS_LOB.LOADFROMFILE(v_dest_blob, v_source_locator1,
        DBMS_LOB.LOBMAXSIZE, 1, 1);
    DBMS_LOB.LOADFROMFILE(v_dest_clob, v_source_locator2,
        DBMS_LOB.LOBMAXSIZE, 1, 1);

    DBMS_OUTPUT.PUT_LINE('Size of BLOB post-load: '
        ||DBMS_LOB.GETLENGTH(v_dest_blob));
```

```
        DBMS_OUTPUT.PUT_LINE('Size of CLOB post-load: '
            ||DBMS_LOB.GETLENGTH(v_dest_clob));

        -- Close the LOBs that we opened
        DBMS_LOB.CLOSE(v_source_locator1);
        DBMS_LOB.CLOSE(v_source_locator2);
        DBMS_LOB.CLOSE(v_dest_blob);
        DBMS_LOB.CLOSE(v_dest_clob);

EXCEPTION
    WHEN OTHERS
    THEN
        DBMS_OUTPUT.PUT_LINE(SQLERRM);
        DBMS_LOB.CLOSE(v_source_locator1);
        DBMS_LOB.CLOSE(v_source_locator2);
        DBMS_LOB.CLOSE(v_dest_blob);
        DBMS_LOB.CLOSE(v_dest_clob);
END;
/
```

Notice that we used DBMS_LOB.LOBMAXSIZE for the AMOUNT parameter. We could have used the length as retrieved by the GETLENGTH function as we did in other examples with the same effect. For all DBMS_LOB.LOAD% procedures, AMOUNT must be less than or equal to the file size or set to LOBMAXSIZE.

TIP
Using LOBMAXSIZE removes the need to retrieve the length of the file, so consider using it. It is not as precise, but it works well and reduces the amount of code.

Our example results in the following output:

```
Length of the BLOB file is: 30731
Length of the CLOB file is: 411
Size of BLOB pre-load: 0
Size of CLOB pre-load: 0
Size of BLOB post-load: 30731
Size of CLOB post-load: 205
```

The size of the CLOB post-load is not the same as the length of the CLOB BFILE. There is *no* implicit character set conversion when using LOADFROMFILE. A select of the description column will show binary characters rather than the text from the file.

```
-- Available online as part of LoadFromFile.sql
SET LONG 64000
SELECT description
FROM book_samples
WHERE book_sample_id = 1;

DESCRIPTION
---------------------------------------
????????????????????????????????4?????????????????/
??????????????4?????????????7??????/
????????????????????????????????????????????????????????????????/
????????????????????????4??????????????????????
```

To avoid this, we would need to do a character set conversion on the BFILE prior to using LOADFROMFILE.

Let's rework the example to use LOADCLOBFROMFILE and LOADBLOBFROMFILE. Oracle added these procedures in 9*i*R2 and recommends they be used instead of LOADFROMFILE. The parameters for the BLOB version are the same as LOADFROMFILE's, while the CLOB version adds character set and language parameters to better handle text.

```
PROCEDURE LOADBLOBFROMFILE
  Argument Name              Type              In/Out Default?
  ---------------  ------------  --- ----
  DEST_LOB                     BLOB              IN/OUT
  SRC_BFILE                    BINARY FILE LOB   IN
  AMOUNT                       NUMBER(38)        IN
  DEST_OFFSET                  NUMBER(38)        IN/OUT
  SRC_OFFSET                   NUMBER(38)        IN/OUT

PROCEDURE LOADCLOBFROMFILE
  Argument Name              Type              In/Out Default?
  ---------------  ------------  --- ----
  DEST_LOB                     CLOB              IN/OUT
  SRC_BFILE                    BINARY FILE LOB   IN
  AMOUNT                       NUMBER(38)        IN
  DEST_OFFSET                  NUMBER(38)        IN/OUT
  SRC_OFFSET                   NUMBER(38)        IN/OUT
  BFILE_CSID                   NUMBER            IN
  LANG_CONTEXT                 NUMBER(38)        IN/OUT
  WARNING                      NUMBER(38)        OUT
```

We mentioned LOADFROMFILE does no character set conversion on load. LOADCLOBFROMFILE, on the other hand, *does* an implicit conversion, as we will see.

```
-- Available online as part of LoadLOBFromFile.sql
DECLARE
    v_dest_blob BLOB;
    v_dest_clob CLOB;
    v_source_locator1 BFILE := BFILENAME('BOOK_SAMPLES_LOC',
        'bfile_example.pdf');
    v_source_locator2 BFILE := BFILENAME('BOOK_SAMPLES_LOC',
        'bfile_example.txt');
    v_source_offset NUMBER := 1;
    v_dest_offset NUMBER := 1;
    v_lang_context NUMBER := DBMS_LOB.DEFAULT_LANG_CTX;
    v_warning PLS_INTEGER;

BEGIN
    -- Empty the description and misc columns
    UPDATE book_samples
    SET description = EMPTY_CLOB(),
        misc = EMPTY_BLOB()
    WHERE book_sample_id = 1;

    -- Retrieve the locators for the two destination columns
    SELECT description, misc
    INTO v_dest_clob, v_dest_blob
    FROM book_samples
    WHERE book_sample_id = 1
    FOR UPDATE;

    -- Open the BFILEs and destination LOBs
    DBMS_LOB.OPEN(v_source_locator1, DBMS_LOB.LOB_READONLY);
    DBMS_LOB.OPEN(v_source_locator2, DBMS_LOB.LOB_READONLY);
    DBMS_LOB.OPEN(v_dest_blob, DBMS_LOB.LOB_READWRITE);
    DBMS_LOB.OPEN(v_dest_clob, DBMS_LOB.LOB_READWRITE);

    DBMS_OUTPUT.PUT_LINE('Length of the BLOB file is: '
        ||DBMS_LOB.GETLENGTH(v_source_locator1));
    DBMS_OUTPUT.PUT_LINE('Length of the CLOB file is: '
        ||DBMS_LOB.GETLENGTH(v_source_locator2));
    DBMS_OUTPUT.PUT_LINE('Size of BLOB pre-load: '
        ||DBMS_LOB.GETLENGTH(v_dest_blob));
    DBMS_OUTPUT.PUT_LINE('Size of CLOB pre-load: '
        ||DBMS_LOB.GETLENGTH(v_dest_clob));

    -- Load the destination columns from the source
    DBMS_LOB.LOADBLOBFROMFILE(v_dest_blob,
                              v_source_locator1,
```

```
                                 DBMS_LOB.LOBMAXSIZE,
                                 v_dest_offset,
                                 v_source_offset);
        DBMS_OUTPUT.PUT_LINE('Size of BLOB post-load: '||(v_dest_offset -1));

        v_dest_offset := 1;
        v_source_offset := 1;

        DBMS_LOB.LOADCLOBFROMFILE(v_dest_clob,
                                  v_source_locator2,
                                  DBMS_LOB.LOBMAXSIZE,
                                  v_dest_offset,
                                  v_source_offset,
                                  DBMS_LOB.DEFAULT_CSID,
                                  v_lang_context,
                                  v_warning);

        DBMS_OUTPUT.PUT_LINE('Size of CLOB post-load: '||(v_dest_offset -1));

        -- Close the LOBs that we opened
        DBMS_LOB.CLOSE(v_source_locator1);
        DBMS_LOB.CLOSE(v_source_locator2);
        DBMS_LOB.CLOSE(v_dest_blob);
        DBMS_LOB.CLOSE(v_dest_clob);

EXCEPTION
    WHEN OTHERS
    THEN
        DBMS_OUTPUT.PUT_LINE(SQLERRM);

        DBMS_LOB.CLOSE(v_source_locator1);
        DBMS_LOB.CLOSE(v_source_locator2);
        DBMS_LOB.CLOSE(v_dest_blob);
        DBMS_LOB.CLOSE(v_dest_clob);

END;
/
```

Execution of this block shows the following:

```
Length of the BLOB file is: 30731
Length of the CLOB file is: 411
Size of BLOB pre-load: 0
Size of CLOB pre-load: 0
Size of BLOB post-load: 30731
Size of CLOB post-load: 411
```

A select of the CLOB column shows a totally different result than our LOADFROMFILE example:

```
-- Available online as part of LoadLOBFromFile.sql
SET LONG 64000
SELECT description
  FROM book_samples
  WHERE book_sample_id = 1;

DESCRIPTION
----------------------------------------
Make certain you have this file saved to your file system in the
location specified in your Oracle Directory. If it is not
there, the examples will not work.

Book Description:
The essential reference for PL/SQL has been revised and
expanded, featuring all new examples throughout based on
the new Oracle Database 10g, plus all the book's code
and expanded topics are included on the website for download.
```

Much better, and we did not have to manually convert the text.

Performance Considerations

By now, you should see that LOBs are far superior to LONG and LONG RAW types in functionality. They also have a leg up in performance as well. In this section we review some features that improve the speed of your code and reduce overhead associated with working with large objects.

Returning Clause

Our examples thus far separate the insertion of LOBs from the retrieval of their locators. Doing this is perfectly fine if you do not need the data immediately. If you require the locator right after the insert, though, it would make sense to *return* the locator you just created at insertion.

We do this with the RETURNING clause. RETURNING is a keyword added to the end of the INSERT statement allowing you to work with the LOB immediately, without any additional steps.

The following example inserts a value into the BOOK_SAMPLES table and immediately returns the LOB locator:

```
-- Available online as part of Returning.sql
SET SERVEROUTPUT ON LONG 64000
DECLARE
```

```
   v_clob CLOB;
BEGIN
   INSERT INTO book_samples (
   book_sample_id,
   isbn,
   description,
   nls_description,
   book_cover,
   chapter)
   VALUES (
   1,
   '72230665',
   'The essential reference for PL/SQL has been revised
    and expanded, featuring all new examples throughout based
    on the new Oracle Database 10g, plus all the book's code
    and expanded topics are included on the website for download.',
   EMPTY_CLOB(),
   EMPTY_BLOB(),
   BFILENAME('BOOK_SAMPLES_LOC', '72230665.jpg'))
   RETURNING description INTO v_clob;
   COMMIT;

   DBMS_OUTPUT.PUT_LINE(v_clob);
EXCEPTION
   WHEN OTHERS
   THEN
      DBMS_OUTPUT.PUT_LINE(SQLERRM);
END;
/
```

The output from this block shows the contents of the description column just inserted:

```
The essential reference for PL/SQL has been revised and
expanded, featuring all new examples throughout based on
the new Oracle Database 10g, plus all the book's code
and expanded topics are included on the website for download.
```

Indexing

Indexing capabilities of LOBs have come a long way since 8.0! Beginning in Oracle 8.1.6, Oracle *inter*Media's text indexing component became standard (meaning you don't have to license it separately). It was an option to select at database creation time that provided full-text search capabilities (text retrieval similar to most Internet search engines) for CLOB and NCLOB columns.

In Oracle 9*i*R1, the text-indexing component was separated from *inter*Media. The name was changed to Oracle Text. Violating Oracle's tradition of changing names every release, the name has remained Oracle Text through release 10*g*R1.

NOTE
From this point forward, we will refer to Oracle's text indexing as Oracle Text, even though the functionality is included in interMedia in Oracle 8i.

Table 16-3 lists the four types of indexes, their descriptions, and which releases first made the index types available.

For the purposes of our discussion regarding LOBs, we will focus on the CONTEXT index.

CONTEXT Index   The CONTEXT index works with the following datatypes:

- CLOB
- NCLOB
- BLOB
- BFILE
- VARCHAR2
- XMLTYPE

Index Name	Primary Use
CONTEXT	Most widely used index with CLOBs/NCLOBs. This index allows full-text retrieval with ranking, stemming, wildcards, and many other advanced features. The CONTEXT index is the oldest of the index types.
CTXRULE	Primarily for classification and routing applications, this index enables you to define RULES or queries that automatically classify documents in your collection.
CTXCAT	Introduced in Oracle 9iR1, this index is for smaller pieces of data than the CONTEXT index. It is intended for catalog applications, as its name implies.
CTXXPATH	Introduced in Oracle 9iR2, this is the first index specifically designed for indexing XML documents. The intent is to improve XPath search performance over what a standard CONTEXT index provides.

TABLE 16-3.   *Oracle Text Indexes*

It can index more than 150 different document types (determined by the built-in INSO Filter), as well as all internal LOBS. Indexing can be done on data stored in the database, across a URL, on a file system, or in another user-defined location.

Refer to Figure 16-3 for a diagram of the indexing process. At index creation, the documents (or data stored in the database) are passed to the FILTER. Text is extracted, and the markup is passed onto a SECTIONER that separates sections from text. The sections are passed directly to the INDEXING ENGINE for later use. The text is passed to a LEXER that generates tokens (words or phrases) based on the appropriate language. The indexing engine creates five tables (four in 8*i*) to support the indexes. The table we will look at later, and the one you will likely use most often, is the DR$...$I table. It contains a list of all tokens generated from the source files/columns.

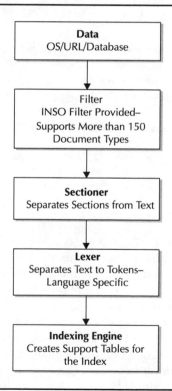

FIGURE 16-3.   *Oracle text indexing*

Using the CONTEXT index, we are able to perform the following types of queries:

- **Boolean searches**   AND, OR, NOT.

- **Exact matches**   Search for the exact word or phrase inside the text.

- **Inexact matches**   Search using stemming (a search for mice finds mouse), wildcard, soundex (one word sounds like another).

- **Proximity**   A word is *near* another.

- **Ranking**   A value is provided based on relevance to the keywords used in the query.

- **Theme searches**   Search on what a document or text is about. The keywords you supply don't even have to exist in the underlying document as long as the theme has been generated and Oracle Text can relate your keyword to the theme or gist of the text.

Let's go ahead and start our example by creating a CONTEXT index on the `DESCRIPTION` column in the `BOOK_SAMPLES` table. The first step in creating the CONTEXT index is to create named preferences. These tell the indexing engine how to process the data when the index is actually created.

```
-- Available online as part of TextIndex.sql
BEGIN
   ctx_ddl.create_preference ('lob_lexer', 'basic_lexer');
   ctx_ddl.set_attribute ('lob_lexer', 'index_text', 'true');
   ctx_ddl.set_attribute ('lob_lexer', 'index_themes', 'false');
END;
/
```

Our LEXER preference, called LOB_LEXER, is using the BASIC_LEXER. If we wished to index text in another language we can specify this here. Japanese, for example, has two possible lexers: JAPANESE_LEXER and JAPANESE_VGRAM_LEXER.

Breaking text into tokens is very different from language to language, yet Oracle provides a MULTI_LEXER in 8*i* and above that can accurately tokenize text in multiple languages stored in the same table and column. You must specify the language of each row in order to use the MULTI_LEXER. Oracle 10*g*R1 includes a lexer called the WORLD_LEXER that can detect the language of the text, so no additional language specification is necessary.

Here we continue our example by creating a wordlist called LOB_WORDLIST:

```
-- Available online as part of TextIndex.sql
BEGIN
```

```
    ctx_ddl.create_preference ('lob_wordlist', 'basic_wordlist');
    ctx_ddl.set_attribute ('lob_wordlist', 'substring_index', 'true');
END;
/
```

We are again using a basic wordlist for our example.

The index creation is fairly straightforward. We index our DESCRIPTION column in the BOOK_SAMPLES table. The type of index is the CONTEXT index, and we pass the two preferences created earlier as parameters.

```
-- Available online as part of TextIndex.sql
CREATE INDEX lob_indx ON book_samples(description)
INDEXTYPE IS CTXSYS.CONTEXT
PARAMETERS ( 'lexer lob_lexer
            wordlist lob_wordlist
            stoplist ctxsys.empty_stoplist' );
```

STOPLIST in this example refers to noise words, or words we do not wish to index. Examples of noise words would be "the," "of," "a," etc. These are words that do not add much of anything to a search and that you see no reason to store as tokens. In this case, we specified EMPTY_STOPLIST, so *all* words are indexed, including noise words.

To examine our tokens, we can select from the DRLOB_INDXI table.

```
-- Available online as part of TextIndex.sql
set pages 9999
SELECT token_text
FROM DR$LOB_INDX$I;
```

This returns 30 rows. A subset of the data appears here:

```
TOKEN_TEXT
-----
10G
ALL
AND
ARE
BASED
BEEN
BOOK
CODE
DATABASE
DOWNLOAD
ESSENTIAL
...
```

Our CLOB column is now indexed and is searchable! To see the difference between an EMPTY_STOPLIST and the DEFAULT_STOPLIST, let's drop the index and recreate it using the DEFAULT_STOPLIST value:

```
-- Available online as part of TextIndex.sql
DROP INDEX lob_indx force;

-- Create an index with the default stoplist
CREATE INDEX lob_indx ON book_samples(description)
INDEXTYPE IS CTXSYS.CONTEXT
PARAMETERS ( 'lexer lob_lexer
             wordlist lob_wordlist
             stoplist ctxsys.default_stoplist' );
```

We can rerun the same select against the DRLOB_INDXI table to see the difference.

```
-- Available online as part of TextIndex.sql
set pages 9999
SELECT token_text
FROM DR$LOB_INDX$I;

TOKEN_TEXT
-----
10G
BASED
BOOK
CODE
DATABASE
DOWNLOAD
ESSENTIAL
...
```

Now only 21 rows are returned from the select statement. This makes a big difference on indexing performance of our LOBs, but also on querying them.

To query the CONTEXT index, we use the CONTAINS operator. The following block searches for the string WEBSITE:

```
-- Available online as part of TextIndex.sql
SELECT SCORE(1), book_sample_id
  FROM book_samples
  WHERE CONTAINS(description, 'website', 1) > 0;

  SCORE(1) BOOK_SAMPLE_ID
  ----- -------
        3              1
```

One very nice feature of the CONTEXT index is that all searches are case-insensitive by default. The TOKEN_TEXT column in the DR$...$I table is in uppercase, so all values for queries are converted to uppercase for comparison. You can always make your indexes case-sensitive by setting your preferences to index that way, but most of the time it is not beneficial.

In addition to the basic querying just shown, you can also do stemming, soundex, and wildcard searches. Of these, stemming is generally the toughest to grasp. For example: A document contains the word "mouse," and you type "mice" in the search window. A normal query, or exact match Text query, would return "no rows." Even though the word mice is the plural of mouse, they do not share the same root, so a wildcard would not be efficient ('M%' would be the only option). With stemming, if you search for mice, you find all documents containing the word mouse.

Oracle Text makes large documentation sets manageable and retrieval and categorization of large volumes of data possible. If you are interested in learning more about Oracle Text, please visit http://otn.oracle.com/products/text/index.html.

Summary

In this chapter we discussed the following:

- BLOBs, BFILEs, CLOBs, and NCLOBs, and the ways we can use them in SQL and PL/SQL

- The differences between LOBs and the LONG and LONG RAW datatypes

- Storage of internal and external LOBs, including in-row and out-of-row LOBs

- The DBMS_LOB package, and how its procedures and functions help us work with LOBs

- Performance considerations for LOBs

- How Oracle Text improves access to LOB data in applications

CHAPTER
17

Scheduling Tasks

cheduling tasks for automated execution can save you time, and your company money. Examples of these tasks include the regular collection of statistics, the purging of interface tables at a specific time, or the execution of any anonymous PL/SQL block, shell script, or stored procedure. Virtually any program or executable can be scheduled for execution using the built-in packages DBMS_JOB and, in Oracle 10g, DBMS_SCHEDULER.

Alas, DBMS_JOB's time is almost up. With Oracle 10g comes DBMS_SCHEDULER, a built-in package that is available from the command line and is fully integrated with the Enterprise Manager utility. While offering all the functionality of DBMS_JOB, it also provides some great new features not available with its predecessor.

In this chapter we discuss both DBMS_JOB and DBMS_SCHEDULER. With DBMS_JOB we discuss some of the key procedures, demonstrating how to create, modify, and remove jobs from the queue. Next, we discuss the new-to-10g scheduling package DBMS_SCHEDULER and provide some insights into the package structure and job creation using this new facility.

The examples for the chapter are included online. To run them, you must do the following:

- Run the examples on a server with a valid e-mail server.

- Modify the seed data in the scripts to provide valid e-mail addresses if you wish to fully test the e-mail functionality.

- Provide your e-mail SMTP server when prompted by the scripts.

- If you are using Oracle 10g, you will need to run the `utlmail.sql` and `prvtmail.plb` scripts in the `$ORACLE_HOME/rdbms/admin` directory.

- Use the `CreateUser.sql` script for the schema creation to ensure all permissions are granted.

NOTE
Not using Oracle 10g yet? You will find the information in this chapter on DBMS_JOB relevant to all releases.

Introducing DBMS_JOB

The DBMS_JOB package was introduced in PL/SQL version 2.2 and is available in all currently supported releases of the Oracle data server, including Oracle 10gR1. It is widely used and recognized as one of the best database features for application developers and administrators alike. With its principal job of running programs on an interval, the ways in which the package is implemented are as varied as the types of programs available. Some common uses include, but are not limited to

- Monitoring session information and logging it to a table

- Scheduling the execution of the UTL_SMTP and UTL_MAIL packages

- Scheduling the gathering of Statspack snapshots

- Replacing OS operations against the database that typically require cron jobs, adding a level of security and exception handling not available with OS jobs

- Running statistics gathering on a regular interval, ensuring consistent explain plan generation by the Cost-Based Optimizer

- Purging interface or staging tables on a regular interval

- Scheduling the execution of time- and resource-intensive programs for off-hours execution

Jobs are scheduled by submitting them to a queue. The Coordinator Job Queue (CJQ) process runs in the background, and when a job is ready to be run, it spawns a job queue process (J*nnn*) to execute the jobs one at a time. Although each job queue process can handle only one request at a time, multiple processes can be spawned to deal with the workload. The number of concurrent processes allowed is controlled by the `init.ora/spfile` parameter JOB_QUEUE_PROCESSES.

If you are unsure what the value is for the JOB_QUEUE_PROCESSES parameter, run the following query:

```
SELECT name||': '||value PARAMETER
FROM v$parameter
WHERE name = 'job_queue_processes';
```

The results on our system are

```
PARAMETER
-----------------------
job_queue_processes: 10
```

One very nice feature of jobs is that they can be exported and imported, maintaining the same job number the whole time. This portability makes tablespace reorganization, or any other process that uses export/import, much less painful.

All jobs are created and maintained using the DBMS_JOB or DBMS_IJOB (not covered here) packages, but information about the jobs is obtained through the following data dictionary views:

- [ALL | DBA | USER]_JOBS

- DBA_JOBS_RUNNING

DBMS_JOB contains eleven procedures and two functions in Oracle 10gR1. We cover the most commonly used procedures in the next few sections in much greater detail.

NOTE
The only procedure that has an implicit commit is the DBMS_JOB.RUN procedure. All other procedures are transactional and require a commit before they can be used. Take note of this in your implementation, as it is quite easy to forget!

SUBMIT

The SUBMIT procedure creates a job by sending it to the job queue. No job can run without being in the job queue. The procedure has the following definition:

```
PROCEDURE SUBMIT
  Argument Name            Type                     In/Out Default?
  -----------------        ----------------------   ------ --------
  JOB                      BINARY_INTEGER           OUT
  WHAT                     VARCHAR2                 IN
  NEXT_DATE                DATE                     IN     DEFAULT
  INTERVAL                 VARCHAR2                 IN     DEFAULT
  NO_PARSE                 BOOLEAN                  IN     DEFAULT
  INSTANCE                 BINARY_INTEGER           IN     DEFAULT
  FORCE                    BOOLEAN                  IN     DEFAULT
```

To execute, use the following syntax:

```
DBMS_JOB.SUBMIT (JOB => job_no,
  WHAT => code_to_run,
  NEXT_DATE => date,
  INTERVAL => schedule,
  NO_PARSE => parse_timing,
  INSTANCE => inst_no,
  FORCE => force_value)
```

Here is how the parameters are defined:

- *Job_no* is the number associated with the job when it is created. The value is derived from the sequence JOBSEQ owned by SYS.

- *Code_to_run* is the task you wish to execute.

- *Date* is the time the job will run next. The default for *date* is SYSDATE.

- *Schedule* is the pattern or frequency of execution. The default is NULL, which means it will run only once.

- *Parse_timing* determines when the job is parsed. The default for *parse_timing* is FALSE, meaning the job is parsed as soon as it is submitted. If it were TRUE, the parse occurs at the time the job is executed by the SNP*n* background process.

- *Inst_no* is the instance number, which can be retrieved from the V$INSTANCE view.

- *Force_value* is related to *inst_no*. They are both added for instance affinity. If FALSE, which is the default, the value provided for *inst_no* must be a valid instance number, and the instance must be running. If TRUE, any positive integer can be provided as the instance number.

In the following set of examples there is a table containing e-mail messages with both sent and unsent messages. The SUBMIT procedure is used to create jobs to process the e-mails.

Example 1: Procedure Execution on 30-Minute Interval

This example creates a job that loops through the EMAIL_TBL table for e-mail messages that still need to be processed. The job executes every half-hour and sends them to the recipients using UTL_SMTP.

```
-- Available online as part of Submit.sql
SET SERVEROUTPUT ON
DECLARE
    v_job_number NUMBER(10);
    v_instance_number NUMBER(10);
BEGIN

    -- Get the instance number for use with DBMS_JOB.SUBMIT
    SELECT instance_number
    INTO v_instance_number
    FROM v$instance;

    -- Submit a job to begin tonight at midnight, and execute
```

```
   --   ever half-hour thereafter
   DBMS_JOB.SUBMIT (JOB => v_job_number,
                    WHAT => 'email_manager.smtp(&mail_server);',
                    NEXT_DATE => TRUNC(SYSDATE + 1),
                    INTERVAL => 'SYSDATE + 1/48',
                    NO_PARSE => TRUE,
                    INSTANCE => v_instance_number,
                    FORCE => NULL);
   COMMIT;
   DBMS_OUTPUT.PUT_LINE('The job number is: '||v_job_number);
END;
/
```

This anonymous block returned a job value of 33 from our system (it will be different in yours). We created the GET_JOB_DETAILS procedure to collect information about jobs:

```
-- Available online as part of Submit.sql
CREATE OR REPLACE PROCEDURE get_job_details(
   i_job_number IN NUMBER,
   cv_job_details IN OUT SYS_REFCURSOR)
IS
BEGIN
   OPEN cv_job_details FOR
   SELECT job, schema_user,
          to_char(next_date, 'dd-mon-yyyy hh24:mi:ss'),
          interval, what, broken
   FROM user_jobs
   WHERE job = i_job_number;
EXCEPTION
   WHEN OTHERS
   THEN
       DBMS_OUTPUT.PUT_LINE(SQLERRM);
END get_job_details;
/
```

We can run this procedure as follows:

```
VARIABLE v_job_details REFCURSOR
EXEC GET_JOB_DETAILS(&job_number, :v_job_details)

COL schema FORMAT A15
COL next_date FORMAT A20
COL interval FORMAT A20
COL what FORMAT A60
PRINT v_job_details
```

Executing this procedure passing 33 in as the job number, we see:

```
          JOB SCHEMA        NEXT_DATE               INTERVAL
---------- ------------ -------------------- --------------------
WHAT                                                                B
---------------------------------------------------------------- -
          33 PLSQL           28-jun-2004 00:00:00 SYSDATE + 1/48
email_manager.smtp('mail.smtp.com');                               N
```

The job is in the queue and scheduled to run at midnight tonight. It will be executed every one-half hour (1/48) thereafter.

Example 2: Purge the E-Mail Table Once Per Week

In this example we create a job that runs a DELETE statement. It is schedule to run every Sunday.

```
-- Available online as part of Submit.sql
SET SERVEROUTPUT ON
DECLARE
    v_job_number NUMBER;
    v_instance_number NUMBER;
    v_statement VARCHAR2(500);
BEGIN
    -- Get the instance number for use with DBMS_JOB.SUBMIT
    SELECT i.instance_number
    INTO v_instance_number
    FROM v$instance i;

    v_statement := 'DELETE FROM email_tbl WHERE date_sent IS NOT NULL;';

    -- Submit a job to begin today, and execute
    --   every Sunday at 11:45 PM.
    DBMS_JOB.SUBMIT (JOB => v_job_number,
            WHAT => v_statement,
            NEXT_DATE => TRUNC(SYSDATE + 1),
            INTERVAL => 'NEXT_DAY(TRUNC(SYSDATE), ''SUNDAY'') + 95/96',
            NO_PARSE => TRUE,
            INSTANCE => v_instance_number,
            FORCE => NULL);
    COMMIT;
    DBMS_OUTPUT.PUT_LINE('The job number is: '||v_job_number);
END;
/
```

In this example we set the interval so that the job would run every Sunday at 11:45 P.M., a time that will allow the snapshots in our first job to start fresh at midnight.

The last example returned a job number of 34 in our instance. We can again execute the GET_JOB_DETAILS procedure.

```
-- Available online as part of Submit.sql
VARIABLE v_job_details REFCURSOR
EXEC GET_JOB_DETAILS(142, :v_job_details)

COL schema_user FORMAT A15
COL next_date FORMAT A20
COL interval FORMAT A20
COL what FORMAT A60
SET PAGES 9999
PRINT v_job_details
```

This prints the following output to the screen:

```
     JOB SCHEMA        NEXT_DATE
---------- ------------ --------------------
INTERVAL
-----------------------------------------------------------
WHAT                                                        B
----------------------------------------------------------- -
        34 PLSQL        04-jul-2004 23:45:00
NEXT_DAY(TRUNC(SYSDATE), 'SUNDAY') + 95/96
DELETE FROM email_tbl WHERE date_sent IS NOT NULL;          N
```

The job was successfully created. Note that the time for the next execution is shown in the interval column as 23:45, or 11:45 P.M.

BROKEN

The Coordinator Job Queue process does not attempt to run any job marked as *broken*. Jobs are marked as broken if they cannot successfully complete after repeated attempts. Oracle also provides a procedure called BROKEN to explicitly mark a job as broken.

The BROKEN procedure has the following definition:

```
PROCEDURE BROKEN
Argument Name                    Type                    In/Out Default?
------------------------------   ----------------------  ------ --------
JOB                              BINARY_INTEGER          IN
BROKEN                           BOOLEAN                 IN
NEXT_DATE                        DATE                    IN     DEFAULT
```

To execute it, use the following syntax:

DBMS_JOB.BROKEN (job => *job_no*,
  broken => *boolean_value*,
  next_date => *date*);

where *job_no* is the number associated with the job when it is created. This number is static. *Boolean_value* can be TRUE, which marks the job as broken, or FALSE, which says the job is not broken. *Date* is the time the job will run next.

This example sets a job created in the *Submit* section (job number 142) as broken:

```
-- Available online as part of Broken.sql
BEGIN
    DBMS_JOB.BROKEN(job => &job_number,
                    broken => TRUE,
                    next_date => sysdate);
    COMMIT;
END;
/
```

We can run this, providing the job number of 34 that we created earlier as part of the *Submit* section, Example 2 (again, your job numbers will be different than ours). To confirm the change, we can check the data dictionary view USER_JOBS using the procedure GET_JOB_DETAILS that we created earlier.

```
-- Available online as part of Broken.sql
VARIABLE v_job_details REFCURSOR
EXEC GET_JOB_DETAILS(&job_number, :v_job_details)

COL schema_user FORMAT A15
COL next_date FORMAT A20
COL interval FORMAT A60
COL what FORMAT A4000
SET PAGES 9999
PRINT v_job_details
```

This returns the following:

```
       JOB SCHEMA        NEXT_DATE
---------- ------------ --------------------
INTERVAL
--------------------------------------------------------
WHAT
--------------------------------------------------------
B
-
        34 PLSQL         01-jan-4000 00:00:00
```

```
NEXT_DAY(TRUNC(SYSDATE), 'SUNDAY') + 95/96
DELETE FROM email_tbl WHERE date_sent IS NOT NULL;
Y
```

Job 34 is marked as broken, as indicated by the Y in the broken column. The Coordinator Job Queue process will not spawn a process to run this job while in this state. Using the BROKEN procedure, we can re-enable the job by passing a value of FALSE to the *broken* parameter.

RUN

Even though job 34 is currently marked as broken, and the job will not be run automatically, the RUN procedure can force the execution of the job regardless of time or status. It has the following definition:

```
PROCEDURE RUN
 Argument Name                       Type                     In/Out Default?
 ------------------------------      ------------------------  ------ -------
 JOB                                 BINARY_INTEGER           IN
 FORCE                               BOOLEAN                  IN     DEFAULT
```

To execute it, use the following syntax:

DBMS_JOB.RUN (JOB => *job_no*,
 FORCE => *force_value*);

where *job_no* is the job number as seen in the USER_JOBS view, and *force_value* is added for instance affinity.

We will test this out by running job 34 that we just disabled in the last section. Checking the record count in the EMAIL_TBL table prior to the job's execution, we can see there are six records.

```
SELECT COUNT(1)
FROM email_tbl;

  COUNT(1)
  -----
        6
```

We can now run the job.

```
-- Available online as part of Run.sql
SET SERVEROUTPUT ON
DECLARE
   v_error EXCEPTION;
   PRAGMA EXCEPTION_INIT(v_error, -23421);
```

```
BEGIN
    DBMS_JOB.RUN(job => &job_number, FORCE => TRUE);
    COMMIT;
EXCEPTION
    WHEN v_error
    THEN
        DBMS_OUTPUT.PUT_LINE('The job number entered was not valid');
END;
/
```

By supplying 34 as the job number, we force its execution. Rerunning the GET_
JOB_DETAILS procedure, notice the change to the value for BROKEN.

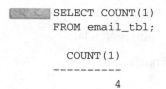

```
      JOB SCHEMA          NEXT_DATE
---------- ------------ --------------------
INTERVAL
--------------------------------------------------
WHAT
--------------------------------------------------
B
-
        34 PLSQL          01-aug-2004 23:45:00
NEXT_DAY(TRUNC(SYSDATE), 'SUNDAY') + 95/96
DELETE FROM email_tbl WHERE date_sent IS NOT NULL;
N
```

Forcing the run marked it as not broken and executed the job. It also performed the
DELETE that is part of the job, as can be seen by a record count.

```
SELECT COUNT(1)
FROM email_tbl;

  COUNT(1)
----------
        4
```

NOTE
*No COMMIT was used with the RUN procedure. It
is the only procedure where the COMMIT is implicit.*

CHANGE

The CHANGE procedure provides a way to modify an existing job in the job queue.
While it is possible to remove and recreate the job, the job number would change
as a result. Using this procedure, the job number remains.

The CHANGE procedure has the following definition:

```
PROCEDURE CHANGE
Argument Name                    Type                       In/Out Default?
------------------------------   ------------------------   ------ --------
JOB                              BINARY_INTEGER             IN
WHAT                             VARCHAR2                   IN
NEXT_DATE                        DATE                       IN
INTERVAL                         VARCHAR2                   IN
INSTANCE                         BINARY_INTEGER             IN     DEFAULT
FORCE                            BOOLEAN                    IN     DEFAULT
```

To execute it, use the following syntax:

EXEC DBMS_JOB.CHANGE (JOB => *job_no,*
  WHAT => *code_to_run,*
  NEXT_DATE => *date,*
  INTERVAL => *schedule,*
  INSTANCE => *inst_no,*
  FORCE => *force_value*);

Here is how the parameters are defined:

- *Job_no* is the number associated with the job when it is created. The value is derived from the sequence JOBSEQ owned by SYS.

- *Code_to_run* is the task you wish to execute.

- *Date* is the time the job will run next. The default for *date* is SYSDATE.

- *Schedule* is the pattern or frequency of execution. The default is NULL.

- *Inst_no* is the instance number, which can be retrieved from the V$INSTANCE view.

- *Force_value* is related to *inst_no.* They are both added for instance affinity. If FALSE, which is the default, the value provided for *inst_no* must be a valid instance number, and the instance must be running. If TRUE, any positive integer can be provided as the instance number.

To test the CHANGE procedure, we will modify job 33 that was created in the "SUBMIT" section.

```
-- Available online as part of Change.sql
DECLARE
   v_instance_number NUMBER(10);
BEGIN
```

```
-- Get the instance number for use with DBMS_JOB.SUBMIT
SELECT instance_number
INTO v_instance_number
FROM v$instance;

DBMS_JOB.CHANGE (JOB => &job_number,
                 WHAT => 'email_manager.smtp(''&mail_server'');',
                 NEXT_DATE => TRUNC(SYSDATE + 1),
                 INTERVAL => 'SYSDATE + 1/24',
                 INSTANCE => v_instance_number,
                 FORCE => NULL);
    COMMIT;
END;
/
```

Now, when we run the GET_JOB_DETAILS procedure, it shows a modified INTERVAL.

```
       JOB SCHEMA           NEXT_DATE
---------- ------------ ----------
INTERVAL
-----------------------------------
WHAT
-----------------------------------
B
-
        33 PLSQL          27-jul-2004 00:00:00
SYSDATE + 1/24
email_manager.smtp('mail.smtp.com');
N
```

The job will be executed every hour, rather than every half-hour.

REMOVE

The last procedure we will cover is the one used to *remove* jobs from the job queue. The REMOVE procedure takes but one argument: the job number. Its definition is as follows:

```
PROCEDURE REMOVE
  Argument Name                         Type                      In/Out Default?
  ------------------------------ ------------------------ ------ --------
  JOB                                  BINARY_INTEGER            IN
```

To execute this procedure, use the following syntax:

DBMS_JOB.REMOVE (JOB => *job_no*);

To illustrate, we will remove job 142 on our system.

```
-- Available online as part of Remove.sql
EXEC DBMS_JOB.REMOVE(JOB => &job_number);
COMMIT;
```

Running the GET_JOB_DETAILS procedure, passing 141 as the job number, results in the following:

```
no rows selected
```

The job was successfully removed.

Oracle Scheduler

Oracle has made it clear that DBMS_JOB will not be around much longer. In fact, the script that creates the DBMS_JOB package specification ($Oracle_Home/ rdbms/admin/dbmsjob.sql) includes a line in the header that says it is present only for backward compatibility and is not used any longer.

What does this mean for application developers and database administrators using Oracle 10g? It means that it is time to migrate those scheduled tasks from using DBMS_JOB to use DBMS_SCHEDULER, and to do it fast!

In this section we provide an overview of the new Scheduler and convert the two jobs created in the section on DBMS_JOB to use DBMS_SCHEDULER instead.

Terminology

If you are familiar with DBMS_JOB (if not, go back and read the last section), you might find the initial terminology quite familiar in meaning, if not name. For instance, Scheduler includes jobs, or tasks to be executed. It includes schedules, similar to the interval specified with the SUBMIT procedure in DBMS_JOB. It also includes *programs,* similar to the value passed to the WHAT parameter of the DBMS_JOB .SUBMIT procedure.

This is really where the terminology parts ways, however. Scheduler includes features and concepts not available with DBMS_JOB, so here we review some of the basics. Refer to Table 17-1 for a list of terms and their definitions.

Using DBMS_SCHEDULER

The DBMS_SCHEDULER package is owned by the user SYS. As you might expect, permissions on a package of this type are not granted to PUBLIC. Rights must be

Term	Definition
JOB CLASS	Job categorization. Similar jobs are grouped together into job classes.
JOB LOGGING	All jobs are logged to the `SYS.SCHEDULER$_EVENT_LOG` and viewed through the `DBA_SCHEDULER_JOB_LOG` view.
RESOURCE CONSUMER GROUP	Defines limits to users and job classes on system resources. It also provides a mechanism for defining job priority, so that the most critical jobs are handled first.
RESOURCE PLAN	Determines limits placed on Resource Consumer Groups.
WINDOW	Schedules resource plan activation. For example, it is possible to have one resource plan in effect during peak hours, and another take over for off-peak times.
WINDOW GROUP	Groups logical windows together.
WINDOW PRIORITY	The order of precedence given to overlapping windows.

TABLE 17-1. *Scheduler Terminology*

specifically granted to use the package. For the examples here we will use the
`SCHEDULER_ADMIN` role that provides the following system privileges:

- CREATE ANY JOB
- EXECUTE ANY PROGRAM
- EXECUTE ANY CLASS

It also includes the MANAGE SCHEDULER privilege that allows our user to
perform most administrative tasks.

DBMS_SCHEDULER.CREATE_JOB

Creating the job with DBMS_SCHEDULER is not so different from using DBMS_JOB.
The CREATE_JOB procedure is actually an overloaded procedure with four definitions.
We are using the following definition for both examples shown here:

```
PROCEDURE CREATE_JOB
 Argument Name                   Type                     In/Out Default?
 ------------------------------  -----------------------  ------ --------
```

JOB_NAME	VARCHAR2	IN	
JOB_TYPE	VARCHAR2	IN	
JOB_ACTION	VARCHAR2	IN	
NUMBER_OF_ARGUMENTS	BINARY_INTEGER	IN	DEFAULT
START_DATE	TIMESTAMP WITH TIME ZONE	IN	DEFAULT
REPEAT_INTERVAL	VARCHAR2	IN	DEFAULT
END_DATE	TIMESTAMP WITH TIME ZONE	IN	DEFAULT
JOB_CLASS	VARCHAR2	IN	DEFAULT
ENABLED	BOOLEAN	IN	DEFAULT
AUTO_DROP	BOOLEAN	IN	DEFAULT
COMMENTS	VARCHAR2	IN	DEFAULT

We are using this procedure because it allows us to create a job without a predefined schedule. The other CREATE_JOB procedures rely on existing schedules and/or programs where the name can be supplied.

The parameters for CREATE_JOB are defined as follows:

- JOB_NAME   The name must be a valid identifier as described in Chapter 3. Unlike jobs created with DBMS_JOB, they can be created in another schema simply by prefixing the JOB_NAME with the name of the schema. Names *must* be unique within a schema.

- JOB_TYPE   The type can be PLSQL_BLOCK, STORED_PROCEDURE, or EXECUTABLE. At the time of this writing, these are the three supported types.

- JOB_ACTION   If the JOB_TYPE is a PLSQL_BLOCK, the string must be an anonymous block. If JOB_TYPE is a STORED_PROCEDURE, the string must be a stored procedure name. If JOB_TYPE is an EXECUTABLE, the action must be a fully qualified string, including filename, pointing to the executable file.

- NUMBER_OF_ARGUMENTS   The default value for this parameter is 0. Provide an integer specifying the number of arguments for an inline program.

- START_DATE   The desired start date and time for the job. Note that the data type is TIMESTAMP WITH TIMEZONE.

- REPEAT_INTERVAL   Provide either a calendar expression or datetime expression specifying the frequency of the execution. This is discussed a little later in this section.

- END_DATE   The date the job will be dropped (if AUTO_DROP is turned on) or stopped. Note that the data type is TIMESTAMP WITH TIMEZONE.

- JOB_CLASS   The class the job should be associated with.

■ ENABLED   If the value is TRUE, the job will be enabled immediately upon creation. If left to the default of FALSE, the job must be explicitly enabled using the DBMS_SCHEDULER.ENABLE procedure.

■ AUTO_DROP   Also a Boolean parameter, if TRUE, the job will be dropped automatically when the date specified for END_DATE is reached. If it is FALSE, jobs must be dropped by running the DBMS_SCHEDULER.DROP_JOB procedure.

■ COMMENTS   This is simply a field to enter text describing the job. We do recommend this field be used to document the jobs to make code maintenance easier.

REPEAT_INTERVAL

The parameter called REPEAT_INTERVAL requires additional explanation, as you might not be familiar with it yet. We mentioned that the parameter accepts either calendar expressions or datetime expressions to determine the frequency of execution. We'll begin with the latter since it matches most closely the examples used for DBMS_JOB.

A valid datetime expression is one that returns a date, but since the parameter is of type VARCHAR2, the expression is enclosed in single quotes. Valid values might include

'SYSTIMESTAMP + 30': Repeat every thirty days.
'SYSDATE + 1/24': Repeat every hour.

Example 1 from the "DBMS_JOB" section sets the interval equal to 'SYSDATE + 1/48'. This is a valid datetime expression to use with DBMS_SCHEDULER.

Calendar expressions, though possibly less cryptic for those new to Oracle, are a big departure from traditional datetime expressions. They are now considered the standard method of setting the REPEAT_INTERVAL, so it is time to get accustomed to the names and conventions.

The syntax for setting the REPEAT_INTERVAL is as follows:

'FREQ=*frequency* [,INTERVAL=*interval* [;*specifier=specifier_value*]]'

Frequency is required and can be any of the following values:

■ YEARLY

■ MONTHLY

- WEEKLY

- DAILY

- HOURLY

- MINUTELY

- SECONDLY

If *frequency* is set to DAILY, for example, and no other parameters are specified, the job will execute one time per day.

Interval operates on the frequency and can be any integer from 1 to 999. The default is 1. If *frequency* were set to DAILY, and *interval* set to 7, the job would be run once every seven days.

Frequency and *interval* give direction to how often a job should be run, but not when it should be run. The *specifier* uses the calendar and clock to provide detailed direction on when the job should run. Valid *specifiers* include

- BYMONTH

- BYWEEK

- BYYEARDAY

- BYMONTHDAY

- BYDAY

- BYHOUR

- BYMINUTE

- BYSECOND

If the specifier is used, so must the *specifier_value*. Valid values are far too numerous to include in this text, but they can be any month abbreviated to three letters (such as JAN or FEB), day of the month, week of the year, etc.

Here are a couple of examples of repeat intervals:

Every 30 minutes

```
'FREQ=MINUTELY; INTERVAL=30;'
```

Every hour at 45 minutes past the hour

```
'FREQ=HOURLY;BYMINUTE=45'
```

Every other Sunday at 8:00 P.M.

```
'FREQ=WEEKLY;INTERVAL=2;BYDAY=SUN;BYHOUR=20'
```

You will no doubt master calendar expressions in no time. We have found it easier to use calendar expressions than datetime expressions when needing to create complex intervals.

Migrating from DBMS_JOB

Migrating from DBMS_JOB to DBMS_SCHEDULER is relatively painless. The new package does not remove functionality, so any additional steps in the creation process go to improve the way the job scheduling works. In this section we recreate the jobs shown in the DBMS_JOB.SUBMIT section, this time using DBMS_ SCHEDULER.CREATE procedure.

Example 1: Procedure Execution on 30-Minute Interval

If you recall, we created a job that executes the EMAIL_MANAGER.SMTP procedure at 30-minute intervals. While we can convert the job to use UTL_SMTP, we will instead use the new UTL_MAIL package provided in Oracle 10*g*. For this example, create the job as the PLSQL user created earlier in the chapter with the *CreateUser.sql* script. If you are not running Oracle 10*g*, the examples will not work in your environment.

```
-- Available online as part of CreateJob.sql
BEGIN
    DBMS_SCHEDULER.CREATE_JOB (JOB_NAME => 'EXAMPLE1',
                JOB_TYPE => 'STORED_PROCEDURE',
                JOB_ACTION => 'EMAIL_MANAGER.INLINE_EMAIL',
                START_DATE => TRUNC(SYSTIMESTAMP + 1),
                REPEAT_INTERVAL => 'FREQ=MINUTELY;INTERVAL=30',
                END_DATE => SYSTIMESTAMP+300,
                ENABLED => TRUE,
                AUTO_DROP => TRUE,
                COMMENTS => 'Send E-Mail on 30 min intervals ');
END;
/
```

This creates the job successfully, but we cannot use the GET_JOB_DETAILS procedure created earlier, since it is specific to data dictionary views for DBMS_JOB. We created a similar procedure called GET_SCHEDULER_DETAILS that we can use instead:

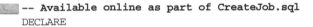

```
-- Available online as part of CreateJob.sql
CREATE OR REPLACE PROCEDURE get_scheduler_details(
    i_job_name IN VARCHAR2,
    cv_job_details IN OUT SYS_REFCURSOR)
IS
BEGIN
    OPEN cv_job_details FOR
        SELECT job_name, state, comments, next_run_date
        FROM dba_scheduler_jobs
        WHERE job_name = UPPER(i_job_name);
EXCEPTION
    WHEN OTHERS
    THEN
        DBMS_OUTPUT.PUT_LINE(SQLERRM);
END get_scheduler_details;
/
```

Using this procedure, we get the following detail:

```
JOB_NAME                           STATE
------------------------------- -----------
COMMENTS
-------------------------------------------
NEXT_RUN_DATE
-------------------------------------------
EXAMPLE1                          SCHEDULED
Send E-Mail on 30 min intervals
28-JUN-04 12.00.00.000000 AM -07:00
```

The start date is at 12 midnight as was expected, and the status is SCHEDULED due to our setting ENABLED=TRUE in the creation.

Example 2: Purge the E-Mail Table Once Per Week

In this example we create a job that runs a DELETE statement. It is scheduled to run every Sunday at 11:45 P.M. We will recreate it using the DBMS_SCHEDULER.CREATE_JOB procedure.

```
-- Available online as part of CreateJob.sql
DECLARE
```

```
    v_instance_number NUMBER;
    v_statement VARCHAR2(500);
    v_dbid NUMBER;
BEGIN
    -- Get the instance number
    SELECT instance_number
    INTO v_instance_number
    FROM v$instance;

    v_statement := 'DELETE FROM email_tbl WHERE date_sent IS NOT NULL;';

    -- Submit a job to begin today, and execute
    --   ever Sunday at 11:45 PM.
    DBMS_SCHEDULER.CREATE_JOB (JOB_NAME => 'EXAMPLE2',
        JOB_TYPE => 'PLSQL_BLOCK',
        JOB_ACTION => v_statement,
        START_DATE => SYSTIMESTAMP,
        REPEAT_INTERVAL => 'FREQ=WEEKLY;BYDAY=SUN; BYHOUR=23; BYMINUTE=45',
        END_DATE => SYSTIMESTAMP+300,
        ENABLED => TRUE,
        AUTO_DROP => TRUE,
        COMMENTS => 'Delete e-mails once per week at 23:45 Sunday');
    COMMIT;
END;
/
```

Checking the job in the using GET_SCHEDULER_DETAILS, we receive the following information:

```
JOB_NAME                          STATE
------------------------------    ---------------
COMMENTS
------------------------------------------------
NEXT_RUN_DATE
------------------------------------------------
EXAMPLE2                          SCHEDULED
Delete e-mails once per week at 23:45 Sunday
04-JUL-04 11.45.58.900000 PM -07:00
```

The time is scheduled correctly, and the job is enabled. Keep in mind that with both Scheduler and DBMS_JOB, all job executions are resource dependent. If there is no available process to execute the job, the NEXT_RUN_DATE does not matter. The advantage to using Scheduler is that we now have the ability to apply resource plans and priority to tasks that were not available previously.

Removing a Job

There are two ways in which a job can be removed from Scheduler. The first depends on the value specified for the AUTO_DROP parameter at job creation. In the two examples shown earlier, AUTO_DROP was set to true. This means that if the END_ DATE is reached, the jobs will be dropped automatically.

In our case, the END_DATE is not close enough. If we need to drop a job right away, we can use the DBMS_SCHEDULER.DROP_JOB procedure. The following example drops both example jobs from the scheduler:

```
EXEC DBMS_SCHEDULER.DROP_JOB('EXAMPLE1');
EXEC DBMS_SCHEDULER.DROP_JOB('EXAMPLE2');
```

That's all there is to it!

Summary

This chapter introduced job scheduling using DBMS_JOB. It included discussions about DBMS_JOB features and demonstrated how to create, modify, and remove jobs from the job queue. The second half of the chapter focused on the new 10*g* scheduling package called DBMS_SCHEDULER that is slated to replace DBMS_JOB. We compared the job creation using both packages and recreated the DBMS_JOB examples using the DBMS_SCHEDULER procedure CREATE_JOB. You also saw examples of UTL_SMTP and UTL_MAIL, and how they can be used to provide e-mail functionality to your applications and database implementation.

PART
III

Appendixes

APPENDIX A

PL/SQL Reserved Words

he words listed in this appendix are reserved by PL/SQL. Reserved words have special syntactic meaning in the language and thus can't be used as identifiers (for variable names, procedure names, and so on). Some of these words are reserved by SQL as well and thus can't be used to name database objects such as tables, sequences, and views.

Table of Reserved Words

The following table lists the reserved words for PL/SQL, up to and including Oracle10*g*R1. The reserved word list was increased for 9*i*R1 and is the same for 9*i*R2 and 10*g*R1. In the table, words not reserved in 8*i*R1 are in bold, while those reserved by SQL have an asterisk (*). You should avoid using any of these words to minimize potential conflicts.

You should also avoid creating a package with the same name as the Oracle predefined packages described in Appendix B, or a procedure with the same name as one defined in the STANDARD package.

ALL*	ALTER*	AND*	ANY*
ARRAY	AS*	ASC*	AT
AUTHID	AVG	BEGIN	BETWEEN*
BINARY_INTEGER	BODY	BOOLEAN	BULK
BY*	**CASE**	CHAR*	CHAR_BASE
CHECK*	CLOSE	CLUSTER*	**COALESCE**
COLLECT	COMMENT*	COMMIT	COMPRESS*
CONNECT*	CONSTANT	CREATE*	CURRENT*
CURRVAL	CURSOR	DATE*	DAY
DECLARE	DECIMAL*	DEFAULT*	DELETE*
DESC*	DISTINCT*	DO	DROP*
ELSE*	ELSIF	END	EXCEPTION
EXCLUSIVE*	EXECUTE	EXISTS*	EXIT
EXTENDS	**EXTRACT**	FALSE	FETCH
FLOAT*	FOR*	FORALL	FROM*
FUNCTION	GOTO	GROUP*	HAVING*

HEAP	HOUR	IF	IMMEDIATE*
IN*	INDEX*	INDICATOR	INSERT*
INTEGER*	INTERFACE	INTERSECT*	INTERVAL
INTO*	IS*	ISOLATION	JAVA
LEVEL*	LIKE*	LIMITED	LOCK*
LONG*	LOOP	MAX	MIN
MINUS*	MINUTE	MLSLABEL*	MOD
MODE*	MONTH	NATURAL	NATURALN
NEW	NEXTVAL	NOCOPY	NOT*
NOWAIT*	NULL*	**NULLIF**	NUMBER*
NUMBER_BASE	OCIROWID	OF*	ON*
OPAQUE	OPEN	OPERATOR	OPTION*
OR*	ORDER*	ORGANIZATION	OTHERS
OUT	PACKAGE	PARTITION	PCTFREE*
PLS_INTEGER	POSITIVE	POSITIVEN	PRAGMA
PRIOR*	PRIVATE	PROCEDURE	PUBLIC*
RAISE	RANGE	RAW*	REAL
RECORD	REF	RELEASE	RETURN
REVERSE	ROLLBACK	ROW*	ROWID*
ROWNUM*	ROWTYPE	SAVEPOINT	SECOND
SELECT*	SEPARATE	SET*	SHARE*
SMALLINT*	SPACE	SQL	SQLCODE
SQLERRM	START*	STDDEV	SUBTYPE
SUCCESSFUL*	SUM	SYNONYM*	SYSDATE*
TABLE*	THEN*	TIME	TIMESTAMP
TIMEZONE_REGION	**TIMEZONE_ABBR**	**TIMEZONE_MINUTE**	**TIMEZONE_HOUR**
TO*	TRIGGER*	TRUE	TYPE
UID*	UNION*	UNIQUE*	UPDATE*

USE	USER*	VALIDATE*	VALUES*
VARCHAR*	VARCHAR2*	VARIANCE	VIEW*
WHEN	WHENEVER*	WHERE*	WHILE
WITH*	WORK	WRITE	YEAR
ZONE			

If you want to use a reserved word, it must be enclosed in double quotation marks, as in this example:

```
DECLARE
  "BEGIN" NUMBER;
BEGIN
  "BEGIN" := 7;
END;
```

Although this block is legal, it is not recommended.

APPENDIX
B

Guide to Supplied Packages

racle-supplied packages, or built-in packages, give programmers access to functionality that greatly improves our ability to perform complex issues. Some of the packages are written in C, providing fast execution and direct access to the kernel (now also available to user-defined packages with Native Compilation). Others are extremely complex, with cross-package dependencies, and would take the best PL/SQL programmers many weeks if they had to write it from scratch.

The first section describes the supplied packages owned by the SYS schema and provides the package descriptions, the scripts used to create them, and the release at which they first became available.

The second section provides information about the packages owned by the CTXSYS user, which is the Oracle Text schema. Oracle Text has become a major component of the database, and a huge feature for Application Developers. The package definitions have the same information as the SYS-owned packages, but we also include descriptions of package procedures and functions. We added this detail to the CTXSYS packages because they are so useful, yet they have very little coverage in other texts.

SYS-Owned Built-in Packages

The built-in packages listed in this section are owned by the user SYS. Each package has a public synonym. The synonym allows you to call the package without using the schema name (SYS) as a prefix. They are created using the catproc.sql script during database creation, which is run automatically if you are using the Database Configuration Assistant (DBCA). In order to use these packages, EXECUTE permissions must be granted to your user.

The list of packages compiled here is based on version 10.1.0.2.0 of the database. To determine the version you have, run the following:

```
SELECT *
FROM v$version;

BANNER
---------------------------------
Oracle Database 10g Enterprise Edition Release 10.1.0.2.0 - Prod
PL/SQL Release 10.1.0.2.0 - Production
CORE    10.1.0.2.0      Production
TNS for 32-bit Windows: Version 10.1.0.2.0 - Production
NLSRTL Version 10.1.0.2.0 - Production
```

While catproc.sql is the script that is run at database creation, it is actually a summary script that calls other files. Catproc.sql and the scripts it calls to create the packages are located in your $ORACLE_HOME/rdbms/admin directory. Each object creation script is stored separately, and the filenames for the specification and body are included with the descriptions that follow. The *.sql scripts used to create the specifications are not encrypted and provide additional descriptive information regarding the package. The *.plb scripts, which create the package bodies, are encrypted.

Not all supplied packages are shown. Many of the packages are covered in detail in the rest of the book, and reference is made to the chapters where they are used. We selected some of the most useful packages related to PL/SQL operation and Application Developer needs. Should you require information that is not included, please refer to the *PL/SQL Packages and Types Reference* available on http://otn.oracle.com.

DBMS_ADVANCED_REWRITE

This package, new to 10*g*R1, is great for third-party applications in particular. It allows you to define source and destination statements, so when a SQL statement is run, it can be changed automatically to be something different. This allows you to redefine how a query runs without changing the source code!

For example, suppose you have an application that has a statement that does not work the way you want it to. Using DBMS_ADVANCED_REWRITE, you can enter this statement as a source query, and create an alternate destination query that works how you want. When the source query is executed, Oracle automatically replaces the source query with your custom destination query.

Creation Scripts
prvtxrmv.plb (includes package spec and body)

Release Available
Oracle 10*g*R1

DBMS_ADVISOR

The new DBMS_ADVISOR package can help tune SQL and materialized views for query rewrite. DBMS_ADVISOR is required for another 10*g* tuning feature, called Automatic Database Diagnostic Monitor (ADDM), that is implemented through 10*g* Enterprise Manager. The DBMS_ADVISOR package can be either used through ADDM in Enterprise Manager, used through the $ORACLE_HOME/rdbms/admin/ addmrpt.sql script, or manually called via SQL (you must have the ADVISOR role granted in order to use this package).

Oracle uses ADDM to analyze SQL and make recommendations on how to tune the statement or dependent objects for optimum performance. Always, always test out the recommendations it makes before implementing!

Creation Scripts
`dbmsadv.sql/dbmsadv.plb`

Release Available
Oracle 10*g*R1

DBMS_ALERT

Use DBMS_ALERT to send event notifications between database sessions. If a session wishes to receive an alert, it must request it using the `REGISTER` procedure. One of the most common uses of this package is to alert a user to a data change. If data is modified, an alert can be issued via a trigger on the modified table. Alerts are transaction based and are not sent until the transaction is committed. This package is discussed and demonstrated in Chapter 11.

Creation Scripts
`dbmsalrt.sql/prvtalrt.plb`

Release Available
Pre–Oracle 8*i*

DBMS_APPLICATION_INFO

This package allows the application developer to assign a module name to a process and an action being performed within that process. The module names and actions can be queried from the `V$SESSION` and `V$SQLAREA` views. This assists the developer and the DBA by allowing module- and action-specific session information to be tracked by name. DBMS_APPLICATION_INFO also allows the registration of a process to `V$SESSION_LONGOP`, which can track the process as a long-running module.

Creation Scripts
`dbmsapin.sql/prvtapin.plb`

Release Available
Pre–Oracle 8*i*

DBMS_APPLY_ADM

The DBMS_APPLY_ADM package is the administration package for an APPLY process. The APPLY process is part of the Oracle Streams functionality. It is a background process that is responsible for handling events that are part of Streams. Additional information regarding streams and the APPLY process can be found in the *Oracle Streams Concepts and Administrator's Guide* at http://otn.oracle.com.

Creation Scripts
dbmsapp.sql/prvtbapp.plb

Release Available
Oracle 9*i*R2

DBMS_AQ

There are actually a number of packages available for Oracle Streams Advanced Queuing. DBMS_AQ is the operational package for Advanced Queuing, and it provides features such as registration for messages and defining listeners for messages in the queue.

Creation Scripts
dbmsaq.plb/prvtaq.plb (In this case, the specification (dbmsaq.plb) is encrypted as well.)

Release Available
Pre–Oracle 8*i*

DBMS_BACKUP_RESTORE

The database consists of redo logs, data files, and control files (the instance is the memory structures). The ARCH background process writes redo logs to archive redo logs for recovery purposes. The DBMS_BACKUP_RESTORE package uses information contained in the control file to create backups of the redo/archive logs and data files, and restore them. This package does not support MTS (Multi-Threaded Server).

Creation Scripts
dbmsbkrs.sql/prvtbkrs.plb

Release Available
Pre–Oracle 8.1.7

DBMS_CAPTURE_ADM

Like the DBMS_APPLY_ADM package, DBMS_CAPTURE_ADM is an administrative package for an Oracle Streams process. The CAPTURE process is an Oracle background process that picks up changes defined by predefined rules, and then acts on them accordingly. Additional information regarding streams and the CAPTURE process can be found in the *Oracle Streams Concepts and Administrator's Guide* at http://otn.oracle.com.

Creation Scripts
`dbmscap.sql/prvtbcap.plb`

Release Available
Oracle 9*i*R2

DBMS_CRYPTO

This package provides industry-standard encryption and is a replacement for the DBMS_OBFUSCATION_TOOLKIT package that was used in Oracle 8*i* and 9*i*. It supports multiple character sets and can use the following algorithms:

- DES (Data Encryption Standard)
- AES (Advanced Encryption Standard, meant to replace DES)
- RC4
- 3DES
- 3DES-2KEY

The following cryptographic and keyed algorithms are also supported:

- MD4
- MD5
- SHA-1
- HMAC_MD5 (MAC stands for Message Authentication Code)
- HMAC_SH1

Creation Scripts
`dbmsobtk.sql/prvtobtk.plb`

Release Available
Oracle 10*g*R1

DBMS_DATA_MINING, DBMS_DATA_MINING_TRANSFORM

These PL/SQL APIs, new to Oracle 10*g*R1, add a PI/SQL interface to the data mining engine. Data mining capabilities include classification and clustering of data. By identifying patterns in text, you can improve the quality of information in your application and turn existing data stores into knowledge repositories.

Creation Scripts

Data mining creation scripts are located in `$ORACLE_HOME/dm/admin`.
   DBMS_DATA_MINING: `dbmsdm.plb/prvtdm.plb`
   DBMS_DATA_MINING_TRANSFORM: `dbmsdmxf.sql` (contains package spec and body)

Release Available
Oracle 10*g*R1

DBMS_DATAPUMP

This new package makes it easy to move data (and metadata) between databases. If you have worked extensively with import/export, you know the problems associated with exporting on one platform and importing to another. DBMS_DATAPUMP allows the movement of all or part of a database from one system to another, regardless of OS and hardware.

Creation Scripts
`dbmsdp.sql/prvtdp.plb`

Release Available
Oracle 10*g*R1

DBMS_DDL

This package includes functions and procedures that give access to a small number of DDL capabilities such as compiling and analyzing objects. Since execution of this package in turn executes other commands, the privileges of the executing user are enforced rather than those of the package owner, SYS.

Creation Scripts
`dbmsutil.sql/prvtutil.plb`

Release Available
Pre–Oracle 8*i*

DBMS_DEBUG

DBMS_DEBUG was designed primarily for vendors wishing to debug server-side code. It is the interface for the PL/SQL Probe debugger. It requires two sessions to work, with one session executing the code to be debugged, and the other producing the debug output. Breakpoints can be set that allow you to step through code.

Creation Scripts
`dbmspb.sql/prvtpb.plb`

Release Available
Oracle 8*i*

DBMS_DEFER

This package is used with Oracle's Advanced Replication option. It is the interface used to create deferred calls to procedures on a remote system (referred to as Remote Procedure Calls, or RPC). With DBMS_DEFER, you can define the target instance for the deferred transaction, call the remote procedure, and commit the work.

Creation Scripts
`dbmsdefr.sql/prvtdefr.plb`

Release Available
Pre–Oracle 8*i*

DBMS_DESCRIBE

The DBMS_DESCRIBE package provides parameter information for other procedures in your database. One procedure in the package, called `DESCRIBE_PROCEDURE`, returns detailed information related to each parameter of the object name passed as an argument.

Creation Scripts
`dbmsdesc.sql/prvtdesc.plb`

Release Available
Pre–Oracle 8*i*

DBMS_DIMENSION

This package is used primarily in the context of a data warehouse and provides a method of displaying dimension information. A dimension is like a category. Real-world terms are used to break data up into logical structures that match real-world business concepts of what the object is. In a data warehouse for a bookstore, for example, a book or CD could be a dimension. Dimensions are also hierarchical, so the dimension book can roll up into the dimension called bookstore. The DBMS_ DIMENSION package retrieves information about the dimension, and validates the defined relationships.

Creation Scripts
`dbmssum.sql/prvtsum.plb`

Release Available
Oracle 10*g*R1

DBMS_DISTRIBUTED_TRUST_ADMIN

This package helps determine whether a database specified by a database link is on the trusted servers list. If a database specified in the link is not on the list, the link is refused. The package is also responsible for maintaining the list.

Creation Scripts
`dbmstrst.sql/prvttrst.plb`

Release Available
Pre–Oracle 8.1.7

DBMS_FGA

FGA stands for Fine-Grained Audit. The DBMS_FGA package provides administrative procedures to add, drop, enable, and disable policies related to auditing. Auditing captures user actions, including SQL that is used by the schema/object being audited.

Creation Scripts
`dbmsfga.sql/prvtfga.plb`

Release Available
Oracle 9*i*R1

DBMS_FILE_TRANSFER

DBMS_FILE_TRANSFER is a great package for those using BFILES. It can create copies of a file and transfer it between the file systems of remote databases. Local and remote copies can be made, and files on a remote database's file system can be retrieved back to the local file system.

Creation Scripts
`dbmsxfr.sql/prvtxfr.plb`

Release Available
Oracle 10*g*R1

DBMS_FLASHBACK

The DBMS_FLASHBACK package provides the ability to restore specific data according to an SCN captured by a snapshot. The flashback is session based and can restore to an SCN that is passed as an argument. This is different from two-phase commit (2PC) and the ability to rollback a change, since flashback can happen even if a commit has been done.

NOTE
SCN, which stands for System Change Number, is an Oracle internal numbering scheme that identifies changes to the database. SCNs allow recovery to a specific change, as each SCN is unique and acts as an identifier for point-in-time recovery.

Creation Scripts
`dbmstran.sql/prvttran.plb`

Release Available
Oracle 9*i*R1

DBMS_HS

Related to Oracle Heterogeneous Services (HS), the DBMS_HS package is an interface to non-Oracle databases. It allows you to run ANSI-standard SQL against supported databases. For additional information on Heterogeneous Services, see the *Oracle Distributed Database Systems* manual on http://otn.oracle.com.

Creation Scripts
dbmshs.sql/prvths.sql

Release Available
Pre–Oracle 8*i*

DBMS_HS_PASSTHROUGH

This package, which is part of the Oracle Transparent Gateway, allows you to send SQL to non-Oracle databases without it being interpreted by the local server. The remote system must be registered with Heterogeneous Services. For additional information on Heterogeneous Services, see the *Oracle Distributed Database Systems* manual on http://otn.oracle.com.

Creation Scripts
dbmshs.sql/prvths.sql

Release Available
Pre–Oracle 8*i*

DBMS_JAVA

PL/SQL can access Java features using the DBMS_JAVA package. Use DBMS_JAVA for loading Java stored procedures into the database and granting permissions on Java objects to users. DBMS_JAVA also helps redirect the display for output using the SET_OUTPUT procedure. Increasing the size of the SQL*Plus buffer, for example, may allow output to display in the SQL*Plus window, where the buffer is quite low by default (2K).

Creation Scripts
initdbj.sql
   The installation of the Oracle JVM actually creates the package.

Release Available
Oracle 8*i*

DBMS_JOB

DBMS_JOB has been deprecated in Oracle 10gR1, though it is still present for backward compatibility. DBMS_SCHEDULER has replaced this heavily used package.

The DBMS_JOB package schedules and runs jobs at predefined intervals. One common use is to schedule a job to automatically execute Statspack snapshots. You submit a job, specifying the task to be performed and the frequency with which it should be executed, and the job is placed in the queue. The `init.ora` parameter `job_queue_processes` controls the number of jobs that can be queued in the system. This package is discussed in depth in Chapter 17.

Creation Scripts
`dbmsjob.sql/prvtjob.plb`

Release Available
Pre–Oracle 8*i*

DBMS_LDAP

The Lightweight Directory Access Protocol, or LDAP, is a communication standard that is used most extensively in Oracle with its Internet Directory. The DBMS_LDAP package allows us to access LDAP servers in SSL or non-SSL modes. If using TCP/IP, non-SSL is used by default.

Creation Scripts
`dbmsldap.sql/prvtldap.plb`

Prior to Oracle 10gR1, this package was not loaded at database creation time. For earlier database releases, the script `$ORACLE_HOME/rdbms/admin/catldap.sql` must be run.

Release Available
Oracle 8*i*

DBMS_LOB

This package is the way to work with LOBs in PL/SQL. It provides capabilities to open, close, load, retrieve, and manipulate all types of LOBs. Please refer to Chapter 16 for complete coverage of the DBMS_LOB package.

Creation Scripts
dbmslob.sql/prvtlob.plb

Release Available
Pre–Oracle 8*i*

DBMS_LOCK

Use DBMS_LOCK to obtain locks in the system. Unlike transaction-based locks, a lock obtained with DBMS_LOCK is not released on commit. You must explicitly release the lock using the RELEASE function.

Creation Scripts
dbmslock.sql/prvtlock.plb

Release Available
Pre–Oracle 8*i*

DBMS_LOGMNR

When Log Miner registers a redo log (done using the ADD_LOGFILE procedure), DBMS_LOGMNR can analyze the log files, extract data from the log files, and populate the database views used by the Log Miner utility.

Creation Scripts
dbmslm.sql/prvtlm.plb

Release Available
Oracle 8*i*

DBMS_METADATA

DBMS_METADATA retrieves metadata from the data dictionary about an object and outputs the information in either XML or DDL. You can then load the XML or run the DDL to re-create that object.

Creation Scripts
dbmsmeta.sql/prvtmeta.plb

Release Available
Oracle 9*i*R1

DBMS_MONITOR

This is useful for providing advanced tracing and statistical data on a client, session, module, or action. These parameter values can be retrieved from the V$SESSION view.

Creation Scripts
dbmsmtr.sql/prvtmtr.plb

Release Available
Oracle 10*g*R1

DBMS_OBFUSCATION_TOOLKIT

The DBMS_OBFUSCATION_TOOLKIT has been deprecated in Oracle 10*g*R1 in favor of the DBMS_CRYPTO package. It is still available for backward compatibility.

This package provides industry-standard encryption. Although it has the ability to encrypt data and generate encryption keys, it cannot maintain them. The keys provide the access to the controlled data, so storage and transport of the keys over the network should be of primary concern when you're using this utility.

Creation Scripts
dbmsobtk.sql/prvtobtk.plb

Release Available
Oracle 8*i*

DBMS_ODCI

The ESTIMATE_CPU_UNITS function in this package provides an estimate for the number of CPU instructions, or cycles, that will be used for the execution of a user function. It calculates the CPU cost in terms of the time it takes to execute (in seconds). The time is passed as input to the function.

Creation Scripts
catodci.sql/prvtodci.plb

Release Available
Oracle 9*i*R1

DBMS_OFFLINE_OG

DBMS_OFFLINE_OG is a replication package that provides the ability to manage replicated environments. Instantiation of master groups is done using this package.

Creation Scripts
dbmsofln.sql/prvtofln.plb

Release Available
Oracle 8*i*

DBMS_OLAP

The DBMS_OLAP package helps you analyze Trace files to help optimize materialized views. As of Oracle 10*g*R1, this package is deprecated. It is actually a synonym in release 10*g*R1 for the replacement package, DBMS_SUMMARY.

Creation Scripts
dbmssum.sql (creates the synonym in Oracle 10*g*R1)

Release Available
Oracle 8*i* (deprecated in release 10*g*R1)

DBMS_OUTLN

DBMS_OUTLN has replaced OUTLN_PKG for the management of stored outlines. The Cost-Based Optimizer (CBO) has been dramatically improved in recent releases, but every once in a while you will find a bad plan being chosen when you know a different plan should be used. Inconsistency of plan choice can also be problematic.

Stored outlines provide a way for you to ensure the plan selection is consistent, and they provide the means through DBMS_OUTLN and DBMS_OUTLN_EDIT to manage the plans.

Stored outlines are different than pinning the statement in a couple of ways:

- Pinning requires you to re-pin the statement when an instance is bounced, but stored outlines do not.

- Pinning still requires that the statement be parsed and the explain plan generated. This is not good if you can't get the correct plan at all. Stored outlines provide the means for you to alter the plan.

Creation Scripts
```
dbmsol.sql/prvtol.plb
```

Release Available
Oracle 8*i*

DBMS_OUTLN_EDIT

This package provides additional stored outline management capabilities than are present with the DBMS_OUTLN package, including the ability to modify the join position of hints for private outlines.

Creation Scripts
```
dbmsol.sql/prvtol.plb
```

Release Available
Oracle 9*i*

DBMS_OUTPUT

DBMS_OUTPUT is great for debugging. Take care to not rely on this package too heavily for reporting or writing to files, however. There is a limitation of 255 characters per line that can cause you some headaches. A simple workaround is to use the SUBSTR function as follows:

```
SET SERVEROUTPUT ON
DECLARE
    v_string VARCHAR2(500);
    v_length NUMBER(10);
BEGIN
    SELECT text, text_length
    INTO v_string, v_length
    FROM dba_views
    WHERE view_name = 'DBA_COL_PRIVS';

    DBMS_OUTPUT.PUT_LINE('View DBA_COL_PRIVS is '||v_length||'
bytes');
    DBMS_OUTPUT.PUT_LINE('TEXT');
    DBMS_OUTPUT.PUT_LINE('====');
    DBMS_OUTPUT.PUT_LINE(SUBSTR(v_string, 1, 250));
    DBMS_OUTPUT.PUT_LINE(SUBSTR(v_string, 251, 500));
END;
/
```

This is a not terribly pretty, but effective way around this problem. It is recommended that you create a custom wrapper for DBMS_OUTPUT to more effectively handle this if you use the package for more than debugging purposes.

Creation Scripts
`dbmsotpt.sql/prvtotpt.sql`

Release Available
Pre–Oracle 8*i*

DBMS_PIPE

DBMS_PIPE provides the ability for different sessions, in the same database, to communicate. Similar to DBMS_ALERT, it is discussed in great detail in Chapter 11.

Creation Scripts
`dbmspipe.sql/prvtpipe.plb`

Release Available
Pre–Oracle 8*i*

DBMS_PROFILER

The DBMS_PROFILER API is used to gather, store, and analyze Profiler data. The Profiler is used by Oracle to track performance of PL/SQL. Before you enable the profiler for application code, it is recommended that your application be run at least once to remove system overhead associated with a first run. Use DBMS_ PROFILER to start the profiler, run your application, and then stop the profiler.

Creation Scripts
`dbmspbp.sql/prvtpbp.plb`

Release Available
Oracle 8*i*

DBMS_PROPAGATION_ADM

DBMS_PROPAGATION_ADM is an Oracle Streams package used to create, alter, and drop propagations. The `CREATE_PROPAGATION` procedure creates a propagation and takes the source and destination queues as well as rule set name to associate with it as an argument. The DROP_PROPAGATION procedure simply drops the propagation. The ALTER_PROPAGATION procedure allows you to add, drop, or modify the rule set assigned to a propagation.

Creation Scripts
dbmsprp.sql/prvtprp.plb

Release Available
Oracle 9*i*R2

DBMS_RANDOM

Oracle includes a C-based random number generator. This built-in package takes advantage of this generator, so it is much faster than PL/SQL-based generators. User-defined PL/SQL-based generators can closely match the speed if native compilation is used.

Creation Scripts
dbmsrand.sql/prvtrand.plb

Release Available
Pre–Oracle 8*i*

DBMS_REDEFINITION

The DBMS_REDEFINITION package is an API that performs online redefinition of tables. The redefinition can include column and column name changes. During the process, interim tables are used. Using the SYNC_INTERIM_TABLE procedure, the interim table that was redefined is synchronized with the original table.

Creation Scripts
dbmshord.sql/prvtbord.sql

Release Available
Oracle 9*i*R1

DBMS_REFRESH

This package creates groups of materialized views for a more consistent (and easier) refresh. Materialized views need to be refreshed in order for their data to be consistent.

Instead of refreshing them independently, risking an out-of-sync situation, create a refresh group and do them at one time.

Creation Scripts
dbmssnap.sql/prvtsnap.plb

Release Available
Pre–Oracle 8*i*

DBMS_REPAIR

Primarily a package for database administrators, the DBMS_REPAIR package detects corrupt table and index blocks and helps to repair them. This is one of the few packages that does not have a public synonym granted to public. It is owned by SYS, and permission must be granted to any other user you wish to have access to it.

Creation Scripts
dbmsrpr.sql/prvtrpr.plb

Release Available
Oracle 8*i*

DBMS_REPCAT

For Oracle Replication, the master site maintains a replication catalog. DBMS_REPCAT is the package to use for maintaining this catalog.

Creation Scripts
dbmshrep.sql/prvtbrep.plb

Release Available
Pre–Oracle 8*i*

DBMS_RESOURCE_MANAGER/ DBMS_RESOURCE_MANAGER_PRIVS

Primarily used by database administrators, these packages provide a way to maintain resource plans.

Creation Scripts
DBMS_RESOURCE_MANAGER: dbmsrmad.sql/prvtrmad.plb
   DBMS_RESOURCE_MANAGER_PRIVS: dbmsrmpr.sql/prvtrmpr.plb

Release Available
Oracle 8*i*

DBMS_RESUMABLE

The DBMS_RESUMABLE package provides you with the ability to manage resources by operation. Limits on space used can be set so that if they are exceeded, the operation/transaction will be suspended for a specified period of time. Should the operation reach the limit and be suspended, the problem can be fixed and the transaction resumed, or it can be aborted.

Creation Scripts
dbmsres.sql/prvtres.plb

Release Available
Oracle 9*i*R1

DBMS_ROWID

Using DBMS_ROWID, you can create ROWIDs or retrieve information about them that would otherwise be very difficult to obtain. Of particular use to us over the years is the ROWID_BLOCK_NUMBER function.

TIP
We've used this function on a number of occasions to track down the block number of a specific row or set of rows. Using this function, you can determine which rows share the same blocks (handy for detecting block contention related to initrans). Select the block number, rowid, and primary key into a temporary table for sorting.

Creation Scripts
dbmsutil.sql/prvtutil.plb

Release Available
Pre–Oracle 8*i*

DBMS_RULE, DBMS_RULE_ADM

The "read" portion of the script names shown here stands for Rules Engine Admin. Rules are defined for Oracle Streams. These packages provide the administrative tools to create and manage the rules and rule sets. They can also be used to monitor the rules that are created for particular events.

Creation Scripts
`dbmsread.sql/prvtread.plb` (creates both packages)

Release Available
Oracle 9*i*R2

DBMS_SCHEDULER

This package supersedes DBMS_JOB. DBMS_SCHEDULER creates, maintains, schedules, and classifies jobs that are needed. Jobs might include user-defined processes such as the collection of statspack snapshots (or ADDM snapshots), or the execution of a specific procedure. DBMS_SCHEDULER can also be used by internal tools, such as Enterprise Manager, for the collection of data on a regular interval. See Chapter 17 for a discussion of this package.

Creation Scripts
`dbmssch.sql/prvtsch.plb`

Release Available
Oracle 10*g*R1

DBMS_SCHEMA_COPY

This package allows you to clone a source schema to a destination schema and clean up after the process is complete. This package is not documented anywhere in Oracle's documentation, so we've played with it a bit more than normal to fully test. It successfully handled everything we threw at it, including executing code in the source schema while running the clone procedure.

Creation Scripts
`prvtupg.plb` (contains both spec and body)

Release Available
Oracle 10*g*R1

DBMS_SERVER_ALERT

This package generates alerts based on predefined thresholds. You can set the critical nature of each threshold so that severe threshold violations are treated differently than warning levels.

Creation Scripts
dbmsslrt.sql/prvtslrt.plb

Release Available
Oracle 10*g*R1

DBMS_SERVICE

This is a Real Application Cluster (RAC) package that lets you maintain services. Capabilities include the ability to create, delete, disconnect, start, and stop services for a single instance.

Creation Scripts
dbmssrv.sql/prvtsrv.plb

Release Available
Oracle 10*g*R1

DBMS_SESSION

This session-specific utility allows you to modify parameters much as you can with the ALTER SESSION command. You can modify NLS settings, turn session tracing on or off, set roles, and more.

Creation Scripts
dbmsutil.sql/prvtutil.plb

Release Available
Pre–Oracle 8*i*

DBMS_SHARED_POOL

This is a memory management package for the shared pool (part of the SGA memory area). DBMS_SHARED_POOL can display SQL that is larger than the size specified, and it can pin (KEEP) or unpin (UNKEEP) SQL in the shared pool.

Creation Scripts
dbmspool.sql/prvtpool.plb

Release Available
Pre–Oracle 8*i*

DBMS_SPACE

The DBMS_SPACE package is useful for trend analysis, providing forecasts of space requirements based on current growth patterns. It also provides current segment space statistics for objects.

Creation Scripts
dbmsutil.sql/prvtutil.plb

Release Available
Pre–Oracle 8*i*

DBMS_SQL

The DBMS_SQL package is useful for executing SQL from PL/SQL (including DDL that cannot be run normally). Native Dynamic SQL (NDS) has reduced the need for this package significantly with its ability to run SQL with the command EXECUTE IMMEDIATE.

Creation Scripts
dbmssql.sql/prvtsql.plb

Release Available
Pre–Oracle 8*i*

DBMS_SQLTUNE

The DBMS_SQLTUNE package creates Profiles and SQL Sets used in analyzing multiple SQL statements for performance. The package can collect statistical information from the Workload Repository regarding SQL statements, and it displays tuning results.

Creation Scripts
dbmssqlt.sql/prvtsqlt.plb

Release Available
Oracle 10*g*R1

DBMS_STANDARD, STANDARD

These packages are very similar to each other. They implement basic built-in functions used by application developers, such as RAISE_APPLICATION_ERROR. To use the functions in these packages, you do not need to prefix the call with the package name!

Creation Scripts
DBMS_STANDARD: dbmsstdx.sql
    STANDARD: stdspec.sql/stdbody.sql

Release Available
Pre–Oracle 8*i*

DBMS_STAT_FUNCS

This package provides data distribution analysis for exponential, normal, Poisson, uniform, and Weibull distributions.

Creation Scripts
dbmsstts.sql/prvtstts.plb

Release Available
Oracle 10*g*R1

DBMS_STATS

The DBMS_STATS package allows you to gather, retrieve, and modify statistics on columns, indexes, tables, schemas, and your entire system. The Cost-Based Optimizer (CBO) uses statistics to evaluate the cost of various explain plans. It is critical that your stats are up-to-date and correct for the CBO to accurately determine the lowest-cost plan. If you are familiar with the Oracle E-Business Suite, you should be using the FND_STATS package or Gather Schema Statistics concurrent program instead.

Creation Scripts
dbmsstats.sql/prvtstats.plb

Release Available
Oracle 8*i*

DBMS_SUMMARY

DBMS_SUMMARY is the replacement for DBMS_OLAP. It helps analyze trace files to optimize materialized views.

Creation Scripts
dbmssum.sql/prvtsum.plb

Release Available
Oracle 10*g*R1

DBMS_TRACE

Stop and start PL/SQL tracing with DBMS_TRACE. Trace output generated by DBMS_TRACE is found in your user_dump_dest location (udump directory). You can also specify the level of the trace, pause the trace while it is running, and then resume it again when you are ready.

Creation Scripts
dbmspbt.sql/prvtpbt.plb

Release Available
Oracle 8*i*

DBMS_TRANSACTION

This package provides transaction control statements such as commit and rollback. There are SQL equivalents for most of the procedures and functions.

Creation Scripts
dbmsutil.sql/prvtutil.plb

Release Available
Pre–Oracle 8*i*

DBMS_TRANSFORM

This is a Oracle Advanced Queuing package that allows you to maintain transformations. Procedures include CREATE_TRANSFORMATION, MODIFY_TRANSFORMATION, and DROP_TRANSFORMATION.

Creation Scripts
dbmstxfm.sql/prvttxfm.plb

Release Available
Oracle 9*i*R1

DBMS_TYPES

The DBMS_TYPES package contains a specification only—no body. It contains constants only and is primarily used with other packages. Use this package in your programs when working with the "ANY" types.

Creation Scripts
dbmsany.sql

Release Available
Oracle 9*i*R1

DBMS_UTILITY

DBMS_UTILITY includes miscellaneous procedures and functions such as COMPILE_SCHEMA, which compiles all objects in the schema, and DB_VERSION, which returns version information for the current instance.

Creation Scripts
dbmsutil.sql/prvtutil.plb

Release Available
Pre–Oracle 8*i*

DBMS_WARNING

This wonderful new package provides advanced warning capabilities for your PL/SQL code. Depending on the warning level you set, you can get informational messages, see warnings of potential performance problems, restrict warnings to severe warnings only, or get *all* warnings, and the package does this at compile time. This is great for code development and unit-testing your code (assuming you do unit-test as all developers should!). It can give you advanced warning on problems that will not show up until execution.

Creation Scripts
`dbmsplsw.sql/prvtplsw.plb`

Release Available
Oracle 10*g*R1

DBMS_WORKLOAD_REPOSITORY

This is an administrative package for the Workload Repository. The AWR, or Automatic Workload Repository, stores snapshots for use in monitoring system performance. The DBMS_WORKLOAD_REPOSITORY package is used to create snapshots and generate reports (text or HTML format) across snapshots.

Creation Scripts
`dbmsawr.sql/prvtawr.plb`

Release Available
Oracle 10*g*R1

DBMS_XMLGEN, DBMS_XMLQUERY

These packages take an SQL statement as input and return XML output as a CLOB (XMLType). Oracle recommends the DBMS_XMLGEN package be used when possible, since it is written in C and precompiled. DBMS_XMLQUERY requires interpretation by the kernel at run time.

Creation Scripts
DBMS_XMLGEN: `dbmsxml.sql/prvtxml.plb`

Release Available
Oracle 9*i*R1

DBMS_XPLAN

The DBMS_XPLAN package provides a number of ways to display explain plan output for a SQL statement. Using this package, you can display the number of rows accessed by each line of the explain plan, the cost (and percent of CPU) associated with each line, the number of bytes accessed by each line, the time associated with each line, and the order of evaluation for each line of the explain plan. In short, it shows you what the Cost-Based Optimizer (CBO) uses to evaluate this plan vs. others it generates.

Creation Scripts
`dbmsxplan.sql/prvtxplan.plb`

Release Available
Oracle 9*i*R2

UTL_COLL

The UTL_COLL package contains a single subprogram. The `IS_LOCATOR` function returns either TRUE or FALSE, depending on whether the collection item is a locator.

Creation Scripts
`utlcoll.plb/prvtcoll.plb`

Release Available
Oracle 8*i*

UTL_COMPRESS

This package provides piecewise compression and uncompression of binary data. Similar in function to Zip or gzip utilities, it is able to compress data of type bfile, blob, and raw.

Creation Scripts
`utlcomp.sql/prvtcomp.plb`

Release Available
Oracle 10*g*R1

UTL_DBWS

This package provides support for database web services. With this package, you can create services, retrieve services as specified by the WSDL document, and remove services.

Creation Scripts
utldbws.sql/prvtdbws.plb

Release Available
Oracle 10*g*R1

UTL_ENCODE

This package includes the ability to encode and decode raw text, such as e-mail messages.

Creation Scripts
utlenc.sql/prvtenc.plb

Release Available
Oracle 9*i*R1

UTL_FILE

Write to and read from files on the operating system. UTL_FILE can write to any directory the Oracle user has write permissions to, as long as the directory is listed as a value for the UTL_FILE_DIR init.ora parameter.

Creation Scripts
utlfile.sql/prvtfile.plb

Release Available
Pre–Oracle 8*i*

UTL_HTTP

Use UTL_HTTP to access data on the Internet. PL/SQL can communicate with web servers with HTTP. It also supports HTTPS and FTP.

Creation Scripts
utlhttp.sql/prvthttp.plb

Release Available
Pre–Oracle 8*i*

UTL_I18N

I18N stands for internationalization (there are 18 letters between the I and N in InternationalizatioN). This package is used for globalization and, more specifically, the Globalization Development Kit. UTL_I18N is useful for character conversions, mapping different types of character sets, and determining the name of an Oracle character set given the language used. It is often used in conjunction with the DBMS_CRYPTO package for encryption.

Creation Scripts
```
utli18n.sql/prvti18n.plb
```

Release Available
Oracle 10gR1

UTL_INADDR

This package includes two functions used with Internet addressing. The first, GET_HOST_ADDRESS, gets the IP address of the machine name specified. The second, GET_HOST_NAME, retrieves the name of the host when provided an IP address.

Creation Scripts
```
utlinad.sql/prvtinad.plb
```

Release Available
Oracle 9iR1

UTL_LMS

This package was designed primarily for globalization support. It includes two functions: one to get a message in another language, and the second to format the message retrieved.

Creation Scripts
```
utllms.sql/prvtlms.plb
```

Release Available
Oracle 10gR1

UTL_MAIL

This is a mail management package that includes standard e-mail features, such as attachments. Use this package whenever you need to design e-mail management features, for example, with a workflow application. UTL_MAIL is demonstrated in Chapter 17.

Creation Scripts
utlmail.sql/prvtmail.plb

Release Available
Oracle 10*g*R1

UTL_RAW

This package provides some SQL function support for the RAW datatype. Supported functions include CONCAT, COMPARE, LENGTH, etc.

Creation Scripts
utlraw.sql/prvtraw.plb

Release Available
Pre–Oracle 8*i*

UTL_RECOMP

This utility provides a means to recompile, by dependency, all objects in the database.

Creation Scripts
utlrcmp.sql/prvtrcmp.plb

Release Available
Oracle 10*g*R1

UTL_REF

The UTL_REF package performs various actions against an object instance given a *reference* to it. The six procedures included in the package perform tasks such as retrieving an object instance, locking an object, updating an object, and more. See Chapter 15 for more information on this package.

Creation Scripts
`utlref.sql/prvtref.plb`

Release Available
Pre–Oracle 8*i*

UTL_SMTP

The UTL_SMTP package is used for PL/SQL programs that must send e-mail using SMTP. This package is demonstrated in Chapter 17.

Creation Scripts
`utlsmtp.sql/prvtsmtp.plb`

Release Available
Oracle 8*i*

UTL_TCP

This package is used primarily with applications that access the Internet. It enables the application to communicate with servers that use TCP/IP as a protocol.

Creation Scripts
`utltcp.sql/prvttcp.plb`

Release Available
Oracle 8*i*

UTL_URL

Two procedures in this package allow you to escape and un-escape when referring to a URL. URLs contain reserved characters, and this provides a means to handle them during both load and read operations.

Creation Scripts
`utlurl.sql/prvturl.plb`

Release Available
Oracle 9*i*R1

CTXSYS-Owned Built-in Packages

CTXSYS is the Oracle Text (formerly called interMedia) schema. Oracle Text provides full-text information retrieval and full text management. It is included with both the Standard and Enterprise editions of the data server at no additional charge.

NOTE
The CTX prefix you see on many Oracle Text objects is a holdover from the early days of the text component. Version 8 of the data server had an option available (which required separate licensing) called ConText, abbreviated as CTX. The ConText Cartridge and ConText Server were rolled into interMedia in Oracle 8i. The text component split out on its own again in Oracle 9iR1, where it was called Oracle Text. One of the indexes still available in Oracle Text is the CONTEXT *index.*

The built-in packages listed here are owned by CTXSYS. In order to use them, EXECUTE permissions must be granted to your user. This list is based on version 10.1.0.2.0 of the context dictionary. To determine the version you have, run the following from the CTXSYS schema:

```
conn ctxsys/<<password>>

SELECT *
  FROM ctx_version;

VER_DICT    VER_CODE
-----  -------
10.1.0.2.0 10.1.0.2.0
```

Scripts used to create the packages are located in your $ORACLE_HOME/ctx/admin directory. Each object creation script is stored separately, and the filenames are included with the descriptions that follow. Package creation scripts are separated between spec and body. Scripts for the spec end in *.plh, while the body scripts have the extension *.plb. The plb files are encrypted so that they cannot be viewed. The plh files are not encrypted.

CTX_ADM

This is the maintenance and administration package for Oracle Text. This has seen a bit of an evolution over time as text indexing operations moved away from the ConText cartridge and server to built-in functionality.

Creation Scripts
dr0adm.pkh/plb

Public Synonym
None

Contents

- *Procedure SHUTDOWN*   This procedure is obsolete in Oracle 10*g*R1 but exists to prevent errors in code that still calls it. It hearkens back to the days of the ConText server and separate administration of the server from the Oracle database.

- *Procedure RECOVER*   The recover procedure recovers the data dictionary.

- *Procedure SET_PARAMETER*   Sets parameters for the system.

- *Procedure TEST_EXTPROC*   Success when running this indicates that extproc can be invoked. For more information on extproc, see the *Oracle Concepts Manual* on the OTN web site (http://otn.oracle.com).

- *Procedure MARK_FAILED*   This procedure is UNPUBLISHED. Use it to mark an index as FAILED if its current status is INPROGRESS. If you try to ALTER an index that is marked as INPROGRESS, it will fail. Marking the index as FAILED allows the ALTER to succeed.

- *Procedure DROP_USER_OBJECTS*   This procedure is used when dropping a user to clean up text objects such as lexers and preferences. It is not generally called individually.

CTX_CLS

This package provides procedures for classification and training. Classification groups similar documents together. Training performs automatic classification based on an initial set of sample documents and categories. Rules are created according to this sample documentation set, and future documents are classified automatically.

Creation Scripts
dr0cls.pkh/plb

Public Synonym
CTX_CLS

Contents

- *Procedure CLUSTERING*   Overloaded procedure that clusters a collection of documents.

- *Procedure TRAIN*   Automatically generates rules based on a training set, or sample set, of documents that are already classified.

CTX_DDL

The most used CTXSYS package, CTX_DDL maintains preferences, policies, stoplists, section groups, and attributes. It provides a means to add sublexers to the multi_ lexer, syncs CONTEXT indexes that may be out-of-sync, and optimizes indexes by reducing fragmentation.

Creation Scripts
dr0ddl.pkh/plb

Public Synonym
CTX_DDL

Contents

- *Procedure ADD_ATTR_SECTION*   Specifies attribute sections that should be indexed within an XML document.

- *Procedure ADD_FIELD_SECTION*   Adds a new field to an existing section group. Sections are detected by tags. Similar to ADD_ZONE_SECTION.

- *Procedure ADD_INDEX*   Adds an index to an existing index set.

- *Procedure ADD_MDATA*   Adds mdata values to documents.

- *Procedure ADD_MDATA_SECTION*   Adds a new mdata section to an existing section group.

- *Procedure ADD_SPECIAL_SECTION* Adds a new special section to an existing section group. Special sections are detected in the text, not the tags.

- *Procedure ADD_STOPCLASS* Adds a new stopclass to an existing stoplist.

- *Procedure ADD_STOP_SECTION* Stop sections define the sections that should not be indexed in a document (HTML or XML, for example). This adds a new stop section to an existing stoplist.

- *Procedure ADD_STOPTHEME* Adds a new stoptheme to an existing stoplist.

- *Procedure ADD_STOPWORD* Adds a new word to an existing stoplist.

- *Procedure ADD_SUB_LEXER* Adds a sublexer under a multilexer. Multilexers allow multiple languages to be indexed in the same index. The sublexers are the individual languages supported by the multilexer.

- *Procedure ADD_ZONE_SECTION* Adds a new section to an existing section group. Sections are detected by tags. Similar to ADD_FIELD_ SECTION.

- *Procedure COPY_POLICY* Creates a new policy based on an existing policy.

- *Procedure CREATE_INDEX_SET* Creates an index set that can have text indexes added to it using the ADD_INDEX procedure.

- *Procedure CREATE_POLICY* Creates a policy for use with the ORA:CONTAINS operator and XML documents.

- *Procedure CREATE_PREFERENCE* Creates preferences that tell Oracle Text how an object is to be customized.

- *Procedure CREATE_SECTION_GROUP* Creates a section group that specifies how document sections are defined (such as HTML and XML). A section group might be the header in an HTML file, for example.

- *Procedure CREATE_STOPLIST* Creates a stoplist or a list of words that should not be indexed.

- *Procedure DROP_INDEX_SET* Drops the supplied index set.

- *Procedure DROP_POLICY* Drops the supplied policy.

- *Procedure DROP_PREFERENCE* Drops the supplied preference.

- *Procedure DROP_SECTION_GROUP* Drops the supplied section group.

- *Procedure DROP_STOPLIST* Drops the supplied stoplist.

- *Procedure OPTIMIZE_INDEX*   Allows index optimization in parallel, and supports full or partial optimization with a limit on the amount of time to devote to the optimization process.

- *Procedure REMOVE_INDEX*   Removes an index from an index set.

- *Procedure REMOVE_MDATA*   Removes mdata values from a document.

- *Procedure REMOVE_SECTION*   Removes a section from a section group without removing the section group.

- *Procedure REMOVE_STOPCLASS*   Removes a stopclass from a section group without removing the section group.

- *Procedure REMOVE_STOPTHEME*   Removes a stoptheme from a section group without removing the section group.

- *Procedure REMOVE_STOPWORD*   Add a new word to an existing stoplist.

- *Procedure REMOVE_SUB_LEXER*   Removes a sublexer without removing the multilexer preference.

- *Procedure REPLACE_INDEX_METADATA*   Removes mdata values from a document. Similar to REMOVE_MDATA.

- *Procedure SET_ATTRIBUTE*   Defines attributes for preferences at preference creation time. The types of attributes available are dependent on the type of preference being created.

- *Procedure SYNC_INDEX*   Synchronizes a CONTEXT index without rebuilding the index. Oracle 10*g* now supports automatic synchronization of CONTEXT indexes.

- *Procedure UNSET_ATTRIBUTE*   Removes an attribute setting from a preference without removing the preference.

- *Procedure UPDATE_POLICY*   Updates the preferences of the supplied policy.

CTX_DOC

This package is used for specialty text indexing and display features such as theme and gist creation, and highlighting of keywords in a search. All POLICY procedures can perform their tasks without an index.

Creation Scripts
dr0doc.pkh/plb

Public Synonym
CTX_DOC

Contents

- *Procedure FILTER*   Overloaded procedure that takes a document or document reference as input and returns the filtered text. The results are returned either to a physical table (the text is stored as a CLOB) or as a CLOB locator. The ability to filter certain documents is controlled by the type of filter you use. The default INSO filter can extract text from more than 150 different document types.

- *Procedure GIST*   Overloaded procedure that generates the theme and gist of a document and returns the results to either a physical table or a CLOB locator.

- *Procedure HIGHLIGHT*   Overloaded procedure that returns offset terms for a document based on the query specified. The results are returned either in-memory or to a physical table.

- *Procedure IFILTER*   Filters binary data to plain text.

- *Procedure MARKUP*   Overloaded procedure that returns the markup of a document to a table or as a CLOB locator. The output can be HTML or a text document.

- *Function PKENCODE*   Used in conjunction with other CTX_DOC procedures, this function creates a composite key based on a list of PK strings.

- *Procedure POLICY_FILTER*   Overloaded procedure that filters policies and returns the text to a CLOB locator. It accepts documents as VARCHAR2 or any type of LOB.

- *Procedure POLICY_GIST*   Overloaded procedure that generates the theme and gist of a document and returns the results to a CLOB locator. The document can be VARCHAR2 or any type of LOB.

- *Procedure POLICY_HIGHLIGHT*   Overloaded procedure that returns offset terms for a document based on the query specified. It allows you to make the terms used in the search stand out from the rest of the text. It accepts documents as VARCHAR2 or any type of LOB and returns the results to a PL/SQL table.

- *Procedure POLICY_MARKUP*   Overloaded procedure returns the CLOB locator of markup text. It takes documents as VARCHAR2 or any LOB type.

- *Procedure POLICY_THEMES* Overloaded procedure that takes documents either as VARCHAR2 or any type of LOB value and returns themes to a PL/SQL table.

- *Procedure POLICY_TOKENS* Overloaded procedure that returns tokens to a PL/SQL table of a document. The document can be VARCHAR2 or any type of LOB.

- *Procedure SET_KEY_TYPE* Changes the value of parameter CTX_DOC_ KEY_TYPE.

- *Procedure THEMES* Overloaded procedure. One version generates themes for documents in the specified index, while the other returns the themes to a PL/SQL table.

- *Procedure TOKENS* Overloaded procedure that returns tokens for a document to either a PL/SQL table or a physical table.

CTX_OUTPUT

Provides output services, including log files and trace files for Oracle Text.

Creation Scripts
dr0out.pkh/plb

Public Synonym
CTX_OUTPUT

Contents

- *Procedure ADD_EVENT* Adds an event to the log creation to improve the level of debug information.

- *Procedure ADD_TRACE* Begins tracing and provides a user-defined trace_id value.

- *Procedure END_LOG* Stops generating logs for index and document service requests.

- *Procedure END_QUERY_LOG* Stops generating logs for queries against Text indexes.

- *Function GET_TRACE_VALUE* Returns the value of the trace_id specified.

- *Procedure LOG_TRACES*   The contents of all traces are placed in a log file.

- *Function LOGFILENAME*   Returns the current log file name.

- *Procedure REMOVE_EVENT*   Stops logging the specified event information to the log file.

- *Procedure REMOVE_TRACE*   Stops tracing the specified `trace_id`.

- *Procedure RESET_TRACE*   Clears the trace, specified by `trace_id`, and resets it to 0.

- *Procedure START_LOG*   Creates a log file in the location specified by the LOG_DIRECTORY parameter for index and document service requests.

- *Procedure START_QUERY_LOG*   Logs queries against Text indexes, including the success or failure of the query in finding results. The results can be used in conjunction with `CTX_REPORT.QUERY_LOG_SUMMARY` to determine the most popular queries that do/do not find the desired information for the user. Queries and data can be adjusted in accordance with the data logged to provide better information for the end user.

CTX_QUERY

CTX_QUERY returns information regarding the query terms you specify. It allows for storage of Text query expressions and returns count information when provided a query expression. One of the more interesting procedures is `HFEEDBACK`, which gives detailed hierarchical information related to the search terms specified. The results are based on the knowledge base of your system.

Creation Scripts
dr0query.pkh/plb

Public Synonym
CTX_QUERY

Contents

- *Procedure BROWSE_WORDS*   Returns the words before, after, or around the word passed to the procedure. It also returns the count of the documents that include each word.

- *Function CHK_TXNQRY_DISBL_SWITCH*   Returns a 0 or 1, depending on the current system value.

- *Function CHK_XPATH*   Oracle Text must process an XPATH expression in a particular format. This function takes an XPATH expression and returns results in a format understood by Oracle.

- *Function COUNT_HITS*   Function that returns the number of hits for a specified query.

- *Procedure EXPLAIN*   Returns the explain plan for a Text query.

- *Function FCONTAINS*   Returns the score of a query using the CONTAINS operator. Works with POLICIES.

- *Procedure HFEEDBACK*   When given a text query, this procedure writes information from the knowledge base to a results table that shows terms and categories related to the terms you specified in your call to the procedure. The results are dependent on your knowledge base.

- *Procedure REMOVE_SQE*   Removes a stored query.

- *Procedure STORE_SQE*   Stores query expressions under the name supplied.

CTX_REPORT

This very useful package retrieves information to assist in both maintenance and tuning of Oracle Text indexes. It retrieves statistical information about existing indexes, including storage and fragmentation details. It delivers summary reports for query logs to determine how frequently certain queries are run, highlighting ways in which we can improve application queries for improved results.

Creation Scripts
dr0repor.pkh/plb

Public Synonym
CTX_REPORT

Contents

- *Procedure/Function CREATE_INDEX_SCRIPT*   Overloaded. This report output includes a script to fully create an index and all preferences, stoplists, and section groups.

- *Procedure/Function CREATE_POLICY_SCRIPT*   Overloaded. Identical to CREATE_INDEX_SCRIPT, but the focus is on POLICIES rather than INDEXES.

■ *Procedure/Function DESCRIBE_INDEX* Overloaded. Use this when troubleshooting indexes. It provides metadata regarding the index, including the type of lexer used, storage clauses, and stoplists. In 10*g*R1, output can be in XML format or formatted text.

■ *Procedure/Function DESCRIBE_POLICY* Overloaded. Identical to `DESCRIBE_INDEX`, but for `POLICIES` rather than `INDEXES`. In 10*g*R1, output can be in XML format or formatted text.

■ *Procedure/Function INDEX_SIZE* Overloaded. Useful for DBAs in monitoring space usage of indexes and index tables. The report displays primarily information about tablespace usage for Text components. In 10*g*R1, output can be in XML format or formatted text.

■ *Procedure INDEX_STATS* One of the most useful reports for tuning Text index performance. It includes statistics about index fragmentation, number of documents indexed, and more. In 10*g*R1, output can be in XML format or formatted text.

■ *Procedure QUERY_LOG_SUMMARY* Analyze the effectiveness of your indexes with this report. You can determine the most common queries made, the most common unsuccessful queries, query frequency, etc. In 10*g*R1, output can be in XML format or formatted text.

■ *Procedure/Function TOKEN_INFO* Overloaded. Provides information to determine if an index is corrupt. In 10*g*R1, output can be in XML format or formatted text.

■ *Function TOKEN_TYPE* Function that returns a number. This function is used with other procedures and functions that have a `TOKEN_TYPE` parameter, like `TOKEN_INFO`.

CTX_THES

This package provides a way to manage thesauri. Oracle Text allows for the creation of thesauri for improved search capabilities. For example, if a term is commonly referred to as a "widget" but the contents are stored as a "gadget" and it means the same thing, a thesaurus can link the two terms together. Search on "widget" and results containing "gadget" are returned.

Creation Scripts
`dr0thes.pkh/plb`

Public Synonym
CTX_THES

Contents

- *Procedure ALTER_PHRASE*   This procedure alters a phrase in a thesaurus.

- *Procedure ALTER_THESAURUS*   Truncate or rename a thesaurus using this procedure.

- *Procedures/Functions BT*   Overloaded. BT stands for Broader Terms. This procedure/function returns the broader terms as defined in the thesaurus. Terms or phrases are related to each other in a hierarchical fashion. This procedure allows you specify the hierarchy level to drill down to.

- *Procedure/Function BTG*   Overloaded. BTG stands for Broader Terms Generic. Similar to BT.

- *Procedure/Function BTI*   Overloaded. BTI stands for Broader Terms Instance. Similar to BT.

- *Procedure/Function BTP*   Overloaded. BTP stands for Broader Terms Partitive. Similar to BT.

- *Procedure CREATE_PHRASE*   This procedure adds phrases to existing thesauri.

- *Procedure CREATE_RELATION*   Phrases can be related to one another.

- *Procedure CREATE_THESAURUS*   The CREATE_THESAURUS procedure creates an empty thesaurus.

- *Procedure CREATE_TRANSLATION*   Phrases can be created in multiple languages and related to each other for cross-language support.

- *Procedure DROP_PHRASE*   This procedure drops the specified phrase from a thesaurus.

- *Procedure DROP_RELATION*   This procedure drops the specified relationship from a thesaurus.

- *Procedure DROP_THESAURUS*   This procedure drops the specified thesaurus.

- *Procedure DROP_TRANSLATION*   This procedure drops the specified translation of a phrase.

- *Function HAS_RELATION*   The HAS_RELATION function tests whether a phrase has the specified relationship. It returns a Boolean value.

- *Procedure/Function NT*   Overloaded. This is the reverse of BT. NT (which stands for Narrower Terms), and it returns the narrower terms of a phrase.

■ *Procedure/Function NTG*   Overloaded. NTG stands for Narrower Terms Generic. NTG is similar to NT.

■ *Procedure/Function NTI*   Overloaded. NTI stands for Narrower Terms Instance. NTI is similar to NT.

■ *Procedure/Function NTP*   Overloaded. NTP stands for Narrower Terms Partitive. NTP is similar to NT.

■ *Procedure OUTPUT_STYLE*   This procedure sets the type of output shown in expansion functions.

■ *Procedure/Function PT*   Overloaded. PT stands for Preferred Term. It returns the preferred term from the thesaurus based on the specified term or phrase.

■ *Procedure/Function RT*   Overloaded. RT stands for Related Terms. It returns the related terms from the thesaurus based on the specified term or phrase.

■ *Function SN*   SN stands for Scope Note. This function returns the scope note or comment.

■ *Procedure/Function SYN*   Overloaded. SYN stands for SYNonym. This function returns the synonyms from the thesaurus based on the specified term or phrase.

■ *Procedure THES_TT*   TT stands for Top Term. This procedure finds all top terms, or terms that have narrower, but not broader, terms. It finds all top terms, not specific to any term or phrase.

■ *Procedure/Function TR*   Overloaded. TR stands for TRanslation. Provided a phrase, this procedure/function finds the foreign language translation based on the language relationships defined in the thesaurus.

■ *Procedure/Function TRSYN*   Overloaded. TR stands for TRanslation and SYN stands for SYNonym. This procedure/function returns the foreign language translation of a given phrase, and the foreign language synonym of that phrase.

■ *Procedure/Function TT*   Overloaded. TT stands for Top Term. This differs from THES_TT in that TT returns the top terms based on a specific term or phrase.

■ *Procedure UPDATE_TRANSLATION*   Procedure to update an existing translation in a thesaurus.

Index

! (exclamation point), 32

F

S

W

X

INTERNATIONAL CONTACT INFORMATION

AUSTRALIA
McGraw-Hill Book Company
Australia Pty. Ltd.
TEL +61-2-9900-1800
FAX +61-2-9878-8881
http://www.mcgraw-hill.com.au
books-it_sydney@mcgraw-hill.com

CANADA
McGraw-Hill Ryerson Ltd.
TEL +905-430-5000
FAX +905-430-5020
http://www.mcgraw-hill.ca

**GREECE, MIDDLE EAST, & AFRICA
(Excluding South Africa)**
McGraw-Hill Hellas
TEL +30-210-6560-990
TEL +30-210-6560-993
TEL +30-210-6560-994
FAX +30-210-6545-525

MEXICO (Also serving Latin America)
McGraw-Hill Interamericana Editores
S.A. de C.V.
TEL +525-1500-5108
FAX +525-117-1589
http://www.mcgraw-hill.com.mx
carlos_ruiz@mcgraw-hill.com

SINGAPORE (Serving Asia)
McGraw-Hill Book Company
TEL +65-6863-1580
FAX +65-6862-3354
http://www.mcgraw-hill.com.sg
mghasia@mcgraw-hill.com

SOUTH AFRICA
McGraw-Hill South Africa
TEL +27-11-622-7512
FAX +27-11-622-9045
robyn_swanepoel@mcgraw-hill.com

SPAIN
McGraw-Hill/
Interamericana de España, S.A.U.
TEL +34-91-180-3000
FAX +34-91-372-8513
http://www.mcgraw-hill.es
professional@mcgraw-hill.es

**UNITED KINGDOM, NORTHERN,
EASTERN, & CENTRAL EUROPE**
McGraw-Hill Education Europe
TEL +44-1-628-502500
FAX +44-1-628-770224
http://www.mcgraw-hill.co.uk
emea_queries@mcgraw-hill.com

ALL OTHER INQUIRIES Contact:
McGraw-Hill/Osborne
TEL +1-510-420-7700
FAX +1-510-420-7703
http://www.osborne.com
omg_international@mcgraw-hill.com

GET YOUR FREE SUBSCRIPTION
TO ORACLE MAGAZINE

Oracle Magazine is essential gear for today's information technology professionals. Stay informed and increase your productivity with every issue of *Oracle Magazine*. Inside each free bimonthly issue you'll get:

IF THERE ARE OTHER ORACLE USERS AT YOUR LOCATION WHO WOULD LIKE TO RECEIVE THEIR OWN SUBSCRIPTION TO ORACLE MAGAZINE, PLEASE PHOTOCOPY THIS FORM AND PASS IT ALONG.

- Up-to-date information on Oracle Database, Oracle Application Server, Web development, enterprise grid computing, database technology, and business trends

- Third-party vendor news and announcements

- Technical articles on Oracle and partner products, technologies, and operating environments

- Development and administration tips

- Real-world customer stories

Three easy ways to subscribe:

① Web
Visit our Web site at otn.oracle.com/oraclemagazine.
You'll find a subscription form there, plus much more!

② Fax
Complete the questionnaire on the back of this card
and fax the questionnaire side only to +1.847.763.9638.

③ Mail
Complete the questionnaire on the back of this card
and mail it to P.O. Box 1263, Skokie, IL 60076-8263

FREE SUBSCRIPTION

○ **Yes, please send me a FREE subscription to *Oracle Magazine*.** ○ **NO**

To receive a free subscription to *Oracle Magazine*, you must fill out the entire card, sign it, and date it (incomplete cards cannot be processed or acknowledged). You can also fax your application to +1.847.763.9638.
Or subscribe at our Web site at otn.oracle.com/oraclemagazine

○ From time to time, Oracle Publishing allows our partners exclusive access to our e-mail addresses for special promotions and announcements. To be included in this program, please check this circle.

○ Oracle Publishing allows sharing of our mailing list with selected third parties. If you prefer your mailing address not to be included in this program, please check here. If at any time you would like to be removed from this mailing list, please contact Customer Service at +1.847.647.9630 or send an e-mail to oracle@halldata.com.

signature (required)   date

X

name   title

company   e-mail address

street/p.o. box

city/state/zip or postal code   telephone

country   fax

YOU MUST ANSWER ALL TEN QUESTIONS BELOW.

① WHAT IS THE PRIMARY BUSINESS ACTIVITY OF YOUR FIRM AT THIS LOCATION? (check one only)
- ☐ 01 Aerospace and Defense Manufacturing
- ☐ 02 Application Service Provider
- ☐ 03 Automotive Manufacturing
- ☐ 04 Chemicals, Oil and Gas
- ☐ 05 Communications and Media
- ☐ 06 Construction/Engineering
- ☐ 07 Consumer Sector/Consumer Packaged Goods
- ☐ 08 Education
- ☐ 09 Financial Services/Insurance
- ☐ 10 Government (civil)
- ☐ 11 Government (military)
- ☐ 12 Healthcare
- ☐ 13 High Technology Manufacturing, OEM
- ☐ 14 Integrated Software Vendor
- ☐ 15 Life Sciences (Biotech, Pharmaceuticals)
- ☐ 16 Mining
- ☐ 17 Retail/Wholesale/Distribution
- ☐ 18 Systems Integrator, VAR/VAD
- ☐ 19 Telecommunications
- ☐ 20 Travel and Transportation
- ☐ 21 Utilities (electric, gas, sanitation, water)
- ☐ 98 Other Business and Services

② WHICH OF THE FOLLOWING BEST DESCRIBES YOUR PRIMARY JOB FUNCTION? (check one only)
Corporate Management/Staff
- ☐ 01 Executive Management (President, Chair, CEO, CFO, Owner, Partner, Principal)
- ☐ 02 Finance/Administrative Management (VP/Director/ Manager/Controller, Purchasing, Administration)
- ☐ 03 Sales/Marketing Management (VP/Director/Manager)
- ☐ 04 Computer Systems/Operations Management (CIO/VP/Director/ Manager MIS, Operations)

IS/IT Staff
- ☐ 05 Systems Development/ Programming Management
- ☐ 06 Systems Development/ Programming Staff
- ☐ 07 Consulting
- ☐ 08 DBA/Systems Administrator
- ☐ 09 Education/Training
- ☐ 10 Technical Support Director/Manager
- ☐ 11 Other Technical Management/Staff
- ☐ 98 Other

③ WHAT IS YOUR CURRENT PRIMARY OPERATING PLATFORM? (select all that apply)
- ☐ 01 Digital Equipment UNIX
- ☐ 02 Digital Equipment VAX VMS
- ☐ 03 HP UNIX
- ☐ 04 IBM AIX
- ☐ 05 IBM UNIX
- ☐ 06 Java
- ☐ 07 Linux
- ☐ 08 Macintosh
- ☐ 09 MS-DOS
- ☐ 10 MVS
- ☐ 11 NetWare
- ☐ 12 Network Computing
- ☐ 13 OpenVMS
- ☐ 14 SCO UNIX
- ☐ 15 Sequent DYNIX/ptx
- ☐ 16 Sun Solaris/SunOS
- ☐ 17 SVR4
- ☐ 18 UnixWare
- ☐ 19 Windows
- ☐ 20 Windows NT
- ☐ 21 Other UNIX
- ☐ 98 Other
- 99 ☐ None of the above

④ DO YOU EVALUATE, SPECIFY, RECOMMEND, OR AUTHORIZE THE PURCHASE OF ANY OF THE FOLLOWING? (check all that apply)
- ☐ 01 Hardware
- ☐ 02 Software
- ☐ 03 Application Development Tools
- ☐ 04 Database Products
- ☐ 05 Internet or Intranet Products
- 99 ☐ None of the above

⑤ IN YOUR JOB, DO YOU USE OR PLAN TO PURCHASE ANY OF THE FOLLOWING PRODUCTS? (check all that apply)
Software
- ☐ 01 Business Graphics
- ☐ 02 CAD/CAE/CAM
- ☐ 03 CASE
- ☐ 04 Communications
- ☐ 05 Database Management
- ☐ 06 File Management
- ☐ 07 Finance
- ☐ 08 Java
- ☐ 09 Materials Resource Planning
- ☐ 10 Multimedia Authoring
- ☐ 11 Networking
- ☐ 12 Office Automation
- ☐ 13 Order Entry/Inventory Control
- ☐ 14 Programming
- ☐ 15 Project Management
- ☐ 16 Scientific and Engineering
- ☐ 17 Spreadsheets
- ☐ 18 Systems Management
- ☐ 19 Workflow

Hardware
- ☐ 20 Macintosh
- ☐ 21 Mainframe
- ☐ 22 Massively Parallel Processing
- ☐ 23 Minicomputer
- ☐ 24 PC
- ☐ 25 Network Computer
- ☐ 26 Symmetric Multiprocessing
- ☐ 27 Workstation

Peripherals
- ☐ 28 Bridges/Routers/Hubs/Gateways
- ☐ 29 CD-ROM Drives
- ☐ 30 Disk Drives/Subsystems
- ☐ 31 Modems
- ☐ 32 Tape Drives/Subsystems
- ☐ 33 Video Boards/Multimedia

Services
- ☐ 34 Application Service Provider
- ☐ 35 Consulting
- ☐ 36 Education/Training
- ☐ 37 Maintenance
- ☐ 38 Online Database Services
- ☐ 39 Support
- ☐ 40 Technology-Based Training
- ☐ 98 Other
- 99 ☐ None of the above

⑥ WHAT ORACLE PRODUCTS ARE IN USE AT YOUR SITE? (check all that apply)
Oracle E-Business Suite
- ☐ 01 Oracle Marketing
- ☐ 02 Oracle Sales
- ☐ 03 Oracle Order Fulfillment
- ☐ 04 Oracle Supply Chain Management
- ☐ 05 Oracle Procurement
- ☐ 06 Oracle Manufacturing
- ☐ 07 Oracle Maintenance Management
- ☐ 08 Oracle Service
- ☐ 09 Oracle Contracts
- ☐ 10 Oracle Projects
- ☐ 11 Oracle Financials
- ☐ 12 Oracle Human Resources
- ☐ 13 Oracle Interaction Center
- ☐ 14 Oracle Communications/Utilities (modules)
- ☐ 15 Oracle Public Sector/University (modules)
- ☐ 16 Oracle Financial Services (modules)

Server/Software
- ☐ 17 Oracle9*i*
- ☐ 18 Oracle9*i* Lite
- ☐ 19 Oracle8*i*
- ☐ 20 Other Oracle database
- ☐ 21 Oracle9*i* Application Server
- ☐ 22 Oracle9*i* Application Server Wireless
- ☐ 23 Oracle Small Business Suite

Tools
- ☐ 24 Oracle Developer Suite
- ☐ 25 Oracle Discoverer
- ☐ 26 Oracle JDeveloper
- ☐ 27 Oracle Migration Workbench
- ☐ 28 Oracle9*i*/AS Portal
- ☐ 29 Oracle Warehouse Builder

Oracle Services
- ☐ 30 Oracle Outsourcing
- ☐ 31 Oracle Consulting
- ☐ 32 Oracle Education
- ☐ 33 Oracle Support
- ☐ 98 Other
- 99 ☐ None of the above

⑦ WHAT OTHER DATABASE PRODUCTS ARE IN USE AT YOUR SITE? (check all that apply)
- ☐ 01 Access
- ☐ 02 Baan
- ☐ 03 dbase
- ☐ 04 Gupta
- ☐ 05 IBM DB2
- ☐ 06 Informix
- ☐ 07 Ingres
- ☐ 08 Microsoft Access
- ☐ 09 Microsoft SQL Server
- ☐ 10 PeopleSoft
- ☐ 11 Progress
- ☐ 12 SAP
- ☐ 13 Sybase
- ☐ 14 VSAM
- ☐ 98 Other
- 99 ☐ None of the above

⑧ WHAT OTHER APPLICATION SERVER PRODUCTS ARE IN USE AT YOUR SITE? (check all that apply)
- ☐ 01 BEA
- ☐ 02 IBM
- ☐ 03 Sybase
- ☐ 04 Sun
- ☐ 05 Other

⑨ DURING THE NEXT 12 MONTHS, HOW MUCH DO YOU ANTICIPATE YOUR ORGANIZATION WILL SPEND ON COMPUTER HARDWARE, SOFTWARE, PERIPHERALS, AND SERVICES FOR YOUR LOCATION? (check only one)
- ☐ 01 Less than $10,000
- ☐ 02 $10,000 to $49,999
- ☐ 03 $50,000 to $99,999
- ☐ 04 $100,000 to $499,999
- ☐ 05 $500,000 to $999,999
- ☐ 06 $1,000,000 and over

⑩ WHAT IS YOUR COMPANY'S YEARLY SALES REVENUE? (please choose one)
- ☐ 01 $500,000,000 and above
- ☐ 02 $100,000,000 to $500,000,000
- ☐ 03 $50,000,000 to $100,000,000
- ☐ 04 $5,000,000 to $50,000,000
- ☐ 05 $1,000,000 to $5,000,000

100103